THE PSYCHOEDUCATIONAL ASSESSMENT OF PRESCHOOL CHILDREN

THIRD EDITION

Edited by

BRUCE A. BRACKEN

University of Memphis

ALLYN AND BACON

Boston • London • Toronto • Sydney • Tokyo • Singapore

In memory of my sister, Robin Rae Madison

To my loving wife, Mary Jo Bracken;
my son, Bruce A. Bracken, Jr.;
and to my brothers,
Jeffrey Allen Bracken
and
Melvin Ernest Bracken

Series editor: Jeff Lasser
Series editorial assistant: Susan Hutchinson
Marketing manager: Joyce Nilsen

Copyright © 2000, 1993, 1983 by Allyn & Bacon
A Pearson Education Company
160 Gould Street
Needham Heights, MA 02494

Internet: www.abacon.com

Library of Congress Cataloging-in-Publication Data

The psychoeducational assessment of preschool children / Bruce A.
    Bracken, editor. — 3rd ed.
        p.   cm.
    Includes bibliographical references and index.
    ISBN 0-205-29021-3 (hard)
    1. Child Development—Evaluation.   2. Ability—Testing.
3. Readiness for school.   I. Bracken, Bruce A.
LB1115.P963   2000
372.126—dc21   99-23802
                                                            CIP

Printed in the United States of America

10   9   8   7   6   5   4   3   2   1   03   02   01   00   99

CONTENTS

The first edition of *The Psychoeducational Assessment of Preschool Children* was conceived in 1979 primarily to meet the needs of the editors and those persons assigned the task of teaching courses in preschool psychoeducational assessment. In preparation for our own teaching assignments, we noted that no broad-spectrum resource books were available to address the theoretical and practical issues, practices, and techniques that would guide students and practitioners toward the meaningful assessment of preschool children. In the late 1970s, the literature was quite limited, generally outdated, and tended to be focused on singular aspects of preschool assessment (e.g., specific instruments, developmental issues).

To acquaint practitioners with the idiosyncratic behavior of preschool children and address the pertinent issues related to the assessment of this unique population, the editors identified and invited a nationally prominent multidisciplinary team of professionals to write chapters that would serve as the foundation for sound psychoeducational assessment of preschool children for the decade to come. The first edition, published in 1983, was adopted nationally as the standard text in preschool assessment courses. Also, the first edition served professionals as the only comprehensive preschool assessment text available.

As the 1980s elapsed, many advancements in preschool assessment and education occurred. Public Law 99-457 brought with it the promise of appropriate assessment and remedial services for exceptional preschool children. Many of the outdated yet venerable preschool assessment instruments, such as the WPPSI and the Vineland Social Maturity Scale, were revised and restandardized. Many new instruments were developed and added to the repertoire of those individuals who assess young children. New theoretical orientations expanded the focus of preschool assessment and combined assessment with instruction (e.g., curriculum-based assessment/intervention and dynamic assessment/intervention). Nationally, universities increased their graduate and undergraduate offerings in early childhood regular and special education, assessment, and therapeutic interventions. Local, state, regional, and national professional organizations and institutions sponsored a truly amazing number and array of skill-building work-shops. Additionally, special topic newsletters were developed, thematic journal issues were published, and lists of consultants were developed and distributed to guide professionals toward sound practice with preschool clients. In light of these remarkable advances, it has been professionally and personally rewarding that the first edition was in the vanguard of this historical preschool movement.

The goal for the second edition was to incorporate the many advances and changes that occurred in the field and continue to serve as a catalyst for future advances in preschool assessment. The second edition continued to be appropriate for school, child clinical, and pediatric psychologists, early childhood educators and diagnosticians, speech and language pathologists, and other professionals who observe and assess preschool children. The second edition also was appropriate for undergraduate and graduate courses devoted to the psychoeducational assessment of preschool children, related special topics courses, and as a "best practices" resource for the practicing professional. Given the legal, ethical, practical, and professional mandates facing those professionals who assess preschool children, the second edition remained in the vanguard as a reliable guide and resource throughout the 1990s.

The third edition of the book was designed to cross over to the twenty-first century and provide professionals with state-of-the-art information about assessing preschool children. This edition of the book discontinued chapters that focused on outdated instrumentation (e.g., the McCarthy Scales) or practices and introduces some new authors who are on the cutting edge of practice and science. For example, Chapter 20 addresses innovative approaches to play-based assessment that provide professionals with a less formal approach to assessing the skills and abilities of young children. Chapter 21, which is also a new chapter, provides an especially helpful approach to interpreting batteries of instruments in a systematic and consistent fashion.

My goal for the third edition was to ensure that the knowledge included in each chapter would provide professionals with useful theory, guidelines, practices, and procedures appropriate for the assessment of preschool children well into the twenty-first century.

B. A. B.

CONTRIBUTORS

Bruce A. Bracken, Ph.D., is a professor at the University of Memphis. He has authored many publications related to psychoeducational assessment and edits the *Journal of Psychoeducational Assessment.* Dr. Bracken is a Fellow in the American Psychological Association and a Diplomate of the American Board of Psychological Assessment.

Darby Abernathy has a master's degree in exercise science with a specialization in motor control/development; she has worked in both clinical and educational settings with young children with developmental coordination disorders, abused children, and children with moderate to severe neurological deficits. Miss Abernathy has broad-based expertise in diagnostic techniques in motor development as well as in program design and implementation.

Michelle Schicke Athanasiou, Ph.D., is an assistant professor of school psychology at the University of Northern Colorado. She received her M.A. degree from the University of Memphis and her Ph.D. from the University of Nebraska–Lincoln. Her teaching and research interests include early childhood assessment and intervention, consultation, and applied behavior analysis.

Andrés Barona, Ph.D., former associate dean for graduate programs and research and currently professor of school psychology at Arizona State University, specializes in service delivery and research related to the assessment of minority language children.

Candace H. Boan, Ph.D., is assistant professor in the department of psychology at Western Carolina University. Her research interests include gender differences and self-concept of children and adolescents.

Ann E. Boehm is a professor of psychology and education at Teachers College, Columbia University. In addition to assessment, her interests include concept acquisition in young children, observation, early reading, and intergenerational literacy. She is the author of such works as *The Boehm Tests of Basic Concepts, The Classroom Observer* (with R. A. Weinberg), and *Literacy Links for Parents and Children* (with K. E. Brobst, in press).

Jonathan M. Campbell is a Ph.D. candidate in child clinical psychology at the University of Memphis. He is interested in the conceptualization and measurement of children's social competence, child and adolescent screening instruments of intelligence, and differential diagnosis and treatment of autism and Asperger's disorder.

Dawn P. Flanagan, Ph.D., is associate professor of school psychology at St. John's University in New York. She conducts research on intelligence and cognitive assessment, is senior editor of *Contemporary Intellectual Assessment,* co-author of *The Intelligence Test Desk Reference (ITDR):* Gf-Gc *Cross-Battery Assessment,* and a recent recipient of APA's Lightner Witmer Award.

Judy L. Genshaft, Ph.D., is provost and vice president for academic affairs at the University at Albany–State University of New York. Dr. Genshaft's areas of interest include psychoeducational assessment, education of gifted and talented students, and professional issues in school psychology. Her articles and chapters on these topics appear in school and clinical psychology journals and books. She is senior editor of *Serving Gifted and Talented Students: A Resource for School Personnel,* co-editor of *Contemporary Intellectual Assessment: Theories, Tests, and Issues,* and co–guest editor of the 1997 *School Psychology Review* mini-series, "Issues in the Use and Interpretation of Intelligence Testing in the Schools." Dr. Genshaft is on the editorial board of *School Psychology Review,* and she cohosts the National Public Radio Show "Best of Our Knowledge."

Kathryn Gerken is the director of training and internship coordinator of the school psychology program at the University of Iowa. She has chaired the Ethics Committee of the Iowa School Psychologists Association since 1989 and has served as the chair (1978–1981) and vice chair (1993–1996) of the Iowa Board of Psychology Examiners.

Gilbert R. Gredler is a professor at the University of South Carolina. Previously he was chair of the department of school psychology at Temple University and director of psychological services with the Atlanta Board of Education. He has published articles in the areas of learning disabilities, personality assessment, and ethical and legal practices in school psychology. He is book review editor for *Psychology in the Schools* and author of *School Readiness: Assessment and Educational Issues.*

James S. Gyurke graduated from Loyola University of Chicago in 1987 with his Ph.D. in developmental psychology. He has worked in both hospital and clinical settings. For the past 11 years, he has worked for the Psychological Corporation as a senior project director in the psychological measurement group and more recently as a senior behavioral healthcare consultant. He also holds a position as an adjunct faculty member in the school psychology program at Trinity University in San Antonio, Texas.

Patti L. Harrison, Ph.D., is professor of school psychology and assistant dean of the graduate school at the University of Alabama. Her chapters and articles on adaptive behavior assessment appear in textbooks and journals in school psychology and special education.

Stephen R. Hooper, Ph.D., is an associate professor of psychiatry and director of psychology at The Clinical Center for the Study of Development and Learning at the University of North Carolina School of Medicine. He also holds appointments as a research associate professor in the department of psychology and as a clinical associate professor in the school of education at the University of North Carolina at Chapel Hill. Research interests have included neuropsychological outcomes and mechanisms in children with learning, behavioral, and pediatric illnesses. He has published numerous books, chapters, and research articles on these topical domains.

Alan S. Kaufman, Ph.D., is professor of psychology at the Yale University School of Medicine, Child Study Center. He is author of *Assessing Adolescent and Adult Intelligence* (1990) and *Intelligent Testing with the WISC-III* (1994), and co-author, with his wife, Nadeen, of the K-ABC, K-TEA, KAIT, K-BIT, and other clinical tests.

Lori Knight Keith is currently a postdoctoral Fellow in Developmental Disabilities at the University of Tennessee Health Sciences Center in Memphis, Tennessee. Dr. Keith's primary research interests include the assessment of social and emotional functioning in children and adolescents, and the study of assessment and primary prevention in young children.

Michael F. Kelley, Ed.D., is an associate professor in early childhood education at Arizona State University–West campus. He has professional experience with fam-

ilies and children ranging from infants through the preschool years. His current scholarship is focused on studying the effects of restructuring early childhood education programs within private and public settings.

Elizabeth Lichtenberger, Ph.D., is a research scientist at The Salk Institute's Laboratory for Cognitive Neuroscience and is an adjunct faculty member of the California School of Professional Psychology–San Diego. Dr. Lichtenberger is also currently co-authoring two books on assessment with the WISC-III and WAIS-III.

Debra S. Marmor graduated with a B.A. in psychology from the University of Texas in San Antonio in 1987. She received an M.A. in school psychology from Trinity University in San Antonio in 1998. She is a research associate at The Psychological Corporation, where she has been employed for 9 years.

Jennifer Mascolo is a doctoral student in school psychology at St. John's University in New York. Her primary areas of interest include psychoeducational assessment, psychometric theories of intelligence, and *Gf-Gc* cross-battery assessment.

R. Steve McCallum, Ph.D., is professor and chair of the Psychoeducational Studies Unit at the University of Tennessee, Knoxville. He is the author of numerous assessment-related publications, directs a grant, supervises students, and provides direct services. He is associate editor of the *Journal of Psychoeducational Assessment* and a Fellow of APA.

Susan E. Melrose obtained her B.A. in psychology from Western Michigan University in 1993 and is nearing completion of the M.A. school psychology program at Trinity University in San Antonio. She is a research associate at The Psychological Corporation, where she has been employed for 5 years.

Richard J. Nagle is Scudder professor of psychology and director of the school psychology program at the University of South Carolina and adjunct professor in the department of pediatrics at the USC School of Medicine. His current research interests involve the early prediction of school learning and adjustment problems and the prevention of behavioral problems among very young children with motor handicaps and developmental delays.

Maryann Santos de Barona, Ph.D., is associate professor in the school psychology training program at Arizona State University. In that capacity, she teaches courses in case-based consultation: interventions in school psychology, individualized intellectual assessment, and preschool assessment. Her research interests include the assessment of culturally and linguistically diverse preschoolers and school-age children.

Elaine Surbeck, Ed.D., is an associate professor in early childhood education at Arizona State University–main campus. She has professional experience with families and children ranging from infants through kindergarten. Her current scholarship is focused on constructivism and its application to teacher preparation and on interprofessional collaboration among human service personnel.

E. Paul Torrance is distinguished professor emeritus of the University of Georgia. He has also held positions at Kansas State University and the University of Minnesota, and has worked with gifted students at all levels, from kindergarten through graduate school. He is the author of over 40 books and 1,500 journal articles. He is also founder of the future problem solving program, and has received many awards for his pioneering work in creativity and gifted education.

Dianne Putman Whitaker, Ph.D., is an assistant professor in the psychoeducational studies unit at the University of Tennessee, Knoxville. She worked with preschool children as a school psychologist in the Broward County, Florida system for many years. She currently teaches as the assessment practicum.

Harriet G. Williams, Ph.D., is professor in the school of public health at the University of South Carolina; she directs the Lifespan Motor Development/Control Laboratories. Dr. Williams is actively involved in clinical service and research with young children; the Perceptual-Motor Development Laboratory, which she directs, assesses, prescribes, and carries out enrichment programs for children with mild/moderate motor, perceptual, and behavioral needs. She has published numerous articles on motor development in children with developmental coordination disorders; her most recent work focuses on the development of bimanual control in young children with normal and delayed motor development.

CHAPTER 1

HISTORY OF PRESCHOOL ASSESSMENT

MICHAEL F. KELLEY
ELAINE SURBECK

Preschool assessment, within the broader context of psychoeducational assessment, is a relative newcomer in the history of testing. Although its history is recent, preschool assessment issues, practices, and techniques have links to practices that began in Europe and the United States more than 150 years ago. This chapter is designed to survey the evolution of the testing movement as it developed over the course of two centuries, and show how this movement affected the current field of preschool assessment in the United States.

Historians have shown that life in Europe and the United States during the eighteenth and nineteenth centuries was difficult for all but a few (Aries, 1962; De Mause, 1974). Disease and famine were commonplace, afflicting young and old alike. Working conditions were difficult and particularly deadly for child laborers. Those who suffered most were young children, the poor, and individuals considered mentally deficient or insane. Schooling was nonexistent for the majority of young people because most schools were private and established for the elite. Virtually all decisions related to societal work or access to educational opportunity were linked to personal or family wealth. Demographically, between 1820 and 1860 U.S. cities grew at a faster rate than during any other period in history, adding an average of 125,000 new immigrants annually to urban areas (U.S. Congress, Office of Technology Assessment, 1992). Many of the cities were overwhelmed by the sheer numbers of people needing education, jobs, and housing.

One of the central educational issues raised during the nineteenth century was the lack of any selection or classification scheme for determining those who might benefit from a proper education and those who were considered uneducable. It was precisely the need for some form of classification of human ability that caused scientists in France, England, Germany, and the United States to formulate the early versions of our present-day assessment devices.

A central theme in the history of assessment is how the early scientists' views of the nature of human development and mental activity influenced the school-age and subsequent preschool testing movement. What is evident in examining the historical antecedents of the preschool testing movement is that each major scientific improvement resulted from cycles of interactions between sociocultural and educational needs of society at a point in time and the prevailing scientific conception of human functioning and ability.

As new views of human functioning and intelligent activity were proposed and challenged during these cycles of intense sociocultural tension and controversy, concomitant changes were reflected in the policies, instruments, and procedures used to measure such ability. In the course of roughly 150 years, current methodological issues such as test validity and reliability, sophisticated sampling techniques, the use of elaborate statistical analyses, and decision utility emerged. These developments can be traced to the pioneering efforts of the nineteenth-century scientists.

NINETEENTH-CENTURY INFLUENCES ON PRESCHOOL ASSESSMENT

The contributions of the great philosophers and educators who lived prior to the twentieth century were instrumental in the formulation of early theories of mental activity and various conceptions of intelligence (Goodenough, 1949). However, because preschool assessment did not begin until the early twentieth century, the focus on nineteenth-century contributions will be limited to those most directly related to contemporary issues of assessment. (For the contributions of the early philosophers and educators, see Braun & Edwards, 1972; Osborn, 1991; and Ulich, 1945, 1947.) Different purposes and methodological issues related to the assessment of human functioning were raised and studied in countries around the world. Foundational contributions came from work done in France, England, Germany, and the United States.

In France, the study and treatment of the insane and the mentally deficient received considerable attention from Esquirol, Itard, Sequin, and Binet. Their contributions included establishing the need for a classification system to diagnose mental retardation, experimenting with sensory training for the mentally deficient, and developing practical diagnostic classification systems for admission to special schools and for selection into professional civil service (Goodenough, 1949; Johnson, 1894).

In England, scientists were struggling with the assessment of inherited mental ability. Sir Francis Galton, a second cousin to Charles Darwin, constructed very simple tests of memory, motor, and sensory functions to differentiate between high and low achievers. Moreover, he advocated studying individual differences between twins and was one of the first scientists to use quantitative methods derived from mathematics and astronomy in analyzing data (Anastasi, 1982), earning him the title of "the father of mental testing" (Goodenough, 1949).

Charles Darwin suggested that the early behaviors of young children might provide relevant information concerning the ontogenesis of human development. Thus, numerous studies of infant behavior were conducted (Darwin, 1877; Preyer, 1882; Shinn, 1900; Stern, 1914, 1924). These early baby biographies were important to the preschool testing movement in that they demonstrated a sequence of early behavioral development and individual differences regarding the rate of development (Goodenough, 1949). Furthermore, the baby biographies extended the span of research to include an age previously neglected. This resulted in a beginning awareness of the importance of infancy and the early childhood years to later development. Some protocols used in early preschool assessment devices to establish developmental sequences were derived, in part, from the work of the baby biographers.

In contrast, German scientists such as Wundt and Cattell were directing their attention toward sensation, perception, and individual differences. Their efforts influenced the emerging testing movement by clearly demonstrating the need for uniform experimental procedures and, more importantly, the existence of age-related individual variations in performance (Goodenough, 1949). The issue of individual differences and instability in test performance among young children proves to be a continuing problem in preschool assessment and educational decision making today.

In the United States a pressing social problem directed investigations of a different nature. Educators were beginning to recognize that the huge population influx of immigrants necessitated new institutional demands for educational efficiency and accountability. What was needed was a system for accurate identification and classification of students that would result in effective mass education. Unfortunately, the U.S. educational institutions of the time were hampered in their goal by the lack of discriminating assessment instruments. Virtually all of the tests constructed were of a highly sensory nature and failed to differentiate individuals of various levels of ability (Goodenough, 1949; Stott & Ball, 1965).

It can thus be seen that the activity of the social scientists during the nineteenth century raised many issues concerning the assessment of children and adults. A primary tension that surfaced was how to respond to the need for efficiency in classification while respecting the need for valid measures that ensured fairness. Questions about test validity and the link to prevalent theories of mental development and human functioning were raised. The changing context of the work during this period is important to recognize. In contrast to earlier periods, the theories generated by the nineteenth-century scientists about intelligence and behavior were more closely linked to phrenology (in which good or base character traits were attributed to physical endowments), experimental psychology, and the systematic study of humans rather than metaphysical notions derived from philosophy and religion. The most prevalent belief was that mental ability was fixed genetically, unalterable from an environmental perspective. Methodological issues such as the need for controlled testing conditions, useful sampling techniques, and test reliability surfaced during the latter part of this period. Finally, how to assess the nonschool-age child began to emerge as a question of study (Senn, 1975).

EARLY TWENTIETH-CENTURY INFLUENCES ON PRESCHOOL ASSESSMENT

The early twentieth century witnessed dramatic developments in technology, medicine, and the behavioral sciences. The major universities in the United States opened psychological clinics with the study of child development as their primary focus (Sears, 1975).

In France and the United States, the enactment of compulsory school attendance laws resulted in numerous school admission problems. Children from all backgrounds and ability levels were rapidly filling U.S. schools so that by the turn of the century, almost 80 percent of children aged 5 to 17 were enrolled in some kind of school (Katz, 1972). Questions about appropriate selection and classification of individuals were being raised, with school personnel relying on best guesses and personal judgments regarding proper academic placement. Eventually, the governments of both France and the United States commissioned groups of scientists to devise tests of mental ability that would assist in differentiating school-age children and allow for appropriate school placement (Goodenough, 1949). The seminal work of Alfred Binet ensued.

THE BINET SCALES AND THEIR INFLUENCE ON PRESCHOOL ASSESSMENT

Alfred Binet and several of his colleagues were asked by the Paris Minister of Public Instruction to construct a means for identifying children in need of special education. Binet, who published numerous studies related to perception and reasoning, eventually became interested in qualitative differences in functioning displayed by young children and adults (Pollack & Brenner, 1969).

As previously mentioned, the commonly held belief of the time was that intelligence (or mental functioning) was a genetically fixed entity manifested behaviorally through the sensory functions of the body. Most of the early influential scientists argued for such a position and constructed sensory tests based on that premise. Binet was one of the first scientists to challenge that belief (Goodenough, 1949). He argued that complex mental functioning could not be determined by a simple test of sensory functioning. Moreover, he believed that intelligence was fluid, shaped by environmental and cultural influences (Fancher, 1985). In contrast, he suggested judgment, reasoning, and comprehension were more adequate dimensions of intellectual ability (Binet & Simon, 1905). With the assistance of Theodore Simon, Binet developed a 30-item test that was administered to a small sample of subnormal and normal children in Paris. The main objective of the test was to determine general mental development rather than simple sensory functioning. The items were arranged in order of difficulty and were scored on a pass/fail basis. Although by today's standards the 1905 scale was quite crude, several important methodological issues were raised by Binet and Simon (1905). They argued that tests of mental ability must be simple to administer and score, must have standard procedures to follow, and should provide re-

sults that distinguish the retarded from the normal (Pinter, 1923).

In 1908, Binet and Simon reported the results of a second test series. They introduced the concept of "mental age" and described the test standardization procedures to determine item placement. Moreover, their work influenced a number of colleagues and former students (including Jean Piaget) to raise substantive methodological questions and pursue them with vigor and scrutiny (Wolf, 1973). In 1911, the year Binet died, a third revision was reported. The 1911 scale was a further refinement of the previous scale with new items added and some of the original items dropped because they did not measure general intelligence.

Numerous translations of the Binet scale appeared, including the English translations provided by Henry Goddard in 1908 and 1910. In response to interest in the scale, Goddard and his associates at Vineland Training School established test administration seminars for teachers and championed the importance of early diagnosis. He advocated the systematic testing of children and the special placement of limited-abilities students in classes especially created and staffed with trained teachers. Thus the seeds of special education classrooms were planted some 65 years prior to the passage of Public Law 94-142, the Education for All Handicapped Children Act (Kelley, Sexton, & Surbeck, 1990). As can be seen by the following quote, Goddard (1920) enthusiastically endorsed the power of systematic testing and its potential impact on human progress and the creation of social order:

> ...it is no longer possible for anyone to deny the validity of mental tests, even in case of group testing; and when it comes to an individual examined by a trained psychologist, it cannot be doubted that the mental level of the individual is determined with marvelous exactness. The significance of all this for human progress and efficiency can hardly be appreciated at once. Whether we are thinking of children or adults it enables us to know a very fundamental fact about the human material. The importance of this in building up the cooperative society such as every community aims to be, is very great. (pp. 28–29)

In addition to the flurry of activity by Goddard and his associates, Kuhlmann (1912, 1914) published two versions of the Binet scales, and it was his second version that extended the test items downward to address intelligent activity at 2 months of age. This was one of the first revised editions designed to test children younger than 3 years of age (Goodenough, 1949).

The work of Binet and Simon, along with the revised scales designed by others, contributed greatly to the impetus for early testing, and more importantly, the emerging preschool assessment efforts. These individuals challenged the widely held beliefs regarding the static nature of intelligent activity. In addition, they described standardization procedures for item placement, documented age-related score variations and other sources of error in test administration, and discussed difficulties in reporting meaningful test results (Goodenough, 1949). Even though Goddard's vision about the benefits of systematic testing was not realized, significant progress was made in establishing the scientific acceptability of psychometric testing (Kelley, Sexton, & Surbeck, 1990). While these important scientific gains were made in Europe, related issues were afoot in the United States.

CHILD STUDY MOVEMENT

In the United States, the child study movement of the early 1900s gained momentum under the leadership of G. Stanley Hall at Clark University. Several influential scientists (e.g., Kuhlmann, Goddard, and Terman) studied under Hall; Arnold Gesell was another influential figure who was his student (Senn, 1975).

Because the vast majority of the tests developed in the early 1900s were for school-age children, it became increasingly apparent to those individuals at Clark University, and to others at Cornell University (Pauline Park and Wilson Knapp), Yale University (Arnold Gesell), the University of Minnesota (John Anderson), the University of Iowa (Bird Baldwin), Teachers College, Columbia (Lois Meeks), Merrill-Palmer Institute in Detroit (Edna Noble White), and the University of California at Berkeley (Herbert Stolz and Nancy Bayley) that additional revisions were needed for the preschool years. This work was facilitated by Lawrence K. Franks, who, through funding provided by the Laura Spelman Rockefeller Memorial, was instrumental in establishing institutes of child welfare for the study of child development in many of these universities. Thus, the preschool assessment movement began in earnest with the study of young children as the primary thrust.

Between the years 1920 and 1940, considerable time and effort went into formulating answers to three major questions in regard to preschool assessment. First, what are the characteristics of normal young children? Second, is intelligent behavior determined by heredity or environment? Third, what can be done to improve assessment devices designed to test the ability of young children? These questions were raised not only by the scientists and academicians of the time but also by the public. In order to understand what occurred during this period of time, consider the sociocultural context and events leading to the intense study of children.

Demographic statistics continued to reflect high infant and maternal mortality among the poor, and the World War I recruits displayed a strikingly poor educational and physical preparedness (Senn, 1975). Moreover, the proliferation of day care, nursery, and kindergarten facilities led to the realization that little was known about the overall development of young children (Sears, 1975).

The baby biographies written in the latter part of the nineteenth century represented the first real attempt at organizing and describing child growth and development. The vast majority of the early scientists and educators directed their attention toward school-age children and the mentally deficient. Although constrained by the theoretical perspective of genetically "fixed" mental ability, several important psychologists and educators of the early 1900s recognized the social and scientific need for relevant information regarding the growth and development of normal young children. (For review, see Sears, 1975, and Senn, 1975.)

In 1916 Lucy Sprague Mitchell and several of her colleagues began a series of experiments at the Bureau of Educational Experiments (presently the Bank Street College of Education) in New York. The research conducted consisted of studying child development and experimental schools. Techniques of recording children's behavior and analyzing and interpreting the data in ways that displayed the interdependent complexities within each child became a primary focus. These efforts were in direct contrast to the work of John B. Watson and colleagues who chose to ignore the issue of context effects for the science of objective observation and measurement (Senn, 1975).

In addition to the work of Mitchell and her colleagues, the behavioristic work of both Thorndike (1921) and Watson (Watson & Watson, 1928) legitimized the study of children by demonstrating that the right stimuli and environment improved children's ability to learn. However, data regarding the typical pattern and sequence of normal behavior of young children were still unavailable. Although testing of school-age children was well established by 1910 (Goodenough, 1949), the preschool child received little attention until Burt (1921), Yerkes and Foster (1923), and Kuhlmann (1914) published versions of intelligence tests that extended downward into the preschool years. Unfortunately, these early tests were considered methodologically lacking in that standardization procedures were poorly defined and reliability and validity data usually were not reported (Stott & Ball, 1965).

GESELL AND THE MATURATIONAL PERSPECTIVE

Perhaps the earliest significant interest in understanding the development of preschool-age children was shown at the Yale Clinic for Child Development. Exceptional children were observed in the Yale Clinic as early as 1911, but by 1916 Gesell had undertaken a project to explore developmental change and growth of normal children under 5 years of age. Operating under the belief that growth and development were biologically predetermined, Gesell (1925) and his colleagues argued for a maturational perspective that incorporated time-bound qualitative change ("ages and stages") in development. This theoretical viewpoint had support among scientists disenchanted with the views and experiments of Watson, and significantly influenced the child study movement and later debates about the impact of environment on intelligent activity (Senn, 1975).

Gesell (1925), a pediatrician by training, began his study with 50 "representative" children; they were examined at each of 10 age levels—birth, 4, 6, 9, 12, 18, 24, 36, 48, and 60 months. A psychological examination and an observational survey of the child's behavior at home were made at each level. Although little attention was paid to precise methodology, the initial results were presented as a "developmental schedule" and contained approximately 150 items in four areas: motor development, language development, adaptive behavior, and personal-social behavior. Gesell's work continued for more than 40 years. Several of the subsequently developed tests for infants and preschoolers used information derived from the Gesell profiles (Stott & Ball, 1965). Innovative techniques for observing children, such as the use of the one-way observation booth, were also developed by Gesell.

While Gesell and his colleagues were gathering normative data on young children at the Yale Clinic, several other assessment instruments were being developed for use with infants and preschoolers. The most notable among these were the Merrill-Palmer Scale of Mental Tests (Stutsman, 1931), the Minnesota Preschool Scale (Goodenough, 1926; Goodenough, Maurer, & Van Wagenen, 1940), the California First Year Mental Scale (Bayley, 1933), and the Iowa Test for Young Children (Fillmore, 1936). (See Stott & Ball, 1965, and Brooks & Weinraub, 1976, for reviews).

Although the reliability and validity data for these early scales would be considered questionable by contemporary standards, the formulation of these tests and their subsequent publication generated considerable research activity on their use as adequate measures (Goodenough, 1949); of central concern was test reliability, predictive validity, and stability of test scores. Moreover, individuals such as Kurt Lewin were proposing naturalistic, ecologically sensitive observational approaches as scientific tools of investigation that would parallel laboratory methods (Senn, 1975).

Although most of these early test developers did not focus on intelligence per se, they were concerned with the mental and physical growth of normal children. Influenced by the theory of maturation of Hall and Gesell, the underlying assumption made by the majority of the test developers and child developmentalists of this period was that mental ability or intelligence was stable and unmodifiable (Stott & Ball, 1965). These assumptions of predetermined development and genetically fixed intelligence established the climate for perhaps one of the best-known controversies in developmental psychology. This controversy was the prelude to major shifts in thinking about the nature of intelligent activity and concomitant preschool test construction.

WELLMAN–GOODENOUGH CONTROVERSY

With the formation of university child development laboratories in the United States, researchers were afforded sizable numbers of preschoolers on which to conduct studies of growth and development. Wellman and her colleagues at the Iowa Child Welfare Research Station administered intelligence tests to the preschool children enrolled in the program. Over a period of several years Wellman (1932b) observed an increase in the IQs of the children and attributed these increases to the stimulating environment in the program. In 1932, Wellman (1932a) published the first of several articles (1932b, 1934, 1940) that challenged the fixed intelligence assumption so prevalent at the time. Several other investigators subsequently conducted longitudinal studies with young children and reported findings that suggested that environment could either increase or decrease IQs (Crissey, 1937; Skeels, 1938; Skodak, 1939). The result of these studies were fiercely attacked by proponents of the fixed intelligence view (Stott & Ball, 1965).

Primary among those who vehemently disagreed with the view of modifiable intelligence were Simpson (1939) and Goodenough (1939). Although Goodenough had earlier (1928) found IQ increases in a study of nursery school children, she dismissed the findings by concluding that the test (1922 Kuhlmann-Binet) was poorly standardized and that any changes in IQ could not be attributed to actual increases in intelligence. In a similar manner, Goodenough (1940) also dismissed the Wellman studies as poorly controlled and methodologically unsound. Finally, Goodenough and Maurer (1940) published another research report that compared IQ changes among nursery school children and nonnursery school children. The result displayed an average IQ gain of 4.6 points for both groups. Thus, as far as Goodenough was concerned, the notion that environment influenced mental development was not tenable. Lewis Terman had reached similar conclusions in his own research (Senn, 1975).

Controversy ensued throughout psychological circles. New studies were designed and conducted with environmentally deprived children (Bradway, 1945; McHugh, 1943). Eventually evidence that supported the conclusion that environment was, indeed, a factor in mental development began to accumulate. The evidence suggested a need for a reevaluation of the structure of intelligence (Stott & Ball, 1965) and the manner in which intelligent activity was assessed.

INTELLIGENT ACTIVITY RECONCEPTUALIZED

While the heredity–environment controversy was raging, Terman and Merrill (1937) published the 1937 revised edition of the 1916 Stanford-Binet. Additional items for the preschool child coupled with more elaborate and carefully designed standardization procedures were introduced. The test incorporated more nonverbal items, had additional memory tests, reported high-reliability coefficients, and could be administered in either of two forms. The 1937 revision was criticized on several grounds (Flanagan, 1938; Krugman, 1939). It took longer to administer than previous editions, it still reflected mostly verbal ability, the standard error of measurement could not be determined, and the notion of one global IQ score did not accommodate the emerging conceptualization of multifactored approaches to intelligence.

Individuals (Hotelling, 1933; Kelley, 1935; Thurstone, 1935) conducted factor analytic studies on the most widely used tests of the day and reported a number of recognizable group factors related to intelligence. These factors included verbal ability, numerical ability, mechanical ability, and attention. Thurstone (1938) reported six primary mental abilities: verbal comprehension, word fluency, space, memory, number, and induction. Thus, it became apparent that the global structure of intelligence was in need of reconceptualization.

The 1930s and 1940s represented a major turning point in the testing movement. Demographically, universal schooling was prevalent for almost all children. Socially and politically, there was the widespread belief that tests would aid in the efficient management of schools. Scientifically, shifts occurred in how intelligent activity was defined and how that information could be used to benefit children. For example, the inherent limitations of the Stanford-Binet concept of global intelligence and the findings of primary mental abilities led Wechsler (1949) to develop the Wechsler Intelligence Scale for Children (WISC), which incorporated subtests to measure the various aspects of intelligence. Subtests allowed for differentiation and interpretation of results leading to greater analysis of performance. Furthermore, social upheaval such as the economic depression and World War II created the need for additional programs for young children including child care facilities (Osborn, 1991). These conditions led to the conduct of longitudinal research programs to investigate the effects of the environment on intelligence. Finally, the older intelligence scales underwent revisions. Throughout the 1940s and into the 1950s the emphasis shifted from intelligence testing to the study of personality, social, and motoric factors related to general functioning.

THE YEARS 1940–1960

Although the previous 20 years had seen increased test construction for preschool-age children and infants, in the years from 1940 to 1960 there was concern over the lack of predictive validity of the existing instruments (Stott & Ball, 1965). Numerous studies reported little correlation between infant and preschool assessment ratings with those gathered at later school-age years (DeForest, 1941; Escalona, 1950; Gallagher, 1953; Goodenough & Maurer, 1942; Mowrer, 1934). These results raised doubts about the generally accepted view of mental development as being genetically endowed, inherently stable, and quantitative in nature (Stott & Ball, 1965). However, these doubts did not stop the designers of tests from continuing their test construction efforts.

NEW TEST DEVELOPMENTS

During the 1940s several tests were published for infant and preschool assessment. These included the Cattell Infant Intelligence Scale (Cattell, 1940), the Northwest Infant Intelligence Scale (Gilliland, 1948), the Leiter International Performance Scale (Leiter, 1948), and the Full Range Picture Vocabulary Test (Ammons & Ammons, 1948). (See Stott & Ball, 1965, for a description of each.) The Cattell scale and the Northwest test were devised to assess infant abilities whereas the Leiter scale and the Full Range Picture Vocabulary Test were concerned with the abilities of preschoolers 2 years of age and older.

The Leiter (1948) scale was devised as a nonlanguage mental test to be as culturally fair as possible. This represented a significant advance in test construction because the Leiter scale proved to be more culture free than the widely accepted Stanford-Binet (Stott & Ball, 1965). However, this finding did not change public opinion; the Stanford-Binet continued to be the most widely used test of mental ability (Goodenough, 1949).

The Full Range Picture Vocabulary Test was novel in that it was a test with high reliability and validity. In addition, care was taken to standardize the test on a sample of preschoolers considered representative of the general population (Ammons & Holmes, 1949). One serious drawback in the standardization procedure, however, was the fact that the entire group of 120 "representative" children was Caucasian.

In 1949, Wechsler published the WISC. The WISC contained 12 subtests applicable to children between 5 and 15 years of age. The subtests included Arithmetic, Vocabulary, Similarities, Picture Completion, Block Design, and Object Assembly, to name a few. Although the WISC was intended for use with children, its application for preschool-age children raised questions. Most of the criticism of the WISC was concerned with its level of difficulty for young children. In spite of this criticism, the WISC was listed as one of the five most frequently used tests to measure mental functioning in preschoolers (Stott & Ball, 1965). This questionable downward extension of tests designed for school-age children into the preschool years was a common practice during this period of time.

During the 1950s two more tests were published: one for infants and another for young children about to enter first grade. The Griffiths Mental Development Scale (Griffiths, 1954) was designed to measure infant mental ability. Constructed under the premise that intelligence is general ability, Griffiths's test consisted of 260 items in five subscales. Although the test-retest reliability coefficient reported was .92 based on 52 cases, no predictive validity coefficients were reported (Stott & Ball, 1965).

The Brenner Gestalt Test (Brenner, 1959) was designed as a screening device to evaluate children's readiness for first grade. The tasks included copying dots, drawing a man, recognizing numbers, and copying sentences. The test correlated .81 with teacher ratings of children's functioning and was easy to administer. It is instructive to point out that during this period of time in the United States many children were denied public school access based on race and/or assessment of potential school success. The questionable ethical and social impact of using screening and readiness tests to determine school placement will be more fully addressed in later sections of this chapter.

Although the tests just mentioned were developed with far greater precision than their earlier counterparts, they still proved inadequate in predicting later mental development. Although factors such as test resistance (Rust, 1931) and individual temperament (Stutsman, 1931) were considered partly responsible for the lack of predictive validity, the idea that intelligence is qualitative in nature was gaining acceptance and a following in the literature.

THEORETICAL REVISIONS REGARDING THE NATURE OF DEVELOPMENT

In the late 1940s and early 1950s Escalona (1950), Garrett (1946), and Piaget (1952), among others, proposed that mental development and intelligent activity were qualitative in nature. Piaget (1952), in his classic work on the origin of intelligence in young children, postulated a fixed sequence of "structures or schemas" that were qualitatively different in composition yet functionally related in that each developed out of the earlier structure. Central to Piaget's theory was the importance of experience. To Piaget, mental development was dependent on the organism's active construction of the invariant aspects of the environment. Thus, the quality of the environment and the nature of the organism's activity were of vital importance. With the publication of *Intelligence and Experience* by J. McVicker Hunt (1961), and the pioneering replication research of Piaget's concepts conducted by David Elkind (Senn, 1975), U.S. psychologists were confronted with a new conceptualization of human experience and intelligent activity. Called into question were the theoretical approaches that viewed intelligent activity as passive and stable.

This alternative view of development coupled with multiple-factor analytical models of intelligence (Guilford, 1956, 1957, 1959) significantly altered the nature of test construction. No longer could intelligence be considered a general unitary ability. Instead, primary mental abilities were seen as constituting a part of intelligence. In addition, it was becoming increasingly apparent that an individual's level of functioning was not dependent solely on mental activity. With the popularization of Freudian theory, psychologists and educators began considering personal and social variables as important components of overall functioning (Stott & Ball, 1965).

The ideas proposed by Piaget (1952) and others (e.g., Escalona, 1950; Hunt, 1961) concerning the qualitative nature of development directly affected subsequent research and educational thought. Research studies demonstrated that the quality of the environment was an important factor in development (Bayley, 1954, 1955; Bradway, Thompson, & Cravens, 1958; Dennis & Najarian, 1957). Educators began calling for social intervention and early education for the economically disadvantaged and for the children of working mothers (Frank, 1938; Hunt, 1964; Hymes, 1944). These ideas were, no doubt, a result of the successes of the war nurseries and child care centers established by the 1940 Lanham Act (Braun & Edwards, 1972). With the successful launching of the Russian spacecraft *Sputnik* in 1957, the U.S. federal government began providing additional education funds for science and math programs (Osborn, 1991). All of these factors contributed to the development of the compensatory early childhood education programs of the 1960s and 1970s. Unfortunately, the previously designed infant and preschool assessment instruments were considered too subjective, culturally outdated, of poor validity, and inadequate in characterizing a child's level of functioning (Stott & Ball, 1965). Hence, new assessment devices that would reflect current theoretical concepts of the qualitative nature of development, contain a child- and family-oriented approach, and provide sufficient diagnostic applications were needed. The period of major developments in preschool assessment was underway.

THE YEARS 1960–1980

Until the 1960s the primary focus of the testing movement was the assessment of school-age children and military inductees (Parker, 1981). Beginning in the early 1960s, remarkable growth occurred in the testing of preschool children. This was primarily because of the significant role the federal government began to play in education. The most influential events were the funding of the 1964 Maternal, Child Health and Mental Retardation Act, the 1964 Educational Opportunity Act, and the 1965 Elementary and Secondary Education Act (Osborn, 1991). These programs provided improved educational and social opportunities for the children of poor families.

Although the period of social and educational concern of the late 1950s and early 1960s generated a few privately funded intervention programs, Headstart and Follow Through programs were the most widely recognized educational experiments. These programs directed attention to the need for effective program evaluation and adequate preschool assessment instruments.

HEADSTART AND TEST DEVELOPMENT

Program orientation and goals in the Headstart models usually reflected one of three philosophies: an emphasis on maturational principles that stressed a nurturant social-emotional environment; a behavioristic approach that emphasized highly structured didactic methods; or a cognitive-interactionist approach that focused on the child's construction of knowledge.

The original Headstart model programs varied in theoretical and instructional orientation; however, they were all required to establish the effectiveness of their program. Primarily through the efforts of Senator Robert Kennedy, a provision was made that federally funded programs have a performance-based evaluation design (Hoepfner, Stern, Nummedal et al., 1971). The continuation of funding was dependent on gains in intelligence scores, academic achievement, or some other measurable dimension. Because most of the measures discussed earlier were imprecise or inappropriate for young children (Stott & Ball, 1965) and often did not reflect program goals, many new measures were developed between 1965 and 1975. Some of the more notable included the McCarthy Scales of Children's Abilities (MSCA) (McCarthy, 1972), the Wechsler Preschool and Primary Scale of Intelligence (WPPSI) (Wechsler, 1967), and the Caldwell Preschool Inventory (CPI). The CPI formed the basis for curriculum objectives and was a forerunner of the criterion-referenced movement (Hoepfner et al., 1971). With program evaluation as a central concern of early childhood education programs in the 1960s and 1970s, the majority of preschool assessment instruments were developed to measure the various goals of the programs. Thus, tests were devised to measure outcomes in the affective domain, the intellectual domain, the psychomotor domain, and the subject-achievement domain. These developments represented a significant shift because overall functioning was seen as a composite of numerous skills, abilities, and aptitudes.

In reviewing several listings of contemporary preschool instruments, one can see the impact of the Headstart movement on preschool test construction (Dykes, Strickland, & Munyer, 1979; Frost & Minisi, 1975; Hoepfner et al., 1971). More than 200 assessment instruments were constructed and published in the years from 1960 to 1980. In 1971, the Center for the Study of Evaluation and the Early Childhood Research Center of the UCLA Graduate School of Education published a comprehensive evaluation guide of more than 120 preschool and kindergarten tests (Hoepfner et al., 1971). Their primary objective was to provide teachers, supervisors, and early childhood specialists with relevant information as to the validity, examinee appropriateness, administrative utility, and normed technical excellence of each test. Of 120 tests comprised of 630 subtests, only seven subtests were rated as providing *good* validity. The ratings for examinee appropriateness and administrative utility were generally higher for most of the tests; however, the general ratings for normed technical excellence were either *poor* or *fair*.

Although additional preschool test construction has continued (Barnes, 1982; Dykes et al., 1979; Wolery, 1994), there are still the age-old measurement problems of inadequate test validity (content, construct, predictive) and inadequate standardization procedures. Such findings, coupled with recent myths of measurement and the social and cultural implications of testing (Bersoff, 1973; Houts, 1977; Laosa, 1991; Meisels, 1987; White, 1977), have raised concern about using test performance as the sole criterion for educational decision making. Indeed, recent concerns have been raised about the use of invalid and unreliable screening and readiness tests for early childhood educational placement (Meisels, 1987, 1992; Shepard, 1992). These issues will be addressed later in this chapter.

IMPACT OF ADDITIONAL FEDERAL SUPPORT AND SPECIAL EDUCATION THROUGH 1990s

With the appropriation of federal funds for Headstart, Follow Through, and the various education acts, university undergraduate and graduate teacher training programs began to proliferate. In addition, the government saw the need for expanding personnel training grants to the field of special education. Prior to 1960, few universities were adequately staffed with professors for training special education personnel (Meyen, 1978). By 1975, 61 federal laws related to children with disabilities had been passed (Weintraub, Abeson, Ballard, & La Wor, 1976), with Public Law (P.L.) 94-142 serving as the cornerstone.

P.L. 94-142 mandated a free and appropriate public education for children with disabilities in the least restrictive environment possible. Included within the provisions were parental input and the requirement that an individualized education program (IEP) be developed and maintained for each child with disabilities. Integral to the development of the IEP is the evaluation and diagnosis of each child's level of functioning. The assessment devices for special education range from informal behavioral checklists to standardized tests (Rotatori, Fox, Sexton, & Miller, 1990). In addition, special education personnel rely on anecdotal information provided by parents and former teachers and observation of the child's behavior in the classroom. Once an adequate diagnosis of functional level has been ascertained, the instructional program is developed based on clearly stated educational objectives.

The mandate for IEPs holds for all exceptional children ages 3 to 21 at various levels of functioning. These include the mentally retarded, hard of hearing, deaf, speech impaired, visually impaired, severely emotionally disturbed, and the gifted and talented. The passage of the 1986 Education of the Handicapped Amendments (P.L. 99-457) required that all preschool children, infants, and toddlers with special needs must be served by the states. Furthermore, identified preschoolers with special needs (including developmental delay) must be placed in the least restrictive environment possible, preferably with peers without disabilities (Wolery & Wilbers, 1994). This provision led many of the states to create interagency agreements between Headstart, child care centers, and the public schools to serve preschool children with special needs.

Unfortunately, some states refused to allow Headstart and child care centers to contract with public school agencies based on the argument that those settings do not meet *regular* educational requirements (Weiner & Koppelman, 1987). Another problem centered around the definition of disability status used by the public schools. By holding to stringent definitions of disabling conditions and requiring significant assessment data, public schools were able to exclude some preschool children with mild to moderate disabilities from being served.

In 1990, P.L. 101-576 reauthorized the Education for All Handicapped Children Act (P.L. 94-142) and renamed it the Individuals with Disabilities Education Act (IDEA); autism and traumatic brain injury were also established as two new categories. This reauthorization clarified special education as specially designed instruction that could be offered in the classroom, in hospitals and institutions, in the home, and in other settings such as community-based early childhood programs. Although states are required to ensure that the services provided are done so by "qualified personnel" who meet state-approved licensing, certification, or other comparable requirements that apply (Bruder, 1994), considerable flexibility is provided to the states in revising or expanding occupational and professional standards for personnel.

The federal government's involvement in establishing educational program guidelines for Headstart and special education and providing substantial dollars for these programs has contributed significantly to the development of assessment devices for the early childhood years. Additionally, this involvement has helped to shape some very important legal parameters related to educational programs, testing, and to parents' rights to participate in the development of educational programs.

The 1975 passage of P.L. 94-142 and subsequent reauthorizations (including the most recent in 1997, P.L. 105-17) specifically established that a free, appropriate public education must be made available to all children with disabilities between birth and age 21 years. These educational opportunity legislative acts mandated formal due process procedures for schools and service entities to follow. These included formal involvement of parents in planning, developing, and implementing educational programs for their children, notice to parents and their children of educational programming changes, the right of the parents and their children to outside legal representation, the right to refuse placement without a full and individual evaluation of each child's educational status and needs (including family needs for children younger than 3 years), and the right to seek outside testing if desired (Prasse, 1983; Wolery & Wilbers, 1994).

With regard to testing specifically, the trends in legislation (P.L. 94-142, P.L. 99-457, P.L. 101-336 [Americans with Disabilities Act], P.L. 101-576, and P.L. 105-17) and court cases (*Hobson v. Hansen,* 1967; *Diana v. State Board of Education,* 1970; *Guadalupe Organization, Inc. v. Tempe School District No. 3,* 1971; *Covarrubias v. San Diego Unified School District,* 1971; *Larry P. v. Riles,* 1979; *PASE v. Hannon,* 1980) have shown clear expectations for special educational assessment requirements. These include:

- Tests and accompanying materials and procedures must be void of racial and cultural bias. Additionally, the child's native language must be considered when administering assessments.

- Tests and accompanying materials and procedures must be valid and administered by trained personnel. This requires the capacity to carefully interpret test results and observed behavior from a culturally and linguistically sensitive perspective (Santos de Barona & Barona, 1991).
- Tests and accompanying materials and procedures must be capable of assessing educational needs.
- Appropriate educational programming for a child must consider multiple assessment procedures including obtaining information from the parent(s) and other significant individuals.
- A multidisciplinary team or group of persons that includes both special and regular education teachers, as well as the parent(s), must be a part of the evaluation.
- The child must be assessed in all areas related to the suspected disability. This is particularly crucial for those children designated as developmentally delayed.

Although these requirements relate to special education, the specific assessment requirements hold utility for all early childhood assessment. As evidence of this, they are in congruence with the American Psychological Association's (1985) standards for educational testing and the curriculum and assessment position statement of the National Association for the Education of Young Children (NAEYC) and the National Association of Early Childhood Specialists in State Departments of Education (NAECS/SDE) (1991). In addition, the Revised Developmentally Appropriate Practices (Bredekamp & Copple, 1997) suggests similar assessment requirements.

THE GROWTH OF PUBLIC SCHOOL PRESCHOOL PROGRAMS AND THE DEVELOPMENTAL ASSESSMENT DEBATES

Considerable debate has been focused on the implementation of preschool programs within public schools (Strother, 1987). A number of national politicians and state legislatures are calling for increased investment in preschool education, while public commitment to early childhood education programs grew considerably during the late 1980s and continues today. Some of the major policy issues that define this period include the matter of funding, where the programs should be located, and which children should be served, and by whom (Kelley, 1996; Kelley & Surbeck, 1991; Schweinhart, Koshel, & Bridgeman, 1987).

The issue of which children should be served has raised numerous concerns. It has been argued that preschool programs are most beneficial for economically disadvantaged children and those "at risk of school failure" (Schweinhart et al., 1987; Zigler & Styfco, 1994). How one determines the "at risk of school failure" child has fueled a major debate in early childhood circles since the 1980s.

In recent publications, Samuel Meisels (1987, 1992) raised several important issues pertinent to the uses and abuses of preschool assessment devices. Specifically, Meisels argued that far too many children are being assessed with screening and readiness tests that have little or no validity and reliability data to support their use. As a result children are being labeled as developmentally immature or not ready for school placement. Meisels (1987) argues, "Tests that exclude children from public education services or that delay their access to the educational mainstream…are antithetical to legal and constitutional rights to free education and equal protection. In addition, such tests and practices are incompatible with the belief systems, theoretical perspectives, and best practices of most early childhood educators" (p. 71).

Specifically, Meisels challenged the use of the Gesell School Readiness Screening Test (Ilg & Ames, 1972), which is linked to the Gesell Preschool Examination (Haines, Ames, & Gillespie, 1980) and the Developmental Assessment (Walker, 1992). Although thousands of public and private schools subscribed to the use of these tests, the Gesell tests have failed to display adequate psychological properties of validity and reliability. Furthermore, the developers of the tests use a concept of developmental age that has never been tested empirically (Meisels, 1987).

The Gesell tests are derived from a theoretical perspective (maturational) that focuses on time as the most important variable in behavior change. Hence, from a Gesellian perspective, young, immature children need only "the gift of time" to develop. This leads to the claim that "perhaps 50 percent of school failures could be prevented or cured by proper placement based on a child's behavior age" (Ames, Gillespie, Haines, & Ilg, 1979, p. 182). Often as many as one-third of the children tested are recommended for "extratime" arrangements such as developmental kindergarten or transitional first grade (Walker, 1992).

The Gesell Institute cites several studies to support its claim that the readiness assessments are reliably predictive of school success (Lichtenstein, 1990; Walker, 1992; Wood, Powell, & Knight, 1984). However, according to Meisels (1987, 1992) and Shepard (Shepard, 1992; Shepard & Smith, 1986), the tests are fraught with error including judgmental bias of examiners, poor predictive power, and lack of evidence of any differential validity. These reviews and others (Bradley, 1985; Kaufman, 1985; Naglieri, 1985) question the use of the tests and cite the potential misuse and misinterpretation that could lead to serious placement problems.

Shepard and Smith (1986) and Shepard (1992) address the issue of assessing readiness. The authors state, "Scientific knowledge underlying readiness assessment is such that none of the existing tests is sufficiently accurate to justify removing children from their normal peer group and placing them in special two-year programs. In part the lack of high correlations with later school success is caused by the instability of the very traits we are seeking to measure" (Shepard & Smith, 1986, p. 83). Thus, extra-year schooling has not shown the achievement-related benefits that many thought would result, and in some cases, children suffer socioemotional harm (Shepard, 1992). Any achievement differences that are shown tend to level off by third grade (Shepard & Smith, 1986).

Unfortunately, the evidence obtained from controlled studies on the lack of academic benefits of extra-year placements does not always coincide with the beliefs of teachers and parents. In a study conducted by Kelley and Surbeck (1987), a small public school district was interested in examining the effects of a developmental kindergarten and first grade program. Specifically, the Early Prevention of School Failure Program (EPSF) was evaluated to determine if children tested for placement in an extra year of schooling benefited academically. School-related test data obtained on children placed in developmental kindergarten were compared to a random sample of children enrolled in regular kindergarten programs. The test results showed that the extra year of schooling did not benefit the developmental kindergarten children academically, yet 90 percent of the teachers and 76 percent of the parents surveyed believed that the EPSF program had helped the young children improve their academic performance. Moreover, most of the teachers and a majority of the parents believed that the children were carefully and accurately identified when placed in the developmental kindergarten. The lack of congruence between teacher and parent perceptions of program placement and impact and actual pupil academic benefits is intriguing. When further probed, the teachers and parents reported being unaware of the research and literature critical of the widespread and unwarranted use of developmental testing devices for placement purposes. The issue of differential validity and use of tests is a continuing problem with preschool assessment. Without evidence that assessment results in direct benefits to the child, the ritual use of even good tests is to be discouraged (NAEYC & NAECS/SDE, 1991).

As suggested earlier, public school preschool programs for both typical and atypical young children are a reality in virtually every state in this country due to the 1997 reauthorization of federal legislation covering children through the Individuals with Disabilities Education Act (IDEA), the recent expansion of Headstart programs, and through state-funded prekindergarten programs. Thus, the need for well-developed preschool assessment instrumentation and processes is apparent. Additionally, with services now mandated for infants and toddlers with special needs and their families, the demand for well-designed assessments for birth to age 3 and family needs assessments is growing considerably.

FUTURE ISSUES IN PRESCHOOL ASSESSMENT

The past two decades have witnessed significant interest in preschool children. Extensive longitudinal research on the effects of the High/Scope Perry Preschool Project has shown significant benefits of high-quality early childhood programs for poor children that extend well into the adult years (Zigler & Styfco, 1994). Moreover, several scientists have extended thinking about intelligent activity that includes multiple information processing components (Sternberg, 1988) and the possibility of separate multiple intelligences that are relatively autonomous and independent of one another (Gardner, 1983). Although these efforts and those of others within the "intelligence" arena may assist in furthering the development of appropriate preschool assessment devices, it is becoming increasingly apparent that we must concentrate on developing an array of reliable and valid indices of social competence that include motivational history, personality, and socioemotional factors (Weinberg, 1989). Preschool children are qualitatively different from young infants and school-age children. Thus, preschool assessment instruments of the 1980s up through the mid-1990s were designed in an attempt to capture that uniqueness and to interpret the findings within contexts of normal preschool development.

Some of the continued work in preschool assessment during this time included the following. During the 1980s, Kaufman and Kaufman (1983) developed the Kaufman Assessment Battery for Children (K-ABC). The K-ABC is designed to measure mental processing and achievement of children ages 2½ to 12½.

The Stanford-Binet Intelligence Scale was revised to produce a fourth edition (Thorndike, Hagen, & Sattler, 1986). This edition assesses the intelligence of children, adolescents, and adults in an age range of 2 years through 24 years.

Additional preschool instruments included the Battelle Developmental Inventory (Newborg, Stock, Wnek, Guidubaldi, & Svinicki, 1984), the Bracken Basic Concept Scale (Bracken, 1984), the Early Screening Inventory (Meisels & Wiske, 1983), and the Peabody Picture Vocabulary Test—Revised (Dunn & Dunn, 1981), to name a few.

Each of these tests serves appropriate functions, yet limitations are also evident. As an example, Bracken (1987) examined many of the commonly used preschool instruments for their technical adequacy. In his study, Bracken examined the subtest internal consistencies, total test internal consistencies, test-retest reliabilities, subtest floors, item gradients, total test floor, and various forms of validity for each of the preschool instruments. By using these criteria, he displayed the psychometric strengths and weaknesses of the various tests. Bracken (1987) concluded, "...preschool assessment below the age of 4 years seems to present the greatest psychometric problems. Selection of tests for use with low-functioning children below age 4 needs to be made with special care. As can be seen, many of these tests designed for preschool use are severely limited in floor, item gradient, and reliability, especially at the lower level" (p. 325). The technical issues raised by Bracken along with continued theoretical developments regarding the nature of intelligent functioning continue to be crucial in the future development of preschool assessment devices.

Much of the work into the 1990s focused on revising many of the standard preschool assessment tests in an attempt to broaden their use with language minority children from other cultures and those children with special needs (Santos de Barona & Barona, 1991; Wolery, 1994). Moreover, revised versions of tests such as the Early Screening Inventory Revised (Meisels, Marsden, Wiske, & Henderson, 1997) have clearly demarcated the preschool years (3 years, 0 months through 4 years, 5 months) as separate from the kindergarten period. Furthermore, standardization, reliability, and validity data are presented separately for the two groups, thereby increasing the utility of the inventory for comparative purposes. Finally, the new versions of the revised instruments are taking a more holistic view of children within a family and cultural context, and typically include parents and other family members as viable and important sources of information (Henderson & Meisels, 1994).

Because the field of early childhood education is evolving into a collaborative enterprise in which multiple human service and educational programs work together to meet the comprehensive needs of children and families (Kagan, Goffin, Golub, & Pritchard, 1995; Kelley, 1996; Kelley & Surbeck, 1991; Surbeck, 1995), the future trends for preschool assessment will undoubtedly focus on a multimethod, multidisciplinary assessment process that includes significant family input. It is certain that technology in its various forms will play an increasing role in comprehensive preschool assessment measures of the future. In addition, questions raised by advancements in brain research offer intriguing ethical and professional challenges as scientists delve further into evidence, collected as early as in utero, of precursors of intelligent functioning. The nature of human development and the measures we create to assess developmental status in the early years may indeed be at a crucial crossroads as we enter the next millenium.

SUMMARY

Many of the theoretical and technical issues that have surfaced within the past 20 years were not seriously considered nor envisioned by individuals engaged in the early stages of development of preschool assessment. Although the primary concern in assessment initially was the identification and classification of those capable and incapable of learning, the tests were of a highly sensory nature. They focused predominantly on the school-age child and ultimately proved incapable of discriminating among various levels of functioning. With the development of the Binet scales and the subsequent construction of related instruments, interest began to shift to the younger child; the issues of simple test validity and reliability, standardization procedures, and the assessment of higher mental abilities were also of concern. Many of the early tests and those that followed were constrained by the view that intelligence and its behavioral manifestations were static. This view of genetically fixed intelligence and performance was predominant until well into the 1950s; resultant test construction reflected this view. Eventually new theories were proposed that posited a qualitative dimension to intelligent activity. Within this new arena, a child's environment and sociocultural experiences were shown to be powerful influences on learning. These changes in the social sciences also mirrored changes occurring in the broader sociopolitical realm. Equity and access to economic and educational opportunities were values espoused by citizens and politicians. Eventually, these values became principles of law, and there followed a decade of compensatory programs and educational intervention.

With millions of dollars in federal support, hundreds of new assessment instruments were constructed to measure the "whole child." Tests were developed to measure achievement, personality, cognitive functioning, adaptive behavior, and specific skills in a variety of areas including music and the arts. However, the majority of these assessment instruments continued to reflect questionable psychometric properties of validity and reliability as well as inadequate standardization procedures.

Today, with the complexities of child and family needs, the demand for additional comprehensive preschool assessment tools and procedures is apparent. Because the educational programs of the recent past were mandated to operate under new social, legal, and educational conditions, it appears that diversity and variation in educational practice will necessitate changes in assessment techniques. Whereas in the past large segments of the population under 5 years of age were typically ignored, current federal and state initiatives now mandate that the needs of children from birth to 5 years of age be addressed. Although the psychometric concerns for validity, reliability, standardization, and utility will continue to be important, the primary thrust for future activity will be how well the assessment instruments and processes assist in planning, monitoring, and evaluating human service and educational programs for children and families.

Because advanced medical breakthroughs are offering new insights into the functioning of the human brain, the media and general population have, in a sense, rediscovered the importance of early stages of life. At this juncture, there are intriguing possibilities for genetic, surgical, environmental, and educational manipulations of human potential, giving new meaning to the concept of early intervention. Such possibilities are fraught with educational, social, and political issues. It is clear that new, comprehensive approaches to the psychoeducational assessment of preschool children (and younger) must reflect the dynamic nature of the young child and his or her sociocultural contexts while respecting the inherent discontinuities in culture and development that prove so difficult to measure. This will be a major challenge for the field of psychoeducational assessment as it moves into the next century.

REFERENCES

American Psychological Association. (1985). *Standards for educational and psychological testing.* Washington, DC: Author.

Ames, L. B., Gillespie, C., Haines, J., & Ilg, F. (1979). *The Gesell Institute's child from one to six.* New York: Harper & Row.

Ammons, R. B., & Ammons, H. S. (1948). *The Full Range Vocabulary Test.* New Orleans, LA: Author.

Ammons, R. B., & Holmes, J. C. (1949). The Full-Range Picture Vocabulary Tests: III, Results for a preschool age population. *Child Development, 20,* 5–14.

Anastasi, A. (1982). *Psychological testing* (5th ed.). New York: Macmillan.

Aries, P. (1962). *Centuries of childhood.* New York: Knopf.

Barnes, K. E. (1982). *Preschool screening: The measurement and prediction of children at-risk.* Springfield, IL: Thomas.

Bayley, N. (1933). *The California First Year Mental Scale.* Berkeley: University of California Press.

Bayley, N. (1954). Some increasing parent–child similarities during the growth of children. *Journal of Educational Psychology, 45,* 1–21.

Bayley, N. (1955). On the growth of intelligence. *American Psychologist, 10,* 805–818.

Bersoff, D. N. (1973). Silk purses into sow's ears: The decline of psychological testing and a suggestion for its redemption. *American Psychologist, 28,* 892–899.

Binet, A., & Simon, T. (1905). Methods nouvelles pour le diagnostic du niveau intellectuel des anormaux. *L'Annee Psychologique, 11,* 191–244.

Bracken, B. A. (1984). *Bracken Basic Concept Scale.* San Antonio, TX: Psychological Corporation.

Bracken, B. A. (1987). Limitations of preschool instrumentations and standards for minimal levels of technical adequacy. *Journal of Psychoeducational Assessment, 5,* 313–326.

Bradley, R. H. (1985). Review of Gesell School Readiness Tests. In J. Mitchell, Jr. (Ed.). *The ninth mental measurements yearbook (Vol I).* Lincoln: University of Nebraska Press.

Bradway, K. P. (1945). An experimental study of the factors associated with Stanford-Binet IQ changes from the preschool to the junior high school. *Journal of Genetic Psychology, 66,* 107.

Bradway, K., Thompson, C. W., & Cravens, R. B. (1958). Preschool IQ's after twenty-five years. *Journal of Educational Psychology, 49,* 278–281.

Braun, S., & Edwards, E. (1972). *History and theory of early childhood education.* Worthington, OH: Jones.

Bredekamp, S., & Copple, C. (Eds.). (1997). *Developmentally appropriate practice in early childhood education programs: Revised edition.* Washington, DC: National Association for the Education of Young Children.

Brenner, A. (1959). A new gestalt test for measuring readiness for school. *Merrill-Palmer Quarterly, 6,* 1–25.

Brooks, J., & Weinraub, M. (1976). A history of infant intelligence testing. In M. Lewis (Ed.). *Origins of intelligence.* New York: Plenum Press.

Bruder, M. B. (1994). Working with members of other disciplines: Collaboration for success. In M. Wolery & J. S. Wilbers (Eds.), *Including children with special needs in early childhood programs.* Washington, DC: National Association for the Education of Young Children.

Burt, C. (1921). *Mental and scholastic tests.* London: King.

Cattell, P. (1940). *The measurement of intelligence of infants and young children.* New York: Psychological Corporation.

Covarrubias v. San Diego Unified School District, Civ. No. 70-394-S. (S.D. Cal., filed Feb. 1971).

Crissey, O. L. (1937). Mental development as related to institutional residence and educational achievement. *University of Iowa Studies in Child Welfare, 13,* 1.

Darwin, C. (1877). A biographical sketch of an infant. *Mind, 2,* 285–294.

DeForest, B. (1941). A study of the prognosis value of the Merrill-Palmer Scale of Mental Tests and the Minnesota Preschool Scale. *Journal of Genetic Psychology, 59,* 219–223.

De Mause, L. (1974). *The history of childhood.* New York: Psychohistory Press.

Dennis, W., & Najarian, P. (1957). Infant development under environmental handicap. *Psychological Monographs, 71* (7, Whole No. 436).

Diana v. State Board of Education, C.A.N. C-70-37 R.F.P. (N.D. Cal., filed Feb. 3, 1970).

Dunn, L. M., & Dunn, L. M. (1981). *Peabody Picture Vocabulary Test—Revised.* Circle Pines, MN: American Guidance Service.

Dykes, J. K., Strickland, A. M., & Munyer, D. D. (1979). *Assessment and evaluation instruments for early childhood programs.* Gainsville, FL: Florida Educational Research and Development Council (Eric Document No. ED 171 378).

Escalona, S. K. (1950). The use of infant tests for predictive purposes. *Bulletin of the Meninger Clinic, 14,* 117–128.

Fancher, R. E. (1985). *The intelligence men: Makers of the IQ controversy*. New York: W. W. Norton & Co.

Fillmore, E. A. (1936). Iowa Tests for Young Children. *University of Iowa Studies in Child Welfare, 22,* 4.

Flanagan, J. S. (1938). Review of Measuring Intelligence by Termin and Merrill. *Harvard Educational Review, 8,* 130–133.

Frank, L. (1938). The fundamental needs of the child. *Mental Hygiene, 22,* 353–379.

Frost, J., & Minisi, R. (1975). *Early childhood assessment list.* Highstown, NJ: Northeast Area Learning Resource Center (ERIC Document No. ED 136 474).

Gallagher, J. J. (1953). Clinical judgment and the Cattell Intelligence Scale. *Journal of Consulting Psychology, 17,* 303–305.

Gardner, H. (1983). *Frames of mind: The theory of multiple intelligence.* New York: Basic Books.

Garrett, H. E. (1946). A developmental theory of intelligence. *American Psychologist, 1,* 372–378.

Gesell, A. (1925). *The mental growth of the preschool child: A psychological outline of normal development from birth to the sixth year.* New York: Macmillan.

Gilliland, A. R. (1948). The measurement of the mentality of infants. *Child Development, 19,* 155–158.

Goddard, H. H. (1920). *Human efficiency and levels of intelligence.* Princeton, NJ: Princeton University Press.

Goodenough, F. L. (1926). *Measurement of intelligence by drawings.* Chicago: World Book.

Goodenough, F. L. (1928). A preliminary report on the effects of nursery school training upon intelligence test scores of young children. *27th Yearbook of the National Society for the Study of Education,* 361–369.

Goodenough, F. L. (1939). Look to the evidence: A critique of recent experiments on raising the IQ. *Educational Methods, 19,* 73–79.

Goodenough, F. L. (1940). New evidence on environmental influence on intelligence. *39th Yearbook of the National Society for the Study of Education* (Part I), 307–365.

Goodenough, F. L. (1949). *Mental testing.* New York: Rinehart.

Goodenough, F. L., & Maurer, K. M. (1940). The mental development of nursery school children compared with that of non-nursery school children. *39th Yearbook of the National Society for the Study of Education* (Part II), 161–178.

Goodenough, F. L., & Maurer, K. M. (1942). *The mental growth of children from two to fourteen years.* Minneapolis: University of Minnesota Press.

Goodenough, F. L., Maurer, K. M., & Van Wagenen, M. J. (1940). *Minnesota Preschool Scales: Manual of instructions.* Minneapolis, MN: Educational Testing Bureau.

Griffiths, R. (1954). *The abilities of babies.* London: University of London Press.

Guadalupe Organization, Inc. v. Tempe School District No. 3, Civ. No. 71-435 (D. Ariz., filed Aug. 9. 1971).

Guilford, J. P. (1956). The structure of intellect. *Psychological Bulletin, 53,* 267–293.

Guilford, J. P. (1957). *A revised structure of intellect* (Report No. 19). Los Angeles: University of Southern California, Psychology Laboratory.

Guilford, J. P. (1959). Three faces of intellect. *American Psychologist, 14,* 469–479.

Haines, J., Ames, L. B., & Gillespie, C. (1980). *The Gesell Preschool Test manual.* Lumberville, PA: Modern Learning Press.

Henderson, L. W., & Meisels, S. J. (1994). Parental involvement in the developmental screening of their young children: A multiple-source perspective. *Journal of Early Intervention, 18*(2), 141–154.

Hobson v. Hansen, 209 F. Supp. 401 (D. D.C. 1967).

Hoepfner, R., Stern, C., Nummedal, S. G. et al. (1971). *CSE-ERIC preschool/kindergarten test evaluations.* Los Angeles: UCLA Graduate School of Education.

Hotelling, H. (1933). Analysis of a complex of statistical variables into principal components. *Journal of Educational Psychology, 24,* 417–520.

Houts, P. L. (Ed.). (1977). *The myth of measurability.* New York: Hart.

Hunt, J. McV. (1961). *Intelligence and experience.* New York: Ronald.

Hunt, J. McV. (1964). The psychological basis for using preschool enrichment as an antidote for cultural deprivation. *Merrill-Palmer Quarterly, 10,* 209–248.

Hymes, J. L. (1944). Who will need a post-war nursery school? *Kaiser Child Services Center Pamphlet for Teachers* (No. 3).

Ilg, F. L., & Ames, L. B. (1972). *School readiness.* New York: Harper & Row.

Johnson, G. E. (1894). Contributions to the psychology and pedagogy of feebleminded children. *Pedagogical Seminars, 3,* 246–301.

Kagan, S., Goffin, S., Golub, S., & Pritchard, E. (1995). *Toward systemic reform: Service integration for young children and their families.* Falls Church, VA: National Center for Service Integration.

Katz, M. B. (1972). *Class, bureaucracy, and schools.* New York: Praeger.

Kaufman, A. S., & Kaufman, N. L. (1983). *Kaufman Assessment Battery for Children.* Circle Pines, MN: American Guidance Service.

Kaufman, N. L. (1985). Review of Gesell Preschool Test. In J. Mitchell, Jr. (Ed.), *The ninth mental measurements yearbook* (Vol. I). Lincoln: University of Nebraska Press.

Kelley, M. F. (1996). Collaboration in early childhood education. *Journal of Educational and Psychological Consultation, 7*(3), 275–282.

Kelley, M. F., Sexton, D., & Surbeck, E. (1990). Traditional psychometric assessment approaches. In A. F. Rotatori, R. A. Fox, D. Sexton, & J. Miller (Eds.), *Comprehensive assessment in Special Education: Approaches, procedures and concerns.* Springfield, IL: Thomas.

Kelley, M. F., & Surbeck, E. (1987). *Evaluation report of the Littleton School District Early Prevention of School Failure Program.* Phoenix, AZ: Michael F. Kelley & Associates.

Kelley, M. F., & Surbeck, E. (1991). *Restructuring early childhood education.* Bloomington, IN: Phi Delta Kappa Educational Foundation.

Kelley, T. L. (1935). *Essential traits of mental life.* Cambridge, MA: Harvard University Press.

Krugman, M. (1939). Some impressions of the revised Stanford-Binet scale. *Journal of Educational Psychology, 30,* 594–603.

Kuhlmann, F. (1912). A revision of the Binet-Simon system for measuring the intelligence of children. *Journal of Psycho-Asthenics Monographs Supplement, 1*(1), 1–41.

Kuhlmann, F. (1914). *A handbook of mental tests.* Baltimore: Warwick & York.

Laosa, L. M. (1991). The cultural context of construct validity and the ethics of generalizability. *Early Childhood Research Quarterly, 6,* 313–321.

Larry P. v. Riles, 495 F. Supp. 96 (N.D. Cal. 1979).

Leiter, R. G. (1948). *International Performance Scale.* Chicago: Stoelting Co.

Lichtenstein, R. (1990). Psychometric characteristics and appropriate uses of the Gesell School Readiness Screening Test. *Early Childhood Research Quarterly, 5,* 359–378.

McCarthy, D. (1972). *The McCarthy Scales of Children's Abilities.* San Antonio, TX: Psychological Corporation.

McHugh, G. (1943). Changes in IQ at the public school kindergarten level. *Psychological Monographs, 55,* 2.

Meisels, S. J. (1987). Uses and abuses of developmental screening and school readiness testing. *Young Children, 42*(2), 4–6, 68–73.

Meisels, S. J. (1992). The Lake Wobegon effect reversed: Commentary on "The Gesell Assessment: Psychometric properties." *Early Childhood Research Quarterly, 7,* 45–46.

Meisels, S. J., Marsden, D. B., Wiske, M. S., & Henderson, L. W. (1997). *Early Screening Inventory—Revised: Examiner's Manual.* Ann Arbor, MI: Rebus, Inc.

Meisels, S. J., & Wiske, M. S. (1983). *Early Screening Inventory.* New York: Teachers College Press.

Meyen, E. L. (1978). *Exceptional children and youth: An introduction.* Denver, CO: Love.

Mowrer, W. M. C. (1934). Performance of children in Stutman tests. *Child Development, 5,* 93–96.

Naglieri, J. A. (1985). Review of Gesell Preschool Tests. In J. Mitchell, Jr. (Ed.), *The ninth mental measurements yearbook* (Vol. I). Lincoln: University of Nebraska Press.

National Association for the Education of Young Children and National Association of Early Childhood Specialists in State Departments of Education. (1991). Guidelines for appropriate curriculum content and assessment in programs serving children ages 3 through 8. *Young Children, 46*(3), 21–38.

Newborg, J., Stock, J. R., Wnek, L., Guidubaldi, J., & Svinicki, J. (1984). *Battelle Developmental Inventory.* Allen, TX: DLM/Teaching Resources.

Osborn, D. K. (1991). *Early childhood education in historical perspective* (3rd ed.). Athens, GA: Daye Press.

Parker, F. (1981). Ideas that shaped American schools. *Phi Delta Kappan, 62* (5), 314–319.

PASE v. Hannon, No. 74-C-3586 (N.D. Ill., July 16, 1980).

Piaget, J. (1952). *The origins of intelligence in children* (M. Cook, trans.). New York: Holt.

Pinter, R. (1923). *Intelligence testing.* New York: Holt.

Pollack, R. H., & Brenner, M. W. (1969). *The experimental psychology of Alfred Binet.* New York: Springer.

Prasse, D. P. (1983). Legal issues underlying preschool assessment. In K. D. Paget & B. A. Bracken (Eds.), *The psychoeducational assessment of preschool children.* Orlando, FL: Grune & Stratton.

Preyer, W. (1882). *The mind of the child.* New York: Springer.

Rotatori, A. F., Fox, R. A., Sexton, J. D., & Miller, J. H. (Eds.). (1990). *Comprehensive assessment in special education: Approaches, procedures and concerns.* Springfield, IL: Thomas.

Rust, M. M. (1931). The effects of resistance on intelligence scores of young children. *Child Development Monographs* (No. 6).

Santos de Barona, M., & Barona, A. (1991). The assessment of culturally and linguistically different preschoolers. *Early Childhood Research Quarterly, 6,* 363–376.

Schweinhart, L. J., Koshel, J. J., & Bridgeman, A. (1987). Policy options for preschool programs. *Phi Delta Kappan, 68*(7), 524–529.

Sears, R. R. (1975). Your ancients revisited: A history of child development. In E. M. Heatherington (Ed.), *Review of child development research* (Vol. 5). Chicago: University of Chicago Press.

Senn, M. J. E. (1975). Insights on the child development movement in the United States. *Monographs of the Society for Research in Child Development, 40* (3–4, Whole No. 161).

Shepard, L. A. (1992). Psychometric properties of the Gesell Developmental Assessment: A critique. *Early Childhood Research Quarterly, 7,* 47–52.

Shepard, L. A., & Smith, M. L. (1986). Synthesis of research on school readiness and kindergarten retention. *Educational Leadership, 44*(3), 78–86.

Shinn, M. (1900). *The biography of a baby.* Boston: Houghton Mifflin.

Simpson, B. R. (1939). The wandering IQ: Is it time to settle down? *Journal of Psychology, 7,* 351–367.

Skeels, H. M. (1938). Mental development of children in foster homes. *Journal of Consulting Psychology, 2,* 33–34.

Skodak, M. (1939). Children in foster homes: A study of mental development. *University of Iowa Studies in Child Welfare, 16,* 1.

Stern, W. (1914). *The psychological methods of testing intelligence.* Baltimore: Warwick & York.

Stern, W. (1924). *Psychology of early childhood up to the sixth year of age.* New York: Henry Hal. (Originally published, 1914).

Sternberg, R. J. (1988). Intellectual development: Psychometric and information-processing approaches. In M. H. Bornstein & M. E. Lamb (Eds.), *Developmental psychology: An advanced testbook* (2nd ed.). Hillsdale, NJ: Erlbaum.

Stott, L. H., & Ball, R. S. (1965). Infant and preschool mental tests: Review and evaluation. *Monographs of the Society for Research in Child Development, 30* (3, Whole No. 101).

Strother, D. B. (1987). Preschool children in the public schools: Good investment? Or bad? *Phi Delta Kappan, 69* (4), 304–308.

Stutsman, R. (1931). *Mental measurement of preschool children.* New York: World Book.

Surbeck, E. (1995). Professionalism in early childhood teacher education: Service integration and interprofessional education. *Journal of Early Childhood Teacher Education, 16* (3), 15–17.

Terman, L. M., & Merrill, M. A. (1937). *Measuring intelligence.* Boston: Houghton Mifflin.

Thorndike, E. L. (1921). Intelligence and its measurement. *Journal of Educational Research, 12,* 124–127.

Thorndike, R. L., Hagen, E. P., & Sattler, J. M. (1986). *Stanford-Binet Intelligence Scale, Fourth Edition.* Chicago: Riverside.

Thurstone, L. L. (1935). *The vectors of the mind.* Chicago: University of Chicago Press.

Thurstone, L. L. (1938). *Primary mental abilities.* Chicago: Unversity of Chicago Press.

Ulich, R. (1945). *History of educational thought.* New York: American Book.

Ulich, R. (1947). *Three thousand years of educational wisdom.* Cambridge, MA: Harvard University Press.

U.S. Congress, Office of Technology Assessment. (1992). *Testing in American schools: Asking the right questions.* OTA-SET-519. Washington, DC: U.S. Government Printing Office.

Walker, R. N. (1992). The Gesell Developmental Assessment: Psychometric properties. *Early Childhood Research Quarterly, 7,* 21–43.

Watson, J. B., & Watson, R. R. (1928). *The psychological care of the infant and child.* New York: Norton.

Wechsler, D. (1949). *Manual for the Wechsler Intelligence Scale for Children.* New York: Psychological Corporation.

Wechsler, D. (1967). *Wechsler Preschool and Primary Scale of Intelligence.* San Antonio, TX: The Psychological Corporation.

Weinberg, R. A. (1989). Intelligence and IQ: Landmark issues and great debates. *American Psychologist, 44* (2), 98–104.

Weiner, R., & Koppelman, J. (1987). *From birth to five: Serving the youngest handicapped children.* Alexandria, VA: Capitol Publications.

Weintraub, F. J., Abeson, A., Ballard, J., & La Wor, M. L. (Eds.). (1976). *Public policy and the education of exceptional children.* Reston, VA: Council for Exceptional Children.

Wellman, B. L. (1932a). Some new bases for interpretation of the IQ. *Journal of Genetic Psychology, 41,* 116–126.

Wellman, B. L. (1932b). The effects of preschool attendance upon the IQ. *Journal of Experimental Education, 1,* 48–49.

Wellman, B. L. (1934). Growth of intelligence under different school environments. *Journal of Experimental Education, 3,* 59–83.

Wellman, B. L. (1940). The meaning of environment. *39th Yearbook of the National Society for the Study of Education* (Part I), 21–40.

White, S. H. (1977). Social implications of IQ. In P. Houts (Ed.), *The myth of measurability.* New York: Hart.

Wolery, M. (1994). Assessing children with special needs. In M. Wolery & J. S. Wilbers (Eds.), *Including children with special needs in early childhood programs.* Washington, DC: National Association for the Education of Young Children.

Wolery, M., & Wilbers, J. S. (Eds.). (1994). *Including children with special needs in early childhood programs.* Washington, DC: National Association for the Education of Young Children.

Wolf, T. H. (1973). *Alfred Binet.* Chicago: University of Chicago Press.

Wood, C., Powell, S., & Knight, R. C. (1984). Predicting school readiness: The validity of developmental age. *Journal of Learning Disabilities, 17,* 8–11.

Yerkes, R. M., & Foster, J. C. (1923). *The point scale for measuring mental ability.* Baltimore: Warwick & York.

Zigler, E., & Styfco, S. J. (1994). Is the Perry Preschool better than Headstart? Yes and no. *Early Childhood Research Quarterly, 9,* 269–287.

CHAPTER 2

ISSUES IN PRESCHOOL ASSESSMENT

RICHARD J. NAGLE

For the past three decades, there has been increasing emphasis on the assessment of preschool children. Many factors have influenced this movement, including the effectiveness of preschool programs, the national agenda of having all children ready for school, and research with young children that has demonstrated the importance of early experiences for later development. Without question the most important influence has been federal legislation. In 1975 the Education for All Handicapped Children Act (Public Law 94-142) was passed and mandated all school-age children with disabilities must receive a free and appropriate education in the least restricted environment. Under Public Law (P.L.) 94-142, schools were also required to provide services to preschool children with disabilities, 3 to 5 years old, to the extent that they served their age mates with disabilities.

P.L. 94-142 was later amended in 1986 with the passage of P.L. 99-457. This legislation required states to provide a free and appropriate public education to children with disabilities from age 3 to 5 (Part B, Section 619). Regulations that governed practices with school-age children were then applied to the assessment of preschool children (McLean, 1996). An additional component of this legislation, Part H, established incentives for states to develop voluntarily services to infants and toddlers with special needs. More recent legislation has reauthorized and changed some portions of the law. P.L. 101-476 (1990) renamed P.L. 94-142 to the Individuals with Disabilities Education Act (IDEA) and P.L. 102-119 (1991) reauthorized and extended Part H of P.L. 99-457 and amended both Parts B and H of Section 619.

Under IDEA, Part B, preschool children are eligible for special and related services under the same disabilities categories as older children. These categories include mental retardation, hearing impairments including deafness, speech or language impairments, visual impairments including blindness, serious emotional disturbance, orthopedic disabilities, autism, traumatic brain injury, other health impairments, or specific learning disabilities. Considerable concerns have been raised in the professional community about how applicable these disability categories are for very young children (Danaher, 1995). According to Danaher, the developmental domains in preschoolers are so interrelated that a disability resulting in developmental delays may not be readily determined. The requirement to identify a disability may also lead to misdiagnosis and inappropriate services. Furthermore, the inherent dangers of premature labeling may have a stigmatizing effect despite appropriate progress in an early intervention program. In view of these concerns, P.L. 102-119 gives states the option of incorporating an additional category for children, ages 3 to 5, who have developmental delays (Danaher, 1995). This preschool-specific categorization includes children experiencing developmental delays in one or more of the following areas: physical development, cognitive development, communication development, social or emotional development, or adaptive development. These developmental delays are defined by the state and are measured by appropriate diagnostic instruments and procedures. The 1997 reauthorization of IDEA extends the definition of preschool children to 9 years for the purpose of providing noncategorical services to these children.

In order to ascertain how states are using the disability categorizations and whether they have incorporated a preschool-specific eligibility category, Danaher (1995) has surveyed special education coordinators in each state and the District of Columbia. She found that only seven states use all Part B categories and no preschool-specific category. Another additional 21 states use Part B categories and a preschool-specific classification with an additional 15 states using some Part B categories and a preschool-specific category that frequently replaces the omitted Part B category. Finally, eight states do not use any Part B categories for preschoolers and have adopted either noncategorical criteria or preschool-specific categories exclusively. These overall findings suggest the increasing use of the preschool-specific category when compared to previous similar surveys conducted in the early 1990s (McLean, 1996). Because states may also develop their own criteria for what constitutes a significant developmental delay that may require special education or related services, a broad range of qualitative and quantitative eligibility requirements has been developed across the country.

These historical and legislative developments have created the need for assessment activities in various areas of early childhood education programming. Nevertheless, issues related to premature labeling, rapid developmental change, and the need to assess within a context of situational specificity make the process of meeting the requirements of legislative mandates for very young children challenging (Paget & Nagle, 1986). Therefore, professionals must enter the assessment process with the understanding that assessments of preschool children are conducted for reasons beyond classification.

The expansion of educational services to young children with disabilities has expanded the role of the school psychologist to include preschool assessment activities (Kelley & Surbeck, 1991; Paget & Nagle, 1986). The National Association of School Psychologists (NASP), recognizing the importance of early identification and intervention for young children's psychological and developmental difficulties, adopted a position statement on early childhood assessment to guide the fair and accurate identification of the developmental needs of young children (Bracken, Bagnato, & Barnett, 1991). The NASP position endorses multidisciplinary team assessments within an ecological model that includes multiple procedures, multiple sources of information, across multiple settings in order to yield a comprehensive viewpoint of the child's abilities. These multidimensional assessments should be linked to intervention strategies and should conceptualize using more than a single methodology or theoretical framework. Furthermore, the position also underscores the importance of the full integration of parents and/or caretakers into the assessment process, including systematic data gathering in the natural environment.

The foundation of the NASP statement on early childhood assessment practices is based on evidence garnered through research and professional practice. This chapter will discuss several critical issues that have emerged as psychologists in preschool settings strive to promote best practice during assessment activities.

PURPOSES OF PRESCHOOL ASSESSMENT

Assessments in educational settings are conducted to gather information, which can be used to make appropriate decisions about children that will promote their educational and psychological development. Within preschool settings, the process of assessment is appropriate when it is systematic, multidisciplinary, and based on the everyday tasks of childhood (Mindes, Ireton, & Mardell-Czudnowski, 1996, p. 10). These assessments should be comprehensive and include information across the developmental areas of motor skills, temperament, language, cognition, and social/emotional development. A preschool child may be assessed for many specific reasons, including eligibility for special programs for developmentally disabled children, kindergarten screening, placement in educationally competitive environments, and evaluation of a community program. For these and other reasons, the purposes of preschool assessment may be grouped into several general areas that include screening, diagnosis, evaluation of the child's progress, and program evaluation (Boehm & Sandberg, 1982). According to Bagnato and Neisworth (1991), these major goals or purposes should be viewed as a continuous process culminating with individualized programming or intervention and ongoing monitoring of the child's progress in the intervention program.

Screening

Screening involves the evaluation of large groups of children with brief, low-cost procedures to identify those children who may need further diagnostic assessment to qualify for special programs or early intervention services from those who do not require follow-up. Because screening activities are designed not to provide an extensive or in-depth evaluation, a primary concern involves the accuracy of decisions based on screening test information. Specifically, these include identifying a child "at risk" when no significant problem exists (false positive) or failing to identify a child with a problem (false negative). The validity of screening devices is usually described in terms of the ratios of sensitivity and specificity. Sensitivity refers to the proportion of those children requiring further services and identified as such, whereas specificity is defined as the proportion of children in the nontarget group who are correctly classified (Lichtenstein & Ireton, 1991). Several recent validity analyses of screening tests (Carran & Scott, 1992; Gredler, 1997) have indicated better specificity than sensitivity indexes. In other words, a high proportion of children performing well at follow-up were children not identified as at risk but a considerable portion of children identified as at risk at screening were performing adequately at follow-up. Beyond validity issues, the impact of misclassifications on children and their parents should be a major concern for professionals. The occurrence of a false positive classification may create substantial anxiety among parents and may result in unnecessary worry and time as well as the expense of further diagnostic work. Perhaps more serious outcomes are involved in cases of false negatives in which the children in need of services lose the opportunity of participating in early intervention services (Lichtenstein & Ireton, 1991).

Diagnosis

Diagnostic assessment usually involves the follow-up evaluation of children identified as having a potential problem during the screening process. The level of assessment is quite comprehensive and should include a broad range of methods, including formal and informal types of data collection, obtained from multiple sources across different settings (Bagnato & Neisworth, 1991; Meisels & Provence, 1989). These procedures usually include norm-based standardized instruments across multiple behavioral domains. The primary objectives of these diagnostic activities are to determine whether a problem or special need exists, ascertain child and family strengths and weaknesses, determine causes of the problem, and to decide what services, interventions, or programs best meet the individual needs of the child (Paget & Nagle, 1986).

Diagnostic assessment may also be focused on determining eligibility for early intervention services. Information gleaned during diagnostic evaluation may also be used to guide in the selection and formulation of intervention programming. Because diagnostic decision making is done prior to entry into early intervention services (Bagnato & Neisworth, 1991) and because preschoolers show rapid developmental changes, frequent reevaluation is commonplace. Consequently, initial diagnostic information and the results from periodic reevaluation are compared to monitor the child's progress and the effectiveness of the child's program in meeting his or her needs (Paget & Nagle, 1986).

Individual Program Planning and Monitoring

It has been stated that intervention starts with the first step in the assessment process (Bagnato & Neisworth, 1991). The link between assessment and intervention is necessary in order to formulate goals and procedures to meet the child's needs. Information gleaned from assessment activities is, therefore, used for program planning and the child's progress is monitored continually by examining the level of attainment of curricular objectives. When the child's progress is summated over the course of the program, these assessment data may be used to document program effectiveness. There is growing support for the use of curriculum-based testing for these activities (Bagnato & Neisworth, 1991, 1994).

Program Evaluation

Program evaluation is the "process which the quality of a program is assessed" (Benner, 1992, p. 300). According to Benner, both accountability and documentation of program efficacy are essential components to program evaluation. A primary focus of program evaluation should be to show which specific features of the program impact program effectiveness. Therefore, not only should emphasis be placed on outcome assessment but also on reasons why changes may have occurred. By studying the processes that underlie program success, evaluations can begin to suggest causal links between program activities and behavior change so that successful preschool programs could be replicated in a variety of settings (Carta & Greenwood, 1985). Program evaluation efforts are also conducted for program justification and improvement (Fitzgibbon & Morris, 1987; Vandiver & Suarez, 1980). Information resulting from program evaluations may be used by agency decision-makers to continue funding and to identify and address elements of the program that require modification.

UNIQUENESS OF PRESCHOOL CHILDREN

Preschool assessment is a complex and challenging professional task (Bracken & Walker, 1997; Lidz, 1991). Effective assessment activities may be bounded by a limited understanding and conceptualization of the growth and development of preschool children (Bailey, 1989). Preschool children comprise a very unique population that is qualitatively different than their school-age counterparts. Many of the characteristics that are typical of preschool children make reliable and valid assessment difficult. One of the most distinguishing features of preschool children is rapid developmental change (Kelley & Melton, 1993). Research suggests that this rapid growth across various domains may be discontinuous and unstable (Bailey, 1989), that many children will show highly diverse rates of maturation (Romero, 1992), and spurts in development are common observations during the preschool years (Culbertson & Willis, 1993). A critical point derived from these developmental issues is understanding the importance of emerging skills as extensions of and complements to acquired skills, and learning processes as vital adjuncts to products of learning (Barnett, 1984; Paget & Nagle, 1986).

The behavior of young children within the testing situation may also affect the accuracy of test results. Preschoolers typically have short attention spans, high levels of activity, high distractibility, low tolerance for frustration, and are likely to fatigue easily. They approach the test session with a different motivational style than older children and tend not to place importance on answering questions correctly, persisting on test items, pleasing the examiner, or responding to social reinforcement. For most preschool children, the test situation represents new surroundings with an unfamiliar adult. Preschool children vary considerably in their experiential and cultural backgrounds and in their levels of exposure to persons and environments outside the home (Romero, 1992). Some children may have prior experience in preschool environments while others have not had comparable experiences. Because of this, the assessor must be vigilant to individual differences in response style and must be sensitive to potential problems with shyness, verbal facility, and interpersonal discomfort (Ulrey, 1982). Several authors (Bracken & Walker, 1997; Paget, 1991; Romero, 1992) provide excellent discussions on facilitating child performance in assessment settings.

The issues of developmental change, emerging skills, behavioral fluctuation, situational variables, and experiential background all strongly influence the psychometric integrity of procedures used at the preschool level. Because of these influences, lower estimates of stability across settings and test intervals (Boehm & Sandberg, 1982; Bracken & Walker, 1997) are more likely to be obtained among preschool populations. These stability data should be viewed as reflections of the rapid developmental change that is characteristic of this population and underscore the necessity of expanding the scope and time frame of assessments to measure these changes. Multimethod-multisource assessments should, therefore, be designed and conducted periodically.

The lower stability estimate of preschool assessment tools also affects the manner in which inferences should be made about future developmental functioning. Because many tests have inherent inadequacies with stability, particularly measures of cognitive ability, test scores are most appropriately interpreted as reflect-

ing current developmental levels (Flanagan & Alfonso, 1995).

ISSUES IN PRESCHOOL INSTRUMENTATION

Technical Adequacy of Preschool Instruments. Selecting assessment devices with adequate psychometric properties is another challenge for professionals involved in the assessment of preschoolers. With changing legal mandates, the number of young children who are referred for psychoeducational assessments will increase. Furthermore, assessors will need to be attentive to the quality of the instruments they use in these activities (Bracken, 1987). Several studies have been directed at evaluating the psychometric properties of commonly used preschool instruments of the post–P.L. 99-457 era.

Bracken (1987) examined 10 preschool instruments. Five that were commonly used for educational placement decisions included the Battelle Developmental Inventory (Newborg, Stock, Wnek, Guidibaldi, & Svinicki, 1984), the Stanford-Binet Intelligence Scale: Fourth Edition (S-B IV; Thorndike, Hagen, & Sattler, 1986), the Kaufman Assessment Battery for Children (K-ABC; Kaufman & Kaufman, 1983), the McCarthy Scales of Children's Abilities (MSCA; McCarthy, 1972), and the Wechsler Preschool and Primary Scale of Intelligence (WPPSI; Wechsler, 1967). Five individual diagnostic instruments used to assess specific skills and/or abilities included the Bracken Basic Concept Scale (BBCS; Bracken, 1984), the Columbia Mental Maturity Scale (Burgemeister, Blum, & Lorge, 1972), the Miller Assessment for Preschoolers (MAP; Miller, 1982), the Peabody Picture Vocabulary Test—Revised (PPVT-R; Dunn & Dunn, 1981), and the Token Test for Children (DiSimoni, 1978).

The technical adequacy of these instruments was evaluated through various indexes of reliability (median subtest reliability, total test internal consistency, and total test stability coefficients), subtest and total test floors, subtest item gradients, and provision of validity information. For each of these areas, Bracken (1987) delineated minimal standards of technical adequacy. These areas were selected because of their central importance in test selection and the interpretation of assessment results.

The reliability of a test refers to the degree to which a child's score is consistent (internal consistency) and stable (test-retest reliability) across time (Anastasi & Urbina, 1997). Adequate internal consistency for subtest and total test scores allows the assessor to assume that the items that comprise the test are highly related and measure a similar domain of behavior. During the assessment process, this permits a more concise and clear interpretation of test scores (Flanagan & Alfonso, 1995). Test-retest reliability or stability is extremely important because it places constraints or limits on the validity of the test. Test-retest reliability for preschool instruments can be affected by a number of variables (Bracken & Walker, 1997). According to Bracken and Walker, the variables that need to be considered in evaluating test-retest reliability include the expected duration of the stability of assessed behavioral levels, whether all assessed skills should be similarly stable over time, the degree that intervening environmental influences will affect the stability of different behavioral domains, and the extent to which normal developmental progression may affect stability.

Another dimension of technical adequacy involves test floors. Test floors refer to the availability of standard scores that are at least two standard deviations below the mean or the presence of a sufficient number of easy items to allow differentiation between levels of test performance. For example, in the assessment of intellectual ability, tests that do not have adequate floor would not be able to discriminate between children with normal abilities from those with mental retardation based on the criteria of the American Association on Mental Retardation (1992). Adequate test floor is also needed to be able to differentiate average, low-average, borderline, and other functioning on a given assessment tool. In instances when poor floor exists, scores may become unduly inflated and, consequently, provide misleading information (Bracken & Walker, 1997). This potential shortcoming is particularly germane for preschool children because many preschool assessment cases have the goal of determining developmental delay based on a significant discrepancy between the referred child's performance from that of same-age peers.

Item gradients are an additional technical quality that is crucial in preschool assessment. An item gradient refers to "how rapidly standard scores increase as a function of a child's success or failure on a single test item" (Bracken, 1987, p. 322). If a single item results in a substantial increment in the child's standard score, the test instrument may not be sensitive to minor differences in the child's ability in the domain being assessed. An acceptable item gradient requires a sufficient number of nonredundant test items placed throughout the test (Bracken & Walker, 1997). Problems with item gradients and floor effects should be considered in conjunction with the mean of the test to guide the interpretation of differentiations in the child's scores. If most of the item gradient violations occur within 1 standard deviation of the mean, then the test will probably show little

sensitivity to differences in ability within the average range of functioning (Flanagan & Alfonso, 1995). This again complicates the accurate detection of children suspected of exhibiting a developmental delay.

Bracken's (1987) analysis of the 10 preschool tests revealed a pattern of psychometric shortcomings, particularly for children below the age of 4 years. Most of the tests evaluated were noted to have problems with limited floor, item gradients, and reliability. Thus, selection of tests for children with significant developmental delays needs to be done with considerable care and attention to the inadequacies of each instrument.

Examining many of the same psychometric properties, Flanagan and Alfonso (1995) sought to determine whether certain technical limitations of previous instruments were improved with the publication of new or recently revised intelligence tests for preschool children. These authors reviewed the following tests: Wechsler Preschool and Primary Scale of Intelligence—Revised (WPPSI-R; Wechsler, 1989); Differential Ability Scale (DAS; Elliott, 1990); Stanford-Binet Intelligence Scale: Fourth Edition (S-B IV; Thorndike, Hagen, & Sattler, 1986); Woodcock-Johnson Psycho-Educational Battery: Tests of Cognitive Ability (WJ-R: COG; Woodcock & Mather, 1989, 1990), and the Bayley Scales of Infant Development—Second Edition (BSID-II; Bayley, 1993).

Similar to Bracken (1987), Flanagan and Alfonso (1995) found that most of the tests showed some of the same inadequacies at the lower end of the preschool age range. Problems with test floors and item gradients, in particular, continued to be evaluated as weaknesses for children below the age of 4 years. Although test-retest reliabilities reported in the respective test manuals appeared satisfactory, Flanagan and Alfonso have pointed out a number of methodological concerns about the design of these test-retest reliability studies. These include small sample sizes as well as the use of samples that were either not representative of preschoolers, comprised of too broad an age range, and/or included children beyond preschool age. According to the authors, stability data should be collected on age-stratified samples that approximate the age ranges for which the test is intended to be used.

Unlike Bracken's findings, Flanagan and Alfonso (1995) found two tests, the BSID-II and the WJ-R: COG, to be technically adequate across most criteria below the age of 4 years. Additionally, the technical qualities of the selected instruments appeared to be superior to those summarized by Bracken. Thus, overall, the technical qualities of the new and recently revised tests for preschoolers have shown improvement.

These evaluative studies (Bracken, 1987; Flanagan & Alfonso, 1995) were limited to tests of cognitive ability. Bracken, Keith, and Walker (1994) examined the quality of 13 commonly used or newly developed instruments designed to assess preschool behavior and social-emotional functioning. Using the same criteria as Bracken (1987), Bracken et al. (1994) found that the 13 social-emotional, third-party assessment devices had more psychometric limitations than preschool cognitive ability measures. When comparing more recently published instruments to others with older publication dates, it was found that the newer instruments were generally more technically sound. This latter finding parallels the work of Flanagan and Alfonso (1995), who also reported a general improvement in quality among newer instruments measuring cognitive abilities. Despite the substantial limitations among existing preschool instruments, there may be some optimism for improved quality assessment tools developed in the future.

Traditional versus Alternative Methods. Considerable debate exists in the professional literature about the most appropriate approaches to be used in preschool assessment activities. In view of the technical inadequacies of many preschool instruments, it has been argued that standardized, norm-based assessment methods should be replaced by a wide range of methods that more clearly meets the various purposes of early childhood assessment (Bagnato & Neisworth, 1991, 1994). These alternative methods may include play-based assessment, direct observation, parent interviews, parent–child interactions, clinical judgment rating scales, and curriculum-based assessment. The strongest criticism lodged by Bagnato and Neisworth (1994) involves the continued use of intelligence tests because of their limited utility in treatment planning. They argue that such testing should be discontinued and replaced by the more dynamic and flexible alternative assessment approaches.

In response to these criticisms, Bracken (1994) acknowledges the technical inadequacies of many preschool instruments, particularly for children younger than 4 years old, and the need for psychologists to use a broad range of techniques in their assessment of preschool children. Bracken argues that the problem is not with intelligence testing but with practices that mandate the administration of an intelligence test when it is incompatible with the nature of the child or the reason for referral. Because standardized assessment data are required by most states in determining eligibility for services, the continued use of measures of intellectual

functioning is likely to remain despite arguments against this practice (Flanagan & Alfonso, 1995; Harbin, Gallagher, & Terry, 1991). The discontinuance of mandated practices would allow psychologists to utilize the full armament of their techniques, procedures, and practices in an unconstrained manner so that assessors can employ all their psychological skills and expertise in promoting the needs of the child (Bracken, 1994).

According to Bracken (1994), preschool assessment does not require choosing between intellectual (traditional) or alternative assessments. He states that rather than conceptualizing these forms of assessment as being mutually exclusive, a better strategy would be to view them as complementary procedures that form a constellation of skills and methods for the psychologist. Gyurke (1994) likewise supports the combined use of both models of assessment but suggests that both approaches are useful for answering different referral questions. If the assessment question focuses on how a child compares to his or her age-mates on a set of defined criteria, then a norm-referenced approach is indicated. In other situations, if the aim of the assessment question is to ascertain the child's relative pattern of strengths and weaknesses or performance limits, alternative strategies are more appropriate.

The development of alternative strategies has been driven by the shortcoming of standardized testing. Many of these procedures were developed with the direct application of creatively meeting the needs of practitioners in early intervention. Although many acknowledge the value of such procedures, there is a need to empirically validate these methods (Bracken, 1994; Bracken & Walker, 1997; Flanagan & Alfonso, 1995; Gyurke, 1994). What is needed is evidence that alternative procedures are "technically adequate, promote meaningful interventions, enhance child development, improve the alliance between parents, educators, professionals, and children" (Bracken, 1994, p. 104) before they can be adopted for widespread application in clinical practice. These research findings would also clarify more fully which relevant dimensions and conditions under these procedures are most effacious.

Issues in Parental Involvement during the Assessment Process

Although P.L. 102-119 only required IFSP development for children up to the age of 2, many service providers opt to maintain the family focus through the age of 5 rather than switching to a strict IEP format when the child turns 3. Therefore, parents of preschool children may be more effectively included if the psychologist interacts with them as they would interact with a parent of an infant (Bailey, 1996; Linder, 1993). From the time of the initial referral, P.L. 102-119 provides opportunities for parents to participate in assessment, interpretation, and intervention planning for their child.

One of the most important ways to include parents in the assessment process is to contact them prior to the evaluation and ascertain their perspective on the child's areas of strength and weakness (Preator & McAllister, 1995). Abilities that are targeted as weaknesses in a preschool or day care setting may be stronger at home. Additionally, the parent may have concerns that the referring agent has not expressed due to lack of importance in that environment or lack of opportunity to see those other skills.

In addition to gathering information about the level of functioning of the child and family, psychologists should be aware that the current evaluation may be the first contact that parents have had with the diverse professionals who work with young children. Three goals may be accomplished during these initial conversations with psychologists. First, early contacts with parents can serve as educational experiences in which the psychologist explains the parents' rights to participate fully in the assessment and intervention process (Linder, 1993). Few parents will be familiar with the extent and nature of their possible participation in their child's evaluation, nor will they recognize the importance of their input in designing interventions. During preliminary conversations, empowering the parents can improve the quality and accuracy of the evaluation process.

A second function of the initial parent contact is to explain the identity and role of the various professionals who may be in contact with the child during the evaluation and intervention phases. A brief summary of the differences between occupational and physical therapists may enlighten parents who are unfamiliar with these professionals. Additionally, parents may not understand the functions of a psychologist in an early childhood assessment. Explaining the types of skills that are likely to be assessed allows parents to offer suggestions about the best way to obtain such information about the child (e.g., if communication will be assessed, parents may know that the child talks a lot with books but less during free play; if motor skills are assessed, parents may report that the child prefers to use his or her right hand for fine motor skills, so the psychologist can present tasks to that hand). Describing the roles of the many professionals

who may be present at the evaluation serves to lessen potential feelings of being overwhelmed by the experts.

The third function of the initial contact is to discuss aspects of the evaluation setting that may affect the child's performance (Linder, 1993; Preator & McAllister, 1995). Parents will be able to report on the child's ability to adapt to new people and materials, allowing the psychologist to prepare for a successful approach to the child and to pace the evaluation appropriately. Parents can also suggest methods of maintaining the child's interest in activities, such as sitting the child at a table or taking breaks to eat a favorite snack. Furthermore, the decision of whether to have the parent present in the room during the evaluation may be explored. Infants and some toddlers perform better when a parent is present; many preschoolers do better if the parent is out of the room or out of sight.

In some cases, the initial contact can serve as the first piece of assessment. Interviewing the parent about the child's adaptive behavior will offer information about specific strengths and weaknesses in the child's daily routine. Parents may also describe physical considerations that could influence test selection. For example, sensory impairments or physical limitations may influence the decision to use a particular measure or to have supportive equipment the child needs in order to complete the tasks.

During the evaluation, parents can serve as valuable sources of information about the representativeness of the child's performance (Bayley, 1993; Linder, 1993). For example, the Behavior Scale of the Bayley Scales of Infant Development: II provides two exemplary questions to be asked of the parent. First, parents are asked if the child's overall behavior was typical, and then parents are asked if the child's performance on the tasks was consistent with what the parents believe the child can do. These two questions are critical because they inform the psychologist of potential problems with the validity of the evaluation results as well as the likelihood that behavioral observations during the session are applicable to intervention planning.

Including a parent in the evaluation process also permits the psychologist to observe parent–child interactions. The child's attachment to the parent, the parent's responsivity to the child's needs, and the verbal and physical interaction between the two provide information about their relationship and the parent's ability to respond effectively. These observations may influence the intensity or breadth of interventions advocated by the assessment team, such as parent training or reliance on the parent to carry out interventions at home.

If the parents are not present during the child's evaluation, they may still provide extensive information about the child's behavior and skills in multiple domains. Checklists and rating scales may give information about adaptive and maladaptive behaviors, temperament, emotional expressiveness, coping skills, and peer relationships that may not be evident during a clinic-based evaluation (see Martin, 1991).

After the evaluation, the psychologist needs to deliver feedback to parents in a way they can understand. With very young children, that feedback session may be the first explicit report of a deficit in their child's functioning. Therefore, psychologists need to present test results clearly and compassionately. The standard scores used in nearly all evaluation scales may confuse most parents. A brief explanation of average scores and cutoffs for significantly impaired performance may help clarify parents' understanding of their own child's relative level of functioning.

Furthermore, parents may need to hear results more than once if they are overwhelmed by test results from multiple professionals and cannot digest everything at once (Parker & Zuckerman, 1990). As a final note, although preschoolers are not required by law to carry a diagnosis in order to be eligible for special services in the schools, it is likely that a specific diagnosis will be applicable to a child after the evaluation. Although sensitivity to parents' feelings is important, psychologists must be honest in their report of the child's abilities. Terms such as *mentally disabled* or *autistic* will most likely upset the parents initially, but psychologists should not avoid using these terms when appropriate. A candid report of the child's status is a first step in the parents' process of accepting their child's disability and later will allow them to participate fully in designing interventions.

PROFESSIONAL COLLABORATION

The development of collaborative relationships during the assessment process is essential for effective program planning and intervention. The problems confronting preschool children with disabilities and vulnerabilities are quite diverse and the range of possible services required to meet these needs is likewise diverse. Because of this, collaborative relationships between disciplines and agencies must be built (McLean & Crais, 1996). Additionally, both the legal mandates and professional guidelines (Bracken, Bagnato, & Barnett, 1991) require that assessment be multidisciplinary in nature. Many

disciplines may be involved in the assessment process (Bondurant-Utz, 1994; Mowder, Widerstrom, & Sandall, 1989), including education, medicine, nursing, psychology, physical therapy, occupational therapy, speech-language pathology, audiology, social work, and nutrition. Professionals in each discipline may have specific questions about the child's level of functioning in their area of specialty, and they may all wish to complete some evaluation with the child. Psychologists must understand the services that each of these professionals can provide and be able to work with them on a team during assessment and intervention planning. In many cases, psychologists will need to become familiar with the terminology used by each profession to describe specific disabilities, therapy techniques, and assistive technology (Preator & McAllister, 1995). The determination of which professionals to include on the team should be made based on the individual needs of the child and family that originated out of their unique home and community environments (Benner, 1992). Although the degree of specific professional involvement will vary, parents should always be central members of the team (Bagnato & Neisworth, 1991; McLean & Crais, 1996). Three models of team functioning have emerged in the early intervention literature.

These models have been labeled multidisciplinary, interdisciplinary, and transdisciplinary, and they vary considerably on the degree of interaction among disciplines represented in the team.

Models of Team Functioning

Multidisciplinary Model.   The multidisciplinary model is the most widely used approach in early assessment settings (Bagnato & Neisworth, 1991). The origins of this approach are rooted in the medical model in which the main premise is that specialists evaluate in areas of their own expertise that parallel suspected areas of dysfunction (Benner, 1992). In the multidisciplinary approach, professionals from each discipline carry out independent assessments and formulate the part of the service plan that is related to their discipline (Bondurant-Utz, 1994). There is little interaction among the disciplines and the results of these independent assessments are reported to the families by each professional separately. This requires family members to integrate meaningfully the information and suggestions given by the different professionals (McLean & Crais, 1996). In the absence of group synthesis, families may find recommendations redundant, confusing, and even conflicting (Bagnato &

Neisworth, 1991). The multidisciplinary approach of meeting with professionals separately is also very time consuming for families. Even in instances when the team provides the assessment results to one professional to summarize the findings and formulate recommendations, the quality of this outcome will be a function of the designated professional's biases and ability to interpret accurately the findings of other professionals (Benner, 1992). The lack of professional communication does not allow for a comprehensive and integrated conception of the child and family. Because many of the developmental problems identified in preschool children are multifaceted and often extend beyond the expertise of any one discipline, professional collaboration is essential (Paget & Barnett, 1990).

Interdisciplinary Model. In the interdisciplinary model professionals also carry out assessments independently. Unlike the multidisciplinary approach, there is a strong emphasis on communication and consultation among team members so that the outcome of the assessment and program planning is more integrated and unified (McLean & Crais, 1996). Interdisciplinary team functioning involves formal channels of communication in which the results of assessment activities across disciplines are shared and used to develop intervention plans. This model also emphasizes group decision making and goal setting with parents as part of the team. Interdisciplinary teamwork results in a more unified view of the needs of the child and family. Interventions are prescribed so that common goals are developed as part of each discipline's program (Bagnato & Neisworth, 1991). The effectiveness of the interdisciplinary model may be limited by communication difficulties across disciplines (Benner, 1992). According to Benner, professionals familiar with the language and terminology of their specialty area may experience difficulty understanding and being understood by other professionals on the interdisciplinary team. Furthermore, disagreement among team members may also emerge over priority areas of intervention. Unlike the multidisciplinary model, the interdisciplinary model represents a true team approach to assessment and program planning (Bagnato & Neisworth, 1991), but team members must be in continual communication with each other to minimize conflict and to ensure that well-coordinated services are received for the child and family.

Transdisciplinary Model. This model attempts to optimize the level of communication and collaboration among team members by crossing disciplinary boundaries (McLean & Crais, 1996). These assessments are frequently conducted as arena assessments. This format of assessment requires considerable preassessment planning by the team members. Typically only one or two of the team members work directly with the child and parent while other team members observe these interactions. During the preassessment phase, team members who will serve as observers consult with the person designated to conduct or facilitate the assessment. At this stage team members coach the facilitator and share information across disciplines to guide the structure of the evaluation. As the assessment is conducted by the facilitator, observers attend to all aspects of the child's behavior and interactions between the child and parent. Team members observe and record across all developmental areas outlined in the assessment plan. Rather than having each professional conduct an assessment independently, they observe each other's assessments and take turns administering items specific to their domain. When possible, a single facilitator may administer items from all domains to take advantage of the rapport established with the child.

In many cases, items from one measure are sufficiently similar to another measure so that more than one person can score an item from a single administration. For example, the psychologist may ask the child to put a block into a cup for the Bayley Scales. The occupational therapist may pay close attention to the child's coordination, grip, and release. The physical therapist may observe the child's ability to balance his or her torso while sitting on the floor during the task. The speech therapist may listen for babbling or attempts at communication. Thus, a single item may provide a wealth of information for multiple professionals. This multidisciplinary approach saves time and reduces stress on the child by minimizing redundancy. Additionally, arena assessments allow the family to answer questions about the child's recent and current performance in one session rather than answering the same questions repeatedly. Following the assessment, team members meet to discuss the results and plan for needed services or interventions. Professionals who undertake arena assessments convey that they are time efficient and with proper training can observe what is needed for their discipline-specific evaluation as well as observe the child's general functioning in other domains (Bondurant-Utz, 1994).

Arena assessments may not be the most appropriate method for some children and families. Bondurant-Utz (1994) has pointed out that some families may feel uncomfortable being in the presence of more than one professional because certain child characteristics such as distractibility or shyness may affect the outcome of the assessment. Before planning an arena assessment, the format should be explained to the parent in order to ascertain the likelihood of the child performing successfully in that environment (McLean & Crais, 1996). A potential drawback of the transdiciplinary model is that it requires a considerable time commitment from multiple professionals (Benner, 1992). According to Benner, professionals are required to attend team meetings, participate in preassessment planning, observe or facilitate the assessment, and attend the final meeting to synthesize the results and formulate recommendations. Thus, this approach can be costly and time consuming. Recently, Myers, McBride, and Peterson (1996) found that transdisciplinary assessments were more time efficient than standardized multidisciplinary assessments. They cited several reasons why multidisciplinary evaluations took longer to complete, including the need to schedule multiple appointments, appointment cancellations, and child health issues. The transdisciplinary approach should be viewed as family-friendly because the family is usually only needed once to complete the assessment. This approach to assessment shows considerable promise for early intervention activities. Whether the assessment takes on an arena format or a more serial format, there will still be opportunities to take advantage of other professionals' skills (Bagnato & Neisworth, 1991). During evaluations for children with physically disabling conditions, a physical therapist may be able to provide appropriate support during testing to optimize the child's ability to complete a task. Occupational therapists are likely to have relevant information for test administration such as handedness, grip strength, and coordination. Speech therapists often have tips for increasing verbalizations during testing by using preferred toys or verbal cues. Physicians or nurses can offer advice on how to work with children who have assistive medical devices such as tracheotomy tubes or gastrointestinal tubes. An initial interview with the parent prior to the evaluation may reveal information that affects evaluation procedures, and psychologists can seek recommendations from relevant colleagues.

Some children may already be receiving therapeutic services from a variety of professionals. They may be accustomed to working with unfamiliar adults and may perform better without their parents present. In these cases, the therapists can answer questions about the representativeness of the child's behavior and tasks performance during testing.

PROFESSIONAL TRAINING IN PRESCHOOL ASSESSMENT

Preschool assessment is a complex and multifaceted process requiring a broad range of skills to meet the purposes of screening, diagnosis, monitoring child progress, intervention design, and program evaluation (Paget & Nagle, 1986). With the passage of federal mandates, it has become apparent that there is a critical shortage of well-trained early interventionists (Klein & Campbell, 1990) and school psychologists (Mowder, 1996). Unfortunately, the availability of training programs has not kept pace with personnel needs. There are few school psychology programs that provide both the didactic and field components of training necessary to prepare school psychologists for their roles in early intervention activities (Epps & Jackson, 1991; McLinden & Prasse, 1991). In addition to school psychology, the application of the discipline of psychology to infants and young children can be found in a small number of specialty areas in university-based training programs such as pediatric psychology, applied developmental psychology, and child-clinical psychology (Poulsen, 1996). In order to meet the challenges of preschool service delivery, professional psychologists will need additional training, and training programs will need to provide specialized coursework and field experiences.

Meisels and Provence (1989) have suggested that extensive and comprehensive training is needed for assessors of very young children. Given the diversity of interlocking roles that psychologists working in preschool settings must assume, a broad range of content and training experiences has been suggested (Flanagan, Sainato, & Genshaft, 1993; Miesels & Provence, 1991; Mowder, 1996; Paget & Nagle, 1986; Poulsen, 1996).

Training should include the mastery of the broad spectrum of techniques involving test and nontest assessment in order to perform comprehensive evaluations that accurately identify child and family strengths and weaknesses to provide useful information in intervention planning. With the proliferation of new preschool methods, it is also important that preschool psychologists be able to evaluate the technical adequacies of assessment tools (Bracken, 1987; Flanagan et al. 1993). Strong psychometric training will ensure that assessors will make sound decisions regarding test selection and interpretation to avoid making misdiagnoses (Bracken, 1987).

Psychologists working in preschool settings also need a background in typical and atypical child development, developmental disabilities, biological and environmental correlates of risk and resilience status, preschool service delivery models for normal children and children with developmental delays, and curriculum programs for preschoolers with disabling conditions. Given the central importance of the family in preschool programming, family systems theory, family life cycles, child–family interactions, and family structure are critical curricular components (Meisels & Provence, 1991). Within this area, it is essential that psychologists develop the skills to build successfully relationships with families throughout the assessment and program planning process. It is likewise important that the preschool psychologist develop a firm understanding of the contributions of other disciplines in preschool programs. In order to develop the groundwork for future collaboration and interdisciplinary functioning, the curriculum should include extensive discussion of the discipline-specific skills of other professionals involved in early intervention programs (Klein & Campbell, 1990; Mowder, 1996). Furthermore, it is also imperative that the skills to establish collaborative relationships with community agencies and programs when seeking additional needed services should be acquired.

Several authors (Mowder, 1996; Paget & Nagle, 1986; Poulsen, 1996) have underscored the importance of field-based practicum and internship experiences. Such experiences are the core to the professional preparation because they afford the opportunity to integrate theory with practice (Mowder, 1996). These activities may also take place across a variety of school, clinical, and medical settings.

Mowder (1996) has discussed several important issues related to the manner in which training may be carried out as a preservice activity or through service, continuing professional development, or postgraduate training formats. With regard to preservice models, it is unclear the time at which specialty training should be introduced. The alternatives involve specialty training following the completion of general training, specialty training in place of program electives, or postgraduate training after the completion of the specialist or doctoral degree. Although Mowder reports much of the literature supports preservice preparation, postgraduate and inservice training experiences will continually need to be developed to meet the needs of practitioners in the field who are presently being asked to provide services to preschoolers. Therefore, it is imperative that training programs and professional organizations develop models of training for practitioners.

As significant advances and innovations are made within the field of early childhood programming, revisions of training content will be necessary to meet the challenges of these new developments. The efficacy of current and future models of training will need to be demonstrated through research (Mowder, 1996) to ensure the delivery of high-quality services to young children and their families.

SUMMARY

The majority of research in preschool assessment has been amassed over the past two decades. The national agenda of having all children ready for school, the effectiveness of early intervention and prevention programs, and legal mandates requiring services to preschool children with disabilities have forced professionals to examine their assessment practices as they relate to the accuracy of identification and the utility of assessment findings for treatment planning and evaluation. As the field of early intervention has advanced, new assessment methods and processes have been developed.

The development of new methods, sometimes referred to as alternative or nontraditional methods (i.e., play-based assessment, judgment-based assessment, etc.), has spawned considerable professional debate over the validity and utility of more traditional assessment approaches such as norm-referenced assessment tools. The selection of which techniques to use in preschool assessment activities must be matched to the purpose for which the assessment is being conducted (Mindes et al. 1996). Why the assessment is being conducted and how the assessment data will be used are critical issues in method selection. Assessment activities should be viewed as a general problem-solving process aimed at identification and intervention. It is time to drop such descriptors as "traditional," "alternative," and so on and view the different methods and approaches to assessment as options the well-trained professional can use to answer the referral problem. Future research should focus on the validity of different assessment approaches with particular emphasis on the comparative validity of different methodologies across various age, sociocultural, and health conditions. This type of research would be especially relevant to support possible changes in eligibility criteria for intervention services.

Training professionals for early child assessment activities will continue to be a critical issue in maintaining high-quality early intervention programs. As discussed earlier, the assessor will need to acquire clinical expertise over a broad range of techniques and knowledge of the contextual influences on child and family development. Progress of our theoretical understanding of early development will also require ongoing specialized training.

REFERENCES

American Association on Mental Retardation. (1992). *Mental retardation: Definition, classification, and systems of supports* (9th ed.). Washington, DC: Author.

Anastasi, A., & Urbina, S. (1997). *Psychological testing* (7th ed.). Upper Saddle River, NJ: Prentice Hall.

Bagnato, S. J., & Neisworth, J. T. (1991). *Assessment for early intervention: Best practices for professionals.* New York: Guilford.

Bagnato, S. J., & Neisworth, J. T. (1994). A national study of the social and treatment "invalidity" of intelligence testing for early intervention. *School Psychology Quarterly, 9*(2), 81–102.

Bailey, D. B. (1996). Assessment and its importance in early intervention. In D. B. Bailey & M. Wolery (Eds.), *Assessing infants and preschoolers with special needs* (pp. 1–21). Columbus, OH: Merrill.

Bailey, D. B. (1996). Assessing family resources, priorities, and concerns. In M. McLean, D. B. Bailey, & M. Wolery (Eds.), *Assessing infants and preschoolers with special needs* (pp. 202–233). Englewood Cliffs, NJ: Prentice Hall.

Barnett, D. W. (1984). An organizational approach to preschool services: Psychological screening, assessment, and intervention. In C. Maher, R. Illback, & J. Zins (Eds.), *Organizational psychology in the schools: A handbook for practitioners* (pp. 53–82). Springfield, IL: C.C. Thomas.

Bayley, N. (1993). *Bayley Scales of Infant Development—II.* San Antonio, TX: Psychological Corporation.

Benner, S. M. (1992). *Assessing young children with special needs: An ecological perspective.* New York: Longman.

Boehm, A., & Sandberg, B. (1982). Assessment of the preschool child. In C. R. Reynolds & T. B. Gutkin (Eds.), *Handbook of School Psychology* (pp. 82–120). New York: Wiley.

Bondurant-Utz, J. A. (1994). The team process. In J. A. Bondurant-Utz & L. B. Luciano (Eds.), *A practical guide to infant and preschool assessment in special education* (pp. 59–72). Boston: Allyn & Bacon.

Bracken, B. A. (1984). *Bracken Basic Concept Scale.* San Antonio, TX: Psychological Corporation.

Bracken, B. A. (1987). Limitations of preschool instruments and standards for minimal levels of technical adequacy. *Journal of Psychoeducational Assessment, 4,* 313–326.

Bracken, B. A. (1994). Advocating for effective preschool assessment practices. A comment on Bagnato and Neisworth. *School Psychology Quarterly, 9*(2), 103–108.

Bracken, B. A., Bagnato, S. J., & Barnett, D. W. (1991). *Early Childhood Assessment.* Position statement adopted by the National Association of School Psychologists Delegate Assembly, March 24, 1991.

Bracken, B. A., Keith, L. K., & Walker, K. C. (1994). Assessment of preschool behavior and socioemotional functioning: A review of thirteen third-party instruments. *Assessment in Rehabilitation and Exceptionality, 1,* 331–346.

Bracken, B. A., & Walker, K. C. (1997). The utility of intelligence tests for preschool children. In D. P. Flanagan, J. L. Genshaft, & P. C. Harrison (Eds.), *Contemporary intellectual assessment: Theories, tests, and issues* (pp. 484–502). New York: Guilford.

Burgemeister, B. B., Blum, L. H., & Lorge, I. (1972). *Columbia Mental Maturity Scale.* New York: Harcourt Brace Jovanovich.

Carran, D. T., & Scott, K. G. (1992). Risk assessment in preschool children: Research implications for the early detection of educational handicaps. *Topics in Early Childhood Special Education, 12,* 196–211.

Carta, J. J., & Greenwood, C. R. (1985). Ecobehavioral assessment: A methodology for expanding the evaluation of early intervention programs. *Topics in Early Childhood Special Education, 5,* 88–104.

Culbertson, J. L., & Willis, D. J. (1993). Introduction to testing young children. In J. L. Culbertson & D. J. Willis (Eds.), *Testing young children: A reference guide for developmental, psychoeducational, and psychosocial assessments* (pp. 1–10). Austin, TX: Pro-Ed.

Danaher, J. (1995). *Preschool special education eligibility classifications.* Chapel Hill, NC: National Early Childhood Technical Assistance System.

DiSimoni, F. (1978). *The Token Test for Children.* Allen, TX: DLM/Teaching Resources.

Dunn, L. M., & Dunn, L. M. (1981). *Peabody Picture Vocabulary Test—Revised.* Circle Pines, MN: American Guidance Service.

Elliot, C. D. (1990). *Differential Ability Scales: Introductory and technical handbook.* San Antonio, TX: Psychological Corporation.

Epps, S., & Jackson, B. J. (1991). Professional preparation of psychologists for family-centered service delivery to at-risk infants and toddlers. *School Psychology Review, 8,* 311–318.

Fitzgibbon, C. T., & Morris, L. L. (1987). *How to design a program evaluation.* Newbury Park, CA: Sage.

Flanagan, D. P., & Alfonso, V. C. (1995). A critical review of the technical characteristics of new and recently revised intelligence tests for preschool children. *Journal of Psychoeducational Assessment, 13,* 66–90.

Flanagan, D. P., Sainato, D. M., & Genshaft, J. L. (1993). Emerging issues in the assessment of young children with disabilities: The expanding role of school psychologists. *Canadian Journal of School Psychology, 9* (2), 192–203.

Gredler, G. R. (1997). Issues in early childhood screening and assessment. *Psychology in the Schools, 24,* 99–106.

Gyurke, J. S. (1994). A reply to Bagnarto and Neisworth: Intelligent versus intelligence testing of preschoolers. *School Psychology Quarterly, 9,* 109–112.

Harbin, G. L., Gallagher, J. J., & Terry, D. V. (1991). Defining the eligibility population: Policy issues and challenges. *Journal of Early Intervention, 15,* 13–20.

Kaufman, A. S., & Kaufman, N. L. (1983). *Kaufman Assessment Battery for Children.* Circle Pines, MN: American Guidance Service.

Kelley, M. P., & Melton, G. B. (1993). Ethical and legal issues. In J. L. Culbertson & D. J. Willis (Eds.), *Testing young children: A reference guide for developmental, psychoeducational, and psychosocial assessments* (pp. 408–426). Austin, TX: Pro-Ed.

Kelley, M. F., & Surbeck, E. (1991). History of preschool assessment. In B. A. Bracken (Ed.), *The psychoeducational assessment of preschool children* (2nd ed., pp. 1–17). Boston: Allyn & Bacon.

Klein, N. K., & Campbell, P. (1990). Preparing personnel to serve at-risk and disabled infants, toddlers, and preschoolers. In S. J. Meisels & J. P. Shonkoff (Eds.), *Handbook of early childhood intervention* (pp. 679–699). New York: Cambridge University Press.

Lichtenstein, R., & Ireton, H. (1991). Preschool screening for developmental and educational problems. In B. A. Bracken (Ed.), *The psychoeducational assessment of preschool children* (2nd ed., pp. 486–513). Boston, MA: Allyn & Bacon.

Lidz, C. S. (1991). Issues in the assessment of preschool children. In B. A. Bracken (Ed.), *The psychoeducational assessment of preschool children* (2nd ed., pp. 18–31). Boston: Allyn & Bacon.

Linder, T. W. (1993). *Transdisciplinary play-based assessment: A functional approach to working with young children.* Baltimore: Paul H. Brookes.

Martin, R. D. (1991). Assessment of social and emotional behavior. In B. A. Bracken (Ed.), *The psychoeducational assessment of preschool children.* (2nd ed., pp. 450–464). Boston: Allyn & Bacon.

McCarthy, D. (1972). *The McCarthy Scales of Children's Abilities.* San Antonio, TX: Psychological Corporation.

McLean, M. (1996). Assessment and its importance in early intervention/early childhood special education. In M. McLean, D. B. Bailey, & M. Wolery (Eds.), *Assessing infants and preschoolers with special needs* (pp. 1–22). Englewood Cliffs, NJ: Prentice Hall.

McLean, M., & Crais, E. R. (1996). Procedural considerations in assessing infants and preschoolers with disabilities. In M. McLean, D. B. Bailey, & M. Wolery (Eds.), *Assessing infants and preschoolers with special needs* (pp. 46–68). Englewood Cliffs, NJ: Prentice Hall.

McLinden, S. E., & Prasse, D. P. (1991). Providing services to infants and toddlers under P.L. 99-457: Training needs of school psychologists. *School Psychology Review, 20,* 37–48.

Meisels, S. J., & Provence, S. (1989). *Screening and assessment: Guidelines for identifying young disabled and developmentally vulnerable children and their families.* Washington, DC: National Center for Infants, Toddlers and Families.

Miller, L. J. (1982). *Miller Assessment for Preschoolers.* Littleton, CO: Foundation for Knowledge and Development.

Mindes, G., Ireton, H., & Mardell-Czudnowski, C. (1996). *Assessing young children.* New York: Delmar.

Mowder, B. A. (1996). Preparing school psychologists. In D. Bricker & A. Widerstrom (Eds.), *Preparing personnel to work with infants and young children and their families: A team approach.* Baltimore: Paul H. Brookes.

Mowder, B. A., Widerstrom, A. H., & Sandall, S. R. (1989). School psychologists serving at-risk and handicapped infants, toddlers, and their families. *Professional School Psychology, 4,* 159–172.

Myers, C. L., McBride, S. L., & Peterson, C. A. (1996). Transdisciplinary, play-based assessment in early childhood special education: An examination of social validity. *Topics in Early Childhood Special Education, 16*(1), 102–126.

Newborg, J., Stock, J. R., Wnek, L., Guidubaldi, J., & Svinivki, J. (1984). *Battelle Developmental Inventory.* Allen, TX: DLM/Teaching Resources.

Paget, K. D. (1991). The individual assessment situation: Basic considerations for preschool-age children. In B. Bracken (Ed.), *The psychoeducational assessment of preschool children* (pp. 32–39). Boston: Allyn & Bacon.

Paget, K. D., & Barnett, D. W. (1990). Assessment of infants, toddlers, preschool children, and their families: Emergent trends. In T. B. Gutkin & C. R. Reynolds, (Eds.) *The handbook of school psychology* (2nd ed., pp. 458–486). New York: Wiley.

Paget, K. D., & Nagle, R. J. (1986). A conceptual model of preschool assessment. *School Psychology Review, 15*(2), 154–165.

Parker, S. J., & Zuckerman, B. S. (1990). Therapeutic aspects of the assessment process. In S. J. Meisels & J. P. Shonkoff (Eds.), *Handbook of early childhood intervention* (pp. 350–369). New York: Cambridge University Press.

Poulsen, M. K. (1996). Preparing pediatric psychologists. In D. Bricker & A. Widerstrom (Eds.), *Preparing personnel to work with infants and young children and their families: A team approach.* Baltimore: Paul H. Brookes.

Preator, K. K., & McAllister, J. R. (1995). Assessing infants and toddlers. In A. Thomas & J. Grimes (Eds.), *Best practices in school psychology—III* (pp. 775–788). Washington, DC: National Association of School Psychologists.

Romero, I. (1992). Individual assessment procedures with preschool children. In E. Vazqez-Nuttal, I. Romero, & J. Kalesnik (Eds.), *Assessing and screening preschoolers: Psychological and educational dimensions* (pp. 55–66). Boston: Allyn & Bacon.

Thorndike, R. L., Hagen, E. P., & Sattler, J. M. (1986). *Stanford-Binet Intelligence Scale, Fourth Edition.* Chicago: Riverside.

Ulrey, G. (1982). Influence of preschooler's behavior on assessment. In G. Ulrey & S. J. Rogers (Eds.), *Psychological assessment of handicapped infants and handicapped children* (pp. 25–34). New York: Thiemme-Stratton.

Vandiver, P., & Suarez, T. M. (1980). *An evaluator's resource handbook.* Chapel Hill, NC: Technical Assistance Development Center.

Wechsler, D. (1967). *Wechsler Preschool and Primary Scale of Intelligence.* San Antonio, TX: Psychological Corporation.

Wechsler, D. (1989). *Manual for the Wechsler Preschool and Primary Scale of Intelligence—Revised.* San Antonio, TX: Psychological Corporation.

Woodcock, R. W., & Mather, N. (1989, 1990). WJ-R Tests of Cognitive Ability—Standard and Supplemental Batteries: Examiner's Manual. In R. W. Woodcock & M. B. Johnson, *Woodcock-Johnson Psychoeducational Battery—Revised.* Allen, TX: DLM Teaching Resources.

CHAPTER 3

MAXIMIZING CONSTRUCT RELEVANT ASSESSMENT
THE OPTIMAL PRESCHOOL TESTING SITUATION

BRUCE A. BRACKEN

The purpose for conducting psychoeducational assessments is to gain information about the child's current level of functioning within any of several important domains (e.g., cognitive, motor, language, personality, academic). Gathering this information enables the examiner to accurately describe and classify the child's abilities within and across the various domains. Assessment information is then used to guide decision makers concerning the need for and types of treatments or interventions that should be implemented.

An assumption made about the psychoeducational assessment process is that examiners have made every effort to eliminate all identifiable construct-irrelevant influences on the child's performance and the resultant test scores. That is, the goal in assessment is to limit assessment to only construct-relevant attributes (e.g., intelligence), while limiting the influences of construct-irrelevant sources of variation (e.g., fatigue, lack of cooperation, emotional lability). Before important decisions can be made with confidence about a child's future educational plans, possible treatments, or medications, examiners must be comfortable with the validity of the assessment results. Only when all construct-irrelevant sources of variation have been eliminated or optimally controlled can examiners attest to the validity of the assessment results.

This chapter will identify common sources of construct-irrelevant influences on young children's assessment performance and will suggest means by which examiners can moderate these unwanted sources of variation by establishing and controlling the examining situation. Many sources of construct-irrelevant variance can be effectively moderated through careful attention; however, some of these influences can never be fully controlled. Examining children's assessment performance in light of these unwanted influences will help explain young children's variable performance on psychometric evaluations and will contribute to a fuller understanding of the child's true skills and abilities.

Conducting assessments in a standardized fashion while employing astute clinical skill and wise selection of instruments will go a long way toward reducing major sources of construct-irrelevant variability in children's test performance. This chapter will address the issue of construct relevance and irrelevance, and suggest means by which examiners can maximize the assessment of the desired construct while controlling threats to validity. That is, this chapter will describe means by which careful attention to the examining situation can facilitate the examiner's valid assessment of preschool children.

CONSTRUCT-RELEVANT VERSUS CONSTRUCT-IRRELEVANT INFLUENCES ON YOUNG CHILDREN'S TEST PERFORMANCE

Examiners should be aware that some influences on a child's test performance may be considered construct relevant, whereas in other instances the same source of variation may be considered construct irrelevant. The examiner must decide when such variation is useful to understanding the child's performance and when it inhibits a clear understanding of the child's abilities. For example, a bilingual child's English language proficiency would be considered construct relevant if the purpose of the evaluation was to determine the child's understanding and use of the English language. However, if the intent of the assessment was to measure the child's visual-spatial skills, use of a test that is heavily laden with verbal directions (e.g., Performance subtests of the WPPSI-R) would produce some degree of construct-irrelevant variance related to English facility and comprehension.

To conduct fair assessments, examiners must decide which constructs are targeted for the assessment and identify the construct-irrelevant variables that threaten the validity of the assessment. Furthermore, examiners should consider and moderate, to whatever extent possible, the influences of these threats to validity. In the previous example, use of a nonverbal test of ability could reduce the language-related threat to validity and allow for a "purer" measure of the construct (i.e., visual-spatial skills) without the confound of language proficiency. In a similar fashion, bicultural children's level of assimilation into the dominant society may constitute a construct-irrelevant influence on their test performance when instruments are heavily loaded with "cultural content" (McGrew & Flanagan, 1998), even when the test is administered without verbal directions.

In addition to linguistic proficiency and enculturation, other variables that may be considered either construct relevant or construct irrelevant, depending on the context, include prior educational and life experiences, exposure to various media, physical and sensory abilities, family socioeconomic status, and many other such influences. When a variable is identified as irrelevant to the assessed construct and yet negatively influences the child's test performance, that variable should be considered as a source of test bias and should be eliminated or moderated to as great an extent as possible. For example, when assessing a visually impaired child's school readiness skills, the examiner should strive to reduce the effects of the visual disability on the child's ability to demonstrate his or her readiness skills. Moderating the effects of the visual impairment might include such situational modifications as arranging seating and lighting to facilitate the child's view of test stimuli (e.g., reducing glare, emphasizing the contrast between light and dark), ensuring that the child wears or uses prescribed corrective devices, and modifying the test stimuli when necessary (e.g., using larger than standard print or stimulus matter).

Although a child's limited range of life experiences cannot be moderated during the assessment process, knowledge of such limitations might temper the examiner's interpretation of the child's test results. A child who has had limited previous experience with the use of puzzles, blocks, and paper and pencil may perform poorly on any of the similar experientially oriented cognitive tasks typically found on early childhood intelligence tests. The child's poor test performance, which is related at least in part to a lack of educational experiences, would negatively influence the child's test performance and lower the child's overall intelligence quotient.

Given typical preschool and primary grade curricular experiences, the assessed experiential weakness may be easily "remediated" once the child is exposed to these activities in a systematic fashion. It would be a mistake to place too much emphasis on the child's artificially lowered overall intelligence, especially on tests that weight heavily educationally related visual-motor skills, when the diminished test performance was due largely to a lack of previous educational opportunity or experience.

MODERATING CONSTRUCT-IRRELEVANT INFLUENCES ON STUDENTS' TEST PERFORMANCE

There are four principal sources of construct-irrelevant influences on children's psychoeducational assessment results: (1) the examinee, (2) the examiner, (3) the environment, and (4) the instrument employed. The remainder of the chapter will address each of these four primary influences and suggest means by which examiners can moderate these unwanted influences by creating an examining situation that facilitates testing and reduces known threats to validity.

Examinee

It may seem odd that a child would be considered a possible source of construct-irrelevant influence on his or her own test performance. However, personal variables and behaviors, both within and outside the child's sphere of control, influence the child's day-to-day demonstration of his or her abilities in ways that can be observed and moderated. To whatever extent possible, these variables should be recognized and controlled during assessments, or at least considered when examiners evaluate the validity of children's assessment results.

Health. In addition to standard examiner inquiries regarding the examinee's health, examiners should be observant of children's apparent health prior to initiating an assessment. Children who show symptoms of an illness, even an illness as mild as the common cold, may experience sluggish mental processing, slower speed of response, diminished ability to find the right word or produce a definition, lessened motivation, and/or decreased energy, concentration, or interest. Children who are ill or who are becoming ill often lack the physical and mental strength and acuity to perform optimally during an evaluation. Such health-related threats to assessment validity should be considered seriously and addressed.

Young children quickly develop physical symptoms and, fortunately, their health often improves just as quickly. When children are not in optimal health or shows signs or symptoms of an oncoming illness (e.g., sniffles, fever, lethargy, complaint of pains, upset stomach), examiners should postpone the evaluation.

If an otherwise healthy child becomes ill shortly after an assessment has been conducted, the examiner should consider whether the child's assessment-related behavior was representative of his or her typical behavior. If the child's assessment behavior was atypical, the examiner should reconsider the validity of the assessment results. Some instruments, for example, the Bayley Scales of Infant Development, have individual rating scales that allow parents to indicate whether the child's assessment-related behavior was typical or atypical.

Importantly, examiners should evaluate children's physical symptoms associated with anxiety (e.g., stomachache, nausea) when considering whether an assessment should be postponed for days or merely delayed briefly until better rapport is established. Children often report somatic complaints when they are fearful or anxious, and examiners should strive to reduce those complaints by alleviating the child's fear and anxiety. In such instances, postponement would not be appropriate, but the expenditure of a little more effort and time to establish a better rapport would be warranted.

Fatigue/Restfulness.   Related to overall health considerations is the child's state of restfulness. With preschool children, it is generally a good idea to conduct assessments as early in the day as possible, within reason. Because young children typically take naps (or need naps) after lunch and then wear themselves out again by late afternoon, assessments are often more easily and validly conducted during the morning hours when children are alert and fresh.

Children who are tired often become "cranky," which can negatively affect their cooperation, motivation, and subsequent test performance. Therefore, examiners should be sensitive to signs of fatigue and offer children breaks in an effort to keep the children's energy level and participation at an optimal level. From a purely behavioral management standpoint, it behooves examiners to assess children who are alert and well rested—or the examiner should be prepared to struggle with the children's misbehavior and diminished effort throughout the assessment.

Fear/Anxiety.   Because young children typically are not experienced with the formal nature of psychoeducational evaluations, fear and anxiety are common examinee reactions at the beginning of assessments. An

optimal level of examinee arousal is highly desired to ensure that the children are sufficiently motivated to perform tasks with their best effort. However, the assessment should not start or continue when children's arousal and anxiety have reached a level that debilitates or impairs the children's spontaneity, concentration, or active participation. The examiner should allay children's fears and anxiety by establishing a comfortable, safe, and engaging environment before initiating testing.

The manner by which examiners greet preschool children can do a lot to initiate a good testing situation. Examiners should meet preschool children by stooping or squatting down to the children's height and offer a friendly, low-key greeting. If a child is reticent and not easily approached, the examiner might stand and shift his or her attention to the parent or guardian who accompanied the child to the evaluation. By addressing the parent, the examiner will allow the child an opportunity to become familiar with the setting and the examiner, and learn a bit about the examiner through the parent–examiner interactions. Gradually the child will become slightly bored by the lack of interaction with the adults, and will become more open to interacting with the examiner.

When the child shows signs of interest in the examiner or the assessment environment, the examiner can re-engage the child by offering to show the child around. Once the child's fears and anxieties have subsided, the examiner should gently "shepherd" the child to the examining room to begin the assessment. Shepherding of this sort is a process by which the examiner guides the child to the examining room by allowing the child to walk in the lead. To effectively shepherd a child, the examiner should place a hand between the child's shoulder blades and gently "steer" the child with slight hand pressure to the desired location. Because children lead the way when shepherded in this fashion, they typically do not feel forced or coerced as when they are led by the hand to the testing location.

Motivation.   Some children are not motivated to demonstrate their potential during psychoeducational assessments for a variety of reasons. Preschool children's limited motivation sometimes is due to insufficient awareness or appreciation of the importance of the test results. Sometimes children do not find the test materials or activities very interesting or engaging, and, on occasion, the examiner or the child's parents have not sufficiently prepared the child for the types of tasks the child will be asked to complete. Also, some children become less motivated as the assessment progresses, and they are faced with tasks that are difficult or particularly challenging or that are not as fun as the child deems they should be.

To overcome initial instances of limited motivation among preschool examinees, the examiner must develop an introduction to the assessment process that prepares the child for what will occur. This introduction should be honest and (1) describe the types of tasks with which the child will be presented; (2) challenge the child to do his or her best on every task; (3) emphasize the importance of effort, persistence, and thoughtful responses; and (4) acknowledge that some of the activities will be difficult and beyond the current abilities of the child. The introduction should not suggest that the examiner and child will be playing games; however, it is fair to say that much of what the child will do will be fun. A sample introduction follows:

> Today we are going to do many interesting and exciting things together. We will work with blocks and puzzles; we'll be looking at some pictures; I'm going to ask you to draw some things for me; and I'll ask you to tell me the answers to some questions. We'll have a good time together. I won't expect you to be able to do everything I ask you to do because some of the things we will do are meant for older children. It's okay if you can't do some of the things I ask you to do, but I want you to try your very best anyway. Let's get going and try some of the fun things I have for you.

During the assessment, if the child's motivation begins to wane, the examiner should remind the child of the salient aspects of the previous paragraph (e.g., "Remember, I told you some of these things would be hard to do." or "That was a tough puzzle wasn't it? I like how well you worked on it even though it was hard for you."). Reinforcing the child's effort is another means of motivating the child to concentrate and give full effort. It is important that the examiner reinforce the child's effort rather than success; otherwise the reinforcement will abruptly end and become painfully absent when the child begins to fail more difficult items. It is also wise to remind the child that some of the items were intended for older children (actually children who are more able, whether due to age or ability), and that the child isn't expected to be successful on every task or item attempted.

Preparing the child in such a fashion before the child begins to experience frequent failure is more timely and helpful than after the child has already failed a succession of items. Warning the child before failure can forestall frustration by challenging the child to attempt the predicted tough problems; reminding the child after failure often is seen as pardoning the child's failures, which can increase the child's frustration and sense of failure.

Temperament. Examiners can facilitate the assessment of preschool children if they accommodate the temperament styles of their examinees. By considering each of the nine temperament characteristics identified by Thomas and Chess (1977), the examiner might better schedule the assessment, approach the examinee, address the child's needs, guide the assessment, and even select the instruments appropriate for administration. In short, the examiner should seek to create the best fit between the child and the assessment situation (Carey & McDevitt, 1995; Chess & Thomas, 1992).

Each child can be expected to demonstrate a *level of activity* that is different from other children the examiner has evaluated. Expecting all young children to sit cooperatively in a chair for an hour or longer and participate actively in an assessment is unrealistic. If the examiner knows before the assessment, either through parent report or observation, that the child is generally active, the examiner can plan ahead to accommodate the child's desire or need to move about. Understanding and accommodating the needs of children by differentially allowing them to stand, move about, handle test materials, and take action breaks can go a long way toward maintaining rapport once it has been established. To be effective, the examiner must note, be sensitive to, and plan ahead for the active child.

Selecting an appropriate time to begin an assessment and being sensitive to children's biological needs should be based on the child's rhythmicity, that is, the predictability of a child's bodily and somatic functions (e.g., times when the child is most alert, responsivity after lunch, how the child interacts after a nap). The examiner should select a window of opportunity for assessment in which the child is predictably in his or her best form.

In addition to children's differential response to routines, children do not all respond in the same manner when approached by others. Some children respond in kind, whereas others withdraw. The child's *approach or withdrawal* tendency should be considered when planning how to best meet and greet the child. If the child is known to respond positively to a forward, gregarious introduction and approach, then the examiner should exude enthusiasm and excitement and boldly introduce himself or herself. However, if the child is more reticent and timid and typically withdraws from strangers, the examiner should proceed slowly and entice the child's participation through subtle engagement. Again, parent or teacher reports or behavioral observations in a classroom can provide information about the child's typical response to being approached by others.

Although some children are very flexible and respond favorably and without comment to unanticipated changes in routines or schedules, some children are hypersensitive to any change in routine or schedule, anticipated or not. Advanced knowledge about the *adaptability* of children to changes in routine will forewarn the examiner about how the child will likely respond to being taken from routine activities for an assessment. The examiner may identify activities that are viewed less favorably by the child than others and plan the assessment at a time when the child will be "excused" from participating in the less desirable activity, thereby lessening the intensity of the child's response to an unpredicted change in routine.

By observing a child in the classroom, examiners can consider the child's unique level of *intensity of reaction* in various situations. Once this information is known, examiners can better anticipate the child's needs and provide as much emotional support, structure, or patience as necessary when the child begins to experience frustration and failure. Similarly, examiners should note the child's *threshold of responsiveness* to stimuli during classroom observations; that is, how much stimulation does it take to evoke a response from the child? The examiner might arrange the instruments and activities in an assessment to accommodate the child as necessary. For example, if the child is slow to warm up and does not respond initially to tasks that require active participation and verbal exchange, the examiner might begin with high-interest, less demanding tasks (e.g., having the child draw pictures as an ice-breaking activity). Once the child becomes more comfortable, the examiner can introduce tasks that are more demanding and require more active participation and social interaction.

The nature and quality of the child's typical *mood* should be considered prior to an evaluation, that is, the sort of mood that characteristically defines the child, such as sadness, anxiety, anger, apathy, happiness, and so on. Anticipating the child's typical mood should help the examiner prepare strategies for working with children who are known or observed to be difficult as opposed to those who are typically positive and cooperative.

Although many preschool children are by nature *distractible* and have short *attention spans* and limited *persistence,* examiners should be prepared to present the assessment according to the pace of the child. By keeping the assessment sufficiently quick-paced, examiners can minimize the effects of a child's short attention span and limited persistence. By organizing and arranging the examining room in a manner to minimize visual and auditory distractions, the examiner also can better limit the distractibility of young examinees.

Examiner Characteristics

Examiners can directly and indirectly influence the examining situation through their appearance, dress, and the manner in which they interact with the child. This section of the chapter addresses examiner characteristics that enhance the examining situation and reduce the potential threats to validity related to unwanted or undesired examiner characteristics.

Approachability/Affect. The examiner must create just the right impression to be perceived as approachable by young children. This impression is a tightrope walk that requires a balance between being formal and business-like on one hand to being fun, interesting, and humorous on the other hand. Young children often "read" examiners and respond according to the behavioral messages communicated by the examiner. When an examiner presents himself or herself in a formal manner, children may perceive the examiner as relatively cold, harsh, or unaccepting—but importantly as someone who cannot be easily manipulated. If the examiner comes across as lively and entertaining, the child may perceive the examiner as someone who will be enjoyable to interact with. But such an examiner may also be seen as a playmate with whom roles can be negotiated, requests can be refused, and who is not necessarily to be taken seriously.

It is important that the examiner balance the need to be approachable with the necessity of communicating that the examiner is the person who is in charge. The examiner can maintain this delicate balance by pleasantly but clearly establishing expectations and firm limits. Clear expectations can be communicated in part by stating directives rather making requests. Requests are polite forms of communication we tend to use with other adults, but requests imply that the other person has the right to refuse. In a testing situation examiners should not give the impression of choice unless choice is truly intended. For example, examiners should say to examinees, "I want you to sit here" rather than "Would you like to sit here?". The former statement is a clear directive to be followed and implies no option, whereas the latter question permits the child to say, "No" or "I want to sit over there." The rule of thumb is that examiners should propose questions or choices only when they are willing to go along with any answer or choice made by the examinee. If the examiner intends no choice, he or she should simply state an unambiguous directive with a warm, engaging smile.

Physical Presence. The examiner should maintain a physical appearance that is conducive to assessing young children. Because many infant and preschool tests require active motor participation on behalf of the examiner, examiners should wear comfortable shoes and clothing that allow for easy performance of motor activities such as skipping, jumping, balancing on one foot, and so on. Also, because young children sometimes will attempt to slide under the examining table to avoid participation, examiners' clothes should readily permit them to crawl, kneel, or sit on the floor.

Examiners should also limit the amount of jewelry they wear during assessments so they do not distract young children with unintended visual or auditory distractions. For example, when performing the Hand Movements subtest of the Kaufman Assessment Battery for Children (K-ABC; Kaufman & Kaufman, 1983), examiners should avoid the distracting clinking sounds that are made when rings, watches, or bracelets come in contact with the table top. Similarly, bright, stimulating earrings, pins, broaches, necklaces, and neckties can create attractive but unwanted visual distractions for young children who would be better served by focusing on test materials rather than the examiner's apparel.

Rapport. Establishing rapport with young children can be challenging for many reasons, but with some flexibility and effort meaningful rapport can be fairly easily established. To establish rapport with young children, examiners have to overcome children's fears, trepidations, shyness, reticence, and reluctance. To overcome these negative conditions, it is imperative that the children quickly develop a sense of physical and emotional safety and comfort. Such conditions can be developed by displaying a personal attitude that is both engaging and sensitive.

To facilitate the maintenance of rapport, examiners should ensure that the testing environment is prepared for a variety of potentially disruptive situations. Plans should be made to ensure that someone is available to assist young examinees in using the bathroom when necessary; tissues should be at hand to dab crying eyes and wipe ubiquitous running noses; play materials should be

available to develop children's interest or to motivate the children when their interests have waned; and examiners should ensure that drawing paper and pencils or coloring materials are available for both informal assessment activities as well as to create a gift the child can proudly hand parents when the assessment is complete. Also, hand puppets, stuffed animals, or other such engaging materials are often useful for establishing rapport or comforting young children because these objects allow examinees to talk indirectly to the examiner. Examiners should anticipate possible situations that could jeopardize rapport and be prepared to deal with these situations proactively and constructively.

Behavior Management. To conduct psychoeducational evaluations with young children, examiners need good behavior management skills. Examiners must know when and how to effectively ask, direct, cajole, tease, laugh, act silly, be stern, reinforce, admonish, talk, be quiet, pat the child's head or hand affectionately, slow down or speed up the administration pace, show genuine empathy, and perform a variety of related behaviors with appropriate timing and sufficient sincerity to maintain the child's motivation, cooperation, and participation.

Preschool children frequently cry when frustrated or when they wish to avoid an activity, and novice examiners often are fearful of crying children. Knowing that a child's crying typically becomes exacerbated when one actively tries to stop the crying, it is usually better to sit back and let children cry until they are ready to stop on their own. With tissue in hand, the examiner should wait until the child stops crying, and then tenderly dab the child's final tears soothingly, and immediately redirect the child to the next assessment task without comment. Mentioning the child's crying frequently results in the child's tears flowing again.

Given the labile emotions, variable activity level, and typical distractibility of preschool children, examiners need well-developed behavior management skills. Examiners also need to recognize which examinee behaviors alert the examiner to potential problems, and the examiner should proactively and subtly change the course of the situation before the child's behavior requires direct intervention. It is always better to maintain rapport than to try to reestablish it once it has been lost.

Psychometric Skill. Proper and well-paced administration of tests during an assessment is essential for maintaining rapport and managing young children's behavior. Whereas adolescents may sit patiently (or sullenly) and wait for the examiner to fumble through the administration of a new instrument, preschool children are not known for their patience. Idle hands do in fact make the devil's work when young children are expected to sit for even brief periods while the examiner readies materials, rereads directions, reviews scoring criteria, or searches for needed stimuli. Therefore, examiners are best served by keeping the child actively engaged in appropriately paced assessment activities.

To facilitate test administration, examiners should be very familiar with the tests they select to administer. Examiners also should prepare the assessment room prior to the child's arrival and have test kits set up for immediate use. The pace of testing throughout the assessment should be controlled by the examiner and should match the characteristics and needs of the examinee. The pace of an assessment can be adequately controlled only when the examiner has mastered its administration features and is familiar with its item content and stimulus materials.

Experience with Preschool Children. Examiners who plan to assess preschool children should be familiar with the developmental characteristics of this age group. Anyone who attributes adult or adolescent motivations to preschool children's behavior simply does not understand how young children operate. If the examiner is to effectively reduce construct irrelevant variance in preschool assessments, he or she must be both comfortable and experienced working with young children and must understand what is typical and atypical preschool behavior.

Environment

A comfortable testing environment sets the stage for a successful assessment, especially for young children. The effective assessment environment should be cheerful, convey safety, capitalize on the child's curiosity, and stimulate the child's participation. For a testing environment to do these things, it must be child oriented and friendly and accommodate the needs of young children.

Furniture. Examining rooms intended for preschool children should include furniture that is appropriately child-sized. Chairs should allow the children's feet to reach the floor; tabletops should be easily reached without straining; and bookshelves should be sufficiently low that the child can readily obtain the books, puzzles, or other objects that may be handled before or after the evaluation. Examining rooms should be furnished appropriately for preschool children rather than forcing preschool children to accommodate to adult-sized furniture and an adult-oriented environment.

Using child-sized furniture is not just a thoughtful consideration, it is an important safety factor. If children's feet do not touch the floor while sitting, circulation to their legs will be reduced, as will the sense of feeling in their legs. Such loss of feeling and the subsequent pins and needles sensation that accompany circulation when it is restored can cause children to wriggle about and increase the risk of their falling off or out of their chairs. Some young children opt to kneel or squat when tested in adult-sized chairs so they can better reach the materials on the tabletop. Squatting and kneeling, while a suitable alternative when necessary, can also lead to a loss of balance and unwanted falls if children are not closely watched. Also, examiners should consider that oversized chairs allow more than ample room for children to escape the assessment by squirming between the chair and table and onto the floor beneath the table.

Decorations. Examining rooms should be cheery, inviting places with interesting and colorful decorations. However, examining rooms should not be so stimulating that examinees will be distracted by the decor. Clean, nicely painted, appropriately furnished, and modestly decorated rooms will provide the desired environment for successful evaluations. When examining rooms include distracting decorations or window scenes, the examiner should arrange the seating to face the child away from the visual distractions. All efforts should be made to ensure that the most stimulating aspect of the examining room is the examiner and the test materials.

Distractions. In addition to limiting visual distractions associated with decorations (e.g., windows, pictures, posters), the examiner should ensure that other distractions are similarly subdued. For example, telephones should be set so they do not ring during assessments; a "Do Not Disturb" sign should be placed on the examining room door; noise from hallways or adjacent rooms should be controlled; and every effort should be made to ensure that the assessment will be conducted in a room that is conducive to concentration. Young children are often easily affected by visual, auditory, or personal distractions, and those children who wish to terminate an evaluation require very little extraneous distraction to direct their attention away from the evaluation.

Climate Control. Examining rooms should be maintained with temperatures that are sufficiently warm so that the children do not sit in a hypothermic stupor, and the rooms should be sufficiently cool so that the children aren't lulled into a drowsy semihypnotic state. Often examiners are required to use rooms (e.g., cloak rooms, closets, boiler rooms) that were not designed for educational or psychological activities, and such examining rooms are frequently too small for adequate or easily moderated climate control. When locating a more suitable room is not possible, the examiner should open windows or keep doors ajar to allow fresh cool (or warm) air to circulate.

Table/Chair Arrangement.   Much can be done to maximize behavior management through the arrangement of office furniture. When examining young, squirmy children, the examiner can maximize control by providing subtle artificial boundaries and structure. To control an active child, especially one who would choose to leave his or her seat on whim, the examiner should place the back legs of the child's chair against a wall—thereby disallowing the child to move his or her chair backward. The table can then be slid gently against the child's abdomen and thus be used as a friendly barrier to keep the child from getting up at unwanted times.

When the room is configured in such a manner that the child's chair cannot be placed against a wall, the examiner should sit across an adjacent corner of the table from the child. This position allows the examiner to sit in close proximity to the child and thereby respond easily and quickly to the child's needs or actions. Such a position also permits the examiner to reposition the child in his or her chair when necessary. For example, a friendly tussle of the child's hair or a tender pat on the shoulder, when done at just the right time, can subtly keep the child from rising in his or her chair. A gentle pat on the back can bring the child closer to the tabletop and work area. Similarly, by placing one foot behind the front leg of the child's chair, the examiner can maintain the position of a squirmy child's chair so it remains in close proximity to the table, workspace, and the examiner.

However the room is situated, the examiner should ensure that the child is positioned farther from the door than the examiner. By carefully arranging the seating, the examiner can forestall the child's efforts to separate from the testing materials and be in a better position to keep the child from leaving the room. By positioning himself or herself closer to the door, the examiner can cut off any attempts by the child to exit the room.

Psychometric Considerations

Although examiners can moderate many of the previously mentioned threats to validity by employing clinical judgment and skill, examiners have no means to control or alter the foibles associated with the various instruments they have available for use. Examiners can and should, however, select instruments for use only after carefully considering each instrument's psychometric properties and unique characteristics.

Bracken (1988) identified 10 common psychometric reasons why similar tests produce dissimilar results. The intent of that article was to reveal common psychometric threats to validity, which may or may not be obvious upon casual viewing of test manuals and materials. In an error-free world, tests that purport to assess the same construct (e.g., intelligence) should produce identical results when administered to the same child. Sometimes, however, tests that purport to measure the same construct produce results that are significantly discrepant from each other, and the reasons for such discrepancies often are related to construct-irrelevant psychometric limitations of the instruments (Bracken, 1987). The remainder of this section will address these construct-irrelevant conditions and recommend possible solutions to these common psychometric limitations.

Test Floors.   The floor of a test is an indication of the extent to which an instrument provides meaningful scores at very low levels of individual functioning. Given that psychoeducational assessments are conducted at times to diagnose delayed or retarded levels of functioning, it is important that examiners use tests that are capable of reliably and accurately assessing such low levels of functioning. Examiners should ensure that the tests they use are in fact capable of producing suitably low scores for the delayed children they serve. Bracken (1987) recommended that a *minimal* standard for subtest, composite, and total test floors should equal or exceed minus two standard deviations (i.e., the minimal level traditionally required to diagnose retarded functioning).

To identify the floor of a subtest, the examiner should locate the lowest possible standard score that would be obtained at every age level, if the examinee were to pass a single item on that subtest. For any age at which a subtest raw score of 1 fails to generate a standard score equal to or greater than −2 standard deviations, the subtest is insufficiently sensitive to accurately identify seriously delayed functioning. To determine the floors of composite or total test scores, the examiner should identify the corresponding standard score associated with an earned raw score of 1 on each of the subtests that contribute to the composite or total test. If five subtests contribute to the composite, the examiner would identify the corresponding standard score associated with a raw score of 5. If the composite standard score is less than 2 standard deviations below the normative mean, the composite has an insufficient floor for identifying retarded-level functioning at the age level considered.

Historically, tests typically have insufficient floors for children below age 4 (Bracken, 1987), which results in construct-irrelevant reasons for the resulting inflated scores. That is, the child's test score would be inaccurate due in part to the psychometric foibles of the instrument used. Examiners must be especially careful to examine floors when conducting assessments on low-functioning young children, especially those younger than 4 years. When composite and total test scores are truncated due to the construct-irrelevant limitations of the instrument employed, that test should not be used to guide decisions about the child's diagnosis and placement. Such a test should be considered biased for children of that particular age and ability level.

Ceilings. Ceilings within tests refer to the extent to which subtest, composite, or total test scores accurately reflect upper extreme levels of functioning among examinees. Because gifted functioning is typically characterized as beginning at 2 or more standard deviations above the normative mean, tests intended for gifted identification should provide accurate scores at and above this criterion level. Ceilings are not generally as relevant among preschool tests as are test floors. It is easier to create suitable items for assessing the upper limits of young children's abilities than it is to develop items that discriminate between the extreme lower limits of ability at this age level. Conversely, it is more difficult to create items that accurately assess the upper extreme abilities of older adolescents than it is to develop items that assess lower limits of abilities among this older population.

Although ceiling limitations are relatively rare in preschool tests, examiners should be watchful just the same. Some tests (e.g., Kaufman Assessment Battery for Children; Kaufman & Kaufman, 1983) include subtests specifically designed for young children, which are discontinued for slightly older children. Subtests typically are discontinued within a battery when the subtests have serious ceiling or floor problems and are no longer appropriate for children at that age level. The Stanford-Binet, Fourth Edition (Thorndike, Hagen, & Sattler, 1986) is another example of a test with subtests that begin or discontinue at different age levels.

Item Gradients. Item gradients refer to how steeply graded standard scores are arranged in relation to their respective raw scores. Ideally, the incremental change in standard scores that results from one raw score unit to another (e.g., a raw score of 5 versus 6) should produce a comparably small standard score increase. Unfortunately, preschool tests are notorious for having steep item gradients, with correspondingly large standard score changes associated with minor increases or decreases in raw scores. When a test has steep item gradients, only a rough discrimination of ability results. Such crude discrimination between levels of ability leads to construct-irrelevant variation in the assessed construct that is related to the instrument rather than true differences in children's individual abilities.

Examiners should carefully examine norm tables for all age levels and determine the ages at which the test or subtests have item gradients that are too steep for accurate and finely graded discrimination of abilities. Bracken (1988) recommended that an increase or decrease of a single raw score should not alter the corresponding standard score by more than $1/3$ standard deviation. That is, a raw score of x (e.g., 25) on a given measure should not produce a standard score that is more than $1/3$ standard deviation greater than that would result from a raw score one integer less (i.e., $x - 1$ or 24). Tests with item gradients that are steeper than these guidelines are too crude to fairly assess individual differences in ability.

Reliability. Tests with low reliability produce proportionately large portions of subtest and composite variability that are due to measurement error rather than true differences in the construct. A test with an alpha coefficient of .80 will produce variance that is 80 percent reliable, while 20 percent of the variance would be related to measurement error. Obviously, error variance is construct irrelevant and examiners should selectively employ only preschool tests that possess reasonable levels of internal consistency and stability. Bracken (1988) suggested that .90 be set as an acceptable level of internal consistency and stability for total test scores. Subtest and composite reliabilities should approximate .80, with median subtest reliabilities equal to .80 or higher. These standards provide a reasonable rule of thumb to apply when selecting tests for individual assessments.

Validity. The essential element of construct-relevant assessment is test validity. Because validity is so important in assessment, test manuals are expected to provide thorough and convincing evidence of content, construct, and criterion-related validity (AERA, APA, NCME, 1985). Because validity is a continuous rather than a dichotomous variable and can range from total absence of validity to perfect validity (both of these absolutes are rare), examiners must determine whether the documentation and level of demonstrated validity justify use of the instrument for the intended purpose. Whenever a test with poor validity is used and contributes to the diagnostic decision-making process, the examiner knowingly introduces variance into the decision-making equation that is to a large extent construct irrelevant. Examiners have an ethical, professional, and legal responsibility to only use instruments of the highest quality, and validity should be the most important aspect of technical adequacy considered.

Norm Tables. Norm tables sometimes are an inadvertent contributor to construct-irrelevant variability in test scores. The norm tables of some preschool tests include age ranges that are too broad to be sensitive to the rapid growth and development that occur during the first 6 years of life (e.g., 6 months or 1 year age ranges). Norm tables for preschool tests should not exceed three-month intervals, and at the youngest age levels (i.e., birth to 2 years) norms should reflect intervals as brief as one or two months.

The easiest way to evaluate the quality of a norm table is to examine the difference in standard scores associated with a given raw score as you progress from one table to the next. If the standard score increases by large amounts (e.g., +1⅓ standard deviation), the test may provide too gross an estimate of ability to instill much confidence in the resultant scores. Consider the importance of norm table sensitivity for a child who is on the very upper cusp of one age level and who is about to "graduate" to the next age level. A good test should not produce a large difference in standard scores based solely on whether the child was tested yesterday, today, or tomorrow, especially when the raw score remains the same across these three days. If a test is sensitive to the construct being assessed, the child's obtained raw score should yield nearly identical standard scores across this hypothetical three-day range. For example, consider a child who is 2 years, 7 months, and 15 days old when tested on the McCarthy Scales of Children's Abilities (MSCA; McCarthy, 1972). If this child obtains a raw score of 37 across the McCarthy's five scales (see Bracken, 1988), her total test score (i.e., GCI) would be 112. However, if the same child earned an identical score on the following day when she was 2 years, 7 months, and 16 days old (i.e., just one day older), her subsequent GCI would be 101—a decrease in functioning by a full ⅔ standard deviation.

Examiners should strive to eliminate or reduce such construct-irrelevant influences in the assessment of pre-

school children by selecting tests with appropriately sensitive norm tables. Sensitivity is needed most at the youngest age levels when children's development occurs at the fastest pace.

Age of Norms. Examiners are ethically bound to use only the most recent editions of tests (e.g., NASP, APA Ethical Guidelines). There are several reasons for using only recent editions of tests, which include the benefits of improved and updated stimulus materials, the inclusion of recent perspectives and theoretical advances in the test, and the application of recent normative samples. This latter reason has direct implications for accurate assessment and decision making.

Flynn (1984, 1987, 1999) has demonstrated that on an international level, the general intelligence of the world's population is increasing at a rate of about 3 IQ points per decade. This increase in population intelligence is related to a variety of hypothesized factors, including improved diet and health care, the positive influences of various media, improved economic conditions among more individuals, and so on. Whatever the reason for this documented longitudinal improvement in intelligence, the implications for using outdated tests are clear. Outdated tests inflate the estimate of children's intelligence in direct proportion to the age of the norms.

Examiners who use tests that are one, two, or three decades old might expect test scores to be inflated by a magnitude of 3, 6, or 9 IQ points, respectively. Such differential effects of test age on assessed intelligence is not related directly to the construct being assessed but rather to the age of the norms. Therefore, examiners should not only be ethically bound but practically and professionally bound also to use only the most recent editions of instruments. When a test has not been revised within the past decade and a half, examiners should question whether to continue using the instrument. The McCarthy Scales of Children's Abilities, for example, was published originally in 1972 and has not been revised since. Examiners would be hard-pressed to defend using such an instrument with norms that are nearly 30 years old, given the construct-irrelevant influences of the age of the norms on the child's estimated level of functioning.

Basic Concepts in Test Directions. Before examiners can effectively assess a child's abilities with standardized instruments, they have to ensure that the child fully understands the test's directions. If a child fails to understand what is required of him or her while taking a test, then the test may assess listening comprehension or receptive vocabulary rather than the intended construct (e.g., intelligence). Researchers have consistently shown that the past several generations of preschool instruments have test directions that are replete with basic concepts beyond the typical child's understanding (Bracken, 1986, 1998; Flanagan & Alfonso, 1995; Flanagan, Alfonso, Kaminer, & Rader, 1995; Kaufman, 1978). When test directions are more complex than the required task, the test will not fairly assess the intended construct.

The relevance of test direction complexity and basic concept inclusion is especially important when assessing children who speak English as a second language or who speak a nonstandard form of English. Children from these linguistic groups may be especially disadvantaged when administered tests with complex verbal directions, especially when the construct purportedly assessed by the instrument is not language facility, fluency, or understanding. To avoid the construct-irrelevant influence of complex test directions, examiners should seek instruments that provide simple test directions, as well as demonstration and sample items that ensure that the child understands the nature of the task requirements before beginning task for credit. In some in which language comprehension is a central referral issue, nonverbal tests of ability may be warranted. Tests such as the Universal Nonverbal Intelligence Test (UNIT; Bracken & McCallum, 1998) or the Leiter International Performance Scale—Revised (Roid & Miller, 1997) were designed to be used when the examinee's language skills represent a construct-irrelevant contributor to test variance.

CONCLUSION

The focus of this chapter has been on creating an examining situation that systematically reduces construct-irrelevant influences in the assessment process and maximizes the examiner's confidence in the accuracy and interpretability of the test results. Examiners should employ clinical skill to reduce threats to the validity of the assessment by creating a safe, secure, and engaging environment. Examiners should also consider the child's current physical condition and health when planning an assessment and decide whether a valid estimate of the child's true abilities can be obtained given the child's current physical state. Finally, examiners should carefully examine and consider the psychometric properties and foibles of the instruments in their psychoeducational batteries. When tests fail to meet psychometric standards that are commonly considered as essential for testing older children, adolescents, and adults, these instruments should not be used for the assessment of preschool children either.

When examiners carefully consider and address these important intrapersonal, interpersonal, environmental, and psychometric issues, they systematically reduce the construct-irrelevant variability in examinees' test scores. By reducing the variability in test scores that is attributable to measurement error, examiners can have more confidence in the test results and thereby make more defensible decisions.

REFERENCES

AERA, APA, NCME. (1985). *Standards for educational and psychological testing.* Washington, DC: Author.

Bracken, B. A. (1986). Incidence of basic concepts in the directions of five commonly used American tests of intelligence. *School Psychology International, 7,* 1–10.

Bracken, B. A. (1987). Limitations of preschool instruments and standards for minimal levels of technical adequacy. *Journal of Psychoeducational Assessment, 4,* 313–326.

Bracken, B. A. (1988). Ten psychometric reasons why similar tests produce dissimilar results. *Journal of School Psychology, 26,* 155–166.

Bracken, B. A. (1998). *Bracken Basic Concept Scale—Revised.* San Antonio, TX: Psychological Corporation.

Bracken, B. A., & McCallum, R. S. (1998). *Universal Nonverbal Intelligence Test.* Itasca, IL: Riverside.

Carey, W. B., & McDevitt, S. C. (1995). *Coping with children's temperament.* New York: Basic Books.

Chess, S., & Thomas, A. (1992). Dynamics of individual behavioral development. In M. D. Levine, W. B. Carey, & A. C. Crocker (Eds.), *Developmental-behavioral pediatrics* (2nd ed., pp. 84–94). Philadelphia: Saunders.

Flanagan, D. P., & Alfonso, V. C. (1995). A critical review of the technical characteristics of new and recently revised intelligence tests for preschoolers. *Journal of Psychoeducational Assessment, 13,* 66–90.

Flanagan, D. P., Alfonso, V. C., Kaminer, T., & Rader, D. E. (1995). Incidence of basic concepts in the directions of new and recently revised American intelligence tests for preschool children. *School Psychology International, 16,* 345–364.

Flynn, J. R. (1984). The mean IQ of Americans: Massive gains from 1932 to 1978. *Psychological Bulletin, 95,* 29–51.

Flynn, J. R. (1987). Massive IQ gains in 14 nations: What IQ tests really measure. *Psychological Bulletin, 95,* 29–51.

Flynn, J. R. (1999). Searching for justice: The discovery of IQ gains over time. *American Psychologist, 54,* 5–20.

Kaufman, A. S. (1978). The importance of basic concepts in individual assessment of preschool children. *Journal of School Psychology, 16,* 207–211.

Kaufman, A. S., & Kaufman, N. L. (1983). *Kaufman Assessment Battery for Children.* Circle Pines, MN: American Guidance Service.

McCarthy, D. (1972). *McCarthy Scales of Children's Abilities.* San Antonio, TX: Psychological Corporation.

McGrew, K. A., & Flanagan, D. P. (1998). *The intelligence test desk reference: Gf-Gc cross-battery assessment.* Boston: Allyn & Bacon.

Roid, G. H., & Miller, L. J. (1997). *Leiter International Performance Scale—Revised.* Wood Dale, IL: Stoelting.

Thomas, A., & Chess, S. (1977). *Temperament and development.* New York: Brunner/Mazel.

Thorndike, R. L., Hagen, E. P., & Sattler, J. M. (1986). *Stanford-Binet Intelligence Scale,* Fourth Edition. Chicago: Riverside.

CHAPTER 4

CLINICAL OBSERVATION OF PRESCHOOL ASSESSMENT BEHAVIOR

BRUCE A. BRACKEN

Anastasi (1988) defined a psychological test as "…an objective and standardized measure of a sample of behavior" (p. 23). Psychoeducational assessment, on the other hand, encompasses much more than the mere administration of tests. Assessment is a multifaceted process that incorporates the use of formal and informal devices such as classroom tests and products, standardized tests, and rating scales, as well as a variety of procedures, including direct test administration, interviews, and clinical observations and judgments. The focus of this chapter is on the importance and use of clinical observations during the assessment of preschool children.

Psychological tests as objective and standardized samples of behavior have many assets. Typically tests provide the examiner with several convenient bits of diagnostic information, including discernible profiles of performance, standard scores, percentile ranks, and age and grade equivalents. Tests also are expected to meet some minimal levels of technical adequacy (AERA, APA, NCME, 1985; Bracken, 1987). Clinical observations and judgments, in comparison, are frequently less objective and standardized than tests, and they allow for much more professional disagreement and debate. Clinically derived observations have no published norms, standard scores, percentile ranks, or age and grade equivalents, and the reliability, validity, and interpretations of assessment observations and interpretations are frequently questioned.

It is much easier for a practitioner to defend decisions made on the basis of test data than it is to defend judgments made on behavior observed and interpreted in a clinical fashion. On the other hand, some concerns with psychoeducational assessment seem to have stemmed from the practice of blindly using test scores for making programmatic and placement decisions about children without the full use of clinical observations, judgments, and common sense.

Clinical observations represent one critical aspect of the assessment process, which can lead to a fuller understanding of the child and the child's test performance. Observations should be employed to describe and explain children's test and nontest behaviors, attest to the validity or invalidity of test scores, at least partially explain children's variable test performance, lend support for diagnoses and remediation strategies made on the basis of standardized test results, and provide the examiner with information needed to develop specific hypotheses concerning a child's learning style and individual strengths and weaknesses.

This focus on clinical observations and judgment does not imply that the issues related to subjectivity, reliability, and validity associated with observations should be ignored; rather, it is recognized that diagnosticians must develop objective, reliable, and valid observational skills. Clinical skill must complement the use of standardized tests if diagnosticians are to make accurate diagnoses, prognoses, and recommendations for the remediation of young children's deficiencies.

NORMAL PRESCHOOL BEHAVIOR

When a child is described by parents and teachers as distractible, impulsive, easily frustrated, and emotionally labile, psychologists frequently consider such tentative diagnostic hypotheses as minimal brain dysfunction, emotional disturbance, learning disabilities, or similar conditions. Although behavioral descriptors of this sort are frequently cited as soft signs for neurological impairment or severe emotional disturbance among older children, the same behaviors often characterize many normal children between the ages of 2 and 6.

Normalcy is especially difficult to define among young children. During the preschool years, social, physical, and cognitive development occurs at a rapid rate and the range of development among normal pre-school children is great. As children grow older, their rate of development decreases and the range of behaviors among normal children likewise decreases. It is sometimes difficult to differentiate preschool children with mild disabilities from normal preschoolers (hence, the preference for such descriptors as developmental delay rather than retardation), whereas older children with mild disabilities are more easily identified. Preschool children, for example, typically exhibit higher energy levels, less self-control, and much more physical activity than socialized school-age children; at what point does an energetic and active preschooler cease being considered normal and begin to be considered abnormal? Because there are no norms that give a clear indication of normal energy levels (or other behaviors) for children of various ages, the question is impossible to answer; experience and "internalized" norms guide most clinicians in the determination of whether the child's behavior is exhibited with more intensity, frequency, or in longer duration than is typical.

ENVIRONMENTAL EFFECTS

It is often assumed that a child's behavior during an evaluation is similar to the child's home or classroom behavior. In many cases this assumption is invalid. Test behavior should never be interpreted unconditionally as being representative of a child's typical behavior in any other setting. The dynamics of an evaluation are much different from those of a typical preschool, day care, kindergarten, or home environment. Even with older children it should not be assumed that assessment behavior is typical behavior. Preschool children especially have had little contact with schools, teachers, authority figures other than parents, and the extensive probing, questioning, and the formality that are part of a psychoeducational evaluation. Thus, the preschool child's test behavior may often be specific to the evaluation and generalize poorly to other assessment sessions or nonassessment situations.

It is not uncommon that when teachers or parents hear the diagnostician's description of the child's behavior during an evaluation, they respond that the examiner must not have seen the child's typical behavior. The evaluation setting provides enough structure and personal attention to keep some children eagerly on task, whereas other youngsters resist the structure and formality and refuse to participate in the assessment process or participate only half-heartedly. The unfamiliar adult–

child interactions, materials, and settings that are part of psychoeducational evaluations may frighten or intimidate some children, whereas other youngsters may respond positively to the novel situation and personal attention.

Psychoeducational evaluations are extremely structured events. Children are directed to do as the examiner instructs; test items, whether enjoyable or not, must be attempted, and the many test rules and directions have an effect on the child's behavior. Although psychoeducational assessments are frequently described by examiners as "fun games," it becomes readily apparent to most preschool children that the examiner is more interested in the child's performance than having fun. There are very few occasions in a preschooler's life when time and behavior are as structured and controlled as during psychoeducational evaluations. Because atypical behavior may be a common occurrence during an evaluation, test behavior should be noted and interpreted cautiously by diagnosticians so that inappropriate generalizations about the child's behavior are not made.

Situational structure and interpersonal interactions are but two possible environmental influences on a child's evaluation behavior. The examiner needs to be sensitive to the effects of a wide variety of environmental influences on the child's performance. To develop a better understanding of the child's typical behavior, the examiner should observe the child in a variety of environments and contrast the child's nonevaluation behavior with behavior observed during testing. The diagnostician should observe the child in the preschool classroom during structured and unstructured activities that require a wide range of behaviors, including quiet listening, active and passive individual and group participation, learning activities, cooperation, sharing, and interactions with peers and adults. Observations should also be made while the child is involved in free play on the playground for a more total picture of the child's typical behavior. If clinical observations are made in a variety of settings, the diagnostician will have a greater sample of behavior from which diagnostic inferences can be more reliably made.

SPECIFIC BEHAVIORS AND BEHAVIORAL TRENDS

To evaluate a child's behavior, the examiner must notice specific behaviors and integrate them into meaningful behavioral trends. Because the length of the evaluation provides a relatively small sample of behavior, the observer must look carefully for noteworthy behavioral trends. Frequently diagnosticians come away from an evaluation with a feeling about the child as a result of observing specific behaviors that together formed a behavioral trend. Undocumented and unsupported feelings about a child's behavior, however, are not enough. It is the task of the diagnostician to observe, note, and integrate assessment and nonassessment behaviors so that when behavioral trends are reported they are sufficiently supported with specific observed behaviors. Rather than merely reporting that a child was fearful during the evaluation, for example, the examiner should support this claim with instances when the child's fearful behavior was exhibited. If the child withdrew from the examiner's touch, began to weep silently during an attempt to build rapport, spoke hesitantly in a shaky and quiet voice, was startled when the examiner placed test materials on the table, and avoided direct eye contact with the examiner, the behavioral trend described as fearful would be well documented and easily supported. Most professionals would agree that a young child who exhibited these and similar behaviors indeed appeared to be frightened.

It is also important to document support of behavioral trends for later reference. If diagnosticians are questioned months later about behavioral judgments, it is much easier to support the existence of behavioral trends if the child's specific behaviors were also observed and recorded during the evaluation. Likewise, when children are reevaluated some time after the initial evaluation, it is helpful to contrast the child's specific behaviors across time.

Specific behaviors should also be examined carefully to identify behaviors that are inconsistent with the general trends. Inconsistent specific behaviors often form subtrends that give an indication of less obvious yet important strengths, weaknesses, fears, likes, dislikes, and so on. A child who smiles frequently, converses freely, jokes and teases with the examiner, readily complies with the examiner's requests, and spontaneously laughs and sings during an evaluation likely would be identified as a friendly and cooperative child. The same child, however, may at times exhibit mild resistance, express a desire to terminate the evaluation, and require occasional redirection and encouragement. If the antecedent conditions for these incongruent specific behaviors are scrutinized, a diagnostically important behavioral subtrend may emerge. For instance, the child might find the verbal exchange with the examiner enjoyable but may have an aversion to tasks that require visual-motor integration. If the pattern of incongruent resistant behaviors is considered in the context of the tasks being performed, the examiner should see that this typically friendly preschooler becomes resistant only when faced with activities requiring visual-motor integration. Observations of this sort, combined with qualitative test data, may provide concomitant evidence for a diagnostic claim of relative weakness in that area.

INABILITY VERSUS UNWILLINGNESS

One distinction that should be made through the use of behavioral observations is whether a child failed individual test items due to an inability to complete the task successfully or due to an unwillingness to attempt the task. It is not uncommon for shy preschoolers to refuse to attempt assessment tasks, especially motor activities that require active physical participation and verbal tasks that require extensive vocalization. In such a case, the diminished subtest score has the effect of lowering the scale score (e.g., Verbal or Performance scale, Simultaneous or Sequential scale) as well as the total test score (e.g., IQ, MPC). Moreover, the skill assessed by the subtest may be identified inappropriately as an area of weakness relative to the child's other abilities because of the low score. An alternative in this instance would be to attest to the invalidity of the subtest, prorate the scale and total test scores, and suggest reevaluation of the skills at a later date.

It is imperative that the diagnostician be more than a test giver. If behavioral observations are used properly to distinguish between a child's inability and unwillingness to perform tasks, the diagnostician will avoid making foolish statements about the child's relative weaknesses and the need for remediation.

DESCRIBING WHAT IS SEEN

Diagnosticians frequently view the purpose of the evaluation as the identification of a child's difficulties so that the child can be properly serviced by the school or agency. In many instances this is the function of a diagnostician because most preschool referrals are made by parents or preschool teachers who have perceived problems in the child's development or adjustment. However, this deficit model of evaluation often results in a biased orientation toward behavioral observations. Rather than observing actual assessment behavior, many diagnosticians observe and report on the absence of behavior: for example, noting that a child was "neither overly active nor impulsive during the assessment process." To say that a child was not overly active nor impulsive provides the parent or teacher with little useful information. It is usually inferred from statements such as these that no problems were noted in the areas mentioned; however, when it is reported that a specific behavior was not observed, the person informed is left to imagine where on a continuum of behavior the child actually performed. If a child is "not overly active," it cannot be safely inferred that the child was moderately active or even appropriately active. Without an accurate description of the child's actual behavior, one cannot safely infer anything except that the child was "not overly active."

Preferably, the examiner should note exactly what the child does and then describe and interpret the behavior in accurate and descriptive terms. Rather than describing a child as neither overly active nor impulsive, a more clear image of the child is communicated when the examiner notes that the child eagerly performed all tasks presented, yet waited patiently for instructions to be read, materials to be readied, and the examiner's direction to begin. In this instance the diagnostician could have characterized the child as interested and patient (or used similar descriptors) and then provided sufficient support for the positively stated clinical judgment.

BEHAVIORAL INFERENCES

Too often, psychoeducational reports contain behavioral observations that are a running chronology that fail to draw any meaningful inferences. Merely reporting what a child did during an evaluation without also providing an interpretation of that behavior in the context of the evaluation environment is insufficient. It is sometimes tempting to cite only what was actually observed during an evaluation rather than interpret the behavior because interpretations and inferences are much more subject to professional disagreement than are behavioral citings, but this temptation should be resisted. The value of behavioral interpretations by far outweighs the difficulties that arise from professional disagreement.

Eye contact, for instance, is a behavior that diagnosticians are fond of reporting but frequently do not interpret. It is fairly common that examiners will state in a psychoeducational report that the child made, or failed to make, eye contact throughout the evaluation. What is the significance of this observation? Alone, it is meaningless, yet when coupled with an inferential interpretation this observation provides relevant and meaningful information. The possible explanations for a child's continued (or absence of) eye contact are numerous, and selecting the appropriate interpretation is important. Did the child make eye contact in an effort to secure assurance from the examiner that the child's test performance was acceptable? Was the eye contact hostile in nature

and used as a nonverbal, passive-aggressive message of resistance? Was eye contact made with teary eyes, suggesting fear and a desire to terminate the evaluation session? Did the child make eye contact with eyes that expressed a lack of understanding and a need for a slower pace and greater explanation? Or did the child's continued eye contact inform the examiner that the evaluation was viewed positively by the youngster? The answers to these questions are not found solely in the observation of eye contact but are answered through the compilation of other specific facial and nonfacial behaviors that form a meaningful behavioral trend.

MEANINGFUL COMMUNICATION OF BEHAVIORAL OBSERVATIONS

The ability to communicate the meaning of a child's behavior to the child's parents, teachers, and others is an important and necessary assessment skill. To do this, examiners must expand their repertoire of behavioral descriptors and describe children's behavior in terms that reflect accurately not only the frequency, intensity, and duration of the child's behavior but also the spirit in which the behavior was performed.

To report that a child walked around the room during the rapport-building phase of the evaluation only minimally describes the child's behavior. The reason for the child's walking and the intensity of the behavior are unclear. Was the child interested in exploring the new environment? Was he afraid and not ready to sit? Was he angry and walking off his anger? It is unclear what the child's intentions were without more detailed information. There are also numerous terms that refer to the nuances in walking behavior that give a clear indication of the child's state of being at the time. If it is reported that the child *darted* around the examining room, this suggests more energy being exerted by the child than if the child is described as *sauntering* around the room. Likewise, *skipping* suggests a lighter mood than *trudging, pacing* connotes a higher level of anxiety than *strolling,* and *stomping* alludes to a greater degree of emotion than *tiptoeing.*

Although there is a greater likelihood of disagreement among professionals over whether a child was sauntering or strolling, marching or stomping, and so on, diagnosticians should not hesitate to describe the behavior in terms that they believe accurately connote the nuance of emotion underlying the child's behavior or the energy with which the behavior was exhibited. As psychologists and educators, our task is to make diagnostic decisions based on the best data available at the time. As mentioned previously, test results are fairly easily defended, but clinical observations are essential for making sense of the test results and providing a clearer understanding of the child.

WHEN TO OBSERVE BEHAVIOR

Behavior is a continuous attribute that flows unendingly. Literally during every moment of an evaluation the child is doing something worth noting. To make sense of the continuous behavior flow, it is necessary to study the child's behavior temporally.

Because much of the child's behavior is a reaction to the examiner or the examining situation, the child's responses to various situations should be studied meticulously to determine possible relationships between the task the child is asked to perform and the child's behavior. Identification of relationships between tasks and resulting behaviors may lead to meaningful hypotheses about the child's abilities. Why might a child kneel and lean forward in anticipation when presented with a verbal memory subtest, yet recoil and become anxious when asked to repeat numbers on a numerical memory task? The child's differential response to the two similar subtests may suggest a tentative hypothesis about the child's relative comfort with verbal as opposed to numerical information.

The examiner's hypothesis should be investigated to determine whether similar responses were made to other memory and nonmemory, verbal and numerical subtests. If the child's response pattern is consistent and verbal items are continually responded to more favorably than numerical items, then information is gained that can be used, along with obtained test scores, to explain the differences in the child's verbal and numerical abilities.

Less contiguous temporal units should also be considered when analyzing trends in a child's behavior. The examiner should compare the child's behavior at the beginning of the evaluation with that near the end of the evaluation. Did the child begin eagerly but finish feeling frustrated? Did the child separate from his or her parents with difficulty but gradually warm in mood so that by the end of the evaluation the examiner and child were mutually comfortable? Does the child work well once he or she gets started but become anxious or frightened when required to cease one activity and initiate another? The child's reaction to transitions in tasks, subtests, tests, and other activities and settings should also be noted by the examiner. By considering temporal units of behavior, whether large or small, the examiner can obtain information that will not only help explain the child's test perfor-

mance but will provide parents and teachers insight into the child's variable behavior at home and in school.

WHAT TO OBSERVE

Although it would be impossible to list all behaviors that are worthy of notice during a diagnostic evaluation, behaviors that should not go unnoticed are discussed next. It is hoped that the reader will become more aware of preschool behavior, expand these suggestions as necessary, and learn to attend selectively to childhood behaviors that provide diagnostically useful information.

Appearance

During the course of an evaluation, the examiner should note with photographic clarity the child's actual physical appearance. This carefully recorded description will prove a useful aid to recall at a later date when the details of the evaluation are no longer vivid. A description of this sort is also useful for professionals who will be working with the child in the future because it provides a concrete referent. Photographic descriptions also humanize the assessment report and make it clear that the report concerns an actual child, not a faceless entity. It is important that future teachers, counselors, and other school personnel see the preschooler as a living, breathing, red-haired, freckle-faced youngster, for example, rather than merely a name–IQ paired association.

Height and Weight

A physical description of a child should include notes about weight and height, especially relative to the child's peers. Height and weight charts are usually available from pediatricians and are also frequently found in books on child development. As with most traits and characteristics, variance for normal height and weight is great during the preschool years. The examiner should take care to note the interaction between the child's size and his or her performance on the assessment tests or how it relates to the child's rate of development. It is more meaningful, for instance, to describe a child as being seriously overweight and discuss the ways in which the child's excess weight interfers with fine and gross motor abilities as measured on a diagnostic evaluation than to cite only that the child's weight is at the 99th percentile when compared to same-age peers.

The examiner needs to be acutely sensitive to the effects that extreme height or weight might have on a youngster's test performance, school performance, self-concept, peer relations, and so on. The question of whether a child's deviant weight is a result of a physiological problem should be investigated by a physician. The diagnostician should be aware that deviancy in a child's physical development may have implications for the emotional, social, and educational well-being of the child and should be considered within the context of the psychoeducational evaluation. As with all areas of development, early intervention for health-related problems is preferred to later interventions.

Physical Abnormalities

The diagnostician should be watchful for physical characteristics that are unusual and/or indicative of insufficient or inappropriate diet, physical or emotional abuse, lack of proper medical or dental attention, improper sleep or rest patterns, and physiological, psychological, or educational disorders.

The child should be surveyed for obvious sensory and motor abnormalities. The child should evidence fairly symmetrical motor development and functioning. Although the young child's movements are typically not as smooth as an older child's, they should be neither jerky nor spasmodic. The child should be observed for tics, tremors, excessive clumsiness, and uncontrolled body movements. The examiner should also be observant for signs of visual and auditory impairments. Visually, the examiner should look for obvious signs, such as red, swollen eyelids, crusty drainage around the eyes, eyes that neither track nor align properly, squinting, excessive blinking, grimacing, or evidence of impaired perception of orientation in space, size, body image, and judgment of distance. The examiner should also watch for signs of auditory impairment such as drainage from the ears, complaints of earaches or itchy ears, repeated requests for questions to be restated, tilting of the head for better reception, and so on. The child's speech should be considered carefully for indications of auditory dysfunction, such as frequent auditory discrimination errors, expressed confusion when there is auditory confusion or commotion, and inappropriate responses to questions, directions, or requests.

Grooming and Dress

Observations of the child's grooming frequently provide the examiner with an indication of the care afforded the child at home. If the child's hands and face are covered with an accumulation of dirt and the clothing bears traces of compounded soil, then it might be safely inferred that little attention has been given to the child's hygiene. A diagnostician should be careful, however, to discern if the child is temporarily disheveled and dirty because of recent play or whether the observed dirt is more permanent and global.

The intent of considering a preschooler's clothing is not to attend to whether the child is stylishly dressed but rather to infer the amount of adult supervision given to the child's daily routines. As with grooming, a child's dress reflects somewhat the attention and care given the child at home. It would be foolish to infer necessarily that a child in old clothes does not have his or her physical needs met; however, a young boy who comes to an evaluation with his shirt buttons and buttonholes misaligned, wearing socks of different colors, and has shoes on the wrong feet obviously had little attention paid to his dress! The examiner should follow up on this observation by asking the parents and preschool teacher about the child's usual dress and dressing routine. It is possible that this situation was unique due to a rushed schedule the day of the evaluation or possibly that the parents are attempting to teach the child to become more independent in his daily functioning. Although the potential explanations for disheveled dress are many, the examiner should pursue the reasons to rule out the possibility of parental neglect.

Children's dress can also be a valuable source of information about their level of dependence on adults. If a child's shoes become untied during the evaluation, does the child immediately ask the examiner to tie them or does the child attempt to tie them without help? Does the child attempt to tuck in a shirt when it comes untucked or does the child obliviously leave it untucked? Does the child attempt to button buttons or snap snaps that have come undone or ask to have them done by an adult? The essence of the observation is whether the child evidences an attempt at independent functioning or is content and used to having others do for him or her. Obviously, the average 2 year-old would be expected to be quite dependent on adults for dressing assistance, but 3- and 4-year-olds should be evidencing attempts at independent functioning even if these attempts prove unsuccessful; and 5- and 6-year-olds should be quite independent in much of their normal daily functioning, requiring assistance much less frequently than their younger peers.

Speech

A preschooler's speech yields a great deal of information about not only the quality of the child's language skills but also the child's overall cognitive ability and level of social-emotional development. Eisenson (1978) provides a useful guide that describes qualitative characteristics of speech in children up to 36 months of age. Also, language development and basic concept attainment for preschool children are discussed in Chapters 9 and 10 of this book. Therefore, little will be added here concerning the specifics of early childhood language development; however, it is important that a child's speech is noted carefully during an evaluation for insight into the child's thought patterns, problem-solving style, tolerance to frustration, awareness and understanding of the examining situation, and ability to communicate needs and follow directions.

Although stuttering, stammering, and mild lisps caused by the loss of baby teeth and imperfect enunciation are common among young children (especially among first graders), the examiner should note the child's speech difficulties and be particularly sensitive to whether the child evidences discomfort over speech production. If the child's speech is unintelligible, is marked by severe stuttering or stammering, or causes concern to the child or parents, then the diagnostician should make a referral for a language assessment and attempt to determine in what ways and to what degree the child's imperfect speech interfered with the test results. In situations in which a child's poor expressive speech results in lowered test scores the examiner should measure the youngster's receptive vocabulary and nonverbal reasoning skills with instruments such as the Peabody Picture Vocabulary Test—Revised (Dunn & Dunn, 1981) or the Columbia Mental Maturity Scale (Burgemeister, Blum, & Lorge, 1972), both of which require no verbal expression and are appropriate for preschool children.

Many preschoolers express their thoughts verbally while attempting to solve problems, which provides the diagnostician with insights into the processes used in obtaining the solution. Although intelligence tests have been criticized historically for measuring intellectual product but not process, the astute diagnostician can infer aspects of the child's cognitive processing from the resultant product and the child's steps taken while working toward producing that product.

During the test administration, when test items become increasingly difficult, the examiner should note the child's response to the increasingly difficult tasks and more frequent item failures. Frequently young children remain on task as long as the task is within their ability. When the tasks become taxing, many children

focus only on particular words within the test questions and respond verbally in an eluding and tangential manner. For example, the examiner who asks a young child to complete the following sentence, "A table is made of wood; a window of…" (Terman & Merrill, 1972, p. 85), might get a response such as "I want to look out the window." Many preschoolers use manipulative ploys in an attempt to avoid failure, whereas others use verbal redirection to avoid participating in the evaluation once they discover that the "games" are not as much fun as they first seemed. A clinician's reported observations about a child's redirective attempts infrequently astonish parents who have been manipulated successfully by their children, though some parents may be unaware that they have been redirected so effectively by their child. An awareness of this sort of observation is all some parents need to begin setting consistent limits and better managing their young children.

A child's level of verbal spontaneity can often be an indication of the child's level of comfort in the examining situation. A verbally expressive youngster who chatters happily throughout the evaluation is visibly more comfortable than a reticent child who speaks haltingly and only when questioned. The examiner should question the validity of evaluation results when it is deemed that the child was overly inhibited during the assessment process. The examiner might contrast the child's performance on subtests that require verbal expression with subtests that require little or none for a better determination of the extent to which the child's shyness affected the test results. If the child scored consistently lower on verbal expressive measures than on verbal receptive items, the examiner should further determine whether the child is reticent due to a verbal deficiency or whether the observed verbal deficiency was a result of reticence. If the child is observed to be verbally fluent and spontaneous in nontest situations, it might be hypothesized that the child's shyness may have been the cause of the poor verbal test performance; in such a case, interventions of an entirely different sort would be warranted.

The examiner should attend to the preschooler's speech for insights into the child's overall affect. Does the child tease, joke, or attempt to be humorous verbally? Does the child use baby talk or regressive language at times of stress or frustration? When tasks become difficult, does the child utter silly nonsense phrases or respond seriously with a relevant response, whether correct or not? Does the youngster become verbally aggressive when faced with failure and petulantly inform the examiner, "I don't like you. I want to go home!'"?

The diagnostician should be watchful for how the child responds verbally as well as nonverbally to the multitude of situations that arise during the evaluation. It is helpful, for example, if a diagnostician notes that a particular child, like many preschoolers, becomes silent when faced with failure, disappointment, embarrassment, or frustration. Many parents react to a young child's silent dejection with overstimulating attention; the diagnostician should advise that increased attention frequently exacerbates the problem and a more relaxed, soothing, and accepting approach may be more helpful in reopening the temporarily closed lines of communication.

The content of a child's verbalizations should be considered carefully, not only to determine the relative maturity of the child's speech, but also to detect emotional projections the child is making while performing tasks during the evaluation. The examiner should listen intently to the young child's interpretations of test pictures, test items, and spontaneous comments. With a verbally expressive preschooler, the examiner frequently has available a great store of additional psychological information; preschoolers typically have not acquired the sophistication to mask their feelings and have not yet developed strong defense mechanisms. Their problems often can be readily detected by a diagnostician who observes as well as tests.

Fine and Gross Motor Skills

Because many early school experiences are motoric in nature, the examiner should pay particularly close attention to the child's motor development. Tests such as the McCarthy Scales of Children's Abilities (McCarthy, 1972) and the Meeting Street School Screening Test (Harnsworth & Siqueland, 1969) have direct measures of motor ability whereas most other preschool tests at least indirectly measure motor skill. The Wechsler Preschool and Primary Scale of Intelligence (Wechsler, 1967) is heavily weighted in fine motor tasks on the Performance scale, and the Stanford-Binet, IV (Thorndike, Hagen, & Sattler, 1986) is also well represented with fine motor tasks.

Formal motor assessment procedures should always be supplemented with direct behavioral observation. The examiner needs to discern the child who performs poorly on formal motor measures for reasons other than poor motor coordination. Children may score low on motor scales because of shyness, an unwillingness to attempt the task, fear of failure, embarrassment, or because motor tasks may lack the necessary structure for some children. Also, one must question whether the child understood the test directions; even subtests that are motoric in nature frequently have long and complex verbal directions (Bracken, 1986; Cummings & Nelson, 1980; Kaufman, 1978).

Children should be watched carefully to note how well they perform nontest motor tasks as well as formal motor tasks. Children who are lacking in educational experiences may look clumsy when drawing, coloring, or cutting with scissors, yet are able to button buttons, zip zippers, and manipulate small objects with obvious facility. The nature of the remediation for a child of this sort should be to engage the child in educationally relevant motor activities as their adaptive behavior type motor skills appear to be well developed already.

When assessing preschoolers, the examiner should observe the child's gross motor abilities, including the ability to climb stairs, walk, run, skip, hop, balance on one foot, walk backward, throw, and catch. Obvious signs of gross asymmetrical development should be noted as possible indicators of neurological impairment, and referrals should be made for a neuropsychological evaluation if warranted. As with fine motor development, the examiner should discern whether the child's gross motor difficulty is due to a lack of meaningful experiences or is due to a physical or perceptual limitation. Although perceptual difficulties may be the cause of poor coordination in the truly awkward and clumsy child and may require educational or physical intervention, the child lacking in experience may need only additional experience to develop better motor skills.

Activity Level

How active a child is during an evaluation has direct implications for the validity of the test results. It is likely that a child who is either lethargic or extremely active is not participating in the assessment process to an optimum degree, thus reducing the test's validity. A child who must be extrinsically motivated to attempt tasks, encouraged to continue the assessment, and prodded to complete test items is problematic. The diagnostician should qualify the reports of the child's poor performance with a note about the child's diminished activity level and reluctance to participate. The examiner should contrast the child's test and nontest behaviors, search for relevant behavioral trends, and watch for instances in which the child displays isolated bursts of interest and energy before making inappropriate diagnoses based on the affected test scores. If a child actively participates in subtests of a particular nature and remains listless for others, the resultant test profile and the examiner's behavioral notes, when coupled, should lead to diagnostically useful information.

The examiner should be aware of whether a child is currently medicated and any effect such medication might have on the child's activity level. If the youngster is taking medication that has a depressant effect, the evaluation should be postponed and rescheduled when the youngster is healthier and better able to give maximum effort. In instances of prolonged medical treatment, the diagnostician should acknowledge that it is likely that the test scores are depressed due to medication and caution the user of the results to consider judiciously the effects of the child's physical condition on the test results. Likewise, ill health may itself adversely affect the child's energy level. The examiner should note symptoms that indicate the onset of an illness and decide whether the evaluation should continue or be rescheduled for a later date.

Similarly, fatigue and drowsiness, common among preschoolers in the early afternoon, should be an indication to the examiner that optimal results on cognitive and achievement measures will not be obtained; upon observing the child's fatigue or sleepiness, the examiner should cease testing for the time being. Fatigue frequently accentuates soft signs of neurological impairment in children and the examiner should be watchful for those signs.

Attention

Artifacts in test results caused by a child's inattentiveness may bring about inappropriate remediation recommendations unless the test results are further explained through behavioral observations. For example, if a child obtains a relatively weak score on the Memory Scale of the McCarthy Scales of Children's Abilities, a diagnostician might conclude that the child's short-term memory is deficient. However, the diagnostician should be able to explain this weakness if the child did not attend fully to the directions or the stimuli on short-term memory items. Because memory items cannot be readministered, as most other items can, the child may

consistently miss the crucial element of test items due to inattentiveness rather than poor memory. The logical recommendation based on this observation would be to ensure that the child is attending carefully before teachers or parents present information they expect the child to recall.

Distractibility

Some children, although attentive during much of the evaluation, miss crucial information because they are easily distracted. These children may be attending appropriately but momentarily discontinue attending to the task and shift their attention to inappropriate stimuli. Distractibility interferes with successful completion of many test activities but is particularly harmful on memory tests and tasks that are timed. The examiner should differentiate a child's failure due to inability and failure due to inconsistent attention. If the child's low scores are properly explained by the examiner, the subsequent recommendations should be more pertinent to the child's actual area of difficulty.

Impulsivity

Like inattentiveness and distractibility, impulsivity can severely limit the child's success on cognitive and achievement tests. If a child blurts out a response before the examiner completes the test question, initiates a task before the directions are finished, or says, "I know how to do it—let me try" as the examiner readies the test materials, the child is likely to fail many times and do poorly on the test overall.

Examiners need to be aware that typical preschoolers are at times inattentive, distractible, and impulsive. However, the crux of the examiner's observations should be to determine the degree to which the child's test performance was adversely affected by extreme behaviors and then judge the usefulness of the test scores. Although the diagnostician may believe that the test results are seriously deflated due to the child's test behavior and may be able to support this belief with a raft of behavioral notes, he or she should be careful when making optimistic claims about the child's likelihood of success in the classroom. If the child's behavior has interfered with the child's performance on the test, it may also interfere with the child's performance in the classroom and indeed may have been the reason for the initial referral.

Affect

Emotional lability is a common characteristic among preschool children. The examiner should become aware of the ways in which a child responds differentially to various situations. It is not uncommon for a young child to be exhilarated by success at one moment and demoralized by failure the next. Unfamiliar tasks may arouse fear and anxiety in a child who had previously completed familiar tasks calmly and confidently. An otherwise compliant and cooperative child may become testy and difficult during the unstructured interim between tests in a battery. A youngster who enters the examining room clinging to doors and furniture in fear may leave the room striding and exuding confidence.

The examiner should attend carefully to shifts in a child's affect as a result of changes in the environment and seek answers to the following types of questions: How does the child respond to structured versus unstructured activities? What is the child's reaction to praise, rebuke, failure, success, redirection, encouragement, and so on? What causes the child to become silent, to start crying, to withdraw, to jump up in excitement, to sing out with pleasure, or strike out in anger? To what test activity is the child most attentive and which activities arouse the least interest? How does the child react to test materials, being timed, the examiner, the examining room, the parents, verbal interaction, and nonverbal, performance-related activity?

Although the examiner may see many mild or even dramatic shifts in the child's mood, the child's general mood should be noted as well. On the whole, did the youngster seem happy? Negative? Fearful? Sullen? Confident? All of the child's affective behaviors should be drawn together diagnostically and inferences should be made about the child's overall mood, level of adjustment, areas of concern, and areas of strength.

Anxiety

Closely associated with affect is the child's level of anxiety. The diagnostician should note what causes the child to become anxious and how the child displays signs of anxiety. When asked several difficult questions near the ceiling of a test, does the youngster begin to suck his thumb while tears well in his eyes? Does the child stare at the floor in silence while sitting on her hands? Does the child giggle nervously, cry, constantly clear her throat, bite her nails, urinate, blush, block while talking, breathe unevenly, or hyperventilate?

Although a psychoeducational evaluation frequently arouses anxiety in preschoolers, some children are more affected than others. Some youngsters are aroused to an optimal level, whereas others are totally debilitated. Some are anxious throughout the evaluation, and others become anxious only in reaction to specific events or situations. By noting the child's behavior in several settings, the diagnostician is better able to determine whether the child's anxiety was specific to the evaluation or more general in nature, and the degree to which the child's anxiety interfered with the evaluation.

Comprehension and Problem Solving

The examiner should attend to the problem-solving approach used while the child seeks solutions to puzzles, mazes, block designs, and similar problems. The approach taken by a youngster yields clues regarding his or her comprehension of the tasks. Does the youngster draw directly through the maze without regard for walls? Remain between the walls yet continually enter blind alleys? Remain within the walls and attempt to avoid blind alleys but proceed too slowly and still fail the task? In each case, the child's earned raw score is zero, but the child's level of comprehension differs dramatically across examples. It is quite likely that the first child did not understand the nature of the task. The second child may have understood the nature of the task, but was not fully cognizant that blind alleys should be avoided. The third child seems to have fully understood the task but was unable to complete the item successfully because of the speeded nature of the task.

The child's reaction to test materials at times provides the diagnostician with surprising insight into the child's level of understanding. In low-functioning, young children, it is fairly common for the child to sniff or suck the mallet of the McCarthy xylophone thinking that it is a lollipop. Similarly, the brightly colored chips that are part of the McCarthy Conceptual Grouping subtest are sometimes mistaken for candy. Observations of this sort, when added to other behavioral notes, yield valuable information about the child's maturity and level of comprehension.

The examiner should be watchful for such events as the following: Does the child make random attempts to solve problems in a trial-and-error fashion or appear to have a strategy? If an attempt is unsuccessful, does the child continue to try the same approach or try other approaches? When solving a puzzle and puzzle pieces do not fit, does the child try a second piece or try to force the first piece into place? Does the child understand that puzzle pieces must be right-side-up in order to fit properly in the puzzle? On simple two- or three-piece puzzles, does the child impulsively shove adjacent pieces together without regard for the total picture? Observations of this sort add a qualitative nature to the test score. Although any two children may obtain the same scores on a given subtest, no two children will exhibit exactly the same behaviors while attempting the subtest items.

Reactions to Other People and Situations

The preschool child's interactions with both parents together and each parent apart, siblings, teachers, classmates, and strangers should be noted. It should be noted whether the child interacts with others by moving forward confidently or timidly holding back. Is the youngster aggressive with classmates or bullied? Does the child seek independence from the teacher or frequently ask for help, reassurance, and support? Does the child obey one parent's commands but ignore the other parent's directions? The child's interactions with the examiner should also be noted. Overall, is the child compliant, manipulative, fearful, confident, respectful, flippant, or otherwise?

In many cases children who have difficulty adjusting come from environments that contribute to their problems. Although teachers and parents mean well and attempt to do what they believe is in the child's best interest, they at times fail to see their role in the child's lack of adjustment. Consider, for example, the father who drops his daughter off at the nursery school. At the moment the father attempts to leave his daughter in her class, she begins to cry. As the daughter cries, her father attempts to console her, yet every time he begins to leave she becomes more upset. This cycle repeats itself daily until the child begins crying before ever leaving her home, and school becomes a negative experience to which she reacts strongly. As any experienced preschool teacher knows, most young children stop crying almost immediately after their parents leave, and the best way to avoid unpleasant separations is to make them warm yet brief.

SUMMARY

Although the administration of psychoeducational tests alone requires a great deal of skill, concentration, and coordination, an effective diagnostician must also have the resources to observe and record the preschool child's behavior. With a carefully collected sample of behavioral observations, the examiner should be able to support or refute test findings, explain a child's variable test performance, and attest to the validity or invalidity of test results. The diagnostician should also note the child's appearance and determine whether signs or symptoms of physical, emotional, or educational difficulties are present. Behaviors that indicate a child's preferred cognitive style, language abilities, problem-solving approach, level of understanding, and reasons for individual item and subtest performance must likewise be observed and interpreted. These behaviors, along with observations of the child's affect, distractibility, dependence, reactions to others, fears, likes, and so on, need to be integrated with obtained test data to formulate accurate diagnoses, prognoses, and remedial recommendations.

REFERENCES

Anastasi, A. (1988). *Psychological testing* (6th ed.). New York: Macmillan.

AERA, APA, NCME. (1985). *Standards for educational and psychological testing.* Washington, DC: American Psychological Association.

Bracken, B. A. (1986). Incidence of basic concepts in the directions of five commonly used American tests of intelligence. *School Psychology International, 7,* 1–10.

Bracken, B. A. (1987). Limitations of preschool instruments and standards for minimal levels of technical adequacy. *Journal of Psychoeducational Assessment, 4,* 313–326.

Burgemeister, B. B., Blum, L., & Lorge, I. (1972). *Columbia Mental Maturity Scale.* New York: Harcourt Brace Jovanovich.

Cummings, J. A., & Nelson, R. B. (1980). Basic concepts in oral directions of group achievement tests. *Journal of Educational Research, 73,* 259–261.

Dunn, L. M., & Dunn, L. M. (1981). *Peabody Picture Vocabulary Test—Revised.* Circle Pines, MN.: American Guidance Service.

Eisenson, J. (1978). Is my child delayed in speech? *School Psychology Digest, 7,* 63–68.

Harnsworth, P., & Siqueland, M. (1969). *Meeting Street School Screening Test.* East Providence, RI: Easter Seal Society.

Kaufman, A. S. (1978). The importance of basic concepts in individual assessment of preschool children. *Journal of School Psychology, 16,* 207–211.

McCarthy, D. (1972). *McCarthy Scales of Children's Abilities.* New York: Psychological Corporation.

Terman, L., & Merrill, M. (1972). *Stanford-Binet Intelligence Scale.* Boston: Houghton Mifflin.

Thorndike, R. L., Hagen, E. P., & Sattler, J. M. (1986). *Stanford-Binet Intelligence Scale: Fourth Edition.* Chicago: Riverside.

Wechsler, D. (1967). *Wechsler Preschool and Primary Scale of Intelligence.* New York: Psychological Corporation.

CHAPTER 5

THE ASSESSMENT OF PRESCHOOL CHILDREN WITH THE WECHSLER PRESCHOOL AND PRIMARY SCALE OF INTELLIGENCE—REVISED

JAMES S. GYURKE

DEBRA S. MARMOR

SUSAN E. MELROSE

The Wechsler Preschool and Primary Scale of Intelligence—Revised (WPPSI-R) (Wechsler, 1989) is a widely used, well standardized, technically sound measure of children's intelligence (Kaufman, 1992). The WPPSI-R, like the WPPSI (Wechsler, 1967), reflects Wechsler's view that intelligence is a global entity that is multidimensional and multifaceted with each ability being equally important. Like other Wechsler scales, the WPPSI-R has a substantial research and clinical foundation supporting its use to accurately measure the intellectual ability of young children.

DESCRIPTION OF THE WPPSI-R

The WPPSI-R is an individually administered clinical instrument for assessing the intelligence of children aged 3 years through 7 years, 3 months. It is organized much like the WPPSI, with one group of primarily perceptual-motor Performance subtests and a second group of Verbal subtests. There are a total of 12 subtests (see Table 5.1), of which 10 are required and two (Animal Pegs and Sentences) are optional.

The 12 subtests are divided into two scales labeled Verbal and Performance. This division has both logical and empirical support. The logical basis for this division rests on the apparent nature of the child's responses to the task: motor responses to the Performance subtests and spoken responses to the Verbal subtests. The empirical rationale for this division comes from the results of several factor analytic studies of both the WPPSI-R and WPPSI structure, consistently finding two subtest clusters within the scale (e.g., Hollenbeck & Kaufman, 1973; Sattler, 1992). The two clusters or factors invari-

TABLE 5.1 WPPSI-R Subtests and Corresponding Scale Placement

PERFORMANCE	VERBAL
1. Object Assembly	2. Information
3. Geometric Design	4. Comprehension
5. Block Design	6. Arithmetic
7. Mazes	8. Vocabulary
9. Picture Completion	10. Similarities
*11. Animal Pegs	*12. Sentences

Source: Wechsler Preschool and Primary Scale of Intelligence—Revised. Copyright © 1989 by The Psychological Corporation. Reproduced by permission. All rights reserved. "WPPSI-R" is a registered trademark of The Psychological Corporation.

*Optional subtests

ably correspond to the Verbal and Performance scales. (A complete review of these studies is provided in the WPPSI-R manual.)

Each of the 12 WPPSI-R subtests produces raw scores that are converted to norm-referenced standard scores ($M = 10$, $SD = 3$). These scaled scores are then summed across the five required subtests within the Verbal scale and the five required subtests within the Performance scale to obtain sums of scaled scores. Each of the individual sum of scaled scores is transformed to an IQ ($M = 100$, $SD = 15$). These two sums of scaled scores—VIQ and PIQ—also are summed to produce a Full scale score that is transformed to an IQ ($M = 100$, $SD = 15$). In addition to the raw-score-to-scaled-score and scaled-score-to-IQ conversion tables, a test-age table that can be used to estimate a child's functional age based on his or her performance also is provided in the manual.

USE OF THE SCALE

The WPPSI-R is intended for use as a measure of intellectual ability in a wide range of educational, clinical, and research settings. In many cases, comparison of intellectual functioning with achievement forms the basis of establishing the existence of learning disabilities. This determination of exceptionality is a common practice in most school settings (Buckhalt, 1990).

Because the upper end of the age range of the WPPSI-R overlaps approximately one year with the lower end of the age range of the WISC-III, examiners have a choice of which scale to use with a child aged 6 years to 7 years, 3 months. In most cases, if the child is expected to be of average or above-average intellectual ability with average communicative ability, the examiner should administer the WISC-III. However, if the child is expected to be below average in either of these areas, the examiner should administer the WPPSI-R. The WPPSI-R's difficulty level is more appropriate for lower-ability children in this age range, and the WISC-III is more appropriate for higher-ability children.

WPPSI-R SUBTESTS

Subtest Description

The following section describes each subtest in detail. Included in this description are the skill measured by the subtest, the format of administration and scoring, and the technical evaluation of the subtest. In the context of describing the subtests, the term *age level* refers to a discrete band of age. For example, the 4-year age level refers to the band of ages from 3 years, 11 months, 16 days to 4 years, 2 months, 15 days. Also, for the purpose of describing the ceiling of the individual subtests, the $6^1/4$-year age level will be used because, from ages 6 years, 6 months through 7 years, 3 months, the WPPSI-R is intended for use only with lower-ability children.

Object Assembly.   This subtest, as with the WISC-III Object Assembly subtest, requires the child to assemble a puzzle picturing a common object. This subtest contains six full-color puzzles of common objects. The child receives credit for both the correct assembly of the puzzle and the speed of performance. This subtest yields a maximum raw score of 32. The summary skills required to

successfully complete the tasks include visual-motor integration, visual perception, and fine motor coordination.

The Object Assembly subtest has adequate floor for young children. A floor or ceiling of a subtest is considered adequate if it produces scores that are 2 or more standard deviations above or below the mean, respectively. A raw score of 0 at the 3-year age level yields a scaled score of 1, which is 3 standard deviations below the mean. The median raw score (raw score that receives a scaled score of 10) is 10 out of a possible 32. The ceiling of this subtest also is adequate. The median raw score at the $6^1/4$-year age level is 25 and the maximum raw score of 32 receives a scaled score of 17. Beyond this $6^1/4$-year age level, the ceiling becomes more limited. In general, this new subtest has sufficient floor and ceiling to test young children and is suitable for use with children across the entire age span of the WPPSI-R.

Information.   The Information subtest requires the child to demonstrate knowledge about events or objects in the environment. This 27-item subtest includes a new set of full-color pictures and requires less advanced verbal skills than its WPPSI counterpart. This set of new picture items was added to a set of items similar to those of the WPPSI Information subtest. Each item is dichotomously scored as 1 (pass) or 0 (failed) with the maximum raw score equal to 27. The skills required to perform this task include long-term memory, verbal fluency, and knowledge of the environment.

As would be expected with a subtest that is primarily verbal, Information has a somewhat weak floor at the youngest ages. At the 3-year age level a raw score of 0 yields a scaled score of 5, a score slightly less than 2 standard deviations below the mean. However, by the 4-year age level this same raw score yields a scaled score of 2, showing that the floor problem is quickly resolved. The ceiling of this subtest is more than adequate because the median raw score at the $6^1/4$-year age level is 22 and the maximum raw score of 27 receives a scaled score of 19.

Overall, the Information subtest has a slightly limited floor but an adequate ceiling. Despite the limited floor, there appears to be a smooth, albeit a slower, progression in the upper age levels of raw scores across the entire age span.

Geometric Design.   The Geometric Design subtest includes two distinct types of tasks among its 16 items. First is a set of visual-recognition tasks that require the child to match a pictured design from an array of four designs. The second type of item requires the child to draw a copy of a geometric figure from a printed model, as in the Geometric Design subtest of the WPPSI. The primary skills required to complete these tasks include visual-perception, visual-motor organization, fine motor coordination, and attention to detail. The scoring of this subtest has been significantly changed in response to criticism regarding the subjective nature of the scoring. Scoring is now based on the critical features of each figure; a child receives credit for each feature of the drawing that he or she has reproduced correctly. These points are summed within an item (drawing) to obtain the raw score for that drawing. With this change in the scoring system, the maximum raw score for the subtest is now 64. By scoring the critical features of each drawing, WPPSI-R scoring accuracy was improved over that of the WPPSI.

The floor of the Geometric Design is slightly weak; a raw score of 0 at the 3-year age level yields a scaled score of 5; however, by the 4-year age level the floor is adequate because a raw score of 0 yields a scaled score of 2. This subtest has an adequate ceiling at all ages. At the $6\frac{1}{4}$-year age level a maximum raw score of 64 yields a scaled score of 17, while at age 7 this same raw score yields a scaled score of 16. At the 7-year level, there are six possible raw score points above the median, suggesting that even at the upper ability levels there is some differentiation among average- to high-ability children.

In summary, the Geometric Design subtest has been changed to include more appropriate items for young children and more objective scoring rules. There is a slightly limited floor for this subtest at the youngest ages, but in general there is ample differentiation across the entire age span.

Comprehension. This subtest requires the child to demonstrate an understanding of the reasons for actions, or of the consequences of certain common events in the environment. The child's responses are scored 2, 1, or 0, depending on the level of understanding the child demonstrates, with a maximum raw score of 30. The primary skills used in completing the Comprehension subtest include verbal ability, logical reasoning, and understanding of relationships.

The floor of this subtest is limited. At the 3-year level, the median raw score is 3 to 4 and a raw score of 0 yields a scaled score of 6. The floor of this subtest is sufficient at the 4-year age level at which the median raw score is 11 to 13 and a raw score of 0 yields a scaled score of 4. Regarding the ceiling at the $6\frac{1}{4}$-year age level, the median raw score is 24 and the maximum raw

score of 30 yields a scaled score of 18, indicating that this subtest possesses a sufficient ceiling at this upper age level. In fact, Comprehension has an adequate ceiling through the 7-year age level at which the maximum raw score of 30 yields a scaled score of 17.

Block Design. The Block Design subtest is similar to the WPPSI version. It requires the child to analyze and reproduce, within a specified time limit, geometric patterns made from flat, two-colored blocks. The child's responses are scored as 2 (correct on first trial), 1 (correct on second trial), or 0 (no correct responses in either trial). For items 8 through 14 the child can obtain up to two additional bonus points for quick, accurate performance on the first trial. The primary skills required by Block Design include visual-motor coordination, visual integration, and synthesis of part–whole information.

The floor of the Block Design subtest is adequate. The median raw score at the 3-year age level is 5 and a raw score of 0 receives a scaled score of 4 at this age. Likewise, this subtest has an adequate ceiling because at the $6\frac{1}{4}$-year age level the median raw score is 26 to 27 and the maximum raw score of 42 receives the maximum scaled score of 19. There is an adequate ceiling through the 7-year age level at which the median raw score is 29 to 30 and the maximum raw score of 42 receives a scaled score of 18.

In conclusion, the WPPSI-R Block Design subtest is much the same as the WPPSI Block Design subtest. There is an adequate floor at the youngest ages and an adequate ceiling at the older ages.

Arithmetic. The Arithmetic subtest assesses the child's understanding of basic quantitative concepts. As in the WPPSI, this subtest begins with pictured stimuli, progresses through simple counting tasks, and ends with more difficult word problems. The 23 items are scored as pass or fail, so the maximum raw score is 23.

The primary skills required for this subtest are visual discrimination, nonverbal reasoning ability, and knowledge of numerical concepts.

The floor of this subtest is more than adequate because the median raw score at ages 3 to 5 and a raw score of 0 receives a scaled score of 3. The ceiling of this subtest also is more than adequate with the median raw score at the $6\frac{1}{4}$-year age level equal to 18 and the maximum raw score of 23 receiving a scaled score of 18. The ceiling remains adequate through the 7-year age level at which the median raw score is 20 and the maximum raw score of 23 receives a scaled score of 16.

To summarize, the Arithmetic subtest on the WPPSI-R is very similar to its counterpart on the WPPSI. The floor and ceiling of this subtest are more than adequate through the entire age span of the scale.

Mazes. The Mazes subtest requires the child to solve pencil-and-paper mazes of increasing difficulty. Although similar to the Mazes subtest on the WPPSI, several new, easier mazes have been added for young children. The child's responses are scored according to the number of errors made on each maze, with the total possible score reduced by each error made. The maximum raw score for this 11-item subtest is 26. The primary skills required by Mazes include attention to detail, planning, perceptual organization, and fine motor control.

Despite the inclusion of easier items, there remains a weak floor for this subtest at the 3-year age level. The 3-year median raw score is 5 and a raw score of 0 receives a scaled score of 5. This weak floor disappears by the 3 1/4-year age level at which the median raw score is 6 to 7 and a raw score of 0 receives a scaled score of 4. The ceiling of this subtest is adequate through the 7-year age level where the median raw score is 20 and the maximum raw score of 26 receives a scaled score of 18.

In summary, the Mazes subtest on the WPPSI-R is similar to that of the WPPSI with the exception of several new, easier mazes for young children. The floor is weak at the 3-year age level but adequate by the 3 1/4-year age level. The ceiling of this subtest is adequate through the 7-year age level.

Vocabulary. The Vocabulary subtest is a two-part subtest. The first part, which is completely new, contains picture identification items, whereas the second part consists of items on which the child is required to provide verbal definitions for orally presented words. The items are scored 2, 1, or 0 depending on the quality of the child's definition. The maximum raw score for this 25-item subtest is 47. The primary skills required by Vocabulary include long-term memory, verbal fluency, and, in some cases, formal education (i.e., items for which the definition of the word has most likely been learned in an educational setting).

The floor of Vocabulary is adequate at the 3-year age level because the median raw score is 8 to 9 and a raw score of 0 receives a scaled score of 3. The ceiling of this subtest is also more than adequate through the 7-year age level with the median raw score being 28 to 29 and the maximum raw score of 47 receiving the maximum scaled score of 19.

In summary, this two-part subtest has both a sufficient floor and a sufficient ceiling across the entire age span of the scale.

Picture Completion. The Picture Completion subtest is similar to that of the WPPSI in that it requires the child to identify what is missing from pictures of common objects or events. The items are scored dichotomously as pass or fail (i.e., 1 or 0) with the maximum raw score being 28. The primary skills required by the subtest include attention to detail, visual organization, and long-term visual memory.

The floor of this subtest is weak at the 3-year age level at which the median raw score is 5 to 6 and a raw score of 0 receives a scaled score of 5. The floor becomes more adequate at the 3 1/4-year age level at which the median raw score is 6 to 7 and a raw score of 0 yields a scaled score of 4. The ceiling of this subtest is adequate through the 7-year age level at which the median raw score is 22 and the maximum raw score of 28 receives a scaled score of 18.

In conclusion, the WPPSI-R Picture Completion subtest is similar to that of the WPPSI. There is a weak floor at the 3-year age level that is corrected by the 3 1/4-year age level. The ceiling of this subtest is adequate through the 7-year age level.

Similarities. The Similarities subtest requires the child to demonstrate an understanding of the concept of similarity in three ways. The first set of tasks requires the child to choose which one of several objects pictured is most similar to a second group of objects. In the second set of items the child must complete a verbally presented sentence that reflects a similarity or analogy between two things. The final set of items requires the child to explain how two verbally presented objects or events are alike. In the first two sections, the child's response is scored as pass or fail. In the third section, the child's responses are scored as 2, 1, or 0 depending on how accurately the child describes the essential nature of the similarity. This 20-item subtest has a maximum raw score of 28. The primary skills required in the first section include visual organization and attention to detail and common features. Logical reasoning, verbal fluency, and concept formation are required skills for success on the last two sections.

The Similarities subtest has a weak floor at the 3-year age level at which the median raw score is 5 and a raw score of 0 receives a scaled score of 6. It is not until the 3 3/4-year age level when the median raw score is 7 to 8 that a raw score of 0 yields a scaled score of 4. The ceiling of this subtest is more than adequate through the $6^{1}/_{4}$-year age level at which the median raw score is 21 to 22 and the maximum raw score of 28 yields a scaled score of 18. In fact, the ceiling is adequate through the 7-year age level, at which the median raw score is 24 and the maximum raw score of 28 receives a scaled score of 17.

In summary, the Similarities subtest requires the child to demonstrate an understanding of the concept of similarity in three different fashions. An adequate floor occurs at the $3^{3}/_{4}$ year age level, and there is sufficient ceiling through the 7-year age level.

Animal Pegs. The Animal Pegs subtest, which was called Animal House in the WPPSI, requires the child to place pegs of the correct colors in holes below a series of pictured animals. The child's performance is scored for both speed and accuracy, with the maximum raw score for this subtest being 70. The primary skills required include memory, attention, concentration, and fine motor coordination.

There is sufficient floor for this subtest at the 3-year age level at which the median raw score is 8 to 12 and a raw score of 0 receives a scaled score of 2. The ceiling of this subtest is adequate through the 7-year age level at which the median raw score is 56 to 58 and the maximum raw score of 70 receives the maximum scaled score of 19.

In summary, the Animal Pegs subtest is the same as the Animal House subtest on the WPPSI. This subtest has sufficient floor and ceiling across the entire age span.

Sentences. The Sentences subtest, similar to that of the WPPSI, requires the child to repeat verbatim a sentence read aloud by the examiner. The number of errors committed in repeating the sentence scores the child's response. The maximum raw score for this 12-item subtest is 37. The primary skills required include verbal facility and memory.

This subtest has a slightly weak floor at the 3-year age level, at which the median raw score is 8 and a raw score of 0 receives a scaled score of 5. This is corrected by the $3^{1}/_{4}$-year age level at which the median raw score is 9 to 10 and a raw score of 0 yields a scaled score of 4. The ceiling of this subtest is adequate through the 7-year age level at which the median raw score is 26 to 27 and the maximum raw score of 37 receives a scaled score of 17.

In summary, the WPPSI-R Sentences subtest is similar to that of the WPPSI. There is an adequate floor from the $3^{1}/_{4}$ year age level and the ceiling is adequate up through the 7-year age level.

Subtest Summary

The subtests of the WPPSI-R are, in general, quite similar to those of the WPPSI and selected subtests of the WISC-III. The floor of a few subtests is weak at the 3-year age level; however, by the $3^{1}/_{4}$-year age level almost all subtests have sufficient floor. As for the ceiling, all subtests have sufficient ceiling through the $6^{1}/_{4}$-year age level and most through the 7-year age level. This suggests that the WPPSI-R subtests provide a suitable assessment of abilities for most children through a majority of the age span of the scale.

CHARACTERISTICS OF THE SCALES

Verbal Scale

The Verbal scale consists of six subtests: Information, Comprehension, Arithmetic, Vocabulary, Similarities, and Sentences. Only five of these subtests (all but Sentences) are required to compute the Verbal sum of scaled scores. For each of the five required subtests, the raw score is transformed into a scaled score ($M = 10$, $SD = 3$). These scaled scores are summed to obtain the Verbal sum of scaled scores (VSS). The VSS is then transformed into a Verbal IQ (VIQ) ($M = 100$, $SD = 15$). The distribution of VIQs ranges from 46 to 160, or approximately $3^{2}/_{3}$ standard deviations below the mean and 4 standard deviations above the mean. This range exceeds that recommended by Bracken (1987) to ensure discrimination among all but the most extreme 1 percent of the population.

Regarding the floor of the Verbal scale, the lowest possible sum of scaled scores at the 3-year age level is 28, which yields a VIQ of 74. Because this score does not exceed the 2 standard deviation criterion, there is a limited floor for the Verbal scale at this age level; however, all subsequent age levels have floors that are at least 2 standard deviations below the mean. The Verbal scale has an adequate ceiling at all age levels because the maximum obtainable sum of scaled scores at the 7-year age level is 86, which is equivalent to an IQ of 152, well above the 2 standard deviation criterion. Overall, the Verbal scale provides a sufficient range of scores to ensure an adequate floor and ceiling for a large majority of the population aged 3 years, 0 months to 7 years, 3 months.

Performance Scale

The Performance scale consists of six subtests: Object Assembly, Geometric Design, Block Design, Mazes, Picture Completion, and Animal Pegs. Only five of these subtests (all but Animal Pegs) are required to compute the Performance sum of scaled scores.

For each of the five required subtests, the raw score is transformed into a scaled score ($M = 10$, $SD = 3$). These scaled scores are summed to obtain the Performance sum of scaled scores (PSS). The PSS is then transformed into a Performance IQ (PIQ) ($M = 100$, $SD = 15$). The distribution of PIQs ranges from 45 to 160, or from 3 standard deviations below the mean to 4 standard deviations above the mean. This range, like that of the Verbal scale, exceeds the recommended 2 standard deviation criterion, assuring discrimination among the most extreme portions of the population.

The Performance scale possesses an adequate floor and ceiling. At the 3-year age level, the lowest possible PSS of 20 yields a PIQ of 63, well beyond the 2 standard deviation criterion. At the 7-year age level, the maximum PSS of 86 translates into a PIQ of 156, well beyond the 2 standard deviation criterion. Therefore, the Performance scale provides a sufficient range of scores to ensure adequate floor and ceiling for the population aged 3 years, 0 months to 7 years, 3 months.

Full Scale

The Full Scale Score (FSS) is the sum of scaled scores from both the Verbal and Performance scales—the sum of the ten required subtest scaled scores. The FSS is transformed into a Full Scale IQ (FSIQ) ($M = 100$, $SD = 15$). The distribution of FSIQs ranges from 41 to 160, or approximately 4 standard deviations below and above the mean, which captures more than 99 percent of the population.

Both the floor and ceiling of the Full scale are more than adequate. For example, at the 3-year age level the lowest possible FSS is 48, which converts to an FSIQ of 65, exceeding the 2 standard deviation criterion. Likewise, the maximum sum of scaled scores obtainable at the 7-year age level is 172, which translates into an IQ of 160, again well beyond the 2 standard deviation criterion.

In summary, the Verbal Performance and Full scales of the WPPSI-R provide sufficient range for both low- and high-ability children across the entire age span.

STANDARDIZATION

The WPPSI-R is appropriate for a majority of children ages 3 years, 0 months through 7 years, 3 months. (See "Uses of the Scale.") The standardization sample included 1,700 children stratified by sex, race (white, black, Hispanic, other), geographic region (Northeast, North Central, South, and West), parents' occupation (Table 5.2), and parent's education (Table 5.3). The quotas for all stratification variables were determined from 1986 U.S. Census Bureau data.

There were 200 children at each of the nine age groups, except the 7-year age group in which there were 100 children. The sample participants were evenly divided by sex. Nineteen percent of the children came from the Northeast, 26.4 percent were from the North Central, 33 percent were from the South, and 21.5 percent were from the West. Children in the sample were 70.3 percent white, 15.1 percent black, 11 percent Hispanic, and 3.5 percent "other." Of the children's parents, 24.3 percent had 16 or more years of education; 22 percent had 13 to 15 years; 38.2 percent had 12 years; 10.2 had 9 to 11 years, and 5.2 percent had 8 or fewer years. This sample also was stratified by parent occupation as follows: 25.1 percent were in managerial/professional positions; 26.2 percent were in farming, forestry and related fields; 10.9 percent were working in precision, production, and related jobs; 11.5 percent were operators, fabricators, and so on; and 12.5 percent were not currently in the labor force.

The match between the obtained sample and the target population is extremely close. The fit is good both for individual stratification variables (e.g., race) and for combinations of variables (e.g., race and region). The

TABLE 5.2 Occupational Categories Used in WPPSI-R Standardization Sample Selection

CATEGORY	DESCRIPTION
I	Managerial and professional worker
II	Technical, sales, and administrative support
III	Service workers
IV	Farming, forestry, and fishing workers
V	Precision, production workers, craftsmen, and repairmen
VI	Operators, fabricators, and laborers
VII	Not currently in the labor force, others

Source: Wechsler Preschool and Primary Scale of Intelligence—Revised. Copyright © 1989 by The Psychological Corporation. Reproduced by permission. All rights reserved. "WPPSI-R" is a registered trademark of The Psychological Corporation.

Occupational categories were derived from 1986 census survey of family heads.

TABLE 5.3   Educational Levels Used in WPPSI-R Standardization Sample Selection

LEVEL	DESCRIPTION
I	8 or fewer years of education
II	9–11 years of education
III	12 years of education
IV	13–15 years of education
V	16 or more years of education

Source: Wechsler Preschool and Primary Scale of Intelligence—Revised. Copyright © 1989 by The Psychological Corporation. Reproduced by permission. All rights reserved. "WPPSI-R" is a registered trademark of The Psychological Corporation.

good fit between the obtained sample and target population indicates that a truly representative sample was used in the standardization of the WPPSI-R.

In addition to obtaining a representative sample, an oversample of approximately 400 minority children was obtained. This oversample, although not used to construct the normative tables, was used to analyze potential item bias. The results of bias analyses were used as part of the item selection procedures.

RELIABILITY

The WPPSI-R is a highly reliable instrument. Three types of reliability are provided in WPPSI-R manual, including internal consistency, stability, and interscorer agreement.

Internal Consistency

The average Verbal, Performance, and Full scale internal consistency coefficients across the nine age groups are .95, .92, and .96, respectively. These high reliabilities exceed the recommended .90 criterion (Bracken, 1987) indicating that, at the scale level, the WPPSI-R is sufficiently reliable for the individual assessment of children aged 3 years to 7 years, 3 months.

The within-age reliabilities also tend to be quite high. The only age at which the .90 criterion is not met is the 7-year age level, for which the Verbal estimates are .86 and .85, respectively. This result was not unexpected because the WPPSI-R is appropriate only for lower-ability children at age 7. Overall, the evidence lends support to interpreting the three scales individually at all age levels.

In addition to being highly reliable at the scale level, the WPPSI-R possesses good reliability at the individual subtest level. The average internal consistency reliability of the six Verbal subtests ranges from .80 for the Arithmetic subtest to .86 for the Similarities subtest. The Performance scale subtests tend to be slightly less reliable than the Verbal scale subtests. The average internal consistency reliability of the Performance subtests ranges from .63 for the Object Assembly subtest to .85 for the Block Design and Picture Completion subtests. Applying the .80 criterion suggested by Bracken (1987) as evidence for sufficient subtest reliability, eight of the 12 WPPSI-R subtests exceed this criterion and two subtests (Geometric Design and Mazes) narrowly miss this criterion. The only subtests that are clearly below the .80 criterion are the Object Assembly and Animal Pegs subtests.

In summary, the WPPSI-R is highly reliable at the scale level, and it also possesses good reliability at the subtest level. Therefore, one may feel confident in interpreting individually the three scales and a large majority of the subtests.

STABILITY

A test-retest study of 175 children in the standardization sample was conducted with an interval of 3 to 7 weeks ($M = 4$ weeks). The sample approximated the standardization sample for ethnicity and geographic region. Using the .90 criterion for the test-retest stability of IQs, the Verbal and Full scale stability meets or exceeds this criterion (correlations of .90 and .91, respectively) and the Performance scale narrowly misses the .90 criterion (.88). These stability coefficients suggest that the WPPSI-R scales are adequately stable over a brief period and provide further evidence of the reliability of this test.

Interscorer Agreement

Most WPPSI-R subtests are objectively scored; however, some subtests are subjectively scored and are, therefore, more vulnerable to scoring error. For these subtests, which include Comprehension, Vocabulary, Similarities, and Mazes, it was necessary to evaluate interscorer reliability. In addition, previous research with the WPPSI indicated a low rate of scoring agreement on the Geometric Design subtest (Sattler, 1976). A more objective set of scoring rules and procedures was created for this subtest, and its effect on scorer agreement also was evaluated.

To assess the interscorer reliability of the Comprehension, Vocabulary, Similarities, and Mazes subtests, a sample of 151 cases (83 males and 68 females) stratified by age was randomly selected from all cases collected for the standardization. For the Geometric Design subtest, a sample of 188 cases (105 males and 83 females) was randomly selected. A group of research scorers was trained and given practice in scoring the subtests. The cases were subdivided by age to control for age effects, and two scorers were selected at random to score all the cases in each age group.

To assess interscorer reliability, a type of intraclass correlation was used that takes account of differences in scorer leniency as well as random error (Shrout & Fleiss, 1979). Interscorer reliability coefficients were as follows: .96 on Comprehension, .94 on Vocabulary, .96 on Similarities, .94 on Mazes, and .88 on Geometric Design. These results indicate that the scoring rules for these subtests are objective enough for different scorers to produce similar results and provide further evidence of the reliability of the WPPSI-R.

VALIDITY

The WPPSI-R manual reports studies of both construct and concurrent validity. Subsequent to publication of the scale, the predictive validity of the WPPSI-R has been examined. Studies by Kaplan (1996, 1993) have established the validity of scores obtained on the WPPSI-R during the preschool years for predicting later school performance. These findings are quite similar to those from studies using the WPPSI (Feshback, Adelman, & Fuller, 1977).

Construct Validity

The construct validity of the WPPSI-R was established through two exploratory factor analytic studies. First, the data from the entire standardization sample were subjected to a principal axis factor analysis with orthogonal rotation. Using an eigenvalue greater than 1 criterion, a two-factor (Verbal–Performance) solution was obtained (Table 5.4). The second study explored the consistency of the two-factor structure across age. A principal axis factor analysis with an orthogonal rotation and eigenvalue greater than 1 criterion was applied to three groups within the standardization sample: 3 years, 0 months to 4 years, 6 months; 4 years, 7 months to 6 years, 0 months; and 6 years, 1 month to 7 years, 3 months. Similar to the results from the entire standardization sample, the by-age results within age groups indicate a two-factor (Verbal–Performance) solution. The one notable exception to these results occurs in the first age group, for which the Picture Completion subtest had

TABLE 5.4   WPPSI-R Principal Axis Factor Matrix with Orthogonal Rotation for Standardization Sample

SUBTEST	FACTOR I	FACTOR II
Comprehension	.75	.19
Information	.74	.33
Vocabulary	.73	.21
Sentences	.65	.24
Similarities	.64	.30
Arithmetic	.57	.44
Block Design	.26	.70
Geometric Design	.20	.64
Object Assembly	.17	.61
Mazes	.19	.59
Picture Completion	.39	.53
Animal Pegs	.25	.41

Source: Wechsler Preschool and Primary Scale of Intelligence—Revised. Copyright © 1989 by The Psychological Corporation. Reproduced by permission. All rights reserved. "WPPSI-R" is a registered trademark of The Psychological Corporation.

$N = 1,700$

equal loadings on both factors. Except for this split loading, all Verbal scale subtests loaded more highly on the verbal factor and all Performance scale subtests loaded more highly on the performance factor at all age levels.

The results of factor analyses for both the entire standardization sample and for three narrower age groups support the conclusion that the WPPSI-R has an underlying two-factor structure. Furthermore, these findings lend support to interpreting the verbal and performance abilities separately at all ages.

Concurrent Validity

Several studies comparing the WPPSI-R to other intellectual assessment scales are reported in the manual. These are summarized in Table 5.5.

As would be expected, the highest correlations obtained across these five studies were between the Wechsler scales, in particular WPPSI-R with the WPPSI. The correlations between the corresponding IQ on these two instruments were all above .80. Given that the WPPSI-R contains many of the same tasks as the WPPSI, these findings were expected. The WPPSI-R also correlates very highly with the WISC-R, with correlations between corresponding IQs ranging from .75 to .85, likewise, an anticipated finding.

TABLE 5.5 Summary of Concurrent Validity Studies with the WPPSI-R

MEASURE	SAMPLE	DESIGN	RESULTS
WPPSI	144 children (73 females, 71 males) ethnic and regional proportions match standardized sample	Tests were administered in alternating order. Between-test interval ranged from 3 to 5 weeks.	Correlations between the scales were: VIQ (.85), PIQ (.82) and FIQ (.87)

	WPPSI-R			WPPSI		
	VIQ	*PIQ*	*FSIQ*	*VIQ*	*PSQ*	*FSIQ*
M	104.0	102.8	103.9	109.1	112.2	111.6
SD	15.9	15.9	16.2	16.9	15.7	16.3

MEASURE	SAMPLE	DESIGN	RESULTS
WISC-R (Urbina & Clayton, in preparation)	50 children (25 females, 25 males), age 72–86 months (mean = 79) from Jacksonville, Florida metropolitan area	Tests were administered in alternating order. Between-test interval ranged from 7 to 8 days.	Correlation between the scales were: VIQ (.76), PIQ (.75), and FIQ (.85)

	WPPSI-R			WISC-R		
	VIQ	*PIQ*	*FSIQ*	*VIQ*	*PSQ*	*FSIQ*
M	106.9	99.8	103.8	111.6	108.7	111.3
SD	11.3	13.1	11.6	15.3	12.3	11.7

MEASURE	SAMPLE	DESIGN	RESULTS
Stanford-Binet Fourth Edition	115 children, age 48–86 months (mean = 70) from 3 of 4 geographic regions (excluding Northeast)	Tests were administered in alternating order. Between-test interval ranged from 1 to 90 days.	Correlation between the WPPSI-R FSIQ and the SB Composite was .74, between PIQ and SB Abstract/Visual Reasoning was .54, and between VIQ and SB Verbal Reasoning was .63.

	WPPSI-R			SB-IV		
	VIQ	*PIQ*	*FSIQ*	*Verb Reas*	*Abst Vis*	*Comp*
M	104.1	104.8	105.3	107.0	106.6	107.2
SD	15.1	13.2	14.0	11.7	15.2	12.8

(continued)

TABLE 5.5 Continued

MEASURE	SAMPLE	DESIGN	RESULTS
McCarthy Scales of Children's Abilities	93 children (49 females, 44 males), ages 48–72 months (mean = 62.5) from the Northeast and North Central regions	Tests were administered in alternating order. Between-test interval ranged from 7 to 21 days.	Correlation between the WPPSI-R FSIQ and MSCA GCI was .81, between the VIQ and MSCA was .75 and between the PIQ and MSCA Perceptual Performance was .71.

	WPPSI-R			MSCA		
	VIQ	PIQ	FSIQ	Verb	Percep Perform	GCI
M	103.3	101.2	102.4	52.1	54.7	104.8
SD	12.9	14.4	13.5	9.8	8.8	14.3

MEASURE	SAMPLE	DESIGN	RESULTS
K-ABC	59 children ages 39 to 76 months (mean = 61) from the Northeast and South regions	Tests were administered in alternating order. Between-test interval ranging from 5 to 15 days.	Correlation between the WPPSI-R FSIQ and K-ABC Mental Processing Score was .49, between the VIQ and Sequential Processing score was .31, between the PIQ and the Simultaneous Processing Score was .37.

	WPPSI-R			K-ABC		
	VIQ	PIQ	FSIQ	Simult	Seq	Mental
M	94.4	100.4	96.8	101.3	104.4	103.1
SD	12.5	13.5	12.6	13.0	14.3	13.1

The lowest correlations obtained were those between the WPPSI-R and the K-ABC (Kaufman & Kaufman, 1983). The correlations between WPPSI-R IQs and K-ABC Processing scores ranged from .31 to .49. These results are not surprising in view of the fact that the K-ABC does not resemble the WPPSI-R in terms of scope or content.

Comparing the mean WPPSI-R IQs with mean scores on other instruments, the mean WPPSI FSIQ was approximately 8 points higher than that for the WPPSI-R, and the WPPSI VIQ and PIQ were 5 and 9 points higher, respectively, than the corresponding WPPSI-R IQs. Differences of this magnitude also were found between the WPPSI-R and the WISC-R. Thus, these discrepancies in mean scores were expected given the 15- to 20-year period between the standardization of these instruments. As the between-standardization interval decreased, so too did the discrepancy between the mean scores. For example, there was a 2- to 3-point mean difference between the three WPPSI-R IQ scales and the corresponding area scores on the *Stanford-Binet, Fourth Edition* (Thorndike, Hagen, & Sattler, 1986), a scale that was standardized within three years of the standardization of the WPPSI-R.

Several studies subsequent to the publication of the manual have supported the concurrent validity of the WPPSI-R. Researchers have found a strong relationship between the WPPSI-R and the McCarthy Scales of Children's Abilities (Oakes & Faust, 1990), the Kaufman Brief Intelligence Test, and the K-ABC (Lassiter, 1995). These findings, in concert with the data presented in the manual, provide strong support for the use of the WPPSI-R.

In summary, the WPPSI-R correlates highly with previous Wechsler scales and, to a somewhat lesser extent, with other measures of intelligence. These correlations provide direct evidence of the concurrent validity of the WPPSI-R. Further evidence for the concurrent validity of the WPPSI-R is found in the fact that the obtained mean differences between the WPPSI-R and the various other instruments are in the direction and of the magnitude one would expect based upon the between-standardization intervals.

INTERPRETING THE WPPSI-R

Interpreting the WPPSI-R is, to a large extent, quite similar to interpreting other Wechsler scales. Kaufman (1994) and Sattler (1992) provide a thorough discussion of the interpretive issues related to the WPPSI-R.

As with any interpretive approach, there are certain limitations and precautions one should take to ensure that conclusions are drawn correctly. The most reliable conclusions can be made at the Full scale level. Conclusions drawn at successively lower levels (e.g., at the scale or subtest levels) have lower reliability because the accuracy of the conclusions drawn is affected by the reliability of the scales or subtests being compared.

The following procedures for interpretation should be treated as general guidelines and not as required procedures. They should serve as an aid to the examiner in generating and testing hypotheses about the child's particular strengths and weaknesses. The procedures recommended here do not include interpretation at the item level. It is believed that item interpretation is risky, given the low reliability of any individual item.

Step 1. Interpreting the Full Scale IQ. Conclusions based on the Full Scale IQ will tend to be the most reliable. Interpretation of the Full Scale IQ can be approached in two ways. The first approach is a quantitative one. The child's Full Scale IQ can be viewed in terms of its deviation from the norm and its percentile rank (Table 5.6). An IQ of 100 on the Full scale defines performance of the average child of a given age. IQs of 85 and 115 correspond to 1 standard deviation below and above the mean, respectively, whereas IQs of 70 and 130 are each 2 standard deviations from the mean. About two-thirds of all children obtain IQs between 85 and 115, about 95 percent score in the 70 to 130 range, and nearly all obtain IQs between 55 and 145 (3 standard deviations on either side of the mean). In addition to determining the distance from the mean, one also can determine the approximate rank of an IQ. Using Table 5.6, which provides selected IQ to percentile rank conversions, the examiner can determine the ranking of the child's IQ relative to the standardization sample.

The second approach is a qualitative system aimed at describing the child's performance. This method might be of most use when describing the child's test performance to someone unfamiliar with the statistical base of the IQ. Table 5.7 presents specific IQ ranges and their corresponding qualitative diagnostic categories. The range provided might not apply to all possible situations; however, if alternative limits are used, the statistical bases for determining the limits must be stated.

Step 2. Comparing the Verbal and Performance Scales. The second step in interpreting a child's performance on the WPPSI-R is to examine the discrepancy

TABLE 5.6 Relation of IQs to Deviation from the Mean and Percentile Ranks

VERBAL PERFORMANCE, OR FULL SCALE IQ	NUMBER OF SDs FROM THE MEAN	PERCENTILE RANK[a]
145	+3	99.9
140	+2²/₃	99.6
135	+2¹/₃	99
130	+2	98
125	+1²/₃	95
120	+1¹/₃	91
115	+1	84
110	+²/₃	75
105	+¹/₃	63
100	0 (Mean)	50
95	−¹/₃	37
90	−²/₃	25
85	−1	16
80	−1¹/₃	9
75	−1²/₃	5
70	−2	2
65	−2¹/₃	1
60	−2²/₃	0.4
55	−3	0.1

Source: Wechsler Preschool and Primary Scale of Intelligence—Revised. Copyright © 1989 by The Psychological Corporation. Reproduced by permission. All rights reserved. "WPPSI-R" is a registered trademark of The Psychological Corporation.

[a]The percentile ranks are theoretical values for a normal distribution.

between the Verbal and Performance Scale IQs. Table 5.8 presents, by age, the differences required for statistical significance at the 15 percent and 5 percent levels.

The information on significance should aid the examiner in determining which differences should be examined in greater detail and which, because they occur by chance, should not be interpreted as meaningful. However, the fact that a difference between the VIQ and PIQ is significant does not tell the entire story. It is also useful to know how frequently a difference of a certain magnitude occurred in the standardization sample. A discrepancy might be statistically significant and still occur frequently in the population. Table 5.9 presents the frequency of VIQ-PIQ differences found in the standardization sample. The following example illustrates the use of the significant difference and frequency of difference information contained in Tables 5.8 and 5.9:

A 5¹/₂-year-old child obtains a VIQ of 105 and a PIQ of 92. A discrepancy of 13 or more points is significant at the .05 level. However, this 13-point discrepancy, according to the frequency table on page 130 of the manual, occurred in approximately 25 percent of the standardization sample, suggesting that a discrepancy of this magnitude is a fairly common occurrence.

Interpretation of differences at the scale level should incorporate information on both the significance and frequency of the discrepancy.

Step 3. Comparing the Mean Verbal and Performance Scaled Score to an Individual Subtest Scaled Score. Comparisons of the scaled scores on individual subtests to the average scaled score of the scale to which those subtests belong provide information on specific strengths and weaknesses within a particular ability domain. Table 5.10 presents the differences between the scaled scores on any individual subtest and the average subtest score required for statistical significance at the .05 and .01 levels. The knowledge that a difference is significant is again only part of the story. It also is important to know the frequency of a discrepancy between a subtest scaled score and the average scaled score.

Table 5.11 provides differences obtained by various percentages of the standardization sample. The following is an example of how to use information on both significance of difference and frequency of this difference.

A 4-year-old child obtains a scaled score of 5 on the Object Assembly subtest. The child's average scaled score for the Performance scale (average of five subtests) is 11. Thus, there is a 6-point difference between the child's subtest scaled core and average scaled score. This 6-point difference exceeds the critical value of 4.88 for the Object Assembly subtest at the .01 level (see Table 5.10). A difference of this magnitude is rare, as evidenced by the fact that it occurred in less than 1 percent of the standardization sample (Table 5.11).

Discrepancies between subtest scaled scores and the average scaled score for the scale to which they belong are interpreted in much the same way as a discrepancy between VIQ and PIQ. Information on both the significance and frequency of the discrepancy is important when determining a child's relative strengths and weaknesses.

TABLE 5.7 Intelligence Classification

		PERCENTAGE INCLUDED	
IQ Range	Classification	Theoretical Normal Curve	Actual[a] Sample
130 and above	Very superior	2.2	2.7
120–129	Superior	6.7	6.5
110–119	High average	16.1	17.3
90–109	Average	50.0	49.4
80–89	Low average	16.1	15.7
70–79	Borderline	6.7	6.4
69 and below	Intellectually Deficient[b]	2.2	2.0

Source: Wechsler Preschool and Primary Scale of Intelligence—Revised. Copyright © 1989 by The Psychological Corporation. Reproduced by permission. All rights reserved. "WPPSI-R" is a registered trademark of The Psychological Corporation.

[a]The percentages shown are for the Full Scale IQ and are based on the total standardization sample ($N = 1,700$). The percentages obtained for the Verbal IQ and Performance IQ are very similar.

[b]In place of the term *mentally retarded* used in the WPPSI, the WPPSI-R uses the term *intellectually deficient*. This practice avoids the implication that a very low IQ is sufficient evidence for the classification of "mental" retardation. The term *intellectually deficient* is descriptive and refers only to low intellectual functioning. This usage is consistent with the standards recommended by the American Association of Mental Deficiency (Grossman, 1983) and the American Psychiatric Association (1980).

Step 4. Comparing Scaled Scores on Individual Subtests. After having compared discrepancies in the VIQ and PIQ and the average subtest scaled score with the individual subtest scaled scores, the examiner frequently seeks more detailed information regarding the child's particular strengths and weaknesses. By comparing the child's scores on individual subtests, the examiner can explore hypotheses about a child's particular strengths and weaknesses.

Tables 5.12 and 5.13 show differences between scaled scores on pairs of WPPSI-R subtests that are required to reach significance at the .15 and .05 levels averaged across the nine age groups. The following example illustrates the use of these tables.

A 5-year-old child obtains a scaled score of 10 on the Block Design subtest and 13 on the Mazes subtest. This 3-point difference is significant at the .15 level (critical value = 2.67) but not at the .05 level (critical value = 3.64).

An important point to remember when interpreting discrepancies between subtests is that the *SEM* varies from subtest to subtest and from age to age within subtests. The lower the subtest reliabilities (and, hence, the higher the *SEM* of the difference), the greater the likelihood that the difference between scores is because of chance rather than a real difference in the child's abilities. For example, for a child aged 3, a larger difference

TABLE 5.8 Differences between WPPSI-R Performance IQ and Verbal IQ Required for Significance at 15 and 5 Percent Levels

Level of Significance	AGE GROUP									Average of Nine Groups
	3	3½	4	4½	5	5½	6	6½	7	
15%	7.30	7.27	7.39	7.56	7.90	8.50	8.34	8.91	10.06	8.13
5%	9.90	9.89	10.06	10.29	10.76	11.56	11.36	12.12	13.70	11.07

Source: Wechsler Preschool and Primary Scale of Intelligence—Revised. Copyright © 1989 by The Psychological Corporation. Reproduced by permission. All rights reserved. "WPPSI-R" is a registered trademark of The Psychological Corporation.

TABLE 5.9 Frequency of Performance IQ–Verbal IQ Difference in the Standardization Sample by Age

Percentage Obtaining Given or Greater Discrepancy	VIQ–PIQ DISCREPANCIES									
	Age									
	3	3½	4	4½	5	5½	6	6½	7	Average[a]
50	8	9	9	8	9	9	9	8	10	9
25	13	14	16	14	16	16	16	15	16	15
20	15	16	17	17	18	18	18	16	17	17
10	19	21	23	22	24	22	23	22	21	22
5	23	28	26	26	28	25	28	28	25	26
2	28	34	31	29	33	38	33	33	32	32
1	35	35	32	35	34	46	38	38	33	36

Source: Wechsler Preschool and Primary Scale of Intelligence—Revised. Copyright © 1989 by the Psychological Corporation. Reproduced by permission. All rights reserved. "WPPSI-R" is a registered trademark of The Psychological Corporation.

[a]Average values have been rounded to the nearest whole number.

is required for statistical significance when comparing the child's scaled scores on Object Assembly and Arithmetic (with reliability coefficients of .63 and .78, respectively) than when comparing scores on Information and Picture Completion (with reliability coefficients of .90 and .78, respectively). Sattler (1992) suggests an additional precaution. He recommends that the values are more accurate when prior rather than post hoc comparisons are made because the use of post hoc comparisons tends to capitalize on chance.

HYPOTHESIS TESTING BASED ON DISCREPANCY INFORMATION

The primary purpose for interpreting discrepancies in a child's performance is to confirm or discount hypotheses about that child's abilities. Statistically significant discrepancies, whether among scales or subtests, indicate real differences in ability.

The Verbal scale measures primarily verbal ability. The questions are presented orally and the child responds orally. On the other hand, the Performance scale consists of primarily perceptual motor tasks. The tasks generally are presented in a nonverbal manner and the child's responses are primarily motoric.

A significant discrepancy between Verbal and Performance scores can be interpreted several ways, including interest patterns, cognitive style, psychopathology or specific deficiencies, or strengths in an ability (Sattler,

1992). It is left to the clinician to determine which of the possible interpretations is feasible in light of the child's performance and clinical history.

When interpreting a significant Verbal–Performance discrepancy, the examiner must determine the clinical significance of the discrepancy. For example, a significant difference exists between a Verbal IQ of 145 and a Performance IQ of 130, yet in reality this difference does not suggest that the child is deficient in the Performance area. Sattler (1992) points out that hypotheses should be formulated in relationship to the child's absolute Verbal, Performance, or Full Scale IQ.

Similar to discrepancies at the Verbal–Performance scale level, discrepancies among the individual subtests from average and pairs of subtests (see section on description of subtests for specific abilities measured by each subtest) should be examined for clinical significance. For example, if a child obtains a scaled score of 8 on Information and has a Verbal scale mean of 13, one can conclude that the child's general knowledge about the environment and long-term memory is significantly less well developed than his or her other verbal skills. Furthermore, if this Information scaled score is compared to the child's scaled score of 12 on both the Comprehension and Vocabulary subtests, one can also conclude that the child's logical reasoning and understanding of relationships is significantly better than his or her knowledge of the environment. In general, the examiner should interpret subtest discrepancy information

TABLE 5.10 Differences Required for Significance between Scaled Scores on Individual Subtests and the Average Subtest Score

Subtest	MEAN OF 5 PERFORMANCE SUBTESTS[a]		MEAN OF 6 PERFORMANCE SUBTESTS		MEAN OF 5 VERBAL SUBTESTS[b]		MEAN OF 6 VERBAL SUBTESTS		MEAN OF 10 SUBTESTS[c]		MEAN OF 11 SUBTESTS[d]		MEAN OF 12 SUBTESTS	
	.05	.01	.05	.01	.05	.01	.05	.01	.05	.01	.05	.01	.05	.01
Object Assembly	4.07	4.88	4.32	5.12	—	—	—	—	4.83	5.68	4.93	5.71	4.99	5.74
Geometric Design	3.20	3.83	3.39	4.02	—	—	—	—	3.65	4.29	3.74	4.32	3.79	4.36
Block Design	2.86	3.43	3.00	3.55	—	—	—	—	3.18	3.73	3.22	3.73	3.27	3.73
Mazes	3.30	3.96	3.47	4.11	—	—	—	—	3.79	4.46	3.85	4.46	3.90	4.49
Picture Completion	2.92	3.49	3.05	3.61	—	—	—	—	3.23	3.8	3.31	3.83	3.33	3.83
Animal Pegs[e]	4.11	—	4.11	4.79	—	—	—	—	—	—	—	—	4.71	5.41
Information	—	—	—	—	2.89	3.46	3.02	3.58	3.34	3.93	3.39	3.93	3.44	3.96
Comprehension	—	—	—	—	2.97	3.55	3.13	3.71	3.46	4.06	3.51	4.06	3.56	4.09
Arithmetic	—	—	—	—	3.10	3.71	3.26	3.86	3.63	4.26	3.71	4.29	3.73	4.29
Vocabulary	—	—	—	—	2.81	3.37	2.97	3.52	3.26	3.83	3.33	3.86	3.36	3.86
Similarities	—	—	—	—	2.81	3.37	2.94	3.49	3.23	3.80	3.31	3.83	3.33	3.83
Sentences	—	—	—	—	—	—	3.10	3.67	—	—	3.51	4.06	3.53	4.06

Source: Wechsler Preschool and Primary Scale of Intelligence—Revised. Copyright © 1989 by the Psychological Corporation. Reproduced by permission. All rights reserved. "WPPSI-R" is a registered trademark of The Psychological Corporation.

Note: To compute the deviations from average that are significant at the .05 and .01 levels, the formula provided by Davis (1959) was used. Values are corrected using Bonferroni adjustment for multiple comparisons.

[a]Animal Pegs excluded. [b]Sentences excluded. [c]Animal Pegs and Sentences excluded. [d]The difference for 11 subtests were calculated with the 10 required subtests and the Sentences subtest. [e]The Average SEM for the Animal Pegs subtest was obtained by averaging the SEMs across the two age groups in the test-retest study.

TABLE 5.11 Differences Obtained by the Various Percentages of the Standardization Sample When Each Subtest Is Compared to the Average Subtest Score

Subtest	PERFORMANCE SCALE (6 SUBTESTS)				VERBAL SCALE (6 SUBTESTS)				FULL SCALE (12 SUBTESTS)			
	10%	5%	2%	1%	10%	5%	2%	1%	10%	5%	2%	1%
Object Assembly	3.5	4.2	4.8	5.3	—	—	—	—	4.0	4.8	5.7	6.1
Geometric Design	3.3	4.0	4.7	5.3	—	—	—	—	3.8	4.4	5.5	6.0
Block Design	3.2	3.8	4.5	5.2	—	—	—	—	3.6	4.3	5.2	5.7
Mazes	3.5	4.2	5.0	5.7	—	—	—	—	4.0	4.8	5.9	6.7
Picture Completion	3.5	4.2	5.0	5.5	—	—	—	—	3.6	4.2	5.1	5.8
Animal Pegs[e]	3.8	4.8	5.7	6.7	—	—	—	—	4.1	5.0	6.2	6.9
Information	—	—	—	—	2.7	3.2	3.8	4.2	3.2	3.8	4.4	4.9
Comprehension	—	—	—	—	2.8	3.7	4.5	5.2	3.6	4.3	5.3	5.9
Arithmetic	—	—	—	—	3.2	3.8	4.5	5.0	3.2	3.9	4.8	5.3
Vocabulary	—	—	—	—	3.0	3.5	4.3	4.7	3.5	4.2	5.1	5.6
Similarities	—	—	—	—	3.0	3.8	4.5	5.0	3.5	4.2	4.9	5.4
Sentences	—	—	—	—	3.2	3.8	4.8	5.3	3.7	4.4	5.2	5.8

Source: Wechsler Preschool and Primary Scale of Intelligence—Revised. Copyright © 1989 by the Psychological Corporation. Reproduced by permission. All rights reserved. "WPPSI-R" is a registered trademark of The Psychological Corporation.

in light of the original hypotheses about the child's strengths and weaknesses. That is to say, one should compare subtests that measure those abilities that are hypothesized to be particularly strong or particularly weak. Whether one's hypotheses about the child are confirmed or discounted, examining discrepancy information will aid the examiner in more fully understanding the child's abilities and devising a set of practical and useful recommendations based on the child's performance. One also should remember that interpretations going beyond the scale level are more subjective and tend to be less reliable and valid. Thus, the wise examiner will interpret the child's performance carefully and in light of all information that is known about the child.

SUMMARY

The revision of the Wechsler Preschool and Primary Scale was undertaken with two primary goals as the focus: to update the norms and extend the age range of the scale both upward and downward. The WPPSI-R has retained many of the features of the WPPSI that made it a highly regarded assessment instrument.

For the most part, the WPPSI-R subtests are similar to those of the WPPSI. A majority of the subtests

have sufficient floor and ceiling to assess children from ages 3 to 6½ years. At the scale level, the floor and ceiling of the Verbal, Performance, and Full scales are sufficient for both low- and high-ability children across the entire age span.

The standardization sample of 1,700 children closely approximates the target population from the 1986 Census Bureau data. In addition to obtaining a representative sample for the standardization, an oversample of minority children also was collected to analyze potential bias.

The reliability of the WPPSI-R is excellent at the scale level with all three scales exceeding the .90 criterion. In addition, a majority of the subtests also exceed the criterion (.80) to be considered reliable. Further evidence of the WPPSI-R's reliability is the fact that the stability estimates obtained in a test-retest study generally met the criterion of .90.

The validity of the WPPSI-R has been established through both concurrent and construct validity research. Studies of the concurrent validity indicate that the WPPSI-R correlates highly with other measures of intellectual ability, particularly other Wechsler scales. The construct validity of the WPPSI-R was established through factor analytic studies that consistently yielded a two-factor solution.

TABLE 5.12 Differences between Scaled Scores Required for Statistical Significance at the 15 Percent Level

SUBTEST	OBJECT ASSEMBLY	GEOMETRIC DESIGN	BLOCK DESIGN	MAZES	PICTURE COMPLETION	ANIMAL PEGS	INFORMATION	COMPREHENSION	ARITHMETIC	VOCABULARY	SIMILARITIES
Geometric Design	3.34	—									
Block Design	3.17	2.61	—								
Mazes	3.39	2.87	2.67	—							
Picture Completion	3.20	2.64	2.42	2.70	—						
Animal Pegs[a]	3.67	3.21	3.02	3.25	3.06	—					
Information	3.23	2.68	2.47	2.74	2.49	3.10	—				
Comprehension	3.28	2.73	2.52	2.79	2.54	3.14	2.58	—			
Arithmetic	3.32	2.79	2.59	2.85	2.62	3.18	2.66	2.71	—		
Vocabulary	3.20	2.65	2.43	2.71	2.46	3.06	2.51	2.56	2.62	—	
Similarities	3.20	2.64	2.43	2.71	2.45	3.07	2.49	2.54	2.62	2.47	—
Sentences	3.26	2.71	2.51	2.77	2.53	3.12	2.58	2.63	2.70	2.55	2.54

Source: Wechsler Preschool and Primary Scale of Intelligence—Revised. Copyright © 1989 by the Psychological Corporation. Reproduced by permission. All rights reserved. "WPPSI-R" is a registered trademark of The Psychological Corporation.

Note: Table 11 is based on average values for nine age groups. To determine whether the difference between two subtests is reliable, the following formula was used:

Where Z is the normal curve value associated with the desired confidence level (i.e., 15 percent level = 1.44). SEM_A and SEM_B are the standard errors of measurement of the two subtests.

[a]The SEM for Animal Pegs was determined from the test-retest study to be 1.74 for the entire retest sample ($N = 175$).

$$\text{Difference Score} = Z \sqrt{SEM_{A^2} + SEM_{B^2}}$$

TABLE 5.13 Differences between Scaled Scores Required for Statistical Significance at the 5 Percent Level

SUBTEST	OBJECT ASSEMBLY	GEOMETRIC DESIGN	BLOCK DESIGN	MAZES	PICTURE COMPLETION	ANIMAL PEGS	INFORMATION	COMPREHENSION	ARITHMETIC	VOCABULARY	SIMILARITIES
Geometric Design	4.55	—									
Block Design	4.31	3.55	—								
Mazes	4.61	3.91	3.64	—							
Picture Completion	4.36	3.59	3.30	3.68	—						
Animal Pegs[a]	4.99	4.36	4.11	4.43	4.15	—					
Information	4.40	3.64	3.36	3.73	3.39	4.21	—				
Comprehension	4.46	3.71	3.43	3.80	3.46	4.27	3.52	—			
Arithmetic	4.52	3.80	3.52	3.88	3.56	4.33	3.62	3.69	—		
Vocabulary	4.35	3.60	3.31	3.68	3.35	4.16	3.41	3.48	3.57	—	
Similarities	4.36	3.60	3.31	3.68	3.34	4.17	3.39	3.46	3.57	3.36	—
Sentences	4.44	3.70	3.41	3.78	3.45	4.25	3.51	3.58	3.67	3.46	3.46

Note: Table 12 is based on average values for nine age groups. The difference required for statistical significance was computed using the following formula:

$$\text{Difference Score} = Z \sqrt{SEM_A^2 + SEM_B^2}$$

Where Z is the normal curve value associated with the desired confidence level (i.e., 5 percent level = 1.96), and SEM_A and SEM_B are the standard errors of measurement of the two subtests.

[a]The SEM for Animal Pegs was determined from the test-retest study to be 1.74 for the entire retest sample (N = 175).

The approach to interpreting the WPPSI-R is quite similar to that of interpreting the WISC-III. The successive levels approach recommended here allows the examiner to generate and test hypotheses at the highest level of certainty first, before proceeding to hypothesis testing at a lower level of certainty. In general, this approach should lead to more systematic and appropriate interpretation of the WPPSI-R.

The WPPSI-R is a well-standardized, reliable, and valid instrument for the assessment of intellectual functioning of children aged 3 years through 7 years, 3 months.

Future research should focus on the issues of predictive and discriminant validity. Also, further work in the area of interpreting the WPPSI-R would aid the clinician using this instrument for diagnostic purposes.

REFERENCES

Bracken, B. A. (1987). Limitations of preschool instruments and standards for minimal levels of technical adequacy. *Journal of Psychoeducational Assessment, 5,* 313–326.

Buckhalt, J. A. (1990). Wechsler Preschool and Primary Scale of Intelligence—Revised (WPPSI-R). *Diagnostique, 15,* 254–263.

Feshback, S., Adelman, H., & Fuller, W. (1977). Prediction of reading and related academic problems. *Journal of Educational Psychology, 69,* 299–308.

Hollenbeck, G. R., & Kaufman, A. S. (1973). Factor analysis of the Wechsler Preschool and Primary Scale of Intelligence (WPPSI). *Journal of Clinical Psychology, 29,* 41–45.

Kaplan, C. (1993). Predicting first-grade achievement from pre-kindergarten WPPSI-R scores. *Journal of Psychoeducational Assessment, 11,* 133–138.

Kaplan, C. (1996). Predictive validity of the WPPSI-R: A four-year follow-up study. *Psychology in the Schools, 33,* 211–220.

Kaufman, A. S. (1992). Evaluation of the WISC-III and WPPSI-R for gifted children. *Roeper Review, 14,* 154–158.

Kaufman, A. S. (1994). *Intelligent Testing with the WISC-III.* New York: John Wiley and Sons.

Kaufman, A. S., & Kaufman, N. L. (1983). *Kaufman Assessment Battery for Children.* Circle Pines, MN: American Guidance Service.

Lassiter, K. S. (1995). The relationship between young children's academic achievement and measures of intelligence. *Psychology in the Schools, 32,* 170–177.

McCarthy, D. (1972). *Manual for the McCarthy Scales of Children's Abilities* . San Antonio, TX: Psychological Corporation.

Oakes, J., & Faust, D. S. (1990, August). *Concurrent validation of the Wechsler Preschool and Primary Scale of Intelligence—Revised (WPPSI-R) with the McCarthy Scales of Children's Abilities and the Peabody Picture Vocabulary Test—Revised.* Paper presented at a meeting of the American Psychological Association, Boston, MA.

Sattler, J. (1976). Scoring difficulty of the WPPSI Geometric Design subtest. *Journal of School Psychology, 14,* 230–234.

Sattler, J. (1992). *Assessment of Children: WISC-III and WPPSI-R Supplement.* San Diego, CA: Author.

Shrout, P. E., & Fleiss, J. L. (1979). Intraclass correlations: Uses in assessing rater reliability. *Psychological Bulletin, 86*(2), 420–428.

Thorndike, R. L., Hagen, E. P., & Sattler, J. M. (1986). *Guide for administering and scoring the Stanford-Binet Intelligence Scale: Fourth Edition.* Chicago: Riverside.

U.S. Bureau of the Census. (1986). *Current population survey,* March 1986 [machine-readable data file]. Washington, DC: Author (Producer/Distributor).

Wechsler, D. (1967). *Manual for the Wechsler Preschool and Primary Scale of Intelligence.* San Antonio, TX: Psychological Corporation.

Wechsler, D. (1989). *Manual for the Wechsler Preschool and Primary Scale of Intelligence—Revised.* San Antonio, TX: Psychological Corporation.

CHAPTER 6

THE ASSESSMENT OF PRESCHOOL CHILDREN WITH THE STANFORD-BINET INTELLIGENCE SCALE: FOURTH EDITION

R. STEVE MCCALLUM

DIANNE P. WHITAKER

In 1986 the Stanford-Binet Intelligence Scale: Fourth Edition (S-B IV) (Thorndike, Hagen, & Sattler, 1986) replaced the Stanford-Binet, Form L-M (Terman & Merrill, 1973). Like its predecessor, the S-B IV contains normative data for children as young as 2 years. Because the Binet L-M was the test of choice for many practitioners, the release of the new Binet was eagerly anticipated and expectations for the new Binet were high. The primary purpose of this revised chapter is to aid practitioners in the intelligent use of the S-B IV—specifically, to aid interpretation of the instrument, and to review current research about the S-B IV and its use with preschool children. Subtest descriptions and general test administration procedures will be presented, followed by a discussion of technical adequacy, including reliability and validity. Other technical characteristics will be considered, such as subtest floors, ceilings, item gradients, and so forth. Various interpretive strategies will be discussed, followed by a limited list of recommendations for use.

TEST DESCRIPTION

Test Model

The authors developed the new Binet according to a hierarchical model of intellectual functioning, using a three-level schemata. The model posits a global-to-specific theoretical structure with *g*, general intelligence, at the apex. Crystallized abilities, fluid and analytic abilities, and short-term memory constructs are at the second level; verbal reasoning, quantitative reasoning, and abstract visual reasoning are at the third level. As is apparent from Figure 6.1, the constructs become more specific at each successive level. The S-B IV's 15 subtests were assigned to the second- and third-level constructs logically, yielding four global scores and a test composite. Three of the global scores are assigned the construct names: Verbal Reasoning, Quantitative Reasoning, and Abstract/Visual Reasoning. The fourth global score, Short-Term Memory, is based on performance on short-term memory subtests.

Although the model is appealing intuitively and logically, it may not provide a foundation for appropriate interpretation. That is, the construct validity of the model is not fully supported by the factor analytic findings from the standardization sample, as shown in the *Stanford-Binet: Fourth Edition Technical Manual* (1986), nor from some of the studies that have been conducted since its introduction. Consequently, the "best-fit" model for the greatest number of children, especially preschool children, might not be the model described by the test authors. Examiners can determine the best interpretive strategy for a given child only after attending to and considering the available interpretative models.

Subtests for Preschool Children

The new Binet is not an omnibus test as was the third edition; that is, dissimilar items or tasks are not assigned to age blocks for administration. Rather, the new Binet follows the test format of the Wechsler scales. The subtests are assigned to more global scales with each subtest containing homogeneous item content of increasing difficulty. Examiners administer each subtest, from start to finish, according to a child's ability.

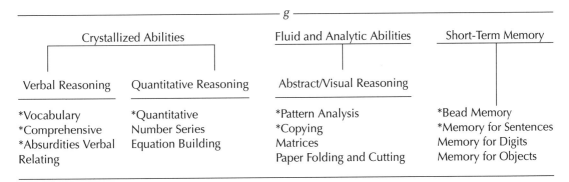

g

| Crystallized Abilities | | Fluid and Analytic Abilities | Short-Term Memory |

| Verbal Reasoning | Quantitative Reasoning | Abstract/Visual Reasoning | |

*Vocabulary	*Quantitative	*Pattern Analysis	*Bead Memory
*Comprehensive	Number Series	*Copying	*Memory for Sentences
*Absurdities Verbal	Equation Building	Matrices	Memory for Digits
Relating		Paper Folding and Cutting	Memory for Objects

Note. The asterisked (*) subtests are appropriate for preschool children. Scores yielded by the Fourth Edition include a composite score, four area scores (for Verbal Reasoning, Quantitative Reasoning, Abstract/Visual Reasoning, and Short-Term Memory), and 15 individual subtest scores.

Making many *unplanned* comparisons capitalizes on chance differences and results in a highly liberal procedure, one in which there is overinterpretation. (A similar phenomenon occurs commonly in research settings when too many unplanned comparisons are made; as you may remember, the Bonferoni *t* procedure provides a correction in the case of too many pairwise comparisons.)

FIGURE 6.1   The Stanford-Binet: Fouth Edition Structure

Source: Copyright © 1987 by the Riverside Publishing Company. Reproduced from the Examiner's Handbook: An Expanded Guide for fourth edition users of *The Stanford Binet Intelligence Scale,* by Elizabeth A. Delaney and Thomas F. Hopkins, with permission of the publisher.

The chronological age of the child and the quality of his or her performance on the router subtest, Vocabulary, determine the particular items administered. Because performance on the Vocabulary subtest aids in the determination of the appropriate starting points on the other subtests, it functions as the router subtest. Chronological age determines the starting item for any child on the Vocabulary subtest. Not all 15 subtests are administered to all children; only six core subtests are appropriate for all examinees. Most preschool children will be given eight subtests, although conversion scores are available for 12 subtests for 5-year-olds. Examiners administer all subtests, except Vocabulary, according to a child's chronological age and cognitive ability (estimated from performance on the Vocabulary subtest). All items are scored dichotomously—correct or incorrect. The examiner is also free to pick and choose certain subtests according to the particular referral reason and needs of the child. For example, the test authors recommend specific subtests for children who may be intellectually gifted, primarily because of the extended ceiling of these subtests. Other subtests, those characterized by an extended floor, are recommended for children suspected of being mentally retarded.

Sattler (1992) suggests a host of variables that impact functioning on the subtests. Some of those influences are listed in Table 6.1. Additional information regarding technical interpretive characteristics is depicted in Tables 6.2 and 6.3. The 15 subtests include four Verbal Reasoning subtests (Vocabulary, Comprehension, Absurdities, Verbal Relations), four Abstract/Visual Reasoning subtests (Pattern Analysis, Copying, Matrices, Paper Folding and Cutting), three Quantitative Reasoning subtests (Quantitative, Number Series, Equation Building), and four Short-Term Memory subtests (Bead Memory, Memory for Sentences, Memory for Digits, and Memory for Objects). The eight subtests administered to preschool children follow.

Test 1: Vocabulary. The Vocabulary subtest is divided into picture vocabulary and oral vocabulary sections. Of 46 items, the first 14 require the child to name a picture. The rest of the subtest requires the examinee to define words presented orally by the examiner. Although the authors are to be commended for addressing the needs of preschool children by including the less difficult picture vocabulary section, the combined format limits interpretability for children who respond to both types of

TABLE 6.1   Possible Abilities Influencing Area, Factor, and Subtest Scores for Preschool Children

AREAS

Verbal Reasoning	Abstract/Visual Reasoning	Quantitative Reasoning	Short-Term Memory
Crystallized skills	Fluid abilities	Crystallized skills	Attention
Formal schooling	Novel problem solving	Formal schooling	Concentration
General life experiences	General life experience	Mathematics	Visual processing and storage
Receptive/expressive language	Visual imagery	Number fluency	Verbal processing and storage
Verbal comprehension	Spatial relationships		
Verbal fluency	Nonverbal concept formation		
Verbal reasoning	Inductive reasoning		
Word knowledge	Visual/motor coordination		

FACTORS

Verbal Comprehension	Nonverbal Reasoning/Visualization
Verbal skills/language facility	Nonverbal concept formation and reasoning
Receptive/expressive language	Fluid ability
Crystallized skills	Visual/spatial skills
Verbal memory	Visual-motor coordination
Formal schooling/life experiences	Visual memory
	Visual analysis/synthesis

SUBTESTS

Vocabulary	Bead Memory	Quantitative	Memory for Sentences	Pattern Analysis	Comprehension	Absurdities	Copying
Expressive language	Visual memory	Number fluency	Short-term auditory memory	Spatialization	Vocabulary skills	Visual perception	Visual-motor coordination
Verbal memory	Visual sequencing	Preschool math	Verbal fluency	Visual-motor coordination	Verbal comprehension and expression	Long-term visual memory	Spatialization
Long-term memory	Chunking	Number facts	Verbal comprehension	Planning	Knowledge of culture	Knowledge of culture	Attention/concentration
Formal schooling	Attention		Syntax	Visual analysis and synthesis	Verbal fluency	Choose essential/nonessential details	Persistence
General life experience	Visual-motor coordination		Attention	Nonverbal concept formation	Long-term verbal memory		
Verbal fluency			Concentration	Resistance to time pressure			

TABLE 6.2   Subtests for Preschool Children

SUBTEST	MEDIAN RELIABILITY	g^2 LOADING (TECHNICAL MANUAL)	g^2 (SATTLER, 1988)	AGES (AMPLE, ADEQUATE) SUBTEST SPECIFICITY
Vocabulary	.78–.85	.42	.64	2
Comprehension	.70–.86	.45	.56	2
Absurdities	.79–.91	.48	.45	all
Pattern Analysis	.80–.91	.48	.45	all
Copying	.74–.88	.38	.36	all
Quantitative	.81–.88	.48	.61	all, except 6
Bead Memory	.83–.89	.34	.48	all
Memory for Sentences	.85–.88	.35	.45	all

items (receptive and expressive vocabulary). Because task demands are different, a single score representing performance on both types of items cannot be given a meaningful interpretation, although all items probably assess verbal comprehension. Furthermore, some preschoolers may not know an appropriate response to "What does 'x' mean?" In a study of linguistically precocious toddlers Robinson, Dale, and Landesman (1990) found that many 24- and 30-month-old youngsters in their study rejected the task when it switched from the colored pictures to purely verbal definitions.

Because the subtest is amenable to administration to a wide range of ages, it is part of the core battery. Technical properties of this subtest are quite good (e.g., the range of Kuder–Richardson 20 formula reliabilities, for ages 2 through 6 is .78 to .85). Vocabulary is a good measure of g; squaring the g loading from the standardization sample shows that 64 percent of its variance is attributed to g. (See Table 6.2 for a minimal description of technical data for all subtests.) The g loading cited in the *Technical Manual* from a factor analysis of 2- through 6-year-old children is .65, yielding a 42 percent estimate of variance attributable to g. Table 6.2 presents g figures from Sattler (1992) and from the *Technical Manual*. They differ because of the different types of factor analytic techniques used to determine g. At age 2, subtest specificity, the extent to which a subtest can be considered a measure of some unique attribute, is adequate (Sattler, 1992). (If the unique variance of a subtest equals at least 25 percent, and is greater than the error variance, the subtest is said to possess adequate subtest specificity.) Vocabulary contributes substantially to the Verbal Comprehension factor at all ages; Verbal Com-

prehension is one of three factors that emerged for most ages from a factor analysis reported by Sattler (1992).

Test 2: Bead Memory. Bead Memory requires the youngest and/or less able children to match beads shown by the examiner to photographs of the beads (items 1 through 10). Older children must place beads onto a vertical rod held in place by a small base platform. The beads are of different shapes (cylindrical, cone, saucer, and round) and colors (red, blue, and white), which complicates recall of the model. The examiner presents the stimulus for 5 seconds and then asks the examinee to duplicate the model. The examinee's beads must match the stimulus picture in color, shape, and juxtaposition. Adding beads to each successive item increases item difficulty. At a minimum the task requires visual discrimination and memory, color vision, and some visual-motor coordination for all but the first 10 items. It is a difficult test for some preschool children. In one study of 121 three-year-old children, 55 percent were unable to obtain a score on some subtests. Bead Memory was one of the two most frequently failed subtests, although the children reported that they liked the colored beads (Johnson, Howie, Owen, Baldwin, & Luttman, 1993). The correlation of Bead Memory with the composite score is .72 (Sattler, 1992). The subtest is a moderate estimate of g. For preschool children this subtest loads on the Nonverbal Reasoning/Visualization factor rather than the Memory factor as it does at some older ages.

Test 3: Quantitative. This subtest requires prearithmetic and arithmetic skills at the preschool level. The difficulty level ranges from basic matching of spots on

TABLE 6.3 Computing Factor Scores

VERBAL COMPREHENSION		NONVERBAL REASONING/VISUALIZATION		MEMORY	
Ages 2 through 7 Score	*Standard Score*	*Ages 2 through 11 Subtest*	*Standard Score*	*Age 7 Subtest*	*Standard Score*
1 Vocabulary (VR)	———	5 Pattern analysis (A/VR)	———	8 Memory for Digits (STM)	———
6 Comprehension (VR)	———	9 Copying (A/VR)	———	10 Memory for Objects (STM)	———
7 Absurdities (VR)	———	3 Quantitative (QR)	———		
4 Memory for Sentences (STM)	———	2 Bead Memory (STM)	———		

Steps (Verbal Comprehension)

1. Sum of standard scores on Vocabulary + Comprehension + Absurdities
2. Verbal Reasoning Area SAS (p. 183 of *Guide* for 3 subtests)
3. Short-Term Memory Area SAS (multiply the standard score by 2)
4. Sum of (2) + (3)
5. Verbal Comprehension Factor Score (p. 187 of *Guide* for 2 area scores)

Steps (Nonverbal Reasoning/Visualization)

1. Sum of standard scores on Pattern Analysis + Copying
2. Abstract/Visual Reasoning Area SAS (p. 187 of *Guide* for 2 subtests)
3. Quantitative Reasoning Area SAS (multiply the standard score by 2)
4. Short-Term Memory Area SAS (multiply the standard by 2)
5. Sum of (2 + 3 + 4)
6. Nonverbal Reasoning/ Visualization Factor Score (p. 187 or 188 of *Guide* for 3 area scores)

Steps (Memory)

1. Sum of standard scores on Memory for Digits + Memory for Objects (STM)
2. Short-Term Memory Area SAS (p. 186 of *Guide* for 2 subtests)
3. Memory Factor Score (p. 187 of *Guide* for 1 area score)

dice and counting to rather complex word problems. This subtest may be the most problematic subtest for preschool children. In one study 70 percent of the children at 24 months and 14 percent of the children at 30 months failed or rejected it (Robinson et al., 1990). In another study of 3-year-olds it was one of the two most frequently failed subtests (Johnson et al., 1993). According to the authors (Lamp and Krohn, 1990), many 4-year-old children from low-SES families in their study were puzzled by the instructions and unable to perform even the simplest items.

In spite of these administration problems with preschoolers, the technical characteristics are good (see Table 6.2). Quantitative correlates .82 with the composite score (Sattler, 1992), and its specificity is ample or adequate at all age levels except 6, and ages 18 to 23. This subtest loads moderately to substantially on the Nonverbal Reasoning/Visualization factor and modestly on the Verbal Comprehension factor (Sattler, 1992).

Test 4: Memory for Sentences. This subtest requires examinees to repeat sentences exactly as read by the examiner. The sentences range from very short two-word phrases to much longer, more convoluted sentences. Auditory short-term memory, verbal facility, and concentration are essential for success on these items. Memory for Sentences is appropriate for all ages, although articulation immaturities are a complication for some, even linguistically precocious, preschoolers (Robinson et al., 1990). Its technical properties are good (see Table 6.2). The correlation coefficient with the composite score is .73 (Sattler, 1992). For preschool children, Memory for Sentences loads on the Verbal Comprehension factor but on the Memory factor for older examinees (Sattler, 1992).

Test 5: Pattern Analysis. This subtest contains items of low difficulty for very young children. Of 42 total items, the first six require use of a form board. The remaining items require examinees to use patterned blocks to copy designs as seen from examiners' models and/or stimulus pictures. The upturned lid from the box of cubes is used to prevent distraction by the appearance of the sides of the cubes at the first entry level after the form boards. However, the child is expected to orient blocks correctly without demonstration or correction. This may be problematic for younger preschoolers (Robinson et al., 1990). This subtest is part of the core battery and is administered to children of all ages. The technical properties are good (see Table 6.2), and the subtest corre-

lates reasonably well with the composite score at .74 (Sattler, 1992). Pattern Analysis is a good measure of *g*. The subtest contributes substantially to the Nonverbal Reasoning/Visualization factor at all age levels.

Test 6: Comprehension. This subtest requires two somewhat different sets of skills. The first six of the 42 Comprehensive items require pointing to body parts; the remaining items require oral responses to aural questions and tap a broad range of knowledge including understanding of basic personal, economic, and social needs and practices. This subtest is part of the core battery and is administered to all examinees. It is usually given after Pattern Analysis, a nonverbal task. However, at least one study found that if it is given after Memory for Sentences, young preschool children tend to mimic the examiner (Robinson et al., 1990). The technical properties of Comprehension are good. (See Table 6.2 for details.) According to Sattler (1992), Comprehension correlates with the composite score moderately highly ($r = .76$), and subtest specificity is adequate at only age 2 for the preschool ages 2 through 6. Comprehension contributes substantially to the Verbal Comprehension factor for preschool children.

Test 7: Absurdities. The Absurdities subtest is not part of the core battery. However, it is recommended for the assessment of preschool children for gifted programs. The first four of a total of 32 items have a multiple-choice pointing administration format; the remaining items require a verbal response. Young children tend to find the initial items confusing, but it is a favorite of brighter preschoolers (Johnson et al., 1993; Robinson et al., 1990). Unlike Vocabulary and Comprehension, this subtest does lend itself to clear interpretation for very young children who respond to both types of items. Even though the response mode changes, all the items require the ability to discern incongruities and absurdities presented visually. This subtest is available for children who range in age from 2 to 14 years. The technical properties are good (see Table 6.2). According to Sattler (1992), its correlation with the composite score is .72. The Absurdities subtest is a good measure of *g* and loads reasonably well on the Verbal Comprehension factor for most ages. However, at some ages it loads on a second factor, referred to by Sattler (1992) as Nonverbal Reasoning/Visualization, which is one of the two primary factors for preschool children.

Test 8: Copying. The Copying subtest is also not part of the core battery but is recommended for preschool youngsters having problems learning in school. As with several other subtests that are available to examinees across the entire age range, Copying requires two somewhat different responses. Of 28 items, the first 12 require the examinee to use three or four blocks to copy a block design constructed by the examiner. The remaining items require the examinee to copy pictured line drawings. This subtest is available for children 2 through 13 years, and the technical properties are good (see Table 6.2). The correlation coefficient with the composite score is .66; Copying loads moderately well on the Nonverbal Reasoning/Visualization factor for preschool children (Sattler, 1992).

When using the S-B IV with preschool children, examiners should keep in mind certain considerations. Glutting and Kaplan (1990) compared directions in the S-B IV to basic concepts in the Boehm Test of Basic Concepts (BTBC; Boehm, 1971). The authors found that preschool children must understand eight basic BTBC concepts to understand the instructions. Robinson et al. (1990) found that at 24 months, even with a precocious sample, very few subtests were applicable because the children could not grasp what they were expected to do. The homogeneity of item types on the S-B IV tends to increase resistance in young preschoolers in comparison to the Binet L-M in which there was rapid movement between favored and unfavored items. Lower-SES children may be especially disadvantaged. Sattler (1992) reported that children in the lowest SES groups scored approximately 14 points lower than children in the highest SES groups. In one study of 121 3-year-olds (Johnson et al., 1993), children who failed at least one subtest had lower scores on the environmental variables (socioeconomic status, verbal and abstract intelligence of the mother, and educational stimulation at home). Thus, examiners should consider carefully not only the child's age but also the child's receptive language skills and background when choosing the S-B IV as the measure of cognitive functioning.

TECHNICAL ADEQUACY

According to *Standards for Educational and Psychological Testing,* published by the American Psychological Association (1985), test publishers should provide enough information for a qualified user to evaluate the appropriateness and technical adequacy of the test. Minimal information includes a discussion of item analysis procedures, relevant standardization data, and appropriate reliability and validity indices. The following discussion includes relevant information from the *Technical Manual,* as well as from other sources, as indicated.

Item Analysis

The authors of the S-B IV tried to maintain continuity with Form L-M. Consequently, they included many of the more popular item types from the old test. According to the authors, item types were retained if they were (1) acceptable measures of verbal reasoning, quantitative reasoning, abstract/visual reasoning, or short-term memory; (2) could be scored reliably; (3) were perceived by experts as being relatively free of ethnic and gender bias; and (4) were functioning across a wide range of ages. Many of the item types were retained (Vocabulary, Comprehension, Verbal Absurdities, Picture Absurdities, Opposite Analogies, Paper Folding and Cutting, Copying, Ingenuity, and Repeating Digits). However, an additional 29 new item types were generated for field testing. Initial item tryouts began in 1979, prior to standardization; items that failed to operate similarly across ethnic groups were eliminated.

Standardization

Stratification variables for the standardization included geographic region, community size, ethnic group, age, and gender. The examinees' socioeconomic status also was obtained. Data from the 1980 U.S. Census were used to stratify variables. Tables in the *Technical Manual* reveal the extent to which the standardization sample conforms to the census figures. In general, the sample was quite representative. Of the four geographical regions, the largest error or misrepresentation was underrepresentation of the Northeast by 5 percent. The South also was underrepresented slightly by about 1.4 percent. The North Central and West were overrepresented by about 3 percent.

Community size representation was similarly impressive. Six "community size" categories were used, ranging from the largest cities (1 million or more) to rural areas (less than 2,500). The largest misrepresentation was 4.1 percent for the rural areas. Ethnic/race representation closely approximated the population according to the census. Whites were underrepresented by about 5 percent; blacks were overrepresented by about 2.9 percent. Other groups were more closely represented. For example, Hispanic examinees comprised 6.3 percent of the sample compared to 6.4 percent of the population. Gender representation was impressive. Males comprised

47.3 percent of the sample and 47.2 percent of the population; females comprised 51.7 percent of the sample and 52.8 percent of the population. Age categories from 2-0 to 23-11 were approximately equally represented, with a few planned exceptions. Extra children were selected for certain transition ages, such as 5-0 to 5-11 and 8-0 to 8-11; these are ages at which children face increased scrutiny and are at increased risk for academic failure.

Although the sampling was generally carefully conducted and accurate, there is one glaring misrepresentation within the sample. The sample was grossly overrepresented in the higher SES categories, as defined by the Parental Occupation and Parental Education criteria. For example, the sample contained 45.9 percent examinees whose parents were described as managerial/professional, compared to 21.8 percent in the population. In contrast, 8.3 percent of the examinees' parents were categorized as operators, fabricators, and laborers, although these occupations comprise 19.5 percent of the population. Similarly, children of college graduates composed 43.7 percent of the sample but only 19 percent of the population. To compensate for these sampling errors the authors used a weighting procedure that overvalued the scores of the lower-SES examinees and undervalued those of the higher-SES examinees. However, the effects of the weighting procedure are unknown; only further research will clarify the possible impact of the misrepresentation.

Reliability

Reliability can be defined as the extent to which scores are free from errors of measurement. Estimates presented in the *Technical Manual* are generally impressive. The authors present two types of reliability estimates—indices of internal consistency and test-retest (stability) coefficients. Internal consistency estimates constitute the bulk of the reliability data (from the Kuder–Richardson 20); test-retest coefficients were obtained from children within two age groups. Internal consistency values are presented initially for preschool-age children, followed by test-retest values. Almost without exception, the KR-20 coefficients are higher. Another general finding, anticipated from the measurement literature, is that the reliabilities increased as a function of age. Younger children yielded lower reliability estimates.

Internal Consistency. According to the authors, the KR-20 estimates should be considered upper-bound val-

ues because the assumption required by the formula—that is, that all items above the ceiling level be failed—cannot be met. KR-20 coefficients range from .95 to .97 for ages 2 through 5 for the composite score. Typically, coefficients get larger as age increases, and the same pattern can be observed for these values; that is, .95 was obtained for 2-year-old children and .97 for 5-year-old children. As can be seen in the *Technical Manual,* this pattern holds for all the estimates across all the various types of standard scores provided. Estimates range from .74 to .91 for the various subtests (see Table 6.2). Because the standard errors of measurement (*SEM-*) are a function of the reliabilities, they fluctuate accordingly. For example, the *SEM* for a reliability coefficient of .80 is 3.6, versus a value of 2.4 for a reliability coefficient of .91.

The *Technical Manual* also contains KR-20 reliability estimates for area scores as well as for the composite and subtest scores. The number of subtests used to calculate area scores varies. For preschool children, one, two, or three scores are used for Verbal Reasoning, one or two scores for Abstract/Visual Reasoning, one score for the Quantitative Reasoning, and one or two scores for Short-Term Memory. When two subtests are used to calculate area scores for Verbal Reasoning, the KR-20 estimates range from .90 to .92 depending on age; when three subtests are used, the values range from .93 to .94. When two subtests are used to calculate the Abstract/Visual Reasoning area score, the KR-20 estimates range from .85 to .93. The Quantitative Reasoning area score is calculated from only one subtest for preschool children; hence, the reliabilities are the same as reported for the Quantitative subtest. However, the *SEM* changes. Because the standard deviation used in the formula to derive *SEM* increases twofold, from 8 to 16, the *SEM* increases proportionately. Finally, the Short-Term Memory area KR-20 reliability estimates range from .90 to .92.

Test-Retest. Although some writers argue cogently that stability is different conceptually from reliability (Jensen, 1980), the S-B IV authors cite test-retest data as evidence for reliability. These reliability data were obtained by retesting 112 children. Fifty-seven of the children were approximately 5 years of age; 55 were approximately 8 years of age. The time between the two administrations varied from two to eight months, with an average test-retest interval of 16 weeks. Subtest test-retest reliability coefficients for the preschool children range from .56 (Bead Memory) to .78 (Memory for Sentences). Area coefficients range from .71 (Quantitative) to .88 (Verbal Reasoning). The composite coefficient .91

is similar, with one notable exception. The test-retest co-efficient for the Quantitative subtest is only .28. According to the authors, limited variability is a possible reason. However, the standard deviations (6 and 6.3) obtained for these children on the two administrations are not appreciably different from some of the other subtests with higher coefficients. (Number Series yielded standard deviation values of 5.4 and 5.3 and a coefficient of .61.) Apparently restriction of range is not the sole explanation for the diminished test-retest reliability.

Although both the preschool and the elementary groups showed higher mean scores on retest, the younger group improved more. The preschoolers improved by an average of 9.2 points on the Abstract/Visual Reasoning but only 4.9 points on the Verbal Reasoning area. Most of the mean subtest increases were from 2 to 4 points. The increases shown for the older group were similar but slightly smaller. Flanagan and Alfonso (1995) have stated that test-retest reliability for the S-B IV is inadequate at the preschool level. They rated the age range as good, although it was limited (4–10 to 5–6). However, the sample size was small (57 subjects) and the sample matched the U.S. population on only two of the five variables originally evaluated. Lamp and Krohn (1990) assessed the stability of the S-B IV by administering the tests to a sample of 71 low-SES children at age 4 and again at age 6. The mean composite scores for the group were very similar at both ages and correlation coefficients between the two sets of scores were moderate to high ranging from .55 to .70. However, the area scores were somewhat less stable. Robinson et al. (1990) point out that because the scoring manual presents four-month age intervals for converting raw scores to scaled scores, reliability is reduced at young ages, which is a time of rapid development. In summary, examiners can be fairly confident of the stability of composite scores at ages 4 and above but should be more cautious about interpretation of area scores and test scores from very young preschool children.

Brief-Form Reliabilities. The authors suggest the use of abbreviated forms of the test for certain purposes and report KR-20 reliabilities for two-, four-, and six-test composite scores. These values range from .88 for the two-test composite at the 2-year age level to .99 for the six-test composite for the 18 to 23 age level. The test authors offer two caveats. First, the two- and four-test batteries should be used for screening only; second, only the composite scores should be used to make decisions from any of the abbreviated batteries. Prewett (1992) evaluated

short forms of the Stanford-Binet with a sample of 150 low-achieving students and found that the six-subtest core battery and the four-subtest short form (Verbal, Quantitative, Pattern Analysis, and Memory for Sentences) had the highest validity coefficients and indicators of *psychometric effectiveness* (the averaged validity and reliability coefficients; Cyr & Brooker, 1984). However, only a small number of this sample was preschool age (below 6). In addition, Glaub and Kamphaus (1991) developed a nonverbal short form of the S-B IV to be used with hearing-impaired, speech/language-disabled, and limited-English-proficient children. They included the Bead Memory, Pattern Analysis, Copying, Memory for Objects, and Matrices subtests. The new composite showed high reliability ($r = .95$) and validity as estimated by its correlation with the test composite from the full battery ($r = .91$). However, this battery would not be appropriate for most children until the age of about 7 and cannot be used until a child is 5 years of age.

Validity

Validity is defined generally as the extent to which a test accomplishes what it purports to do, or, more technically, the extent to which evidence is available to support inferences made from test scores. Test validity is specifically defined as content validity (the extent to which a test assesses some predetermined content area), concurrent validity (the extent to which a test assesses the content assessed by a second test), construct validity (the extent to which a test assesses some hypothetical construct), predictive validity (the extent to which a test predicts some future performance), and treatment validity (the extent to which test results contribute to interventions). Content validity is especially relevant for academic achievement tests but less so for constructs such as intelligence. Predictive and treatment validities are determined over time as a test is available for research over the years. Some predictive validity data are cited in the new *Examiner's Manual,* from the publishers of the S-B IV, and in Table 6.5. The authors could find no treatment validity studies.

There is considerable evidence available addressing construct validity, including factor analytic data focusing on the test structure, concurrent validity studies focusing on the relationship of the new Binet to other tests that assess similar constructs, and studies of Binet performance groups of individuals who are high or low on the construct presumably assessed by the Binet (i.e., intelligence). Some of the currently available evidence has been summarized by the Stanford-Binet authors and is presented in the *Technical Manual*. Evidence from other sources is beginning to surface.

Construct Validity. The structure of the Stanford-Binet, as determined by factor analytic results, provides some limited support for the logically derived model adopted by the authors. The model originally suggested by the authors promotes the notion of a first-level *g* factor, followed by a second level of general or pervasive abilities, namely, fluid and crystallized abilities, and short-term memory. The third, more specific level of abilities includes verbal reasoning and quantitative reasoning, both subsumed under the superordinate *crystallized ability*. Abstract/Visual reasoning is the other third-level category and is subsumed under the superordinate *fluid analytic abilities*. Figure 6.1 depicts the relationship among the various categories, levels, and subtests.

Factor Analytic Results. Evidence for construct validity can be provided by results of confirmatory factor analytic procedures using the entire standardization sample. If the subtests load as predicted, the structure is supported. The confirmatory factor analysis used by the Stanford-Binet authors for the entire standardization sample required extraction of a general factor first (using median correlations among the subtests), followed by extractions of group factors. Although the analysis provides limited support for the organizational scheme as shown in Figure 6.1, there are considerable discrepancies.

In support of the model, all subtests load significantly on *g;* the loadings range from .51 (Memory for Designs) to .79 (Number Series) for the total standardization sample. For the preschool sample the *g* loadings range from .58 (Bead Memory) to .69 (Absurdities, Quantitative, and Pattern Analysis). Most of the subtests load appreciably on predicted factors. For the entire sample all the Verbal Reasoning subtests load more highly on the verbal factor than on any other factor (except the first large *g* factor). The loadings on the verbal factor by verbal subtests range from .26 to .47. Similarly, all the Short-Term Memory subtests load more highly on the memory factor than on any other factor, with one exception. Bead Memory loads modestly (.13) on the memory factor as well as the abstract/visual factor (.13). Memory factor loadings from other Short-Term Memory subtests range from .29 to .48. The three Quantitative Reasoning subtests load more heavily on the quantitative factor than on any other, with loadings ranging from a very modest .21 to a moderate .49. With one

exception, the four Abstract/Visual subtests load more heavily on the abstract/visual than on any other factor. The Matrices subtest loads most highly on the quantitative factor (.11), though it fails to load appreciably on any one of the four area factors. Furthermore, although Copying and Paper Folding and Cutting yield their highest loadings on the appropriate Abstract/Visual factor, both loadings are low. Only the Pattern Analysis produces a robust loading in this factor (.65).

Thorndike, Hagen, and Sattler (1986) conclude from the factor structure that there is "... positive support for the rationale underlying the battery" (p. 55). The support should be considered modest. There is a strong *g* factor loading; also the subtest variance attributable to some unique characteristic or ability, the subtest specificity, is very large for almost all the subtests. The median subtest specificity loading is .53. Consequently, there is little variance remaining to be invested in the more specific area constructs for most subtests. Of course, the type of factor analysis used can affect the solution; that is, a factor solution emphasizing the independence of factors, rather than their interdependence, can reflect more robust area loadings. However, the authors offer the solution as presented in the *Technical Manual* as the most appropriate as it apparently emphasizes the interdependence of the subtests rather than their independence.

Another factor analysis is also presented in the *Technical Manual* that has implications for the construct validity, especially for preschoolers. The solution was obtained from only preschool children, those ranging in age from 2 to 6 years. As is apparent, only two factors emerged other than the large general factor; Thorndike, Hagen, and Sattler (1986) identify these factors as Verbal and Abstract/Visual. This solution is partially a function of the eight subtests that are appropriate for the children in this age range. According to the test authors, the fact that only one quantitative subtest is included in the battery for children this age precluded the emergence of a separate quantitative factor. In addition, of the four short-term memory subtests included on the complete battery only two are included on the battery for this age group—Bead Memory and Memory for Sentences. According to the authors, Bead Memory loaded on the Abstract/Visual factor; Memory for Sentences loaded on the Verbal factor. The authors note that these loadings could be anticipated because of the content of the two tests. Consequently, the emergence of a two-factor structure was not surprising. Sattler (1992) also presents a two-factor structure for young children, as reflected in the factors depicted in Table 6.3.

Since its introduction, a number of other validity studies have been conducted with the SB-IV. One (Boyle, 1989) unconditionally confirmed the model, but this study has been criticized for methodological problems (Laurent, Swerdlik, & Ryburn, 1992; Thorndike, 1990). Using confirmatory factor analysis, McCallum (1990) found support for a four-factor structure for the entire standardization sample, and Keith, Cool, Novak, White and Pottebaum (1988) found support for the four-factor structure after age 6. For the preschool group the Short-Term Memory factor correlated perfectly ($r = 1.0$) with both the Verbal and Abstract/Visual Reasoning factors in the Constrained model. In a No-Memory model, Memory for Sentences loaded with Verbal Reasoning and Bead Memory with Abstract/Visual Reasoning, supporting a three-factor test at this age. Research from a number of other studies supported the original study and Sattler's conclusion that the S-B IV is a two-factor test with a verbal and a nonverbal component for the 2 through 6 age groups (Kline, 1989; Molfese, Yaple, Helwig, Harris, & Connell, 1992; Ownby & Carmin, 1988; Reynolds, Kamphaus, & Rosenthal, 1988; Thorndike, 1990), although Thorndike found that the three-factor solution gave the best results for the 2-year-old sample and Ownby and Carmin noted that a four-factor solution was appropriate for 3-year-olds. When the General Purpose Abbreviated Battery (GPAB) of six core tests is used with preschool children, there is evidence that only the composite score should be interpreted, representing general intelligence or g (Riccio, Platt, Kamphaus, Greer, & Elksnin, 1994).

For whatever reason, the most parsimonious explanation of what the test assesses for preschoolers should rely on an estimate of g and the two other constructs defined by this two-factor structure (Verbal Comprehension and Nonverbal Reasoning/Visualization). More specific explanations should follow, only if these initial models fail to explain a particular pattern of scores.

Concurrent Validity.   Another source of support for claims of construct validity comes from results of studies comparing the S-B IV to existing measures of general intellectual ability. This includes comparisons to the Kaufman Assessment Battery for Children (Kaufman & Kaufman, 1983), the Wechsler Preschool and Primary Test of Intelligence—Revised (Wechsler, 1972), and the Peabody Picture Vocabulary Test—Revised (Dunn, 1965). Table 6.4 summarizes some of the studies that included preschool-age children.

Several of the concurrent validity studies present data comparing the S-B IV to the S-B III. Thorndike, Hagen, and Sattler (1986) report that area and composite scores from the S-B IV correlate moderately to strongly with global scores from the third edition, and the means are generally similar. Table 6.5 also presents summaries of these studies that included preschool children.

In summary, for older preschool-age and elementary-age children, both Binets yield similar mean scores. When differences occur, they are more apparent at the extreme ranges, with the Binet III yielding slightly more extreme scores. However, some of the differences appear to be because of regression to the mean effects, as well as to any standardization sample differences. Correlations between the two are moderate to strong. This relationship is less strong for populations showing restriction in range, such as gifted children. Also, on a more molecular level, the Verbal Reasoning area score for the S-B IV seems to be more closely related to the total Form L-M IQ than any of the other three area scores, at least for the ages studied thus far. The relationship between the two tests is not well defined for young preschool children, those ranging in age from 2 to 5. More research is needed to clarify the relationship for these children. Of course, the psychometric limitations of the tests for that age, such as a limited floor, will reduce the magnitude of the relationship between the two tests.

One of the most relevant concurrent validity studies compares the S-B IV to the WPPSI. According to the Binet authors, the most meaningful mean comparisons might not be across the existing similar-named scales. Because the Verbal Scale of the WPPSI includes the Arithmetic Test and sometimes the Sentences Test, in addition to other verbal tests, an average of the Binet areas of Verbal Reasoning and Quantitative Reasoning *or* an average of these two plus Short-Term Memory might be more appropriate when comparing Binet performance to the WPPSI Verbal Scale. The Binet authors note that several of their predictions were supported by the data from this study. For example, the composite score on the S-B IV was expected to correlate more highly with the WPPSI Verbal Scale IQ and Full Scale IQ than with the Performance Scale IQ. Also the Verbal Reasoning, Quantitative Reasoning, and Short-Term Memory areas of the S-B IV were expected to correlate more highly with the Verbal Scale of the WPPSI than with the Performance Scale. This conjecture has been supported by at least one other study comparing the S-B IV and the WPPSI-R (McCrowell and Nagle, 1994). The results from a study of 30 preschool children indicated

TABLE 6.4   Concurrent Validity Studies

STUDY	SAMPLE	RESULTS
Thorndike, Hagen, & Sattler, 1986	139 Nonexceptional Mean age = 6-11, *SD* = 30 months	Correlations between S-B III and IV range from .56 to .76; S-B III Mean, 108.1 vs. 105.8 from S-B IV composite.
Thorndike, Hagen, & Sattler, 1986	14 LD children Mean age = 8-4, *SD* = 34 months	Correlations between S-B III and IV range from .54 to .86; S-B III Mean is slightly lower (76.9) than all S-B IV mean global scores (79.9 to 87.6).
Livesay & Mealor, 1987	120 gifted referrals Mean age = 6.81, *SD* = 6 months	Correlations between S-B III and IV range from .24 to .57; S-B III Mean (130.45) is higher than S-B IV means (IV composite, 122.46).
Thorndike, Hagen, & Sattler, 1986	75 exceptional children Mean age = 5-6, *SD* = 6 months	Correlations among global WPPSI and S-B IV scores range from .46 to .80; months WPPSI means (108.2 to 110.3) are slightly higher than S-B IV (100.4 to 109.8).
McCrowell & Nagle, 1994	30 nonexceptional children Mean age = 5-0 (Range 4-1 to 6-7)	Correlations among S-B IV and WPPSI-R scores range from .32 to .77 (S-B IV 92.07 to 101.57; WPPSI 93.87 to 95.50).
Prewitt & Matavich, 1994	73 low-SES referred students Mean age = 9-8, *SD* = 21.6 months	Correlations among S-B IV and WISC-III from .21 to .78 (S-B IV mean 81.97 to 86.37; WISC III 74.08 to 79.07).
Thorndike, Hagen, & Sattler, 1986	175 nonexceptional children Mean age = 70, *SD* = 29 months	Correlations among K-ABC and S-B IV range from .68 to .89, means are similar (K-ABC, 107.4 to 112.3; S-B IV, 110.2 to 112.7).
Thorndike, Hagen, & Sattler, 1986	Not apparent	Correlations among K-ABC and S-B IV range from .28 to .74; means from the K-ABC are from 91.1 to 97.5, and for the S-B IV, 88.6 to 99.1.
Hendershott et al., 1990	36 white, middle class 12 3-yr-olds 12 4-yr-olds 12 5-yr-olds	Correlations between S-B IV and K-ABC range from .25 to .65 (S-B IV from 108.8 to 116.4; K-ABC from 112.8 to 118.2).
Molfese, Helwig, & Holcomb, 1993	129 3-yr-olds	Correlations between S-B IV and MSCA range from .23 to .57 (S-B IV 102.8 to 107.6, MCSA 109.4) correlations between S-B IV and PPVT range from .36 to .62 (PPVT X = 99.0).

that the composite SAS of the S-B IV and the Full Scale IQ of the WPPSI-R yield similar scores. No significant differences existed between the Abstract/Visual scales of both measures, although adding the Quantitative and Bead Memory subtests to the S-B IV Abstract/Visual Reasoning SAS increased its correlation with the WPPSI-R Performance IQ from .59 to .72. However, when the verbal scales were compared, the S-B IV Verbal Reasoning score was significantly greater than the WPPSI-R Verbal IQ.

TABLE 6.5   Predictive Validity Studies

STUDY	SAMPLE	RESULTS
Delaney & Hopkins, 1987	30 nonexceptional children, Mean age = 5-4, *SD* = 2 months	Correlations among scores from the Woodcock–Johnson (WJ Achievement) range from .36 to .92; means from the WJ and Binet are similar (WJ, 97.5 to 104.8; S-B IV, 96.9 to 109.0).
Delaney & Hopkins, 1987	30 nonexceptional children, Mean age = 5-4, *SD* = 4 months	Correlations among scores from the Woodcock–Johnson (WJ Achievement) range from .36 to .92; means from the WJ and Binet are similar (WJ, 97.5 to 104.8; S-B IV, 96.9 to 109.0).
Hendershott et al., 1990	36 white, middle class 12 3-yr-olds 12 4-yr-olds 12 5-yr-olds	Correlations among scores from the S-B IV and K-ABC range from .43 to .74 (S-B IV 108.8 to 116.4; K-ABC 112.87).

When the relationship between WISC-R (Wechsler, 1974) and Binet scores are depicted from studies in the *Technical Manual*, the following patterns seem to emerge. Scores from the Verbal Reasoning and Quantitative Reasoning areas correlate more highly with WISC-R Verbal IQs than with scores on the other areas of the S-B IV. Scores on the Abstract/Visual Reasoning area correlate more highly with the WISC-R Performance Scale IQs than do scores from the other Binet areas. Finally, scores from the Abstract/Visual Reasoning area correlate more highly with the WISC-R Performance IQ than with the Verbal IQ.

Of interest are studies with special populations. Thorndike, Hagen, and Sattler (1986) found correlations ranging from .46 to .80 among global WPPSI and S-B IV scores for 75 exceptional preschool children. Means for the WPPSI were slightly higher. An independent study (McCallum & Karnes, 1987) comparing the WISC-R to the S-B IV for 38 older gifted children (ages 9–5 to 12–6, mean age = 10–10) reported relatively low correlation coefficients (ranging from .02 to .49). The coefficients are higher for the WISC-R Full Scale IQ and the various Binet scores than for the Verbal and Performance IQs and the Binet global scores. The mean Binet scores range from 116.87 (Verbal Reasoning) to 124.08 (Quantitative Reasoning), with a composite of 125.03. Contrast these means with those from the WISC-R, which range from 124.80 to 129.28. However, according to the authors of the study, the mean differences could result partially from regression to the mean because the WISC-R was administered first to all children. These authors caution practitioners that the regression effect operates in daily practice and should be considered when gifted children are reevaluated for placement after a period of service. A study by Prewett and Matavich (1994) administered the WISC-III and S-B IV to 73 low-SES, inner-city referred students. In this study the WISC-III Full Scale IQ averaged 9.4 points lower than the S-B IV Test Composite, and the WISC-III Verbal IQ averaged 13.1 points lower than the S-B IV Verbal Reasoning area score. The nonverbal scales differed by an average of 8.1 points. Although the two tests were highly correlated (*r* = .81), they did not give the same diagnostic impressions. For example, only 21 percent of the subjects who scored in the mentally retarded range on the WISC-III (IQ < 70) scored in this range on the S-B IV.

Two studies from the *Technical Manual* report data comparing the S-B IV to the K-ABC. The first study, reported in Table 6.5, reveals high correlation coefficients depicting the interrelationships among the various global scores. According to the Binet authors, the most meaningful mean difference comparisons should be between areas that purport to assess similar constructs or cognitive skills. For example, the following comparisons seem most reasonable: K-ABC Sequential Processing and Binet Short-Term Memory; K-ABC Simultaneous Processing and Binet Abstract/Visual Reasoning; K-ABC Mental Processing Composite and Binet Composite; and K-ABC Achievement and Binet Verbal Reasoning/Quantitative Reasoning. All these various pairwise comparisons reveal very similar mean scores. The difference between the two composites was only .4. Another study comparing the K-ABC and the S-B IV reveals very similar mean scores across the two tests, but the correlation coefficients are lower in general than those from the first study. The reduced coefficients might be a function of restriction in range; standard deviations were all below the population standard deviations for both tests, typically by about 3 to 4 points. A third study with the K-ABC (Hendershott, Searight, Hatfield, & Rogers, 1990) compared scores for 36 white, middle-class preschoolers (aged 3 through 5) and found no significant mean difference between composite scores. However, it should be noted that the highest correlation was between the Kaufman Achievement scores and the S-B IV Composite.

In an effort to examine multiple operationalizations of verbal ability, Molfese, Helwig, and Holcomb (1993) examined three measures of verbal intelligence obtained from the S-B IV, the McCarthy Scales of Children's Abilities (MSCA; McCarthy, 1972), and the Peabody Picture Vocabulary Test (PPVT: Dunn, 1965). The means and standard deviations for all three tests were similar (MSCA mean of 109.4, PPVT mean of 99.0, and S-B IV mean of 105.7). Biomedical measures (perinatal risks and child health) were not correlated with verbal scores, but socioeconomic status and the child's home environment were correlated ($r = .49$, $p < .01$). Johnson et al. (1993) in their study of 121 three-year-olds found that scores for the S-B IV and PPVT-R were moderately correlated.

Performance of Exceptional Groups. The performance of exceptional groups is sometimes used to provide evidence of construct validity. The reasoning is as follows. If exceptional groups perform as predicted on some new test, then the new test is said to be sensitive to the exceptionality in question. That is, if the exceptionality is defined in part by modified cognitive functioning, and the new test is sensitive to and reflects the modified cognitive functioning, this evidence supports use of the new test with that exceptional group. The *Technical Manual* of the Binet reports three such studies, and all are somewhat supportive of the construct validity of the S-B IV. For example, for 217 gifted students (mean age = 9-0, standard deviation = 2-10), the means were all well above average, ranging from about 1.2 to 1.5 standard deviations above the population mean of 100. On the other end of the continuum, mean scores were all well below the population mean of 100 for 223 students labeled as mentally retarded by their schools (mean age = 14-4, standard deviation = 6-1). Means ranged from 54.9 to 61.9. Finally, for a sample of 227 learning disabled children (mean age = 10-7, standard deviation = 2-10),

mean scores ranged from 84.7 to 89.1. An independent study of 24 young children with autism (aged 35 to 84 months) yielded a distinct profile with the subscale of Absurdities consistently the lowest and Pattern Analysis as the highest subtest (Harris, Handleman, & Burton, 1990). Autistic children might be expected to perform better on tasks relying on nonverbal reasoning and spatial relations in comparison to verbally laden tasks.

Predictive Validity. Although the *Technical Manual* includes several studies describing construct validity, there are no predictive studies cited. As the Binet authors note, predictive validity studies are available for new instruments over time as practitioners use them. Predictive validity studies are just now beginning to appear for the S-B IV. Several appear in the *Examiner's Handbook: An Expanded Guide for Fourth Edition Users,* authored by Delaney and Hopkins (1987). Three of these report data from samples of nonexceptional children; two of these are particularly useful for those who specialize in preschool assessment (see Table 6.5).

One study reported in Delaney and Hopkins (1987) used a test-retest interval of about six months, comparing the S-B IV to the Wide Range Achievement Test—Revised (WRAT-R). Correlations ranged from .33 to .58 over the interval. With a second older sample, the correlations were slightly higher (.36 to .74). The larger coefficients reported for these older children are reasonable, given that older children obtain less error in their scores. In general, the strongest correlation coefficients were obtained from the analyses comparing the Binet Composite and WRAT-R subtests, ranging from .55 to .61. Slightly lower values were obtained when the relationship between Verbal Reasoning area scores and WRAT-R subtests was explored. Values of similar magnitude were obtained when the Short-Term Memory area scores and WRAT-R subtests were analyzed. Somewhat lower values resulted from analysis of the relationship between the Abstract/Visual Reasoning area scores and the WRAT-R subtests. Similarly low coefficients were obtained from analysis of the relationship between the Quantitative Reasoning area scores and the WRAT-R subtests.

A third study exploring the relationship between the Binet and the WRAT-R included older children still. The test-retest interval was again about six months. In general, the results from these 46 children were consistent with expectations. That is, just as with the younger children, the means from the WRAT-R tend to be slightly lower than those from the Binet, and the correlation coefficients are moderate.

A fourth predictive validity study to use the WRAT-R as the criterion, reported in the *Handbook*, reveals a similar pattern of means but a pattern of correlation coefficients slightly lower than the one obtained from the 12-year-old children. A possible explanation might be the nature of the sample—all the children had been designated by their schools as emotionally disturbed. There is some evidence that emotionally disturbed children are more erratic in performance, which contributes to test error and ultimately to reduced estimates of relationships. Another difference between this study and the three others reported is that the test-retest interval for this study was only one month. However, this reduced time interval between administration of the two tests probably did not reduce the magnitude of the coefficients.

Three additional predictive validity studies reported in the *Handbook* use the *Woodcock-Johnson Psycho-educational Battery Part Two: Tests of Achievement* (WJ; Woodcock & Johnson, 1977) as the criterion measure. Table 6.5 reveals summary data. One study of 30 preschool children found correlations among scores from the Woodcock-Johnson Achievement ranging from .36 to .92, with most correlations in the .50s for the interrelationships between the area and composite Binet scores and the Reading, Mathematics, Written Language, and Knowledge subtests of the WJ. The highest correlation coefficients generally were obtained for the relationships between the Verbal Reasoning and WJ subtests, ranging from .53 to .92. The coefficients defining the relationships between the composite Binet scores and the WJ subtests rank second in magnitude, ranging from .57 to .84. The coefficients defining the relationship between the Short-Term Memory area from the Binet and the WJ subtests rank third in magnitude; values range from .51 to .72. In general, the Quantitative Reasoning and WJ subtests relationships ranked next (ranging from .40 to .56), followed in magnitude by the coefficients describing the relationships among the Abstract/Visual Reasoning area and WJ subtests (ranging from .36 to .53). A consistent finding is that the Knowledge subtest of the WJ shares more test variance with the various Binet area scores than any of the other WJ subtests. That is, the Knowledge subtest appears to have more in common with the Binet areas than the other WJ subtests. Means from the WJ and the Binet are very similar. The WJ means range from 97.5 to 104.8; means from the Binet range from 96.9 to 109.0. Two other studies designed to explore the predictive relationship between the Binet and the WJ are reported in the *Handbook;* both report data from older, nonexceptional children. Moderate to moderately strong correlations were obtained.

Hendershott et al. (1990) administered the S-B IV and the K-ABC to 36 middle-class, white children, aged 3 to 5 years. They found the highest correlation between the S-B IV and the K-ABC was on the Achievement scores. Correlations with Achievement scores ranged from .43 to .74. The mean K-ABC Achievement score for the sample was 112.8 compared to 108.8 to 116.4 on the S-B IV.

Technical Adequacy: Additional Considerations and Summary Analysis. Overall, the technical adequacy of the Binet is impressive. However, the technical properties, such as reliabilities, are less impressive for preschool children than for older children. Because reliability affects various other statistics, the interpretation for young examinees is affected. Bands of error are larger because the standard errors of measurement are increased. Differences between various global and subtest scores have to be larger to be significant. Also, validity indices are depressed. Even so, many of the Binet characteristics do meet minimum standards for preschoolers. For example, the median subtest reliabilities (internal consistency estimates) do meet the criterion recommended by Bracken (1987) as minimal (.80). In addition, the Total Test internal consistency coefficients are adequate at all preschool ages and meet Bracken's criterion of .90.

Although some of the test-retest stability estimates are low and unimpressive for subtests, the Total Test estimate is slightly better than Bracken's recommended minimum of .90. On the other hand, some of the technical properties are problematic. For example, some subtest floors are inadequate for very young examinees, specifically, Vocabulary, Comprehension, and Abstract/Visual Reasoning until age 3–4, Short-Term Memory until 3-8, and Quantitative Reasoning until 5-0 (Flanagan & Alfonso, 1995). The average subtest floor for the Binet is so high that it fails to differentiate among approximately the lowest 37 percent of the children in the normal population (Bracken, 1987). In fact, the Binet fails to produce subtest scores that are at least 2 standard deviations below the mean through age 3-6, and again fails to meet this criterion at age 5-0 when new subtests with weak floors are introduced. Limited ability to discriminate is the result. For a hypothetical 2-year-old examinee, a raw score of 1 on the subtest Bead Memory produces a standard score of 53, which is slightly above average ($X = 50$, $SD = 8$). Raw scores of 1 on each of the Verbal Reasoning subtests lead to a Verbal Reasoning area score of 86, which is about 1 standard deviation below the mean ($X = 100$, $SD = 16$). Raw scores of 1 on each of the Abstract/Visual Reasoning subtests yield an area score of 91, about $2/3$ standard deviation below average for the population. A raw score of 1 on the Quantitative subtest yields a Quantitative Reasoning area score of 104, slightly above the population average. Raw scores of 1 on each of the Short-Term Memory subtests yield an area score of 101, just about the population average. This examinee would have earned a composite score of 95, an average score, even though only 1 raw score point was earned per subtest. The Test Composite scores show that moderate mental retardation cannot be diagnosed in 4-year-olds and that mild mental retardation in 4-year-olds and moderate mental retardation in 5-year-olds can be diagnosed only tentatively. Severe retardation cannot be diagnosed at any age except with the statement that results indicate an IQ "below 36." This has lead some authors (Flanagan & Alfonso, 1995; Wilson, 1992) to question the use of the S-B IV with children suspected of being mentally disabled. Wilson (1992) concluded that the S-B IV is unsuitable for the intellectual assessment of children less than 5 years old who are thought to have mild mental retardation and for persons of any age who are thought to have severe mental retardation.

Two related technical considerations include the item analysis quality and the item gradient levels as described in the Binet manual. Much attention was paid to the item analysis procedures, but there is a lack of specific information describing item parameters. Users must depend on the wisdom of the authors in making the best selections; however, this state of affairs is fairly typical. Flanagan and Alfonso (1995) used the item gradient criterion that was set by Bracken (1987). An item gradient was considered to be violated each time a one-unit increase in raw score points made a change of more than $1/3$ standard deviation. At first glance, the item gradient appears adequate. That is, each item is worth no more than $1/3$ standard score standard deviation. However, Flanagan and Alfonso (1995) found item gradients to be inadequate for all core subtests for ages 2-6 to 3-5, inadequate for all but Comprehension for ages 3-6 to 4-5, and inadequate for all but Comprehension and Absurdities for ages 4-6 to 5-5. Item gradients were determined to be inadequate when all or any portion of violations occurred between the mean and −1 standard deviation. Items that are too steeply graded reduce precision and

lead to gross discriminations. It should be noted that their method results in a conservative calculation because $1/3$ standard deviation is three points.

A final technical consideration to be addressed is subtest specificity. Subtest specificity is the proportion of the variance accounted for by a subtest that is unique, that is, not attributed to error or to some other construct measured in common. For example, the Vocabulary subtest of the Binet measures the Verbal Comprehension construct in common with the other subtests included in that "factor," but it measures something that is unique to it, discounting error. If this unique variance is equal to at least 25 percent of the total subtest variance and is larger than error variance, the subtest is said to possess adequate subtest specificity for interpretation (of this unique ability or abilities). According to Sattler (1992), the following subtests have inadequate subtest specificity for preschoolers at the ages indicated: Vocabulary, ages 3 through 9; Comprehension, ages 3 through 6; and Quantitative at 6 years of age (see Table 6.2).

Test Interpretation

The ultimate worth of a test is determined by the wealth and quality of information it provides. Such information is obtained from knowledgeable test interpretation. Competent interpretation requires a particular plan of action, a scheme, or framework for making sense of the variability from the myriad of subtest scores a test typically produces. There are two primary approaches to subtest analyses: ipsative and baserate interpretation. Baserate interpretation developed in reaction to the perceived limitations of ipsative interpretation (Glutting, McDermott, & Konold, 1997) and allows users to compare the profile of each examinee to common population profiles, or to profiles common to particular disorders. To use baserate interpretative strategies, common patterns must be made available from the standardization sample. These data are not available in the literature and our interpretation will focus on ipsative strategies only as first popularized by Kaufman (1979). There are several ipsative approaches for attacking subtest scatter, or subtest patterns. Three of these seem particularly reasonable and defensible and will be presented in this section. An examiner can start by using any one of the three. If the first procedure tried fails to provide a satisfactory interpretive solution, one of the others can be chosen.

The three interpretative strategies will be labeled the *pooled or g-factor* procedure, described by Delaney and Hopkins (1987) in the *Examiner's Handbook,* the *rational-intuitive* procedure, and the *independent factors* procedure. All three approaches make use of the standard scores, such as the composite score, the area scores, and subtest scores; subtest scores are referred to in the Binet manual as Standard Age Scores (SAS). Although percentile ranks and age equivalents are available, these are not amenable to scatter analysis.

The three specific interpretative procedures are addressed in detail. First, however, some general interpretive strategies are presented. After presentation of the three interpretative procedures, there is a discussion of interpretive limitations. The interpretation of choice for each child must be designed to avoid limitations or pitfalls such as overemphasis of small subtest differences when multiple comparisons are made, inattention to subtest specificity, and inattention to poor floor and ceiling effects. The final section of the chapter presents some interpretive recommendations for preschoolers.

General Interpretive Strategies.   Primary goals of this section are to describe general interpretive strategies and to introduce three specific interpretive strategies. This focus requires consideration of the technical adequacy of the S-B IV. Because the test manual presents basic administration instructions, we devote little attention to them. However, the "adaptive testing" format, using the establishment of a starting point from the examinee's chronological age and Vocabulary score, and the use of a basal and ceiling to reduce testing time are particularly laudatory, even though they occasionally produce administrative difficulties. It is noteworthy that the *Handbook* devotes several pages to clarifying some of the administration problems not addressed in the original manual, such as the need to present lower-level task "orientation" directions when examiners must move below the original starting point to establish a basal.

The most effective test interpretation relies on a formal and an informal database. Informal assessment requires the observation and recording of characteristic problem-solving strategies employed by the examinee, such as the level and number of anxiety indicators displayed, the extent of enthusiasm displayed for the different tasks, the amount of support required, attention span, and so on. Honzik (1976) points out examiners of young children need a high skill level because of the shorter attention spans, the greater distractibility, and the occasional reluctance to follow instructions by preschoolers. This type of qualitative assessment can never be replaced by use of quantitative methods that rely only on the use of scores to characterize performance. The ex-

aminer must be able to provide elaboration and clarification of scores based on these kinds of observations. In other words, does the interpretation make sense in terms of the other known data, which include observation of behavior? Consequently, a quality interpretation relies on both qualitative and quantitative data. Because qualitative assessment is described elsewhere in this book, the following discussion focuses primarily on building quantitative interpretive skills. It is noteworthy that the authors of the S-B IV retain a brief checklist of test behavior to aid qualitative assessment; the examiner can use this to characterize the performance of the examinee.

Meaningful quantitative interpretation requires analysis of standard scores. The S-B IV retains the global scale properties of the old Form L-M. That is, the total or composite score for the S-B IV uses a standard score population mean of 100, and a standard deviation of 16, rather than 100 and 15, as do most of the more recently developed tests (e.g., K-ABC, Wechsler Scale revisions). The SAS assigned by the new Binet are somewhat atypical. That is, the subtest population is set to 50, and the standard deviation to 8, rather than the more conventional 10 and 3, or 50 and 10. Some mental adjustment is necessary for those examiners who are familiar with the more conventional score schemes.

The first step in the quantitative interpretation process is the transformation of raw scores to standard scores. Once raw scores have been transformed, there are some general guidelines to follow, no matter which type of subtest pattern analysis procedure an examiner chooses. Although these strategies are appropriate for examinees of all ages, special attention is devoted to making the interpretive strategies useful for preschool children. These strategies include:

1. *Interpret the composite score in some context.* Typically the composite score is related to the normative sample by describing how the score ranks relative to the population (typically by providing a percentile rank). Also, occasionally the score is interpreted relative to previous scores, other test scores, and so on.

2. *Discuss the composite score briefly within a band of error.* This band of error is described as a function of the SEM of the instrument for that child's age. The composite score is placed within the band of scores, and the probability of the examinee's "true score" falling within that band is presented. (The true score can be conceptualized as the average score an examinee would obtain upon repeated testing using the same instrument, minus the effects of practice, fatigue, and other sources of test

error.) The *Handbook* presents the confidence bands by ages and confidence levels, including 99 percent, 95 percent, 90 percent, and 85 percent. An additional confidence band table is provided for a "General Purpose Abbreviated Battery" for the examiner's convenience.

3. *Compare the global scores.* The area scores or factor scores are compared to each other. The area scores are available from straightforward raw to standard score transformations using calculations and tables, as described in the *Administration and Scoring Manual* of the S-B IV. The factor scores are available by following a set of instructions described by Sattler (1992) and reproduced here by permission in Table 6.3. (Table 6.3 contains steps for calculating factor scores for children ranging in age from 2 to 7; factor scores for older children can be calculated by relying on the directions provided in Sattler's textbook.)

Whether an examiner uses area scores or factor scores as a point of departure for analyzing subtest patterns is somewhat arbitrary and depends on the examiner's preference for the Rational-Intuitive or the Independent Factors subtest analysis procedures described shortly. In any case, if the global scores are not significantly different from each other, then the composite score is very likely a good estimate of the child's overall performance. That is, there is likely little variability in performance, and the composite score can be considered a good reflection of overall ability. Of course, a highly variable set of scores can be taken to mean highly variable underlying abilities and a composite score that is less meaningful. A highly variable performance cannot be summarized very well by any single composite score. The level of significance required to establish clinically meaningful differences among scores is not clearly established in the literature, but differences that occur less than 1 percent, 5 percent, or 15 percent of the time by chance are typically interpreted as "meaningful," even though differences of this magnitude can occur fairly often in the population. Differences that occur relatively often in the normal population can still reflect real differences in abilities for a given child and, consequently, might have implications for intervention. For example, a 10-point or larger difference between the Binet Verbal Reasoning and composite score occurs for about 20 percent of the population, yet a difference of that magnitude would not be expected *by chance* more than five times out of 100. Hence, the difference might require interpretation from a clinical standpoint even though it is a relatively common occurrence. The table describing differences required for significance among the various global scores and the "base rates" for actual differences in the population are presented in the *Handbook*. A portion of this table depicting differences between area and composite scores required for statistical significance is reproduced in Table 6.6. Differences between the composite scores and factor scores required for significance for various comparisons, by age, have been developed by Rosenthal and Kamphaus (1988) and reproduced here as Tables 6.7 and 6.8; and by Sattler (1992), and reproduced here as Table 6.9. These tables present values for preschool children, taking into consideration the varying SEMs.

TABLE 6.6 Differences between the Area and the Composite Required for Statistical Significance at the 15% and 5% Levels of Confidence for Preschool Children

BETWEEN AREAS	CONFIDENCE LEVEL	AGES				
		2	*3*	*4*	*5*	*6*
Verbal Reasoning and Composite	15%	8	7	7	8	8
	5%	11	10	10	10	11
Abstract/Visual Reasoning and Composite	15%	10	10	8	8	8
	5%	14	13	11	10	11
Quantitative Reasoning and Composite Short-Term Memory and Composite	15%	11	10	9	9	11
	5%	15	14	13	12	15
	15%	9	8	8	8	9
	5%	12	11	11	10	12

Source: Reproduced from *Technical Manual,* Thorndike, Hagen, and Sattler (1988).

TABLE 6.7   Differences between Subtest Scores Required for Statistical Significance at the 1% and 5% Levels of Confidence for: (A) 2- to 5-Year-Olds (B) 6- to 10-Year-Olds

(A) 2- TO 5-YEAR-OLDS

	Voc	Comp	Abs	PA	Copy	Quant	B-Mem	MemS
Voc	—	12	11	12	12	12	11	11
Comp	9	—	11	11	11	11	11	11
Abs	9	8	—	11	11	11	10	10
PA	9	9	9	—	12	12	11	11
Copy	9	9	8	9	—	11	11	11
Quant	9	8	8	9	9	—	11	11
B-Mem	9	8	8	9	8	8	—	10
MemS	9	8	8	9	8	8	8	—

(B) 6- TO 10-YEAR-OLDS

	Voc	Comp	Abs	PA	Copy	Mat	Quant	NS	B-Mem	MemS	MemD	MemO
Voc	—	12	13	11	12	11	12	11	12	12	12	14
Comp	9	—	13	11	12	11	12	11	12	12	12	14
Abs	10	10	—	11	12	12	13	12	12	12	13	14
PA	8	8	9	—	10	9	11	9	10	10	11	12
Copy	9	9	9	7	—	10	12	10	11	11	11	13
Mat	8	8	9	7	8	—	11	9	10	10	11	13
Quant	9	9	10	8	9	8	—	11	12	12	12	14
NS	8	8	9	7	8	7	8	—	10	10	11	13
B-Mem	9	9	9	8	8	8	9	8	—	11	12	13
MemS	9	9	9	7	8	8	9	8	8	—	11	13
MemD	9	9	10	8	9	8	9	8	9	9	—	14
MemO	11	11	11	9	10	10	11	10	10	10	10	—

Note: Values above the diagonal line are at the .01 level; values below the diagonal line are at the .05 level. Voc = Vocabulary, Comp = Comprehensive, Abs = Absurdities, PA = Pattern Analysis, Copy = Copying, Mat = Matrices, Quant = Quantitative, NS = Number Series, B-Mem = Bead Memory, MemS = Memory for Sentences, MemD = Memory for Digits, MemO = Memory for Objects.

One caveat is necessary. Even if the composite and area or factor scores are similar, there still can be considerable variance in performance. For example, subtest scores can differ from each other significantly but still occur in such a pattern as to render area or factor scores similar. That is, assuming more than one subtest is administered to obtain an area or factor score, subtest highs and lows can cancel, leaving a type of average area or factor score. So Step 3 is not complete until the possibility of subtest variability is checked, even though the area or factor scores look flat. (Because there is only one

Quantitative subtest for preschool children, and it produces the Quantitative area score, there can be no within-area scatter.)

A general rule for determining subtest variability is simply to observe whether there is at least one significant difference between or among subtests. An 8-point difference is recommended as the criterion for significance for this purpose, which is slightly more rigorous than the 7-point difference recommended by Delaney and Hopkins (1987). The additional rigor is suggested to compensate for the greater error in scores of very young

TABLE 6.8   Differences between Area Scores Required for Statistical Significance at the 1% and 5% Levels of Confidence for: (A) 2- to 5-Year-Olds (B) 6- to 10-Year Olds

(A) 2- TO 5-YEAR-OLDS

	VR 2	VR 3	A/V 2	Q 1	STM 2
VR 2	—	16	18	20	17
VR 3	13	—	17	19	16
A/V 2	14	13	—	21	18
Q 1	15	15	16	—	20
STM 2	13	13	14	15	—

(B) 6- TO 10-YEAR-OLDS

	VR 2	VR 3	A/V 2	A/V 3	Q 1	Q 2	STM 2	STM 3	STM 4
VR 2	—	18	18	17	23	19	20	19	18
VR 3	14	—	16	15	22	17	18	17	16
A/V 2	14	12	—	14	21	16	18	17	16
A/V 3	13	11	11	—	21	15	17	16	15
Q 1	18	17	16	16	—	22	23	23	22
Q 2	14	13	12	12	17	—	19	17	16
STM 2	15	14	14	13	18	14	—	19	18
STM 3	15	13	13	12	17	13	15	—	17
STM 4	14	12	12	11	16	12	14	13	—

Note: Values above the diagonal line are at the .01 level; values below the diagonal line are at the .05 level. VR = Verbal Reasoning, A/V = Abstract/Visual Reasoning, Q = Quantitative Reasoning, STM = Short-Term Memory.

children. (Spruill, 1988, has produced a table of differences required for significance across ages; for the younger children the differences average 8.5 at the .05 level of confidence.) If there is not at least one subtest difference that reaches statistical significance, then interpretation stops. If there is, one of the three specific interpretative strategies should be applied. A flat profile, one with no subtests that deviate significantly from their cohort mean, indicates that the composite score is a good estimate of the child's ability.

Each of the three of the scatter analysis procedures is similar in that they all represent a systematic and logical strategy for attacking subtest scatter. Each one describes an averaging strategy, although for preschoolers the averaging process is limited. The averaging process prevents haphazard pairwise comparisons. Except for the Verbal Reasoning area, which contains three subtests designed for preschool children, the averaging strategy becomes problematic for *preschool* examinees. Both the Abstract/Visual Reasoning and the Short-Term Memory

area include (only) two subtests for preschoolers. For scatter analysis of these two areas, rather than averaging, determine whether the two subtests are significantly different from each other. If the two are significantly different, and again an 8-point difference seems reasonable, the area is not uniformly or homogeneously developed. (See Table 6.7 for specific differences required at the .01 and .05 levels for preschool children.) Consequently, the area score is not definitive and requires elaboration. Remember the Quantitative Reasoning area includes only one subtest for preschool examinees; consequently, this area score should be interpreted cautiously for this age group.

All three of the scatter analysis procedures are ipsative; they allow conclusions to be drawn about relative strengths and weaknesses within the individual's performance. SAS scores are compared to an individual's personal subtest average. This ipsative approach lends itself more easily to the development of interventions. The extent to which Binet scores impact intervention, referred

TABLE 6.9 Differences Required for Significance When Each S-B IV Subtest Scaled Score Is Compared to the Respective Mean Factor Scaled Score For Any Individual Child

SUBTEST	(AGES 2 THROUGH 7)	
	.05	.01
Verbal Comprehension		
Vocabulary	6.18	7.51
Comprehension	5.74	6.99
Absurdities	6.18	7.51
Memory for Sentences	5.74	6.99
Verbal Relations	—	—

SUBTEST	(AGES 2 THROUGH 11)	
	.05	.01
Nonverbal Reasoning/Visualization		
Pattern Analysis	5.30	6.44
Copying	6.15	7.41
Quantitative	6.02	7.33
Bead Memory	6.15	7.41
Matrices	—	—

to as treatment validity, is the topic of discussion later in this chapter.

4. *The final general step is a transition step.* This step leads directly into the scatter analysis and cannot be separated from that procedure; this step is necessary if there are differences among the area factor scores or among the subtests. Otherwise, statistically based interpretation stops. If there is no appreciable test variability, that is, there are no significant differences among the global scores, and if subtest variability is not apparent, the interpretation ends with a statement describing the composite score as a good estimate of overall ability. If there is evidence of variability among the global scores, those significant global score differences should be discussed, including some presentation of the general abilities assumed to be assessed by the areas or factors. (See Table 6.1 for a presentation of the general abilities purported to be assessed by the area or factors, as described in the various Binet manuals by Sattler and others.) Of course, if there is considerable variability within a given area or factor (characterized by several within-area or within-factor significant differences), then any discussion of the abilities assessed by a given area or factor must be tempered accordingly. In such cases, specific subtest interpretation will be required. Certain limitations should be

kept in mind, such as whether adequate subtest specificity exists for relevant subtests, and the hazard of overinterpreting when there are several significant differences.

Three Specific Interpretive Strategies. The following three scatter analysis procedures are offered as aids to developing interpretive strategies. Any one might be appropriate, depending on the examiner's orientation and the pattern of scores obtained.

The Pooled or g-*Factor Procedure.* The pooled procedure is described by Delaney and Hopkins in the *Handbook* for the S-B IV. Delaney and Hopkins adapted the technique from a procedure first described by Davis in 1955. The procedure is described as pooled because all the subtests from the entire test are pooled to obtain an average, rather than averaging subtests within areas or factors. After focusing on the global scores, the relationship of the composite score to global scores, and other indicators of test variability, the examiner must make a decision. If the area scores do not differ significantly among themselves, none of them is likely to differ from the composite, yet there may be subtest scatter. In this situation, the pooled procedure can be used to determine the presence of meaningful subtest scatter.

Use of the pooled procedure to determine the existence of meaningful scatter requires an averaging of all the subtests administered; the number and choice of subtests administered depends on the child's age, ability, and whether a brief form is used as opposed to the full battery. After the full complement of subtests is averaged, each subtest score is compared to this average subtest score. Based on the degree of difference from the mean subtest scores, each subtest is designated as being average, a strength, or a weakness. The criterion difference recommended by Delaney and Hopkins is a 7-point deviation from the average subtest score. An 8-point difference should be used as the criterion for preschoolers because the psychometric properties of the subtests are less impressive for that age examinee (Spruill, 1988). Particular abilities presumably assessed by the subtests are noted. When conflicts arise, as when some subtest assessing a given ability is deemed a strength and another subtest assessing the same ability is judged a weakness, the conflict is resolved by qualitative analysis, by evaluating the particular task demands of the subtests, and by evaluating scores and information from other sources (e.g., other tests and teacher and parent reports).

To provide aid in developing hypotheses regarding abilities assessed by the subtests, Delaney and Hopkins provide an "Inferred Abilities and Influences Chart" in the *Examiner's Handbook.* This chart lists subtests across the top and various abilities and influences suspected of impacting performance on subtests along the left margin. The juxtaposition of a particular subtest and some ability forms a cell, which can be designated a strength or a weakness, or neither, as is appropriate. Use of the chart is helpful in making a tentative hypothesis about the test performance of any examinee. Examiners should note that the particular abilities and influences listed are somewhat arbitrarily determined; that is, many of the entries are determined by logic rather than by empirical findings. Consequently, not all practitioners will agree with the rationale used to construct the existing chart. There is considerable evidence available to suggest that practitioners do not agree totally with test authors' analysis of such hypothesis-generating aids (Bracken & Fagan, 1988). Practitioners can choose to construct a separate chart for themselves, using the one provided by Delaney and Hopkins as a beginning point. Table 6.1, which describes some of the abilities and influences thought to impact each of the subtests appropriate for preschoolers, should help that process. After determining the abilities that are specific strengths and weaknesses for the examinee, from whatever source, the next step is to reconcile the specific strengths and weaknesses with the more general ones identified earlier from analysis of the global scores (area or factor scores).

Use of the pooled procedure rests on the assumption that the total test is designed to assess g and that subtests are primarily a measure of that underlying ability. Consequently, the extent to which any subtest measures other constructs should depend on (1) the distance of that subtest from an estimate of whatever the total test assesses, in this case defined by the subtest average, and (2) whether the subtest possesses adequate subtest specificity. Also intrasubtest scatter might be informative in some situations, for example, when there is wide variability of item performance within a subtest. Because of the relatively strong reliance on g as the interpretive basis, this procedure is sometimes referred to as the *g-factor* procedure. As a final consideration in the interpretive process, the examiner must consider how identified strengths can be used to guide interventions for those identified weaknesses.

The interpretive steps for the pooled procedures are:

1. Average all subtest scaled scores.
2. Identify strengths by identifying subtest scaled scores that are eight or more points higher than the subtest average scaled score.
3. Identify weaknesses by identifying subtest scaled scores that are eight or more points below the subtest average scaled score.
4. Identify abilities and influences from tables and task analysis, which correspond to the strong and weak subtests, remembering subtest similarities (clusters of ability) and specificity data.
5. Resolve conflicting scores; that is, task analyze and cross-reference subtest demands and review strong and weak abilities.
6. Reconcile strong and weak subtest abilities with general strong and weak abilities identified from either global scores from the Binet or from other tests.
7. Consider intrasubtest scatter by examining specific item responses and patterns of subtest responses.
8. Conceive of intervention strategies and steps to evaluate the recommended strategies. Intervention would take advantage of identified strengths to guide educational instruction.

The Rational-Intuitive Procedure. This scatter analysis procedure is referred to as the rational-intuitive procedure because it takes into account the theoretical model upon which the new Binet is based, which is rationally and intuitively derived. This procedure allows for analysis using the areas defined by the test model, that is, Verbal Reasoning, Quantitative Reasoning, Abstract-Visual Reasoning, and Short-Term Memory. After the general steps are completed, and assuming variability has been identified (area scores are significantly different among themselves), the meaningfulness of area score differences is discussed. If an examiner accepts the test model of the new Binet as described by Thorndike, Hagen, and Sattler, General Step 4 requires the use of area scores to describe functioning rather than factor scores. The examiner would describe abilities presumed to underlie the area scores in interpreting test performance, and specifically, significant area differences. Further subtest scatter would be defined from within each area by using area means as a point of departure. For preschool children, scatter would be defined for two of the areas by simply comparing the two subtest scores for the two relevant subtests included for examinees of that age. These two areas are Abstract/Visual Reasoning and Short-Term Memory. Because the Quantitative Reasoning area includes only one subtest for preschoolers, the issue of scatter within that area is moot. Subtests' strengths and weaknesses and their corresponding "abilities" would be determined by establishing whether an 8-point (for preschoolers) difference occurred for the relevant scatter analyses. Specific subtest strengths and weaknesses and the unique and idiosyncratic abilities assessed by them become grist for scatter interpretation if significant differences are found. If differences occur, and the particular subtests have adequate subtest specificity at the particular age in question, then unique abilities as defined on the examiner's "Inferred Abilities and Influences Chart" could be meaningfully interpreted. Finally, checks and balances are required to validate the hypotheses raised by the interpretive procedure. Strengths must be verified by other subtest scores, or other sources, as must weaknesses. Finally, strengths are "wedded" to interventions in a meaningful way, and the efficacy of the resultant recommendations determined. (To determine strengths and weaknesses use Tables 6.7 and 6.8.)

The interpreted steps for the rational-intuitive procedure are:

1. Use the Binet model to interpret abilities that underlie area scores. Area scores become the focus initially.
2. Average the within-area subtest scores. For preschool children this requires only one average, an average of the three subtests comprising Verbal Reasoning; all other areas are assessed by two or fewer subtests. In the case of a two-subtest area, simply check to determine if the two subtests are significantly different.
3. Interpret significant scatter comparing unique abilities and influences to area constructs, remembering subtest specificity data.
4. Validate strengths and weaknesses, and resolve apparent conflicts by task analysis and cross-referencing scores.
5. Evaluate intrasubtest scatter, characteristics, and patterns of responses.
6. Begin to think of intervention strategies and steps to evaluate these strategies.

The Independent Factors Procedure. This procedure is referred to as the independent factors procedure because it relies on the factor analytic structure of the Binet, obtained by using a principle factors approach, varimax rotation. That is, the analysis sought to maximize the independence of the constructs that underlie the Binet, rather than maximize the commonality of the largest underlying construct, or *g*. This approach has been described by Kaufman for the WISC-R and the K-ABC, and by Sattler for use with the Binet. Scatter analysis based on this procedure is much like the analysis described for the rational-intuitive approach, except rather than relying on area scores and the Binet model for interpretive direction, this procedure relies on the factor

structure obtained empirically by factor analysis. For preschool children, there are two basic factors that underlie Binet performance—a Verbal/Comprehension factor and a Nonverbal/Visual factor. For older children there are three factors, the two just mentioned and a separate Memory factor. This Memory factor emerges for 7-year-old children and consists of the Memory for Sentences, Memory for Digits, and Memory for Objects subtests. See Table 6.3 for description of the factors, as defined by their subtests, and Table 6.1 for a list of possible abilities and influences that impact the factors. The logic for this scatter analysis procedure is similar to that defined in the rational-intuitive approach, except that the term factor should be substituted for area, and the procedure for calculating factor scores is slightly different from the procedure for calculating area scores. Factor scores are determined by a procedure described by Sattler (1992) and presented in Table 6.3. A set of criteria values of such a magnitude as to be significantly different for factor scores also is provided by Sattler and is reported in the next paragraph. Subtest scatter is facilitated by examining the values reproduced in Table 6.9, which provide the magnitudes required for a particular subtest to be significantly different from the *mean* of the particular factor. That is, the mean for each factor is determined, and each subtest score is compared to that mean to determine significant subtest strengths and weaknesses. Scatter is evaluated by hypothesis generation, as dictated by the subtest profile.

Table 6.3 described the procedures for calculating scores. Sattler (1992) provides some tentative hypotheses for greater Verbal Comprehension than Nonverbal Reasoning/Visualization factor scores, as well as for the reverse pattern. For example, for preschoolers a greater Verbal Comprehension than Nonverbal Reasoning/ Visualization pattern might suggest relatively stronger verbal fluency skills as compared to performance-type skills, or perhaps that the child's crystallized abilities are better than novel problem-solving abilities. Factor score differences large enough to be statistically significant are at age 2, 13/18; at age 3, 10/14; at age 4, 10/13; at age 5, 9/12; at age 6, 12/15; and at age 7, 12/16 for the .05/.01 level of confidence levels for the Verbal Comprehension versus Nonverbal Reasoning/Visualization factors. Factor score differences required for significance are 15/19 for the Verbal Comprehension versus Memory Factor Comparison for 7-year-old children, and 14/19 for the Nonverbal Reasoning/Visualization versus Memory Comparison for 7-year-old children (Sattler, 1992).

The steps for the interpretive approach for the independent factors procedure are:

1. Use the factor structure defined by a principle factors solution, varimax rotation, to identify factors. These factors, calculated as described in Table 6.3, become the basis for interpreting Binet performance rather than area scores.
2. Calculate the factor scores and interpret any differences, taking into account subtest scatter.
3. Examine significant subtest scatter using Table 6.9.
4. Interpret strengths and weaknesses, assuming adequate subtest specificity, relative to constructs identified by the factor structure.
5. Validate apparent strengths and weaknesses by task analyzing and cross-referencing strengths and weaknesses.
6. Determine relevance of intrasubtest scatter characteristics.
7. Consider appropriate intervention strategies and evaluation of those strategies.

SUMMARY

All three of the procedures just described are valuable approaches for Binet interpretation. All are systematic and offer hypothesis-generating strategies. Consider all three procedures for every examinee. Any one of these procedures might be the most appropriate depending on the particular child; use the most appropriate procedure under the circumstances. Evaluate each procedure for each examinee, and choose the one that fits your examinee best. For example, for examinees that exhibit little global score scatter, as evidenced by a lack of significant differences among the area or factor scores, the pooled procedure seems most reasonable. When there are differences, use the independent factors procedure first. If the factor scores fail to offer a satisfactory interpretation, then try the rational-intuitive procedure. Perhaps for a particular examinee, that model will provide the best fit.

Finally, there are many interpretive schemes available. The three described here seem reasonable; others can be chosen to supplement them. Subtests can be grouped according to any number of constructs or skills. Consider the following dichotomies: verbal versus nonverbal; timed versus untimed; simultaneous versus successive; left-brain versus right-brain; memory versus no memory; abstract versus concrete; motoric versus non-motoric, and so on. As is apparent, subtests can be rearranged according to any reasonable model. Of course, examiners of preschool children have less latitude be-

cause there are fewer subtests available for that age group. Remember, no matter what scheme is employed, the ultimate purpose is to aid and improve the examinee's life. For many practitioners, that translates into making test information relevant for educational program planning or for developing classroom management strategies.

Psychologists and educators have not been very successful in developing effective treatment strategies from tests of cognitive abilities, despite all the optimism generated by discussions of uncovering appropriate *Aptitude by Treatment Interactions* (Reynolds, 1981). To date, if academic program planning is the goal of evaluation, the most relevant and useful test is one designed to discover educational strengths and weaknesses, that is, a criterion-referenced test of specific academic content. The more closely the test is tied to the curriculum, the more relevant and useful the test information is for academic planning. Nonetheless, tests of general cognitive ability can provide a wealth of useful information. Even hypothetical constructs or aptitudes might prove useful in educational program planning, assuming they are carefully identified, tied to instruction, and used as a basis to develop hypotheses designed to aid instruction; those hypotheses should be tested with the help of classroom teachers. Perhaps the search for the aptitude treatment interaction has failed so far because of gross measurement techniques, or inappropriate research designs, rather than the inability of aptitudes to impact performance. As professionals continue to try to bridge the gap between direct assessment and cognitive assessment, and continue to improve the treatment validity of existing instruments, remember an old line—do not throw out the baby with the bathwater. But if, as practitioners, we continue to make recommendations for educational or behavioral programming—from the Binet or some similar instrument—let us be rigorous in the assessment of the abilities and constructs, let us be diligent and creative in working with teachers in devising directly applicable educationally relevant recommendations, and let us be willing to evaluate the success of the intervention strategy employed. Practitioners must be accountable; the time is long past when poorly conceptualized and irrelevant recommendations will impress teachers, parents, and other consumers. Recommendations from testing must be academically relevant and amenable to evaluation.

RECOMMENDATIONS FOR PRACTICE

The following list of recommendations covers a range of topics but certainly is not exhaustive; rather it is offered as a beginning. Examiners are encouraged to add to this list to build test interpretation knowledge. After all, interpretation leads to information, and information sharing is the main reason for tests such as the Binet:

1. Some subtests can be grouped to make a battery amenable for administration to special populations. For example, the Nonverbal Reasoning/Visualization subtests can provide a rough index of ability for hearing-impaired examinees; for most preschoolers this battery would consist of three or four subtests. Several of the verbal subtests can be grouped for a similar battery for the visually impaired examinees, although for severely visually impaired young preschoolers only Memory for Sentences has no visual component.

2. Remember the instruments' technical limitations and their effect on interpretation (e.g., limited floors for children for Vocabulary, Comprehension and Abstract/Visual Reasoning until age 3-4, Short-Term Memory until 3-8, and Quantitative Reasoning until 5-0).

3. Interpret the unique variance of subtests if the subtests have adequate subtest specificity, and if their scores differ significantly in magnitude from the average of the global constructs or from each other. Patterns of scores should be combined into clusters of abilities as is possible.

4. Remember that the test does not contain the same subtests across the age range; consequently, the same abilities might not be assessed to the same degree on reevaluations.

5. Check the *Technical Manual* for suggestions regarding short forms when available testing time is limited. The authors report various short forms for specific purposes (e.g., assessment of gifted children, using the subtests with the best ceiling).

6. Be careful of administrative error; the S-B IV administration directions are somewhat unwieldy. Check the *Handbook* for additional clarification of administration details.

7. Consider and report bands of error for global scores.

8. Keep in mind that Binet score parameters are somewhat atypical, especially the scores for the subtests (population means of 50 and standard deviations of 8).

9. When interpreting scores, if the pooled approach is not appropriate, try next the independent factors procedure; it has better empirical support.

10. Develop relevant recommendations from a rigorous interpretation strategy and evaluate the success of recommendations.

REFERENCES

American Psychological Association. (1985). *Standards for educational and psychological testing*. Washington, DC: Author.

Boehm, A. E. (1971). *Boehm Test of Basic Concepts: Manual*. New York: Psychological Corporation.

Boyle, G. J. (1989). Confirmation of the structural dimensionality of the Stanford-Binet Intelligence Scale (Fourth Edition). *Personality and Individual Differences, 10,* 709–715.

Bracken, B. A. (1987). Limitations of preschool instruments and standards for minimal levels of technical adequacy. *Journal of Psychoeducational Assessment, 5,* 313–326.

Bracken, B. A., & Fagan, T. K. (1988). Abilities answered by the K-ABC Mental Processing subtests: The perceptions of practitioners with varying degrees of experience. *Psychology in the Schools, 25,* 22–34.

Cyr, J. J., & Brooker, B. H. (1984). Use of appropriate formulas for selecting WAIS-R short forms. *Journal of Consulting and Clinical Psychology, 52,* 903–905.

Delaney, E. A., & Hopkins, T. F. (1987). *Examiners' handbook: An expanded guide for fourth edition users*. Chicago: Riverside.

Dunn, L. (1965). *Peabody Picture Vocabulary Test*. Circle Pines, MN: American Guidance Service.

Flanagan, D. P., & Alfonso, V. C. (1995). A critical review of the technical characteristics of new and recently revised intelligence tests for preschool children. *Journal of Psychoeducational Assessment, 13,* 66–90.

Glaub, V. E., & Kamphaus, R. W. (1991). Construction of a nonverbal adaptation of the Stanford-Binet Fourth Edition. *Educational and Psychological Measurement, 51,* 231–242.

Glutting, J. J., & Kaplan, D. (1990). Stanford-Binet Intelligence Scale: Fourth Edition; Making the case for reasonable interpretations. In C. R. Reynolds & R. W. Kamphaus (Eds.), *Handbook of psychological and educational assessment of children*. New York: Guilford.

Glutting, J. J., McDermott, P. A., & Konold, T. R. (1997). Ontology, structure, and diagnostic benefits of a normative subtest taxonomy from the WISC-III standardization sample. In D. P. Flannagan, J. L. Genshaft, & P. L. Harrison (Eds.), *Contemporary intellectual assessment: Theories, test, and issues.* New York: Guilford.

Harris, S. L., Handleman, J. S., & Burton, J. L. (1990). The Stanford-Binet profiles of young children with autism. *Special Services in the Schools, 6,* 135–143.

Hendershott, J. L., Searight, H. R., Hatfield, J. L., & Rogers, B. J. (1990). Correlations between the Stanford-Binet, Fourth Edition and the Kaufman Assessment Battery for Children for a preschool sample. *Perceptual and Motor Skills, 71,* 819–825.

Honzik, M. P. (1976). Value and limitations of infant tests. In M. Lewis (Ed.), *Origins of Intelligence* (pp. 59–95). New York: Plenum.

Jensen, A. R. (1980). *Bias in mental testing.* New York: Free Press.

Johnson, D. L., Howie, V. M., Owen, M., Baldwin, C. D., & Luttman, D. (1993). Assessment of three-year-olds with the Stanford-Binet Fourth Edition. *Psychological Reports, 73,* 51–57.

Kaufman, A. S. (1979). *Intelligent testing with the WISC-R.* New York: Wiley.

Kaufman, A. S., & Kaufman, N. L. (1983). *Kaufman Assessment Battery for Children.* Circle Pines, MN: American Guidance Services.

Keith, T. Z., Cool, V. A., Novak, C. G., White, L. J., & Pottebaum, S. M. (1988). Confirmatiory factor analysis of the Stanford-Binet Fourth Edition: Testing the theory-test match. *Journal of School Psychology, 26,* 253–274.

Kline, R. B. (1989). Is the fourth edition Stanford-Binet a four-factor test? Confirmatory factor analysis of alternative models for ages 2 through 23. *Journal of Psychological Assessment, 7,* 4–13.

Lamp, R. E., & Krohn, E. J. (1990). Stability of the Stanford-Binet Fourth Edition and K-ABC for young black and white children from low-income families. *Journal of Psychological Assessment, 8,* 139–149.

Laurent, J., Swerdlik, M., & Ryburn, M. (1992). Review of validity research on the Stanford-Binet Intelligence Scale: Fourth Edition. *Psychological Assessment, 4,* 102–112.

Livesay, K. K., & Mealor, D. J. (1987). *A comparison of the Stanford-Binet Intelligence Scale (3rd) to the Stanford-Binet (4th).* Unpublished manuscript.

McCallum, R. S. (1990). Determining the factor structure of the Stanford-Binet: Fourth Edition—the right choice. *Journal of Psychoeducational Assessment, 8,* 436–442.

McCallum, R. S., & Karnes, F. A. (1987). Comparison of the Stanford-Binet Intelligence Scale (4th ed.), the British Ability Scales and the WISC-R. *School Psychology International, 8,* 133–139.

McCarthy, D. A. (1972). *McCarthy Scales of Children's Abilities.* San Antonio, TX: The Psychological Corporation.

McCrowell, K. L., & Nagle, R. J. (1994). Comparability of the WPPSI-R and the S-B: IV among preschool children. *Journal of Psychoeducational Assessment, 12,* 126–134.

Molfese, V. J., Helwig, S., & Holcomb, L. (1993). Standardized assessments of verbal intelligence in 3-year-old children: A comparison of biomedical and psychoeducational data in a longitudinal sample. *Journal of Psychoeducational Assessment, 11,* 56–66.

Molfese, V., Yaple, K., Helwig, S., Harris, L., & Connell, S. (1992). Stanford-Binet Intelligence Scale (Fourth Edition): Factor structure and verbal subscale scores for three-year-olds. *Journal of Psychoeducational Assessment, 10,* 47–58.

Ownby, R. L., & Carmin, C. N. (1988). Confirmatory factor analyses of the Stanford-Binet Intelligence Scale: Fourth Edition. *Journal of Psychoeducational Assessment, 6,* 331–340.

Prewett, P. N. (1992). Short forms of the Stanford-Binet Intelligence Scale: Fourth Edition. *Journal of Psychoeducational Assessment, 10,* 257–264.

Prewett, P. N., & Matavich, M. A. (1994). A comparison of referred students' performance on the WISC-III and the Stanford-Binet Intelligence Scale: Fourth Edition. *Journal of Psychoeducational Assessment, 12,* 42–48.

Reynolds, C. R. (1981). Neuropsychological assessment and the habilitation of learning: Considerations in the search for the aptitude × treatment interaction. *School Psychology Review, 10,* 343–349.

Reynolds, C. R., Kamphaus, R. W., & Rosenthal, B. L. (1988). Factor analysis of the Stanford-Binet Fourth Edition for ages two years through twenty-three years. *Measurement and Evaluation in Counseling and Development, 21,* 52–63.

Riccio, C. A., Platt, L. O., Kamphaus, R. W., Greer, M. K., & Elksnin, N. (1994). Principal components analysis of the general abbreviated battery of the Stanford-Binet, Fourth Edition, for young children. *Assessment, 1,* 173–178.

Robinson, N. M., Dale, P. S., & Landesman, S. (1990). Validity of the Stanford-Binet IV with linguistically precocious toddlers. *Intelligence, 14*, 173–186.

Rosenthal, B. L., & Kamphaus, R. W. (1988). Interpreting tables for test scatter on the Stanford-Binet Intelligence Scale: Fourth Edition. *Journal of Psychoeducational Assessment, 6*, 359–370.

Sattler, J. M. (1992). *Assessment of children: Revised and updated third edition.* San Diego: Author.

Spruill, J. (1988). Two types of tables for use with the Stanford-Binet Intelligence Scale: Fourth Edition. *Journal of Psychoeducational Assessment, 6*, 76–86.

Terman, L. M., & Merrill, M. A. (1973). *The Stanford-Binet Intelligence Scale.* Boston: Houghton Mifflin.

Thorndike, R. L. (1990). Would the real factors of the Stanford-Binet Fourth Edition please come forward? *Journal of Psychoeducational Assessment, 8*, 412–435.

Thorndike, R. L., Hagen, E. P., & Sattler, J. M. (1986). *The Stanford-Binet Intelligence Scale: Fourth Edition.* Chicago: Riverside.

Thorndike, R. L., Hagen, E. P., & Sattler, J. M. (1986). *The Stanford-Binet Intelligence Scale: Fourth Edition. Technical Manual.* Chicago: Riverside.

Wechsler, D. (1972). *The Wechsler Preschool and Primary Scale of Intelligence.* San Antonio, TX: Psychological Corporation.

Wechsler, D. (1974). *The Wechsler Intelligence Scale for Children—Revised.* San Antonio, TX: Psychological Corporation.

Wilson, W. M. (1992). The Stanford-Binet: Fourth Edition and Form L-M in assessment of young children with mental retardation. *Mental Retardation, 30*, 81–84.

Woodcock, R. W., & Johnson, M. B. (1977). *Woodcock–Johnson Psycho-Educational Battery.* Allen, TX: DLM/Teaching Resources.

CHAPTER 7

THE ASSESSMENT OF PRESCHOOL CHILDREN WITH THE KAUFMAN ASSESSMENT BATTERY FOR CHILDREN

ELIZABETH O. LICHTENBERGER
ALAN S. KAUFMAN

There are many uses of the K-ABC with a preschool population, as well as other populations (Kaufman, 1984). This is by no coincidence, as the K-ABC was especially developed to make it appropriate for use with preschoolers (Kaufman & Kaufman, 1983). The K-ABC shares a great deal of overlap with existing measures of childhood cognitive assessment (Kamphaus & Reynolds, 1987), and like many assessment instruments, it has its strengths and weaknesses. However, the K-ABC differs from many other intelligence tests because it measures two constructs: intelligence and achievement. For researchers and clinicians alike, guidance as to the utility of the K-ABC for particular populations is available in the research literature. This chapter highlights the use of the K-ABC with preschoolers and can be used to guide clinical assessment practice.

For those readers who are unfamiliar with the K-ABC, there are a number of sources that provide basic information about the test. A great deal of information, both psychometric and introductory, is provided in the test manuals themselves (Anastasi, 1984), and several chapters have provided integrated interpretations of the large body of research that has accumulated on the K-ABC (Kamphaus, Beres, Kaufman, & Kaufman, 1996; Kaufman & Lichtenberger, 1998; Kaufman, Lichtenberger, & Naglieri, 1999). Two chapters specifically present concise information on theoretical, empirical, and practical applications of the K-ABC in a cross-cultural setting (Lichtenberger & Kaufman, 1998; Lichtenberger, Kaufman, & Kaufman, 1998). In addition, a book by Kamphaus and Reynolds (1987) provides more detailed information for experienced K-ABC users, encouraging comprehensive psychometric and clinical interpretation of the battery and promoting its intelli-

gent application for preschool and elementary school children.

Following is a brief overview of the K-ABC's structure for the preschool population, the underlying theory of the K-ABC, and the features of the K-ABC that were included specifically for preschoolers. A number of research studies that have used the K-ABC with preschoolers will be examined and some conclusions regarding the use of the K-ABC with preschoolers will be drawn. Finally, a clinical case report using the K-ABC will be presented. In general, for the chapter, *preschool* is defined as 2 years, 6 months to 4 years, 11 months—the age range that is administered the preschool level of the K-ABC.

K-ABC STRUCTURE

The K-ABC is a battery of tests that taps both intelligence and achievement. The Achievement scale of the K-ABC is analogous to the Verbal scale of the WISC-III (Wechsler, 1991). Tests of vocabulary, oral arithmetic, and general information appear on the Achievement scale in alternate forms to similar subtests on the WISC-III. Kaufman and Kaufman (1983) believe that these tests are certainly influenced by intelligence, but they are also influenced by so-called nonintellective factors such as English language proficiency, acculturation, and quality of school experiences. The K-ABC Achievement scale correlates highly with the Verbal scale of the WISC-III and "behaves" very similarly in clinical evaluations.

The K-ABC measures intelligence and achievement constructs with 16 subtests that span the age range of 2½ through 12½ years. From the ages of 2½ to 3 years, 11 months, the preschool battery consists of five mental processing tests. At age 4, two more mental processing tests are added to the battery. The achievement battery is relatively small for preschoolers, consisting of only two subtests at ages 2½ through 2 years, 11 months, and four subtests at ages 3 through 4. The subtests are described here (see Figure 7.1) in a similar manner to the descriptions given in the K-ABC *Interpretative Manual* (Kaufman and Kaufman, 1983); however, Figure 7.1 includes only the subtests that comprise the preschool level of the K-ABC.

The K-ABC subtests have many unique characteristics in comparison to their predecessors. This is not surprising because the most popular IQ tests, such as the WISC-III, are not theoretically driven and have subtests selected prior to World War II. One of the more important criteria for mental processing subtest selection was that the subtest not be too heavily influenced by nonintellective factors. Hence, subtests that have been traditionally included as measures of verbal intelligence are not included on the Mental Processing (intelligence) scale of the K-ABC. This dramatic departure from practice has led to both criticism (Sternberg, 1984) and praise (Telzrow, 1984). These efforts to eliminate nonintellective factors were taken, in part, to limit cultural influences. In the development of subtests, further efforts were taken to identify any culturally inappropriate subtests or items. Minority group reviewers were employed to identify any such items and these items were subsequently removed (Kaufman & Kaufman, 1983). The minority group reviewers did not, however, identify any entire mental processing subtests as inappropriate. Yet, this is not to say that the K-ABC mental processing subtests are immune to cultural or linguistic differences. Rather these subtests are *less influenced* by these variables (Lichtenberger & Kaufman, 1998; Lichtenberger et al., 1998). It is quite likely that a child's performance on tests such as Gestalt Closure and Magic Window is affected by English language proficiency, as discussed in a later section. Additionally, K-ABC subtests were selected on the basis of their ability to assess sequential and simultaneous processing.

As noted in the description of the K-ABC subtests included in the preschool battery, the tests administered differ across ages. The developers of the K-ABC recognized that a bright 4½-year-old may not be challenged by the subtests designed solely for preschool-age children (Magic Window, Face Recognition, Expressive Vocabulary). Therefore, the K-ABC's authors designed the test so that examiners are permitted to administer the "age 5" level of the K-ABC to children ages 4 years, 6

months through 4 years, 11 months, who are known or believed to be gifted or precocious in their learning ability. The K-ABC *Administration and Scoring Manual* (Kaufman & Kaufman, 1983) details the procedure for conducting and scoring out-of-level testing.

The battery that is designed to be administered to a 5-year-old consists of two additional mental processing subtests and one additional achievement subtest; the three subtests designed only for preschool children, listed in the previous paragraph, are removed from the battery. The first mental processing subtest added is a Simultaneous Processing task named Matrix Analogies. In this task, the child has to select the picture or abstract design that best completes a visual analogy. The second mental processing subtest added is another Simultaneous Processing task named Spatial Memory. In this task, the child must recall the placement of pictures on a page that was exposed briefly. The added Achievement test at age 5 is Reading/Decoding, which requires the child to name letters and read words.

K-ABC THEORY

The theory underlying the K-ABC reflects the coming together of information about mental processing from numerous laboratory and clinical settings within the domains of neuropsychology, psychobiology, and experimental psychology. The K-ABC theory has roots with those such as Luria, Das, Sperry, Gazzaniga, Neisser, and others. Thus, the theory of sequential and simultaneous processing underlying the K-ABC represents the Kaufmans' fusion of a variety of theories and research findings.

Simultaneous processing refers to the mental ability to integrate and synthesize multiple pieces of input to solve a problem correctly. This type of holistic processing is achieved by processing many stimuli all at once rather than bit by bit. Simultaneous processing frequently involves spatial, analogic, or organizational abilities (Kaufman & Kaufman, 1983). A K-ABC subtest that involves constructing an abstract design from several identical triangles (an analog of Wechsler's Block Design task) is a prototypical measure of simultaneous processing. To solve these items correctly, one must mentally integrate the components of the design to see the whole. Another K-ABC subtest that taps a child's ability to form a gestalt is titled Spatial Memory. This novel task requires the child to memorize the spatial locations of stimuli and then identify the correct locations of the stimuli on a blank grid but in no particular

MENTAL PROCESSING SCALE		AGES		
		2-6 through 2-11	*3-0 through 3-11*	*4-0 through 4-11*
Sequential Scale Subtests				
Hand Movements	The child is required to imitate a series of movements in the same sequence as the examiner performed them.	X	X	X
Number Recall	The child must repeat a series of digits in the same sequence as the examiner said them.	X	X	X
Word Order	The examinee is required to touch a series of pictures in the same sequence as they were named by the examiner, with more difficult items using a color-interference task.			X
Simultaneous Scale Subtests				
Magic Window	The child must identify a picture that the examiner exposes moving it past a narrow slit, making the picture only partly visible at any one time.	X	X	X
Face Recognition	The child must select, from a group of photographs, the one or two faces that were exposed briefly in the proceeding photograph.	X	X	X
Gestalt Closure	The child must name the object or scene pictured in a partial drawing.	X	X	X
Triangles	The child is required to assemble several identical triangles into an abstract pattern that matches a model.			X
Achievement Scale Subtests				
Expressive Vocabulary	The child has to name the object in a photograph.	X	X	X
Faces & Places	The child must name a well-known person, fictional character, or place pictured in a photograph or illustration.	X	X	X
Arithmetic	The child is required to answer a question that requires the knowledge of math concepts or the manipulation of numbers.		X	X
Riddles	The child must name the object or concept described by a list of three characters.		X	X

FIGURE 7.1   The K-ABC Subtests Administered to Each Age in the Preschool Range

Source: Interpretive manual for the Kaufman Assessment Battery for Children, by A. S. Kaufman & N. L. Kaufman, 1983.

sequence. Whether the tasks are spatial or analogic in nature, the unifying characteristic of simultaneous processing is the mental synthesis of stimuli to solve the problem independently of the sensory modality of the input. Even a verbal test such as Riddles can have a substantial loading on the Simultaneous factor (Kaufman & Kamphaus, 1984). This K-ABC Achievement task requires a child to integrate multiple pieces of verbally presented information to determine what whole object is being described.

The second form of mental processing measured by the K-ABC is sequential processing. It emphasizes the arrangement of stimuli in serial order for successful problem solving. In every instance, each stimulus is linearly or temporally related to the previous one (Kaufman & Kaufman, 1983) creating a form of serial interdependence. An example is the Word Order subtest, a task that requires the child to point to a series of silhouettes of common objects (e.g., tree, shoe, hand) in the same sequence that the objects were named by the examiner—sometimes following a color-interference activity. In this task, and in other Sequential Processing subtests, the child has to place the stimuli in their proper order; it is not acceptable merely to reproduce the input without regard to the serial order. Other Sequential Processing tasks include Hand Movements, which involves visual input and a motor response, and Number Recall, which involves auditory input and a verbal response. As is the case with the Simultaneous subtests, neither the modality of presentation nor the mode of response determines the scale placement of a task, but rather it is the mental processing demands of the task that are most salient (Kaufman & Kaufman, 1983).

In solving problems, neither simultaneous nor sequential processing is used in isolation. These two types of information processing are constantly interacting, though one approach usually will take a lead role in processing. Which method takes the lead role can change according to the problem or, as is the case with some individuals, persist across problem type (i.e., forming what Das, Kirby, & Jarman, 1979, refer to as habitual modes of processing). In fact, almost any problem can be solved through either method of processing. In most cases, one method is clearly superior to another and when the appropriate method is used to complete a task, superior results are obtained.

A separate component of the K-ABC is the Achievement scale. This scale measures abilities that serve to assess knowledge and skills usually obtained through alertness to the environment and formal educa-

tion. These measures serve as a complement to the intelligence scales. Although verbal concept formation and vocabulary are usually equated with verbal intelligence, the K-ABC's authors found them to fit more appropriately in a measure of achievement. Also included on the Achievement scale are measures of general information, arithmetic, and language development. Performance on the Achievement scale is viewed as an estimate of the child's success in the application of his or her mental processing skills to the acquisition of knowledge from the environment (Kaufman, Kaufman, & Kamphaus, 1985). Knowing all the while that it is not possible to separate completely what you know (achievement) from how well you think (intelligence), the Kaufmans tried to distinguish the two variables better than in the past. For example, the Wechsler intelligence scales and the Peabody Individual Achievement Test—Revised (PIAT-R), although supposedly measures of different constructs, overlap on two subtests: measures of arithmetic ability and general information.

FACTOR ANALYTIC SUPPORT OF THE THEORY

Studies of the factorial validity of the K-ABC for preschoolers at least partially support the scale division of the K-ABC. The national standardization sample was used to evaluate the factor structure of the K-ABC (Kaufman & Kamphaus, 1984). In this study, the authors concluded that the K-ABC produces only two meaningful factors at ages 2 and 3; a third (Achievement) factor does not emerge until age 4. Moreover, this Achievement factor becomes even more distinct shortly after the onset of formal schooling.

Easily identifiable Sequential and Simultaneous factors are produced for preschoolers at ages 2½, 3, and 4 years in factor analysis of all K-ABC subtests (Mental Processing and Achievement). The subtests that have their highest loadings on these factors, almost without exception, are the subtests that are included on the Sequential and Simultaneous Processing scales, respectively (Kaufman & Kamphaus, 1984). Even when a third (Achievement) factor is extracted for age 4, the Sequential and Simultaneous dimensions remain robust. Not one mental processing task for children in the 4-year-age range has a factor loading on the Achievement factor that is .40 or above. However, the subtests that comprise the K-ABC Achievement scale all have an average loading above .50 at age 4 years on the Achievement factor. Thus, even though the third factor is only partially supported for preschool children, and it is not as robust for

4-year-olds as it is for school-age children, the factor analyses of all K-ABC tasks for preschool children do provide good support for the validity of the sequential and simultaneous dichotomy for all age groups. The factor analyses of these tasks also support the validity of the three-scale structure of the K-ABC for children who have reached their fourth birthday. When only the Mental Processing subtests are factor analyzed, the varimax-rotated solutions correspond quite closely to the Sequential and Simultaneous Processing scale for ages 2½, 3, and 4 (see Table 7.1; see Kaufman & Kamphaus, 1984). Similar data have been also found by Gridley, Miller, Barke, and Fischer (1990) in an at-risk population: "The structure of the K-ABC for the present at risk sample is similar to the empirically derived structure for the standardization sample" (p. 46).

Many foreign adaptations and translations of the K-ABC have appeared throughout Europe and Asia, for example, in France, Germany, Spain, Japan, Korea, Israel, and Jordan. Test manuals for these foreign versions sometimes include factor analysis data of portions of their standardization samples, thereby permitting cross-cultural comparisons of the K-ABC factor structure. Tables 7.2 and 7.3 present factor analytic data for preschool children in three countries: France (Kaufman & Kaufman, 1993), Germany (Melchers & Preuss, 1991), and Japan (Matsubara et al., 1994). Two foreign *K-ABC Interpretive Manuals* present two-factor solutions of the Sequential and Simultaneous Processing subtests for age 2½ (France)

and for ages 2½, 3, and 4 (Germany). These data, all based on principal factor analysis followed by varimax rotation, are shown in Table 7.2. Additionally, three-factor, varimax-rotated solutions of all age-appropriate K-ABC subtests are presented in the *K-ABC Interpretive Manuals* for Japan (age 3), France (age 4), and Germany (age 4). These data are presented in Table 7.3.

Table 7.2 reveals that two clear-cut Sequential and Simultaneous factors emerged in France at age 2½ and in Germany for all three preschool-age groups studied. All subtests loaded above .30 on their designated factor and, in those instances in which they had meaningful loadings on both factors, they loaded more highly on their designated factor. These results support the construct validity of the preschool version of the K-ABC Mental Processing scales in France and Germany and support the cross-cultural consistency of the Sequential and Simultaneous Processing dimensions identified for the U.S. version of the K-ABC.

In Table 7.3, three factors emerged for young children in Japan, Germany, and France, and these factors are compatible with the labels Sequential, Simultaneous, and Achievement. As was true for the U.S. version of the K-ABC, the factorial purity of the three factors for preschool children was not optimal in these three foreign countries. As in the United States, there was a decided overlap between the subtests that are labeled "Simultaneous" and "Achievement." (In agreement with Kaufman & Kamphaus's, 1984, interpretation of the data for

TABLE 7.1 Varimax-Rotated Factor Loadings of the K-ABC Mental Processing Subtests on the Sequential and Simultaneous Factors for Preschool Children (Ages 2½ to 4 Years) in the United States

K-ABC Subtest	AGE 2½ (N = 100)		AGE 3 (N = 200)		AGE 4 (N = 200)	
	SEQ	SIM	SEQ	SIM	SEQ	SIM
Sequential						
Hand Movements	**.60**	.12	**.57**	.19	**.62**	.25
Number Recall	**.59**	**.38**	**.74**	**.31**	**.58**	.16
Word Order	—	—	—	—	**.69**	**.32**
Simultaneous						
Magic Window	.17	**.80**	.17	**.62**	**.30**	**.47**
Face Recognition	**.36**	**.34**	.23	**.37**	.24	**.50**
Gestalt Closure	**.36**	**.48**	.20	**.50**	.14	**.79**
Triangles	—	—	—	—	**.36**	**.47**

Loadings > .30 appear in bold print. SEQ = Sequential; SIM = Simultaneous.

TABLE 7.2 Varimax-Rotated Two-Factor Solutions of the Preschool Sequential and Simultaneous Processing Subtests in the French and German Adaptations of the K-ABC

K-ABC Subtest	FRANCE AGE 2½ (N = 57)		GERMANY AGE 2½ (N = 97)		GERMANY AGE 3 (N = 295)		GERMANY AGE 4 (N = 336)	
	SEQ	SIM	SEQ	SIM	SEQ	SIM	SEQ	SIM
Sequential								
Hand Movements	**.71**	.09	**.95**	.12	**.46**	.21	**.48**	**.30**
Number Recall	**.85**	.06	**.61**	.26	**.72**	.11	**.61**	.17
Word Order	—	—	—	—	—	—	**.68**	**.68**
Simultaneous								
Magic Window	**.43**	**.73**	.23	**.64**	.19	**.66**	.08	**.50**
Face Recognition	**.35**	**.77**	**.47**	**.50**	.29	**.38**	.19	**.33**
Gestalt Closure	.21	**.71**	.11	**.78**	.11	**.63**	.15	**.62**
Triangles	—	—	—	—	—	—	**.32**	**.40**

Loadings > .30 appear in bold print. SEQ = Sequential; SIM = Simultaneous.

TABLE 7.3 Varimax-Rotated Three-Factor Solutions of the Preschool Sequential, Simultaneous, and Achievement Processing Subtests in the Japanese, German, and French Adaptations of the K-ABC

K-ABC Subtest	JAPAN AGE 3 (N = 160)			GERMANY AGE 4 (N = 295)			FRANCE AGE 4 (N = 119)		
	SEQ	SIM	ACH	SEQ	SIM	ACH	SEQ	SIM	ACH
Sequential									
Hand Movements	**.77**	.29	.20	**.45**	.28	.18	**.68**	.16	.20
Number Recall	**.84**	.09	.15	**.56**	.15	.15	**.70**	.00	.00
Word Order	—	—	—	**.70**	.11	.09	**.80**	.04	**.35**
Simultaneous									
Magic Window	.26	**.40**	**.57**	.04	.20	**.54**	.02	**.35**	**.54**
Face Recognition	.17	**.89**	.02	.19	.11	**.33**	**.48**	**.40**	.06
Gestalt Closure	.10	**.55**	**.63**	.11	**.51**	.27	.00	**.86**	.19
Triangles	—	—	—	.27	**.55**	.10	**.45**	**.50**	**.33**
Achievement									
Expressive Vocabulary	.18	.02	**.90**	.11	.06	**.75**	.19	.07	**.82**
Faces & Places	—	—	—	**.41**	**.34**	**.44**	.12	.28	**.76**
Arithmetic	**.66**	.07	**.44**	**.58**	**.50**	.16	**.48**	.05	**.65**
Riddles	**.41**	.01	**.74**	**.32**	**.44**	**.49**	.21	.09	**.80**

Loadings > .30 appear in bold print. SEQ = Sequential; SIM = Simultaneous; ACH = Achievement.
The Japanese version of the K-ABC does not include Faces & Places.

preschool children, Melchers & Preuss, 1991, extracted only two factors for children ages 2½ and 3 years.) Nonetheless, the factor solutions shown in Table 7.3 do offer construct validity support for the three K-ABC scales at ages 3 and 4, and this support is strongest in Japan at age 3 and France at age 4. Again, the analyses of all K-ABC subtests for preschool children in these foreign countries are reasonably similar to the results in the United States, suggesting the cross-cultural generalizability of the K-ABC for children between the ages of 2 years, 6 months and 4 years, 11 months.

The most important finding from factor analyses of the K-ABC in the United States and other countries is the consistent emergence of Sequential and Simultaneous factors for preschool children, both normal and exceptional, from a variety of cultures. This result had been well established for elementary school children prior to the development of the K-ABC (Das, Kirby, & Jarman, 1979). Yet, evidence of this processing distinction for preschool youngsters was scarce prior to the research leading up to the construction of the K-ABC (Kaufman, Kaufman, Kamphaus, & Naglieri, 1982). Therefore, support for the theoretical constructs underlying the K-ABC was essential because of the theoretical underpinnings claimed for the battery, and it was especially invaluable for ages 2½ through 5 years because of the unavailability of previous construct validity data for that age group.

Evidence of construct validation for both preschool boys and girls was provided by Kamphaus and Kaufman (1986) in their study of 2,000 children from the normative sample. Their data included a substantial number of preschoolers, namely 300 from ages 2½ to 3 years, 11 months, and 200 children from ages 4 years to 4 years, 11 months. Data were analyzed for this combined group of 500 preschool children, and, with one exception, the Sequential and Simultaneous subtests behaved exactly as predicted; Triangles for the sample of males loaded more highly on the Sequential factor (.39) than on the Simultaneous factor (.27). Thus, when comparing the mean varimax-rotated loadings for boys and girls ages 2 years, 6 months to 4 years, 11 months, the coefficent of congruence is not as strong for the Simultaneous factor (.61) because it contains Triangles. However, the congruence of the Sequential dimension for boys and girls was demonstrated by the strong coefficient of congruence (.96).

The data for preschool children in Kaufman and Kamphaus's (1984, 1986) studies attest to the robust nature of the processing constructs defining the K-ABC intelligence subtests for preschool children, and that ro-

bustness is further reinforced by the data from France, Germany, and Japan. The fact that Face Recognition (a memory test) loads decisively on the Simultaneous factor for boys and girls and for virtually all age groups discourages interpretation of the factor pattern from a Jensen (1973) memory-reasoning hierarchy. Similarly, Keith and Dunbar's (1984) alternative interpretation of the K-ABC's two-factor solution as Verbal Memory and Nonverbal Reasoning seems far less defensible than a mental processing orientation. Keith and Dunbar's approach is arguable for school-age children but pales in comparison to the Sequential–Simultaneous model for preschool youngsters. The nonverbal Hand Movements task loads so well on the Sequential factor for preschoolers (it is the *best* measure for girls) that the label Verbal Memory for that factor seems unwarranted. Similarly, the perceptual nonreasoning Gestalt Closure subtest (a paradigm of simultaneous processing) is the best measure of the Simultaneous factor for boys *and* girls, making Keith and Dunbar's (1984) Nonverbal Reasoning label seem unjustified.

Goldstein, Smith, and Waldrep (1986) factor analyzed data on the K-ABC Mental Processing Composite, along with other instruments, for a small group of 40 three-year-olds. The two Sequential subtests at age 3 loaded together, as did two of the three Simultaneous tasks (Magic Window, Gestalt Closure); Face Recognition loaded by itself on a third factor. Magic Window and Gestalt Closure, which both require verbal responses, loaded on a factor that the authors interpreted as Verbal Ability. Indeed, for a sample as young as age 3 (all subjects were between 35 and 38 months), it is quite possible that vocabulary will be a crucial determinant of performance on Magic Window and Gestalt Closure, as Goldstein and coworkers suggest. Indeed, the latter two subtests commonly load substantially on Achievment factors for preschool children (e.g., see Table 7.2).

Kaufman and Kaufman (1983) state that some Mental Processing subtest scores might be depressed by poor language development. In the case study of 4-year-old Jack in the *K-ABC Interpretive Manual*, they say, "His great deficiency in basic labeling vocabulary is conceivably the cause of his below normal performance on Magic Window, Gestalt Closure, and Word Order. For Jack, these subtests functioned more as vocabulary and achievement tests than as measures of his mental processing skills. Consequently, his standard score on the Mental Processing scales are likely to be underestimates, perhaps even gross underestimates, of his true intellectual functioning" (p. 215).

Kaufman and Kaufman (1983) suggest that examiners can gain insight into the nature of a young child's language problem by studying his or her responses to Magic Window, Gestalt Closure, Expressive Vocabulary, Riddles, and Faces & Places. Many of the suggestions made by German (1983) concerning the identification of possible word-finding disorders are especially helpful, for example, noting a child's tendency to describe words instead of naming them ("that monkey thing" for "banana" on Expressive Vocabulary) or to substitute a wrong word for the correct word ("caw" for "saw" on Magic Window, or "ring" for "key" on Riddles).

Goldstein et al.'s (1986) study is a good reminder that some K-ABC Mental Processing subtests might be measuring vocabulary for very young or language disabled children. Their factor analysis does not at all establish that fact, although their results make it clear that verbal ability is certainly involved in the 3-year-olds' performance on Magic Window and Gestalt Closure. Unfortunately, those researchers excluded the K-ABC Achievement scale from their study, preventing follow-up of their specific hypotheses about the two Simultaneous Processing subtests. Also, Goldstein et al. (1986) analyzed 12 variables with only 40 subjects, a ratio of subjects to variables of only about 3:1; the desired ratio is 10:1 to reduce to influence of chance factors on the obtained factor structure.

FEATURES OF THE K-ABC FOR PRESCHOOLERS

Developmentally Appropriate Materials

Upon administering the K-ABC, one can see the game-like nature of the tasks, which are quite enjoyable for preschoolers (and to examiners who administer them). The K-ABC was designed to attract the interest of preschoolers by using colorful and true-to-life materials. Tests such as Magic Window, Face Recognition, Expressive Vocabulary, and Arithmetic use either full-color artwork or photographs. These features are helpful in maintaining rapport with a young child and facilitate a valid administration. As Telzrow (1984) notes, "Unlike other measures of preschool intelligence…the K-ABC utilizes marvelous color photographs in place of static (and often too unfamiliar) line drawings" (p. 312). Although the K-ABC is clearly tailored to the preschool level, some clinicians feel that it could benefit from having more objects to manipulate to further interest young children. The Triangles subtest, which is not administered until age 4, is a good example of such a manipulative task.

The child's developmental level at each of the age ranges tested with the K-ABC preschool battery was taken into account in its development. A thorough item analysis helped to tailor the battery to make each of the items developmentally appropriate. Because the items are so well selected for the child's developmental level, this prevents the frustration that often occurs when too many difficult items are presented and also prevents boredom when too many easy items are administered.

Sensitivity to Attention Span

The attention span of a very young child can be notably short. In light of this, the K-ABC shows an awareness of developmental changes in attention span as children get older. The length of time to administer the K-ABC increases as the age of the child and the child's attention span increase. Thus, instead of requiring all preschoolers to take the same number of subtests, the number of K-ABC subtests that a child must take begins at seven for age 2½ and progresses to nine at age 3, and 11 at age 4. Although even seven subtests can be interminable for a 2½-year-old (or for the examiner!), the K-ABC still makes more reasonable requirements of the attention of young children than do either similar tests. Additionally, Telzrow (1984) remarks, "The easel format facilitates the direction of attention where it should be—on the child—instead of on myriad boxes, manuals, and test materials. And the child's attention is easy to maintain, given the attractiveness of the materials and their appeal to children" (pp. 311–312).

Clear Instructions

The K-ABC authors took great care to ensure that young children are able to understand the test instructions. If it is not certain that a child understands what he or she is to do, then the obtained score may not be valid, and the K-ABC authors wanted to avoid this. Creating understandable directions for the preschool child was accomplished by removing potentially difficult verbal concepts from the examiner's instructions. Such concepts as "middle" and "after," which Boehm (1971) found to be difficult for young disadvantaged children, appear commonly in the directions spoken by the examiner when administering various standardized preschool instruments (Kaufman, 1978). Many examiners have asked why, for example, the Photo Series instructions do not use the words *sequence* or *order*. (Photo Series is a Simultaneous Processing subtest for ages 6 and above.) These words were not used because it was felt that they would be difficult for some 6-year-olds to understand. In the K-ABC, however, there is an additional fallback position if a young child does not understand even these simplified directions.

Sample and Teaching Items

Every Mental Processing scale subtest begins with an unscored sample item in which, if the child fails the item, the examiner can use his or her own words to explain the nature of the task. The examiner then can give the child a second trial, and, if necessary, explain the demands of the task to the child again. This same procedure is applied to the teaching items (the first two items administered to the child after the sample item) with the exception that the first trial of each teaching item is scored. Examiners should consult the K-ABC test manuals for more information on the use of sample and teaching items. Some practitioners have expressed concern that the introduction of flexibility into the use of test instructions can adversely affect the reliability of the obtained scores. Although this seems to be a logical concern, it does not have any support to date. If this flexibility was a problem of significant magnitude, the K-ABC subtests would not show such good evidence of internal consistency, stability, and construct validity. For the time being, it appears that examiners should not be concerned about these flexible test administration procedures as a problem unless they have some difficulties of this nature in their everyday practice with the K-ABC.

Adequate Floor

Kamphaus and Reynolds (1987) note that the K-ABC has a number of easy items for preschoolers that mitigate against the problem of having a number of zero raw scores. Although the K-ABC has a sufficient floor for most preschoolers, there are not enough easy items on the K-ABC to permit evaluation of the profiles of preschool children with abilities that are well below average (Bracken, 1987). Unfortunately, this problem affects virtually all preschool multiscore intelligence batteries.

Telzrow (1984) described several potential uses of the K-ABC with preschoolers. She proposed that the Nonverbal scale is a needed addition for young children and noted deficiencies in other available measures. The Nonverbal scale should be given a trial by those charged with the evaluation of hearing-impaired and severely speech-impaired preschoolers. Telzrow cautioned that some severely language disordered children might be misidentified, possibly as mentally retarded, by many existing measures of intelligence that depend heavily on the assessment of verbal skills and knowledge.

Telzrow also argued that the K-ABC offers two advantages in the identification of preschool gifted children. One of these advantages is the availability of an Achievement scale that is normed down to age $2^{1}/_{2}$. She noted that academic achievement has been proposed as an important measure of early academic potential and that the K-ABC is unusual in that it possesses one of the few Achievement scales that is appropriate for this age group. Furthermore, the K-ABC out-of-level norms allow the examiner to administer tests designed for school-age children (such as Reading/Decoding) to bright $4^{1}/_{2}$-year-olds, as mentioned previously. The interested reader can find other advice regarding the use of K-ABC with preschoolers in Telzrow's (1984) article.

RELIABILITY AND VALIDITY OF THE K-ABC FOR PRESCHOOLERS

Reliability

The internal consistency of a test evaluates the degree to which a score represents a homogeneous ability or trait. The *K-ABC Interpretive Manual* (Kaufman & Kaufman, 1983) reports mean internal consistency scores ranging from .86 to .91 on the preschool Mental Processing global scales. The mean internal consistency of the preschool Achievement scale was .93. Test-retest or stability coefficients are also reported in the *K-ABC Interpretive Manual* (Kaufman & Kaufman, 1983), which are quite useful to practitioners. For the Mental Processing subtests for preschool children, these coefficients range from .77 (Sequential and Simultaneous Processing) to .83 for the Mental Processing Composite. The stability coefficients are generally higher (.95) for the Achievement scale. This is an interesting finding in that the K-ABC Achievement scale is very similar to traditional measures of verbal intelligence (Kamphaus & Reynolds, 1987). Furthermore, the K-ABC Achievement scale is the best predictor of future achievement on the battery. Because prediction of future achievement is one the central purposes of preschool intelligence testing, it is fortuitous for practitioners that the best predictor on the K-ABC clearly possesses the best reliability.

In comparison to other tests of preschool-age children, the Achievement scale of the K-ABC yields comparable or higher stability coefficients. At the preschool level, tests such as the Binet IV do not demonstrate test-retest reliability as highly as the Achievement scale of the K-ABC (see Bracken, 1987, for a review of the stability of several other scales and the Mental Processing scales of the K-ABC).

The reliability of the K-ABC also appears to remain strong in the transition between the preschool and early elementary years. In a study of 25 preschool children without disabilities, Smith, Bolin, and Stovall (1988) found a high level of stability between and among scores on the global scales of the K-ABC at ages 4, 5, and 6. They reported that all stability correlations were significant in the comparison between age 4 and age 6: Achievement = .80, Sequential = .73, and Simultaneous = .76. These test-retest results compare favorably with the data presented in the *K-ABC Interpretive Manual*.

Similar to the preceding study with preschool children without disabilities, in a two-year study of the stability of the K-ABC, Lamp and Krohn (1990) found that the K-ABC was "highly stable" from ages 4 to 6 for children from low-income families. They reported the stability of the Mental Processing Composite (MPC) scores from ages 4 to 6 for the entire group to be .82, and for the Achievement scale to be .84. They additionally compared subgroups of white and African American children and found no significant differences between the populations. The authors concluded that if children are tested at the end of their preschool year, their global or composite scores would likely remain relatively stable through the end of the first grade year.

The long-term stability of the K-ABC with at-risk preschoolers was assessed by Lyon and Smith (1986). The K-ABC was administered at a nine-month interval to 53 children between the ages of 49 and 73 months. The stability coefficients ranged from .83 for the MPC to .73 for the Sequential scale. The coefficient was .76 for the Simultaneous scale and .82 for the Achievement scale. Although these results support the overall accuracy of the K-ABC, an equally useful finding for practitioners was the level of gain over this time period. The Simultaneous scale was the big gainer (87.9 on test 1 to 97.2 on test 2 for a 9-point increase), which is highly consistent with the test-retest data presented in the *K-ABC Interpretative Manual* (Kaufman & Kaufman, 1983). The Sequential and Achievement scale each improved by about 3 points. The MPC improved about 8 points over the nine-month period.

Relationship of the K-ABC to Other Tests

The K-ABC exhibits considerable overlap with other measures of intelligence, yet also contributes something new. Evidence of this is available in looking at correlations between the K-ABC and other popular measures, and by examining differences between standard scores. The *K-ABC Interpretive Manual* (Kaufman & Kaufman, 1983) and Kamphaus and Reynolds's (1987) book on the K-ABC both provide numerous comparisons between the K-ABC and other tests, as do recent chapters on the K-ABC (Kamphaus et al., 1996; Kaufman et al., 1999; Kaufman & Lichtenberger, 1998).

When examining differences between standard scores, some of the variation in scores can be accounted for by the fact that, on the average, intelligence test norms get about 3 standard score points tougher with each decade (Flynn, 1984). The relationship between the K-ABC norms and norms for the WISC-R, the Binet L-M, and Binet IV demonstrates that these changes over the years do predictably occur (Kamphaus & Reynolds, 1987). Kamphaus and Reynolds (1987) found the K-ABC norms to be about 2 points lower than those for the WISC-R and 1972 Binet. This is consistent with Flynn's prediction because these two measures were normed about a decade prior to the K-ABC. Similarly, the Binet IV norms (Thorndike, Hagen, & Sattler, 1986) are slightly tougher than those of the K-ABC. In a study of 89 preschool children, the Binet IV Composite was 93.4 and the K-ABC MPC was 96.0 (Krohn & Lamp, 1989). As these two tests were normed within the same era, the similarity in the scores is also predicable.

One of the few studies comparing the K-ABC with another test for a normal sample of preschoolers was conducted by Lampley and Rust (1986). They administered the K-ABC and Slosson Intelligence Test to a group of 50 preschoolers between the ages of 2½ and 4. In this study the K-ABC Mental Processing Composite (MPC) ($M = 108.7$) was predictably lower than the Slosson ($M = 123.2$). Although the Slosson Intelligence Test lacks the more sophisticated psychometric properties of the K-ABC, it does appear to produce lawful differences (i.e., higher scores) in at least this one investigation.

This trend for the K-ABC to produce lower scores than previous measures is, however, moderated by ethnic and linguistic differences. One of the few studies comparing different ethnic groups of preschoolers that sheds some light on this issue was conducted by Valencia (1984). In this study, a group of 42 Mexican American children from a Headstart program was administered the K-ABC and WPPSI in counterbalanced fashion. The K-ABC mean (104.1) was slightly higher than the WPPSI mean (102.4). For most children administered these two tests, it would be expected that the K-ABC would give lower scores than the WPPSI by almost 5 points (the WPPSI was normed about 15 years before the K-ABC). However, this trend is reversed for a sample of Mexican American children. On the other hand, this finding is consistent with research showing that the K-ABC produces smaller ethnic group differences (Kaufman & Kaufman, 1983). It is reasonable to expect a linguistically different population such as the one used in the Valencia (1984) investigation to score more highly on the K-ABC than the WPPSI because the WPPSI requires more English language proficiency. It appears that the tendency for more modern tests, such as the K-ABC, to produce lower scores holds—except when cultural variables such as dominant primary language exert an influence.

Predictive Validity

An important finding for clinicians to remember is that measures of achievement, basic concepts, readiness skills, and related measures are likely to be better predictors of future school achievement than intelligence measures. In fact, the K-ABC Achievement scale, like the Verbal scale of the WISC-III, is the best predictor of subsequent school achievement (Kamphaus & Reynolds, 1987). Thus, it is very important to administer more than just an intelligence test to assess a preschooler, because an incomplete picture of the child will be drawn.

Williams, Voelker, and Ricciardi (1995) completed a five-year follow-up study examining the predictive validity of the K-ABC for 39 children identified during preschool as exhibiting language impairment, behavior control deficits, or normal language and behavioral development. The K-ABC MPC and Achievement scales were administered at baseline and at follow-up times. Also administered at follow-up were the Peabody Individual Achievement Test—Revised (PIAT-R; Markwardt, 1989), the Peabody Picture Vocabulary Test—Revised (PPVT-R; Dunn & Dunn, 1981), and the Test for Auditory Comprehension of Language—Revised (TACL-R; Carrow-Woolfolk, 1985). Results provided evidence of the long-term predictive validity of the K-ABC for a sample of normal and at-risk preschool children. The baseline K-ABC MPC for the total sample correlated from .58 with the TACL-R to .73 with the PPVT-R. The baseline K-ABC Achievement correlations ranged from .74 with the PIAT-R to .56 with the TACL-R. The findings from the study provide support for the usefulness of the K-ABC in assessment of preschoolers.

To better understand the child's at-risk status, preschool assessment batteries should include measures such as the K-ABC Achievement scale and related measures in addition to simply measuring cognitive ability. Because of the strong predictive validity of the Achievement scale, it is recommended that it be administered routinely when assessing preschoolers. Indeed, Kaufman and Kaufman (1983) recommend that the Achievement scale always be administered with the Mental Processing scales of the K-ABC for children of all ages.

IDENTIFICATION OF AT-RISK PRESCHOOLERS WITH THE K-ABC

Studies of children who are susceptible to future academic and cognitive difficulties provide evidence that the K-ABC is a useful tool for diagnostic evaluations of preschoolers. All K-ABC scales appear capable of differentiating normal children from those with disabilities and high-risk groups of preschoolers.

Research with at-risk preschoolers has compared the K-ABC to other popular tests. Lyon and Smith (1986) compared the K-ABC, Stanford-Binet, Form L-M, and McCarthy Scales (McCarthy, 1972) for a group of 72 children referred for early intervention. The children ranged in age from 49 to 73 months. The correlation between the K-ABC and other tests was moderate: .59 with the McCarthy General Cognition Index (GCI) and .45 with the Binet IQ. The correlation between the K-ABC Achievement scale and the GCI was also .59. The correlation between the K-ABC Achievement scale and Binet IQ, however, was higher (.71). This strong relationship between achievement and the Binet Form L-M is consistent with early research on the K-ABC (Kaufman & Kaufman, 1983). In the Lyon and Smith study, the K-ABC MPC ($M = 85.0$) and McCarthy GCI were highly consistent ($M = 86.3$). The Binet mean IQ of 82.4 was somewhat lower.

Bing and Bing (1985) compared the K-ABC and PPVT-R for a group of predominantly African American children enrolled in a Headstart program. Given knowledge of the K-ABC regarding reduced differences in the scores earned by African Americans and whites, we would expect the PPVT-R scores to be lower than the K-ABC scores. This discrepancy would be expected despite the fact that these two tests were normed within five years of each other. These predictions were realized. The PPVT-R means of 75.0 for Form L and 73.5 for Form M were significantly lower than the K-ABC MPC mean of 90.2 and the Achievement scale mean of 86.8. The correlations between the MPC and PPVT-R Forms L and M were .50 and .58, respectively. The correlations between the Achievement scale and PPVT-R were considerably higher: .76 and .70, respectively. A similar coefficient between the K-ABC Achievement scale and PPVT-R $(r = .66)$ was reported by McLoughlin and Ellison (1984) for 32 nonreferred, white, middle-class 3- and 4-year-olds.

The K-ABC was used to differentiate normal from high-risk preschoolers in a comparison of the performance of 49 normal and 44 high-risk children between the ages of 4 and 70 months (Lyon, Smith, & Klass, 1986). They found all of the K-ABC global scales to be excellent discriminators between the normal and high-risk groups. On every scale the high-risk group mean was below average. The mean scores for this group ranged from 89.3 on the MPC to 92.5 on the Achievement scale. The means for the normal group were considerably higher, ranging from 107.0 on the Simultaneous scale to 111.8 on the Achievement scale. The mean scores for the normal group raise the question as to how "normal" this group is. Whether or not the normal sample is well matched to the high-risk sample does not detract, however, from the ability of the K-ABC to discriminate those in the high-risk group; their means were still well below the national norm.

In a similar fashion, Smith and Lyon (1987) compared McCarthy and K-ABC performance on groups of repeating and nonrepeating preschoolers. One group had been recommended for kindergarten $(N = 27)$ and a second group had been recommended for retention in the preschool program $(N = 13)$. Both the K-ABC and McCarthy scores discriminated between the two groups. The mean GCI for the repeaters was 67.0, whereas for the nonrepeaters the mean GCI was 86.5. In parallel fashion the MPC for the repeaters was 76.2 as opposed to 91.4 for the nonrepeaters. All of the K-ABC scales discriminated between the two groups. The mean scores for the repeaters were uniformly lower (Sequential $M = 80.3$, Simultaneous $M = 77.5$, Achievement $M = 80.5$) than for the nonrepeaters (Sequential $M = 91.3$, Simultaneous $M = 93.4$, and Achievement $M = 94.7$). In this study the McCarthy scores are lower for both the repeater and nonrepeater groups.

Ricciardi, Voelker, Carter, and Shore (1991) examined the discriminative power of the K-ABC for groups of children with language impairment, behavioral problems, or a combination of the two, and normal controls. Their study included 59 children between the ages of 40 and 73 months. They reported that an overall correct classification rate of 61 percent, on the basis of a weighted combination of K-ABC Simultaneous, Sequential, and Achievement scale scores. Seventy-nine percent of the controls, 85 percent of the language-impaired subjects, and 42 percent of the subjects with both language impairment and behavioral problems were correctly classified. The Simultaneous Processing scale was found to maximally contribute to discrimination between groups, accounting for 45 percent of the variance. Ricciardi et al. (1991) found that the control group ($M = 102.9$) obtained higher scores than the other experimental groups (means ranged from 76.0 to 90.6) on the Achievement scale. For the Mental Processing Composite, the control group ($M = 104.0$) and children with behavioral problems ($M = 95.3$) also scored significantly higher than the two language-impaired groups ($M = 83.1$ and 77.0).

IMPLICATIONS FOR PRACTITIONERS

There are many practical implications derived from the research available on use of the K-ABC with preschoolers. This chapter has outlined many important aspects of the K-ABC research, but to make practical suggestions clear, this section will review issues on its clinical use.

Generally speaking, the K-ABC produces lower than average scores for preschool children who are at risk for learning problems in school. In this regard the K-ABC serves the same identification purpose as other intelligence tests.

Many tests of preschool intelligence have been found to have some floor problems. The K-ABC's floor problems are, in large part, because of having new subtests introduced at a variety of ages. As a result, K-ABC users have to be wary of obtaining too many zero raw scores when assessing children with disabilities. Because populations vary so greatly, it is recommended that examiners try the K-ABC with their population and see if it is a frequent or infrequent problem. The K-ABC has plenty of difficulty to challenge precocious preschoolers, especially beginning at age $4^1/2$, for whom tests such as Reading/Decoding and Matrix Analogies can be administered via the out-of-level norms procedure.

In attempting to remove the nonintellective factors of acculturation, formal schooling, and related issues from their measure of intelligence, the Kaufmans minimized the impact of verbal ability on the K-ABC Mental Processing scales. This feature is especially notable in comparison to tests such as the Wechsler scales or the Binet-IV, which demand extensive verbalization. In fact, none of the K-ABC subtests, including those on the Achievement scale, require a multiple-word response. Data from recent studies reported in the *Stanford-Binet Fourth Edition Technical Manual* (Thorndike, Hagen, &

Sattler, 1986), for example, show a great deal of overlap between the Verbal scale of the WISC-R, the Verbal Reasoning scale of the Binet IV, and the Achievement scale of the K-ABC. All of the intercorrelations of these verbal scales are well above .70 with some being in the high .80s, which are considered high. Despite the fact that K-ABC Achievement subtests require only one-word or few-word responses, the wealth of data (including data on non-English speakers as reported by Kamphaus & Reynolds, 1987) imply that the Achievement scale might—like other verbal scales of intelligence—serve as a screening for language abilities. Based on this screening, further evaluation with a language assessment battery might be advised. A local trial of the test would help determine if these data apply.

The factorial validity has begun to be established for the applicability of the K-ABC Sequential and Simultaneous Processing model with preschoolers. In studies of this age group, the Simultaneous and Sequential factors consistently appear, but under age 4, the Achievement tests also load on the Mental Processing scales. Thus, there is a need for further research to determine the utility of this model for the understanding of preschool children's cognitive performance. More research with preschoolers would be beneficial.

INTERPRETATION

Practical Aspects

The "intelligent testing" approach to test interpretation first introduced in Kaufman's (1979) text, *Intelligent Testing with the WISC-R,* and further developed in Kaufman's (1994) text, *Intelligent Testing with the WISC-III,* is applied to the K-ABC. This system of interpretation examines the test data from a global level down to the specific subtest level. Looking at each individual's unique profile rather than trying to apply the same global interpretation to many profiles has been considered by some as an advance in clinical assessment, although this approach is not without criticism or controversey (Kaufman, 1994, Chapter 1). Anastasi (1982) writes of Kaufman's book:

> [T]he most important feature of [Kaufman's] approach is that it calls for individualized interpretation of test performance, in contrast to the uniform application of any one type of pattern analysis.... The basic approach described by Kaufman undoubtedly represents a major contribution to the clinical use of intelligence tests. (p. 466)

The *K-ABC Interpretive Manual* (Chapter 5) details the steps needed to interpret a profile from the most global scores to the pattern of more specific subtest scores. The steps, adapted from the manual, are presented as follows:

Step 1. Describe the derived scores with descriptive categories, bands of error, percentile ranks, and age equivalents.

Step 2. Compare standard scores on the two global processing scales: Sequential and Simultaneous.

Step 3. Compare standard scores on the Mental Processing scales and the Achievement scales.

Step 4. Determine strengths and weaknesses among the Mental Processing subtests.

Step 5. Determine strengths and weaknesses among the Achievement subtests.

   Step a. After steps 4 and 5 are completed, try to interpret the significant strengths and weaknesses from the vantage point of the Sequential–Simultaneous model.

   Step b. Select a significant strength or weakness. Write down all shared abilities and influences affecting performance on this subtest.

   Step c. Evaluate, one by one, the merits of each ability and influence that was written down.

   Step d. Repeat steps B and C for every significant strength and weakness, taking each in turn.

   Step e. Identify the most appropriate hypotheses about strengths and weaknesses by integrating K-ABC data with background information, test behaviors, and scores on other tests.

To help in the process of hypothesis generation, the Kaufmans provide several tables of shared and unique abilities of the subtests (Kaufman & Kaufman, 1983). It is important to note that when practitioners use the various tables for the steps, they need to go beyond just subtest scores and utilize clinical observation and background information to support hypotheses. Essentially this process involves virtually the same steps that many psychologists have been taught to use through Kaufman's (1979, 1994) books on the WISC-R and WISC-III. Consequently, there is considerable transfer of training from Weschler scales to K-ABC interpretation for many practitioners.

The theory underlying the K-ABC adds a great deal to the interpretation of the test. With the extensive explanations of these two constructs provided in the K-ABC manuals, even clinicians unfamiliar with the theory can feel reasonably comfortable in its application. In addition, it is possible that other existing theoretical explanations be utilized in interpretation of the K-ABC through profile analysis and recategorizations of K-ABC subtests because of the multisubtest format of the K-ABC. This notion of applying alternate theories also is entirely consistent with Kaufman's (1979, 1994) popular approach to intelligence test interpretation.

CLINICAL CASE REPORT

The case report that follows demonstrates the use of the K-ABC in the assessment of a boy who is almost 4 years old. Pertinent information has been changed to protect the confidentiality of the client and his family.

Identifying Information and Reason for Referral

Michael A is a 3-year, 11-month-old boy who lives with his parents, Mr. and Mrs. A. Michael's parents are particularly concerned about his language development because he was initially delayed in his speech production and his language is now difficult to understand when he speaks. He was referred for a psychological evaluation as part of the process of determining eligibility for specialized services to help his cognitive and language development.

Relevant History

Michael is the only child in his family. Mr. A is employed as a salesman in a retail furniture store and Mrs. A is a full-time mother. Mrs. A reported that she was 28 years old when Michael was born. He was born two weeks prematurely, but no complications were noted with the birth. Weighing 6 pounds, 5 ounces and being 21 inches long, Michael was found to be a healthy newborn according to doctors' records.

Michael's medical history contains no significant injuries or illnesses, other than ear infections from 12 to 18 months. According to Michael's mother, he had a series of ear infections during this period requiring him to be on antibiotics nearly every other month. Mrs. A re-

ported that he "recently had a wax build-up removed from his ears," and his physician has ordered a hearing test for Michael, which is to be completed soon. According to Mrs. A, Michael achieved his motor milestones within the normally expected time frame, but his speech seemed to be delayed. Michael rolled over at 7 months, sat unsupported at 6 months, walked with help at 9 months, and walked unassisted at 14 months. Mrs. A noted that Michael did not begin to approximate words until 36 months. Most of his words at that time were unintelligible. Recently he has begun putting combinations of words together, sometimes in an understandable manner. She stated that he seems to utilize nonverbal gesturing to communicate his needs quite often.

Michael has attended a preschool three days a week since age 30 months. Mrs. A reported that he seems to enjoy the social aspect of the school and the physical activity. However, she also remarked that he becomes physically aggressive with his peers when he is frustrated in his attempts to communicate. At home when he exhibits these types of aggressive behaviors, Michael's parents stated that they utilize behavioral modification and "time-outs" to stop his aggression.

According to Michael's mother, there is a history of mental retardation and learning disabilities in the family. She reported that Michael's father received special help throughout his schooling for a reading disability. A maternal aunt of Michael's also struggles with reading. In addition, Michael's paternal uncle is "mentally disabled."

Tests Administered and Scores

(When applicable, 90% confidence intervals were used in reporting scores in Table 7.4.)

Behavioral Observations

Michael is a cute, friendly, 3-year, 11-month-old Caucasian boy of average size, with dark hair and brown eyes. Michael and his mother were greeted in the waiting area by the examiner. Michael did not appear shy upon meeting the examiner, as he appropriately greeted her with a bold "Hi," displayed a large smile, and readily followed the examiner to the examination room after being asked if he wanted to see some toys. Both Michael and his mother were initially in the examination room, where he began eagerly exploring a box of toys and showing them to his mother. Michael demonstrated the ability to share toys with his mother but at times became possessive and

TABLE 7.4   Michael A. Psychometric Summary

KAUFMAN ASSESSMENT BATTERY FOR CHILDREN (K-ABC)

	Scaled Score	Percentile Rank
Sequential Scale Subtests		
Hand Movements	8	25
Number Recall	7	16
Simultaneous Scale Subtests		
Magic Window	9	37
Face Recognition	9	37
Gestalt Closure	6	9

	Standard Score	Percentile Rank
Achievement Scale Subtests		
Expressive Vocabulary	66±11	1
Faces & Places	77±14	6
Arithmetic	89±10	23
Riddles	82±10	12
Global Scales		
Sequential Processing	84±8	14
Simultaneous Processing	86±10	18
Mental Processing Composite	83±8	13
Achievement	76±7	5

LEITER INTERNATIONAL PERFORMANCE SCALE

IQ	Percentile Rank
107	68

PEABODY PICTURE VOCABULARY TEST—REVISED (PPVT-R)

Standard Score	Percentile Rank
80	9

VINELAND ADAPTIVE BEHAVIOR SCALES

	Standard Score	Age Equivalent	Adaptive Level
Communication	73±7	2 yr., 3 mo.	Moderately low
Daily Living Skills	114±7	4 yr., 9 mo.	Adequate
Socialization	106±8	4 yr., 5 mo.	Adequate
Motor Skills Domain	91±11	2 yr.,11 mo.	Adequate

irritated if his mother directed the play. When the standardized testing began, Mrs. A left the examination room because she did not want him to be distracted by her presence. Michael was not disturbed by his mother leaving; rather, he displayed a high level of comfort with the separation and in his interaction with the examiner.

Michael's expressive language was very difficult to understand. He had difficulty articulating many words, making his speech indistinct. Examples of his speech included, "Wher di doe?" (Where's this go?); "Ear i doe" (Here it goes); "burr" (bird); "do kee" (doggy); and other words which were not interpretable such as, "pee," and "boebay." He was noted to have difficulty articulating consonant endings of words. His verbal expression was aided by nonverbal communication, such as pointing, gesturing, and pantomiming. His indistinct speech did not impede him from talking, however. His pattern of speech flowed smoothly, and he continued to speak at a normal pace, using more nonverbal communication when the examiner stated that she did not understand. When his mother was present in the room, she was able to translate many of Michael's words that were not understandable to the examiner. Mrs. A had clearly become accustomed to his speech, which enabled her to more readily understand him.

Michael was very cooperative, helpful, and followed directions throughout the evaluation session. He was attentive and enthusiastic with each new test that was presented to him. In a playful manner he helped the examiner return the parts of the test back to the appropriate spot and helped set up a new test when he could. For example, when items that involved blocks were completed, he handed the blocks to the examiner to put away by pretending they were an airplane and saying, "vroom," as he made the blocks fly under the table to the examiner's hands. When Michael began to get off-task, he was quickly and easily redirected with just a couple of words by the examiner. Michael's cooperativeness and helpfulness were also evident when he put toys away without being asked before the testing began and at the end of the session.

Test Interpretation

Michael was administered the Kaufman Assessment Battery for Children (K-ABC), on which he earned a Simultaneous Processing standard score of 86 ± 10, and a Sequential Processing standard score of 84 ± 8, both in the Below Average Range of Intelligence. Michael's Sequential and Simultaneous scores were not significantly different, rendering the K-ABC Mental Processing Composite of 83 ± 8 (13th percentile) an accurate representation of his overall ability. It is important to note that some of Michael's global scores may be an underestimate of his true cognitive ability because certain subtest scores on each scale may have been lowered by his difficulty with verbal expression.

The Simultaneous Processing scale measures a child's ability to process many stimuli at once, using holistic problem solving. Within the Simultaneous Processing scale, Michael demonstrated no significant strengths or weaknesses. On one task he demonstrated average holistic processing ability in identifying and naming an object whose picture was rotated behind a narrow slit. On this task, in particular, Michael supplemented his verbal expression a great deal with pointing and gesturing to help communicate what he meant. On another task of holistic processing, one that required no

verbal expression, Michael performed at an average level when required to attend closely to a picture of a person's face and then select the correct face later shown in a different group. Michael demonstrated more difficulty, scoring in the Below Average range, on a Simultaneous task that required him to name a partially completed inkblot drawing. Many of his responses on this task were not clearly articulated words; thus, his expressive difficulty may have lowered his score. Therefore, his scores on this Gestalt Closure task (although not technically a significant weakness) should be interpreted with caution.

The Sequential Processing scale of the K-ABC measures a child's ability to process information in a step-by-step manner, and solve problems that present stimuli in serial order. Within the Sequential Processing scale, Michael demonstrated no significant strengths or weaknesses. On a nonverbal test that required him to copy a series of hand gestures, Michael demonstrated average short-term visual memory abilities (scoring at the 25th percentile). On a task that required him to use short-term auditory memory to repeat a series of numbers said to him aloud, Michael scored at about the same level as he did on the nonverbal memory test. Although the number memory subtest may have been partially reflecting his articulation difficulties, as he said numbers such as, "nun, two, pee" (one, two, three), and "nen, pie" (ten, five), he was able to say most numbers in a manner that was understandable to the examiner. Therefore, this test is believed to be a valid measure of his rote short-term auditory memory.

As a result of Michael's noted language difficulties and because of his demonstrated understanding of nonverbal tasks, testing was continued with the nonverbal Leiter International Performance Scale. On the Leiter, Michael achieved a basal score at the 2-year level and went on to pass items into year 5, but was not able to pass any items in year 6 or beyond. Falling in the Average Range of intelligence (68th percentile), his Leiter IQ of 107 score was higher than his performance on cognitive tasks that required verbal expression. Michael readily completed tasks that required exact matching of color or form. He was also successful on number-matching up to two, but demonstrated difficulty on a simple picture completion task. At the 4-year level of the test, Michael was able to complete a matching task that required attention to both color and form, together, and was also able to match more complicated geometric forms. However, he was not able to demonstrate the ability to count to four; rather, he appeared to place blocks randomly in the slots. At the 5-year level, Michael was able to complete items that required conceptual understanding to match the correct blocks, but was he not able to match forms with two colors to complete an item.

Michael was also administered the Achievement scale of the K-ABC to measure more specifically his verbal and preacademic skills. It was again noted that his difficulty in pronouncing words negatively impacted his performance on all the tasks. He earned an overall Achievement standard score of 76 ± 7 (5th percentile), but no significant relative strengths or weaknesses were noted within the Achievement scale. On a test measuring expressive vocabulary, which required Michael to say the names of pictures he was shown, he performed in the Lower Extreme category (1st percentile). He was able to pronounce, "do kee" (doggy) and "tee bee" (TV). However, attempts at all other words of this subtest were unintelligible. When required to utilize expressive and receptive understanding of language, Michael was clearly challenged by his speech but seemed to understand what was said. On a test of verbal reasoning, Michael scored at the 12th percentile (a score that was felt to be negatively impacted by his verbal expression). On a test measuring Michael's knowledge of familiar storybook characters and other well-known characters, his speech difficulties hampered his ability to respond. He earned a score at the 6th percentile on this subtest, able to proudly say, "Ernieeee" when he saw the Sesame Street character. Michael's ability to count and recognize shapes was measured in a manner that was not as significantly impacted by his poor verbal expression. Michael is able to approximate many numbers in his speech (i.e., "nun, two, pee," for one, two, three). Though not a significant strength, he earned a score in the area of Arithmetic at the 23rd percentile. Overall, Michael's Achievement standard score of 76 did not differ significantly from his scores on the Mental Processing, or intelligence, scales (83–86).

Michael was administered the Peabody Picture Vocabulary Test—Revised (PPVT-R) to assess his receptive vocabulary skills. On this task, he was required to point to a picture of the word said to him; no verbal expression was needed. Michael's standard score on the PPVT-R was 80 (9th percentile), which was just about the same as his cognitive standard score of 83 on the Mental Processing Composite of the K-ABC and significantly lower than his IQ of 107 on the Leiter. His receptive vocabulary skills also appeared stronger than his expressive language skills, as evidenced by his K-ABC Expressive Vocabulary score of 66. His performance on the PPVT-R shows some delays in receptive vocabulary. However, within the very structured one-on-one evaluation situation, Michael had no difficulty understanding and following directions spoken by two adults, his mother and the examiner.

According to Mrs. A's report on the Vineland Adaptive Behavior Scales, Michael has difficulty in the Communication Domain (standard score of 73 ± 7) but average skills in other areas of adaptive development, namely Daily Living Skills (114 ± 7), Socialization (106 ± 8), and Motor Skills (91 ± 11). Michael is able to communicate with difficulty verbally, and better nonverbally, but is not performing at an age-expected level. Michael can deliver a simple message such as "Dinner time," but rarely speaks in full sentences, nor does he use articles such as "a" or "the" in phrases. According to Mrs. A, Michael is beginning to ask questions that use words such as "what" or "why" but has not mastered their use. He has great difficulty articulating and frequently uses sound substitutions.

According to Mrs. A, Michael has good daily living skills, as he is able to take care of his toileting needs, he can put his shoes on the correct feet, and can help clean around the house. Michael is beginning to understand how to tell time, he can fasten buttons, but not zip zippers or tie shoelaces, and he can make his own bed when asked. In the social realm, Mrs. A reported that Michael also has good abilities. She indicated that he likes to participate in games and activities, especially outside. He is able to follow rules when at school or in other facilities. However, he occasionally exhibits behavioral difficulties when frustrated with communicating verbally. When introduced to strangers, he responds appropriately and will shake hands and behaves in a friendly manner. Mrs. A stated that Michael shares toys most of the time, returns things that he has borrowed, and is very honest and will communicate when he has made a mistake.

Diagnostic Impressions

Michael is a friendly, 3-year, 11-month-old boy who was referred for a psychological evaluation to provide information that will be used to assist in determining eligibility for services to advance his cognitive and language development. Michael was found to have difficulty with verbal expression, including indistinct articulation of many words and frequent sound substitutions. Although he attempts to aid his verbal expression through nonverbal communication, such as pointing, gesturing, and pantomiming, he is not easily able to communicate what he means. Because of his expressive difficulties, some of the Below Average scores on the K-ABC may be an underestimate of his true cognitive abilities.

His cognitive abilities fall in the Below Average to Average Range according to his standard scores on the K-ABC Mental Processing Composite (83 ± 8) and the Leiter (IQ = 107), a test of nonverbal cognitive ability. Michael's articulation difficulties appeared to impact his overall scores on the K-ABC Achievement scale (5th percentile). His expressive language appears slightly more delayed than his receptive understanding of language (1st percentile on Expressive Vocabulary versus 9th percentile on PPVT-R). Michael's receptive vocabulary also appears to be slightly lower than his overall cognitive ability, when compared to his nonverbal skills. Commensurate with observations of Michael during the evaluation, Mrs. A indicated on the Vineland Adaptive Behavior Scales that his communication abilities are moderately low (2 year, 3 month range). However, the rest of his adaptive behavior, including Daily Living Skills, Socialization Skills, and Motor Skills, are at an age-appropriate level. A diagnosis of Phonological Disorder (DSM-IV 315.39) is made at this time, as Michael demonstrates failure to use developmentally expected speech sounds that are appropriate for his age, which significantly interferes with his social communication.

Recommendations

Following Michael's assessment, the following recommendations were made:

1. With speech and language difficulties, and a history of ear infections during the second year of life, it is important to have a child's hearing thoroughly evaluated. Thus, it is recommended that if such an exam has not yet been completed, Michael should be taken to a pediatrician who can refer him to an audiologist to have a comprehensive hearing evaluation.

2. In light of Michael's extreme difficulty with verbal expression, it is recommended that he have a comprehensive speech and language evaluation completed to determine what his specific strengths and weaknesses are in his language ability. Such an evaluation will help to determine what special services are necessary. Periodic developmental assessments are also recommended to help monitor the rate and continuity of Michael's cognitive and language development.

3. Mr. and Mrs. A should be assisted in applying to schools for consideration of inclusion in a preschool that can provide Michael with additional assistance in speech and language development.

4. It is important that the family be provided with information about language delays and related problems. Often children with communication difficulties are at risk for behavioral problems and need special assistance to learn alternative ways of how to express feelings in a socially appropriate manner. Through the help of their Regional Center social worker, Mr. and Mrs. A should be assisted in finding other appropriate community resources and support to help them with the difficulties related to raising a child with such communication difficulties.

5. Michael reportedly exhibits aggressive behavior at times when he is frustrated with his inability to communicate. His parents and teachers are encouraged to help Michael develop alternative ways of communicating his frustration (until his speech ability is improved). Such alternatives may include nonaggressive gesturing, creating a picture board to which he can point, or drawing a picture to express himself. These alternatives will help provide a socially acceptable means of communication.

Examiner: Liz Lichtenberger, Ph.D.

Supervisor: Carren J. Stika, Ph.D.

CONCLUSIONS

The K-ABC possesses similarities and differences to its predecessors. Its differences, such as its theoretical underpinnings and deemphasis on the impact of language, are unique strengths, and the K-ABC's similarity to obtained global scores on other measures of intelligence is also a strength. Having a measure of achievement available to assess preschoolers is also appealing to many clinicians. This particular aspect of the test makes it a useful tool in evaluations of at-risk children.

The K-ABC has a number of characteristics to recommend its use with preschoolers. The K-ABC has proved to be a widely accepted measure of preschool intelligence. The K-ABC is among the most frequently used tests in handicapped children's education programs (HCEEP) (Lehr, Ysseldyke, & Thurlow, 1987), and in programs for preschool children with learning disabilities (Esterly & Griffin, 1987). Of the instruments used by five or more HCEEP demonstration projects, the K-ABC was one of the only three instruments (the McCarthy Scales and Vineland were the others) to be rated by Lehr and coworkers as possessing technical adequacy in all five selected areas pertaining to norms, reliability, and validity. Interestingly, the K-ABC was one of the 12 tests used in various preschool programs for children with learning disabilities (Esterly & Griffin, 1987), but it was the only multisubtest intelligence test on the list (the WPPSI and McCarthy were excluded).

Each unique testing situation dictates how useful a particular instrument will be in answering the referral question. In assessment of preschoolers with the K-ABC, its strengths and weaknesses and the research supporting it are some factors that should be taken into account when deciding whether it should be used. In addition, the clinician should take into account his or her own level of training with the instrument. Since its development, much has been published on the K-ABC. Much information about the K-ABC is provided in chapters such as this one, and the ones by Kamphaus et al. (1990), Kaufman et al. (1999), and Kaufman and Lichtenberger (1998). Specific information on cross-cultural use of the K-ABC is available in Lichtenberger and Kaufman (1998) and Lichtenberger et al. (1998). In addition, the book by Kamphaus and Reynolds (1987) can supplement practical experience with research findings for a variety of populations. The K-ABC can be utilized as a tool by itself and can also be effectively used by supplementing its administration with other measures of cognitive, academic, and language ability, as each individual case necessitates. Using this approach of gathering information from many different data sources is very effective in creating the best understanding of the young child.

REFERENCES

Anastasi, A. (1982). *Psychological testing* (5th ed.). New York: Macmillan.

Anastasi, A. (1984). The K-ABC in historical and contemporary perspective. *Journal of Special Education, 18,* 357–366.

Bing, S. B., & Bing, J. R. (1985). Comparison of the K-ABC and PPVT-R with Headstart children. *Psychology in the Schools, 22,* 245–249.

Boehm, A. E. (1971). *Manual for the Boehm Test of Basic Concepts.* San Antonio, TX: Psychological Corporation.

Bracken, B. A. (1987). Limitations of preschool instruments and standards for minimal levels of technical adequacy. *Journal of Psychoeducational Assessment, 5,* 313–326.

Carrow-Woolfolk, E. (1985). *Test for Auditory Comprehension of Language—Revised.* Allen, TX: DLM Teaching Resources.

Das, J. P., Kirby, J. R., & Jarman, R. F. (1979). Simultaneous and successive processes, language and mental abilities. *Canadian Psychological Review, 20,* 1–11.

Dunn, L. M., & Dunn, L. M. (1981). *Peabody Picture Vocabulary Test—Revised.* Circle Pines, MN: American Guidance Service.

Esterly, D. L., & Griffin, H. C. (1987). Preschool programs for children with learning disabilities. *Journal of Learning Disabilities, 20,* 571–573.

Flynn, J. R. (1984). The mean IQ of Americans: Massive gains 1932 to 1978. *Psychological Bulletin, 95,* 29–51.

German, D. (1983). Analysis of word finding disorders on the Kaufman Assessment Battery for Children (K-ABC). *Journal of Psychoeducational Assessment, 1,* 121–133.

Goldstein, D. J., Smith, K. B., & Waldrep, E. E. (1986). Factor analytic study of the Kaufman Assessment Battery for Children. *Journal of Clinical Psychology, 42,* 890–894.

Gridley, B. E., Miller, G., Barke, C., & Fischer, W. (1990). Construct validity of the K-ABC with an at-risk preschool population. *Journal of School Psychology, 28,* 39–49.

Jensen, A. R. (1973). Level I and level II abilities in three ethnic groups. *American Educational Research Journal, 10,* 263–276.

Kamphaus, R. W., Beres, K., Kaufman, A. S., & Kaufman, N. L. (1996). The Kaufman Assessment Battery for Children (K-ABC). In C. S. Newmark (Ed.), *Major psychological assessment instruments* (2nd ed.) (pp. 348–399). Boston: Allyn & Bacon.

Kamphaus, R. W., & Kaufman, A. S. (1986). Factor analysis of the Kaufman Assessment Battery for Children (K-ABC) for separate groups of boys and girls. *Journal of Clinical Child Psychology, 3,* 210–213.

Kamphaus, R. W., & Reynolds, C. R. (1987). *Clinical and research applications of the K-ABC.* Circle Pines, MN: American Guidance Service.

Kaufman, A. S. (1978). The importance of basic concepts in the individual assessment of preschool children. *Journal of School Psychology, 16,* 207–211.

Kaufman, A. S. (1979). *Intelligent testing with the WISC-R.* New York: John Wiley & Sons.

Kaufman, A. S. (1984). K-ABC and Controversy. *The Journal of Special Education, 18,* 409–444.

Kaufman, A. S. (1994). *Intelligent testing with the WISC-III*. New York: John Wiley & Sons.

Kaufman, A. S., & Kamphaus, R. W. (1984). Factor analysis of the Kaufman Assessment Battery for Children (K-ABC) for ages 2½ through 12½ years. *Journal of Educational Psychology, 76,* 623–637.

Kaufman, A. S., & Kaufman, N. L. (1983). *Interpretive manual for the Kaufman Assessment Battery for Children*. Circle Pines, MN: American Guidance Service.

Kaufman, A. S., & Kaufman, N. L. (1993). *K-ABC batterie pour l'examen psychologique de l'enfant*. Paris: ECPA.

Kaufman, A. S., Kaufman, N. L., & Kamphaus, R. W. (1985). The Kaufman Assessment Battery for Children (K-ABC). In C. S. Newmark (Ed.), *Major Psychological Assessment Instruments*. Boston: Allyn & Bacon.

Kaufman, A. S., Kaufman, N. L., Kamphaus, R. W., & Naglieri, J. A. (1982). Sequential and simultaneous factors at ages 3–12½: Developmental changes in neuropsychological dimensions. *Clinical Neuropsychology, 4,* 74–81.

Kaufman, A. S., & Lichtenberger, E. O. (1998). Intellectual assessment. In A. S. Bellack & M. Hersen (Series Eds.) & C. R. Reynolds (Vol. Ed.), *Comprehensive clinical psychology, Volume 4: Assessment (pp. 187–238)*. New York: Pergamon.

Kaufman, A. S., Lichtenberger, E. O., & Naglieri, J. A. (1999). Intelligence testing in the schools. In C. R. Reynolds & T. Gutkin (Eds.), *The handbook of school psychology* (3rd ed.) (pp. 307–349). New York: Wiley.

Keith, T. Z., & Dunbar, S. B. (1984). Hierarchical factor analysis of the K-ABC: Testing alternate models. *The Journal of Special Education, 18,* 367–375.

Krohn, E. J., & Lamp, R. E. (1989). Concurrent validity of the Stanford-Binet Fourth Edition and K-ABC for Headstart children. *Journal of School Psychology, 27,* 59–67.

Lamp, R. E., & Krohn, E. J. (1990). Stability of the Stanford-Binet Fourth Edition and K-ABC for young black and white children from low income families. *Journal of Psychoeducational Achievement, 8,* 139–149.

Lampley, D. A., & Rust, J. O. (1986). Validation of the Kaufman Assessment Battery for Children with a sample of preschool children. *Psychology in the Schools, 23,* 131–137.

Lehr, C. A., Ysseldyke, J. E., & Thurlow, M. L. (1987). Assessment practices in model early childhood special education programs. *Psychology in the schools, 24,* 390–399.

Lichtenberger, E. O., & Kaufman, A. S. (1998). The K-ABC: Recent Research. In R. J. Samuda (Ed.), *Advances in cross-cultural assessment* (pp. 56–99). Thousand Oaks, CA: Sage.

Lichtenberger, E. O., Kaufman, A. S., & Kaufman, N. L. (1998). The K-ABC: Theory and Application. In R. J. Samuda (Ed.), *Advances in cross-cultural assessment* (pp. 20–55). Thousand Oaks, CA: Sage.

Lyon, M. A., & Smith, D. K. (1986). A comparison of at-risk preschool children's performance on the K-ABC, McCarthy Scales and Stanford-Binet. *Journal of Psychoeducational Assessment, 4,* 35–43.

Lyon, M. A., Smith, D. K., & Klass, P. D. (1986, April). A comparison of K-ABC performance between at-risk and normal preschoolers. Paper presented at the meeting of the National Association of School Psychologists, Hollywood, FL.

Markwardt, F. C., Jr. (1989). *Peabody Individual Achievement Test—Revised manual*. Circle Pines, MN: American Guidance Service.

Matsubara, T., Fujita, K., Maekawa, H., Ishikuma, T., Kaufman, A. S., & Kaufman, N. L. (1994). *Interpretive manual for the Japanese K-ABC*. Tokyo: Maruzen Mates.

McCarthy, D. (1972). *McCarthy Scales of Children's Abilities*. New York: Psychological Corporation.

McLoughlin, C. S., & Ellison, C. L. (1984). Comparison for normal preschool children on the Peabody Picture Vocabulary Test—Revised and the Achievement Scales of the Kaufman Assessment Battery for Children. *Psychological Reports, 55,* 107–114.

Melchers, P., & Preuss, U. (1991). *K-ABC Interpretationshandbuch*. Amsterdam: Swets & Zeitlinger.

Ricciardi, P. W., Voelker, S., Carter, R. A., & Shore, D. L. (1991). K-ABC sequential simultaneous processing and language-impaired preschoolers. *Developmental Neuropsychology, 7,* 523–535.

Smith, D. K., Bolin, J. A., & Stovall, D. L. (1988). K-ABC stability in a preschool sample: A longitudinal study. *Journal of Psychoeducational Achievement, 6,* 396–403.

Smith D. K., & Lyon, M. A. (1987, March). K-ABC/McCarthy performance of repeating and nonrepeating preschoolers. Paper presented at the meeting of the National Association of School Psychologists, New Orleans, LA.

Sternberg, R. J. (1984). The Kaufman Assessment Battery for Children: An information processing analysis and critique. *The Journal of Special Education, 18,* 269–279.

Telzrow, C. F. (1984). Practical applications of the K-ABC in the identification of handicapped preschoolers. *The Journal of Special Education, 18,* 311–324.

Thorndike, R. L., Hagen, E. C., & Sattler, J. M. (1986). *Technical manual of the Stanford-Binet Intelligence Scale: Fourth Edition.* Chicago: Riverside.

Valencia, R. R. (1984). Concurrent validity of the Kaufman Assessment Battery for children in a sample of Mexican-American children. *Educational and Psychological Measurement, 44,* 365–371.

Wechsler, D. (1991). *Manual for the Wechsler Intelligence Scale for Children—Third Edition (WISC-III).* San Antonio, TX: Psychological Corporation.

Williams, J. M., Voelker, S., & Ricciardi, P. W. (1995). Predictive validity of the K-ABC for exceptional preschoolers. *Psychology in the Schools, 32,* 178–184.

CHAPTER 8

ASSESSMENT OF ADAPTIVE BEHAVIOR

PATTI L. HARRISON
CANDACE H. BOAN

Does Jessie eat with a spoon? Is Mickey toilet trained? Does Jonathan open a door on his own? Does Betsy play games with her friends? Does Antonia speak in full sentences? These questions represent activities of adaptive behavior, or children's ability to take care of themselves and get along with others. Assessment of adaptive behavior is an extremely important aspect of the multidimensional assessment and the development of interventions for preschool children. The purpose of this chapter is to explore the uses of adaptive behavior assessment for diagnosing possible disabilities and developmental problems of preschoolers and planning effective home, family, and school programs. Major adaptive behavior scales, as well as informal assessment techniques, are reviewed. Finally, because adaptive behavior assessment has traditionally been problematic and controversial, some of the issues facing professionals who assess adaptive behavior are discussed.

DEFINITION OF ADAPTIVE BEHAVIOR

The American Association on Mental Retardation (AAMR; 1992) defines adaptive behavior as the skills needed for successful life functioning and indicates that deficits in adaptive skills, in addition to subaverage intellectual functioning, are essential requirements for a classification of mental retardation. Deficits in adaptive behavior are not limited to individuals with mental retardation but may also impact the functioning of individuals with developmental delays, emotional disturbances, learning disabilities, physical disabilities, sensory disabilities, or other disabilities and learning and behavior problems (Harrison, 1984, 1985, 1990; Holman & Bruininks, 1985; Reschly, 1990; Sparrow, Balla, & Cicchetti, 1984a, 1984b). Traditionally, the definition of adaptive behavior has focused on both personal independence and social responsibility (AAMR, 1992; Horn & Fuchs, 1987). Adaptive behavior is based on the degree

to which an individual takes care of himself or herself and gets along with others.

Adaptive behavior has been incorporated into Greenspan's broader model of *personal competence* (AAMR, 1992; Greenspan & Driscoll, 1997; Greenspan & Granfield, 1992). In one of the latest descriptions of the model, Greenspan and Driscoll outlined four major divisions of personal competence: physical competence, affective competence, everyday competence, and academic competence. Everyday competence includes practical intelligence, or the ability to understand technical, mechanical, and physical problems encountered in daily settings, and social intelligence, the ability to understand daily problems encountered in relationships with other people. Research has yielded some support for using a personal competence model (Greenspan & Driscoll, 1997; McGrew & Bruininks, 1989; McGrew, Bruininks, & Johnson, 1996; Widamin & McGrew, 1996).

Critics of adaptive behavior have argued that it is not as clearly defined as other constructs assessed for children, for instance, intelligence and achievement (e.g., Clausen, 1972; Gresham & Elliott, 1987; Zigler, Balla, & Hodapp, 1984). Others have pointed out the many consistencies in definitions of adaptive behavior and the close correspondence among the structures of different adaptive behavior scales (e.g., Holman & Bruininks, 1985; Kamphaus, 1987; Meyers, Nihira, & Zetlin, 1979; Reschly, 1982). Kamphaus (1987) argued that definitions of adaptive behavior have the homogenizing influence of the AAMR definition of adaptive behavior. Other constructs, such as intelligence, do not have the support of a broad unifying definition such as the AAMR's definition of adaptive behavior. Common elements in definitions and measures of adaptive behavior include the developmental nature of the construct; the basic dimensions of adaptive behavior; and an emphasis on cultural influences, situational specificity, and performance rather than ability (AAMR, 1992; Bruininks, Thurlow, & Gilman, 1987; Harrison, 1990; Holman & Bruininks, 1985;

Kamphaus, 1987; Meyers et al., 1979; Reschly, 1982; Witt & Martens, 1984).

Developmental Nature

Most definitions indicate that adaptive behavior is developmental in nature, increasing in complexity and number as children grow older. This increase in the number and complexity of adaptive skills is in part related to the demands and expectations that are encountered in new environments or situations (AAMR, 1992; Boan & Harrison, in press; Harrison, 1990; Harrison & Robinson, 1995). As the child encounters different experiences, his or her adaptive behaviors will broaden to meet the demands of the new environment. The child will acquire new adaptive skills that allow him or her to function in the new situation. In addition, adaptive skills that the child has already acquired will become more complex as the social and environmental demands become more abstract. The determination of appropriate adaptive behavior is typically based on sociocultural expectations about how an individual of a certain age should behave in a given situation (Salvia & Ysseldyke, 1995). Thus, a child's adaptive skills always must be examined in the context of a typical age peer. For instance, adaptive skills such as brushing teeth without assistance, pouring a glass of milk, or answering the telephone may be deemed appropriate for preschool or school-age children, while not expected of infants or toddlers. Ultimately, the decision of appropriate and typical behaviors for a given age is a reflection of the cultural standards and social norms within a community.

Some researchers have suggested that specific age groups or developmental periods are characterized by certain types of adaptive behavior. According to Grossman (1983), the infancy and early childhood periods emphasize sensorimotor, communication, self-help, and socialization skills. Later childhood and adolescence are characterized by the acquisition of basic academic skills necessary for daily life activities, judgment and reasoning in the mastery of the environment, and social skills necessary for interacting with others. Vocational and social skills are required for late adolescents and adults. Other descriptions of adaptive behaviors characteristic of various ages or developmental levels have been provided. For example, Salvia and Ysseldyke (1995) suggested that for infants and young children, adaptive behavior is centered around reflexive behaviors or maturational processes; however, as an individual gets older, typical adaptive skills begin to focus more on learned be-

haviors. They indicated that adaptive behaviors of preschool children are characterized by social use of language, appropriate play, and increasing levels of responsibility and independence. They suggested that, with typical school-age children and adolescents, there is a continued increase in independence and responsibility across a number of settings. Understanding the developmental nature of adaptive behavior is imperative for determining the needs of an individual child. When assessing the adaptive behavior strengths and limitations of a child, it is important to consider the adaptive skills that are typical of age peers and to explain what should be expected of the child to parents and teachers.

Basic Dimensions

Definitions and measures of adaptive behavior typically include two major components: independent or personal functioning and social responsibility. Furthermore, analysis of adaptive behavior scales indicates that the items typically assess relatively similar domains of adaptive behavior (Holman & Bruininks, 1985; Kamphaus, 1987; Reschly, 1982). The skill areas identified by the AAMR (1992) include the following:

- self-care skills (e.g., eating, toileting, dressing, hygiene)
- communication skills (e.g., expressive and receptive language skills, basic reading, writing)
- social skills (e.g., interacting with others, cooperating, playing)
- health and safety skills (e.g., eats only edibles, communicating sickness or injury, following safety rules)
- leisure skills (e.g., playing with toys or games, watching television videos)
- home living skills (e.g., clothing care, food preparation, housekeeping)
- community use skills (e.g., traveling in the community, using the library, attending church)
- self-direction skills (e.g., using a schedule, purchasing needed items, managing time)
- functional academic skills (e.g., managing money, reading directions for cooking, writing a business letter)
- work skills (e.g., job-related skills)

However, the domains that are assessed are generally influenced by the age of the child (Kamphaus & Frick, 1996). Self-care, communication, social skills, health and safety skills, and leisure skills are emphasized for younger children. Older children, adolescents, and adults add home living skills, community use skills, self-direction skills, functional academics, and work skills to their array of skills needed for daily functioning. The AAMR (1992) cautions that specific skill areas should be given attention only when they are relevant to the age of the child.

According to the AAMR (1992), individuals can have coexisting strengths and limitations in the adaptive behavior domains. For example, a child may have a strength in self-care skills and a coexisting limitation in social behavior. This child may also have other strengths or limitations within his or her adaptive behavior profile. The existence of strengths does not imply that interventions are not needed to address limitations. For this reason, the selection of an adaptive behavior instrument as well as other informal methods of assessing adaptive skills should ensure a comprehensive assessment of an individual child's adaptive behavior profile. This assessment should identify the child's strengths and limitations across all the age-relevant adaptive behavior domains. Developing an understanding of the child's adaptive behavior profile is critical for determining needs and developing interventions.

Cultural Influences

In various conceptualizations of adaptive behavior, the construct is recognized as being dependent on the expectations of the culture to which a person belongs. Undoubtedly, different cultures have different expectations for the behavior of children. Cultural norms and expectations determine what behaviors are considered adaptive skills (AAMR, 1992). These norms are specified by members of the community and are used to judge the adaptive skills of a particular child.

The cultural and ethnic makeup of a community must be examined when assessing adaptive behaviors. Expectations about adaptive behavior are determined within the context of the community. The culture of the community, the ethnicity of the family and team members, the culture of the classroom, and the dynamics of the family are all important considerations when examining the child's adaptive skills. As indicated by Leland (1983), it is perfectly acceptable for children to urinate in public in some countries. In other countries, this practice is unacceptable. There are also different expectations for children within the different subcultures of the same country. For example, different subcultures within the United States place varying amounts of emphasis on dress, hygiene, and other variables related to adaptive behavior. Cultural expectations about age-appropriate behavior may also influence parental expectations for children's adaptive skills. Tonya, a preschool child, may not be allowed to use a knife to spread jelly on bread because her parents feel that using knives is unsafe for preschool children. Tonya's performance of this skill may be more a reflection of parent expectations than of her ability. Other parents may have different expectations for their preschool children.

Considerations of a child's adaptive skills must recognize that adaptive behavior does not occur in a vacuum. Thus, assessment of adaptive behavior must also explore environmental, cultural, and familial contexts that influence the behavior of the child. Developing an understanding of the cultural, linguistic, and behavioral factors that influence an individual's behavior is an imperative part of making decisions about his or her adaptive behaviors (AAMR, 1992). This emphasis on developing a contextual understanding of the individual's adaptive behavior provides information about the skills of the individual, as well as information about possible support systems and resources within the environment that can be utilized in the development and implementation of interventions.

Situational Specificity

A child's adaptive behavior is very much influenced by the demands and expectations of the setting in which the child is involved. Different situations demand different adaptive behaviors or skills. Andy, a preschool child, may not perform the expected behavior of sharing toys with other classmates at school because at home he has no siblings or others that he is expected to share toys with on a regular basis. In Andy's case, the adaptive skills required in the classroom may be quite different from those expected at home. Other examples of the adaptation process occur when children enter preschool and are expected to acquire the adaptive skills of taking turns or waiting in line. Children learn adaptive skills through their interactions with teachers and classmates in the new environment.

When children encounter these new expectations in ever-expanding settings and situations, their adaptive skills will increase and become more complex. Adaptation occurs through interactions with significant people in children's environments (Horn & Fuchs, 1987; Leland, 1983). Children's development of adaptive behavior is influenced by the expectations of the significant others and the situations in which they must interact with others. Assessment of children's adaptive behavior must take into account the situational specificity of different skills. Developing interventions to address limitations in children's adaptive skills may involve nothing more than providing a context for new skills or allowing sufficient time to naturally develop these skills within the new situation. Preschool children who have had no exposure to sharing or taking turns may develop these skills upon entering school as a process of their adaptation to the new environment with little need for an intense intervention.

Performance versus Ability

Adaptive behavior is defined as the *performance* of daily activities required for personal and social self-sufficiency. An implicit assumption is that children must have the *ability* to perform daily activities. However, the concept of adaptive behavior stresses the observable performance of these activities and places less emphasis on the ability necessary to perform them. Adaptive behavior measures typically focus on what children *usually do* rather than what *they are capable of doing,* and adaptive behavior is considered to be deficient if children have a skill but do not routinely perform it. For example, Molly may be able to tie her shoes but does not routinely do so, perhaps because she does not want to or prefers a parent to do it. In addition, having the knowledge of how to engage in a specific adaptive behavior does not demonstrate that an individual actually behaves in such a manner on a regular basis (Salvia & Ysseldyke, 1995). This emphasis on performance, not ability, implies that the concept of adaptive behavior includes the *motivation* for performing activities. This emphasis also requires a method of assessment that measures what children do daily rather than what they can do. Most adaptive behavior scales utilize a *third-party informant* approach, and individuals familiar with children's daily activities are questioned about their performance. It is important to ensure that the individual rating the child's adaptive behavior understands the difference between performance and ability and rates the child based on this understanding. Although adaptive behavior focuses on performance rather than ability, knowledge of an individual's capabilities is also useful for developing interventions. Determination of typical performance of a child is used to identify limitations, whereas knowledge about ability provides a basis for targeting the limitations. The limitations can be addressed as either lack of ability, lack of knowledge about the skills, or lack of motivation.

THE IMPORTANCE OF ADAPTIVE BEHAVIOR ASSESSMENT FOR PRESCHOOL CHILDREN

The ability to take care of oneself and get along with others represents important goals for everyone, regardless of age or disability. Traditionally, adaptive behavior assessment was emphasized due to the needs for nonbiased assessment and training of individuals with mental retardation. Nonbiased assessment and training obviously have implications for young children but typically have been focused on school-age children and adults. The developmental characteristics and needs of preschool children are quite different from those of older individuals and the assessment of adaptive behavior takes on new and increased importance during the preschool years. In this section of the chapter, the traditional importance for adaptive behavior assessment and the specific importance of adaptive behavior assessment for preschool children are discussed.

Traditional Importance

Adaptive behavior assessment has its roots in the field of mental retardation. Legislation and litigation during the past 30 years have established the importance of adaptive behavior in the diagnosis, assessment, and intervention plans for individuals with mental retardation (AAMR, 1992; Harrison, 1990; Harrison & Robinson, 1995; Horn & Fuchs, 1987). One reason for the inclusion of adaptive behavior assessment when diagnosing an individual with mental retardation was to ensure that assessment involved a nonbiased and comprehensive examination of the individual. Several lawsuits in the 1970s focused on the use of intelligence test scores as the sole criterion for placing children into programs for mental retardation. These lawsuits identified disproportionate placement of children from minority groups as a result of the reliance on a single intelligence test score. Because many of the children from minority groups had adequate adaptive behavior outside of school, the appropriateness of using intelligence tests to classify children as having mental retardation was questioned. Critics of intelligence tests claimed that the instruments did not provide a nonbiased and "culture-fair" assessment of the individual's skills. These lawsuits resulted in an emphasis on adaptive behavior assessment as one method for promoting the nonbiased assessment of children from minority groups.

Legislation has also stressed the importance of adaptive behavior assessment for individuals with mental retardation. Federal laws such as the Education for

All Handicapped Act in 1975, the Individuals with Disabilities Act in 1991, and the reauthorization of the Individuals with Disabilities Act in 1997 have defined mental retardation as including below-average intelligence and significant deficits in adaptive behavior. These legislative acts also center on the notion that assessment of an individual should be nonbiased, comprehensive, and linked to interventions.

A final reason for increased interest in the assessment of adaptive behavior was the need to develop interventions for individuals with mental retardation and other disabilities that would enable them to live more independently. A critical assumption of the AAMR (1992) definition of mental retardation is that, with appropriate supports and interventions, the adaptive skills of an individual with mental retardation will improve. Thus, interventions targeting the adaptive skills of individuals with disabilities such as mental retardation may facilitate increased levels of inclusion in regular education programs and enhance the individual's involvement in the community. In order to develop interventions for adaptive skill areas, assessment must provide a complete picture of the individual's adaptive behavior strengths and limitations.

Importance for Preschool Assessment

The reauthorization of the Individuals with Disabilities Act in 1997 provides guidelines for early educational services for preschool and school-age children with a disability. This law expands the definition of developmental delay to allow for the inclusion of children ages 3 years through 9 years in the category. The 1991 Individuals with Disabilities Education Act specified that developmental delay only included children ages 3 through 5 years. The expansion of this category allows for more flexibility in classification, placement, and educational services for preschool and young school-age children. This flexibility in the new definition of developmental delay avoids labeling a child with a specific disability at a young age and may reduce the stigmatization that occurs with some special education classifications. It also promotes educators' examination of the needs of the child and prevents a focus only on a specific disability classification.

Other components of the Individuals with Disabilities Education Act in 1991 and 1997 outline the need for early intervention for children with disabilities. These interventions should address the needs of young children *and* their families. Major requirements of the laws also include assessment and intervention in all developmental areas (physical, cognitive, communication, social or emotional, and adaptive). Current legislation recognizes adaptive behavior as an integral part of preschool children's development and indicates that remediation of deficits in adaptive behavior represents an important goal for early intervention programs. Thus, adaptive behavior assessment is an important component of the flexible, multidimensional assessment process recommended for evaluating the development of preschool children. Characteristics of this process include assessment of multiple domains, assessment from multiple sources, the involvement of parents in the assessment, ecologically valid assessment, and assessment that leads to early intervention (Barnett, 1984; Benner, 1992; Paget, 1987; Paget & Nagle, 1986; "NASP Position Statement," 1987; Telzrow, 1992).

Multiple Domains

The first requirement of preschool assessment is that information should be obtained about multiple domains of development. Adaptive behavior measures typically assess activities in several areas. Definitions and measures of adaptive behavior include the domains of communication, self-care, home living, social skills, community use, self-direction, health and safety, functional academics, leisure, and work (AAMR, 1992). Decisions about which domains are particularly relevant depend to a certain extent on the individual child being assessed. For instance, when examining the adaptive behavior of a preschool child, the work domain has little relevance or validity. The selection of the domains to be assessed should be tailored to the developmental level of the child, the culture of the community, the dynamics of the family, the structure of the school environment, and the individual characteristics of the child. For preschool children, assessment of adaptive behavior domains usually allows a sampling of behavior from a number of developmental areas. Although adaptive behavior assessment should not, of course, be the only type of measure used with a preschool child, it does offer information about several important areas of functioning. This information can be used to develop interventions for needed adaptive skill areas and ultimately improve the child's functioning within the environment.

Multiple Sources

The second requirement of the preschool assessment process is that information should be obtained from multiple sources. Most adaptive behavior scales utilize one or more third-party informants (e.g., parent, teacher, caregiver) to describe children's adaptive behavior instead of using structured, individual testing of children. This format provides a source of information other than structured testing of children, as well as a way of gathering information from several informants.

Information from multiple sources increases the understanding of the child, the environment, and the interaction between the child and the environment. Multiple sources also allow for validity and reliability checks as well as an opportunity to compare discrepant viewpoints (AAMR, 1992; Sattler, 1992). The information provided by informants may be based on familiarity with the child, personality traits, expectations, reference group, previous experience with an instrument, and knowledge of the child in a variety of settings. The use of multiple sources helps ensure that a preschool child's adaptive behavior is not biased or skewed by a single rater or single context and, thus, provides a comprehensive description of the child's strengths and limitations.

Parental Involvement

The third requirement of preschool assessment is that parents should be involved in every phase (Paget, 1992). The importance of parental involvement in the assessment and intervention process is emphasized in the Individuals with Disabilities Act, other legislative acts, and professional guidelines. Parents may provide information about a child's behavior at home, such as his or her sleeping habits, which may not be observed at school (Sattler, 1992). Again, the third-party method of administration used in adaptive behavior assessment provides an excellent opportunity to tap the rich store of information that parents have about their children. It also allows parents to express their concerns about their children and discuss issues about parenting, schooling, and other important factors.

Ecologically Valid Assessment

Preschool assessment must be ecologically valid or sample behavior appropriate to the various environments (e.g., home, school, community) in which preschool children must function (Barnett, 1984; Benner, 1992; Paget, 1987). Third-party adaptive behavior assessment is based on informants' observations of children's activities in the real world, rather than being based on observations of children in an artificial, structured testing situation. In addition, informants can provide information about behavior in a variety of different environments and specific situations.

The administration of a structured test to a preschool child, especially one who has a disability, often presents problems not typically encountered with a school-age child and is impossible in some cases (Paget, 1983). Third-party adaptive behavior assessment provides a unique solution to this problem. Developmental assessment is possible without the administration of a structured test to children because informants, rather than children, are used as the sources of information.

Assessment That Leads to Early Intervention

Adaptive behavior influences not only the ability to succeed in school but the ability to succeed in the environment (Weller & Strawser, 1987). This basic assumption is seen in the Individuals with Disabilities Education Act and professional guidelines that include adaptive behavior skills as an integral part of early intervention programs for preschool children with disabilities. Adaptive behavior, unlike intelligence, is considered to be modifiable and interventions targeting specific areas can result in increases in adaptive behavior of the child (AAMR, 1992; Keith, Harrison, & Ehly, 1987; Meyers et al., 1979). A critical assumption of the AAMR definition of mental retardation is that with appropriate supports and interventions, the adaptive skills of an individual can improve. Furthermore, deficits in adaptive behavior may be related to home, family, and school factors that are amenable to change. Interventions to promote changes in the child's environment may result in increased adaptive functioning. An examination of the different domains of an individual's adaptive skills may provide information about the needs of the child and the types of interventions that may be most appropriate.

In the past, early intervention programs attempted to measure outcomes by determining increases in intelligence test scores. Zigler (Zigler & Seitz, 1980; Zigler & Trickett, 1978) suggested that intelligence was emphasized because intelligence test scores are typically the best predictors of school performance. However, he criticized the use of intelligence for training and measuring outcomes because intelligence test scores provide little information about how people function in everyday life. He supported the inclusion of adaptive behavior in early intervention programs when he indicated that social competence might be a viable alternative to intelligence. In addition, recent legislation and litigation have emphasized the role of adaptive behavior assessment in ensuring that assessment is nonbiased. As indicated earlier in this chapter, the concept of social competence, although not equivalent to adaptive behavior, includes both the components of adaptive behavior and intelligence. Basing intervention outcomes solely on intelligence test scores results in the same potential for bias as using intelligence test scores as the sole criterion for classifying an individual for special education.

SELECTED ADAPTIVE BEHAVIOR SCALES FOR USE WITH PRESCHOOL CHILDREN

There are many different instruments used to assess the adaptive behavior strengths and limitations of children. In this section of the chapter, adaptive behavior scales that can be used with preschool children are described. The scales selected to be discussed in this chapter are those that are standardized and readily available. There are many other scales that are not standardized or were developed for in-house use by specific organizations. The more well-known scales are described in detail and, at the end of this section, a brief summary of scales that are less well known or have more limited use with preschoolers is provided.

Scales of Independent Behavior—Revised (SIB-R)

The SIB-R (Bruininks, Woodcock, Weatherman, & Hill, 1996) provides a norm-referenced assessment of adaptive behavior for infants through 80 years of age. It consists of four adaptive behavior skill clusters encompassing 14 subscales, as seen in Table 8.1. (The domestic skills, time and punctuality, money and values, work skills, and community orientation subscales are not comprehensively assessed for preschoolers.) The four adaptive behavior clusters are combined to form the Broad Independence scale. The SIB-R also contains a problem behavior scale that has the following subscales: asocial, internalizing, externalizing, and a general maladaptive behavior index. The SIB-R can be administered to a parent or caregiver as an interview, or as a checklist to be completed by a person who has sufficient knowledge of the individual and the instrument. An easel may be used during administration and the informant is shown possible responses to items on the easel pages.

The SIB-R yields a wide variety of derived scores, including age equivalents, percentile ranks, standard scores with a mean of 100 and standard deviation of 15, and normal curve equivalents. A sample of 2,182 individuals was used for standardization; the sample was stratified according to gender, race, Hispanic origin, occupational status, occupational level, geographic region, and community type. Internal consistency estimates us-

TABLE 8.1   Content of the Scales of Independent Behavior—Revised (SIB-R)

CLUSTERS	SUBSCALES
Motor Skills	Gross Motor
	Fine Motor
Social Interaction and Communication Skills	Social Interaction
	Language Comprehension
	Language Expression
Personal Living Skills	Eating and Meal Preparation
	Toileting
	Dressing
	Personal Self-Care
	Domestic Skills
Community Living Skills	Time and Punctuality
	Money and Value
	Work Skills
	Home/Community Orientation

Broad Independence (Full Scale)

Internalized Maladaptive Behavior	Hurtful to Self
	Unusual or Repetitive Habits
	Withdrawal or Inattentive Behavior
Asocial Maladaptive Behavior	Socially Offensive Behavior
	Uncooperative Behavior
Externalized Maladaptive Behavior	Hurtful to Others
	Destructive to Property
	Disruptive Behavior

General Maladaptive Behavior (Full Scale)

ing a median-corrected, split-half reliability ranged from .67 to .98 for the cluster scores across the various age groups, test-retest reliability estimates from .80 to .97, and interrater reliability estimates from .58 to .98. Reliability estimates for both test-retest and interrater were based on samples of school-age children (ages 6 to 13) and did not include specific estimates for preschool children. The internal consistency for the clusters for children ages 3 years, 11 months through 9 years ranged from .67 to .98. The SIB-R technical manual reports a respectable amount of validity evidence including developmental progression of scores, differences between scores of individuals with disabilities and individuals without disabilities, and correlations with other adaptive behavior scales and intelligence tests.

A particularly useful feature of the SIB-R for preschool assessment is the Early Development scale. This scale includes a sample of items from developmental areas of the Full scale. It is designed for children and infants through 6 years of age or individuals who are older and have severe disabilities and adaptive behavior limitations.

Vineland Adaptive Behavior Scales

The Vineland (Harrison, 1985; Sparrow, Balla, & Cicchetti, 1984a, 1984b), a revision of the Vineland Social Maturity Scale (Doll, 1935, 1965), consists of three versions. The *Survey Form* is administered to parents and caregivers of infants, children through 18 years of age, and low-functioning adults and provides a norm-referenced assessment of adaptive behavior. The *Expanded Form* also is administered to parents and caregivers of infants through adults and provides a norm-referenced assessment. However, the primary purpose of the Expanded Form is to provide detailed information about specific deficits in adaptive behavior and a sequential guide for planning intervention programs. The *Classroom Edition* is administered to teachers of children aged 3 through 12 and provides a norm-referenced assessment of adaptive behavior in the classroom.

All three versions of the Vineland measure adaptive behavior in four domains and 11 subdomains of adaptive behavior, as seen in Table 8.2. (The written and domestic subdomains will typically be assessed fairly briefly for preschool-age children). The four domains are combined to form a general measure of adaptive behavior, the adaptive behavior composite.

The Survey Form and Expanded Form include a maladaptive behavior domain. This domain is only administered for children aged 5 and older because many of the behaviors assessed by this domain (e.g., thumb sucking, bed wetting) are usually not considered maladaptive for preschool-age children.

The Survey Form and Expanded Form are administered to parents and caregivers during a semistructured interview. Although this type of interview requires a trained professional, its flexible nature allows clinicians

TABLE 8.2   Content of the Vineland Adaptive Behavior Scales

DOMAIN	SUBDOMAINS
Communication	Receptive Expressive Written
Daily Living Skills	Personal Domestic Community
Socialization	Interpersonal Relationships Play and Leisure Time Coping Skills
Motor Skills	Gross Fine
Adaptive Behavior Composite Maladaptive Behavior	

to make valuable observations about parental concerns. The Classroom Edition is administered with a questionnaire completed by teachers.

The Survey Form was standardized with a stratified sample of 3,000 individuals selected on the basis of sex, race, socioeconomic status, geographic region, and community size. The Expanded Form was not standardized but an equating study allowed the generation of norms using Survey Form standardization data. The Classroom Edition was standardized with a sample of 2,984 children, also stratified according to sex, race, socioeconomic status, geographic region, and community size. Standard scores with a mean of 100 and standard deviation of 15, percentile ranks, stanines, and age equivalents are yielded by all three versions of the Vineland.

Internal consistency estimates range from .83 to .94 for the Survey Form, .86 to .97 for the Expanded Form, and .80 to .98 for the Classroom Edition. Test-retest reliability coefficients for the Survey Form range from .81 to .88 and interrater reliability coefficients for the Survey Form range from .62 to .75. Internal consistency estimates for the domains of children ages 3 years through 9 years range from .88 to .98. The manuals for the three Vineland versions report an impressive array of validity data including factor analyses, developmental progression of scores, differences between scores of individuals with disabilities and individuals without disabilities, and correlations with other adaptive behavior scales and intelligence tests.

AAMR Adaptive Behavior Scale—School Edition, (2nd edition; ABS-SE2)

The ABS-SE2 (Lambert, Nihira, & Leland, 1993) is a norm-referenced instrument designed for children 3 through 21 years of age. The ABS-SE2 is divided into two parts. Part I explores adaptive behaviors and Part II examines maladaptive behaviors. Nine behavior subdomains comprise Part I and are listed in Table 8.3. Scores in Part I are combined for three broad factors: Personal Self-Sufficiency, Community Self-Sufficiency, and Personal-Social Responsibility. Part II includes measures for nine domains, listed in Table 8.3. Scores for two broad factors are results from Part II: Social Adjustment and Personal Adjustment. The ABS-SE2 can be administered by asking a parent, teacher, or other informant to complete a questionnaire booklet or by conducting an interview with the informant.

TABLE 8.3 Content of the AAMR Adaptive Behavior Scale—School Edition (2nd edition)

FACTORS	DOMAINS
Part I	
Personal Self-Sufficiency	Independent Functioning
	Physical Development
Community Self-Sufficiency	Economic Activity
	Language Development
Personal-Social Sufficiency	Numbers and Time
	Prevocational/Vocational Activity
	Self-Direction
	Responsibility
	Socialization
Part II	Social Behavior
Social Adjustment	Conformity
Personal Adjustment	Trustworthiness
	Stereotyped and Hyperactive Behavior
	Self-Abusive Behavior
	Social Engagement
	Disturbing Interpersonal Behavior

The ABS-SE2 was standardized with 1,254 individuals without mental retardation and 2,074 individuals with mental retardation. Groups without mental retardation were stratified on the following variables: age, gender, geographic region, domicile, ethnicity, parent education, instructional setting, and place of residence. The group with mental retardation was stratified on additional variables of IQ, other disabling conditions, and etiology. Percentile ranks can be obtained and factor scores are reported as scaled scores with a mean of 10 and a standard deviation of 3.

Internal consistency reliability estimates for Part I range from .81 to .98 and .80 to .96 for Part II. For preschool children, estimates range from .81 to .98 for Part I and .84 to .98 for Part II. Interrater reliability estimates for Part I range from .95 to .98, and for Part II range from .96 to .99. No information on the interrater reliability is provided specifically for preschool children. Test-retest corrected coefficients ranged from .72 to .99 for Part I and .80 to .99 for Part II; however, no specific information is provided for preschool children. Validity data consist of correlations with other adaptive behavior instruments, developmental analysis, comparison of children with disabilities and children without disabilities, and factor analyses.

Battelle Developmental Inventory

The Battelle (Newborg, Stock, Wnek, Guidubaldi, & Svinicki, 1984), although not called an adaptive behavior scale, is included in this chapter because it measures several areas typically associated with adaptive behavior assessment. The Battelle is used with children from birth to age 8 and assesses five domains of development (personal-social, adaptive, motor, communication, and cognitive). Each domain consists of two to six subdomains, listed in Table 8.4. The five domains are combined to yield a total measure of development. The Battelle is administered in three ways: structured testing, observation, and parent/teacher interview. Some of the items in the battery can be administered with another procedure if the suggested procedure is not possible.

The Battelle was standardized with a stratified sample of 800 subjects selected according to region of the country, race, and sex. No information about the socioeconomic status of the sample is reported. Percentile ranks, age equivalents, and several standard scores (z scores, T scores, deviation quotients, and normal curve equivalents) can be determined. Test-retest reliability coefficients range from .84 to .99 and interrater reliability coefficients range from .85 to .99. Limited validity data, primarily factor analysis, and differences between children with disabilities and children without disabilities are reported.

Pyramid Scales

The Pyramid Scales (Cone, 1984), for infants to adults, are quite different from the previously discussed adaptive behavior scales. They consist of 20 scales, listed in Table 8.5, tied to three sensory areas. No norm-referenced scores are provided; instead, the percentage of items usually performed on each of the scales is computed for a criterion-referenced assessment. The Pyramid Scales are tied to 5,000 specific objectives and a complete curriculum for training adaptive behavior (Cone, 1986). The scales can be administered either through a structured interview with an informant or questionnaire.

TABLE 8.4   Content of the Battelle Developmental Inventory

DOMAINS	COMPONENTS
Personal-Social	Adult Interaction
	Expression of Feelings/Affect
	Self-Concept
	Peer Interaction
	Coping
	Social Role
Adaptive	Attention
	Eating
	Dressing
	Personal Responsibility
	Toileting
Motor	Muscle Control
	Body Coordination
	Locomotion
	Fine Muscle
Communication	Receptive
	Expressive
Cognitive	Perceptual Discrimination
	Memory
	Reasoning and Academic Skills
	Conceptual Development

TABLE 8.5   Content of the Pyramid Scale

ZONE	AREA
Sensory Zone	Tactile Responsiveness
	Auditory Responsiveness
	Visual Responsiveness
Primary Zone	Gross Motor
	Eating
	Fine Motor
	Toileting
	Dressing
	Social Interaction
	Washing/Grooming
	Receptive Language
	Expressive Language
Secondary Zone	Recreation/Leisure
	Writing
	Domestic Behavior
	Reading
	Vocational
	Time
	Numbers
	Money

Others

Several scales may provide useful information with specific preschool children. The Adaptive Behavior Inventory (ABI; Brown & Leigh, 1986) is administered as a questionnaire for teachers. It can be used for assessing the adaptive behavior of individuals ages 3 through 17 years. The ABI measures academic skills, self-care skills, occupational skills, communication skills, and social skills.

The Inventory for Client and Agency Planning (ICAP; Bruininks, Hill, Weatherman, & Woodcock, 1986) measures maladaptive and adaptive skills of infants through adults. The ICAP is a questionnaire that is completed by an individual who is familiar with the person being assessed. The domains included on the ICAP are as follows: community living skills, motor skills, personal living skills, and social and communication skills. The ICAP elicits additional information about the individual, including a general description, diagnostic status, needed assistance, functional limitations, residential placement, support services, daytime program, social involvement, and leisure activities. The

ICAP can provide a comprehensive picture of the child being assessed.

The Adaptive Behavior Evaluation Scale (ABES; McCarney, 1983) involves the completion of a rating scale by a teacher or parent. The instrument can be used with children in kindergarten through twelfth grade. The ABES contains three domains of adaptive behavior, task-related behaviors, self-related behaviors, and environmental/interpersonal behaviors. The Learning Accomplishment Profile (LAP; LeMay, Griffin, & Sanford, 1983) requires the direct administrations of tasks to children. Physical, psychomotor, cognitive, linguistic, and self-management skills are assessed for children ages 2½ to 6 years. Standardization of the LAP was conducted with a small sample of Headstart children.

Information obtained from other instruments such as the Behavior Assessment System for Children (BASC; Reynolds & Kamphaus, 1992), the Social Skills Rating System (SSRS; Gresham & Elliott, 1990), and various others may provide supplemental information about the adaptive behavior of the preschool child. The BASC has a preschool and school-age rating scale for both parents and teachers. It measures functioning in areas such as social skills, leadership, and adaptability. The SSRS also includes both parent and teacher ratings for preschool and school-age children. It measures the social skills of a child as well as his or her externalizing, internalizing, and problem behaviors. Other instruments may provide important information about the adaptive behaviors of an individual. When selecting the instruments or methods for assessing the adaptive skills of the preschool child, it is important to ensure that a comprehensive assessment provides a clear profile of the child and that this profile can be used to develop needed interventions.

INFORMAL ADAPTIVE BEHAVIOR ASSESSMENT

The scales discussed in the previous section can only provide a limited amount of information about preschool children's adaptive behavior. Standardized procedures are an integral part of the assessment of preschoolers but fail to take into account a variety of factors necessary to obtain a complete picture of adaptive functioning (Leland, 1983). The informants used in a third-party assessment of adaptive behavior may present biased information or may not have the knowledge of a child's activities necessary for a valid assessment of adaptive behavior (Boan & Harrison, 1997; Harrison & Robinson, 1995; Harrison & Sparrow, 1981; Holman & Bruininks,

1985). For example, teachers completing adaptive behavior instruments are often forced to make estimations about a child's behavior at home. These estimates may not reflect knowledge of the actual behavior of the child but are based on perceptions of the teacher. The reference group of the person completing the instrument may result in a skewed picture of the adaptive behavior of the child. The ratings of a regular education teacher may differ significantly from those provided by a special education teacher because the students who serve as the comparison group may have different levels of adaptive behavior. If, on the other hand, a direct assessment such as the CABS or LAP is used, children's performance may indicate what they can do in a structured testing situation but may not generalize to other situations. Although adaptive behavior scales contribute to the ecologically valid assessment (Barnett, 1984; Benner, 1992; Paget, 1987), they cannot sample children's adaptive activities in every possible situation encountered in daily life. Finally, standardized adaptive behavior scales measure behavior up to a given point in time. Like instruments that measure other constructs, such as intelligence and achievement, they neglect the rapid behavior and developmental changes that characterize preschool children (Mcmann & Barnett, 1984; Paget, 1987; Telzrow, 1992).

Given these limitations of standardized adaptive behavior scales, informal assessment of adaptive behavior should always be conducted to supplement and expand the information obtained from the scales. As is true with any type of assessment with preschoolers, adaptive behavior assessment must depend as much on non-test-based assessment as it does on test-based assessment. Alternative methods of assessing the adaptive behavior of preschool children should supplement formal assessment procedures to provide a comprehensive understanding of the child's adaptive skill strengths and limitations (Benner, 1992; Boan & Harrison, 1997; Harrison & Robinson, 1995). Informal observation techniques, informal assessment with parents and teachers, assessment in a variety of settings, and ongoing assessment are described in this section of the chapter.

Informal Observation Techniques

Informal observations of adaptive behavior provide opportunities for assessing behaviors in a variety of settings and situations. Although adaptive behavior scales yield a fund of information about children's activities, they are usually limited to behaviors that can be reliably and validly measured in an interview, questionnaire, or direct testing format. When the third-party informant method of assessment is used, there is a great reliance on respondents' memory of a wide variety of activities. Informal observations of children's adaptive behavior by a psychologist, counselor, teacher, or other professional allows them to see, firsthand, children's responses to the environment.

Informal observation also provides an opportunity to examine the child's behavior in the natural environment. This type of observation, referred to as functional assessment or ecological assessment, provides an examination of a child's performance in a typical setting (Benner, 1992; Downing & Perino, 1992). The activities being observed are meaningful to the child, parent, and teacher. Functional assessment may be used to examine the child's strengths and weaknesses within the natural environment (Boan & Harrison, 1997). This profile of the strengths and limitations can be used to develop relevant interventions for a preschool child. According to Downing and Perino (1992), functional-ecological assessment can be used as a formative evaluation that targets specific activities, environments, and generates potential interventions. The use of functional assessment may provide additional information about the adaptive skills of the child, the role of environmental variables in strengths and limitations, and target areas for intervention. It may also provide information about resources and supports that can be used during the intervention.

Informal Assessment with Parents and Teachers

The third-party interview used with many adaptive behavior scales also presents a means of discussing, on an informal basis, issues that are related to adaptive behavior.

Parent and teacher responses to these informal types of questions may assist in the development of a comprehensive assessment plan for a child. The information may suggest possible areas of strength and limitation in the child's adaptive behavior profile that should be thoroughly investigated. Informal discussions and interviews may also provide some insight into environmental factors or parenting and teaching styles that may influence the adaptive behavior of a preschool child. An informal discussion with parents and teachers may provide details about parenting and teaching techniques that are being used with children. Deficits in children's adaptive behavior may be more of a function of teaching, parenting, or

environmental factors rather than delayed development. Informal discussions can often serve as a foundation for parent and teacher education and change parenting and teaching to meet the needs of a particular child.

A second important function of informal discussions is to disseminate the results of assessment activities to parents and teachers. After the administration of an adaptive behavior scale, it is important to discuss the activities or behaviors of the child that parents and teachers find worrisome (Leland, 1983). Parents and teachers often have limited knowledge of normal child development and they may be expecting more of the child than a child of that age is capable of doing. For example, a parent of a 3-year-old child may be concerned that the child continues to wet the bed occasionally and will be relieved to know that this is typical of many 3-year-old children. In other cases, the worries of parents and teachers may be well founded, and informally discussing the issue with them may yield information that is important for planning interventions. Additionally, informal discussions should center around the implications of assessment results. In particular, parents and teachers should be involved in a discussion of types of support services available, possible interventions, and needs of the child.

Assessment in a Variety of Settings

Several topics were discussed earlier in this chapter that are relevant to the need for informally assessing adaptive behavior in a variety of situations. First, one characteristic of the construct of adaptive behavior is its situational specificity; children's adaptive behavior changes to meet the demands of different situations. Second, adaptive behavior scales, when used with parents, teachers, and other informants, can provide information about children's behavior in different settings, such as home and school. However, the response to an adaptive behavior scale by parents or teachers is often a generalized response; the informants are required to indicate what children usually do across *all* situations in that environment. Informal assessment of children's behavior in response to different situations is needed to allow a more comprehensive assessment of adaptive behavior.

There are many specific situations in which children's adaptive behavior can be observed. For example, children can be observed on the playground interacting with younger versus older peers. They can be observed meeting new people and going to places they have never been before. Their interactions with parents and teachers can be compared. An astute observer should also assess the *situation,* in addition to assessing the child. For instance, what characteristics of a situation are preventing a child from exhibiting an adaptive behavior in that situation but not in another? What interactions seem to motivate the child and promote adaptive behavior? What interactions appear to threaten the child and impede adaptive behavior? How does adaptive behavior change as the child gains more experience with the situation?

Most children are evaluated with an adaptive behavior scale as a prerequisite for entering a preschool program. An important area to informally assess is children's reactions to the new program and changes in adaptive behavior that occur as a result of the program. School or day care may result in increases in adaptive behavior or, with some children, may extinguish previously acquired skills.

Informal Assessment and Ongoing Evaluation

Informal assessment procedures can provide supplemental information to the results of standardized assessments. This supplemental information enhances the understanding of the child. It also helps ensure that the comprehensive assessment provides a profile of the adaptive behavior strengths and limitations of the child. Information obtained during the assessment is then used to develop interventions and facilitate the needed supports in the environment. Another function of informal assessment is to monitor, evaluate, and modify implemented interventions. Informal assessment may provide information about a specific skill that a preschool child needs to function in the classroom. This skill can then be targeted using an intervention. The intervention is aimed at improving the child's performance of this skill. Informal assessment can be used at several times during the implementation to examine the effectiveness of the particular intervention. If it is determined that the intervention needs modification, informal assessment may yield information about what types of changes may improve the intervention.

The role of informal assessment in the ongoing evaluation of preschool children is imperative. A critical assumption of the AAMR (1992) definition of mental retardation is that with needed supports, an individual's adaptive skills will improve. Thus, the focus of assessment should extend beyond identifying strengths and limitations. It should also be used to evaluate programs

and interventions. Modifications of interventions and programs can be developed from the information obtained using informal and formal assessment procedures. There should be continuous assessment of the intervention and program to ensure that supports being provided are effective at improving skill deficits.

USES OF ADAPTIVE BEHAVIOR ASSESSMENT

Information obtained from adaptive behavior assessment can be used for diagnosis and classification, placement decisions in special education, intervention planning, and determining needed supports in the environment (AAMR, 1992; Salvia & Ysseldyke, 1995). One major function of adaptive behavior assessment is to provide information that leads to decisions about the nature, diagnosis, and classification of disabilities. This information is often the basis of placement decisions for special education. A second use of adaptive behavior assessment is to acquire information that will assist in the determination of needed supports and the development of appropriate interventions.

Diagnosis/Classification

Historically, adaptive behavior assessment has been used to diagnose and classify individuals with mental retardation. The AAMR (1992) definition of mental retardation requires that deficits in adaptive behavior, as well as in intellectual functioning, must be substantiated before a person can be classified as having mental retardation. Most states use the concept of adaptive behavior in their definitions of mental retardation and require assessment of adaptive behavior to determine eligibility for special services for individuals with mental retardation (Patrick & Reschly, 1982).

Adaptive behavior assessment can also be used for the identification of disabilities or problems other than mental retardation because it is reasonable to expect that many disabilities will be related to deficits in personal and social functioning. It has been suggested that children with emotional and behavioral disturbances are characterized by average intelligence and deficits in adaptive behavior (Coulter, 1980; Mercer, 1973) and research supports that children with emotional disturbances can be distinguished from normal children by their deficits in adaptive behavior (e.g., Mealor, 1984; Sparrow & Cicchetti, 1987). Although adaptive behavior assessment may not be necessary for the identification of sensory and physical disabilities, it is important for determining the effects these disabilities have on daily functioning (e.g., Meacham, Kline, Stovall, & Sands, 1987; Pollingue, 1987; Sparrow et al., 1984a, 1984b). There is evidence to support that different subtypes of children with learning disabilities have characteristic patterns of adaptive behavior and that children with learning disabilities exhibit adaptive behavior that is lower than that of normal children but higher than that of children with mental retardation (e.g., Rainwater-Bryant, 1985; Weller & Strawser, 1987). Research reviewed by Harrison (1990) suggested that individuals with learning disabilities, emotional disturbances, and sensory impairments experienced deficits in adaptive behavior areas. Furthermore, she stressed that children with these disabilities, regardless of exceptionality, could benefit from training and interventions in the specific adaptive behavior area.

Special education and disability categories such as mental retardation, emotional disturbance, and so on may not be used with preschool children, depending on the guidelines of the state in which they reside. Instead of using categories, the 1997 reauthorization of the Individuals with Disabilities Education Act expands the definition of children with developmental delays to include ages 3 years through 9 years. Essentially, this law provides for early intervention services for children with developmental delays, with conditions that may result in developmental delay, or who are at risk of developmental delay. These children are eligible for early intervention services under this legislation.

Adaptive behavior assessment may be used for determining children who may be classified as having a developmental delay, as defined by the Individuals with Disabilities Education Act. Deficits in adaptive behavior, along with deficits in other developmental areas, may supply evidence of delay or possible delay. However, children who do not have deficits in adaptive behavior may have deficits in other developmental areas. School-age children with these characteristics face the risk of *declassification,* or the denial of special services, because they cannot be classified with mental retardation (Reschly, 1985). Early intervention services for preschoolers with deficits in intellectual functioning, but average adaptive behavior, may be justified because these children may be at risk of developing deficits in adaptive behavior without early home and school intervention (Leland, 1983). However, determination of the necessity of early intervention should be based on the needs of the individual child and not solely on level of cognitive functioning.

Intervention Planning

All assessment of preschoolers must lead to appropriate intervention plans. Verhaaren and Conner (1981) indicated that the results of assessment have three major purposes. Assessment should lead to education, or the teaching of skills to children that enable them to achieve their potential. Assessment should lead to prevention, or keeping any further problems or disabilities from occurring. Finally, assessment should lead to correction, or the reduction of any disabilities.

The important link between assessment and intervention aimed at adaptive skill areas is stressed in the AAMR (1992) manual. The AAMR describes the expanded role of an assessment team as a multidisciplinary group that explores not only the strengths and limitations but also identifies supports and services that can address the adaptive skill needs of the individual. Additionally, this assessment should be an ongoing, problem-solving process that meets the needs of the individual. The AAMR suggests that the purpose or function of the assessment may involve identifying priorities for interventions targeting adaptive behavior skills, to explore vocational programs, to evaluate progress following the implementation of an intervention, and to identify factors that may decrease the effectiveness of an intervention. Ultimately, the AAMR suggests that the intervention developed from the comprehensive and ongoing assessments of the individual's strengths and limitations should result in increased independence for the individual, levels of integration into the community, and higher levels of productivity.

Adaptive behavior scales have several features that are useful for planning intervention programs for preschool children. Most adaptive behavior scales yield scores in several domains of adaptive behavior, indicating children's strengths and weaknesses. Intervention programs can be planned to enhance strengths and remediate weaknesses. Items on adaptive behavior scales can be reviewed to determine specific adaptive activities and these activities can become goals in intervention programs (Witt & Martens, 1984). Informal assessment of adaptive behavior can also be used to determine strengths and weaknesses and evaluate the effectiveness of intervention programs.

Langone and Burton (1987) suggested that adaptive skills training requires carefully designed task sequences. These task sequences should be hierarchically arranged, from the simplest component of an activity to the most difficult. Three adaptive behavior scales, the

ABS-SE2, Vineland Expanded Form, and Pyramid Scales, list activities in hierarchical sequences. The Pyramid Scales also have the advantage of a well-designed, comprehensive curriculum as their base.

Adaptive skills training programs will be more effective when they occur in the environments in which the children are expected to exhibit the skills (AAMR, 1992; Langone & Burton, 1987). Thus, interventions for preschool children must involve parents as well as teachers because many activities, such as dressing and hygiene, occur more often at home than school. Other adaptive activities, such as eating and interpersonal skills, occur both at home and school. Doll (1953) reported that parental education was one of the primary uses of assessment with the Vineland Social Maturity Scale, the first major measure of adaptive behavior.

Training of adaptive behavior should be an ongoing process and not limited to structured training situations. Certain skills can be learned by children through direct teaching, but efforts should be made to foster generalization of the skills to daily activities. For example, using dolls or other toys to teach dressing skills should be accompanied by teaching that occurs when children are actually dressing themselves.

Cone (1987) listed a series of steps to be used for planning adaptive behavior intervention programs. The first step is to determine a long-range goal for the child, which, according to Cone, should be the behavior that is required for a specific situation, such as entry into the next less restrictive program. The second step is to determine the child's performance of that activity. The third step is to determine the skills needed by the child to achieve the long-range goal. The fourth step is to estimate the amount of time it will take for the child to achieve the long-range goal. The final steps are to establish annual goals, monthly goals, short-term goals, and immediate instructional objectives.

Similarly, the AAMR (1992) provides the following guidelines for prioritizing skills that should be addressed in interventions goals, which are guidelines that have special relevance for preschool children:

- skills needed for the child to function in the same way as age peers
- skills needed for the child to function in targeted settings
- skills preferred by the child
- skills that will contribute to happiness of the child and acceptance by others

- skills critical to the physical safety and health of the child
- skills that will promote the child's independence in the community and other settings

ISSUES IN ADAPTIVE BEHAVIOR ASSESSMENT

Adaptive behavior assessment, like any other area of assessment, is not without its inherent problems. These problems are of both of a conceptual and methodological nature. Three major issues in adaptive behavior assessment are reviewed: differences in adaptive behavior and cognitive functioning, the limitations of the third-party assessment technique, and psychometric problems with many adaptive behavior scales.

Adaptive Behavior versus Cognitive Functioning

A common misconception about adaptive behavior is that adaptive behavior and cognitive functioning are equivalent (Coulter, 1980). Research has demonstrated a moderate correlation between intelligence test scores and adaptive behavior scores (Harrison, 1990). Harrison indicated that correlations between adaptive behavior and intelligence test scores were in the low to moderate range for a number of reasons, including the following: (1) Intelligence is conceptualized as a thought process whereas adaptive behavior emphasizes everyday behavior; (2) intelligence scales measure maximum performance (potential) whereas adaptive behavior scales measure typical performance; and (3) intelligence scales assume a stability in scores whereas adaptive behavior scales assume that performance can be modified. Research by Keith, Fehrmann, Harrison, and Pottebaum (1987) provided support for these suggestions by investigating three hypotheses: Intelligence and adaptive behavior are components of the same underlying construct; intelligence and adaptive behavior are two separate but related constructs; and intelligence and adaptive behavior are two unrelated constructs. The results of their investigation supported the hypotheses that intelligence and adaptive behavior are two separate but related constructs.

The correlations between scores from intelligence tests and adaptive behavior scales tend to be low to moderate. Harrison (1987) reviewed a number of studies investigating the relationship between intelligence and adaptive behavior and found that the majority of correlations were in the low to moderate range. For example, Arffa, Rider, and Cummings (1984) reported correlations of .25 to .49 between intelligence and adaptive behavior scores of Headstart students, and Harrison and Ingram (1984) found a correlation of .41 between intelligence and adaptive behavior scores of preschoolers with developmental delays.

The obvious implication of the low to moderate correlations between adaptive behavior and intelligence scales is that children's adaptive behavior scores, in many cases, will not be equivalent to their intelligence test scores. Practitioners may find that one child has a below-average adaptive behavior score and average intelligence test score whereas another child has an average adaptive behavior score and below average intelligence test score. It is the latter example that results in declassification of mental retardation, according to AAMR guidelines. As stated earlier, declassification may not be as much of an issue under the reauthorization of the Individuals with Disabilities Education Act, in which developmental delay is used instead of categories such as mental retardation for ages 3 years through 9 years.

Adaptive behavior scales usually have low to moderate correlations with achievement test scores as well. In a review of research with adaptive behavior scales, Harrison (1987) reported correlations with achievement tests that ranged from −.18 to .57. Harrison (1981) and Oakland (1983), using multiple regression analysis, found that although adaptive behavior exhibited a significant, but moderate, correlation with school achievement, it did not significantly improve the prediction of achievement beyond that accounted for by intelligence. Keith et al. (1987), in a study using path analysis instead of regression analysis, reported that adaptive behavior had a small, but significant, effect on achievement beyond that accounted for by intelligence. Adaptive behavior scales appear to have a very modest effect on school achievement, but as suggested by Kamphaus (1987), perhaps a more important criterion for adaptive behavior is life achievement. Several studies support the positive relationship between adaptive behavior and measures of life achievement (e.g., Malgady, Barcher, Davis, & Towner, 1980; Irvin, Halpern, & Reynolds, 1977).

Third-Party Assessment

Throughout this chapter, the third-party assessment used with many adaptive behavior scales has been described. This method of assessment is deemed the most appropriate and efficient way of assessing adaptive behavior because it measures what children do daily to take care of themselves and get along with others (e.g., Adams, 1986; Harrison, 1985; Holman & Bruininks, 1985). Less efficient alternatives to third-party assessment include direct assessment of children, which determines what they can do instead of what they usually do, and observation of children day after day in home and school by a trained observer. Although the third-party method is attractive, it presents several problems for professionals who assess adaptive behavior.

Parents and teachers are the two primary informants for third-party adaptive behavior scales. Parents may lack objectivity and overestimate their children's adaptive behavior, whereas teachers may not have enough information about adaptive behavior to give valid information (Harrison & Sparrow, 1981; Holman & Bruininks, 1985). Harrison (1985) reported that preschool teachers usually have more information about adaptive behavior than teachers of school age children. Furthermore, many studies report low correlations between adaptive behavior and other behavior rating scores of parents and teachers (Harrison, 1987; Mayfield, Forman, & Nagle, 1984). For example, Ronka and Barnett (1986) reported correlations as low as .06 between parents and teachers of children classified with educable mental retardation and Arffa et al. (1984) reported a correlation of −.05 between parents and teachers of Headstart children. Gresham and Elliott (1990) reported a median correlation of .18 between parent and teacher SSRS ratings of preschool children. Reynolds and Kamphaus (1992) reported a median correlation of .24 between parent and teacher BASC ratings of preschool children. Overall, research has suggested that adaptive skill ratings made by parents may be higher on some skill areas than those made by teachers (Heath & Obrzut, 1984; Mealor & Richmond, 1980; Spivack, 1980). Such findings led Salvia and Ysseldyke (1995) to conclude that interrater agreement is poor and Bracken and Barnett (1987) to suggest that adaptive behavior scales lack interrater reliability and convergent validity.

Salvia and Ysseldyke's (1995) and Bracken and Barnett's (1987) conclusions are certainly warranted but another alternative should be considered when interpreting low correlations between parents and teachers on adaptive behavior scales. The issue of low correlations between parents and teachers may be a conceptual, rather than psychometric, issue. Bracken and Barnett's conclusion assumes that parent and teacher scores should correlate highly, but the definition of adaptive behavior suggests that it is feasible to assume that they should not. Adaptive behavior is situationally specific and influenced by cultural expectations; parents and teachers observe children in different situations and may have different expectations.

It is suggested that research reporting low correlations between parents and teachers may support the necessity of using both parents and teachers as informants in adaptive behavior assessment. If parents and teachers disagree in their estimates of a child's adaptive behavior, important information may be gained. Informal assessment should be conducted to answers questions such as the following: Do the parents and teachers have different expectations? What implications do the different expectations have for the development of the child? Is the child behaving differently at home and school? How are parents and teachers affecting the child's behavior at home and school? Research has demonstrated that controlling the familiarity and administration of the instrument may decrease the discrepancy between parent and teacher ratings (Foster-Gaitskell & Pratt, 1989).

Psychometric Standards

Many adaptive behavior scales fail to meet basic psychometric standards (AAMR, 1992). A large number of scales were normed on unrepresentative samples and the manuals for the scales often report limited reliability and validity data. Earlier in this chapter, several adaptive behavior scales were described but a complete evaluation of their psychometric properties is beyond the scope of this chapter. The brief descriptions provided in this chapter contain enough details about psychometric properties to observe that, for several of the scales, standardization was conducted with samples from one or two states, important stratification variables such as socioeconomic status were not used, and basic reliability and validity data are not reported. These scales are often used for placement decisions, but as indicated by Kamphaus (1987), it is difficult to imagine using an intelligence test with such poor psychometric properties. Kamphaus specifically discussed the problem of inadequate norms for adaptive behavior scales and cautioned practitioners against using scales for placement of children when they were poorly standardized. Kamphaus

cited the Vineland and SIB (and the new SIB-R also has adequate sampling) as scales with adequate samples. Review of the psychometric properties of these two scales clearly shows that their manuals also report more detailed information about reliability and validity scales than do manuals for other scales.

CONCLUSION

The importance of adaptive behavior assessment in developing a comprehensive understanding of preschool children has become widely accepted. Improvements in the psychometric standards of adaptive behavior instruments and the development of other informal assessment techniques has increased the popularity of adaptive behavior assessment as a means of expanding the knowledge about a young child. Formal and informal adaptive behavior assessment provides information about the strengths and limitations of a child. This profile can be directly used to develop interventions and support services for needed areas. Adaptive behavior assessment also has a major role in the ongoing evaluation of the needs of preschool children and the success of interventions. Modifications of interventions can develop naturally during the ongoing assessment process.

Adaptive behavior assessment has become an integral part of early childhood intervention programs. Legislation has emphasized assessment and intervention of all developmental areas and the needs of families and children and, thus, increased the importance of adaptive behavior assessment. In addition, the Individuals with Disabilities Act of 1991 and its 1997 reauthorization have widened the scope of adaptive behavior beyond the field of mental retardation and supports the use of the construct with children with other disabilities. The 1997 legislation expands the age limits for developmental delay and places the emphasis on determining the needs of the child, not the classification of the child. The most important factors to address when examining the adaptive behavior of a child are that the assessment must provide information that enhances the understanding of the strengths and limitations of the child and, ultimately, facilitates the development of interventions and support systems that address the needs of the child.

REFERENCES

Adams, G. L. (1986). *Comprehensive Test of Adaptive Behavior and Normative Adaptive Behavior Checklist technical manual.* Columbus, OH: Charles E. Merrill.

American Association on Mental Retardation. (1992). *Definitions, classifications, and systems of supports* (9th ed.). Washington, DC: Author.

Arffa, S., Rider, L., & Cummings, J. (1984). *An investigation of cognitive and adaptive functioning of Head Start children.* Unpublished manuscript, Indiana University, Bloomington.

Barnett, D. W. (1984). An organizational approach to preschool services: Psychological screening, assessment, and intervention. In C. Maher, R. Illback, & J. Zins (Eds.), *Organizational psychology in the schools: A handbook for practitioners* (pp. 53–82). Springfield, IL: Thomas.

Benner, S. M. (1992). *Assessing young children with special needs: An ecological perspective.* New York: Longman.

Boan, C. H., & Harrison, P. H. (1997). Adaptive behavior assessment and individuals with mental retardation. In R. Taylor (Ed.), *Assessment of individuals with mental retardation* (pp. 33–53). San Diego, CA: Singular.

Bracken, B., & Barnett, D. (1987, June). The technical side of preschool assessment: A primer of critical issues. *Preschool Interests, 6–7,* 9.

Brown, L., & Leigh, J. E. (1986). *Adaptive behavior scale.* Austin, TX: PRO-ED.

Bruininks, R. H., Hill, B. K., Weatherman, R., & Woodcock, R. W. (1986). *Inventory for client and agency planning.* Chicago: Riverside.

Bruininks, R. H., Thurlow, M., & Gilman, C. J. (1987). Adaptive behavior and mental retardation. *Journal of Special Education, 21,* 69–88.

Bruininks, R. H., Woodcock, R. W., Weatherman, R. F., & Hill, B. K. (1996). *Scales of independent behavior, revised.* Chicago: Riverside.

Clausen, J. (1972). The continuing problem of defining mental deficiency. *Journal of Special Education, 6,* 97–106.

Cone, J. D. (1984). *The pyramid scales.* Austin, TX: PRO-ED.

Cone, J. D. (Ed.). (1986). *The pyramid system: Comprehensive assessment and programming for handicapped persons.* Morgantown, WV: Pyramid Press.

Cone, J. D. (1987). Intervention planning using adaptive behavior instruments. *Journal of Special Education, 21,* 127–148.

Coulter, W. A. (1980). Adaptive behavior and professional disfavor: Controversies and trends for school psychologists. *School Psychology Review, 9,* 67–74.

Doll, E. A. (1935). A generic scale of social maturity. *American Journal of Orthopsychiatry, 5,* 180–188.

Doll, E. A. (1953). *Measurement of social competence.* Circle Pines, MN: American Guidance Service.

Doll, E. A. (1965). *Vineland Social Maturity Scale.* Circle Pines, MN: American Guidance Service.

Downing, J., & Perino, D. M. (1992). Functional versus standardized assessment procedures: Implications for educational programming. *Mental Retardation, 30,* 289–295.

Foster-Gaitskell, D., & Pratt, C. (1989). Comparison of parent and teacher ratings of adaptive behavior of children with mental retardation. *American Journal of Mental Retardation, 94,* 177–181.

Greenspan, S., & Driscoll, J. (1997). The role of intelligence in a broad model of personal competence. In D. P. Flanagan, J. L. Genshaft, & P. L. Harrison (Eds.), *Contemporary intellectual assessment: Theories, tests, and issues* (pp. 131–150). New York: Guilford.

Greenspan, S., & Granfield, J. M. (1992). Reconsidering the construct of mental retardation: Implications of a model of social competence. *American Journal of Mental Retardation, 96,* 442–453.

Gresham, F. M., & Elliott, S. N. (1987). The relationship between adaptive behavior and social skills: Issues in definition and assessment. *Journal of Special Education, 21,* 167–182.

Gresham, R. M., & Elliott, S. N. (1990). *Social skills rating system.* Circle Pines, MN: American Guidance Service.

Grossman, H. J. (1983). *Classification in mental retardation.* Washington, DC: American Association on Mental Deficiency.

Harrison, P. L. (1981). Mercer's adaptive behavior inventory, the McCarthy scales, and dental development as predictors of first grade achievement. *Journal of Educational Psychology, 73,* 78–82.

Harrison, P. L. (1984). The application of the Vineland Adaptive Behavior Scales in educational settings. *Techniques: A Journal for Remedial Education and Counseling, 7,* 101–112.

Harrison, P. L. (1985). *Vineland Adaptive Behavior Scales, Classroom Edition manual.* Circle Pines, MN: American Guidance Service.

Harrison, P. L. (1987). Research with adaptive behavior scales. *Journal of Special Education, 21,* 37–68.

Harrison, P. L. (1990). Mental retardation, adaptive behavior assessment, and giftedness. In A. S. Kaufman (Ed.), *Assessing adolescent and adult intelligence* (pp. 533–585). Boston: Allyn & Bacon.

Harrison, P. L., & Ingram, R. P. (1984, May). Performance of developmentally delayed preschoolers on the Vineland Adaptive Behavior Scales. In S. S.

Sparrow (Chair), *The Vineland Adaptive Behavior Scales: Results of national standardization and clinical and research applications.* Symposium conducted at the meeting of the American Association on Mental Deficiency, Minneapolis, MN.

Harrison, P. L., & Robinson, B. (1995). Best practices in the assessment of adaptive behavior. In A. Thomas & J. Grimes (Eds.), *Best practices in school psychology* (3rd ed., pp. 753–762). Washington, DC: National Association of School Psychologists.

Harrison, P. L., & Sparrow, S. S. (1981, April). *Adaptive behavior: What teachers know.* Paper presented at the meeting of the National Association of School Psychologists, Houston, TX.

Heath, C. P., & Obrzut, J. E. (1984). Comparison of three measures of adaptive behavior. *American Journal of Mental Deficiency, 89,* 205–208.

Holman, J., & Bruininks, R. (1985). Assessing and training adaptive behaviors. In K. C. Lakin & R. H. Bruininks (Eds.), *Strategies for achieving community integration of developmentally disabled citizens* (pp. 73–104). Baltimore, MD: Paul H. Brookes.

Horn, E., & Fuchs, D. (1987). Using adaptive behavior assessment and intervention: An overview. *Journal of Special Education, 21,* 11–26.

Irvin, L. K., Halpern, A. A., & Reynolds, W. M. (1977). Assessing social and prevocational awareness in mildly and moderately retarded individuals. *American Journal of Mental Deficiency, 82,* 266–272.

Kamphaus, R. W. (1987). Conceptual and psychometric issues in the assessment of adaptive behavior. *Journal of Special Education, 21,* 27–36.

Kamphaus, R. W., & Frick, P. J. (1996). *Clinical assessment of child and adolescent personality and behavior.* Boston: Allyn & Bacon.

Keith, T. Z., Fehrmann, P. G., Harrison, P. L., & Pottebaum, S. M. (1987). The relationship between adaptive behavior and intelligence: Testing alternative explanations. *Journal of School Psychology, 25,* 31–43.

Keith, T. Z., Harrison, P. L., & Ehly, S. W. (1987). Effects of adaptive behavior on achievement: Path analysis of a national sample. *Professional School Psychology, 2,* 205–216.

Lambert, N., Nihira, K., & Leland, H. (1993). *AAMR adaptive behavior scale—school edition* (2nd edition). Austin, TX: PRO-ED.

Langone, J., & Burton, T. A. (1987). Teaching adaptive behavior skills to moderately and severely handicapped individuals: Best practices for facilitating independent living. *Journal of Special Education, 21,* 149–166.

Leland, H. (1983). Assessment of adaptive behavior. In K. D. Paget & B. A. Bracken (Eds.), *The psychoeducational assessment of preschool children* (pp. 191–206). New York: Grune & Stratton.

LeMay, D. W., Griffin, P. M., & Sanford, A. R. (1983). *Learning Accomplishment Profile—Diagnostic Edition.* Winston-Salem, NC: Kaplan Press.

Malgady, R. G., Barcher, P. R., Davis, J., & Towner, G. (1980). Validity of the Vocational Adaptation Rating Scale: Prediction of mentally retarded workers' placement in sheltered workshops. *American Journal of Mental Deficiency, 84,* 633–640.

Mayfield, K. L., Forman, S. G., & Nagle, R. J. (1984). Reliability of the AAMD Adaptive Behavior Scale, Public School Version. *Journal of School Psychology, 22,* 53–61.

McCarney, S. B. (1983). *Adaptive behavior evaluation scale.* Columbia, MO: Hawthorne Educational Service.

McGrew, K., & Bruininks, R. (1989). The factor structure of adaptive behavior. *School Psychology Review, 18,* 64–81.

McGrew, K. S., Bruininks, R. H., & Johnson, D. R. (1996). A confirmatory factor analysis investigation of Greenspan's model of personal competence. *American Journal on Mental Retardation, 100,* 533–545.

McMann, G. M., & Barnett, D. W. (1984). An analysis of the construct validity of two measures of adaptive behavior. *Journal of Psychoeducational Assessment, 2,* 239–247.

Meacham, F. R., Kline, M. M., Stovall, J. A., & Sands, D. I. (1987). Adaptive behavior and low incidence handicaps: Hearing and visual impairments. *Journal of Special Education, 21,* 183–196.

Mealor, D. J. (1984). *An analysis of intellectual functioning and adaptive behavior of behaviorally disordered students.* Unpublished manuscript, University of Central Florida, Orlando.

Mealor, D. J., & Richmond, B. O. (1980). Adaptive behavior: Teachers and parents disagree. *Exceptional Children, 46,* 386–389.

Mercer, J. R. (1973). *Labeling the mentally retarded child.* Berkeley: University of California Press.

Meyers, C. E., Nihira, K., & Zetlin, A. (1979). The measurement of adaptive behavior. In N. R. Ellis (Ed.), *Handbook of mental deficiency: Psychological the-*

ory and research (2nd ed., pp. 215–253). Hillsdale, NJ: Lawrence Erlbaum.

NASP position statement and supporting paper on early intervention services in the schools. (1987, November). *Communique, 4*–5.

Newborg, J., Stock, J. R., Wnek, L., Guidubaldi, J., & Svinicki, J. (1984). *Battelle Developmental Inventory examiner's manual.* Allen, TX: DLM Teaching Resources.

Oakland, T. (1983). Joint use of adaptive behavior and IQ to predict achievement. *Journal of Consulting and Clinical Psychology, 51,* 298–301.

Paget, K. D. (1983). The individual examining situation: Basic considerations for preschool children. In K. D. Paget & B. A. Bracken (Eds.), *The psychoeducational assessment of preschool children* (pp. 51–62). New York: Grune & Stratton.

Paget, K. D. (1987). Preschool assessment. In C. R. Reynolds & L. Mann (Eds.), *Encyclopedia of Special Education* (pp. 1237–1239). New York: John Wiley.

Paget, K. D. (1992). Parent involvement in early childhood services. In T. R. Kratochwill, S. N. Elliott, & M. Gettinger (Eds.), *Preschool and early childhood treatment directions* (pp. 89–112). Hillsdale, NJ: Lawrence Erlbaum.

Paget, K. D., & Nagle, R. J. (1986). A conceptual model of preschool assessment. *School Psychology Review, 15,* 154–165.

Patrick, J. L., & Reschly, D. J. (1982). Relationship of state educational criteria and demographic variables to school system prevalence of mental retardation. *American Journal of Mental Deficiency, 86,* 351–360.

Pollingue, A. (1987). Adaptive behavior and low incidence handicaps: Use of adaptive behavior instruments for persons with physical handicaps. *Journal of Special Education, 21,* 117–126.

Rainwater-Bryant, B. J. (1985). *Comparisons of parent obtained and teacher obtained adaptive behavior scores for handicapped children.* Unpublished doctoral dissertation, Memphis State University, Memphis, TN.

Reschly, D. J. (1982). Assessing mild mental retardation: The influence of adaptive behavior, sociocultural status, and prospects for nonbiased assessment. In C. R. Reynolds & T. B. Gutkin (Eds.), *The handbook of school psychology* (pp. 209–242). New York: John Wiley.

Reschly, D. J. (1985). Best practices: Adaptive behavior. In A. Thomas & J. Grimes (Eds.), *Best practices in school psychology* (pp. 353–368). Stratford, CT: National Association of School Psychologists.

Reschly, D. J. (1990). Best practices in adaptive behavior. In A. Thomas & J. Grimes (Eds.), *Best practices in school psychology—II* (pp. 29–42). Washington, DC: National Association of School Psychologists.

Reynolds, C. R., & Kamphaus, R. W. (1992). *Behavior assessment system for children.* Circle Pines, MN: American Guidance Service.

Ronka, C. S., & Barnett, D. (1986). A comparison of adaptive behavior ratings: Revised Vineland and AAMD ABS-SE. *Special Services in the Schools, 2,* 87–96.

Salvia, J., & Ysseldyke, J. E. (1995). *Assessment* (6th ed.). Boston: Houghton Mifflin.

Sattler, J. M. (1992). *Assessment of children, revised and updated* (3rd ed.). San Diego, CA: Author.

Sparrow, S. S., Balla, D. A., & Cicchetti, D. V. (1984a). *Vineland Adaptive Behavior Scales, Expanded Form manual.* Circle Pines, MN: American guidance Service.

Sparrow, S. S., Balla, D. A., & Cicchetti, D. V. (1984b). *Vineland Adaptive Behavior Scales, Survey Form manual.* Circle Pines, MN: American Guidance Service.

Sparrow, S. S., & Cicchetti, D. V. (1987). Adaptive behavior and the psychologically disturbed child. *Journal of Special Education, 21,* 89–100.

Spivak, G. M. (1980, April). *The construct of adaptive behavior: Consistency across raters and instruments.* Paper presented at the meeting of the National Association of School Psychologists, Washington, DC.

Telzrow, C. F. (1992). Young children with special educational needs. In T. R. Kratochwill, S. N. Elliott, & M. Gettinger (Eds.), *Preschool and early childhood treatment directions* (pp. 55–88). Hillsdale, NJ: Lawrence Erlbaum.

Verhaaren, P., & Conner, F. P. (1981). Physical disabilities. In J. M. Kauffman & D. P. Hallahan (Eds.), *Handbook of Special Education.* Englewood Cliffs, NJ: Prentice-Hall.

Weller, C., & Strawser, S. (1987). Adaptive behavior of subtypes of learning disabled individuals. *Journal of Special Education, 21,* 101–116.

Widamin, K. F., & McGrew, K. S. (1996). The structure of adaptive behavior. In J. W. Jacobson & J. A. Mulick (Eds.), *Manual of diagnosis and professional practice in mental retardation* (pp. 97–110). Washington, DC: American Psychological Association.

Witt, J. C., & Martens, B. K. (1984). Adaptive behavior: Tests and assessment issues. *School Psychology Review, 13,* 478–484.

Zigler, E., Balla, D., & Hodapp, R. (1984). On the definition and classification of mental retardation. *American Journal of Mental Deficiency, 89,* 215–230.

Zigler, E., & Seitz, V. (1980). Early childhood intervention programs: A reanalysis. *School Psychology Review, 9,* 354–368.

Zigler, E., & Trickett, P. K. (1978). IQ, social competence, and evaluation of early childhood intervention programs. *American Psychologist, 33,* 789–798.

CHAPTER 9

ASSESSMENT OF COMMUNICATION, LANGUAGE, AND SPEECH
QUESTIONS OF "WHAT TO DO NEXT?"

CANDIS WARNER
NICKOLA WOLF NELSON

Shannon, Zachary, and Max are enrolled in a preschool program designed for children with speech-language impairments. Shannon, age 3½, speaks with enthusiasm and in long, seemingly complex utterances consisting of mostly unintelligible consonant-vowel combinations. She uses a complicated system of gestures and sophisticated facial expressions to assist her numerous communication attempts. She seems to comprehend the language expected of a 3-year-old, and her use of nonverbal language is exceptional. She works hard to engage all of the adults present and expects them to share her attention and interpret her utterances. Shannon's parents note that she is sometimes an exhausting communicative partner, but they enjoy her need to interact with them. They are pleased with her tenacious, high-spirited nature but are concerned that she will lose her outgoing personality if she continues to experience difficulty in communicating.

Zachary, also 3½, has perfect articulation. He often uses complex sentences, is beginning to "read" snatches of print, such as videotape labels and warnings, sings along with the radio, and can operate the most complex computer software. However, when asked to talk about the book about the dog "Spot" just read to him, he responds with a long statement about his father's workshop. Zachary's parents report that he talks incessantly, but communicating with him is very difficult. He rarely stays on a topic for more than one or two conversational turns and seems to enjoy one-to-one communication with adults, but only when he chooses the topic. Zachary also withdraws from group activities with peers and from situations in which he is expected to respond to questions. Zachary seems attached to his parents. He runs to greet them when they return home, and takes them by the hand when he wants something, but they wish he were more interactive with them and with other children.

Max, age 4, rarely initiates conversations but does respond to direct questions. He uses short, one- or two-word utterances, omits all forms of the verb "to be," substitutes "me" for "I," and has a limited expressive vocabulary for his age. He correctly points to pictured items when asked but has difficulty naming the pictures. He follows orally presented directions well and is eager to participate in all planned activities in preschool. He positions himself in the middle of the group but never chooses to be a leader. Max's parents express concern that Max will not be accepted by his peers at school. They have decided not to have other children because they believe he needs all of their attention.

All of these children have normal hearing and are from families in which English is the only language spoken. None of these children has been identified as developmentally delayed by the school psychologist. The results of the assessments for these three children revealed very different profiles; yet each has been diagnosed with a language impairment. Their disparate skills and needs illustrate the complexities of assessing the communication, language, and speech of toddlers and preschoolers.

WHY ASSESS COMMUNICATION, LANGUAGE, AND SPEECH?

The overriding purpose for assessing the language development of children such as Shannon, Zachary, and Max is to yield an accurate picture of their communicative abilities and needs. This is not done in the abstract

TABLE 9.1   Definitions of Communication, Language, and Speech

TERM	DEFINITION
Communication	The broadest term. Essentially, it means "getting the message across." Messages can be communicated through language (spoken or written), but communication can also occur without language. Many animal species communicate but do not have language. No human being can be too impaired to communicate.
Language	A language is built through orderly combinations of linguistic symbols into words, sentences, and discourse. All peoples of the world have spoken languages, but not all languages have a written form. To "know" a language means to be able to apply the rules of five linguistic subsystems for comprehending and formulating messages: • a *phonological system* for representing the sounds • a *morphological system* for forming words and inflectional endings that have meaning • a *syntactic system* for combining words into sentences • a *semantic system* for representing meaning • a *pragmatic system* for using language in contextually and socially appropriate ways
Speech	To be shared, language must be transformed into speech, print, or sign language. Speech production is a complex motor act, directed by the brain. It requires: • a respiratory system to provide the airstream • a vocal tract to shape the airstream into sounds by manipulating the larynx, teeth, tongue, jaw, and soft palate

but in the contexts of families and preschool experiences. Although the assessment tools and techniques vary depending on individual needs and the point in the intervention process, the general purpose of all assessment activities is to address the question of "what to do next." For Shannon, Zachary, and Max, assessment results confirmed their parents' concerns regarding communicative development. Each of them can be identified as having a speech-language impairment, and each has been found in need of a speech-language intervention program.

Underlying the question of "what to do next" are several more specific reasons to assess the speech-language performance of a preschool child. A basic reason is to determine whether the child has a problem understanding or using language that could be considered a disorder of speech-language development. This is the diagnostic purpose. Three other specific purposes for assessment are to establish intervention targets, to determine baseline functioning prior to intervention, and to measure change within an intervention program. The questions underlying these four purposes all relate in

some way to planning "what to do next" in treatment (Schiefelbusch & McCormick, 1984) and to documenting outcomes.

Relationships among Communication, Language, and Speech

Communication, language, and speech (defined in Table 9.1) are typically intertwined and supportive of each other; however, each may be relatively spared or impaired in children with atypical developmental patterns. Thus, assessment must consider the relative involvement of each of these three systems for a particular child.

Although Shannon's pattern appears to represent a problem of speech development, further assessment reveals that Shannon's communicative difficulties primarily stem from delayed acquisition of the phonological rules of language. Her expressive syntax may be marginally affected as well, particularly verb tense and plural endings, but it is difficult to tell because the language she produces is only partially intelligible, even to those who know her well. She is apparently using real words (although they are not pronounced clearly) to formulate sentences with a variety of linguistic rules. She communicates a variety of functions and uses complex sentence structures. Another important note about Shannon's language is that she understands age-appropriate linguistic messages, an observation that was confirmed in assessment tasks using few nonverbal communicative cues. In the area of communication, Shannon has exceptional strengths, using gestures and other communicative strategies to get her message across. She is an active communicator (Fey, 1986), both initiating and responding in communicative exchanges and completing multiple communicative circles with her parents (Greenspan, 1992). In the past, a high use of gestural communication might have been viewed as a concern in itself, and treatment might have involved warning Shannon's parents not to respond to her gestural communication but to insist on producing clearer words. More recent approaches emphasize the positive prognostic value of a good gestural communication system (Thal & Tobias, 1992), which can help Shannon experience communicative success while she receives specialized attention to learn the phonological intricacies of her language and to speak clearly. Shannon's educational team also recognizes that helping her to sort out the phonological rules of English in her auditory perceptual and motor production systems as a preschooler will help her have the phonological awareness capabilities that are critical to the early stages of learning to read and write (Kamhi & Catts, 1989; Stanovich, 1985).

Zachary shows a different pattern of relationship among the three elements, communication, language, and speech. For him, communication is the major concern. Not only his verbal interactions but his use of gestures to communicate are atypical. For example, Zachary rarely uses distal gestures, such as pointing, to guide his parents' attention or to accompany the requests he makes by pulling them by the hand toward desired objects. Zachary's perceptual-motor grasp of the surface features of both speech and written language is exceptional. When assessment probes beneath the surface, however, not only is Zachary's understanding of how to communicate with others impaired, but his difficulty in comprehending the conceptual aspects of language also becomes apparent. Zachary is a verbal noncommunicator (Fey, 1986). He chatters but has marked difficulty completing "communicative circles" (Greenspan's [e.g., 1992] term to highlight how children learn to signal and respond purposefully in exchanges with another person)

and participating in play. In addition, Zachary's symptoms of early reading without comprehension might be described as hyperlexia, but the label does not fully convey the problems that Zachary has in the broader aspects of language and social communication. Zachary's unusual social interactions, in particular, reflect his difficulties in learning linguistic rules and communicative expectations for participating in meaning making.

Like Shannon, Max has a strength in communication relative to his expressive language capabilities, but for him the contrast is less dramatic. Max is demonstrating significant delays of speech and language development that are concentrated in his difficulty in acquiring the linguistic rules of language, to some extent for comprehension, but most clearly involving impaired language expression. Max completes communicative circles (Greenspan, 1992) by responding to turns initiated by others, but he rarely initiates them. Thus, he can be described as a passive communicator (Fey, 1986). He has fewer strategies than Shannon for compensating communicatively for his limited speech-language skills. He does have strengths for comprehending linguistic vocabulary relative to his production of it. Comprehension difficulties are often associated with cognitive deficits, but psychometric assessment ruled out generalized developmental delay for Max. Max is different from Shannon in another way as well. We wonder if Max might be having word-finding difficulties. Although Shannon lacks the speech capabilities to be understood, she seems to retrieve words easily and to have the linguistic rules to formulate them into sentences. Max's problems are more focused in learning the rules of language and retrieving the words to convey complex meanings linguistically. For Max, the risks in school when it comes to reading and writing are that he will have difficulty comprehending when he reads and formulating when he writes. Getting his oral language going now will serve an important role in secondary prevention of educational problems in the future.

Screening, Referral, and Interviewing

Before the process of diagnosis, someone must identify a reason for concern. Concern might be raised either through screening or referral. Either intake procedure suggests that a problem may exist. Thus, the answer to the first question about "what to do next" is to engage in further assessment.

Screening is the preliminary assessment process used to identify children for whom a more complete speech-language evaluation is warranted. Although screenings can take place in physicians' offices or other settings, the most common example of mass screening of speech-language skills occurs as five-year-olds are screened before entering kindergarten. Screening implies quick and efficient sampling of several areas of language functioning. Often language is just one of many developmental areas screened.

In contrast to a mass screening, a referral of a child for an initial assessment suggests that someone in the child's environment is already concerned about the child's development. The chances that preliminary screening activities will reveal a reason for the concern are greater in cases of referral.

Answers about "what to do next" based on administration of standardized screening procedures are usually presented as "pass" or "fail" (sometimes termed *refer*). Children who pass are thought not to have a language disorder; those who fail might have a language disorder, but they also might not. It is wise for examiners to beware of the potential for cultural bias because the screening process may identify those children with cultural and linguistic differences, as well as those with a potential language disorder. In any case, it is critical that screening not be used to diagnose. Particularly, screening results must not be used inappropriately to diagnose children whose developmental experiences are unlike those of middle-class children on whom most tests are standardized. For example, low scores on screening tests might indicate only that a test is biased against a particular child's prior experiences, or in some cases, that a child's speech-language development should be monitored and fostered by regular or bilingual educators.

In addition to avoiding the pitfalls of cultural and linguistic bias when using screening tools, professionals should take care to consider how screening decisions might be perceived by parents. An atmosphere of overconcern might contribute to reduced expectations by the parents and others in the child's environment, leading to the well-known "Rosenthal effect" (Rosenthal & Jacobson, 1968), in which lowered expectations contribute to reduced achievement. Each case is different, however. For some concerned parents, the results of a screening process might provide reassuring evidence that their child's worrisome speech "errors" are actually developmentally appropriate. For others, whose concerns are validated by the results of screening, it might come as a relief that professionals are listening to them and planning to help them address the concerns.

Ideally, the child's relationship and interaction with the parents or primary caregivers should be the corner-stone of all stages of the assessment process, including the initial screening and history gathering. Every interaction between parents and professionals is an important event (Berman & Shaw, 1996). Families are always affected by an assessment of their preschool child, whether or not they have actively sought it (Popper, 1996), and no matter how comprehensive the assessment is.

The parents of Shannon, Zachary, and Max provided information and actively participated in the testing activities. Thus, they were instrumental in determining the results of the initial broad screening as well as in the more focused activities of the diagnostic process. They responded to "grand tour" interview questions about the nature of their concerns and their child's strengths and preferences (Westby, 1990). Then they provided prioritized lists of their specific concerns and answered the question, "If you could change just one thing for your child, what would that be?" They also shared anecdotes that illustrated the source of their concerns. They now expect to be active members of the intervention team because they have been involved from the beginning of their children's assessment process. They have been encouraged to enjoy and nourish their children's strengths while directly addressing their concerns.

If the screening results indicate that further speech-language evaluation be conducted due to a possible disorder, not a dialectal or cultural difference, the goals of further assessment ("what to do next") are to determine and describe the child's communicative functioning across all areas of language development and to yield a diagnosis if warranted. Answers to the diagnostic question, "Does the child have a language disorder?" are based on one's definition of language disorder and the policy-driven procedures used to operationalize it.

WHAT IS A LANGUAGE DISORDER?

The American Speech-Language-Hearing Association (ASHA, 1982) defined *language disorder* as:

> *the impairment or deviant development of comprehension and/or use of a spoken, written, and/or other symbol system. The disorder may involve (1) the form of language (phonologic, morphologic, and syntactic systems), (2) the content of language (semantic system), and/or (3) the function of language in communication (pragmatic system) in any combination. (p. 949)*

This definition addresses the form, content, and use of language, but like many other definitions, it is not explicit about how to determine "any disruption in the learning or use" (Lahey, 1988, p. 21) or "deficits in comprehension, production, and/or use of language" (Bashir, 1989, p. 181). Hence, most definitions by themselves do not operationalize criteria for diagnosing language disorder for a specific child. Generally, in order to diagnose an impairment or disorder of language development, a speech-language pathologist (SLP) must find a child's language performance on formal tests to be significantly lower than the performance of a comparison group of children either of the same chronological age (CA) or mental age (MA) (Nelson, 1998). The fact is, however, that children in comparison groups frequently are not comparable in terms of background experiences; thus, many children from minority groups, different cultures, or families who are poor receive biased assessments in spite of policies intended to avoid bias.

Chronological and Mental Age Referencing

CA referencing involves comparing a child's scores on normative language measures to data collected on children of the same age group. MA, or cognitive referencing, involves comparing a child's scores on language tests against a standardized measure of cognitive ability, usually a formal intelligence test.

The *DSM-IV* (American Psychiatric Association, 1994) uses nonverbal MA as a reference point in the identification of language disorders. The use of either CA or MA referencing to diagnose language disorders is not agreed on by all speech-language pathologists, and requirements vary across state policies. The problems associated with both CA and MA referencing include the fact that normative data on minority groups are not typically collected in sufficient numbers to exclude bias when evaluating children from diverse cultural backgrounds (Lahey, 1992; Seymour, 1992; Terrell & Terrell, 1983). In addition, CA referencing may be inappropriate because of difficulties comparing the language abilities of children with slower overall development to typically developing, same-aged peers.

MA referencing is also questionable because many intelligence tests are, to a large extent, language based. Therefore, the language disorder evident on formal language measures may also negatively affect the scores on tests of intelligence; this double jeopardy can make MA referencing inappropriate (Francis, Fletcher, Shaywitz, Shaywitz, & Rourke, 1996). To compound the problem, children with language disorders may not have normal use of verbal strategies that allow them to identify, retain, and manipulate nonverbal symbols, thus placing them at a disadvantage even when nonverbal intelligence tests are

used to compare language abilities with overall cognitive functioning. Other evidence suggests that some combinations of language tests and cognitive tests may show a discrepancy when others do not, and that results may vary at different points of development (Cole, Dale, & Mills, 1990, 1992; Cole, Mills, & Kelley, 1994).

Whenever policies allow, professionals should seek to limit their dependence on discrepancy criteria for diagnosing language disorder or learning disability. For purposes of describing participants in research studies, it may be important to compare MA and scores from formal language tests, but for clinical purposes such practices may exclude children from receiving the services they need (Francis et al., 1996). In fact, several studies have shown that preschool age children can benefit equally from language intervention services whether or not they show discrepancies between MA and LA (language age) (Cole & Harris, 1992; Fey, Long, & Cleave, 1994).

Intralinguistic Profiling as an Alternative to CA or MA Referencing

Intralinguistic profiling can be used to compare the child's language skills in one aspect of language development to other aspects of language development. This approach may reveal the scattered patterns of development that have been reported as characterizing the language of children with specific language impairment (Leonard, 1980). Intralinguistic profiling, in particular, may provide justification for diagnosing those children who should be eligible for speech-language services based on need but who may be excluded if discrepancy between MA and language test scores is used as the only criterion for service eligibility. A combination of formal and informal measures may also overcome the limitations of formal tests for assessing needs for language intervention in everyday contexts (Westby, StevensDominguez, & Oetter, 1996).

Needs-Based Assessment as an Alternative to CA or MA Referencing for Preschoolers

The basic criterion for determining disability within the Individuals with Disabilities Education Act (IDEA; Public Law 105-17) is that a child needs specialized intervention in order to benefit from general education experiences. At the preschool level, this means that the diagnostic team finds that a child has not developed language normally in spite of adequate experience with it and, thus, is not likely to catch up without special help, indicating a need for speech-language intervention.

In determining whether prior experiences have been adequate, it should not be assumed automatically that children who come from backgrounds impoverished in material things have been impoverished in relational experiences as well. On the other hand, one reason that children from poor families score lower on standardized tests is that many are exposed less frequently to vocabulary that preschoolers are expected to know (Hart & Risley, 1995). Also, children from minority populations are more likely to produce language with dialectal features that could be inappropriately categorized as errors if test designers and examiners are not sensitive to the potential for bias. For such children, the most appropriate diagnostic approach might be to provide an enriched language and communication learning environment and then observe how quickly the child acquires language features associated with the experiences. Such dynamic assessment strategies (discussed later in this chapter) involve assessing "a child's immediate ability to change or advance when provided with guided experience by a more experienced person" (Olswang & Bain, 1996, p. 415). However, if a child continues to experience difficulty acquiring linguistic concepts and forms, including those of his family's primary cultural and linguistic systems, it may be that the problem is best understood as a language disorder.

The data on whether to risk overidentification by recommending early diagnosis and intervention for all children who are late talkers or to take a more conservative "watch and see" approach (Paul, 1996) are still mixed. The key question is whether early diagnosis is justified or whether it might lead to the inappropriate labeling of children who are really developing at the low end of the range considered typical.

Questions about Labels

The diagnostic question is based on the examiner's definition of speech-language disorders, what to call them, measures to employ, and the criteria used for diagnosis. Several authoritative sources, including the *Diagnostic and Statistical Manual of Mental Disorder, fourth edition* (*DSM-IV;* American Psychiatric Association, 1994) and the *International Code of Diseases* (ICD-10; World Health Organization, 1992), require two primary diagnostic criteria for language impairments: (1) scoring significantly low on standardized language testing, and (2) being perceived by others as having a problem. As noted previously, more specific operational definitions for diagnosing speech-language impairment are contro-

versial, and they are often influenced by inconsistent policies at the local, state, and federal levels. Table 9.2 provides generally accepted definitions for a variety of currently used identifying labels for toddlers and preschoolers with atypical language development.

Being a "late talker" or having a "delay" in communicative development is less likely to have devastating implications for parents than labels of *impairment* or *disability*. Parents may understand and respond with agreement more frequently when the examiner makes statements such as, "It feels like I'm talking to a 4-year-old rather than a 6-year-old. Does it feel like that to you when you communicate with him?" One mother emphasized her reasons for this preference:

> I was devastated when I first heard the word *impaired* to describe my sweet little Jacob. The speech pathologist said he was delayed in language development. Delayed. OK, I know that. We can deal with a delay. We can work hard to help him with a delay. I'm not so sure about an impairment.

Words are powerful. For all difficulties, including atypical development of communication, language, and speech, the optimism of family members is critical to good outcomes; thus, professionals should try to be accurate, but sensitive, when choosing words to define problems with families, especially those of very young children.

Advocacy for Early Response to Concerns

The authors of this chapter support an inclusive definition of preschool-age children who should be eligible for consultative, if not direct, intervention from a specialist in communicative development and disorders. To receive such services in the contexts of their families or preschools, such children might not have to be burdened with the label of having a *disorder*. Under the 1997 Amendments to the Individuals with Disabilities Education Act, Part C (formerly Part H), states are given the responsibility to define developmental delay and the option to define what it means to be *at risk*. According to the statutory language in IDEA, "infant or toddler with a disability"

(A) means an individual under 3 years of age who needs early intervention services because the individual—

   (i) is experiencing developmental delays, as measured by appropriate diagnostic in-

TABLE 9.2 Definitions of Commonly Used Terms

TERM(S)	DEFINITION
Typical language development	Describes the condition in which a child's language is developing at an expected pace (see Table 9.3).
Late talker	Describes toddlers who: • are slow at producing first words (expected at 12 to 18 months). • are still producing few words (less than 50) and limited word combinations by 24 months. • show no other signs of developmental delays, such as cognitive, emotional, or sensory problems.
Specific language impairment—expressive (SLI-E) Slow expressive language development (SELD)	Describes young children with age-appropriate cognitive and receptive language skills whose "late talker" symptoms persist or are especially marked.
Specific language impairment	Describes children or adults who have age-appropriate (nonverbal) cognitive ability in combination with atypical expressive and receptive language development.
Language disorder Nonspecific language impairment Speech-language impairment Communication disorder	Describes children or adults with atypical language development, whether or not they have co-occurring special needs (e.g., cognitive, emotional, or sensory).

struments and procedures in one or more of the areas of cognitive development, physical development, communication development, social or emotional development, and adaptive development; or

(ii) has a diagnosed physical or mental condition which has a high probability of resulting in developmental delay; and

(B) may also include, at a State's discretion, at-risk infants and toddlers. [Sec. 632(5)]

The rationale for an inclusive definition is that those preschool children who demonstrate uneven patterns of language development, are atypical or slow in their acquisition of language skills, or have other conditions commonly associated with communicative difficulties should not be excluded from receiving intervention because of restrictive eligibility criterion based on a narrow definition of specific language impairment or SLI-E. Language disorders can (and often do) co-occur with such conditions as hearing impair-

ment, neurological impairment, speech-motor control impairment (apraxia or dysarthria), learning disabilities, mental retardation, emotional disturbance, and reading difficulties (Nelson, 1998). Atypical language development is an identifying characteristic of autism and other pervasive developmental disorders (Wetherby, Prizant, & Hutchinson, 1998).

Either over- or underidentification of children as speech-language impaired should be avoided. Cognitive (MA) referencing may underidentify children who need and can benefit from speech-language intervention services. CA referencing may overidentify children with language differences rather than disorders. It may also overidentify children with low cognitive abilities and commensurate language levels. The fact remains, however, that MA or CA referencing is often required by state policy for diagnosing disorder. It is up to the diagnostician to select language assessment tools and procedures that will provide the most accurate, unbiased picture of the language development of a particular child.

WHAT IS TYPICAL COMMUNICATIVE DEVELOPMENT?

The process of assessing young children is complex because the development of young children is complex. In order to decide "what to do next" when choosing appropriate assessment tools and procedures for a particular child, professionals must understand children's communicative developmental products and processes (Anstey & Bull, 1991). The following sections provide a brief review of developmental expectations for communication, speech, and language, first at the toddler level of emerging language and then at the preschool level of developing language. These expectations are summarized in Table 9.3.

Toddler Level: The Stage of Emerging Language

The range of speech-language and communication skills that can be considered "normal" for very young children is relatively large. However, research has helped to identify some language skills that mark typical development in early childhood.

The presence of a preverbal system of communicative gestures and vocalizations is an important precursor of language development. Frequency of use is important too. By 18 months of age, most children express an average of two communicative acts per minute. These include intentional use of vocalizations, verbalizations, gestures, or gesture sequences. By 24 months, children typically produce an average of five communicative acts per minute. These consist primarily of words and word combinations, accompanied by some nonverbal acts (Paul & Shiffer, 1991; Wetherby, Cain, Yonclas, & Walker, 1988).

Comprehension of a first word usually occurs about three months ahead of the production of a first word. Comprehension of 50 different words usually occurs about five months before the productive lexicon reaches this size (Benedict, 1979). Most 18- to 24-month-old children probably comprehend only two or three words out of each sentence they hear (Chapman, 1978). They depend on nonverbal and contextual cues to help them respond appropriately to longer utterances.

The age of acquisition of first words is 12 to 18 months. This well-known developmental milestone is important, but the rate of acquisition of additional words is also meaningful. At 18 months, 84 percent of children produce a wide variety of words; by 24 months, more than 150 words; and by 30 months, more than 450 words (Stoel-Gammon, 1991). As Table 9.3 indicates, this ex-

plosion includes words that represent a variety of semantic categories, for example, not only agents and actions but also words to signify recurrence (e.g., *more*) and disappearance (e.g., *allgone*). Furthermore, such words are put to varied pragmatic uses, such as *more* + extending arm with cup to request more juice, and *more* + finger point to comment on more ducks in the park.

Focusing for a moment on speech, the words toddlers produce should also be clear enough that adults can understand them. By age 2 years, the "typical" child matches the consonant phonemes of adult words with at least 70 percent accuracy (Stoel-Gammon, 1987).

The transition from single-word production to two-word phrases occurs for most middle-class toddlers by 18 months of age. The mean length of utterance (MLU) at 24 months is between 1.5 and 2.4 morphemes (Miller, 1981). An MLU of 1.5 indicates an equal number of one- and two-word utterances. An MLU of 2.4 indicates that children are producing a high proportion of three-word utterances as well.

To summarize, by 24 months, the vast majority of children produce correct phonemes, communicate frequently, have large vocabularies, and combine words into sentences. However, assessment at this stage is still difficult because normal development varies considerably. Some children who are slow in early speech-language development do catch up. The question of "what to do next" is not easily answered when assessment reveals slow speech-language development for toddlers. The goal is to identify all and only those children who truly need intervention and who will not reach typical milestones without it.

Preschool Level: The Stage of Developing Language

Once a child begins to form three-word utterances, grammatical development takes off like a rocket in typically developing children. Communicative usage and speech production skills also advance at a remarkable pace, but the rapid acquisition of language rules is what has prompted many, including Chomsky (1968) and Pinker (1994), to attribute language learning to an innately programmed acquisition module or "instinct."

The growing sophistication of language form during the preschool years allows children to produce and comprehend a wide variety of sentence structures (outlined in Table 9.3). Previous developmental specialists, in fact, claimed that language acquisition was nearly complete by age 5. Language specialists now know that that claim is exaggerated because it fails to take into

TABLE 9.3 Development Expectations from 12 Months to 7 Years

AGE RANGE	RECEPTIVE LANGUAGE	EXPRESSIVE LANGUAGE	SOCIAL PLAY AND INTERACTION

12 to 18 months	**Comprehension**
	__ Understands one word in some sentences when referents are present
	__ Points to objects in response to "Show me—" (e.g. body parts)
	__ Follows simple one step commands
	
	Nonverbal comprehension strategies
	__ Attends to object mentioned
	__ Gives evidence of notice
	__ Does what is usually done in a situation
		Transition to first words
		__ Gestures accompany vocalization or word
		  __ Hi/bye routines common
		  __ Request object or attention
		  __ Communicates immediate needs by pulling or pointing
		  __ Makes comments
		  __ Labels
		  __ Indicates personal feelings
		__ First words represent varied semantic content (recurrence, existence, nonexistence, rejection, denial, agent, object, action or state, location)
			__ Reacts to emotions of others
			__ Prefers solitary or onlooker play with peers
			__ Scribbles spontaneously with crayon
			__ Points to objects he or she wants and claims certain objects as own
			__ Acts out single pretend actions (sweeping, hair combing, hugging doll, pulling toy, eating, sleeping, drinking from a cup, using phone)
			__ Attention shifts frequently
			__ Completes 3 or more consecutive communicative exchanges about varied intentions (protest, comfort, notice)

18 to 24 months	**Comprehension** __ Understands words when referent is not present __ Understands action verbs out of routine context __ Carries out two-word commands but often fails to understand three lexical elements __ Understands routine forms of questions for agent, object, locative, and action **Nonverbal comprehension strategies** __ Locates the objects mentioned __ Gives evidence of notice __ Does what is usually done: objects into containers, conventional use __ Acts on the objects in the way mentioned __ Acts as agent of action (When told, "Show me 'Bear kisses kitty,'" child kisses kitty)	**Transition to two-word combinations** **12–26 mos Brown's stage I MLU 1.5** *New semantic roles* __ Early: action–object relations, agent, action, object, recurrence, disappearance __ Later: object–object relations, location, possession, nonexistence *Other new developments* __ Asks "What's that?" questions __ Answers some routine questions __ Acquires vocabulary rapidly __ Produces successive one-word utterances __ Talks more frequently __ Refers to people or objects not present	__ Engages in parallel play (early play is near others but not with them) __ Talks to self while playing __ Combines two actions or toys in pretend (rocking doll and putting to bed, feeding doll with spoon) __ Relates action to object or another person (washes, feeds doll in addition to self) __ Demonstrates pleasure in make-believe games (two sticks to represent "airplane") __ Initiates and completes 10 or more consecutive communicative exchanges as part of dealing with emotional issues

(continued)

TABLE 9.3   Continued

AGE RANGE	RECEPTIVE LANGUAGE	EXPRESSIVE LANGUAGE	SOCIAL PLAY AND INTERACTION
2 to 2½ years	**Comprehension** Understands and responds to: —What for object __ What-do for action __ Where for location (place) __ Concepts of one/all **Comprehension strategies** __ In response to yes/no questions, accepts or rejects, confirms or denies __ Does what is usually done with object — Uses probable location strategy for in, on, under, beside (when told "Put the ball under the box," puts ball in box) — Uses probable event strategy for simple active reversible sentences (when told "Show me, 'The wagon pushes the boy,'" acts out the boy pushes the wagon) __ Supplies missing information to wh-questions *Other new developments* __ Has complex sequenced routines for daily activities (bedtime, meals)	**Expressive Language** **2 yrs Brown's stage I** **MLU 1.75** Basic semantic relations __ Agent–action __ Action–object __ Agent–object __ Possessive __ Entity–locative __ Action–locative __ Existence __ Recurrence __ Nonexistence __ Rejection __ Denial __ Attributive **2 yrs Brown's stage II** **MLU 2.25** *Grammatical inflections* __ Some articles, plurals, possessives __ -ing on verbs __ In/on __ Some memorized contractions (don't, can't, it's, that's) __ What doing? questions **2½ yrs Brown's stage III** **MLU 2.75** *Differentiation of sentences* __ Modalities __ Possession __ Number (noun plural) *Question formation* __ Asks simple wh-questions (What's that?) __ Asks simple yes/no questions (Is he sleeping?)	**Social Play and Interaction** __ Parallel play predominates (24 mos) __ Begins elaborated pretend schemas (24 mos) (e.g., puts lids on pan, puts pan on stove, turns on stove; collects items associated with cooking/eating) __ Begins dramatization, imagination, and symbolic play (make-believe and pretend) __ Takes turns __ Watches cartoons on TV __ Listens to short story — Begins to engage in cooperative play (small group play) __ Imitates drawing of lines, circles
3 to 3½ years	**Lexical Comprehension** — Whose for possessor — Who for person — Why for cause or reason — How many for number	**Expressive Language** **3 yrs Brown's stage IV** **MLU 3.50** __ Sentence embedding __ Immediate future (gonna) __ Regular past –ed	**Social Play and Interaction** __ Uses doll as participant in play, talks for doll __ Organizes doll furniture accurately and plays imaginatively

AGE RANGE	RECEPTIVE LANGUAGE	EXPRESSIVE LANGUAGE	SOCIAL PLAY AND INTERACTION
3 to 3½ years (cont)	**Lexical Comprehension (continued)** — Understanding of gender contrasts in third person pronouns __ Understanding of hard/soft, rough/smooth **Comprehension strategies** — Supplies explanation for why and how questions __ Infers most probable speech act in context *Spatial prepositions* __ In __ In front of __ Beside __ Next to __ On __ Over __ Out __ Under	**Expressive Language (continued)** __ Inflects verb be (am, was, are) __ Articles (a, the) **3½ yrs Brown's stage V MLU 3.75** —Sentence conjoining —Regular past –ed __ Future aspect forms (gonna) __ Third person singular __ Irregular (does, has) __ Copula "be" __ Auxiliary "be" *Other new developments* __ Projects thoughts and feelings onto others __ Changes speech depending on listener __ Metalinguistic and metacognitive language (e.g., "I know," "He said") __ Descriptive vocabulary	**Social Play and Interaction (continued)** __ Builds bridge from model __ Begins associative group play (3½ yrs) __ Uses one object to represent another (e.g., a stick for a comb) __ Acts out observed events __ Conveys 2 or more logically connected emotional ideas with words or unverbally
4 to 4½ years	**Comprehension** Understands and responds to: __ How much __ How long (duration) __ How far __ How often __ When **Comprehension strategies** __ Comprehension of word order as cues to understand agent-object in active sentences (word order strategy) *Spatial prepositions* __ On top __ Between	**Expressive Language** **4 yrs. Brown's stage V+ MLU 4.5+** Modals (can, may, might, will, would, could) *Event relations (sequence of emergence)* — And (coordinate and temporal) — Because, so (causal) — Why, what for (causal) — But (contrastive) — When (conditional) *Some immature forms remain* — Noninversion of aux/modal (Where daddy is?) — Aux/modal + aux modal (How can he can look? Is that's a rocket?)	**Social Play and Interaction** __ Increased dramatization in play __ Narrates and tells stories __ Uses language to invent props and scenes __ Suggests turns but often bossy __ Plays in group of 2 to 3 children __ Child or doll has multiple roles (mother, secretary) (3½–4 years) __ Shows off __ Friendships stronger

(continued)

TABLE 9.3 Continued

AGE RANGE	RECEPTIVE LANGUAGE	EXPRESSIVE LANGUAGE	SOCIAL PLAY AND INTERACTION
4 to 4½ years (cont)	*Other new developments* __ Responds to two stage action commands __ Understands concept of numbers	— Continued use of double negation; some problems in the truth value of negatives — Continued regularization of irregular forms	
5 to 7 years	***Comprehension*** __ "What happens if_" questions *Spatial prepositions/lexical items* __ Behind __ Below __ Above (6;6) __ Opposites __ Yesterday/tomorrow __ More/less __ Some/many __ Most/least __ Before/after __ Across *Other new developments* __ Understands and differentiates coins, numbers __ Knows right from left __ Understands seasons of the year, what to do in each, and days of the week __ Can classify and shift classifications (sort by shape, then sort by color)	***Syntactic Rule Emergence from 4 to 6 years*** *Phrase development* __ Adjectives __ Possessives __ Compound nouns *Event relations (sequence of emergence)* — While (simultaneity) — After — Before __ Then __ Next __ Last — Past time (-ed) — Possibility (might) ***Syntactic Rule Emergence from 6 to 7 Years*** — Passive (The boy was hit by the girl) — If…then (If it rains, we won't go) — S/V agreement (He likes candy) — Inversion of aux/modal + main V (When's going to be the party?) *Other new developments* __ Can state differences and similarities in objects __ Recites alphabet, numbers, days of week, seasons __ Is aware of mistakes in others' speech __ Apt to use slang	***Social Play and Interaction*** __ Combines known schemas with novel schemas invented by the child (age 5) __ Plans and organizes objects and children for pretend play __ Able to play games by rules (by age 6) __ Spends hours at one activity __ Demands more realism in play (age 7) __ Dramatizes experiences and stories __ Uses language totally to set scenes, actions, roles

AGE RANGE	RECEPTIVE LANGUAGE	EXPRESSIVE LANGUAGE	SOCIAL PLAY AND INTERACTION
5 to 7 years (cont)		*Syntactic Rule Emergence from 6 to 7 Years (continued)* Other new developments (cont) __ Pronouns used consistently __ If…so developed __ Superlatives (biggest) used	

account the complexities of abstract and academic language usage. Development of grammatical knowledge during the preschool years is nevertheless astounding. Knowledge of syntax is what allows individuals to formulate and comprehend an infinite variety of sentences to communicate intricate descriptions; convey complex logical, temporal, or causative relationships; or to perform many other complex communicative functions.

Before children learn to comprehend the various syntactic forms of their language, they employ a number of other cognitive and nonlinguistic strategies to respond to commands and requests (Edmonston & Thane, 1992). For example, English-speaking children rely on canonical word order to identify the subject in passive sentences at age 4. Thus, when asked to use stuffed animals to show "The pig is kissed by the dog," 4-year-olds are likely to have the pig do the kissing, although they would not make this mistake for nonreversible passives such as "The present was opened by the boy." By age 5, most children can use syntactic strategies to comprehend passives, even when canonical order is violated, as in "The mother was fed by the baby." Other transitions from nonlinguistic to linguistic comprehension strategies are summarized in Table 9.3.

During the preschool years, children also begin to vary their language use to be appropriate in different conversational contexts. The typically developing child, for example, explores "the options for getting and constructing his turns at talk and for exploiting the conversational subsystems in negotiating his power and solidarity" (Dore, 1986, p. 36). Typically developing children also can make a balanced number of assertive and responsive conversational moves (Fey, 1986). Compared with their abilities between 2 to 4 years of age, children in the age range from 4 to 8 become more capable of: (1) getting attention specifically and effectively,

(2) taking into account the listener's prior knowledge, (3) being sensitive to the effects of interruption and formulating polite indirect requests, (4) supplying reasons when attempting to persuade peers to comply with requests, and (5) using obligation, justification, or bribery, in addition to urgency when their requests are not met (Ervin-Tripp & Gordon, 1986).

Word knowledge continues to develop from ages 2 to 7 years at a remarkable rate. The body of research suggests that children between 18 months and 6 years add an average of five word roots per day, allowing them to comprehend around 14,000 words by the time they are 6 (Crais, 1990). In fact, vocabulary acquisition is one aspect of language development that continues across the life span. As young as age 3 to 4 years, children can use contextual cues to "fast map" information about novel words into semantic memory with only one exposure (Carey & Bartlett, 1978). The fact that children can recognize new words as they encounter them provides additional evidence of an amazing auditory discrimination system that is tuned at birth to discriminate the sounds of speech (Eimas, 1975).

Speech production improvements also result in children's words becoming clearer and easier to understand during their preschool years. By age 7 years, most children produce all of the speech sounds of their language clearly and are able to blend them smoothly to produce clearly intelligible words and sentences with only minor disfluencies. Children who persist in substituting /w/ for /r/ or /l/, or who produce /s/ with the tongue between the teeth as a lisp may be identified as needing speech therapy, but not until the second or third grade unless other communicative symptoms justify the need.

To summarize, by the early elementary years, the majority of children can produce and understand most of the grammatical structures of their language, talk about a wide variety of concrete and abstract topics, and use diverse strategies for communicating appropriately in a variety of contexts. Their increased vocabulary, increased knowledge of syntax, and increased understanding of what adults want when they give commands to point to pictures or manipulate objects all contribute to increased demonstration of language comprehension. They tell stories, follow multiple-step directions, and participate in conversations. They also enjoy jokes, although the retelling may still leave something to be desired. This is because children at this age have not yet mastered dual word meanings and other metalinguistic skills necessary for appreciating the subtleties of linguistic humor. Children developing typically use phonological awareness skills to help them with the early stages of reading and writing, and they are able to understand the increasingly decontextualized language of school settings. Children who cannot demonstrate such abilities are at risk for social disvalue and academic failure. They need specialized intervention.

TECHNIQUES OF LANGUAGE ASSESSMENT

Formal or Informal?

Assessment procedures can be divided into two broad categories—formal and informal. Formal assessments use standardized tests that yield specifically defined information to be compared to normative data. Thus, the evaluator has control of the sequence of the assessment, the materials used, and the expected responses. Informal assessments are systematic observations of behaviors within meaningful, context-bound activities (e.g., conversations, dramatic play, storytelling, nonverbal interactions).

The term *informal* does not mean casual, however. In fact, Notari-Syverson and Losardo (1996) preferred the term *nonformal assessment* to represent the structure and purpose of the ongoing information collection process. If the purpose of assessment is screening or diagnostic assessment, formal, norm-referenced tests are often used. Traditional norm-referenced instruments, although commonly used, may not be as helpful as some informal methods for choosing "what to do next" regarding program decisions, curricular content, or intervention strategies (Darby, 1979; Garwood, 1982; Muma, 1978).

Formal Assessment Procedures. Formal instruments are often helpful for screening and developing a general picture. Some tools are specifically designed to assess speech, language, and communication; however, many screening tools focus more on general development. Some assessment instruments designed for assessing the

language of both toddlers and preschoolers are listed in Table 9.4. Many of these tools are designed for children starting at age 3 years. Others are intended for use with children ages 4 through 9 years.

Informal Assessment Procedures. Formal assessment procedures should be augmented by informal assessment strategies whenever a child is suspected of a delay in language development (Crais & Roberts, 1991). The question of "what to do next" is more easily answered when intervention is recommended if informal procedures have been conducted that reveal information about how a child learns best and specific forms, content, or functions that are not as developed as they should be. Because infants and toddlers are typically not required to have a specific diagnostic label to be eligible for intervention services, clinicians are more free to use informal procedures with younger children. Such strategies have the advantage of integrating assessment and intervention. For children at the prelinguistic or one-word stage, formal procedures may not offer broad enough samples of early language, speech, and communication to provide evidence that a need for intervention services exists. Broader views of communicative processes are needed (Nelson, 1998). A profile of communication and related abilities can be derived by using a set of informal assessment methods that can help identify specific intervention targets in nonverbal communication, expressive language, receptive language, and phonology (Paul, 1991).

Parent Report Measures

Parental report is commonly used in the earliest stages of development. Because parents have experience with their children throughout the full range of life experiences, "Parental report is likely to reflect what a child knows, whereas [a sample of] free speech reflects those forms that she is more likely to use" (Bates, Bretherton, & Snyder, 1988). According to Dale (1996), parent report is most likely to be accurate under three general conditions: (1) when assessment is limited to current behaviors, (2) when assessment is focused on emergent behaviors, and (3) when a primarily recognition format is used. Expressive vocabulary can be monitored by parents until about 2 years, six months (2-6) to 3 years, after which it becomes too large. It is better to ask parents to report on their child's vocabulary by selecting words from a comprehensive list rather than by having them generate a list from memory.

Tools for parent report include vocabulary checklists that parents use to indicate the receptive and

TABLE 9.4 Formal Tests to Assess Communication Skills of Toddlers and Preschoolers

TEST AUTHORS	AGE SPAN	DESCRIPTION	PUBLISHER
Ages and Stages Questionnaire (ASQ): A Parent Completed, Child-Monitoring System Bricker, D., Squires, J., Mounts, L., Potter, L., Nickel, R., & Farrell, J. 1997	4 months to 4 years	Identifies children who have developmental delays, or are at risk for developmental delays. Actively involves parents and family members in assessment, intervention, and evaluation.	Paul H. Brookes Baltimore, MD
Assessing Prelinguistic and Early Linguistic Behaviors in Developmentally Young Children Olswang, L. B., Stoel-Gammon, C., Coggins, T. E., & Carpenter, R. L. 1987	0 to 3 years	Includes five scales of cognitive antecedents to word meaning, play, communication intention, language comprehension, and language production. A training videotape is also available. Based on 3-year longitudinal study of prelinguistic and early linguistic behaviors of 37 normally developing children.	University of Washington Press Seattle, WA
Assessment of Children's Language Comprehension (ACLC) Foster, R., Giddan, J., & Stark, J. 1983	3 to 7 years	Establishes recognition of single-word vocabulary, then uses this vocabulary to test comprehension of 2-, 3-, and 4-word phrases (e.g., "Happy little girl jumping"), using picture-pointing task.	Consulting Psychologists Press Palo Alto, CA
Assessment of Phonological Processes—Revised (APP-R) Hodson, B. 1986	3 to 12 years	Can be administered in 15 to 20 minutes and scored in 30 minutes. Results in categorization of phonological processes that is useful for intervention planning.	Pro-Ed Austin, TX
Bankson Language Text (2nd ed.) (BLT-2) Bankson, N. W. 1990	3 to 8 years	In the revised version, test results may be reported as standard scores or percentile ranks. Assesses semantic knowledge, morphological/syntactic rules, and pragmatics. Standardized on 1,200 children in 19 states.	Pro-Ed Austin, TX
Bankson-Bernthal Test of Phonology (BBTOP) Bankson, N. W., & Bernthal, J. E. 1990	3 to 9 years	Assesses articulation and phonological processes.	Applied Symbolix Chicago, IL
Boehm Test of Basic Concepts—Preschool Version Boehm, A. 1986	3 to 5 years	The preschool version is individually administered to test comprehension of basic relational concepts.	The Psychological Corporation San Antonio, TX

(continued)

TABLE 9.4   Continued

TEST AUTHORS	AGE SPAN	DESCRIPTION	PUBLISHER
Bracken Basic Concept Scale—Revised (BBCS-R) Bracken, B. A. 1998	Preschool and primary age	Designed to be used with children with receptive language difficulties. Items require either short verbal responses or pointing. Yields percentile ranks, z-scores, and standard scores with a mean of 10 and standard deviation of 3 based on national norms.	The Psychological Corporation San Antonio, TX
Clinical Assessment of Language Comprehension Miller, J. F., & Paul, R. 1995	8 months to 10 years	Provides informal assessment tools for use with children who are very young or difficult to test. Designed to supplement formal measures. Response types include pointing, object manipulation, conversation, and behavioral compliance. Includes score sheets for use with procedures.	Paul H. Brookes Publishing Co. Baltimore, MD
Clinical Evaluation of Language Fundamentals—3rd ed. (CELF-3) Semel, E., Wiig, E., & Secord, W. 1995 CELF-Screening Test 1996 and CELF-Preschool Wiig, E. H., Secord, W., & Semel, E. 1992	6 to 22 years Preschoolers	CELF-preschool includes 6 diagnostic subtests for preschoolers. CELF-Screening Test yields criterion scores in 10 minutes. CELF-3 expressive subtests include Word Structure, Formulated Sentences, Sentence Assembly, Recalling Sentences, Word Associations, and Rapid, Automatic Naming. Receptive subtests include Sentence Structure, Concepts and Directions, Semantic Relationships, Word Classes, and Listening to Paragraphs.	The Psychological Corporation San Antonio, TX
Communication and Symbolic Behavior Scales (CSBS) [Norm-referenced ed.] Wetherby, A. M., & Prizant, B. M. 1991	9 months to 2 years	Uses a caregiver questionnaire, direct sampling of verbal and nonverbal communicative behaviors, and observation of relatively unstructured play activities. Scoring is based on a rating of 1 to 5 for each of 20 separate scales. Includes 16 communication scales (subdivided into 4 areas) and 4 scales for rating symbolic behavior (subdivided into 2 areas).	Applied Symbolix Chicago, IL
Comprehensive Receptive and Expressive Vocabulary Test (CREVT) Wallace, G., & Hammill, D. D. 1994	4 to 18 years	Assesses receptive and expressive oral vocabulary strengths and weaknesses. Identifies students significantly below their peers in oral abilities. Scores from this tests are correlated with scores from the TOLD:P-2, PPVT-R, EOWPVT-R, and the CELF.	Pro-Ed Austin, TX

TEST AUTHORS	AGE SPAN	DESCRIPTION	PUBLISHER
Denver Developmental Screening Test (DDST) Frankenburg, W. K., Dodds, J. B., & Fandal, A. W. 1969 (Manual revised, 1970) (Revised again in 1990; now called Denver II)	0 to 6 years	Designed to screen children from the general population in 4 areas, including language, who need further evaluation. Standardized on 1,036 Denver children. Items are marked as to when 25%, 50%, 75%, and 90% of the normative sample passed them.	University of Colorado Medical Center Denver, CO
Developmental Indicators for the Assessment of Learning—Revised (DIAL-R) Mardell-Czudnowski, C., & Goldenberg, D. S. 1990	2 to 6 years	A preschool and prekindergarten screening instrument that screens children in 3 developmental skill areas (motor, concepts, and language) in 20 to 30 minutes. Includes statistical data from three norming groups (1990 census, Caucasian, and minority.) Results can be compared with cutoff scores at +1, +1.5, or +2 SD.	AGS Circle Pines, MN
Early Language Milestone Scale (2nd ed.) (ELM Scale-2) Coplan, J. 1993	0 to 36 months	Designed to measure auditory expressive, auditory receptive, and visual skills. May be used in 1–10 minutes with older children whose development falls within this range. Can be scored as pass/fail or with a point system. Yields percentile and standard score equivalents.	Pro-Ed Austin, TX
Early Screening Profiles (ESP) Harrison, P., Kaufman, A., Kaufman, N., Bruininks, R., Rynders, J., Ilmer, S., Sparrow, S., & Cicchetti, D. 1990	2 to 7 years	Comprehensive screening instrument. Yields screening indexes or standard scores in 3 areas: cognitive/language, motor, and self-help social. Identifies at-risk or gifted children.	AGS Circle Pines, MN
ECO Scales MacDonald, J. D., & Gillette, Y. 1989	Infants and toddlers	Uses five separate scales to assess the areas of social play, turn taking, preverbal communication, language, and conversation. Takes 10 to 30 minutes.	Applied Symbolix Chicago, IL
Evaluating Acquired Skills in Communication (EASIC) (Revised) Riley, A. M. 1984	3 months to 8 years	Can be used with severely impaired clients to rate behaviors at the levels: prelanguage, receptive I (noun labels, action verbs, and basic concepts); expressive I (emerging modes of communication); receptive II (more complex language forms); and expressive II (using more complex communication). Criterion referenced.	Communication Skill Builders, The Psychological Corporation San Antonio, TX

(continued)

TABLE 9.4 Continued

TEST AUTHORS	AGE SPAN	DESCRIPTION	PUBLISHER
Expressive One Word Picture Vocabulary Test—Revised (EOWPVT-R) Gardner, M. 1990	2 to 12 years	Assesses expressive vocabulary in children (can be administered with ROWPVT).	Pro-Ed Austin, TX
Functional Emotional Assessment Scale for Infancy and Early Childhood (FEAS) Greenspan, S. I. 1992	0 to 48 months	Uses a free-play situation for observing children's abilities to attend and interact with parents and includes a rating scale for emotional development based on the levels of communication.	In *Infancy and Early Childhood*, International Universities Press, P.O. Box 524, Madison, CT 06643
Goldman-Fristoe Test of Articulation (GFTA) Goldman, R., & Fristoe, M. 1972, 1986	2 to 16+ years	Measures articulation of sounds-in-words, sounds-in-sentences, and stimulability. Yields percentile ranks for the sounds-in-words and stimulability subtests.	AGS Circle Pines, MN
Grammatical Analysis of Elicited Language (GAEL) Moog, J. S., & Geers, A. E. 1980	3 to 6 years normal-hearing children and 8 to 12 years hearing impaired	Manipulable toys are used to elicit and evaluate important elements of spoken and signed English in children. The assessment focuses on 16 grammatical structures.	Central Institute for the Deaf St. Louis, MO
Hawaii Early Learning Profile (HELP) Furuno, S., O'Reilly, K., Inatsuka, T., Hosaka, C., Allman, T., & Zeisloft-Falbey, C. 1979	0 to 3 years	Criterion-referenced charts are provided for 650 skills in the 6 areas of cognitive, language, gross motor, fine motor, social, and self-help. A sequenced checklist can be used to select objectives.	VORT Corporation Palo Alto, CA
Kaufman Survey of Early Academic and Language Skills (K-SEALS) Kaufman, A. S., & Kaufman, N. L. 1993	3-0 to 6-11 years	Nationally normed measure that assesses children's expressive and receptive language skills, preacademic skills, and articulation.	AGS Circle Pines, MN
MacArthur Communicative Development Inventories (CDI) Fenson, L., Dale, P. S., Resnick, J. S., Thal, D., Bates, E., Hartung, J. P., Pethick, S., & Reilly, J. S. 1993	1 to 3 years	Uses a parental checklist format to assess first signs of understanding, comprehension of early phrases, and starting to talk. Vocabulary checklist (for both understanding and saying) includes lists of words in categories. Early gestures, play, pretending, and imitating behaviors are also probed.	Singular Publishing Group San Diego, CA

TEST AUTHORS	AGE SPAN	DESCRIPTION	PUBLISHER
MacArthur Communicative Development Inventories (CDI) (Continued)		The Words and Sentences CDI probes sentences and grammar, including morphological endings and varied expressions of two-word meanings. Can be used with older children at early stages.	
Miller-Yoder Language Comprehension Test (MY) Miller, J. F., & Yoder, D. 1984 (Manual by G. Gill, M. Rosin, N. O. Owings, & K. A. Carlson).	4 to 8 years	Includes three sets of pictures to assess comprehension of short simple sentences with a variety of grammatical structures. Can be administered to normally developing, developmentally delayed, or mentally retarded children. Results allow comparison to performance of same-age peers.	Pro-Ed Austin, TX
Observation of Communicative Interactions (OCI) Klein, M. D., & Briggs, M. H. 1987	Infants	Designed specifically to measure caregiver responsivity to infant's communicative cues. Includes a continuum of 10 categories of responsiveness ranging from basic caregiving responses to more sophisticated efforts to facilitate language and conceptual development. It can also be used to guide intervention efforts.	Mother–Infant Communication Project, California State University Los Angeles, CA
Oral and Written Language Scales (OWLS) Carrow-Woolfolk, E. 1995, 1996	3 to 21 years	Offers a quick measure of receptive and expressive language through comprehensive examination of semantic, syntactic, pragmatic, and supralinguistic aspects of language.	AGS Circle Pines, MN
Oral-Motor/Feeding Rating Scale Jelm, J. M. 1990	All ages	Observational scale for combined assessment and intervention purposes. Summarizes oral-motor and feeding functioning in 8 areas: breast feeding, bottle feeding, spoon feeding, cup drinking, biting (soft cookie), biting (hard cookie), chewing, and straw drinking.	Communication Skill Builders, The Psychological Corporation San Antonio, TX
Parent–Infant Interaction Scale Clark, G. N., & Seifer, R. 1985	Infants	Areas addressed include caregiver interaction behaviors, caregiver and child social referencing, reciprocity, and caregiver affect.	Assessment of parents' interaction with their developmentally delayed infants. *Infant Mental Health Journal, 6* (4), 214–225.

(continued)

TABLE 9.4   Continued

TEST AUTHORS	AGE SPAN	DESCRIPTION	PUBLISHER
Peabody Picture Vocabulary Test (3rd ed.) (PPVT-III) Dunn, L. M., Dunn, L. M., & Williams, K. T. 1997	2 to 85+ years	A quick measure of receptive hearing vocabulary for Standard American English.	AGS Circle Pines, MN
Photo Articulation Test (3rd ed.) (PAT-3) Lippke, B. A., Dickey, S. E., Selmar, J. W., & Soder, A. L. 1997	3 to 9 years	Uses 72 color photographs to assess initial, medial, and final position articulation errors in children.	Pro-Ed Austin, TX
Preschool Language Assessment Instrument (PLAI) Blank, M., Rose, S., & Berlin, L. 1978	3 to 6 years	Not a standardized test but can be used to assess a variety of language skills; labeling objects and actions, role play, responding to conversational interactions, describing object functions, solving problems, defining, and performing other language skills related to academic success. Can be used with Spanish-speaking children.	The Psychological Corporation San Antonio, TX
Preschool Language Scale (3rd ed.) (PLS-3) Zimmerman, I. L., Steiner, V. G., & Pond, R. E. 1992	0 to 7 years	Takes 20 to 30 minutes and yields total language, auditory comprehension, and expressive communication standard scores, percentile ranks, and language-age equivalents. A Spanish-language version, has norms based on Spanish-speaking children throughout the United States.	The Psychological Corporation San Antonio, TX
Preverbal Assessment Intervention Profile (PAIP) Connard, P. 1984	All ages	Standardized Piagetian assessment of sensorimotor stages of prelinguistic behavior I to III. It can be used with individuals with severe, profound, and multiple disabilities.	Pro-Ed Austin, TX
Prueba del Desarrollo Inicial del Lenguaje (PDIL) Hresko, W. P., Reid, D. K., & Hammill, D. D. 1982	3 to 7 years	Standardized test of the Spanish spoken language for children. Includes 38 items used to assess receptive and expressive language through a variety of semantic and syntactic tasks.	Pro-Ed Austin, TX
The Receptive-Expressive Emergent Language Scale (2nd ed.) (REEL-2) Bzoch, K., & League, R. 1991	0 to 3 years	Designed to help public health nurses, pediatricians, and educators identify children who have specific language problems based on interview of significant others (usually a parent). Results are presented as expressive, receptive, and combined language ages.	Pro-Ed Austin, TX

TEST AUTHORS	AGE SPAN	DESCRIPTION	PUBLISHER
Receptive One Word Picture Vocabulary Test (ROW-PVT) Gardner, M. 1985	2 to 12 years	Assesses receptive vocabulary in children (can be administered with EOWPVT).	Pro-Ed Austin, TX
Reynell Developmental Language Scales Reynell, J. K. 1985	1 to 5 years	Uses observation, picture identification, object identification, and object manipulation to measure general receptive and expressive skills.	Webster Psychological Services Los Angeles, CA
Rhode Island Test of Language Structure (RITLS) Engen, E., & Engen, T. 1983	3 to 20 years	Primarily designed for use with children with hearing impairments but can also be used with other children, including those who have mental retardation or learning disabilities or who are bilingual. Emphasizes understanding of language structure.	Pro-Ed Austin, TX
The Rossetti Infant-Toddler Language Scale Rossetti, L. 1990	0 to 3 years	Criterion-referenced assessment scale. Covers multiple developmental areas: interaction and attachment, gestures, pragmatics, play, language comprehension, and language expression. Includes 3 to 7 items for each domain at each 3-month interval.	LinguiSystems East Moline, IL
Screening Kit of Language Development (SKOLD) Bliss, L. S., & Allen, D. V. 1983	2 to 5 years	Screening tests that can be administered to children in 15 minutes by paraprofessionals. Assesses preschool language development in 6 areas: vocabulary, comprehension, story completion, individual and paired sentence repetition without pictures, and comprehension of commands. Norm-referenced for both Black English- and Standard English-speaking children.	Slosson Educational Publications Aurora, NY
Screening Test for Developmental Apraxia of Speech (STDAS) Blakely, R. W. 1980	4 to 12 years	Assists in differential diagnosis of speech apraxia with 8 subtests: expressive language discrepancy, vowels and diphthongs, oral-motor movement, verbal sequencing, motorically complex words, articulation, transposition, and prosody.	Pro-Ed Austin, TX
Sequenced Inventory of Communication Development (2nd ed.) (SICD) Hedrick, D. L., Prather, E. M., & Tobin, A. R. 1984	4 months to 4 years	Includes receptive and expressive scales. Cuban-Spanish edition (by L. R. Rosenberg) available.	University of Washington Press Seattle, WA

(continued)

TABLE 9.4 Continued

TEST AUTHORS	AGE SPAN	DESCRIPTION	PUBLISHER
Smit-Hand Articulation and Phonology Evaluation (SHAPE) Smit, A. B. & Hand, L. 1997	3 to 9 years	Nationally norm-based measurement of speech sound acquisition. Uses photo cards of common objects to assess the production of initial and final consonants and initial two- and three-consonant blends; grouped by semantic categories.	Western Psychological Services Los Angeles, CA
Spanish Structured Photographic Expressive Language Test (Spanish SPELT-Preschool) (Spanish SPELT-II) Werner, E. O., & Kresheck, J. D. 1989	3 to 6 years (SSPELT-P) 4 to 10 years (SSPELT-II)	Uses snapshots to elicit early developing Spanish morphological and syntactic forms. It can be administered in 10 to 15 minutes. The manual addresses issues in assessing children with limited English proficiency and provides developmental guidelines for Spanish morphology and syntax.	Janelle Publications Sandwich, IL
Structured Photographic Expressive Language Test (SPELT-P) (SPELT-II) Werner, E. O., & Kresheck, J. D. 1983	3 to 6 years (SPELT-P) 4 to 10 years (SPELT-II)	Uses snapshots to elicit early developing morphological and syntactic forms. Can be administered in 10 to 15 minutes. Guidelines are provided for analyzing productions from speakers of Black English.	Janelle Publications Sandwich, IL
Test for Examining Expressive Morphology (TEEM) Shipley, K. G., Stone, T. A., & Sue, M. B. 1983	3 to 8 years	Evaluates use of expressive morphemes in 7 minutes. Assesses present progressives, plurals, possessives, past tenses, third-person singulars, and derived adjectives. Norms based on more than 500 children.	Communication Skill Builders Tucson, AZ
Test of Auditory Comprehension of Language—Revised (TACL-R) Carrow-Woolfolk, E. 1985	3 to 10 years	Assesses auditory comprehension of word classes and relations, grammatical morphemes, elaborated sentence constructions. Yields standard scores, percentile ranks, age equivalents. (A computerized scoring system is also available.)	Pro-Ed Austin, TX
Test of Awareness of Language Segments (TALS) Sawyer, D. J. 1987	4 to 7 years	A screening test. Includes 46 items distributed across 3 subtests: sentences-to-words, words-to syllables, and words-to sounds. Cutoff scores permit inferences about readiness for beginning reading programs and which types of introductory reading approach might be easier for a child.	Pro-Ed Austin, TX

TEST AUTHORS	AGE SPAN	DESCRIPTION	PUBLISHER
Test of Early Language Development (2nd ed.) (TELD-2) Hresko, W. P., Reid, D. K., & Hammill, D. D. 1991	2 to 8 years	Measures expressive and receptive language form and content. Includes expanded diagnostic profile, extended age range, and two alternative forms.	Pro-Ed Austin, TX
Test of Early Reading Ability—2 (TERA-2) Reid, D. K., Hresko, W. P., & Hammill, D. D. 1989	3 to 10 years	Measures reading abilities of children. Items measure knowledge of contextual meaning, alphabet, and conventions. Standard scores have a mean of 100 and standard deviation of 15.	Pro-Ed Austin, TX
Test of Early Written Language (TEWL) Hresko, W. P. 1988	3 to 8 years	Measures emerging written language. Standard scores and percentiles may be particularly helpful for identifying students with mild disabilities.	Pro-Ed Austin, TX
Transdisciplinary Play-Based Assessment (Rev. ed.) (TPBA) Linder, T. W. 1993	6 months to 6 years	Set of criterion-referenced informal assessment scales. A 1-hour to 1½-hour session of videotaped play interaction with facilitator, parent, and peer is observed and scored by multiple professionals in four domains: social-emotional, cognitive, language and communication, and sensorimotor. No standardized scores. Results in analysis of developmental level, learning style, interaction patterns, and other relevant behaviors, which can become an integral part of intervention planning.	Paul H. Brookes Baltimore, MD

expressive vocabularies of their infants and toddlers (Fenson et al., 1993; Rescorla, 1989; Rosetti, 1990). From a list of commonly used words, parents are asked to check those words their child uses or comprehends. Results of studies of concurrent validity of parent report instruments such as the MacArthur Communication Development Inventory (CDI) have been encouraging (Dale, 1996; Miller, Sedey, and Miolo, 1995). In addition to those instruments that focus only on language development, other instruments that attempt to evaluate a broad range of ability domains in addition to language include the Denver Developmental Screening Test (DDST) (Frankenburg, Dodds, & Fandal, 1969), the Child Development Inventory (Ireton, 1992), the Vineland Adaptive Behavior Scales (Sparrow, Balla, & Cicchetti, 1984), the Ages and Stages Questionnaires (ASQ) (Bricker, Squires, Mounts, Potter, Nickel, & Farrell, 1997), and the Assessment, Evaluation and Programming System (AEPS) (Bricker, 1993). Parent report tools save time and increase the ecological and sociocultural validity of procedures conducted with children's own toys and in natural contexts. The caution is that parents must understand this role and want to take a formal part in the assessment process (Crais, 1995).

Dynamic Assessment

Dynamic assessment is an interactive approach to the assessment process based on direct intervention. It yields predictive and prescriptive information (Lidz, 1991) that typically is limited in traditional, static testing. In static assessment, the role of the examiner is that of neutral observer and recorder; the child is viewed as a passive respondent (Meyers, 1987). An assumption of static assessment is that variation in performance represents variation in ability (McCauley & Swisher, 1984b).

In contrast to static assessment, dynamic assessment is an interactive process that deliberately fosters change and assesses ability based on how easy it is to facilitate change. Based on a view that language learning is primarily a socially mediated process, dynamic language assessment involves structured observation of language learning during mediation. The process of inducing change and then measuring it is the core of dynamic assessment (Pena, 1996). According to Lidz (1991), dynamic assessment should (1) profile the learner's abilities or performance strengths and identify weak processing areas; (2) document the learner's modifiability; (3) induce active, self-regulated learning; and (4) point to recommendations for interventions that will benefit performance.

Language Sampling Techniques

The spontaneous language sample affords the richest opportunity to observe a preschool child's integrated communicative, speech, and language skills within relatively naturalistic communicative interactions. The language sampling process can be used to answer the question of "what to do next" at the time of diagnosis, baseline assessment, or progress reporting (Fey, 1986; Miller, 1981; Roberts & Crais, 1989).

Language sampling procedures are implemented in several stages. Most clinicians start by gathering a sample themselves or tape-recording the child interacting with a peer or parent. They transcribe the sample as soon as possible to accurately reflect the child's utterances. Next, many perform a general analysis of language form, content, and use. Analysis results provide evidence of features most in need of intervention, either because they should have developed earlier or should be appearing more frequently. (Table 9.3 can assist in defining expectations.) Later, it may be possible to conduct a more focused analysis of particular features that have been targeted in intervention. For example, the clinician might count the number of times a child initiates or completes a communicative turn within a specified time frame directly from the audiotape or videotape. These data can then be compared with baseline data to document progress and to decide "what to do next."

When gathering the sample, the context must be considered. With all children, but especially with younger children or with children from cultures different than the examiner's, sampling in a familiar context is more likely to provide better verbal interaction. In addition, for many children physical aspects of the setting (e.g., the temperature, lights, ambient noise, number of persons present, color and detail of the room) can affect the success of all aspects of assessment but especially the representativeness of the language sample.

No standard language sampling procedure has been proven to be most effective for all children. Some children respond to specific toys, games, or storytelling with zest and enthusiastic verbalizations, whereas others, depending on their culture or past experiences, find the same objects or activities frightening, uninteresting, or overstimulating. For those children who have experienced abuse or unpleasantness in their lives, the sight of some objects may cause them to withdraw. One preschool girl put her head down on the table and refused to speak again in the session when a family of dolls was brought into the assessment. Her mother later reported that the dolls were similar to the ones used by the psychologist when the child first described being sexually abused. It is important to remember that a child's apparent communicative skill or lack of skill may be directly related to the time, context, tools, and strategies of the language sampling experience.

A child must experience a sense of warmth from an adult, and feel calm and connected, to achieve the full engagement, shared attention, and verbal exchanges necessary for the gathering of a good language sample. First, the adult must physically get down to the child's eye level—for a preschooler that is likely on the floor—and follow the child's lead playing or exploring the environment. Adults should try to capture the child's emotional tone as well (Greenspan, 1992). A child who feels understood and connected is more likely to stay engaged and to demonstrate his or her communicative abilities. In an assessment process, time constraints may tempt adults to try to get the child to match their own pace and emotional tone for expedient test results. This temptation must be avoided so as not to compromise the language sampling process.

Direct questioning, especially yes and no questions, should be avoided unless questions occur naturally in play such as, "I'm afraid Pooh Bear was hurt in the crash. What do you think we should do?" Small figures of people, animals, or television and storybook characters often provide children with ideas for representational play and rich language interaction. Such objects can be springboards for narrative discourse and interactive play, as can wordless picture books. Stockman (1996) used race cars and interactions with books to gather language samples from African American preschool children. Computerized or motorized toys and other manipulative materials (e.g., play dough, art supplies) may not be optimal for eliciting good language interaction because children, especially those with motor or language impairments, may become so involved in manipulating the objects that they cease talking. Although materials are important in gathering a rich language sample, they provide only the props for shared attention and interaction. It is the adult's ability to provide a warm, responsive context that is the key to eliciting optimal two-way communication exchanges.

CONTEXTS OF LANGUAGE ASSESSMENT

Assessments are most valid when they are comprehensive and based on multiple methods of data gathering, including observations of communicative interactions in multiple contexts with more than one partner (Crais, 1995; Westby et al., 1996). Assessing and intervening across contexts calls for a comprehensive plan that uses multiple methods and sources across multiple contexts. To be effective, contextualized assessments involve collaboration among disciplines and with the family (Neisworth & Bagnato, 1988; Silliman & Wilkinson, 1991; Thomas, 1993). The frequency, diversity, and even the mode with which communicative intents are expressed may vary considerably depending on the context (Coggins, 1991). To be representative, children's language and communication abilities across settings must be sampled. The context of the assessment is a key variable.

Family-Sensitive Assessment

Traditionally, assessment has focused on the appropriate use of specific tools and procedures. Yet, the most important aspect of the assessment process is communication—the sharing of meaning—between the child and the examiner and the family members and the examiner. When clinicians and families bring different world views, expectations, values, and behaviors to the assessment process, the complexity of the process increases (Anderson & Goldberg, 1991; Barrera, 1996; Lynch & Hanson, 1992). Although ethnic and racial affiliations are often considered to be primary markers of diversity, even members within identified groups may differ widely in their perceptions, values, and behaviors. Barrera (1996) clarified the need for a balanced perspective:

To view a child's individuality without considering his or her group affiliation is to deny the reality of culture. On the other hand, to see only group membership is to deny the rich variability among human beings, that is, to stereotype. Socioculturally competent assessment requires the integration of both perspectives. (p. 72)

Cultures often have diverse linguistic backgrounds that influence children's responses to specific assessment strategies and techniques. For example, native Hawaiian children may understand written texts better when read in the "talk story" conversational format often used in their homes than in a turn-taking reading group (Au & Mason, 1981). African American children may be more likely to tell topic associative narratives than narratives using traditional European-influenced structures (Hester, 1996).

Socioculturally competent assessment of the communication, speech, and language of young children would include an understanding by professionals of some key dimensions of the sociocultural context of the family. This often may only be accessed through a culture-language mediator (i.e., someone who is familiar with both the environment of the child and family and the assessment environment) (Barrera, 1996), or an "auxiliary examiner." For many families from cultures that are unfamiliar to the examiner, especially when a different language is spoken, a culture-language mediator can be indispensable, not only to interpret the families' messages to the professionals but also to interpret the assessment situation to the families. For children who are bilingual, it is critical that information about their knowledge of languages other than English be gathered so that the assessment of language development is not compromised through the second-language learning process. Barrera (1993) found that children with disabilities responded differently when their non-English home language was introduced into the intervention setting. Assessment can likely also be enhanced with such modifications.

Families of young children, even those of mainstream culture, often dread the assessment process in spite of their awareness that something is "not right" with their children. They fear being judged in the process, and they fear that the diagnosis will have long-standing negative implications for their child. Sometimes parents carry with them unpleasant memories from their own school years related to the terms *special education* or *special needs,* and they worry that entering into the assessment process will place them into a bureaucratic maze of powerlessness. Some have heard stories of professionally insensitive treatment from other parents of children who have received special services. Unfortunately, the assessment process can be unpleasant for many parents. Janice Fialka's poem (1997) in Box 9.1 illustrates her response to the assessment process of her son.

Professionals must remember that their words are powerful. Nonverbal behavior sends equally powerful messages to parents. Variations in posture, smiles, gestures, and openness to listening can facilitate or impede the relationship-building process critical to accurate data collection. One mother said:

> I just knew when I met the woman who tested my preschool child that I would not go back there. She was just not tuned in to me. She was focused on her own agenda of what she thought was wrong with my child's communication. She asked questions I did not think were important, didn't ask what I thought was important, and when she finally smiled, it just didn't seem genuine.

Box 9.1

Advice to Professional Who Must Conference Cases

JANICE FIALKA, PARENT, MSW, ACSW

Before the case conference.
  I would look at my almost five-year-old son
  And see a golden hair boy
  Who giggled at his new baby sister's attempts to
    clap her hands.
  Who charmed adults by his spontaneous hugs and
    hello's.
  Who captured his parents with his rapture with
    music and
  his care for white-haired people who walked a
    walk
  a bit slower than younger folks.
  Who often became a legend in places visited be-
    cause of his
  exquisite ability to befriend a few special souls.
  Who often wanted to play "peace marches."
  And who, at the age of four
  went to the Detroit Public Library
  requesting a book on Martin Luther King.

After the case conference.
  I looked at my almost five-year-old son.
  He seemed to have lost his golden hair.
  I saw only words plastered on his face.
  Words that drowned us in fear and revolting nausea.
  Words like:
  Primary expressive speech and language disorder
  severe visual motor dysfunction
  sensory integration dysfunction
  fine and gross motor delay
  developmental dyspraxia and RITALIN now.

I want my son back. That's all.
  I want him back now. Then I'll get on with my life.
  If you could see the depth of this wrenching pair.
  If you could see the depth of our sadness
  then you would be moved to return
  our almost five-year-old son
  who sparkles in the sunlight despite his faulty
    neurons.

Please give me back my son
  undamaged and untouched by your label, test
    results,
  descriptions and categories.
  If you can't, if you truly cannot give us back our son
  Then just be with us quietly,
  gently and compassionately as we feel.
  Just sit patiently and attentively as we grieve and
    feel powerless.
  Sit with us and create a stillness
  known only in small, empty chapels at sundown.
  Be there with us
  As our witness and as our friend.

Please do not give us advice, suggestions, compari-
  sons or another appointment. (That's for later.)
  We want only a quiet shoulder upon which to rest
    our too-heavy heads.
  If you can't give us back our sweet dream
  then comfort us through this nightmare.
  Hold us. Rock us until morning light creeps in.
  Then we will rise and begin the work of a new day.

Reprinted by permission of the author. Janice Fialka, MSW, ACSW is a national speaker and mother of two children, Micah (who has developmental disabilities) and Emma. This poem is published in a collection of her writings called "It Matters: Lessons from My Son." To obtain a copy or to receive information about her speaking engagements on parent–professional partnerships, contact her at 10474 LaSalle Boulevard, Huntington Woods, Michigan 48070 or by e-mail: ruaw@aol.com.

Although the mother complained about the examiner's lack of warmth, the key to this mother's dissatisfaction was that she perceived that her concerns were not important to the examiner. Parents are the experts on their children, and good examiners will tap into that expertise at every stage of the assessment process.

Assessment of a child at this stage of development often is initiated because of a parent's uneasy feelings about the child's communication compared to other children. Pediatricians may be the first to be consulted by the parent regarding the development of a child's speech and language. A recent trend is for pediatricians to refer late-talking children to speech-language pathologists earlier, but some still hold a "wait and see" attitude for preschool children. Parents often report that they count with worry the days until the child reaches the age, usually 3 or 4 years, at which point the pediatrician will refer them to a speech-language pathologist for an assessment. Because parents often know that something is amiss with their child's development early on, they frequently express anger at themselves and their pediatrician when they delay assessment and the implementation of intervention.

Prior to assessment, concerned parents of children with delayed speech and language development have, consciously or unconsciously, already begun to think about "what to do next." What they do intuitively, however, may not be optimal for facilitating the development of communication skills. Evidence suggests that parents tend to become more directive and less semantically contingent when their children experience difficulty learning to talk (Cross, 1984; Lasky & Klopp, 1982). In their efforts to do something, some parents may develop an interrogative style of interacting with their children, whereas others may rarely ask questions (Cross, 1984). In either case, the naturally rewarding back-and-forth circles of communication between parent and child that foster the development of good speech and language skills are compromised. This is not to blame parents for their child's speech and language delays. Parents seem to alter their communicative style in response to a child's delays and vice versa (Cross, 1984; Leonard, 1987) in circular patterns of cause and effect. Many parents fear, however, that they are at some level responsible for their child's delays in development. Thus, an important component of the assessment process can be to reassure concerned parents that their communication style did not cause the child's disorder, but that together, the professional and the parent will look for ways to optimize communicative interactions to benefit the child's language development.

Home Assessment

Home assessment offers a practical solution for assessing children in the context of families when transportation or other physical difficulties make access to center-based facilities difficult. Home-based assessment is recommended by Bailey and Simeonsson (1988) because in the home parents are likely to assume the role of primary interventionists for their children. The interaction between parent and child, which should be the cornerstone of every assessment with young children, may be more readily observed and assessed in the home. Professionals are likely to find that such assessments reveal samples of communication that are more typical than in clinical settings, and that family concerns are more clearly illustrated. In addition, recommendations resulting from home assessments are likely to be relevant to the daily lives of families.

Some disadvantages are also associated with home-based assessment services. Some parents may not wish to participate in the assessment activities (Crais, 1995), and some homes do not provide access to a wide range of toys or to specialized tools or equipment (Bailey & Simeonsson, 1988). In addition, many families express concern about housekeeping issues, and there may be insufficient space to allow simultaneous observation by multiple professionals.

Center- or Clinic-Based Assessment

Advantages of center-based assessments include the availability of multiple professionals and opportunities for peer interaction (Bailey & Simeonsson, 1988). In some centers, children can receive medical examinations and a hearing evaluation, as well as integrated evaluations from multiple professionals, such as educators, physical therapists, occupational therapists, social workers, speech-language pathologists, and psychologists. Parents who bring their child to a center may become educated about helpful programs and find the center to be a supportive environment for them as they attend to their child's developmental needs. Centers also may provide opportunities for observing peer interactions, and these may be critical for helping professionals and parents design the best intervention program for meeting a particular child's communicative development and social interaction needs. Transportation to an assessment center may pose a barrier for some families, but agencies responsible for implementing IDEA must help parents and guardians overcome these barriers.

Team Assessment

Regardless of setting, children cannot be adequately assessed and treated in isolation. They are members of whole systems, and it is their own cultural, family, and educational systems that will support the child's ongoing development. Families provide the system that serves a child's primary needs and, therefore, act as the cornerstone of the assessment process. Thus, parents should be integral members of any assessment team. In addition, members from several professional disciplines may be needed to provide assessment services for families with young children.

Child care providers often are also important contributors to the assessment process. In some cases, parents or guardians are not aware of communicative delays, and the first person to become aware of them may be the child care provider or the preschool teacher. This person may provide important insights about a child's variation from typical communicative expectations for interacting with peers and unfamiliar adults in settings outside the home.

Team organization for assessment takes three typical forms—multidisciplinary, interdisciplinary, or transdisciplinary. In multidisciplinary assessment, each professional carries out a relatively independent assessment and reports findings separately. An interdisciplinary assessment team may be guided by a case manager, but its members come together at the end of the assessment process to discuss findings with the family and plan "what to do next" jointly.

Transdisciplinary assessment is unique in that members of several disciplines collaborate in a single set of evaluation activities, during which they teach each other about their disciplines and release aspects of their roles to each other. Typically, the child interacts with just one adult who performs some formal and informal assessment tasks. The other members of the team may observe the examiner's interactions with the child. They provide information and recommendations for assessment to the examiner and use the information collected by the examiner. This approach, which is sometimes call arena assessment (Linder, 1993), is useful for those children who may have difficulty interacting with more than one unfamiliar adult (Paul, 1995). More collaboration tends to occur among professionals and families in transdisciplinary assessment, and decisions are made though consensus (Notari-Syverson & Losardo, 1996). On the other hand, if surrounded by a group of visible adults, the child may be just as intimidated as if seeing them all in a series of separate appointments. Also, if the lack of face-to-face interaction compromises the assessment, speech-language pathologists and other professionals may find it necessary to conduct more specific assessments separately over time.

Play-Based Assessment

During the early stage of development, observable play behaviors tend to co-occur with relatively predictable communicative developments. The development of these play abilities and language skills seems to occur in parallel fashion and, thus, may reinforce or complement each other (Paul, 1995). So, for children in the early stages of language development, particularly those between 18 and 36 months of age, an assessment of play can provide another means to compare nonlinguistic and linguistic development. It can also lead to a better understanding of how to reach the child for assessment and intervention of communicative skills. Several relatively formal tools have been designed for assessing the play skills of young children. Table 9.3 includes a listing of markers of typical development of play, as well as of related expressive and receptive communicative abilities.

One relatively formal tool, Transdisciplinary Play-Based Assessment (Linder, 1993), uses a play interaction context to provide opportunity for developmental observations in four domains: (1) social-emotional, (2) cognitive, (3) language and communication, and (4) sensorimotor. It uses a transdisciplinary format with a single play facilitator and a group of observing professionals. The outcome is a criterion-referenced analysis of developmental level, learning style, interactions patterns, and other behaviors relevant to intervention planning. The "what to do next" question is answered with a set of recommendations for intervention designed to fit the child's current set of performance.

Another tool, the Communication and Symbolic Behaviors Scales (CSBS; Wetherby & Prizant, 1993), uses direct sampling of interactive verbal and nonverbal play behaviors, a caregiver questionnaire, and observation of relatively unstructured play activities. It is designed for children whose functional communication ages are between 9 months and 2 years. The CSBS includes normative data and uses communicative temptations, such as wind-up toys, balloons, and bubbles, to encourage the child to communicate. Four areas—communicative function, communicative means, reciprocity, and social affective signaling—are each rated on scales of 1 to 5; four scales are also included for rating symbolic behavior.

Carpenter's (1987) Play Scale was designed to assess symbolic behavior among nonverbal children, whose parents are asked to engage them in four play scenes. The parents are directed to respond to their child in a natural way, to follow the child's lead, and to be a quiet, nondirective partner for eight minutes with each set of toys. Norm-referenced data are provided for comparison.

In another detailed method of analyzing play behavior (McCune, 1995), the child is given a standard set of toys (e.g., cars, telephone, dolls, tea set, foods) and is invited to play with a familiar adult. A hierarchy of behaviors reveals the current and emerging levels of symbolic play that can be used to assist in planning intervention.

ASSESSING THE EMERGING LANGUAGE OF TODDLERS

Whenever a child's communicative development is in question, a thorough audiometric examination is warranted. The language assessment should also involve multiple opportunities to observe both receptive and expressive language abilities. Wetherby, Yonclas, and Bryan (1989) recommended using information from four categories: (1) communicative functions, (2) discourse structure, (3) communicative means, and (4) syllabic shape. Wetherby and her colleagues suggested that the prognosis for children might be worse if more parameters are atypical or if particular parameters are significantly different than expected. For example, the ability to establish joint attention may be more important than correct articulation.

Assessing Caregiver–Child Interactions: The Discourse of Emergent Language

Assessment of the range of communicative functions, frequency of communication, and diversity of forms can be coded and charted for evaluating the child's communication across time and in varied contexts, always including observations of the caregiver and child interaction. Some informal assessment tools for communicative development for infants and toddlers have been devised specifically to look at the interactions between caregivers and children.

The scale for Observation of Communicative Interactions (OCI; Klein & Briggs, 1987) was designed to measure caregiver responsivity to the infant's communicative cues. It includes a continuum of ten categories of responsiveness, ranging from basic caregiving responses to more sophisticated facilitation of language and conceptual development. The Parent-Infant Interaction Scale (Clark & Seifer, 1985) assesses caregiver interaction behaviors, caregiver and child social referencing, caregiver and child reciprocity, and caregiver affect. This instrument allows for a rating of the caregiver's relative sensitivity to the child's cues along a continuum of sensitivity. Even though these tools were designed to be used with infants, they can be used to assess interactions of caregivers with toddlers and older children as well.

The answer to the "what to do next" question following the assessment of a caregiver–child interaction should never be to place blame on the parents or indicate that they are responsible for their child's communication difficulties. Paul and Elwood (1991) indicated that parental input is generally well matched to the child's language level, and for those parents who do not have a good communicative fit with their child, it is unlikely that they will be helped by hearing negative feedback. Parents are the child's primary developmental guides and they must be encouraged, not negatively judged, in their efforts to provide a facilitative environment for good communicative development.

Many parents of children with communication difficulties do lack confidence in their abilities to provide maximally effective experiences for their child's communicative development. Even the most competent parents may feel uneasy when they believe that their interactions with their child are being judged. For example, one highly educated, verbal university professor accompanied her son, her fourth child, to a speech-language evaluation. The examiner said, "Please, just play with your son for a few minutes while I watch. I want to get a sample of the words he uses when he plays with you." Following the play, the examiner said, "I noticed he has a good sense of humor. He really seemed to enjoy the play with you." At which point the professor mother replied, "I don't remember, I was so nervous about my saying and doing the right things."

The speech-language pathologist may help parents recognize their own strengths and more finely hone their skills for providing a stimulating environment tailored to the needs of the child as they work together as respectful collaborators. Sometimes, simply by witnessing the way the examiner interacts with the child and by participating in the assessment, parents or caregivers may alter their own behaviors while interacting with the child, which in turn may alter the child's behavior. The assessment of the communicative environment should provide information that can be used to increase opportunities for communicating and to enhance the reciprocity of communicative interactions between children and caregivers. The fine line between assessment and intervention is especially blurred as parents and professionals interact during the assessment of communication of young children.

Assessing Communicative Expression as Language Emerges

Before they say their first word, children have been communicating for at least a year through nonverbal gestures, facial expressions, and vocalizations. During the second and third years of life, they become more verbal as well as increasing the range of intentions they express. When toddlers are referred for evaluation, it is likely that they are late in using words to communicate and have fewer resources for acquiring them.

The MacArthur Communicative Development Inventories (CDI; Fenson et al., 1993) are frequently used at this stage to judge early vocabulary use and preverbal indicators, such as gestures, play, pretending, and imitating. Parents are asked to check off specific vocabulary items they have observed their children using.

When considering expressive communication limitations, it is critical that the child's nonverbal and gestural system of communication also be assessed in order to discern whether the child has a more pervasive deficit in communication. The key question is whether the child has a problem with communication in general or is experiencing difficulty only in the area of speech-language development. If a child is showing few examples of nonverbal communication and is not engaging with others to complete circles of communication (Greenspan, 1992), the child may not yet recognize what communication is about and the value it can have for him or her.

Assessing Communicative Functions as Language Emerges

As these observations suggest, language expression is thoroughly intertwined with communicative functions, especially in the toddler years. Assessing communicative functions involves asking about (1) the range of communicative functions, (2) their frequency, and (3) the means the child uses to communicate them (Paul, 1995).

Early communication between infants and caregivers begins as two-way, presymbolic exchanges. These lay the groundwork for later conversations. The child's earliest communicative functions are termed *protoimperatives* or *protodeclaratives* (Bates, 1976). Pro-

toimperatives get an adult to do something. They include conventional gestures to request objects or express rejection. Protodeclaratives draw adults' attention to something. They include showing or pointing gestures.

As toddlers develop, a wider range of discourse functions (Chapman, 1981) emerges, indicating that the child recognizes some basic rules of conversation and can incorporate them into a communicative repertoire. Discourse functions for toddlers include (1) requests for information about their world, (2) acknowledgments of previous messages sent to them, and (3) answers to requests for information from them. Failure to produce a full range of early intentions, particularly comments (Paul & Shiffer, 1991), may indicate a risk for future communicative development (Wetherby & Prutting, 1984). Assessment of the range of functions can be completed informally while keeping a tally of the child's communicative intentions over time and in different contexts. The answer to the "what to do next" question for a child who is not using a full range of communicative intentions would include recommendations to assist the child directly to increase the range of functions used in a variety of contexts.

The frequency with which a child makes expressive communicative attempts also should be assessed. The expectation is for 18-month-olds to produce approximately two intentional communication moves per minute. This increases to an expectation for more than five examples per minute by 24 months of age. Even those children with limited speech production should communicate nonverbally at the expected rates. A child who does not initiate interactions in play with his parents or with examiners at these frequencies may have a problem with the expression of communicative intention. To assess communicative act frequency, speech-language pathologists tally the number of times a child initiates communication in a set period of time. The answer to the "what to do next" question for a child who is not using an expected frequency of communicative intentions would include dynamic assessment activities and recommendations about how to persuade the child to engage adults in actions and to share attention with others.

Assessing the forms of communicative intentions is important as well. Young children should decrease their reliance on presymbolic, nonverbal vocalizations and gestures and increase their use of verbal symbols during the toddler stage. Gestures are typically combined with vocalizations that sound increasingly like words from 12 to 18 months of age. From 18 to 24 months, conventional words or word combinations are used with increasing frequency to express a range of communicative intentions (Chapman, 1981). An assessment of the toddler's primary means of communication can help determine "what to do next" in intervention. A well-developed gestural system is important in the development of overall communicative skills; however, if a child's communication is limited to gestures, a speech-language pathologist may need to assist the family and child to develop strategies for emphasizing the functionality of vocalizations and words and for assisting the child to acquire a broader range of spoken language possibilities. When speech production capabilities seem to be unusually limited, the assessment should consider whether limitations of speech motor control, as described subsequently, might provide a partial explanation.

Assessing Comprehension as Language Emerges

Understanding the meaning of words is a benchmark indicator of the beginnings of language. Toddlers can lead their parents and others to overestimate their comprehension abilities by responding to complex directions while understanding only one or two key words. Children learn early to follow gestures and other nonlinguistic cues to discern what is expected of them. Therefore, it is important to assess directly the receptive language skills of any child at risk for language delay.

The first question to be asked in an assessment of receptive language is "Does the toddler with emerging language understand words without nonlinguistic cues?" Few formal tests of receptive language exist for toddlers that are useful for attaining specific information about comprehension of words and sentences. Standardized tests of receptive language such as the Peabody Picture Vocabulary Test—III (Dunn, Dunn, & Williams, 1997) only assess understanding of single-word vocabulary. Because toddlers often understand a unique set of vocabulary words peculiar to their individual families, standardized tools for children with emerging language may be problematic. Persistence of such patterns past toddlerhood can signal the presence of disorder, however. For example, Zachary, described at the beginning of this chapter, pointed correctly when asked, "Where is the computer?" but he did not respond to "Show me doggie," or "Where is puppy?" When asked, "Where is dolly?" however, he pointed to a toy dog because Dolly happened to be the name of his family's collie. Parents can be indispensable in helping to identify such idiosyncratic vocabulary associations during the assessment of comprehension of language.

Miller and Paul (1995) described nonstandardized comprehension assessment activities for toddlers with emerging language. They suggested using objects to ask the child to identify several nouns and verbs at random intervals. Comprehension of single words without the support of nonlinguistic cues is taken to indicate performance expected at the 12- to 18-month level in normally developing children (Chapman, 1978). Expectations are for the child to demonstrate linguistic comprehension of three to five nouns and three to five verbs at the 12- to 18-month level. Expectations for the 18- to 24-month level are for the child to understand two-word instructions. Miller and Paul suggested using unusual combinations of action (verb)-object (noun) combinations, such as "Hug the shoe," or "Push the baby," to assure that the child is not just doing what usually is done with the object.

Following success on a majority of the 18- to 24-month items, toddlers are asked to process agent-action-object instructions typical for children in the 24- to 36-month old age range. The children are asked to perform probable and improbable actions with agents and objects, such as to show "The mommy feeds the baby," and "The baby feeds the mommy." Miller and Paul (1995) provided a worksheet for charting the developmental levels of comprehension reached on this nonstandardized measure. If toddlers succeed at the 24- to 36-month level, formal assessment measures such as the PPVT-III (Dunn, Dunn, & Williams, 1997), the Assessment of Children's Language Comprehension (ACLC; Foster, Giddan, & Stark, 1983), the Test for Auditory Comprehension of Language—Revised (TACL-R; Carrow-Woolfolk, 1985), or the Test of Early Language Development (TELD; Hresko, Reid, & Hammill, 1991), or a number of other instruments listed in Table 9.4 might be administered.

The "what to do next" question again is important for planning intervention following assessment. When poor comprehension is observed in a variety of contexts over time, an intervention program is designed with enhanced input and adult mediation to help the child discover meaning through child-centered activities. For children with a deficit in comprehension as well as expression, it is particularly critical to assess the child's communicative strengths. The complete picture will help the intervention team plan strategies to assist the child in both input and output areas of development.

Assessing Speech as Language Emerges

Analysis of a recorded speech sample of toddlers can help to answer the "what to do next" question about speech development. These samples may be gathered in the clinical setting or in a home assessment context. Parents can also help by producing video or audio recordings of their toddler's verbalizations at times when they are most talkative, such as at bedtime.

When speech development is delayed, a critical question is whether the child can hear. Even a mild impairment in only the high frequencies can impede the acquisition of speech and language (Northern & Downs, 1984). Intermittent hearing loss due to fluid in the middle ear can also cause difficulty in learning to perceive and produce all of the sounds of language (Gravel & Wallace, 1995; Klein, Chase, Teele, Menyuk, & Rosner, 1988).

Another possible explanation for slow speech development is impairment of the oral motor mechanism structure and function. Performing the oral motor examination can be challenging with toddlers, who are notorious for their resistance to opening their mouths on request. Bright young children with oral motor difficulties are often keenly aware that they are not able to speak as well as others. They may become more and more reticent to imitate speech or oral motor movements. Even after weeks of developing a good relationship with a toddler, a request for imitation of an oral motor movement may be met with a firm "no." Thus, clinicians who wish for a good assessment of oral motor skills must be unusually creative in setting a relaxed, playful tone, and they must be quick. Sometimes play with a penlight, modeling a playful look into a mirror or the parent's mouth, or performing "magic" to find a small block or coin in unlikely places with amateur slight of hand will convince the child that no harm will be incurred by allowing the examiner a quick examination of the oral cavity.

There the clinician looks for normal eruption and alignment of teeth, intact hard and soft palates, elevation and retraction of the soft palate when the child vocalizes, and a symmetrical and mobile tongue. The child may or may not permit the clinician to use a tongue blade to hold the tongue down for a better look at the posterior oral cavity and to check for normal muscle tone. Some are more likely to do so if first allowed to peek into the examiner's mouth. If a child's speech is hypernasal, the clinician looks for evidence of a submucous cleft. This is sometimes signaled by an area at the juncture of the hard and soft palates that is not normally pink, or the presence of a bifid uvula (split in the little piece of tissue that dangles from the soft palate).

When speech motor control problems are suspected, activities are designed to contrast the symptoms of dysarthria with those of developmental apraxia. Contrasts are drawn between reflexive and voluntary movements and between speech and nonspeech movements. Dysarthria describes articulatory difficulties associated with general weakness or incoordination of reflexive neural-motor control. It is associated with problems involving eating or respiratory behavior. *Dysarthria* is the descriptive term for the speech distortions associated with cerebral palsy and other forms of direct neuromotor impairment. Drooling often accompanies dysarthria. Oral-motor apraxia, on the other hand, is a motor programming problem that only appears during voluntary movement attempts. It is diagnosed when normal reflexive breathing, chewing, and swallowing are observed, but the child cannot coordinate movements of the tongue, lips, jaw, and teeth for voluntary acts such as blowing or kissing. Developmental apraxia of speech (DAS) is often, but not always, linked to oral-motor apraxia. Either condition may occur separately. DAS involves excessive difficulties with the initiation and production of speech articulation shapes, sequences, and transitions. Dysarthria and both forms of apraxia are symptoms of central nervous system dysfunction, but apraxias are thought to involve a problem of motor programming at the cortical level, and dysarthrias may be caused by impairments at the subcortical level or even at the final connection of neuron to muscle.

Sometimes parents can provide the information about early babbling or feeding, which may reveal helpful cues as to a possible connection between motor development and slow speech development related to either of these diagnoses. Formal instruments such as the Preschool Oral Motor Examination (Sheppard, 1987) or the Pre-Speech Assessment Scale (Morris, 1982) involve direct clinical assessment of oral motor behaviors for infants and young children. They can help identify causal physical factors for late developing speech for toddlers with emerging language. If formal methods or parent reports regarding present or past babbling or feeding behaviors indicate problems with weakness or paralysis, dysarthric conditions may be suspected, and a more in-depth motor speech assessment can be completed as the intervention process begins. To rule out or confirm suspicion of DAS (also called dyspraxia), formal and informal assessment tools can be combined to compare voluntary with involuntary movements of the oral motor mechanism.

Another option for explaining atypically limited speech production and intelligibility among toddlers with emerging language is rooted in limitations of linguistic rule learning rather than in limitations of speech motor control. Children with normal oral motor structure and function may still experience specific difficulty in learning the linguistic rules of phonology. In some cases, a child's limitations of speech production are best described as problems of persistent immature phonological processes. Children with this condition seem to have a limited internal representation of the abstract range of phonemic distinctions that signal differences in the meaning of words. They may think they are producing words like those of their parents and peers, but actually may be attempting to "make do" with an extremely limited set of vowel and consonantal contrasts (Hodson, 1986).

Although phonological difficulties are not generally included in the criteria for a diagnosis of SLI, young children with SLI often demonstrate phoneme production similar to younger children (Paul & Jennings, 1992; Rescorla & Ratner, 1996). In other words, the phonological systems of these children appear to be delayed and less systematic in development. Late talking toddlers diagnosed with SLI-E at age 2 years represent a discrete diagnostic group with the potential for continuing difficulty with phonological and language skills. Roberts, Rescorla, Giroux, and Stevens (1998) found that children with SLI-E at age 2 had significantly fewer vocalizations than typically developing children, but there was no difference in frequency of vocalization at age 3. For many, however, there continued to be differences in other areas of articulation and language development, including overall intelligibility and mean length of utterance (MLU). Because the development of a productive phonetic inventory and grammatical skills continue to pose problems for toddlers with SLI as they move into later stages of development, comprehensive assessment may help determine "what to do next" in intervention. On the other hand, several research studies have suggested that 50 percent of late talkers do "catch up," justifying a "watch and see" (not wait and see) policy of reassessment every 3 to 6 months for 2- to 3-year-olds, and at every 6 to 12 months for 3- to 5-year-olds (Paul, 1996). During this period, consultative services may provide parents with suggestions for facilitating their child's language and speech acquisition.

ASSESSING THE LANGUAGE DEVELOPMENT OF PRESCHOOLERS

Children in the preschool stage of language development are primed for acquiring the rules of the grammatical code. This is the stage during which children combine words into complete sentences and express ideas about a wide variety of concepts. It is the stage during which they are able to vary their language to fit specific contexts and to use comprehension strategies that are more linguistic than nonlinguistic. It is the stage when most children become adept at producing all the phonemes of their language and at speaking with a reasonable degree of fluency.

Table 9.3 summarizes indicators of normal development for preschoolers as they continue to develop communication, speech, and language beyond the toddler years. For children with language-learning difficulties, however, the process of moving through these stages may be more protracted than the table's ages suggest, and it may involve unusual mixtures of more and less mature developments across receptive/expressive and speech/language/communication domains.

The assessment process for 3- to 7-year-olds starts with a thorough assessment of the child's hearing. It also requires gathering language samples using formal and/or informal techniques across a variety of contexts, including at least conversation, preacademic activities, and play. Then the child's observed responses are compared with a set of expected responses outlined in the quantitative tables provided with formal tests or with the descriptors provided with informal assessment tools, such as those summarized in Table 9.3.

Comprehensive assessment tools often used with preschoolers include the Clinical Evaluation of Language Fundamentals—3rd edition (CELF-3; Semel, Wiig, & Secord, 1995), the Test of Early Language Development—2nd edition (TELD-2; Hresko et al., 1991), the Test of Language Development—Primary; 3rd edition (TOLD-P:3; Newcomer & Hammill, 1997), and the Preschool Language Scale—3rd edition (PLS-3; Zimmerman, Steiner, & Pond, 1992). Many formal assessment tools used with preschoolers have been criticized for their psychometric flaws (McCauley & Swisher, 1984b; Plante & Vance, 1994), and examiners are urged to read manuals carefully and to use the data from formal tests with a degree of caution. When the "what to do next" question involves issues of diagnosis, it is desirable for the test to demonstrate sensitivity in identifying *all* the children with potential language disorders, as well as specificity in identifying *only* the children with actual language disorders. Plante and Vance (1994) studied several tests and found that the Structured Photographic Expressive Language Test—II (SPELT-II; Werner & Kresheck, 1983) achieved these purposes best.

Assessing Language Expression in the Preschool Years

Most formal and informal language assessment procedures for preschoolers depend heavily on the observation of expressive language abilities. The primacy of grammatical acquisition during this stage makes it an important indicator for discriminating atypical language development. Spontaneous language sampling techniques are essential for observing acquisition of the syntactic rules for formulating increasingly lengthy sentences and the lexicon and semantic strategies for conveying increasingly abstract meanings.

Tape-recorded samples should be gathered during play interactions with parents and peers and well as from conversational interactions with the clinician. Transcription should occur as soon as possible after the sample is gathered to facilitate accurate recall of the interaction, and the child's utterances should be transcribed exactly as spoken, although not necessarily phonetically.

Transcribed samples are analyzed for length and complexity of utterances. Mean length of utterance (MLU) is an especially powerful indicator of a child's expressive language development during the preschool years. MLU is computed by counting the number of morphemes (words and word endings, such as plurals, possessives, and tense markers) in a sample of 100 or more utterances, then dividing this total by the number of utterances to arrive at the mean. The resulting MLU in morphemes is compared with data for expected ranges associated with normal development using sources such as Brown (1973) or Miller (1981). Table 9.3 includes general age-related expectations for MLU development.

It is also helpful to look for the productive use of certain morphemes that have an expected order of emergence, starting with the inflectional rule for adding -ing, the early production of in and on, and the regular plural -s, and moving to inflected auxiliary and main verb forms of to be, as well as possessive and past-tense endings (Brown, 1973; De Villiers & De Villiers, 1973). The typically developing child goes through a period of over-generalizing rules for adding bound morphemes at this point, and that is a good sign. In other words, when a child regularizes the use of plural and past-tense endings (e.g., *feets* and *goed*), the clinician can conclude that the child is attending to the regularities of language. The irregular forms may appear early as unanalyzed forms but then disappear temporarily. Most children do not figure out the full set of irregular forms until they are well into their elementary school years, and adults may even struggle with irregular forms of a few infrequently used

words. On the other hand, persistence of immature forms of irregularly inflected words, such as *me/I* pronoun confusion persisting into kindergarten, can signal cause for concern (Leonard, 1980).

Some techniques for assessing the acquisition of particular grammatical forms and sentence structures are hybrids between formal and informal procedures. Developmental Sentence Scoring (Lee, 1974), in particular, has been used over several decades now because it can capture a set of indicators with a single score, which can be compared with normative data. Such tools provide clinicians with a means for assessing quantitatively how a child is doing relative to Standard English–learning peers and also describing qualitatively which structures a child is or is not using when obligated by linguistic context.

A caution for using grammatical assessment checklists and similar tools is that they are particularly biased against children who are not learning Standard English. A child's acquisition of grammatical rules should always be analyzed with reference to the linguistic community in which the child is immersed. Children learning English as a second language may use a mixture of forms from their first language (L1), at the same time they are beginning to incorporate the rules of English (L2). A child's language should always be evaluated in the system in which the child is most fluent and comfortable, especially for purposes of determining disorder, and if the clinician is not fluent in the child's language, an examiner assistant must be located who is.

Particular care should also be taken when a child is learning a dialectal variant of Standard English. For example, children learning African American English (AAE; also called Ebonics or Black English Vernacular) often use different set rules for forming some sentence structures, such as questions (*What that is? Where you work? Do he still have it?*), complex sentences (*I aks him, do he want some more. Why he's in there cause baby scared the dog.*), and negatives (*Can't nobody make me. He not a baby.*). Primary verb inflectional rules may differ for main verb and auxiliaries, such as forms of to be (*That boy my friend. The girl singin'.*). Children using later developing AAE forms also have options for conveying temporal relations not available in Standard English, such as the invariant be (*He be my friend*) and the remote past aspect (*She been whuptin' the baby. I been wanted this*). Several systems have been described for analyzing language samples of children learning AAE (Hyter, 1984; Nelson, 1998; Washington & Craig, 1994). Stockman (1996) suggested a minimal competency core (MCC) to be used for criterion reference for 33- to 36-month old African American children, looking for developmental evidence in four areas of language development—a phonological feature core, a pragmatic functions core, a semantic relations core, and a morphosyntactic core. This tool has the advantage of assessing more areas of language development than syntax and morphology.

In addition to assessing the child's expressive language at the level of the sentence, larger units of discourse should also be considered. Preschoolers should be developing skill for telling and retelling events with an emerging narrative organizational structure. Two systems are often used for assessing narrative maturity among children (Nelson, 1998). The descriptors proposed by Applebee (1978) look for the developing ability to maintain a central focus while chaining together a set of events using both temporal and logical links. Hedberg and Westby (1993) adapted this system and story grammar analysis (Stein & Glenn, 1979) to describe a developmental sequence in which the child starts with (1) an *isolated description* with little relationship among elements, (2) then learns to produce a *descriptive sequence* with related statements, (3) followed by a more mature *action sequence* with temporal links, (4) then a *reactive sequence* with cause and effect, (5) an *abbreviated episode* with an implied goal for addressing a central problem, (6) a *complete episode* with planning to achieve the goal, and (7) eventually a *complex episode,* in which the main character overcomes obstacles while implementing the plan. Most preschoolers do not advance beyond the level of reactive sequence or abbreviated episode, and even when children can produce more mature narratives under optimal conditions, most children move up and down the narrative maturity scales, depending on the context. That is, a child typically does not master a higher level of narrative maturity and then abandon all earlier levels. Narrative discourse analysis is thus better at answering questions about "what to do next" in intervention than answering diagnostic questions about whether or not the child has a language disorder.

Assessing Communicative Functions in the Preschool Years

It is difficult to assess pragmatic functions with a formal test because the essence of pragmatic use is the ability to modify how one says things to achieve varied communicative purposes (e.g., requesting actions or objects, making descriptive comments or evaluative statements) to fit particular social contexts. The ability to interpret social meanings by using nonverbal communicative cues such

as tone, facial expression, and body posture, as well as the words spoken, is also an important part of pragmatic assessment. Such abilities are best observed in naturalistic contexts. Therefore, spontaneous language samples gathered in social interactions with peers, particularly during symbolic and creative play, often provide the richest opportunities to judge the adequacy of a child's repertoire of communicative acts. Table 9.3 can serve as an observational guide about what to look for in the areas of social interaction and play as the child develops over the preschool and early elementary school years.

Concern is noted particularly when a child is observed to have an imbalance of assertive and responsive communicative acts. In the case examples discussed in the early sections of this chapter, we used a system for characterizing four patterns of balance and imbalance suggested by Fey (1986). Fey's system works by coding varied assertive forms of requests, comments, statements, and disagreements initiated by the child, and comparing them with a varied set of responsive forms the child produces in response to questions or statements initiated by an adult communicative partner. There are no hard and fast rules for identifying patterns, but the examiner compares numbers of assertive and responsive acts, considering whether the adult provided ample opportunities for both when gathering the sample. A pattern of balanced assertives and responsives indicates an *active conversationalist;* a pattern with more assertives than responsives indicates a *verbal noncommunicator;* a pattern with many responsives and few assertives indicates a *passive conversationalist;* and a pattern with few assertives or responsives indicates an *inactive communicator* (Fey, 1986).

Assessing Language Comprehension in the Preschool Years

A formal test often used for assessing language comprehension in the preschool years is the Test of Auditory Comprehension of Language—Revised (TACL-R; Carrow-Woolfolk, 1985). This test involves pointing to pictures with foils designed to test understanding of particular lexical and syntactic relationships. It can be useful for assessing the comprehension skills of children learning standard English, although it did not fare as well as the SPELT-II (Werner & Kresheck, 1983) in Plante and Vance's (1994) study of test specificity and sensitivity for identifying specific language impairment. In fact, children with comprehension deficits are more likely to have associated cognitive difficulties with nonverbal as well as with verbal understandings. The

Bracken Basic Concept Scale (BBCS; Bracken, 1998) provides a means for systematic assessment of key relational concepts and vocabulary important for understanding school discourse in kindergarten and first grade.

Informal assessment of a child's language comprehension can be accomplished by playing with the child and looking for opportunities to probe for understanding of varied lexical items and syntactic relationships. The context of playfulness is especially important when assessing the comprehension of children who are reluctant to cooperate with more formal measures. Probes should be presented without gestural cues, direct commands, or questions. For example, to assess comprehension of prepositional concepts, a probe embedded in play might be, "I think the baby's bottle is under the chair," or "Let's put the cookies in the refrigerator." The possibility that the child might be using earlier developing nonlinguistic strategies should also be considered. For example, a probe for assessing whether a child is using the do-what-you-usually-do strategy might be, "Put the cookies under the table." A probe for assessing whether a child has moved beyond the order-of-mention strategy might be, "Before you feed the baby, let's give her a bath." Correct response to such comprehension probes usually indicate linguistic comprehension, but an incorrect response or no response may indicate only that the preschooler had different intentions. In such cases, additional probes are needed, perhaps further into an interactive play sequence.

Assessing Speech in the Preschool Years

If a child is not speaking clearly enough to be understood by most adults by age 3, a formal articulation test and assessment of the child's use of immature phonological processes is warranted. Several frequently used tools for doing so are included in Table 9.4.

Speech-language pathologists use tables of developmental expectations to judge whether difficulty in producing particular phonemes should be considered atypical. Generally speaking, children with articulatory difficulties on the sounds /s/, /l/, /r/, or /th/ are not seen as needing articulation therapy unless the difficulties persist into second or third grade. Children may need help earlier if they have difficulties with all of these phonemes and have marginal intelligibility as a result, or if they have concurrent language problems.

When a child's phonological system for representing the speech sounds of language is limited, the child is particularly at risk for developing sound awareness, which is one of the key indicators that a child can learn to read (Blachman, 1994; Kamhi & Catts, 1989). The assessment process for preschoolers should focus primarily on the productive use of the phonological rules for articulating words in sentences with relative completeness, if not full correctness. When a child is in kindergarten, first, or second grade, the assessment should extend to the child's awareness of phonemes in the contexts of rhyming, segmenting, and combining sounds in isolated words or nonsense words. The ability to connect sounds to print in both reading and writing modes might also be considered when assessing how the child is able to use speech capabilities to support the acquisition of written language.

SUMMARY AND CONCLUSIONS

This chapter has presented a view of language, speech, and communication assessment guided by the recursive question, "What to do next?" The answer to the question depends on many factors, including how a child is identified or referred, one's place in the assessment cycle, the complexity and multiplicity of potential diagnoses, and whether intervention appears necessary. Choices differ for children who are just beginning to acquire and combine words in prelinguistic or toddler stages of language development and those who are in the rapid period of language learning during the preschool stage. A child's interaction in social exchanges and play can yield information essential to both accurate diagnosis and program planning during both developmental stages.

The chapter has emphasized the importance of using a family-sensitive process to make choices about assessment contexts, strategies, and tools. The entire assessment process works best when it occurs as a joint enterprise, including professionals from several disciplines and the family as full members of the team. As a team, the group considers initial evidence and priorities. As a team, they decide on a set of formal and informal assessment tools to gather evidence about how a child is currently functioning within familial and cultural contexts. Finally, as a team, they consider jointly "what to do next." Choices may include further assessment, the initiation of intervention services, or to watch and see whether problems persist. Regardless, any time a parent raises concerns about a child's communicative development, the team should consult regarding the best strategies for optimizing opportunities for positive communication interactions and fostering normal language development for the child.

REFERENCES

American Psychiatric Association. (1994). *Diagnostic and statistical manual of mental disorders* (4th ed.). Washington, DC: Author.

American Speech-Language-Hearing Association. (1982). Committee on language, Speech and Hearing Services in the Schools. Definitions: Communicative disorders and variations. *American Speech-Language-Hearing Association, 24,* 949–950.

Anderson, P. P., & Goldberg, P. G. (1991). *Cultural competence in screening and assessment.* Minneapolis, MN: Pacer Center.

Anstey, M., & Bull, G. (1991). From teaching to learning: Translating monitoring into practice. In E. Daly (Ed.), *Monitoring children's language development: Holistic assessment in the classroom* (pp. 3–15). Portsmouth, NH: Heinemann.

Applebee, A. N. (1978). *The child's concept of story.* Chicago: University of Chicago Press.

Au, K. H., & Mason, J. M. (1981). Social organizational factors in learning to read: The balance of rights hypothesis. *Reading Research Quarterly, 17,* 115–152.

Bailey, D., & Simeonsson, R. (1988). *Family assessment in early intervention.* Columbus, OH: Charles. E. Merrill.

Barrera, I. (1993). Effective and appropriate interaction for all children: The challenge of cultural/linguistic diversity and young children with special needs. *Topics in Early Childhood Special Education, 13*(4), 461–487.

Barrera, I. (1996). Thoughts on the assessment of young children whose sociocultural background is unfamiliar to the assessor. In S. J. Meisels & E. Fenichel (Eds.), *New visions for the developmental assessment of infants and young children* (pp. 69–84). Washington, DC: Zero to Three: National Center for Infants, Toddlers, and Families.

Bashir, A. S. (1989). Language intervention and the curriculum. *Seminars in Speech and Language, 10*(3), 181–191.

Bates, E. (1976). *Language in context: Studies in the acquisition of pragmatics.* New York: Academic Press.

Bates, E., Bretherton, E., & Snyder, L. (1988). *From first words to grammar: Individual differences and dissociable mechanisms.* New York: Cambridge University Press.

Benedict, H. (1979). Early lexical development: Comprehension and production. *Journal of Child Language, 6,* 183–200.

Berman, C., & Shaw, E. (1996). Family-directed child evaluation and assessment under the Individuals with Disabilities Education Act (IDEA). In S. J. Meisels & E. Fenichel (Eds.), *New visions for the developmental assessment of infants and young children.* Washington, DC: Zero to Three: National Center for Infants, Toddlers, and Families.

Blachman, B. A. (1994). Early literacy acquisition: The role of phonological awareness. In G. P. Wallach & K. G. Butler (Eds.), *Language learning disabilities in school-age children and adolescents* (pp. 253–274). Boston: Allyn and Bacon.

Bracken, B. A. (1998). *Bracken Basic Concepts Scale—Revised.* San Antonio, TX: Psychological Corporation.

Bricker, D. (1993). *Assessment, evaluation and programming system for infants and toddlers.* Baltimore: Paul H. Brookes.

Bricker, D., Squires, J., Mounts, L., Potter, L., Nickel, R., & Farrell, J. (1997). *Ages and Stages Questionnaire (ASQ): A parent-completed, child-monitoring system.* Baltimore: Paul H. Brookes.

Brown, R. A. (1973). *A first language: The early stages.* Cambridge, MA: Harvard University Press.

Carey, S., & Bartlett, E. (1978). Acquiring a single new word. *Papers and Reports in Child Language Development, 15,* 17–29.

Carpenter, R. (1987). Play scale. In L. Olswang, C. Stoel-Gammon, T. Coggins, & R. Carpenter (Eds.), *Assessing prelinguistic and early behaviors in developmentally young children* (pp. 44–77). Seattle: University of Washington Press.

Carrow-Woolfolk, E. (1985). *Test for Auditory Comprehension of Language—Revised.* Austin, TX: Pro-Ed.

Chapman, R. (1978). Comprehension strategies in children. In J. Kavanagh & P. Strange (Eds.), *Language and speech in the laboratory, school and clinic.* Cambridge, MA: MIT Press.

Chapman, R. (1981). Exploring children's communicative intents. In J. Miller (Ed.), *Assessing language production in children* (pp. 111–138). Baltimore: University Park Press.

Chomsky, N. (1968). *Language and mind.* New York: Harcourt, Brace & World.

Clark, G. N., & Seifer, R. (1985). Assessment of parent's interactions with their developmentally delayed infants. *Infant Mental Health Journal, 6*(4), 214–225.

Coggins, T. E. (1991). Bringing context back into assessment. *Topics in Language Disorders, 11,* 43–54.

Cole, K. N., Dale, P. S., & Mills, P. E. (1990). Defining language delay in young children by cognitive referencing: Are we saying more than we know? *Applied Psycholinguistics, 11,* 291–302.

Cole, K. N., Dale, P. S., & Mills, P. E. (1992). Stability of the intelligence quotient–language quotient relation: Is discrepancy modeling based on a myth? *American Journal on Mental Retardation, 97,* 131–143.

Cole, K. N., & Harris, S. R. (1992). Instability of the intelligence quotient–motor quotient relationship. *Developmental Medicine and Child Neurology, 34,* 633–641.

Cole, K. N., Mills, P. E., & Kelley, D. (1994). Agreement of assessment profiles used in cognitive referencing. *Language, Speech, and Hearing Services in Schools, 25,* 25–31.

Crais, E. R. (1990). World knowledge to word knowledge. World knowledge and language: Development and disorders. *Topics in Language Disorders, 10*(3), 45–62.

Crais, E. R. (1995). Expanding the repertoire of tools and techniques for assessing the communication skills of infants and toddlers. *American Journal of Speech-Language Pathology, 4*(3), 47–59.

Crais, E., & Roberts, J. (1991). Decision making in assessment and early intervention planning. *Language, Speech and Hearing Services in Schools, 22,* 19–30.

Cross, T. G. (1984). Habilitating the language impaired child: Ideas from studies of parent–child interaction. *Topics in Language Disorders, 4*(4), 1–14.

Dale, P. S. (1996). Parent report assessment of language and communication. In K. N. Cole, P. S. Dale, & D. J. Thal (Eds.), *Assessment of communication and language* (pp. 161–182). Baltimore: Paul H. Brookes.

Darby, B. L. (1979). Infant cognition: Considerations for assessment tools. In B. L. Darby & M. J. Mays (Eds.), *Infant assessment: Issues and applications* (pp. 103–111). Seattle, WA: WESTAR.

De Villiers, J., & De Villiers, P. (1973). A cross-sectional study of the development of grammatical morphemes in child speech. *Journal of Psycholinguistic Research, 2,* 267–268.

Dore, J. (1986). The development of conversational competence. In R. L. Schiefelbusch (Ed.), *Language competence: Assessment and intervention* (pp. 3–60). Austin, TX: Pro-Ed.

Dunn, L., Dunn, L., & Williams, K. T. (1997). *Peabody Picture Vocabulary Test—3rd edition.* Circle Pines, MN: American Guidance Service.

Edmonston, N. K., & Thane, N. L. (1992). Children's use of comprehension strategies in response to relational words: Implications for assessment. *American Journal of Speech-Language Pathology, 1*(2), 30–35.

Eimas, P. D. (1975). Developmental studies in speech perception. In L. B. Cohen & P. Salapatek (Eds.), *Infant perception: From sensation to cognition* (Vol. 2, pp. 193–231). New York: Academic Press.

Ervin-Tripp, S., & Gordon, D. (1986). The development of requests. In R. L. Schiefelbusch (Ed.), *Language competence: Assessment and intervention* (pp. 61–95). Austin, TX: Pro-Ed.

Fenson, L., Dale, P. S., Resnick, J. S., Thal, D., Bates, E., Hartung, J. P., Pethick, D., & Reilly, J. S. (1993). *MacArthur Communicative Development Inventories (CDI).* San Diego, CA: Singular Publishing Group.

Fey, M. E. (1986). *Language intervention with young children.* San Diego, CA: College-Hill.

Fey, M. E., Long, S. H., & Cleave, P. L. (1994). Reconsideration of IQ criteria in the definition of specific language impairments. In R. V. Watkins & M. L. Rice (Eds.), *Specific language impairments in children.* Baltimore: Paul H. Brookes.

Fialka, J. (1997). *It matters: Lessons from my son.* Huntington Woods, MI: Author.

Foster, R., Giddan, J., & Stark, J. (1983). *Assessment of Children's Language Comprehension.* Palo Alto, CA: Consulting Psychologists Press.

Francis, D. J., Fletcher, J. M., Shaywitz, B. A., Shaywitz, S. E., & Rourke, B. P. (1996). Defining learning and language disabilities: Conceptual and psychometric issues with the use of IQ tests. *Language, Speech, and Hearing Services in the Schools, 27,* 132–143.

Frankenburg, W., Dodds, J., Archer, P., Bresnick, B., Maskchka, P., Edelman, M., & Shapiro, J. (1990). *Denver II: Screening Manual.* Denver, CO: Denver Developmental Materials.

Frankenburg, W., Dodds, J., & Fandal, A. W. (1969). *Denver Developmental Screening Test* (Manual revised, 1970). Denver: University of Colorado Medical Center.

Garwood, S. G. (1982). (Mis)use of developmental scales in program evaluation. *Topics in Early Childhood Special Education, 1*(4), 61–69.

Gravel, J. S., & Wallace, I. (1995). Early otitis media, auditory abilities, and educational risk. *American Journal of Speech-Language Pathology, 4*(3), 89–94.

Greenspan, S. (1992). *Infancy and early development.* Madison, CT: International Universities Press.

Hart, B., & Risley, T. R. (1995). *Meaningful differences.* Baltimore: Paul H. Brookes.

Hedberg, N. L., & Westby, C. E. (1993). *Analyzing storytelling skills: Theory to practice.* Tucson, AZ: Communication Skill Builders.

Hester, E. J. (1996). Narratives of young African American children. In A. G. Kamhi, K. E. Pollack, & J. L. Harris (Eds.), *Communication development and disorders in African American children: Research, assessment, and intervention* (pp. 227–245). Baltimore: Paul H. Brookes.

Hodson, B. (1986). *Assessment of phonological processes—Revised.* Austin, TX: Pro-Ed.

Hresko, W. P., Reid, D. K., & Hammill, D. D. (1991). *The Test of Early Language Development* (2nd ed.). Austin, TX: Pro-Ed.

Hyter, Y. (1984). *Reliability and validity of the Black English sentence scoring system.* Unpublished master's thesis, Western Michigan University, Kalamazoo.

Ireton, J. (1992). *Child Development Inventory Manual.* Minneapolis, MN: Behavior Science Systems.

Kamhi, A. G., & Catts, H. (1989). *Reading disabilities: A developmental language perspective.* Austin, TX: Pro-Ed.

Klein, J., Chase, C., Teele, D., Menyuk, P., & Rosner, B. (1988). Otitis media and the development of speech, language, and cognitive abilities at seven years of age. In D. Lim, C. Bluestone, J. Klein, & J. Nelson (Eds.), *Recent advances in otitis media* (pp. 396–400). Toronto: B. C. Decker.

Klein, M. D., & Briggs, M. H. (1987). Facilitating mother–infant communicative interaction in mothers and high-risk infants. *Journal of Communication Disorders, 10,* 95–106.

Lahey, M. (1988). *Language disorders and language development.* New York: Macmillan.

Lahey, M. (1992). Linguistic and cultural diversity: Further problems for determining who shall be called language disordered. *Journal of Speech and Hearing Disorders, 56,* 638–639.

Lasky, E. Z., & Klopp, K. (1982). Parent–child interactions in normal and language-disordered children. *Journal of Speech and Hearing Disorders, 47,* 7–18.

Lee, L. L. (1974). *Developmental sentence analysis.* Evanston, IL: Northwestern University Press.

Leonard, L. B. (1980). The speech of language-disabled children. *Bulletin of the Orton Society (now Annuals of Dyslexia), 30,* 141–152.

Leonard, L. B. (1987). Is specific language impairment a useful construct? In S. Rosenberg (Ed.), *Advances in applied psycholinguistics. Vol. 1: Disorders of first language acquisition* (pp. 1–39). New York: Cambridge University Press.

Lidz, C. S. (1991). *Practitioner's guide to dynamic assessment.* New York: Guilford Press.

Linder, T. W. (1993). *Transdisciplinary play-based assessment: A functional approach to working with young children* (Rev. ed.) Baltimore: Paul H. Brookes.

Lynch, E. W., & Hanson, M. (1992). *Developing cross-cultural competence.* Baltimore: Paul H. Brookes.

McCauley, R., & Swisher, L. (1984b). Use and misuse of norm-referenced tests in clinical assessment: A hypothetical case. *Journal of Speech and Hearing Disorders, 49,* 338–348.

McCune, L. (1995). A normative study of representational play at the transition to language. *Developmental Psychology, 31*(2), 206.

Meyers, J. (1987). The training of dynamic assessors. In C. S. Lidz (Ed.), *Dynamic assessment: An interactional approach to evaluating learning potential* (pp. 288–326). New York: Guilford Press.

Miller, J. F. (1981). *Assessing language production in children: Experimental procedures.* Austin, TX: Pro-Ed.

Miller, J. F., & Paul, R. (1995). *The clinical assessment of language comprehension.* Baltimore: Paul H. Brookes.

Miller, J. F., Sedey, A. L., & Miolo, G. (1995). Validity of parent report measures of vocabulary development for children with Down Syndrome. *Journal of Speech and Hearing Research, 38,* 1037–1044.

Morris, S. (1982). *Pre-speech Assessment Scale.* Clifton, NJ: J. A. Preston.

Muma, J. R. (1978). *Language handbook: Concepts, assessment, intervention.* Englewood Cliffs, NJ: Prentice-Hall.

Neisworth, J. T., & Bagnato, S. J. (1988). Assessment in early childhood special education: A typology of dependent measures. In S. L. Odom & M. B. Karnes (Eds.), *Early intervention for infants and children with handicaps: An empirical base* (pp. 23–49). Baltimore: Paul H. Brookes.

Nelson, N. (1998). *Childhood language disorders in context: Infancy through adolescence.* Boston: Allyn and Bacon.

Newcomer, P. L., & Hammill, D. D. (1997). *Test of Language Development—Primary* (3rd ed.). Austin, TX: Pro-Ed.

Northern, J. L., & Downs, M. P. (1984). *Hearing in children* (3rd ed.). Baltimore: Williams and Wilkins.

Notari-Syverson, A., & Losardo, A. (1996). Assessing children's language in meaningful contexts. In K. N. Cole, P. S. Dale, & D. J. Thal (Eds.), *Assessment of communication and language* (pp. 257–279). Baltimore: Paul H. Brookes.

Olswang, L. B., & Bain, B. A. (1996). Assessment information for predicting upcoming change in language production. *Journal of Speech and Hearing Research, 39*(2), 414–423.

Paul, R. (1991). Profiles of toddlers with slow expressive language development. *Topics in Language Disorders, 10*(3), 63–75.

Paul, R. (1995). *Language disorders from infancy through adolescence.* St. Louis, MO: Mosby-Year Book.

Paul, R. (1996). Clinical implications of the natural history of slow expressive language development. *American Journal of Speech-Language Pathology, 5*(2), 5–21.

Paul, R., & Elwood, T. (1991). Maternal linguistic input to toddlers with slow expressive language development. *Journal of Speech and Hearing Research, 34,* 982–988.

Paul, R., & Jennings, P. (1992). Phonological behaviors in toddlers with slow expressive language development. *Journal of Speech and Hearing Research, 35,* 99–107.

Paul, R., & Shiffer, M. (1991). Communicative initiations in normal and late-talking toddlers. *Applied Psycholinguistics, 12*(4), 419–431.

Pena, E. D. (1996). Dynamic Assessment: The model and its language applications. In K. N. Cole, P. S. Dale, & D. J. Thal (Eds.), *Assessment of communication and language* (pp. 281–307). Baltimore: Paul H. Brookes.

Pinker, S. (1994). *The language instinct.* New York: William Morrow.

Plante, E., & Vance, R. (1994). Selection of preschool language tests: A data-based approach. *Language, Speech, and Hearing Services in Schools, 25,* 15–25.

Popper, B. K. (1996). Achieving change in assessment practices: A parent's perspective. In S. J. Meisels & E. Fenichel (Eds.), *New visions for the developmental assessment of infants and young children* (pp. 59–66). Washington, DC: Zero to Three: National Center for Infants, Toddlers, and Families.

Rescorla, L. (1989). The Language Development Survey: A screening tool for delayed language in toddlers. *Journal of Speech and Hearing Disorders, 54,* 587–599.

Rescorla L., & Ratner, N. B. (1996). Phonetic profiles of toddlers with specific expressive language impairment (SLI-E). *Journal of Speech and Hearing Research, 39,* 153–165.

Roberts, J. E., & Crais, E. R. (1989). Assessing communication skills. In D. G. Bailey, Jr. & M. Wolery (Eds.), *Assessing infants and preschoolers with handicaps* (pp. 339–389). Columbus, OH: Merrill.

Roberts, J., Rescorla, L., Giroux, J., & Stevens, L. (1998). Phonological skills of children with specific expressive language impairment (SLI-E): Outcome at age 3. *Journal of Speech and Hearing Research, 4,* 374–384.

Rosenthal, R., & Jacobson, L. (1968). *Pygmalion in the classroom: Teacher expectation and pupils' intellectual development.* New York: Holt, Rinehart & Winston.

Rosetti, L. (1990). *The Rossetti Infant-Toddler Language Scale.* East Moline, IL: LinguiSystems.

Schiefelbusch, R. L., & McCormick, L. (1984). *Early language intervention.* Columbus, OH: Charles E. Merrill.

Semel, E., Wiig, E. H., & Secord, W. (1995). *Clinical evaluation of language fundamentals* (3rd ed.). San Antonio, TX: Psychological Corporation.

Seymour, H. N. (1992). The invisible children: A reply to Lahey's perspective. *Journal of Speech and Hearing Disorders, 56,* 640–641.

Sheppard, J. (1987). Assessment of oral motor behaviors in cerebral palsy. In E. D. Mysak (Ed.), *Seminars in speech and language* (pp. 57–70). New York: Thieme-Stratton.

Silliman, E. R., & Wilkinson, L. C. (1991). *Communicating for learning: Classroom observations and collaboration.* Gaithersburg, MD: Aspen Publishers.

Silliman, E. R., Wilkinson, L. C., & Hoffman, L. P. (1993). Documenting authentic progress in language and literacy learning: Collaborative assessment in classrooms. *Topics in Language Disorders, 11*(3), 58–71.

Sparrow, S. S., Balla, D. A., & Cicchetti, D. V. (1984). *Vineland Adaptive Behavior Scales.* Circle Pines, MN: American Guidance Service.

Stanovich, K. E. (1985). Explaining the variance in reading ability in terms of psychological processes: What have we learned? *Annals of Dyslexia, 35,* 67–96.

Stein, N., & Glenn, C. (1979). An analysis of story comprehension in elementary school children. In R. Freedle (Ed.), *New directions in discourse processing* (Vol. 2, pp. 53–120). Norwood, NJ: Ablex.

Stockman, I. J. (1996). The promises and pitfalls of language sample analysis as an assessment tool for linguistic minority children. *Language, Speech, and Hearing Services in Schools, 27,* 355–366.

Stoel-Gammon, C. (1987). Phonological skills of two-year-olds. *Language, Speech, and Hearing Services in Schools, 18,* 323–329.

Stoel-Gammon, C. (1991). Normal and disordered phonology in two-year-olds. *Topics in Language Disorders, 11*(4), 21–32.

Terrell, S. L., & Terrell, F. (1983). Distinguishing linguistic differences from disorders: The past, present, and future of nonbiased assessment. *Topics in Language Disorders, 3*(3), 1–7.

Thal, D., & Tobias, S. (1992). Communicative gestures in children with delayed onset of oral expressive vocabulary. *Journal of Speech and Hearing Research, 35,* 1281–1289.

Thomas, S. (1993). Rethinking assessment: Teachers and students helping each other through the "sharp curves of life." *Learning Disability Quarterly, 16*(4), 257–279.

Washington, J. A., & Craig, H. K. (1994). Dialectal forms during discourse of poor, urban, African American preschoolers. *Journal of Speech and Hearing Research, 37,* 816–823.

Werner, E., & Kresheck, J. D. (1983). *Structured Photographic Expressive Language Test-II.* Sandwich, IL: Janelle Publications.

Westby, C. E. (1990). Ethnographic interviewing: Asking the right questions to the right people in the right ways. *Journal of Childhood Communication Disorders, 13,* 101–111.

Westby, C. E., StevensDominguez, M., & Oetter, P. (1996). A performance/competence model of observational assessment. *Language, Speech and Hearing Services in Schools, 27,* 144–156.

Wetherby, A. M., Cain, D., Yonclas, D., & Walker, V. (1988). Analysis of intentional communication of normal children from the prelinguistic to the multiword stage. *Journal of Speech and Hearing Research, 31,* 240–252.

Wetherby, A. M., & Prizant, B. M. (1993). *Communication and Symbolic Behavior Scales.* Chicago: Applied Symbolix.

Wetherby, A. M., Prizant, B. M., & Hutchinson, T. A. (1998). Communicative, social/affective, and symbolic profiles of young children with autism and pervasive developmental disorders. *American Journal of Speech-Language Pathology, 7*(2), 79–91.

Wetherby, A. M., & Prutting, C. (1984). Profiles of communicative and cognitive-social abilities in autistic children. *Journal of Speech and Hearing Research, 27,* 364–377.

Wetherby, A. M., Yonclas, D., & Bryan, A. (1989). Communication profiles of preschool children with handicaps: Implications for early identification. *Journal of Speech and Hearing Disorders, 54,* 148–158.

World Health Organization. (1992). *International code of diseases* (10th ed.). 10. New York: Author.

Zimmerman, I. L., Steiner, V. G., & Pond, R. E. (1992). *Preschool Language Scale* (3rd ed.). San Antonio, TX: Psychological Corporation.

CHAPTER 10

ASSESSMENT OF BASIC RELATIONAL CONCEPTS

ANN E. BOEHM

An understanding of basic concepts is necessary for the young child to deal with the demands of everyday living and to build upon in later learning. *Basic concepts,* as the term is used here, involve the child's ability to make relational judgments, either among objects, persons, or situations, or in reference to a standard. Basic concepts help the child understand and describe relationships between and among objects, locations of objects and persons, characteristics of objects (dimensions, positions, movements, quantity, and presence), and sequences of events. Basic concepts are called upon early in the child's life as interactions take place in situations, such as the child pointing to a table and saying, "Cookie *on* table," or with the mother responding to the child and saying, "Look *under* the bed for the ball." As the child develops, basic concepts are used to order, to make comparisons, to classify, to conserve, and to solve problems. All these abilities are applied in a wide variety of situations (Boehm, 1976). As deVilliers and deVilliers (1979) pointed out when describing the development of word meaning, "Still more complex are the meanings of relational words, such as the dimensional adjectives big and little, tall and short or thick and thin. Their correct use depends on reference to some standard that varies with the object described and with the context in which it is placed" (p. 123).

As Flavell (1970) noted, there is no one universally accepted definition of a concept. Contributing to the diversity of definitions is the fact that concepts vary in their inclusiveness, generalizability, preciseness, and importance. Consistent with this observation, there is no one definition of what constitutes a basic concept. A writer's definition thus determines the scope and range of possible concepts included on a particular assessment instrument. This definition can be more delimited such as that used by Boehm (1969, 1971, 1976, 1986a,b) to include the relational concepts of size, distance, position

in space, time, and quantity. Or it can be used more generally to include all receptive concept areas likely to be encountered by young children including color, shape, letter identification, numbers and counting, social and emotional concepts, and textural material, along with relational concepts, such as that used by Bracken (1984, 1998). Many preschool assessment tasks encompass such a broad definition. Some examples will be presented later in this chapter.

The term *basic concepts,* as used in this chapter, refers only to relational concepts of size, distance, position in space, time, and quantity. These basic concepts differ from other concepts the young child is called upon to use. For example, when the child has developed a concept of an object such as a table, the internal image of a table—that of an object with a flat surface on four legs—soon becomes fairly stable. As the child encounters new objects that are tables, he or she can make a match between the new object and the internal image (concept) of a table. In contrast, consider the basic concept pairs *first–last* and *near–far.* The child will not easily form a stable image of these concepts, for they are shifting in nature and must be applied to new and different situations. In addition, they can be applied at different levels of complexity. *First* and *last* can be used to designate positions in space and in time. The car *first* in line on one occasion can be *last* on another. The *last* thing a child worked on yesterday might be the *first* thing he or she worked on today. Likewise with *near* and *far,* which help describe distance in space or time and illustrate other levels of complexity. We can speak of the animal *near* or *far* away from a tree that we can see, a friend who lives *far* away whom we cannot see, and a planet so *far* away we may never be able to see it.

The child's ability to make such relational decisions is necessary at the preschool level to do the following: follow instructions ("Justin, go to the *front* of the line"); comprehend stories ("When the dog was frightened, she hid '*under* the bed'"); describe situations or events to others ("I went to bed *early* because I was tired"); facilitate communication with others ("I want the *long* jump rope"); and describe thoughts and feelings ("My friend moved *far* away").

As children engage in early learning activities that prepare them for school and later in the formal learning of reading and arithmetic, they increasingly need to draw upon their fund of basic concepts to follow directions and understand instructions such as "Mark all the words that *begin* with the letter b," or "Which is *more,* 5 + 2 or 3 + 7?" Given these examples, it readily becomes apparent that the assessment of basic concepts among preschool children, age 2 to 6 years, is of importance and interest. This assessment needs to focus on at least two dimensions of basic concept use: the child's understanding of these terms as demonstrated through action, manipulation of objects, or in response to pictured situations; and the child's use of these concepts in his or her everyday language.

The set of basic concepts of concern in this chapter includes relational terms such as *top–bottom, same– different, in front of–behind, near–far,* and *right–left,* many of which have been identified in the Boehm Test of Basic Concepts—Revised (Boehm-R, 1986) and Boehm Test of Basic Concepts—Preschool Version (1986), which measure 50 and 26 basic relational terms, respectively. Bracken (1984, 1990, 1998) also includes relational concepts on the Bracken Basic Concept Scale-R. Other tests include a subsample of basic relational concepts, a selection of which will be detailed later.

IMPORTANCE OF BASIC RELATIONAL CONCEPTS

Instruction

The importance of understanding basic concepts can be documented in a number of ways. Studying the complexity of verbal directions used by teachers in grades K through 5, Kaplan (1978) recorded the verbal interactions of three teachers at each of these grade levels while engaged in different areas of instruction; each teacher was recorded for a total of one hour. The level of complexity of teacher directions (number of behavior steps to be followed and qualifying statements such as "put the big ball on the small box") was found to be similar across the grade levels studied, with 82 percent of all teacher directions containing no more than two behaviors and two qualifiers. Kaplan then developed "the directions game," a task designed to assess the extent to which children understood teacher directions. Of the qualifiers contained in "the directions game," at least 41 percent were basic concepts as defined in this chapter. The better the performance on the Boehm-R, the better the performance was on "the directions game" ($r = .71$).

Reanalysis of Kaplan's transcripts of teacher verbal directions (Boehm, Kaplan, & Preddy, 1980) revealed that 33 of the 50 Boehm-R terms (plus 18 antonyms, synonyms, or other comparative forms of these terms) were used by grade K through 2 teachers. Of the teacher directions recorded, 34.7 percent contained at least one Boehm-R term, its synonym, antonym, or comparative form. This count did not include the use of other basic concepts or "easier" basic concepts such as *in* and *on,* which occurred frequently. These findings highlight the importance of basic concepts in following teachers' directions. Using a similar approach, Boehm, Classon, and Kelly (1986) recorded the basic concepts used by prekindergarten teachers in their verbal directions. One-hour samples of two teachers of 3-year-old children and of four teachers of 4-year-old children were included. These teachers used 47 of the relational concepts assessed by the BTBC-PV or BTBC-R, plus 10 synonyms of these terms: (e.g., *apart* for *separated*). These findings help highlight the importance of basic concepts in following teacher directions, both during a child's preschool and early school experiences.

The frequency with which basic concepts appeared in current reading and mathematics curricula was also studied by Boehm and coworkers (1980). Counting all words (on a 20-page sample from five reading series and five arithmetic series) read by teachers to children or by the children themselves in workbooks at each grade level, K through 2, revealed that all Boehm-R words were used; they accounted for 9.5 percent and 8.8 percent of all words presented in the reading and arithmetic workbooks sampled, respectively. Antonyms, synonyms, and comparative forms of the Boehm-R terms accounted for another 9.7 percent and 6.8 percent of the words used, and easier basic concepts (especially *in* and *on*) for a further 11.1 percent and 8.1 percent.

This review helps underscore the importance of basic concepts in understanding early instruction. At the time of school entrance, however, many school children have not yet learned the meaning of many of these concepts (Boehm, 1966, 1969, 1971, 1986a,b), which might place them at a disadvantage in their early school experience. Therefore, assessment of children's understanding of basic concepts during the preschool years is an important consideration.

Test Taking

The importance of basic concepts in following directions on standardized tests was reported by Kaufman (1978), who reviewed the directions on four individual tests of ability: the ITPA, McCarthy Scales (Cognitive Scale), Binet L-M (years 2 through 7), and WPPSI. Kaufman found that these tests often assumed children's understanding of basic concepts as measured by the Boehm-R. On the four tests, respectively, 0, 7, 5, and 14 basic concepts were required to comply with the directions. In addition, easier concepts that could be troublesome for preschoolers (3, 10, 10, and 10 easier concepts for the four tests, respectively) were included.

Kaufman concluded that it is important for the assessor to review what the child is *required to do to comply with test directions.* Kaufman's findings relative to tests of ability were confirmed by Bracken (1986a), who studied the incidence of 258 concepts from the Bracken Scale in 11 categorized areas (color, shape, letter identification, numbers and counting, social/emotional and textural material along with comparison, direction/position, size, quantity, and time) in the directions of five intelligence tests commonly used in the United States. Many of these concepts appeared frequently in the verbal directions.

Cummings and Nelson (1980) extended Kaufman's conclusions regarding the understanding of basic concepts to verbal directions of achievement tests. These researchers analyzed the incidence of the Boehm-R concepts in the oral directions of four commonly used achievement measures: The California Achievement Tests, Iowa Tests of Basic Skills, Metropolitan Achievement Tests, and the Stanford Diagnostic Reading Test. Each of these tests assumed children's understanding of basic concepts (11, 8, 15, and 8, respectively) in addition to easier relational concepts assessed on the BTBC-PV (1986). Across tests, a child needs to understand basic concepts, however they are defined, to comply with test demands. This finding clearly needs to be a concern for professionals who work with preschool children. Kaufman (1978) recommended that assessors working with preschool children need to determine children's knowledge of basic concepts, teach those concepts needed to comply with the administrative aspects of test directions, and question results from individual tests already administered that contain many basic concepts in the test directions, a concern underscored by Cummings and Nelson (1980) and Bracken (1986a). Some tests, such as the Gates-MacGinitie Reading Tests (MacGinitie, 1989) and the K-ABC (Kaufman & Kaufman, 1983), alert test users to basic concepts needed to comply with directions.

Kennedy (1970) pointed out other problems children encounter in following language used in test instructions and items: the use of the passive voice, the order of presentation in directions not following the order of actions called for, long sentences placing severe demands on memory, and functional words, which include relational terms, not being stressed despite their importance.

In addition, to assess children's understanding of individual basic concepts, assessors need to consider children's ability to use the concepts in combination with other concepts. In samples of verbal statements of first grade teachers collected by Kaplan (1978), 29.9 percent included two or more relational concepts. Thus, an application's booklet was introduced with the Boehm-R to assess concepts in combination and as tools of thinking in making higher-order relational decisions.

DEVELOPMENT OF BASIC CONCEPTS

Developmental Framework

The ways in which children learn the use of basic concepts and the developmental order of their acquisition have important implications both for assessment and instruction. Our understanding about concept acquisition comes largely from the fields of cognitive development and language acquisition. The typical stages children pass through as they acquire individual concepts, the types of errors they make, and some of the reasons that have been offered to explain the stages of acquisition are considered next.

The work of Piaget and his associates has given us important insight into how the young child's thinking develops (Flavell, 1970; Piaget, 1967). These researchers emphasized that a young child does not perceive the world in the same way as does an adult but progresses through a sequential order of developmental stages in solving problems. Of the four stages detailed, the first two have particular relevance to assessing concept understanding in the 2- to 6-year-old child (Table 10.1).

Another avenue for understanding basic concept development is the child's development of language. Among the earliest words used by the child, according to deVilliers and deVilliers (1979), are those used "to regulate his interaction with his parents—'in, more, no, up, out, open, and the like'" (p. 31). Relational words are used by 18- to 24-month-old children, and their correct

TABLE 10.1   Assessment Features at Early Developmental Stages

BEHAVIORS	IMPLICATIONS FOR ASSESSMENT
Sensorimotor stage (0 to 2 years)	
Child reacts to the world through motor behavior	Observation of child's manipulation of objects
Child observes the world around and develops rudimentary concepts	Imitation of assessor's behaviors
Child learns that objects have permanence and looks for hidden objects	Response to assessor's verbal requests, including concept labels
Child engages in trial-and-error play and looks for hidden objects	
Preoperational stage (2 to 7 years)	
Language plays an increasingly important role	Observation of child's manipulative and verbal response to questions
Child's perspective continues to be egocentric observation of child's ability to take the perspective of another	
Child focuses on visual appearance of objects	
Child begins to be able to group on the basis of one characteristic	Grouping of objects together based on one common characteristic assessed
Child follows sequence of events	Child's ability to sequence events assessed
Child begins to reverse	Observation of child's ability to reverse a procedure
One-to-one correspondence is developed	Observation of child's ability to engage in one-to-one correspondence

and incorrect usage has been traced in many studies. For example, the young child might overextend a word beyond its appropriate application by calling any moving vehicle a "car." The earliest uses of words made by the child refer to a variety of objects or situations, and the very young child probably understands more than he or she is able to communicate.

Going beyond single words to two-word utterances and phrases, the 2-year-old child is able to communicate relationships that express location (e.g., "ball *in* box"), recurrence (e.g., "*more* cookie"), and negation (e.g., "*no more* cookie"), all of which are related to basic concepts. Examples cited by deVilliers and deVilliers (1979) included the relational terms *all, again, outside, more, some, in, off, another,* and *on.*

From the ages 2 to 4, children's ability to express themselves expands greatly as they learn to respond to different types of questions and relational terms. Some

relational terms can have the same meaning for the child of 2½ or 3 years as for the adult (E. Clark, 1978). E. Clark (1973) traced a number of stages in the development of the easiest relational terms, *in, on,* and *under.* These stages, along with those noted in other studies, apply to the acquisition of basic concepts in general:

1. The child does not know the concept or its term.
2. The child knows something about the object, attribute, or event the concept designates; this understanding is gained through general experience.
3. The child has partial knowledge of a specific concept or concept pair.
4. The child might have certain preferences (nonlinguistic strategies) by which he or she responds to a task, for example, liking to put things in other things or choosing things with more, irrespective of the concepts. [Clark (1973, 1980) clarified this

issue by noting that the child's response preferences might make it appear that the child understands or knows what he or she really does not. For example, the tendency to put things on other things conforms to the correct position of *top* and might make it appear that the child knows *top* versus *bottom* when given a task tapping this concept pair. It also might facilitate learning the concept *top*. When this response tendency does not conform, however, it might appear that the child does not understand the concept, whereas the child might actually have some partial understanding.]

5. The child uses the positive or most extended member of a concept pair before the negative or least extended member so that it is likely the child will learn *top* before learning *bottom*.

6. The child might overextend the concept term to include other similar concepts (*big* is used to refer to things that are *tall*).

7. The child confuses the positive member of a concept pair with its opposite (*much* is also used to refer to *less*).

8. The child understands and can use the concept in the same way as an adult would but not at all levels of complexity.

9. The child might know a concept in some contexts and not be able to apply it in others.

In addition to basic concepts that denote location, deVilliers and deVilliers (1978) reviewed the development of many spatial concepts from the more general *big–little* to the more specific *tall–short, long–short, high–low, wide–narrow,* and *thick–thin.* As terms become more specific, they become more difficult because more components of meaning are associated with them. A number of other researchers have explored the acquisition of relational concepts and have contributed to the understanding of their development; among these are Blewitt (1982), Clark (1983), French and Nelson (1985), Richards and Haupe (1981), and Richards (1982).

The perspective summarized thus far reflects E. Clark's (1971) "semantic features" model of concept acquisition in which meaning components of concepts are acquired over time, which can result in partial knowledge of these concept terms. French (1985) disagrees with this position and argues that young children can demonstrate the full lexical meanings of terms such as *before* and *after* depending on the context of the task. French proposes a "context-sensitive" model for understanding children's comprehension of relational terms in which children gradually extend the contexts to which they can apply their knowledge (p. 326). Assessment of relational concepts at the preschool level, therefore, needs to consider children's knowledge of these concepts across contexts and to identify the conditions under which children can display their knowledge. For example, French and Nelson (1985) demonstrated that when asked to *describe* familiar events (such as eating at a restaurant), children as young as 3 years used the temporal terms *before* and *after* correctly. From my perspective, both models are useful in helping assessors translate outcomes into intervention with the decontextualized use of concepts as the ultimate goal.

Individual Basic Concepts

In relation to concept attainment in general (see D. Clark, 1971 and E. Clark, 1983, for helpful reviews), it is known that children's understanding increases with age and progresses from general application to specific, precise application, and from concrete to abstract levels of application. This developmental progression occurs at different age levels and rates for different concepts. The concepts learned can be applied more accurately in some contexts or situations than others. Children might have partial rather than complete mastery of more complex concepts by the time they enter school. Furthermore, children might have some understanding of the concepts but not have the words for them, even by 8 or 9 years (deVilliers & deVilliers, 1978; Meisner, 1973).

The types of errors children make on concept tasks provide us with insights into how they think. A review of studies exploring the acquisition of some relational terms uncovers a number of rather systematic errors. Most studies have focused on preschool children who attend university-based nursery schools or who come from middle-class backgrounds (the assessment of concepts among children from many backgrounds is discussed later). Implications for the assessor based on these studies include the following:

- By the age of 5 or 6 years, children have a fairly complete mastery of most basic concept terms.
- There are systematic, sequential stages of acquisition of meaning of a concept.
- Different basic concepts are the sources of different types of errors.
- Acquisition of one member of a concept pair usually precedes acquisition of the other.

- The context in which a concept is used influences a child's performance.
- With development, children are able to use concepts across contexts.

Different studies have assessed the acquisition of the same concepts in different ways (pantomime, imitation, spontaneous speech, acting out, elicitation, teaching comprehension, reaction time, and opposite games). In addition, basic concepts have been assessed in different contexts from study to study and at different levels of complexity. These comparative studies have revealed the following:

- Relational concepts apply to a series of shifting referents.
- The nature of the task and the familiarity of the context affect the ease of the concept.
- Words that have both spatial and temporal meanings are not learned at the same time to apply to both contexts.
- Some tasks present a greater demand on the child's memory load.
- Some concepts are more abstract and difficult than others and require the child to learn more components of meaning (such as cross laterality with the concepts *right* and *left*).

The use of most basic concepts develops gradually over time and is not an all-or-none process. Some of the major findings are highlighted next to provide a focus for the assessor of the preschool child. The examples given typify problems children encounter as they acquire different basic concepts.

Before–After **(First–Last).**   Many studies (Amidon & Carey, 1972; Beilin, 1975; Carni & French, 1984; E. Clark, 1970, 1971; Coker, 1978; French & Brown, 1977; French & Nelson, 1985; Friedman & Seely, 1976; Johnson, 1975; Richards & Haupe, 1981) have revealed the following patterns among children 2 years, 11 months to 8 years of age: *Before* and *after* are easier for the child to respond to when the order of mention corresponds to the order of their occurrence. For example, "drink your milk *before* you eat the cake" is easier to follow than "*before* you eat the cake, drink your milk." Although omissions and/or reversals can occur, acquisition seems to proceed in the following order: understanding neither *before* nor *after;* understanding the concept term *before;* possibly overgeneralizing the concept term *before* to refer to *after;* and understanding both *before* and *after.*

Moreover, some words are understood in the spatial sense first, whereas others are understood in their temporal sense first. The complexity of modifiers and subordinate clauses can increase the difficulty of a task involving these concepts (e.g., "Put the blue box on the line *after* you put the red car on the line"). French (1985) and French and Nelson (1985) point out, however, that very young children can use these concepts as would an adult to describe familiar events. French found that in her tasks children acquired *before* and *after* at about the same time.

In Front of–Behind **(Ahead of, Front, Back of, Beside, Side).**   In addition to the problems common to the acquisition of other relational terms, *in front of* and *behind* present additional problems (Harris & Strommen, 1971; Kuczaj & Maratos, 1975; Levine & Carey, 1982). Objects with defined front and back features are easier to respond to than nonfeatured objects for which the child has to use himself or herself as the point of reference. Therefore, it is easier to respond to the back and front of a car than the back and front of a block. *Front* and *back* are acquired at about the same time, but *side* is more difficult, probably because *side* lacks specificity. The child needs to be able to take the perspective of another to understand how that person sees the *back* and *front* of objects.

More–Less.   The considerable interest in the concepts *more–less* (Donaldson & Balfour, 1968; Donaldson & Wales, 1970; Gathercole, 1985; Kavanaugh, 1976; Palermo, 1973, 1974; Trehub & Abramovitch, 1978; Weiner, 1974) has been an important stimulus to our present understanding of basic concept acquisition. More specifically, these studies have shown that a response preference for *more* might make this concept appear easier than *less,* when in fact this might not be the case, and the frequently observed confusion of *less* or *more* might be related to the number of response options presented in the task (often only two).

Same–Different.   Fewer studies have focused on the concepts *same–different* than on some others (Blake & Beilin, 1975; Fein & Eshleman, 1976; Glucksberg, 1975; Josephs, 1975), but their findings provide insight into the problems confronting the learner. They have shown that the context of the task, as well as singular and plural referents, are related to complexity. When attributes such as size and color are named, the child is better able to respond, so that the direction "Point to the boxes that are the *same* size" is easier than "Point to the boxes that are the *same.*"

The correct application of basic concepts takes place gradually and is dependent on the nature and complexity of the task and the context in which it is presented, as well as the developmental level of the child.

Assessment Procedures

Procedures currently available for the assessment of basic concepts, from informal observation to formal standardized tests, typically are not intended to and do not assess the breadth and scope of the preschool child's concept understanding; instead, they serve as guideposts for assessing general understanding of individual basic concepts. The tasks and tests presented here are designed to assess the level of a child's basic concept knowledge for the purpose of curriculum planning. All can be followed up by more intense observations of child behavior as demonstrated in sequentially ordered series of tasks that break down concepts into their different components and levels of complexity and that view concept use across contexts. The information yielded can be very useful for informing instruction.

Informal Measures

Observation is the essential beginning point for understanding children's thinking. Kamii (1971) stressed the need for observation of child behavior, with teachers probing to get at a child's meaning. This exploratory method can be used to record the child's spontaneous and elicited use of basic concepts. Cazden (1971) also stressed that assessment must relate to teaching goals and pointed to the importance of enriching the child's receptive and productive use of words. Children's understanding can be observed, according to Cazden, as they repeat sentences or phrases, describe and explain activities and events, retell stories, engage in classification activities, play games that involve following directions of increasing length, and so forth. Cazden presented a unit on relational words and exemplified a formative evaluation for each unit objective; this perspective might be useful to the assessor interested in observing the child's basic concept understanding. The assessor should take into account the child's comprehension and production of both positive and negative applications of the concept in relation to objects and pictures, simple uses as well as uses in multiple-part directions, viewing objects from different vantage points, and understanding opposites.

Systematic observation is the only practical way currently available to assess the breadth and scope of concept understanding and development over time. Many behaviors associated with basic concept acquisition can be viewed through observation (Boehm, 1976). Although simpler applications of concepts can be developed during the preschool years, the child's ability to apply these concepts to situations and events that represent increasing levels of complexity continue to develop during the elementary grades. Therefore, assessment of basic concepts should take place from different perspectives over time and should take into account both the receptive and expressive use of these concepts. A sample checklist for the development of basic concept is presented in Table 10.2.

Lidz (1983) urged that observation be used to observe the process and/or the style children use to solve problems in addition to the adequacy of their responses. Such observation focused on process has important implications for basic concept assessment and intervention.

Other informal measures are available that ask the assessor to observe the presence or absence of a broad range of specified behaviors on the part of the child; a number of basic concepts can be among the behaviors covered. Although the assessor's attention might be directed to individual basic concepts, more frequently concepts are used in combination with other concepts, such as "Point to the star in the *top left-hand corner.*" Two examples of informal measures follow:

1. Preschool Attainment Record (Doll, 1966a): This extension of the Vineland Social Maturity Scale is used with children to 7 years old. The presence or absence of several basic concepts such as *right* and *left* is assessed through interviewing the parent or other child care workers along with other concepts children need to deal with their environment.
2. Meeting Street School Screening Test (Hainsworth & Siqueland, 1969): On this test children are requested to act out concepts, such as *right* and *left* or *above* and *below,* by following multiple-part directions such as "Put (body part/object) above your head and *in front of you.*"

In addition, the Meeting Street School Screening Test assesses children's motor patterning abilities; visual, perceptual, and motor skills; language memory of words and sentences; counting of numbers forward, backward, and by twos; and ability to tell a story from a picture. Each of these areas is assessed to identify children in kindergarten and first grade who do not possess

TABLE 10.2 Basic Concept Development Checklist

Name of child _____

Concept pair _____

   I. Levels of development/concept differentiation
      A. No understanding of the concept pair
      B. Responds correctly to one number of the concept pair (indicate which)
      C. Confuses one member of the concept pair with its opposite (indicate which is confused)
      D. Can respond correctly when order of mention corresponds to order of presentation (for terms such as *before* and *after*)
      E. Omits part of longer concept directions (give example)
      F. Reverses parts of concept directions (give example)
      G. Responds correctly when features or attributes of objects are named
      H. Responds correctly when nonfeatured objects are named or objects are named without attributes
      I. Responds correctly to both members of a concept pair
      J. Can produce the opposite of a concept pair when asked to
  II. Use of verbal label for concept
      A. No spontaneous use of concept term
      B. Concept term used by child in natural communications with others to
          1. Describe events or objects
          2. Respond to general questions
          3. Express desires or needs
          4. Gain information
      C. Concept term used to respond to specific questions that are asked to elicit term
      D. Responds appropriately depending on the context of the task; i.e., may be able to use a term when describing a familiar activity
 III. Response through actions in situations structured to elicit such response
      A. Can respond appropriately using concept in relation to self, objects, and pictures
      B. Can respond when the concept is used in combination with other concepts
      C. Can respond to the concept used in its comparative forms
      D. Can use the concept to order
      E. Can use the concept to classify
      F. Can perceive the concept relation from another person's perspective
      G. Can respond to the moral as well as spatial use of the concept term

---

adequate language, visual, and motor skills to deal adequately with the symbolic information of traditional school curriculum and who might be at risk for learning disability. The test, which is individually administered, was developed for use with children 5–0 to 7–5 years.

Other informal measures are tied to teaching activities, some of which center around basic concepts. Two examples follow:

  1. Revised Brigance Diagnostic Inventory of Early Development (Brigance, 1991, 1978): This inventory assesses readiness and entry skills related to the subjects covered in grades K through 6. The outcomes of informal assessment lead to instructional objectives and guides to instruction. At the readiness level, directional and positional concepts are assessed in relationship to the children's own bodies (e.g., children identify their own *right* and *left* hands or place their hand *behind* or *next to* another body part).

  2. Portage Guide to Early Education, Revised (Bluma et al., 1976): This guide includes a checklist of 580 behaviors in six areas that are organized sequentially and are tied to activities. It was developed to be used by home-based teachers working with parents of very young children (birth to 6 years of age identified as having disabilities in one or more areas). Its purpose is to assess children's behavior and plan learning programs. Among the activities included are those involving cognitive and thinking skills, and seeing relationships. Some basic concepts are included.

Formal Assessment

Although numerous tests are available to assess the child at the preschool level, few of these have as their major focus specific assessment of basic concepts. Basic concepts are incorporated within some subtest items, but the intent of these subtests is to get at functions other than basic relational concept understanding. For example, the Detroit Tests of Learning Aptitude (DTLA-2) (Hammill, 1985) are used to assess children from age 6 through high school. Basic relational concepts are included on a Word Opposites subtest that requires children to give words that mean the opposite of the stimulus words. In another subtest, Oral Directions, children need to respond to complex multiple-part directions, many of which contain basic concepts such as *right, under, first,* and *last.* Thus, although basic concepts are involved both in the items and instructions of this test, the child's specific strengths or difficulties in dealing with basic concept terms are not assessed.

Tests of reading readiness include some assessment of basic concepts. It is important to note, however, that it is the total readiness score that is the focus of these tests and individual items are infrequently reviewed. In addition, the small size of the items and the child's familiarity with the objects or situations depicted in the pictures present a further problem in assessing concept understanding (see, for example, the Metropolitan Readiness Test, Nurss & McGauvran, 1986).

Other tests focus on the preschool and early school years and either specifically or along with other skills and objectives include the assessment of some basic concepts measured individually or in combination with other concepts. The following are some examples:

1. *Clinical Evaluation of Language Fundamentals— Preschool (CELF-Preschool):* The purpose of the test is to assess receptive and expressive language ability and explore language form and content. The CELF-Preschool, a downward extension of the CELF-3 (viewed as prerequisite for those skills covered on the CELF-3), is appropriate for children 3-0 to 6-11 years. The test consists of six subtests, three receptive language subtests (Linguistic Concepts, Sentence Structure, and Basic Concepts), and three expressive language subtests (Recalling Sentences in Context, Formulating Labels, and Word Structure). The record form includes a "Behavioral Observation Checklist" for recording behaviors observed during testing as well as an item analysis for each subtest to assist in the review of error patterns. The authors also recommend a "Quick Test" consisting of the Linguistic Concepts and Recalling Sentences in Context subtests when time is limited and the test is used as a preliminary step for classification and diagnostic decisions. The Linguistic Concepts subtest includes three levels of oral directions, which embed spatial, order, temporal, and quantitative concepts. The Basic Concepts subtest covers 18 relational concepts.

2. *The Boehm Test of Basic Concepts—Revised (Boehm-R, 1986):* This test surveys the kindergarten through second grade child's understanding of 50 basic relational concepts of position in space, direction, quantity, sequence, time, and size for the purpose of instructional planning. A total score can be obtained, and norms are provided for both Forms C and D of the test. However, the child's performance on each item serves as the major basis for interpretation, with information presented on items by grade, socioeconomic status, and time of year used. The items, in which pictures are named, focus on the child's understanding of the basic concepts being tapped. The Boehm-R was normed on children in kindergarten through second grade. An *Applications* booklet that assesses mastery of concepts used in combination, used in sequences, and used to make comparisons is available. A Spanish version is available as well as instructional activities detailed in the *Boehm Resource Guide for Basic Concept Teaching.*

The Boehm Test of Basic Concepts—Preschool Version (Boehm-PV, 1986): This test extends downward the Boehm-R and surveys the 3- to 5-year-old child's understanding of 26 easier basic relational concepts that help children understand and describe the world around them. The test is individually administered. The results are intended to be used by teachers to plan instruction and as indicators of school readiness.

3. *The Bracken Basic Concept Scale (Bracken, 1984):* This scale assesses 258 concepts in 11 categorical areas (color, letter identification, numbers/counting, comparison, shapes, direction/position, social-emotional, size, textural/material, quantity, and time/sequence. The test was developed to be used with children 2-6 to 8-0 years. Bracken divides his scale into two instruments: a diagnostic full-scale instrument and an alternate form screening test. The diagnostic scale is administered individually and assesses the full range of concepts included. The screening test, which can be administered individually or in small groups, consists of 30 items to identify children who might benefit from more intensive assessment. The primary use of the screening test is with kindergarten and first grade children. Thus, relational concepts, along with concepts in other skill areas such as color knowledge and letter identification, are included. An instructional program also has been developed to accompany the test, *The Bracken Concept Development Program* (Bracken, 1986b). This scale assesses 301 concepts in 11 categories (colors, letters, numbers/counting, sizes, comparisons, shapes, direction/position, self-/social awareness, texture/materials, quantity, and time/sequence). The first six subtests (Colors, Letters, Numbers and Counting, Sizes, Comparisons, and Shapes), which comprise the "School Readiness Composite," can be used for purposes of screening. A Spanish Edition is also available, which can be used as a criterion-referenced measure.

   4. *Circus (Anderson et al., 1974, 1976, 1979):* Circus was developed to provide prekindergarten and kindergarten teachers with comprehensive assessment information to help them diagnose children's instructional needs and evaluation programs. Level A covers the pre-primary level; Level B, grade 1; Levels C and D extend the test through grades 3 through 5. Circus consists of 17 instruments. Six of these assess basic concepts along with other concepts and areas of understanding. What Words Mean assesses understanding of nouns, verbs, and modifiers. How Much and How Many assesses counting skills, number concepts, and relational terms. How Words Work includes verbs, prepositions, and conjunctions. Listen to the Story assesses story comprehension and includes the terms *first* and *last*. Do You Know…? assesses picture recognition and comprehension that includes concept understanding, such as *most* (in relationship to money). Think It Through assesses understanding of group membership, sequences, and classification. The assessor can choose to use all or several of the 17 measures and a total score is obtained for each subtest. Teachers are encouraged to examine errors made by items and by children. A set of instructional activities, *After the Circus,* also has been developed.

   5. *The Cognitive Skills Assessment Battery, Second Edition (CSAB, Boehm & Slater, 1981):* The CSAB was developed to provide a profile of strengths and weaknesses of the prekindergarten and kindergarten child in the cognitive skills area and simultaneously a profile for the class as a whole. The skills areas included cover orientation to one's environment; large muscle and visual

motor coordination; discrimination of similarities and differences; auditory, visual, picture, and story memory; comprehension; and concept formation. Each task area is divided by levels of difficulty, providing teachers important information for program planning. Some relational concepts are included in the multiple directions task.

   6. *Developmental Tasks for Kindergarten Readiness-II (Lesiak & Lesiak, 1994):* The test was developed to screen children for purposes of instructional planning. It consists of 15 subtests that cover four skill areas (Oral Language, Visual-Motor Skills, Cognitive Skills, and Social Development).

   7. *Stanford Early School Achievement Test (Madden, Gardner, & Collins, 1983):* This group-administered test was developed to be used in kindergarten and beginning first grade and includes among its items the basic concepts *longest* and *beginning.* Concepts assessed when used in combination with other concepts include basic concepts such as *after, of, most, same, farthest,* and *third.*

   8. *Tests of Basic Experiences-2 (TOBE-2; Moss, 1979):* The purpose of this group-administered test is to assess the child's conceptual understanding to plan curricular experiences. It has two overlapping levels, one appropriate for preschool and kindergarten, and the other for kindergarten or grade 1. Each level consists of a battery of four tests: Mathematics, Language, Science, and Social Studies. Each of the four area tests include a breakdown of concepts and skills. Throughout the focus is on the child's conceptual understanding gained through experience rather than on facts. Some basic relational concepts are assessed individually or in combination with other concepts, along with other areas of understanding, on each test. Different tests can assess the same concept from different perspectives. In many cases the child needs to be familiar with the function of the picture depicted to respond to the concept terms. Mathematics assesses fundamental quantitative operations and terms, including basic concepts of size and quantity. Language assesses vocabulary and sentence structure, including position terms and identification of "same" sounds. Science assesses understandings gained through observation. It includes concepts that denote quality, such as *hardest,* and comprehension of objects and their functions, such as determining which ship is heaviest by its level in the water. Social Studies assesses children's understanding of social groups and roles, safety facts, and emotions and includes the relational concepts, such as *slow* and *fast.* The Test of Basic Experiences yields scores for each test in the battery and item scores can be obtained if desired.

Prepositions and adjectives, some of which are basic relational concepts, can be tapped to some extent on these measures. For example, the ability of the child to note similarities and differences and to produce opposites among the items presented is often assessed. In addition, understanding of basic concepts might be required to comply with task directions.

In this section a sample of preschool assessment tasks has been presented to illustrate how basic relational concepts are measured and the extent to which they are covered among commonly used tests. Boehm (1990) recommends a multiple-step model for assessing basic concepts, which includes:

1. *Standardized testing that covers the broad range of relational concepts and is used as a starting point for interpretation including those concepts the child knows and may not know.*
2. *Review of errors to identify patterns.*
3. *Observation over time of the child's use of concepts in everyday activities of the classroom environment.*
4. *A brief post-test interview to identify the strategies children use to arrive at answers.*
5. *A mini-teach to help determine how ready the child is to acquire the concept.*
6. *Observation of children's use of concepts as tools of thinking such as combining concepts and using them for comparing, classifying, and problem solving. (p. 658)*

In addition, assessors can provide information about children's production and comprehension as well as (where appropriate) their use of concepts across spatial and temporal contexts.

IMPLICATIONS FOR DIAGNOSIS AND REMEDIATION

Because the author is most familiar with the BTBC, this section focuses on results that have been evidenced through the use of that test. The issues raised, however, can be addressed to other formal and informal measures of concepts as well.

Basic concept assessment is used to determine the extent to which children understand those relational terms that are essential for complying with teacher directions and meeting the demands of early reading and mathematics tasks. The preschool child 3 to 6 years of age is in the process of acquiring these basic concepts. Although the child understands and is able to use few relational words

at age 3, most children of normal ability acquire the majority of these concepts by the time they enter grade 1. The child's understanding, however, probably does not encompass the many levels of concept application that will be called upon in reasoning tasks that involve ordering, classifying, talking, and later inductive reasoning.

Norms for both Forms C and D of the Boehm-R and the Boehm-PV increase with increasing grade level, and from the beginning to midyear within grade levels. Children from lower socioeconomic levels perform on the test in grades 1 and 2 as do children from more advantaged backgrounds at the end of kindergarten. The same concepts, however, are relatively easy or difficult across socioeconomic levels. The concepts *top, through, away from, next to,* and *first* are among the easiest, whereas the concepts *pair, fewest, left,* and *right* are among the most difficult. The major focus is on identifying concepts with which children are familiar and those in which they need instruction. Increased concept understanding by age was also evidenced on the BBCS (Bracken, 1984).

During the past 10 years increasing research attention has been directed toward understanding the cognitive processes that underlie task performance and the strategies children use to solve problems. This information can be useful for informing intervention and is particularly relevant to the assessment of basic concepts. In order to be successful at following directions including basic concepts, the child needs to:

- pay attention to the direction
- remember the direction
- be familiar with the objects or situations referred to
- focus on critical components and process this information
- scan pictorial representations
- recall from working memory key components
- respond appropriately based on this information

The assessor needs to identify which of these processes might be influencing performance. This can be accomplished in part through observation and follow-up tasks that measure such areas as memory span, vigilance, and breaking down tasks into smaller units.

Increasing evidence also exists to indicate that children's errors in general are not random. The research literature has helped us understand the kinds of errors children make in the process of learning basic concepts. A number of considerations include:

- To what extent is the child's use of a concept tied to a particular context?
- Can the child use a concept term spontaneously when describing objects or talking about events?

- To what extent can the child answer questions that include different levels of linguistic complexity?

There is invaluable benefit in exploring children's concept understanding through interviewing (Boehm, 1990). Children as young as 3 in day care centers can respond if questions are posed in ways they can understand and if they are given time to respond. Such interviews can yield information about related concepts a child knows, reasons for errors, and strategies used to arrive at answers (such as the elimination of choices).

Basic concepts are used in different ways to solve different cognitive tasks, from simple to complex. For example, words that *begin* with the same sound, responding to a question such as "What happened at the *beginning* of the story?" or identifying a child who is not at the *beginning* or *end* of the line. Basic concept understanding, therefore, needs to be considered from multiple perspectives and as applying to multiple levels of complexity. Assessing these multiple levels of use needs to be built into both informal and formal assessment procedures, which are used over time, such as using basic concepts:

- in combination with each other
- to make comparisons to a standard or with each other
- to classify
- to follow multiple-step instructions
- to order

The *Applications* booklet of the Boehm-R begins to address these issues.

Special Needs Children

The results of studies of basic concept understanding and development in special needs populations help us understand how these children develop relational concepts and have important implications for remediation.

Blind Children. A tactile analogue to the BTBC, called the Tactile Test of Basic Concepts, was developed by Caton (1976, 1977) using raised geometric forms that paralleled all BTBC (1971) items. Using it with a sample of 25 blind children, at each grade level from kindergarten through grade 2 attending residential and public schools in 1974, Caton found that the blind children performed in a manner generally similar to lower socioeconomic level children in the normative sample; those enrolled in public schools performed somewhat better than those in residential schools. When the understanding of individual concepts of blind children was compared to that of sighted children in the normative

population, a moderately similar concept difficulty was seen in kindergarten, but 11 and 12 concepts were more difficult in grades 1 and 2, respectively. The easiest concepts were those that required the child to use himself or herself as the reference, such as *behind* and *next to.* The most difficult concepts were those that required comparative judgments, such as *third* and *in order.* Caton pointed to the need for continued emphasis on basic relational concepts in instruction after kindergarten.

Educable Mentally Retarded Children. BTBC performance of 100 EMR children from middle-class backgrounds was studied by Chin (1976). All attended public schools in a large urban setting. Four age groups were studied, with mental-age equivalents generally comparable to those of children in kindergarten through third grade (mean mental ages of 4-6, 6-6, 7-3, and 8-6 corresponding to chronological ages of 6-7, 9-7, 11-5, and 13-2, respectively). The mean BTBC scores for each of these groups were 20.0, 34.2, 38.1, and 43.0, respectively. The 9- and 11-year-old EMR children responded like normal kindergarten children, and 13-year-old EMR children like normal first graders. Although a four- to seven-year lag was demonstrated when chronological age was used as the basis for comparison, the difference was less pronounced when mental age was used as the basis of comparison. EMR children do acquire basic concepts, although the rate of development is slower than among normal children, suggesting the importance of early instruction. The order of concept difficulty largely paralleled that found in the normative population.

Nelson and Cummings (1981) also demonstrated a significant developmental trend in basic concept understanding among 45 EMR black and white children in a semirural area of northeastern Georgia. The children studied ranged in age from 7-0 to 10-7. Although significant gains were demonstrated, the oldest group continued to demonstrate a gap in their concept repertoire, incorrectly responding to a mean of 10.2 concepts. The four most difficult concepts for this group were *in order, least, pair,* and *third.* These authors also underscored the importance of systematic instruction of basic concepts.

Hearing-Impaired Children. When the BTBC was used with hearing-impaired children, Davis (1974) found that those of normal intelligence fell increasingly behind their normal-age mates; more than two-thirds of the 24 children age 6-0 to 8-1 whom I studied fell below the first percentile. The greater their hearing loss, the poorer their performance was on the BTBC. Although there was no overall pattern of errors over the concept types, the most difficult concepts were generally the same for these children as for those in the normal-hearing group studied by Davis, and included *between, always, medium-sized, separated, left, pair, skip, equal, third,* and *last.* Davis stressed the need for specific instruction of basic relational concepts with these children.

Brown (1976), who studied 30 hearing-impaired children aged 7-1 to 11-11, found that deaf children who are taught signed English acquired basic relational concepts at an earlier age than those taught speech reading only. Brown also documented error patterns exhibited by hearing-impaired children as contrasted with normal hearing children. Results of Dickie's (1980) study supported a total communication approach over the aural/oral approach in instruction of basic concepts with 30 severely and profoundly hearing-impaired children.

Bracken and Cato (1986) compared the rate of concept development across two samples of children, those diagnosed as deaf and those with normal hearing abilities. The sample of 34 subjects was matched on the basis of age, sex, race, and geographic region. It was found that the deaf children performed consistently more poorly than the hearing children on each of the BBCS (Bracken, 1984) subtests and Total Test. In fact, the deaf children scored approximately 2 standard deviations below the nonimpaired children on each of the subscales and the total scale and consistently showed retardation in their conceptual development, though none was intellectually impaired and none was diagnosed as exceptional in any way other than hearing ability.

Syntactically Deviant Children.   Spector (1977) studied the BTBC performance of syntactically deviant kindergarten children with normal intelligence. Generalized weakness was noted when they were compared to their normal age-mates, and 16 of the concepts assessed were much more difficult for these children. Spector's findings with kindergarten children were consistent with the work of Wiig and Semel (1976), who also reviewed the research relevant to language-processing problems among LD school-age children. These authors stressed that although LD children can have an adequate vocabulary, the task of processing spoken language is a complex one involving auditory memory, understanding of syntax, and comprehension of concepts. Each of these areas can present problems for the LD child and decrease the rate at which spoken language is processed. Adjectives and prepositions that designate location, space, time, quantity, and quality (many of which are ba-

sic relational concepts) present special problems. Therefore, concepts that are conveyed in verbal teacher directions would be poorly processed by these children. Spector (1979) speculated on possible difficulties syntactically deviant children might encounter when responding to directions containing relational concepts. She elaborated strategies and the cognitive abilities language therapists needed to consider during instruction with basic concepts.

Learning Disabled Children.   There is consistent evidence that young children who have been classified as learning disabled also have difficulty with many basic relational concepts. When compared with their peers who do not demonstrate problems, LD children demonstrated both lower mean scores and greater score variability on the BTBC (Di Napoli, Kagedan-Kage, & Boehm, 1980; Kavale, 1982). In both of these studies LD children lagged behind their peers in their understanding of basic concepts.

Children from Non-English-Speaking Backgrounds.
A Spanish version of the BTBC (Form A, 1971; Form B, 1973) was normed on 1,292, 1,280, and 1,279 pupils at the beginning of the year, midyear, and end of year, respectively, in Puerto Rico (Preddy, Boehm, & Shepherd, 1984). Achievement data were collected one year later. The results, which largely paralleled the mainland U.S. norms, demonstrated both increasing mastery with age and a similar relative order of concept difficulty. The BTBC results showed a strong predictive relationship one year later with language and mathematics as measured by two Spanish-Language achievement tests. Translated versions of the BTBC used with other cultural groups repeatedly have pointed to the need for basic concept instruction in bilingual programs (Mickelson & Galloway, 1973; Patterson, 1981).

The procedures for translation of the BTBC into Spanish were repeated with the Spanish translation of the Boehm-R (1987). These included (1) an initial translation from English to Spanish, (2) a blind back-translation, (3) repetitions of steps a and b until the back-translation resembled the original English version, (4) a review by a national bilingual committee of teachers, and (5) field testing with bilingual children from Texas, California, and Missouri. The validation of the Spanish translation of the Boehm-R (1987) is currently in progress.

BBCS has also been translated into Spanish, and has been partially validated in the United States, Puerto

Rico, and Venezuela (Bracken et al., in press). Bracken and Fouad (1987) conducted a comprehensive multistep translation and validation process that included (1) an initial translation from English to Spanish, (2) a blind back-translation, (3) repetitions of steps a and b until the back-translation was very similar to the original English version, (4) review by a multinational bilingual committee, (5) pilot field testing, and (6) a more extensive pilot testing and item analysis.

After this initial translation and validation project, the BBCS was further validated through a large-scale administration (approximately 300 subjects) of the instrument in Puerto Rico, Venezuela, and the southwestern United States (Bracken et al., 1990). The results of this large-scale validation evidenced high age–score subtest developmental correlations across the three samples (median correlations, Puerto Rican = .76, Venezuelan = .55, and Mexican American = .71); subtest intercorrelations across the three samples were consistently as high or higher than the U.S. Anglo standardization sample intercorrelations by age; and item rank-order correlations between the three samples and the U.S. Anglo standardization sample were fairly uniformly moderate to high (with a few low and negative correlations); and coefficient alpha reliabilities for the Total Test exceeded .90 for all samples and all age levels.

The study by Bracken and coworkers (1990) demonstrated that across cultural samples, the basic concept construct is quite similar in its sequence of acquisition and age-related progression. The comparability of the intercorrelations across the three Latin samples and the U.S. Anglo standardization sample demonstrates a similar construct structure across the samples. Cross-cultural equivalence of the BBCS for the three distinct Latin samples and the U.S. Anglo sample was supported.

The studies cited all indicate that within a broad range of special populations there is delayed acquisition of basic concepts. For many children, their lack of concept mastery becomes more pronounced with time in school. Although the relative ease or difficulty of individual concepts tends to vary in the normative population, specific concepts can present special problems for different groups of children.

The poorer performance among these groups suggests that children with special learning needs are likely to have difficulty processing teacher directions and learning materials that involve basic concepts. Furthermore, because the complexity of concept use increases with time in school to include multiple-part directions and more abstract applications, the assessor can antici-

pate that the difficulty these children encounter will be compounded.

Although the need for remedial instruction is clear, it is necessary to question whether specific instruction in basic concepts is effective. Studies have suggested two benefits of such training. Thai (1973) reported that nursery school children who participated in a concept-learning program made significant improvement on the BTBC from pre- to posttesting. Concept instruction was also reported to result in significant improvement with Headstart children (Levin et al., 1975). Instruction, then, seems to benefit preschool children's understanding of basic concepts.

Moers and Harris (1978) reported a study of two groups of children from low-middle to middle-class backgrounds. The experimental group participated in an organized sequence of concept instruction that lasted for 15 weeks, while the control group was engaged in placebo activities. Both the experimental and control groups were then tested and received increased scores on the BTBC. After a semester of no specific training, however, the experimental group performed better on both the reading and mathematics sections of the Stanford Achievement Test. The authors concluded that the concept-training program resulted in a generalized improvement in academic functioning. First grade, low- to middle-class children at the Central Arkansas Education Center (1972) who received enrichment experience based on the BTBC also achieved higher BTBC scores and reading scores than children taught by traditional methods. These results were corroborated by Nason (1986) who studied the effects of systematic instruction of basic concepts using a translated version of the *Boehm Resource Guide for Basic Concept Teaching* (Boehm, 1976) on achievement of first grade children from low-income families in Puerto Rico. Not only did systematic instruction improve children's understanding of basic concepts, but children receiving such instruction also demonstrated significantly higher scores on tests of achievement in language and mathematics.

A number of major reviews suggest considerations to be taken into account when planning concept instruction (see, for example, D. C. Clark, 1971; Klausmeir, 1976, 1992; Tennyson & Cocchiarella, 1986; Tennyson & Park, 1980).

SUMMARY

Assessment of the preschool child's understanding of basic relational concepts can supply the classroom teacher and specialist with important information about the child. From a developmental perspective, a child's ability to identify basic concepts and/or produce their labels provides cues as to his or her concept and language acquisition. Formal testing can serve only as the beginning point for understanding concept development; it can be followed up by tasks devised to determine specific levels of responding, which can be compared with those levels noted in the literature. Ongoing, systematic observation can help us understand the breadth and scope with which specific concepts are applied.

Because basic concepts occur frequently in teachers' verbal directions and in directed learning experiences in reading and mathematics, assessment of basic concepts can help in planning instruction. Instruction and remediation are the primary uses of assessment procedures that measure basic concepts. Children who have special learning needs also have more pronounced gaps in their basic concept repertoire. Special attention needs to be given to basic concepts when teaching or testing these children.

Finally, the use of basic concepts in the administrative sections of other tests underscores the need to determine which of these terms children need to know to comply with the demands of the tests. Because it is difficult to present verbal directions without using basic concepts, their assessment should be an integral component of assessment procedures used with young children.

REFERENCES

Amidon, A., & Carey, P. (1972). Why five year-olds cannot understand before and after. *Journal of Verbal Learning, Verbal Behavior, 11*, 417–423.

Anderson, S. B., Bogatz, G. A., & Draper, T. (1974, 1979). *Circus*. Princeton, NJ: Educational Testing Service.

Anderson, S. B., Bogatz, G. A., & Draper, T. (1976). *Circus: Levels A and B* (Teacher's ed. of the manual and technical report). Menlo Park, CA: Addison-Wesley.

Ault, R. L., Cromer, C. C., & Mitchell, C. (1977). The Boehm Test of Basic Concepts: A three-dimensional version. *Journal of Educational Research, 70*(4), 186–188.

Beilin, H. (1975). *Studies in the cognitive basis of language development*. New York: Academic Press.

Blake, J., & Beilin, H. (1975). The development of "same" and "different" judgments. *Journal of Experimental Child Psychology, 19*, 177–194.

Blewitt, P. (1982). Word meaning acquisition in young children: A review of theory and research. In H. W. Reese & L. P. Lipsitt (Eds.), *Advances in child development and behavior* (Vol. 17, pp. 139–195). New York: Academic Press.

Bloom, L. (1991). *Language development from two to three*. New York: Cambridge University Press.

Bloom, L., & Lahey, M. (1978). *Language development and language disorders*. New York: Wiley.

Bluma, S., Shearer, A., Frohmann, A., & Hillard, J. (1976). *Portage guide to early education* (Rev. ed.). Portage, WI: Portage Project.

Boehm, A. E. (1966). *The development of comparative concepts in primary school children*. Unpublished doctoral dissertation, Columbia University.

Boehm, A. E. (1969, 1971). *Boehm Test of Basic Concepts*. New York: Psychological Corporation.

Boehm, A. E. (1970, 1973). *Prueba Boehm de Conceptos Basicos*. New York: Psychological Corporation.

Boehm, A. E. (1976). *Boehm resource guide for basic concept teaching*. New York: The Psychological Corporation.

Boehm, A. E. (1986a). *Boehm Test of Basic Concepts—Revised*. San Antonio, TX: Psychological Corporation.

Boehm, A. E. (1986b). *Boehm Test of Basic Concepts—Preschool Version*. San Antonio, TX: Psychological Corporation.

Boehm, A. E. (1987). *Prueba Boehm de Conceptos Basicos* (Rev. ed.). New York: Psychological Corporation.

Boehm, A. E. (1990). Assessing children's knowledge of basic concepts. In C. R. Reynolds & P. W. Kampaus (Eds.), *Handbook of psychological and educational assessment of children: Intelligence and achievement* (pp. 654–670). Austin, TX: Psychological Corporation.

Boehm, A. E., Classon, B., & Kelly, M. (1986). *Preschool teachers' spoken use of basic concepts*. Unpublished manuscript, Teachers College, Columbia University, New York.

Boehm, A. E., Kaplan, C., & Preddy, D. (1980). *How important are basic concepts to instruction: Validation of the Boehm Test of Basic Concepts*. Unpublished paper, Teachers College, Columbia University, New York.

Boehm, A. E., & Slater, B. R. (1981). *The Cognitive Skills Assessment Battery* (2nd ed.). New York: Teachers College, Columbia University.

Bracken, B. A. (1984). *Bracken Basic Concept Scale.* San Antonio, TX: Psychological Corporation.

Bracken, B. A. (1986a). Incidence of basic concepts in the directions of five commonly used American tests of intelligence. *School Psychology International, 7,* 1–10.

Bracken, B. A. (1986b). *The Bracken Concept Development Program.* San Antonio, TX: Psychological Corporation.

Bracken, B. A. (1998). *Bracken Basic Concept Scale—Revised.* San Antonio, TX: Psychological Corporation.

Bracken, B. A., Barona, A., Bauermeister, J. J., Howell, K. K., Poggioli, L., & Puente, A. (1990). Multinational validation of the Spanish Bracken Basic Concept Scale for cross-cultural assessments. *Journal of School Psychology.*

Bracken, B. A., & Cato, L. A. (1986). Rate of conceptual development among deaf preschool and primary children as compared to a matched group of non-hearing-impaired children. *Psychology in the Schools, 23,* 95–99.

Bracken, B. A., & Fouad, N. (1987). Spanish translation and validation of the Bracken Basic Concept Scale. *School Psychology Review, 16,* 94–102.

Brigance, A. H. (1991, 1978). *Revised Brigance Diagnostic Inventory of Early Development.* North Billerica, MA: Curriculum Associates.

Brown, D. (1976). Validation of the Boehm Test of Basic Concepts. (Doctoral Dissertation, University of Wisconsin). *Dissertation Abstracts International, 36,* 4338A.

Carni, E., & French, L. A. (1984). The acquisition of *before* and *after* reconsidered: What develops? *Journal of Experimental Child Psychology, 37,* 394–403.

Caton, H. (1976). *The Tactile Test of Basic Concepts.* Louisville, KY: American Printing House for the Blind.

Caton, H. (1977). The development and evaluation of a tactile analogue to the Boehm Test of Basic Concepts, Form A. *Journal of Visual Impairment and Blindness, 71,* 382–386.

Cazden, D. (1971). Evaluation of learning in preschool education: Early language development. In B. Bloom, J. Hastings, & G. Madaus (Eds.), *Handbook on formative and summative evaluation of student learning* (pp. 345–398). New York: McGraw-Hill.

Central Arkansas Education Center. (1972). *The detection and remediation of deficiencies in verbal understanding of first grade students.* Little Rock, AR: Central Arkansas Education Center. (ERIC Document Reproduction Service No. ED 080 967, EC 000 705).

Chin, J. (1976). The development of basic relational concepts in educable mentally retarded children (Doctoral dissertation, Teachers College, Columbia University, 1976). *Dissertation Abstracts International, 36,* 4338.

Clark, D. C. (1971). Teaching of concepts in the classroom: A set of teaching prescriptions derived from experimental research. *Journal of Educational Psychology Monograph, 63*(3), 253–278.

Clark, E. (1970). How young children describe events in time. In G. Flores D'Arcais & W. J. Levelt (Eds.), *Advances in Psycholinguistics.* New York: American Elsevier.

Clark, E. (1971). On the acquisition of the meaning of before and after. *Journal of Verbal Learning, Verbal Behavior, 10,* 266–275.

Clark, E. (1973). Non-linguistic strategies and the acquisition of word meanings. *Cognition, 2,* 161–182.

Clark, E. (1978). In, on, and under revisited again. *Papers and Reports in Child Language Development from Stanford University, Palo Alto, 15,* 38–45.

Clark, E. (1980). Here's the top: Nonlinguistic strategies in the acquisition of orientation terms. *Child Development, 51,* 329–338.

Clark, E. (1983). Meanings and concepts. In P. H. Mussen (Ed.), *Handbook of Child Psychology.* P. H. Flavell & E. M. Markman (Eds.), Vol. 3: *Cognitive development* (pp. 787–840). New York: Wiley.

Coker, P. I. (1978). Syntactic and semantic factors in the acquisition of *before* and *after. Journal of Child Language, 5,* 261–277.

Cummings, J. A., & Nelson, R. B. (1980). Basic concepts in oral directions of group achievement tests. *Journal of Educational Research, 73,* 259–261.

Davis, J. (1974). Performance of young learning-impaired children on a test of basic concepts. *Journal of Speech and Hearing Research, 17,* 342–351.

deVilliers, J. G., & deVilliers, P. A. (1978). *Language acquisition.* Cambridge, MA: Harvard University Press.

deVilliers, J. G., & deVilliers, P. A. (1979). *Early language.* Cambridge, MA: Harvard University Press.

Dickie, D. C. (1980). Performance of severely and profoundly hearing impaired children on aural/oral and total communication presentations of the Boehm Test of Basic Concepts (Doctoral dissertation, Michigan State University). *Dissertation Abstracts International, 49,* 6227–6228A.

Di Napoli, N., Kagedan-Kage, S. M., & Boehm, A. E. (1980). Basic concept acquisition in learning-disabled children. (ERIC Document Reproduction Service No. ED 240 718).

Doll, E. (1966a). *Preschool Attainment Record.* Circle Pines, MN: American Guidance Service.

Donaldson, M., & Balfour, G. (1968). Less is more: A study of language comprehension in children. *British Journal of Psychology, 59,* 461–472.

Donaldson, M., & Wales, R. (1970). On the acquisition of some relational terms. In J. Hayes (Ed.), *Cognition and the development of language* (pp. 235–268). New York: Wiley.

Fein, G., & Eshleman, S. (1976). Individuals and dimensions in children's judgment of "same" and "different." *Developmental Psychology, 10,* 793–796.

Flavell, J. (1970). Concept development. In P. H. Mussen (Ed.), *Carmichael's manual of child psychology.* New York: Wiley.

French, L. A. (1985). Acquiring and using words to express logical relationships. In S. A. Kuczaj & M. D. Barrett (Eds.), *The development of words meaning* (pp. 307–338). New York: Springer-Verlag.

French, L., & Brown, A. (1977). Comprehension of before and after in logical and arbitrary sequences. *Journal of Child Language, 4*(2), 247–256.

French, L. A., & Nelson, K. (1985). *Young children's knowledge relational terms: Some ifs, ors, or buts.* New York: Springer-Verlag.

Friedman, W., & Seely, P. (1976). The child's acquisition of spatial and temporal word meanings. *Child Development, 47,* 1103–1108.

Gathercole, V. C. (1985). More and more and more about more. *Journal of Experimental Child Psychology, 40,* 73–104.

Glucksberg, S. (1975). *Word versus sentence interpretation: Do adults overextend the meaning of "different"?* Paper presented at the meeting of the Society for Research and Development, Denver.

Hainsworth, P., & Siqueland, E. (1969). *Meeting Street School Screening Test.* East Providence, RI: Crippled Children and Adults of Rhode Island.

Hammill, D. D. (1985). *Detroit Tests of Learning Aptitude (DTLA-2).* Austin, TX: Pro-Ed.

Harris, L., & Strommen, E. (1971). The role of front-back features in children's "front, back, and beside" placement of objects. *Merrill-Palmer Quarterly, 18,* 259–271.

Johnson, H. (1975). The meaning of before and after for preschool children. *Journal of Experimental Child Psychology, 19,* 88–99.

Josephs, J. (1975). *Children's comprehension of same and different in varying contexts.* Unpublished doctoral dissertation, Columbia University.

Kamii, C. (1971). Evaluation of learning in preschool education: Socio-emotional, perceptual-motor, and cognitive development. In B. Bloom, J. Hastings, & G. Madaus (Eds.), *Handbook on formative and summative evaluation of student learning* (pp. 281–344). New York: McGraw-Hill.

Kaplan, C. (1978). *A developmental analysis of children's direction following behavior in grades K-5.* Unpublished doctoral dissertation, Columbia University.

Kaufman, A. (1978). The importance of basic concepts in individual assessment of preschool children. *Journal of School Psychology, 16,* 207–211.

Kaufman, A. S., & Kaufman, N. L. (1983). *Kaufman Assessment Battery for Children.* Circle Pines, MN: American Guidance Service.

Kavale, K. A. (1982). A comparison of learning disabled and normal children on the Boehm Test of Basic Concepts. *Journal of Learning Disabilities, 15,* 160–161.

Kavanaugh, R. (1976). Developmental changes in preschool children's comprehension of comparative sentences. *Merrill-Palmer Quarterly, 22,* 309–318.

Kennedy, G. (1970). *The Language of Tests for Young Children* (CSE Working Paper 7). Los Angeles: Center for the Study of Evaluation, UCLA Graduate School of Education.

Klausmeier, H. J. (1976). Instructional design and the teaching of concepts. In J. R. Levin & V. I. Allen (Eds.), *Cognitive learning in children.* New York: Academic Press.

Klausmeier, H. J. (1992). Concept learning and concept teaching. *Educational Psychologist, 27,* 267–286.

Kuczaj, S., & Maratos, M. (1975). On the acquisition of front, back, and side. *Child Development, 4,* 202–210.

Lahey, M. (1988). *Language disorders and language development.* New York: Macmillan.

Lesiak, W. J., & Lesiak, J. L. (1994). *Kindergarten tasks for kindergarten readiness-II.* Brandon, VT: Clinical Psychology Publishing.

Levin, J., Henderson, B., Levin, A. M., et al. (1975). Measuring knowledge of basic concepts in disadvantaged preschoolers. *Psychology in the Schools, 12,* 132–139.

Levine, S., & Carey, S. (1982). Up front: the acquisition of a concept and a word. *Journal of Child Language, 9,* 645–657.

Lidz, C. S. (1983). Issues in assessing preschool children. In K. D. Paget & B. A. Bracken (Eds.), *The* psychoeducational assessment of preschool children. New York: Grune & Stratton.

MacGinitie, W. H. (1989). *Gates-MacGinitie Reading Tests*. Boston: Houghton Mifflin.

Madden, R., Gardner, E. F., & Collins, C. S. (1983). *Stanford Early School Achievement Test* (2nd ed.). Cleveland, OH: Psychological Corporation.

Meisner, J. (1973). Use of relational concepts by inner city children. *Journal of Educational Psychology, 46,* 22–29.

Mickelson, N. I., & Galloway, C. G. (1973). Verbal concepts of Indian and non-Indian school beginners. *Journal of Educational Research, 67,* 55–56.

Moers, F., & Harris, J. (1978). Instruction in basic concepts and first grade achievement. *Psychology in the Schools, 15,* 84–86.

Moss, M. (1979). *Test of Basic Experiences 2: Norms and technical data book.* Monterey, CA: CTB/McGraw-Hill.

Nason, F. O. (1986). *Systematic instruction of basic relational concepts: Effects on the acquisition of concept knowledge and of language and mathematics achievement of Puerto Rican first graders from low income families.* Unpublished doctoral dissertation, Teachers College, Columbia University.

Nelson, R. B., & Cummings, J. A. (1981). Basic concept attainment of educably mentally handicapped children: Implications for teaching concepts. *Education and Training of the Mentally Retarded, 16,* 303, 306.

Nurss, J. R., & McGauvran, M. (1986). *Metropolitan Readiness Tests* (5th ed.). San Antonio, TX: Psychological Corporation.

Palermo, D. S. (1973). More about less: A study of language comprehension. *Journal of Verbal Learning and Verbal Behavior, 13,* 211–221.

Palermo, D. S. (1974). Still more about the comprehension of "less." *Developmental Psychology, 10,* 827–829.

Patterson, M. C. (1981). Performance of Hutter children in English and Hutterish versions of the Boehm Test of Basic Concepts. *Dissertation Abstracts International, 41,* 2987.

Piaget, J. (1967). *Six psychological studies.* New York: Random House.

Preddy, D., Boehm, A. E., & Shepherd. M. J. (1984). PBCB: A norming of the Spanish translation of the Boehm Test of Basic Concepts. *Journal of School Psychology, 22,* 407–413.

Richards, M. M. (1982). Empiricism and learning to mean. In S. Kuczaj (Ed.), *Language development, Vol. 1: Syntax and semantics.* Hillside, NJ: Erlbaum.

Richards, M. M., & Haupe, L. S. (1981). Contrasting patterns in the acquisition of spatial/temporal terms. *Journal of Experimental Child Psychology, 32,* 485–512.

Spector, C. C. (1977). *Concepts comprehension of normal kindergarten children with deviant syntactic development.* Unpublished doctoral dissertation, New York University.

Spector, C. C. (1979). The Boehm Test of Basic Concepts: Exploring the test results for cognitive deficits. *Journal of Learning Disabilities, 12,* 564–567.

Tennyson, R. D., & Cocchiarella, M. J. (1986). An empirically based instructional design theory for teaching concepts. *Review of Educational Research, 86,* 40–71.

Tennyson, R. D., & Park, D. (1980). The teaching of concepts: A review of instructional design research literature. *Review of Educational Research, 50,* 55–70.

Thai, B. (1973). Concept learning-mastery in Harcum Junior College Laboratory Nursery School/Kindergarten. *Psychology, 10*(2), 35–36.

Trehub, S., & Abramovitch, R. (1978). Less is not more: Further observations on nonlinguistic strategies. *Journal of Experimental Child Psychology, 25,* 160–167.

Weiner, S. (1974). On the development of more and less. *Journal of Experimental Child Psychology, 17,* 271–287.

Wiig, E., & Semel, E. (1976). *Learning disabilities in children and adolescents.* Columbus, OH: Merrill.

CHAPTER 11

ASSESSMENT OF GROSS MOTOR DEVELOPMENT

HARRIET G. WILLIAMS
DARBY ABERNATHY

Motor development has been considered an important part of child development and is a universally recognized means for assessing the overall rate and level of development of the child during the early months and years after birth (Gesell, 1973; Illingworth, 1975). Motor development can be defined as the gradual acquisition of control and/or use of the large and small muscle masses of the body (neuromuscular coordination). The development and assessment of the young child's use of the large muscle masses of the body is the primary focus of this chapter.

A major function of the human nervous system is the coordinated control of movement. Evidence is overwhelming that the acquisition of coordinated movements is inextricably linked to the development of the brain and that perception and action are intricately intertwined early in life (Sporns & Edelman, 1993). Coordinated motor responses enable the young child to explore his or her environment and to sample and process a variety of different sensory stimuli. This promotes brain development and perceptual function. Thus, movement appears to be crucial to the development of perceptual categorization and to the development of fundamental concepts such as unity, boundedness, persistence of objects, construction of spatial maps of the environment, and so on (Spelke, 1990; Sporns & Edelman, 1993). It is a widely held belief that motor development may, in part, determine the nature and sequence in which certain perceptual and cognitive abilities unfold. If a child is unable to engage in a motor behavior that is prerequisite to the acquisition or practice of certain perceptual or cognitive abilities, that lack of motor competence may block the emergence of those abilities (Bushnell & Boudreau, 1993).

The years from 2 to 6 are considered the "golden years" for motor development (Flinchum, 1975; Gesell, 1973; Williams, 1983). During this period, most children acquire their basic repertoire of manipulative and locomotor skills, develop goal-directed motor behaviors, and learn to put together two or three movement sequences to accomplish specific end goals (Bruininks, 1978; Piaget, 1963; Sporns & Edelman, 1993). All of these behavioral achievements are forerunners of important aspects of adult functioning and are contingent upon the child's acquiring an adequate base of motor development. The early years of motor development set the foundation of neuromuscular coordination that will be used by the individual throughout life to deal with a multitude of different mental, social, emotional, and recreational dimensions of living.

Learning in the early years centers around play and physical activity (Flinchum, 1975; Riggs, 1980). Most children have a natural tendency to seek stimulation and to learn about themselves and their environment. They spend many hours actively exploring and examining both their bodies and the physical environment that surrounds them. Such activities necessarily involve and rely upon the use of fundamental motor skills. Adequate motor development is important in optimizing this early concrete and sensorimotor-based learning. A process instrumental in the child's development from early primitive levels of thinking to those of higher abstraction is that of the symbolization of objects and events and the relationship between the two (Piaget, 1963). Physical activity provides the basis for such important symbolic activities as imitation (use of the body to represent objects and events), symbolic play (use of objects to represent other objects), and modeling, drawing, and cutting (construction of objects in two and three dimensions). Motor development and the physical activity associated with it, thus, are integral to promoting selected aspects of the early, active learning process.

Motor development also is linked during the early years to general psychological health, to social and emotional adjustment, and to educational achievement (Cantell, Smyth, & Ahonen, 1994; Henderson, Knight, Losse, & Jongmans, 1990; Lyytinen & Ahonen, 1989). Underachievement in school, lack of concentration, low self-esteem, poor social competence, and behavioral problems have all been linked to or associated with deficits in motor development in early and later years of childhood (Geuze & Borger, 1993; Henderson et al., 1990; Lyytinen & Ahonen, 1989). For example, there is a greater incidence of difficulty in making appropriate social and emotional adjustments to both play and learning situations in children whose motor development is below that of other children of similar chronological age. Lack of physical or motor skill often prevents children from joining in group games and other sports that encourage social interaction and personal growth.

Successful motor development is important not only in early development; it also has important implications for development in adolescence. Cantell, Smyth, and Ahonen (1994), in a 10-year follow-up study, reported that, when compared to a group of age-matched peers, children who exhibited motor development problems at age 5 were still significantly poorer in performance of motor skills at age 15. These children, now adolescents, also had less social interaction with peers, participated less in team games, and had lower academic ambitions and future goals than other children. Losse et al. (1991) also reported that in addition to continuing motor problems at age 16, children with motor difficulties early in life (6 years) also had a variety of educational, social, and emotional problems. The inability to perform basic motor skills, thus, can have long-term negative effects on the individual; the potential implications for adult behavior, although not well studied, seem clear.

Motor development delays frequently accompany a number of potentially serious health conditions and are often associated with lack of integrity of neurological functioning (e.g., prematurity, mental subnormality, emotional disturbances, cerebral palsy, etc.). These are conditions that may require medical and/or other special professional attention, and motor development needs or difficulties accompanying these conditions need to be identified early. Recent evidence suggests that some 57 percent of children born prematurely and who showed some minor neurological impairment early in life continue to show deficits in motor functions (balance, gross motor coordination, etc.) as well as in other school-related behaviors into the preschool years (Lane, Attanasio, & Huselid, 1993). Assessment of motor development in these cases may be integral to help circumvent

potential problems that may accompany school-related stresses.

Most tests of mental development in infants and young children include a large number of items that essentially are neuromuscular coordination or motor development tasks (Bayley, 1965; Cratty, 1972; Stott & Ball, 1965). Gesell (1973) grouped such items into a separate "motor category" in his developmental schedules. Pediatric neurologists often use, as a part of their assessment of the neurological status of the young child, items that directly involve neuromuscular coordination (e.g., evaluation of posture, gait, balance, alternating movements of the limbs, etc.). In general a child whose motor development is considerably below that observed in children of similar chronological age is more likely than others to exhibit soft and/or hard neurological signs—an indication that systems that provide support for the growth and refinement of neuromuscular coordination are not functioning appropriately (Capute & Accardo, 1996; Paine & Oppe, 1966; Precht, 1977; Precht & Beintema, 1964; Touwen, 1976). Still many children do not show classical neurological signs and their difficulties cannot be linked to an identifiable neurological disease; yet they exhibit significant difficulty performing tasks that require motor coordination (e.g., writing, catching a ball, riding a bicycle). Several terms have been used to describe this condition; these include *developmental agnosia* and *apraxia* (Gubbay, 1975), *developmental dyspraxia* (Denckla, 1984) and most recently *developmental coordination disorder* (DSM-IV, 1993). Most simply refer to this condition as the "clumsy child syndrome." The motor problems of these children are of concern not only because they are stressful to the children themselves but also because they are often associated with higher incidences of learning difficulties, school failure, and psychological problems (Losse et al., 1991). For these reasons, assessment of gross motor development in the preschool-age child is an essential component in planning for and providing optimal conditions for development and learning during one of the most significant periods of growth in the life of the child.

OVERVIEW OF GROSS MOTOR DEVELOPMENT IN YOUNG CHILDREN

Gross motor development in the preschool years is characterized by the appearance and mastery of a number of fundamental motor skills. These gross motor skills include body projection (locomotor movements), body manipulation (nonlocomotor movements), and object manipulation (ball handling) skills. Body projection or locomotor skills include running, jumping, hopping, skipping, galloping, leaping, and sliding (DeOreo & Keogh, 1980). These skills all focus on the use of the large muscle masses of the body in moving the total body horizontally through space. Body manipulation skills, on the other hand, are concerned with moving the body and/or body parts within a well-defined but small area of space and include stretching, curling, twisting, rolling, bending, and balancing skills. Universally recognized object manipulation skills include throwing, catching, striking, kicking, and ball bouncing (Roberton & Halverson, 1984). Not all of the skills included under the heading of fundamental motor skills can be addressed here. This discussion focuses primarily on the locomotor skills of running, jumping, hopping, and skipping; the object projection skills of throwing, catching, and striking; and that dimension of body control concerned with balance.

Some general parameters that describe the development of selected locomotor and ball-handling skills are given in Table 11.1. More specific developmental changes typically observed in gross motor development during the preschool years are given in Table 11.2. The list of steps in the development of skill mastery describes the qualitative changes that occur in children's gross motor development during this period. Quantitative changes are listed as general accomplishments. There is a striking lack of convergent information about developmental changes that occur in gross motor control in the preschool child. It is important to note that although the steps that are described for each skill can be loosely associated with chronological age, the relationship between the steps and chronological age per se is at best a tenuous one. One of the most dramatic characteristics of gross motor development in the preschool child is its great variability (Garfield, 1964; Keogh, 1975). Some children fall nicely into a rather traditional age-step association, but most do not. It is for this reason that ages have been intentionally deemphasized in the discussion of developmental changes in gross motor skills in the preschool child. The steps described in Table 11.2 are typically achieved by children during the period from 2 to 6 years.

The reader also should be aware that the steps identified for individual skill sequences are not mutually exclusive; that is, it is not unusual for children to display characteristics from more than one step at any given time in their development (Roberton & Langendorfer, 1980). Children typically display characteristics from steps that are adjacent to one another, although they also might ex-

hibit characteristics of performance that are from nonadjacent steps. This is uncommon and is usually a reflection of special developmental difficulties.

Running. (Gallahue & Ozmun, 1998; Wickstrom, 1977; Williams, 1983; Williams & Breihan, 1995) In general the early running pattern resembles a fast walk. The base of support is wide (feet are shoulder-width apart) and there is little or no use of the arms. The feet tend to toe-out and the child receives the body's weight on a flatfoot (little foot control). As control and coordination increase, the base of support narrows (feet are placed one in front of the other), rhythmical arm/foot opposition is integrated into the run, and the body weight is received in a heel-to-toe fashion (slow running). Quantitatively, the length of stride steadily increases as does the speed and versatility of the running pattern (the child starts, stops, turns, and runs at a variety of speeds and in a variety of directions).

Jumping. (Gallahue & Ozmun, 1998; Wickstrom, 1977; Williams, 1983; Williams & Breihan, 1995) Jumping proceeds developmentally from a one-foot step down from a low object to a skillful execution of a standing broad (long) jump that covers a distance of about 44 inches. In the beginning, the arms are used very little and when they are used, they are used ineffectively (the arms are moved but not in conjunction with the legs). Skillful jumping is manifested most clearly in the smooth coordination of arm and leg movements. In early jumping patterns leg movements are characterized by incomplete flexion and extension. That is, the young or inexperienced jumper fails to assume a semicrouched position in jumping and at take-off fails to fully extend the body. The accomplished 6-year-old jumper assumes a flexed (semicrouched) position prior to jumping and fully extends the ankles, knees, and hips at take-off. In actuality the body of the mature jumper at take-off forms a straight line that extends from the ankle to the fingertips. Last but not least, young jumpers tend to lose balance upon landing and often fall backward or in general lose control. The skillful jumper flexes (most obviously at the knees) to absorb the momentum of the body upon landing and rarely loses balance. Quantitatively, the distance of the jump (vertical, running broad, or standing broad) increases from step to step in a nonlinear fashion.

Hopping. (Gallahue & Ozmun, 1998; Williams, 1983; Williams & Breihan, 1995) Early hopping patterns are characterized by little or no elevation of the body (the

TABLE 11.1   General Parameters of Typical Motor Development

LOCOMOTOR/BODY PROJECTION SKILLS

Walking, Running, and Jumping

Children easily walk or run a straight path before a circular or curved one.
Children progress from a stage of aided jumping, to jumping alone with one foot in front of the other, to jumping alone with a two-foot propulsion.
Children pass through the same progression as noted above at each height from which a jump is attempted.
Children execute jumps from lower heights before attempting jumps from higher heights.
Children jump down from something before they jump up onto something.

Hopping, Skipping, and Galloping

Children gallop before they hop or skip.
Children hop on both feet prior to the development of a true hopping movement on one foot.
Skipping progresses from a shuffle to a skip on one foot to skipping on alternate feet.

Climbing

Marking time (both feet placed on rung or step before next step is attempted) precedes alternation of feet in climbing.
Use of alternating feet appears first in ascending skills, later in descending skills.
Children will ascend a set of stairs or object before they will descend it.
Children acquire proficiency in climbing a short flight of stairs or a ladder with the rungs close together before they gain proficiency in climbing a long flight of stairs or a ladder with the rungs farther apart.
Children alternate feet to climb short flights of stairs but still mark time on longer flights of stairs.

BALL-HANDLING/OBJECT CONTROL SKILLS

Throwing

Children progress from anteroposterior plane movement to horizontal plane movement.
There is a progression from an unchanging base of support (body fixed in space) to a changing base of support (an appropriately timed transference of weight).
There is a progression toward shorter periods of acceleration; that is, the necessary joint actions occur in shorter periods of time, thus aiding in increased force development.
At a given age, children throw a smaller ball farther than a large one.

Catching

Attempts to intercept a ball rolling on the ground usually precede attempts to intercept a bounced or aerial ball.
Bounced balls are caught more easily than aerial balls.
Children progress from using hands and arms as a single unit to trap the ball against the body to contacting and controlling the ball with hands and fingers only.

(continued)

TABLE 11.1   Continued

BALL-HANDLING/OBJECT CONTROL SKILLS

Catching

Children progress from minimal attempts to track or judge the speed or direction of a
   moving ball (child does not move to the ball) to definite attempts to judge speed and
   direction of the moving ball and to move the body to the oncoming ball.
Children successfully intercept a large ball before successfully intercepting a small ball.
Children revert to using the hands and arms as a single unit when first attempting to
   intercept a small ball, while they easily coordinate the use of hands and arms in
   catching a large ball.

Striking

Children begin by using a one-arm strike and gradually develop a two-arm striking
   pattern.
Children are successful in hitting a stationary ball before a moving ball.

Ball Bouncing

Children attempt a two-hand bounce before a one-hand bounce.
Children skillfully bounce a small ball before a large ball.
Children perform a series of "bounce-and catches" before they perform a continuous
   bounce.
Children successfully bounce a ball in a stationary position before they bounce a
   moving ball.

child doesn't get very high off the ground if at all), little or no arm usage, and limited use of the nonsupport leg. Early hopping patterns are jerky, staccato, and arrhythmic. Gradually the arms and nonsupport leg are used to add to force production, and, thus, to the elevation of the body; the nonsupport leg actually "pumps" (flexes and extends rapidly) to aid in the forward momentum of the hopping action. The hop becomes smoother with practice and the child advances from being unable to execute a hop, to hopping in place, to carrying out a short series of coordinated hopping movements, to hopping a 25-foot distance skillfully in 5 seconds. The versatility of the hopping pattern also increases. The child can hop backward and sideward and can alternate hops between right and left feet.

Skipping. (DeOreo & Keogh, 1980; Espenschade & Eckert, 1980; Williams & Breihan, 1995) The early skip is a shuffle step. The shuffle step is followed by a one-sided skip; the final step in development is a step-hop on alternate sides of the body (the true skip). Early skipping

patterns are characterized by a lack of use of the arms, a toeing out of the feet, and a lack of ability to maintain a continuous skipping sequence. Skillful skipping involves smooth and consistent arm/leg opposition (the arms move in opposition to the legs). The toes point forward and the body's weight is received on the ball of the foot. Mastery of a continuous skipping action is seen in the growing capacity of the child to skip long distances in less time. The more skillful 6-year-old skipper can cover a distance of 25 feet in approximately 4 seconds.

Throwing. (Gallahue & Ozmun, 1998; Wickstrom, 1977; Wild, 1938; Williams, 1983; Williams & Breihan, 1995) The earliest beginning of a throwing pattern is simply the release of an object from the hand. The early overarm throwing pattern consists largely of flexion and extension of the trunk and arm (elbow). There is little or no weight shift or trunk rotation. Gradually a shift of weight and trunk rotation appear and help to increase the force or velocity of the throw. The weight shift is first seen as a shift of weight forward onto the foot on the

TABLE 11.2 Developmental Changes in Gross Motor Skills

STEPS IN DEVELOPMENTAL SEQUENCE	GENERAL ACCOMPLISHMENTS

Running: Moving the body through space by alternate shifting of weight from one foot to the other with a period of nonsupport

Step 1

Rudimentary run resembles fast walk	Takes walking/running steps on toes
Series of hurried steps is taken without a nonsupport phase	Walks a straight line
	Walks backward
Knees are moved high and quickly	Walks 10-ft pathway (1-in wide) without stepping off
Movement of body is more vertical than horizontal	Has difficulty walking circular path
Arms swing randomly at sides; gait is uneven and jarring	

Step 2

True run has definite nonsupport phase	Walks 2.25-in board partway before stepping off
Elbows are slightly flexed and at low-guard position	Walks circle (1-ft wide, 4-in circumference)
Forward/backward arm swing is limited	Run improves in form and power
There is occasional arm–foot opposition	
Stride is stiff and uneven in length and timing	
Legs may swing out, around, and forward	
Base of support is wide (feet about shoulder width)	
Feet tend to toe out	
Child has difficulty stopping, starting, and turning	
Weight shifts onto flat foot	

Step 3

Running speed increases	Runs forward effectively
Elbows are flexed; arms at high-guard	Runs backward with hesitancy
Arms swing through larger arc	Runs 25 ft in 2.8 sec
Arms tend to swing across body	Runs 30-yd dash in 6–7 sec
Arm–leg opposition is evident	Completes 40-yd agility run in ~ 15 sec
Some rotation of the trunk may be present	
Length of stride increases	
Legs flex and extend more fully	
Body weight is received on a flat foot	
Child has better control in stopping, starting, and turning	

Step 4

Running speed is increased	Runs 25 ft in 2.5 sec
Running pattern is more automatic	Changes directions easily
Elbows are flexed at right angles	Uses running skills in games
There is consistent arm–foot opposition	Performs 10-ft shuttle run (5 trips in 17.5 sec)
Arm action is used to aid forward motion	Runs 30-yd dash in 5–6 sec
Weight is received in a heel-to-toe fashion (slow run)	Completes 40-yd agility run in ~ 14 sec
Run is even and smooth (little vertical motion)	

(continued)

TABLE 11.2   Continued

STEPS IN DEVELOPMENTAL SEQUENCE	GENERAL ACCOMPLISHMENTS

Jumping: Projection of the body into the air from a two-foot take-off and a two foot landing

Step 1

Jump is a step down from a low object	Steps down aided onto one foot
Jump is a bounce up and down vertically	Steps down unaided onto one foot
Feet are parallel or in slight side stride	Steps down aided onto two feet
Flexion is primarily at knees	Steps down unaided onto two feet
Leg extension (knees) is uneven (first one leg and then the other extends)	
Arms are at sides; used in limited ways	

Step 2

Two-foot take-off and landing is used	Jumps down from 8-in height alone
Arms are not coordinated with the legs	Jumps over an 8-in piece of paper
Arms swing back and forth before take-off but are not used at take-off	Jumps distance of 14–24 in
	Steps over rope approximately 7 in high
Knee/hip flexion increase to add force to take-off	Jumps down from 28-in height with help
Legs are not fully extended at take-off	
Thighs are perpendicular to the ground during flight	
Knee/hip flexion increase to absorb momentum ~ landing	
Balance may be lost on landing	

Step 3

Distance and height of jump increase	Jumps distance of 23–36 in
Arms are used to initiate take-off	Attempts jumps over low barriers (1–3 in)
Knee and hip flexion are increased (deeper crouch)	Jumps down from 12–18 in in height without help
Legs extend fully at take-off	Performs vertical jump of 17 in
Thighs are more parallel to ground during flight	
Arms brought down/forward to maintain balance ~ landing	

Step 4

Preparatory crouch is deeper	Jumps distance of 28–35 in
Arms action is coordinated with leg action	Performs vertical jump of 19 in
Hips, knees, and ankles fully extend at takeoff	Jumps down from 28-in height without help
Hips and knees flex during flight (thighs are parallel to ground)	
Legs reach out, arms are brought down, knees flex to aid in landing	
Balance is maintained on landing	
True broad jump is present	

Hopping: Projection of the body into the air from one foot and landing on same (one) foot

Step 1

Arms are raised to sides	No true hopping present
Nonsupport leg is lifted in attempt to hop	
Trunk is bent slightly forward	

STEPS IN DEVELOPMENTAL SEQUENCE	GENERAL ACCOMPLISHMENTS

Hopping: Projection of the body into the air from one foot and landing on same (one) foot

Step 1 (continued)
Support leg flexes slightly
May be momentary retraction of support foot
   from ground

Step 2
Arms are held in high-guard, elbows flexed
Nonsupport leg (hip and knee) is held high and
   flexed at right angle
Body weight is suspended momentarily
Little or no elevation is present

Performs 1–3 consecutive hops
Hops forward but not backward

Step 3
Child leans forward and shifts weight to balls of feet
Arms are held at middle-guard position for balance
Nonsupport leg is less flexed
Body weight is suspended for longer time
Hops are more horizontal

Hops lowly and deliberately
Hops forward and backward
Hops 4–6 times consecutively
Hops 2–16 ft with variable skill
Hops better on preferred side

Step 4
Arms are used to assist in projection of body
Nonsupport leg swings to aid in take-off
Swing leg is more fully extended at knee/ankle
Weight is received on ball of foot

Performs up to 10 consecutive hops
Hops arrhythmically
Hops 25 ft in approximately 17 sec
Speed of hopping is increased
Has difficulty but can occasionally can hop on right
   and left feet

Step 5
Arms are used to aid in force production
Range of motion of arms and legs is increased
Nonsupport leg flexes and extends to aid in
   force production
Trunk is inclined forward
Support leg flexes on landing to absorb body weight
Weight is received on ball of foot

Hops smoothly and rhythmically
Hops 25 ft in 5 sec
Hops 50 ft in 8 sec
Can alternate hops on right and left feet

Skipping: Projection of the body through space using a step-hop on one side followed by a step-hop on the opposite side

Step 1
Skip is a shuffle on one of both feet
No hop is present
Arms are not used

Performs shuffle step
No true skip present

Step 2
Skip is a step-hop on one side and a walk on the other
Arms are held out to sides and slightly flexed
Hands may be stiff and tense
Movement is arrhythmical

Performs one-sided skip
Performs 4 one-sided skips in sequence
No true skip present

(continued)

TABLE 11.2   Continued

STEPS IN DEVELOPMENTAL SEQUENCE	GENERAL ACCOMPLISHMENTS

Skipping: Projection of the body through space using a step-hop on one side followed by a step-hop on the opposite side

Step 3

Skip is a step-hop on alternate sides	Performs alternate skipping action
Running or walking steps maybe interspersed into skipping pattern	True skip is present
	Skips 25 ft in approximately 4 sec
Length of skips is short; elevation of body is minimal	
Arms not used in opposition and may swing randomly	
Some toeing out of feet might occur	
Movements are still arrhythmical and slow	

Step 4

Support leg quickly flexes to receive weight	Skips 25 ft in ~ 3.5 sec
Support leg extends to produce force for take-off	
Nonsupport leg is flexed and swings forward to aid in momentum of skip	
Body may be turned from side to side	
Arms are used in opposition to the legs	
Arms are flexed at elbows and held at middle-guard position	
Base of support is reduced	
Skipping action is smoother, more rhythmical	

Throwing (overarm): Ability to project an object through space with speed and accuracy

Step 1

Body faces direction of throw	Simply drops/tosses objects
Feet are stationary; no weight shift occurs	Often throws underhand
No body or shoulder rotation is present	
Movement is primarily in the vertical plane	
Arm movement is largely elbow flexion and extension	
Trunk moves backward and forward in vertical plane	
Ball is released before elbow is extended	

Step 2

Feet are stationary (either together or spread)	Is fascinated with throwing
No weight shift is present	Throws ball 4–5 ft using one or two hands
Some block rotation is present	Throws without losing balance
Trunk rotates backward toward throwing side and then forward	
Arm initiates throwing action, which is in a flat or oblique plane	

Step 3

Weight shift is present	Successfully tosses ring at a peg 4 feet away
Step-out is on foot on side of throwing arm	Throws a distance of over 10 ft
Body rotation may decrease	
Range of arm–trunk movement is limited by forward position of throwing foot	

STEPS IN DEVELOPMENTAL SEQUENCE	GENERAL ACCOMPLISHMENTS

Throwing (overarm): Ability to project an object through space with speed and accuracy

Step 3 (continued)
Trunk flexion and extension increases
Arm follows through across body

Step 4
Step-out is on foot opposite throwing arm   Throws a distance of 17+ ft at velocity ~ 27 ft/sec
Body rotation increases
Trunk rotates as unit
Shoulder rotation is present
Elbow lags behind as trunk rotates forward
Wrist snaps to release ball
Arm follows through across body

Step 5
Differentiated trunk rotation appears (pelvic   Throws a distance of 20+ ft at velocity of ~ ft/sec
    followed by spinal rotation)
Ball is released from fingertips

Catching: Ability to contact, stop, and control aerial objects

Step 1
Rolling ball is stopped or trapped
Aerial ball is not responded to

Step 2
Arms are held out straight in front of body
Elbows are stiff; forearms supinated
Timing is off—ball often rebounds off arms, trunk,
    or hits face
Fear reaction is present: child turns head, closes
    eyes, leans back, tenses fingers
Catching is passive and often by chance

Step 3
Arms are held in front of body with elbows
    slightly flexed
Active attempt is made to catch ball
Ball is scooped or trapped between arms and
    chest or between arms
Attempt is made to trap ball with clapping
    motion
Timing is still awkward but improved

Step 4
Arms are held at sides, hands are cupped   May catch large ball thrown from 5 ft 1 of 3 times
Fingers are pointed at oncoming ball
Arms and hands are used to stop catch the ball
Arms and hands adjust to meet oncoming ball
Arms and hands give to absorb momentum of ball
Child watches ball as it approaches

(continued)

TABLE 11.2   Continued

STEPS IN DEVELOPMENTAL SEQUENCE	GENERAL ACCOMPLISHMENTS

Catching: Ability to contact, stop, and control aerial objects

Step 5
Fingers and hands adjust to close around ball
   at contact

Catches large ball 50 percent of time
Catches 8-in ball bounced from 15 feet 3 of 5 times
Catches small balls with varying degrees of skill
Attempts one-hand catch
Catches ball bounced from 10 ft 4 of 10 times

Step 6
Entire body adjusts to receive balls thrown at various
   speeds and from different directions

Catches balls of various sizes skillfully
Catches balls bounced from 10 ft 7 of 10 times

Two-arm strike: Ability to make contact with a stationary or moving object using the hands and/or other implements

Step 1
Child faces oncoming ball
Implement is held and swung in vertical plane
Attempt is made to contact stationary object using
   a one-arm pattern

Step 2
Child experiments with using two hands
Swings bat in vertical plane
Flexes trunk as swings implement
Action is a vertical chopping motion

Step 3
Child stands with side to oncoming ball
Bat rests on or near back shoulder
Weight is shifted in a kind of rocking motion
Two hands are used to hold implement
Swing is made with sidearm motion in flat arc
Arms, hands, and wrists are held stiffly
Swing is adjusted to height of ball by flexion at waist

Step 4
Child stands with side to oncoming ball
Bat rests on or near back shoulder
Weight is shifted to forward foot
Weight shift occurs prior to arm action
Trunk rotates as unit (backward and forward)
Range of arm motion is increased

Projects ball with two-arm strike: velocity ~ 3 ft/sec

Step 5
Child stands with side to oncoming ball
Weight is shifted to opposite foot
Differentiated trunk rotation is present
Bat is swung on horizontal plane
Bat is swung with greater force

Hits stationary ball 17 of 20 times
Hits moving ball 27 of 40 times
Projects tennis ball: two-arm strike:
   velocity ~ 26–31 ft/sec
Projects whiffle ball: two-arm strike:
   velocity ~ 17–20 ft/sec

STEPS IN DEVELOPMENTAL SEQUENCE	GENERAL ACCOMPLISHMENTS

Balance: Ability to maintain the body in state of equilibrium whether stationary or moving

Step 1
Balances on all fours
Balances on knees
Maintains standing position

Step 2
Attempts to stand on objects (e.g., balance beam)
Attempts to walk beam (2¼ in wide), one foot on,
    one foot off
Arms flail; hands and face tense

Step 3
Attempts to walk beam (2¼ in wide), alternating
    feet
Walks 1-in line for 10-ft distance

Step 4
Stands heel to toe, eyes closed, hands on hips
    (on floor)
Walks 1 inch circular line
Slowly walks entire length of beam (2¼ in)
Tension and flail of arms diminished

Step 5
Balances on preferred foot minimum of 3–5 sec
Walks standard-length beam using natural gait
    with relative ease
Walks 12 ft on 4-inch beam before stepping off
Walks 10–11 ft on 3-inch beam before stepping
    off
Walks 5–8 ft on 2-inch beam before stepping off
Balances on unstable platform 8–9 sec

Step 6
Balances on preferred foot, eyes open,
    54 sec (average)
Balances on nonpreferred foot, eyes open,
    41 sec (average)
Balances on preferred foot, eyes closed,
    7 sec (average)
Balances on one foot on 1-inch stick,
    3 sec (average)
Walks balance beam in heel-to-toe controlled
    manner, 23 sec (average)

Primary sources: Problems of Movement Skill Development, by J. Keogh and D. Sudgen, 1991, Columbia: University of South Carolina Press and *Perceptual and Motor Development in Young Children,* by H. Williams, 1983, Englewood Cliffs, NJ: Prentice-Hall.

same side as the throwing arm; later the skillful thrower steps onto the foot opposite the throwing arm. Trunk rotation first occurs in block form (the lower and upper trunk, e.g., pelvis and spine) rotate as a single unit. Later trunk rotation is differentiated (the lower trunk or pelvis rotates first; this is followed by upper trunk or spinal rotation). Quantitatively, developmental changes are seen primarily in increases in the distance and velocity of the throw. Increases in both distance and velocity from one step in the developmental sequence to the next are nonlinear in nature. There are dramatic quantitative changes in throwing in the fourth and fifth steps.

Catching. (DeOreo & Keogh, 1980; Gallahue & Ozmun, 1998; Wickstrom, 1977; Williams, 1983; Williams & Breihan, 1995) Early and/or immature catching patterns are characterized by lack of skillful use of the arms, hands, and fingers. Initially the arms and hands are held stiffly in front of the body with the elbows extended. The ball often rebounds off the outstretched arms. Later the arms are held at the sides with the hands relaxed and cupped. The arms, hands, and fingers of more accomplished catchers are positioned according to the flight of the oncoming object. The fingers and hands are pointed toward the ball. For balls above the waist, the fingers and hands point upward; for balls below the waist, the fingers and hands point downward. When ball contact is made, the fingers close around the ball. Young or inefficient catchers rarely display this fingertip control in making contact with the ball. Another aspect of the child's early catching response is a fear reaction in which the child turns the head, closes the eyes, and fails to track the ball as it comes toward him or her. This reaction disappears as skill and confidence increase; the child watches the ball intently as it approaches. The major characteristic of the highly proficient catcher is his or her ability to adjust the total movement of the body to receive balls bounced or thrown at different speeds and from varying distances and directions. Young catchers are unable to do this. Quantitatively the number of successful catches (ball skillfully contacted with hands and fingers) slowly increases. Changes in catching skills have not been quantified to any great extent in children of preschool age.

Striking. (DeOreo & Keogh, 1980; Gallahue & Ozmun, 1998; Wickstrom, 1977; Williams, 1983; Williams & Breihan, 1995) The development of striking skills is an important part of early gross motor development. Although there is not much normative or descriptive data available on developmental changes in striking

skill in young children, the little that is available suggests that striking patterns proceed from one-arm attempts at contacting stationary objects to skillful two-arm striking patterns made in an effort to contact objects moving at different speeds and in different directions. Initially, the striking movement is a vertical chopping motion; later it becomes a sidearm motion executed in the horizontal plane (the swing is flat). Early in the development of the striking pattern (as in throwing), the trunk rotates as a single unit; later, differentiated or two-part trunk rotation occurs. Another important developmental change in striking behavior is the appearance of a definite shift of weight onto the forward (opposite) foot prior to the beginning of the arm swing. The child will also gradually change from assuming a position facing the oncoming ball to one in which the side of the body is placed toward the ball. Quantitatively, with advancing development, the bat is swung with greater force (the range and timing of the movement of the body are improved) and the ball is projected with increasingly greater velocity.

Balance. (Gallahue & Ozmun, 1998; Williams, 1983; Williams & Breihan, 1995) Early balance development is manifested in the child's ability to maintain equilibrium in a variety of positions (e.g., on all fours, on the knees, in a standing position). This is followed by attempts to stand, to walk, and to navigate around objects in the environment. Once some success is achieved in these behaviors, the child will attempt to walk on narrow objects (e.g., balance beams, rails, lines) and shows some beginning ability to maintain balance on one foot. By 6 years most children can balance for fairly long periods of time on the preferred foot with the eyes open (M = 22 sec). Balancing on the nonpreferred foot is more difficult (M = 14 sec) and balancing with the eyes closed is just beginning to be mastered (M = 7 sec). Most children can, at this age, walk a balance beam (2½ inches wide) in a controlled heel-toe manner in 23 seconds.

ASSESSMENT OF GROSS MOTOR DEVELOPMENT

Gross motor development is most effectively evaluated by considering both process and product characteristics of the child's movement (Williams, 1983). Process characteristics address qualitative aspects of movement and have to do with how a child moves the body in performing a motor task. Thus, evaluation of process characteristics is concerned with assessing the form or quality of the movement itself (e.g., observing how the body is positioned, which limbs are moved, how movements are sequenced, etc.). Product characteristics of movement, in contrast, have to do with the end product or outcome of the movement and usually are more quantitative in nature. Evaluation of product characteristics of movement answer such questions as: How far did the child run? How high did he jump? How fast did she move? Techniques used for assessing gross motor development often incorporate measures of both process and product aspects of movement performance. Most motor development scales or tests available for use with younger children tend to emphasize process characteristics; tests for older children tend to emphasize product measures. Both types of information are needed at all ages if a complete and comprehensive assessment of the motor development of the child is to be made. An example of a simple checklist that includes both process and product characteristic items is Cratty's Perceptual-Motor Behaviors Checklist (Cratty, 1970). See Table 11.3. Examples of items that emphasize process characteristics are: "can walk rhythmically at an even pace" (2 to 3 years), "can step off low objects, one foot ahead of the other" (2 to 3 years), and "walks and runs with arm action coordinated with leg action" (4 to 4^1/$_2$ years). Items that are more product-oriented include: "can walk a 2-inch-wide line for 10 feet" (2 to 3 years), "can jump 8 inches or higher" (5 to 5^1/$_2$ years), and "can run 50 feet in 5 seconds" (6 to 6^1/$_2$ years).

Product Measures

The most common approach to the evaluation of motor development is to use product assessment. Normative data for such test batteries usually are given in standard scores, percentiles, or some other quantitative form derived from means, standard deviations, and/or standard errors. Normative data generally are used for comparing individual children to standards typical for children of comparable chronological ages. There are no comprehensive, published test batteries of this type for very young children (2- to 3-year-olds); several are available for assessing 4-, 5-, and 6-year-old children. Seven of the more widely used product-oriented motor performance test batteries are reviewed here; all are formal, standardized measures of motor development. Only brief mention is made of informal measures of product characteristics.

Movement Assessment Battery for Children. The
Movement Assessment Battery for Children is the most recent and comprehensive test battery for assessing mo-

tor development in children. It is generally referred to as the Movement ABC (Henderson & Sudgen, 1992) and was designed to provide both process and product information about children's motor development. It includes an objective "test," which includes both a product and process component and a "checklist." The checklist is more general and asks questions about what tasks a child can perform in different settings. The former is used for more detailed diagnosis of motor development needs; the latter is used primarily for classroom or clinically based screening. The "test" component is divided into different age bands; the youngest age band is from 4 to 6 years. Each age band consists of eight tasks. Tasks in each age band are categorized as follows: manual dexterity (fine motor tasks), ball skills, and static and dynamic balance. The latter three categories assess gross motor development. For each task there is a quantitative or product score (e.g., time in balance, number of steps, etc.) and a series of process characteristics to be checked. Some selected examples of process characteristics for each of the gross motor tasks are given in Table 11.4. The process characteristics listed in the table are, for the most part, paraphrased and do not represent the verbatim wording found in the battery.

The "checklist" consists of 48 items divided into four sections; each section addresses the child's performance in progressively more complex situations (child stationary/environment stable, child moving/environment stable, child stationary/environment changing, and child moving/environment changing). There is also a section that focuses on the child's attitudes and feelings about motor skills. Sample "checklist" questions are paraphrased and given in Table 11.5. Normative data for both the "test" and "checklist" components are based on 1,200 children from 4 to 12 years of age; the sample in the age range from 4 to 6 years was 493 children. Boys and girls of different ethnic origins and from diverse regions of the United States were included.

Denver Developmental Screening Test. The Denver
test (Frankenburg & Dodds, 1967; Frankenburg, Dodds, Archer, Bresnick, & Shapiro, 1990) is one of the most universally recognized and widely used standardized procedures for assessing gross motor development in young children. It uses simple tasks that are essentially product characteristic measures; the tasks are ones that look at minimal levels of motor skill achievement. The items in this battery are helpful to the educator and clinician in that they provide information about whether certain common gross motor skills are within the behavioral

TABLE 11.3 Cratty's Perceptual-Motor Behaviors Checklist

2–3 Years
Displays a variety of scribbling behaviors
Can walk rhythmically at an even pace (process)
Can step off low object, one foot ahead of the other (process)
Can name hands, feet, head, and some face parts
Opposes thumb to fingers when grasping objects and releases objects smoothly from finger thumb grasp (process)
Can walk a 2-in wide line 10 ft long placed on ground (product)

4–4½ Years
Can forward broad jump both feet together and clear ground at same time (process)
Can hop 2 or 3 times on one foot without precision or rhythm (product and process)
Walks and runs with arm action coordinated with leg action (process)
Can walk a circular line a short distance (product)
Can draw a crude circle
Can imitate a simple line cross using a vertical and horizontal line

5–5½ Years
Runs 30 yds in just over 8 sec (product)
Balances on one foot; girls 6–8 sec; boys 4–6 sec (product)
Catches large playground ball bounced to him or her chest high from 15 ft, 4–5 of 5 times (product)
Draws rectangle and square differently (one side at a time)
Can high jump 8 in or more over bar with simultaneous two-foot take-off (product and process)
Bounces playground ball using one or two hands a distance of 3–4 ft (product)

6–6½ Years
Can block print first name in letters 1½–2 inches high
Can gallop if it is demonstrated (product)
Can exert 6 lb or more of pressure in grip strength measures (product)
Can walk a balance beam 2 in wide, 6 in high, and 10–12 ft long (product)
Can run 50 ft in about 5 sec (product)
Can arise from ground from backlying position in 2 sec or less (product)

Source: From B. J. Cratty, *Perceptual and Motor Development in Infants and Young Children.* Copyright © 1986 by Allyn & Bacon. Adapted by permission.

The tasks described above are usually performed by 70–80 percent of children of the ages indicated. The database for the checklist was from children from white middle-class neighborhoods. A child who fails to master four of six of the tasks for his or her age may need a more thorough evaluation and possibly remedial help. Gross motor skills are indicated in italic.

repertoire of a child at a given age. They do not, however, provide information about why a given motor skill is not a part of the child's set of behavioral skills. Thus, this test is most properly used as a screening device (for which it was designed) and not for detailed diagnosis of motor development difficulties.

The Denver Developmental Screening Test (DDST) can be used to outline the general nature and/or level of motor skill development in children from birth to 6 years. Standards for passing items on the test are described in simple language and are based on normative data gathered on 1,036 children. The major gross motor

TABLE 11.4   Sample Process Characteristics: Movement ABC Gross Motor Tasks

CATEGORY	ITEM/TASK	SAMPLE PROCESS CHARACTERISTICS
Ball Skills	Bean bag catch	Body is rigid/floppy Closes eyes as object approaches Fingers close too early/too late
	Roll ball to goal	Doesn't fixate object Releases ball too soon/too late Can't maintain balance
Static Balance	One leg balance	Looks at feet Sway is extreme Doesn't use arms to aid balance
Dynamic Balance	Jump over cord	Doesn't use arms No preparatory crouch Nonsimultaneous two-foot take-off
	Walk on heels	Body is tense/floppy Arm movements are exaggerated Balance wobbly as put feet on line

items included in the test and the age at which 90 percent of children pass these items are given in Table 11.6.

Peabody Developmental Motor Scales and Activity Cards.   A very widely used tool for assessing motor development in young children is the Peabody Developmental Motor Scales (Folio & Fewell, 1983). The scales were designed to evaluate gross and fine motor skills in both children with and without disabilities from birth to 6

years. The Gross Motor Scale consists of a total of 170 items, 10 items at each of 17 age levels. Items are grouped at six-month intervals beginning at 2 years. The areas of gross motor development that are considered include reflexes (in children up to 1 year of age), balance, nonlocomotor behaviors, locomotor skills, and object receipt and propulsion skills. Examples of each of these skill areas and the criteria for passing (for 4-year-olds) are provided in Table 11.7. The gross motor development

TABLE 11.5   Sample Checklist Questions: Movement ABC for Children

	ENVIRONMENT STABLE	ENVIRONMENT CHANGING
Child Stationary	Has good posture ~ standing Stands on one leg ~ is stable Throws ball to stationary target*	Intercepts moving object Catches small ball ~ 1 hand Kicks rolling ball Throws ball to moving child
Child Moving	Runs, stops, avoids objects Skips or gallops specified distance Hops on either foot	Moves or avoids other moving children Runs to kick a ball Moves to catch a ball Rides tricycle

*Authors' example; not included in actual battery.

TABLE 11.6 Selected Gross Motor Items: Denver Development Screening Test

ITEM	AGE*
Walks backward	21 mo
Walks up steps	22 mo
Kicks ball forward	2 yrs
Throws ball overhand	2½ yrs
Jumps in place	3 yrs
Pedals tricycle	3 yrs
Performs broad jump	3½ yrs
Balances on 1 foot for 1 sec	3½ yrs
Balances on 1 foot for 5 sec 2 of 3 times	4¼ yrs
Hops on 1 foot	4¾ yrs
Performs heel-toe walk 2 of 3 times	5 yrs
Catches bounced ball 2 of 3 times	5½ yrs
Balances on 1 foot for 10 sec 2 of 3 times	5¾ yrs
Performs backward heel-toe walk 2 of 3 times	6 yrs

Source: Adapted from "The Denver Developmental Screening Test," by W. K. Frankenburg and J. B. Dodds, 1967, *Journal of Pediatrics, 71,* p. 181.

*Age at which 90 percent of children pass individual items.

scale requires approximately 30 minutes to administer and is straightforward in administration, scoring, and interpretation. All items are scored 0 (the child cannot or does not perform the task), 1, or 2 (the child performs the task according to the differential criteria listed). Basal and ceiling ages are determined, and raw scores can be converted into percentile ranks, standard scores, and a developmental motor quotient. Normative data on 617 children (85.1 percent Caucasian) from a wide variety of geographical locations (northeastern, northern central, southern, and western United States) are provided. Of the total number of children in the standardization sample, there were 92 2-year-olds, 103 3-year-olds, 50 4-year-olds, and 55 5-year-olds.

Williams-Breihan Motor Control Test Battery.
The Williams-Breihan test (Williams & Breihan, 1995) was originally developed in 1979 and revised in 1995 (Will-

iams, 1995). It is designed for use in assessing product characteristics of motor performance in 4-, 6-, and 8-year-old children. Tasks in this battery were designed to assess both fine and gross motor skills; normative data are presented in the form of percentile ranks for boys and girls at 4 and 6 years of age. Once the child's raw score on a given task is obtained, it can be compared to an average percentile score, and a determination can be made as to whether or not the child's level of skill mastery compares to other children of similar chronological ages. By using percentile rank information, simple but informative profiles of motor development can be outlined for the young child. One of the difficulties with tests based on normative data lies in the interpretation of the outcomes on those tests. What exactly does it mean to have a score above or below the 50th percentile? Even the experts cannot say for certain. In addition, norms established on one population of children often are not applicable to other groups of children. Caution should always be exerted in using and interpreting normative data for comparative purposes.

Bruininks-Oseretsky Test of Motor Proficiency.
The Bruininks-Oseretsky test (Bruininks, 1978) is designed for use with children 4½ through 14½ years of age. It consists of eight subtests (46 separate items) that provide a broad index of the child's proficiency in both gross and fine motor skills. A short form of the test (14 items) provides a brief overview of the child's general motor proficiency. Four of the subtests measure gross motor skills: Running Speed and Agility, Balance, Bilateral Coordination, and Upper Limb Coordination. Selected items used to assess these four aspects of gross motor development are described in Table 11.8.

Raw scores on gross motor items are converted to point scores that are then converted to standard scores. The standard scores are summed to give a gross motor composite; this is converted into a composite standard score. The standard score is used to determine a percentile rank for the individual child. Some age-equivalent data are provided, and norms are established for six-month intervals. The standardization sample was based on 68 children for the 4 year, 6 month to 5 year, 5 month range and 82 children for the 5 year, 6 month to 6 year, 5 month range.

Cashin Test of Motor Development.
The Cashin Test (Cashin, 1975; Williams, 1995) was designed for use with 4- and 5-year-olds and its database is approximately 1,000 children. This test assesses five different gross mo-

TABLE 11.7   Examples of Items from the Peabody Gross Motor Scale (4-year-olds)

SKILL AREA	ITEM	CRITERION FOR PASSING
Balance	Walks a 4-in balance beam	Completes 4 steps without support Stands on tiptoes with hands over head Maintains position for 8 sec with good stability
Nonlocomotor	Performs sit-ups	Performs 3–4 sit-ups in 30 sec
Locomotor	Jumps up with hands overhead as high as possible	Jumps 3 ft beyond normal reach
	Jumps down from 32 in	Jumps without support, leading with one foot
	Jumps forward as far as possible	Jumps forward 16 in on one foot Jumps forward on opposite foot Jumps forward 12 in on opposite foot
	Rolls forward (somersault)	Rolls forward over head without turning head 15 to either side
Receipt and Propulsion	Throws ball	Throws ball 10 ft on 1 of 2 trials

tor skills: static balance, dynamic balance, agility, throwing (overarm), and catching. General task descriptions, testing procedures, and some normative data are given in Table 11.9. The Cashin Test was developed with ease of administration in mind. Space requirements are minimal and, on the average, a child can complete the entire test in 20 minutes. Some minimal training or experience in observing process characteristics of throwing and catching patterns in young children is necessary to use the battery successfully. Young children often have difficulty understanding exactly what to do on the agility task, and several practice trials might be needed if an accurate assessment of the child's agility is to be made. The normative data provided are a rough standard for assessing the level of motor development in individual children. Three categories of development are identified: *average, accelerated,* and *developmental lag.* The score(s) corresponding with these three levels of motor development are based on group means and standard deviations (average level of development is within ±1 standard deviation; accelerated development is at least +2 standard deviation; developmental lag is at least –2 standard deviation). Important male-female differences are also noted in Table 11.9.

McCarthy Scales of Children's Abilities.   Another example of a product approach to the evaluation of young children's motor development is the McCarthy Scales of Children's Abilities. This test battery was designed to

help fulfill the need for a single instrument to evaluate strengths and weaknesses of young children's abilities (McCarthy, 1972). The McCarthy scales involve systematic observation of a variety of cognitive and motor behaviors that are subdivided into six scales. The Motor Development Scale assesses gross and fine motor skills through the following subtests: Leg Coordination, Arm Coordination, Imitative Action, Draw-A-Design, and Draw-A-Child. The latter two tasks are fine motor tasks and are included in the Perceptual-Performance and General Cognitive Scales.

Leg Coordination is examined using the following tasks: walk backward, walk on tiptoes, walk on a straight line, stand on one foot, and skip. Arm Coordination involves three tasks: bouncing a ball, catching a bean bag, and throwing a bean bag at a target. Four tasks are included in the Imitative Action sequence: crossing feet at the ankles, folding hands, twiddling thumbs, and sighting through a tube. In the Draw-A-Design task, the child is asked to reproduce various geometric designs including a circle, vertical and horizontal lines, a parallelogram, and so on. In the Draw-A-Child task, the child is asked to draw a picture of a boy or girl according to the gender of the child. During performance of the motor items, observations concerning hand usage and eye preferences also are made.

For each of the scales, including the Motor Scale, the child's raw scores are converted into T-scores based

TABLE 11.8 Gross Motor Skills Subtest from the Bruininks-Oseretsky Test of Motor Proficiency

Running Speed Agility
Child runs from a start line to an end line 15 yd away, picks up a block, runs back across
  the start line (time to nearest .2 sec)

Balance
Child stands on preferred leg on floor and holds position for 10 sec
Child stands on preferred leg on balance beam and holds position for 10 sec
Child stands on preferred leg on balance beam with eyes closed (time to nearest sec)
Child walks line on floor in normal stride for 6 steps
Child walks forward on balance beam in normal stride for 6 steps
Child walks forward in heel-to-toe fashion on line on floor for 6 steps
Child walks forward in heel-to-toe fashion on balance beam for 6 steps
Child walks forward on balance beam (normal gait) and steps over a stick held at knee
  height; hands are on hips

Bilateral Coordination
Child taps feet alternately while making circles with index fingers (must complete 10
  consecutive foot taps in 90 sec)
Child simultaneously taps foot and index finger on one side of body and then on the
  opposite side (must complete 10 consecutive taps in 90 sec)
Child simultaneously taps right foot and left index finger and then taps left foot and right
  index finger on opposite side of body
Child jumps in place with leg and arm on opposite sides of body—right leg, left arm
  together, then left leg and right arm together (must complete 10 consecutive jumps
  in 90 sec)
Child jumps as high as possible and touches heels (pass or fail)

Upper Limb Coordination
Child bounces tennis ball on floor and catches it using both hands (number of correct
  catches in 5)
Child uses preferred hand and bounces tennis ball on floor and catches it (number of
  correct catches in 5)
Child catches tennis ball tossed from 10 ft using two hands (number of correct catches
  in 5)
Child catches tennis ball tossed from 10 ft in preferred hand (number of correct catches
  in 5)
Child throws ball overarm at target 4 ft away (number of points in 5 trials)
Child attempts to touch with the index finger a ball swung horizontally in front of him or
  her (number of points in 5 trials)

Source: Adapted from *Bruininks-Oseretsky Test of Motor Proficiency: Examiner's manual,* by Robert H. Bruininks, 1978, Circle Pines, MN: American Guidance Service, Inc.

on the child's chronological age. Percentile ranks are also presented for purposes of interpretation. The scales are based on normative data gathered on 1,032 children ages 2½ through 8½ years.

The Vulpe Assessment Battery. The Vulpe Assessment Battery (Vulpe, 1982) was developed by physical and occupational therapists to assess a wide variety of behaviors using a clinical approach. Among the areas of

TABLE 11.9 Cashin Test of Motor Development

TASK*	SCORING	AGE/SEX	AVERAGE	ACCELERATED	LAG
Agility (obstacle course)	One practice and 3 trials are given; time to nearest .l sec; score ~ average of 3 trials	4/M/F 5/M 5/F	9.5–10.2 8.1–8.6 9.0–10.2	Below 9.0 Below 7.9 Below 8.5	Above 11.0 Above 9.0 Above 11.0
Static Balance (stork stand)	One practice and 3 trials are given; time to nearest .1 sec; score is average of 3 trials; 30 sec maximum	4/M 4/F 5/M 5/F	13.7–16.9 17.6–21.1 20.3–22.5 20.3–22.5	Above 19.0 Above 23.0 Above 24.0 Above 24.0	Below 12.0 Below 15.0 Below 19.0 Below 19.0
Dynamic Balance (plank walk)	Three trials are given; each trial ~ 2 trips of 10 steps. Child is allowed 2 errors per trip; score is average number steps in 3 trials	4/M 4/F 5/M 5/F	5.8–7.9 11.9–14.2 13.2–14.8 13.2–14.8	Above 9.0 Above 15.0 Above 16.0 Above 16.0	Below 4.7 Below 10.7 Below 12.0 Below 12.0
Throwing	Two trials of 12 throws are given; score is total points for 2 trials; an overarm rating scale is used to determine points; maximum 50 points per trial/5 points per throw	4/M 4/F 5/M 5/F	55–59 45–48 56–58 46–49	Above 59 Above 49 Above 59 Above 51	Below 53 Below 43 Below 55 Below 45
Catching	Two trials of 12 tosses each are given; score ~ average points in 2 trials; a catching rating scale is used to determine points; maximum 50 points/5 points per toss	4/M 4/F 5/M 5/F	30–32 30–32 34–36 34–35	Above 33 Above 33 Above 37 Above 36	Below 29 Below 29 Below 30 Below 30

*Agility: On the signal go, the child follows the path below. **Static Balance:** Child places hands on hips and foot of choice against the inside part of supporting leg just below the knee. **Dynamic Balance:** Child places hands on hips and steps on beam 2-inch wide and walks 10 steps (heel to toe), stops, returns to end of beam and repeats task. **Throwing:** Child stands behind a line 13 feet from a wall and throws the ball, overarm, as hard as possible against the wall. **Catching:** Child stands on an "x" 13 feet from the examiner and attempts to catch an 8½-inch playground ball; 4 tosses to the child, 4 tosses to the child's right, and 4 tosses to the child's left are given in random order in each trial.

behavior that are evaluated are basic sensory functions, expressive and receptive language, object, body, size, space, time, and number concepts as well as gross and fine motor skills. The test, which is a product-oriented assessment tool, also includes tests of muscle strength, motor planning, reflex development, and balance. These are useful tools for conducting a comprehensive analysis of the young child's gross motor development. With regard to specific gross motor skill development, significant individual motor development achievements are identified for different ages beginning at 1 month and extending to 6 years of age. Skills are organized in an age-based sequence, and criteria for assessing mastery of each skill at each age are provided. The gross motor skills assessed by the Vulpe include sitting, kneeling, standing, walking, stair climbing, running, jumping, kicking, throwing, and balancing. A number of different tasks (usually one to three) are used to assess each motor skill; performance is judged on a number of dimensions ranging from whether the child requires physical or verbal assistance to perform the tasks to whether the child can perform the skill alone and/or can transfer the skill to a different task or environmental context. Overall the test is most useful as a source of information about age-related motor development and other behavioral achievements in young children. An important limitation is that there has been no formal standardization of the test.

Process Measures

A popular and useful approach to the assessment of gross motor development in young children focuses on observing and evaluating process characteristics of movement performance (i.e., motor development). This involves assessing the quality, form, and/or action sequence of the motor response. These techniques focus on how the child moves his or her body to perform a given motor skill. Process evaluation instruments usually are informal in nature; they rely on subjective analyses and are rarely based on large standardization populations. The process approach to the assessment of gross motor skill in young children often is used in clinical settings to provide initial screening of children's movement problems as well as to give insight into possible factors contributing to movement problems that already have been diagnosed. Most of these instruments require some understanding of the developmental steps involved in the acquisition of motor skills in young children as well as some experience in observing children's movement behavior in play or other naturalistic environments. Most process assessment techniques are organized in a checklist format that contains a series of descriptive statements designed to identify important aspects of movement performance. The interpretation of the information from the checklists is usually simple and varies from one instrument to another.

Ulrich Test of Gross Motor Development. The Ulrich Test of Gross Motor Development (Ulrich, 1985) is an excellent example of a battery that emphasizes process characteristics of movement and is both norm and criterion referenced. It is one of very few standardized tests that uses a quantitative approach to evaluating process aspects of gross motor skill development in young children (data are provided on children between the ages of 3 and 10 years). The battery is designed to, among other things, identify children who are significantly behind age-expected levels of motor development. It also has the potential, because of its quantitative approach, to be an excellent research tool for individuals interested in the scientific study of motor skill acquisition in young children.

Two areas of gross motor development are evaluated: locomotion (body projection) and object control (ball handling). Locomotor skills that are evaluated include running, hopping, leaping, jumping, skipping, and sliding. Object control skills include two-hand striking, bouncing, catching, kicking, and throwing. Each skill is scored according to the presence or absence of selected movement process characteristics. An example of the specific locomotor and object control skill process characteristics are described in Table 11.10. If the process characteristic is present, a score of 1 is given; if it is absent, a score of 0 is given. Scores are summed for each skill and can be converted into percentile ranks (recommended for parental use) or standard scores (recommended for educational or clinical program planning). A scale is provided for arranging individual skill standard scores into seven steps ranging from very poor to very superior. Standard scores for each of the areas of locomotion and object control are summed to arrive at a Gross Motor Development Quotient. This quotient provides an estimate of the child's overall gross motor development and is interpreted in the same way (very poor to very superior) as individual standard scores. Normative data for the battery are based on 909 children from a variety of racial backgrounds from eight states; a careful analysis of reliability and validity issues also is provided.

Williams's Preschool Motor Development Checklist. Williams's checklist (Williams, 1995) is an informal measure of process characteristics of motor development in children ages 3 to 6 years. This checklist deals with basic motor development immaturities in six important gross motor skills. It includes four locomotor skills (running, jumping, hopping, skipping) and two ball-handling or object projection skills (throwing and catching). Williams's checklist uses a question format and presents some simple guidelines for determining the presence or absence of developmental lags in each skill area. This checklist is best used for screening potential movement control problems in young children. Information provided by this checklist can indicate whether the child has isolated motor control problems (e.g., difficulty executing the movements involved in hopping but not in skipping, jumping, or running), general locomotor control difficulties (e.g., immaturities in the movements involved in three or more of the four locomotor skills), or ball-handling problems (e.g., poor control in throwing and catching movements). Data from the checklist provide some insight into the nature of the general gross motor control profile of the young child. Information about the nature of the movement control difficulty is detailed enough that beginning enrichment programs can be planned.

TABLE 11.10   A Locomotor and Object Control Example from Ulrich's Test of Gross Motor Development

SKILL	DESCRIPTION	PROCESS CHARACTERISTICS (PC)	AGE AT WHICH 60 PERCENT OF CHILDREN ACHIEVE PC
Hop	Child hops 3 times on each foot	Foot of nonsupport bent Carried in back of body	5 years
		Nonsupport legs swings in pendular fashion	7 years
		Arms bent at elbows; swing forward on take-off	7 years
		Able to hop on right and left feet	4 years
Bounce	Child bounces ball 8–10 feet 3 times/3 trials	Contacts ball with 1 hand at hip height	7 years
		Pushes ball with fingers	6 years
		Ball contacts floor in front of foot on side of hand used for bouncing	7 years

This checklist was developed from published research as well as from data on clinical observations of motor development characteristics of young children. It can be used in both clinical and educational settings. The checklist items and score sheet are given in Table 11.11 and guidelines for interpreting the information gathered are given in Table 11.12.

Motor Control Process Checklists.   In the revised Motor Control Process Checklists, Williams and Breihan (1995) have attempted to create a standardized approach to the assessment of process characteristics of movement control in young children. The 16 checklists in the battery describe, in simple language, movement characteristics of selected gross and fine motor skills and are based on data from 150 children 4 and 6 years of age. The statements in each checklist are descriptions of the actions required for mastery of each skill. Typically, full mastery of most of the tasks included in this battery is not expected until after 6 years of age.

Ten of the gross motor skill checklists are presented in Table 11.13. Each checklist consists of four to six statements about pertinent process characteristics to look for in the movement behavior of the child during performance of the task. Percentages of 4- and 6-year-old children who show various process characteristics in their motor performances are given to the right of each statement. The statements in these checklists are more detailed than those discussed earlier and allow the evaluator to assess more precisely the quality of the child's movement as well as to identify the nature of the motor control problem if one is present. The child performs the skill at least four times, preferably in a naturalistic setting. While the child moves, the evaluator checks those statements that typify or characterize the movement behavior of the child. The general rule of thumb is that the child must display a given process characteristic at least 75 percent of the time if that characteristic is to be considered typical of his or her movement behavior. In addition, if the child does not exhibit two or more of the process characteristics that 70 percent of same-age children display, he or she might be experiencing some motor development problems. This child should receive further assessment of motor skills and some consideration should be given to providing enrichment activities to support development in the area(s) of delay.

Other Multidomain Tests.   Zittel (1994) reviews important considerations in selecting an instrument for assessing gross motor development in preschool children with special needs. This work provides an excellent overview of several test batteries that could be used with preschoolers with special motor development needs; these include the I CAN Preprimary Motor and Play Skills (Wessel, 1980), Battelle Developmental Inventory (Newborg, Stock, Wnek, Guidubaldi, & Svinicki, 1984),

TABLE 11.11 Williams Preschool Motor Development Checklist

Directions: Carefully observe the child perform each skill several times in different settings. Ask the following questions about the "way" the young child performs each motor skill. Try to answer "yes" or "no" to each question.

Running
1. Does the child experience difficulty in starting, stopping, or making sudden turns?
2. Does the child run using a flatfoot; that is, does he or she receive the body weight on the whole foot?
3. Does the child run with toes pointed outward?
4. Do the arms move back and forth in a sideways motion across the body?

Jumping
1. Does the child fail to flex hips, knees, and ankles in preparing to jump?
2. Does the child fail to extend hips, knees, and ankles in initiating the jump?
3. Does the child fail to execute a two-footed take-off?
4. Does the child fail to swing the arms back in preparing to jump and then forward and upward as he or she initiates the jump?
5. Does the child land with the hips and knees straight (extended and stiff)?
6. Does the child lose balance on landing?

Hopping
1. Does the child hop two or three steps and lose control?
2. Are the hopping movements staccato and/or arrhythmical?
3. Are the hands and fingers tense and/or extended?
4. Do the arms flail?
5. Is the nonsupport foot kept in contact with the floor?

Skipping
1. Does the child fail to skip a 20-ft distance maintaining smooth, sequential, rhythmical action?
2. Does the child skip on one foot while the other foot executes a walking or running step?
3. Does the child skip using a flatfooted pattern?
4. Does the child skip with the toes turned outward in duck-walk fashion?
5. Does the child fail to use arm-foot opposition?

Throwing
1. Does the child's arm move primarily in the anteroposterior plane?
2. Is there any trunk rotation?
3. Does the child hold the ball in the palm of the hand?
4. Does the child show no evidence of weight transfer?
5. Does the child throw by stepping on the same foot as the throwing arm?
6. Does the child fail to follow through?

Catching
1. Does the child attempt to catch the ball with arms outstretched and straight?
2. Does the child use the arms, hands, and body as a single unit to trap the ball?
3. Does the child turn his or her head away from the ball as he or she catches it?
4. Does the child seem to let the ball bounce off the outstretched arms?
5. Does the child only catch balls bounced from close distances (5 ft or less)?
6. Does the child fail to watch or track the flight of the ball?

Source: Williams' Preschool Motor Development Checklist, by H. Williams, 1996. *The Perceptual-Motor Development Laboratory Protocols,* University of South Carolina–Columbia.

TABLE 11.12 Interpretation of *Williams' Preschool Gross Motor Development Checklist*

SKILL	GUIDELINE
Running	If three of the four questions are answered yes, there may be a developmental lag in running.
Jumping	If four of the six questions are answered yes, there may be a development lag in jumping.
Hopping	If four of the five questions are answered yes, there may be a developmental lag in hopping.
Skipping	If the child is 5 to 6 years old and the answer to all five questions is yes, there may be a developmental lag in skipping.
Throwing	If a child is 4 or 5 years old and the answer to five of the six questions is yes, there may be a developmental lag in throwing.
Catching	If the child is 3 years old, and the answer to questions 2, 3, 4, and 5 is yes, keep a watchful eye on this aspect of motor develpment. If the child is 5 years old, and the answer to any question is yes, there may be a developmental lag in catching.

Source: Williams' Preschool Motor Development Checklist, by H. Williams, 1995, *The Perceptual-Motor Development Laboratory Protocols,* University of South Carolina–Columbia.

Brigance Diagnostic Inventory of Early Development (Brigance, 1978), Miller Assessment for Preschoolers (Miller, 1988), and Developmental Indicators for the Assessment of Learning—Revised (Mardell-Czudnowski & Goldenberg, 1983). These are all multidomain tests and, thus, do not focus primarily on assessment of gross motor development.

USE OF ASSESSMENT RESULTS

Because we know that children who experience lags in motor development are more likely than their peers to display difficulties in adapting to both school and play environments, information about the level and nature of motor skill development is of major importance to the parent, the teacher, the school psychologist, and the family physician. A scientifically sound and insightful diagnosis of gross motor development must be based on information from formal and informal product and process assessments of the child's gross motor behavior. Formal measures of gross motor development are needed to support, clarify, and extend observations of motor behavior made with informal instruments. Formal product measures of motor development are valuable because they provide a frame of reference for interpreting the current status of the child's motor development. It is important to note, however, that it is imprudent and unfair to act as though figures or descriptions in a table or on a chart are an irrefutable indication of whether or not a child is "normal."

Process information is used to elaborate on the product frame of reference. Process information is especially important because it considers directly how the body is moved and attempts to determine what is missing from or contributing to the child's lack of adequate motor control. Informal process assessment techniques are particularly important for gaining insight into how the child attempts to solve the problem of performing a motor task. These techniques often provide information about the child's level of understanding of the task to be performed. This type of information is integral to an accurate diagnosis of the level of gross motor development because lags in motor development can be as much a function of the young child's understanding of the what and how of a task as they are of the child's ability to perform the task. The most significant, direct, and immediate uses that can be made of information from gross motor development screening and evaluation include the following:

1. *Planning and evaluating effective gross motor curricula for young children.* To individualize early sensory and motor learning experiences for young children, professionals need to be able to group or to identify children according to motor development levels. When specific aspects of the gross motor behavior of the child are known, basic tasks can be modified in a variety of ways to encourage individual refinement of and success in motor skill performance at the child's present level of development as well as to promote growth toward higher levels of skill mastery.

2. *Early identification of motor dysfunctions.* Motor dysfunctions can impede the child's physical, mental, social, and emotional development. Information about gross motor development can be valuable to the teacher

TABLE 11.13   Motor Control Process Checklists

Skills	PERCENTAGE OF AGE*	
	4	6
Locomotor Skills		
Running		
1. Arms and legs used in opposition	74	84
2. Extension and flexion evident in both legs during running cycle	86	90
3. Arms swing freely, close to body in vertical plane	54	68
4. Arms are bent at the elbow	64	82
5. Support foot hits floor heel first	5	64
6. Trunk is inclined slightly forward	56	70
7. Head is held erect, facing forward	66	88
Galloping		
1. Lead foot absorbs body's weight on heel; weight is transferred to the toes; there is heel-to-toe action in lead foot	48	66
2. Trail foot moves toward lead foot but does not pass lead foot	34	64
3. Extension and flexion are evident in both legs during complete	56	76
4. Trunk is extended and inclined slightly forward	52	76
5. Arms swing freely from shoulder in the vertical plane	34	60
6. Body is momentarily suspended in air	58	72
7. Child continually leads with same foot	66	80
Hopping		
1. Weight is balanced easily on one foot	68	84
2. Nonsupport foot is flexed at the knees; does not touch the floor	58	88
3. Arms either held out to sides to assist with balance or moved up and down to help lift the body	56	74
4. Body weight is received on ball of foot and is immediately shifted to entire foot	42	62
5. Hips and knees flex on landing to absorb momentum of body	54	74
6. Head and trunk are held erect	48	84
Skipping		
1. A normal walking step is combined with a hop; a forward step-hop on one foot is followed by a forward step-hop on the opposite foot	34	86
2. There is a continuous sequential and alternating step-hop action	32	80
3. Arms swing freely in opposition to leg movements	8	48
4. Knee and hip of the nonsupport leg are flexed to aid in action	40	84
5. The body is suspended in the air momentarily	42	86
6. There is obvious smoothness and rhythm in the total skipping action	12	50
Balance Beam Walk		
1. Child alternates feet and can execute a simple walking pattern	94	96
2. Child can maintain a heel-toe walking sequence	24	60
3. Arms are carried; held below shoulder height; there is no flailing	24	54
4. Movement is smooth; there is no exaggerated body sway	26	50
5. Feet are placed with toes pointing forward on the beam	42	62
6. Head is erect, facing forward	0	20

Skills	PERCENTAGE OF AGE*	
	4	*6*

Object Projection Skills

Throw

	4	6
1. Trunk is rotated backward; weight is shifted to back foot	44	52
2. Throwing arm is moved backward with rotation occurring at the shoulder joint	66	66
3. A step is taken toward the intended target	52	74
4. The step is on the foot opposite the throwing arm	44	54
5. Body weight is shifted forward: the arm lags behind and begins moving in the horizontal plane, the elbow leads	40	56
6. Medial rotation of the shoulder and elbow extension occur; the elbow is close to complete extension at the time of release	56	82
7. Wrist is flexed rapidly just before ball is released	32	62
8. On the follow-through the body and arm continue to rotate forward	18	48

Kick

	4	6
1. A preliminary step is taken on the support leg toward the ball	30	54
2. The kicking leg swings backward	56	74
3. The kicking leg swings forward with flexion in the lower leg	88	92
4. Body is inclined slightly backward	22	44
5. As the upper leg becomes perpendicular to the floor, lower leg extends (at knee)	30	74
6. The opposite arm swings forward	44	60
7. The kicking leg extends and makes contact with the ball	62	90
8. The contact is made with the toes; the ankle is slightly flexed	40	64
9. The opposite arm swings forward/upward in the follow-through	10	20
10. Trunk becomes slightly more vertical	12	42

Stationary Catch

	4	6
1. Arms move to a position in front of the body, hands juxtaposed, the palms of the hands facing each other	72	90
2. Hands are turned to accommodate the high or low trajectory of ball	8	42
3. Hands and fingers are "loose" but slightly cupped and pointed in direction of the oncoming ball	26	62
4. Eyes pick up and follow the flight of the ball until ball contact is made	62	88
5. Initially, the ball contact is made with both hands simultaneously	34	68
6. Adjustments in the elbow and shoulder joint positions are made to accommodate "changes" in the flight of the ball	12	48
7. Fingers close immediately around the ball and the arms "give" to absorb momentum of ball	14	36

Two-Arm Strike

	4	6
1. Feet are positioned approximately shoulder width apart	56	62
2. Trunk is rotated backward and the weight is shifted onto the back foot	32	36
3. Lead elbow is held up and out from the body with bat off the shoulder	50	48
4. Eyes follow the flight of the ball until just before contact is made	44	72
5. Body weight is shifted forward (onto the opposite foot) in the direction of the intended hit	38	58
6. Hips and trunk rotate in the direction of intended hit; hips lead	14	34
7. Arms move forward independent of hip action	42	76

(continued)

TABLE 11.13 Continued

Skills	PERCENTAGE OF AGE*	
	4	6
Object Projection Skills		
Ball-Bounce		
1. Body is flexed at knees, hips, waist	28	28
2. Child uses fingertip control, does not slap at ball	6	40
3. Eyes track the ball	24	84
4. Ball is bounced to waist level	12	50

Source: Motor Control Tasks for Young Children, by H. Williams and S. Breihan, 1995, *The Perceptual-Motor Development Laboratory Protocols.* University of South Carolina–Columbia.

*Percentage of children at specified age who show the process characteristic in their skill performance.

of the young child for maximizing early learning potential and for educational counseling. Such information is vital when making decisions about whether the child possesses the basic skills needed to succeed in simple classroom activities. The child who devotes a major share of his or her energy to assuming and maintaining basic postures or to controlling movements of the body will have much less energy to devote to other important activities that are integral to optimal development. Data about the child's level of gross motor development are important in determining when and/or if a child should enter school or whether he or she should be placed in a developmental enrichment environment.

3. *Design of individual programs of enrichment activities.* Motor skill deficiencies often accompany and contribute to other learning, behavior, and attention problems of the young child. When this is the case, some attention almost always is required to improve the motor capacities of the child before other learning and behavior problems can be effectively addressed. If, on the other hand, the young child has learning, memory, and/or attentional problems but no accompanying motor development difficulties, gross motor activities may be used in creative ways to help stimulate improvement in other dimensions of development.

Results of gross motor skill screening and evaluation of the preschool child are most useful as a part of a comprehensive, multidimensional assessment of the young child. At a minimum, information about the child's fine motor control or eye–hand coordination

(e.g., cutting, peg manipulation, pencil or crayon usage), simple perceptual skills (e.g., identification of colors, color matching, visual, verbal, and tactile-kinesthetic discrimination of shapes and sizes, as well as figure–ground perception), and general characteristics of eye movement control ought to accompany the child's motor development record. It is only when information from gross motor development testing is used or viewed in conjunction with information about these other aspects of sensory and motor development that appropriate prognostic statements and remediation techniques for gross motor and other dimensions of development can be established or prescribed.

If the child has gross motor deficiencies only (e.g., no accompanying deficits in other sensory and motor behaviors), it is more likely that the motor development problems observed are temporary and simply reflect an uneven growth process that will self-correct with time. If, on the other hand, gross motor deficits are accompanied by fine motor and/or other sensory-perceptual difficulties, there may be underlying neurological problems. In this case, referral to a pediatric neurologist and/or other appropriate medical personnel for further evaluation is appropriate. The motor system (including the control of eye muscles) is more likely than other systems to show deficits when something has gone awry with basic central and/or peripheral neurophysiological processes. At a behavioral level, information-gathering behaviors (e.g., the way children use their eyes to pick up information from the environment) and information interpretation skills (e.g., figure–ground perception) can contribute significantly to the lack of refined fine and gross motor skills. Gross motor deficits are often, at least in part, a reflection of inadequate support skills in visual perception. Therefore, remediation and enrichment programs for children with both gross motor and simple perceptual deficits need to focus on improving the supporting perceptual behaviors as well as the movement behaviors themselves. Professionals working in educational settings with preschool children should use the following guide to gross motor development:

- Screen all children in gross motor development prior to or early in their entry into the preschool program.
- For initial screening, use a simple motor development checklist such as those developed by Ulrich (1985) or Williams (1995).
- Observe the children in naturalistic play settings.

- Use this information to determine which children might need closer observation.
- Use a formal instrument to screen more carefully the children identified as potentially having gross motor process and product deficiencies.
- Examiners who must choose one measure over another should be sure to include some evaluation of the process characteristics of the child's motor behavior.
- Children with questionable abilities should be referred to a motor development specialist, physical education teacher, or school psychologist for a more formal and comprehensive evaluation.
- When in doubt about the child's motor development difficulties, talk to or refer the child to the appropriate personnel within or outside the school setting.

REFERENCES

American Psychiatric Association. (1993). *Diagnostic and Statistical Manual of Mental Disorders* (4th ed.). Washington, DC: Author.

Bayley, N. (1965). Comparisons of mental and motor test scores for ages 1–15 months by sex, birth order, race, geographical location and education of parents. *Child Development, 36,* 379–411.

Brigance, A. (1978). *Brigance Diagnostic Inventory of Early Development.* North Billerica, MA: Curriculum Associates.

Bruininks, R. (1978). *Bruininks-Oseretsky Test of Motor Proficiency. Examiner's Manual.* Circle Pines, MN: American Guidance Service.

Bushnell, E., & Boudreau, J. (1993). Motor development and the mind: The potential role of motor abilities as a determinant of aspects of perceptual development. *Child Development, 64,* 1005–1021.

Cantell, M., Smyth, M., & Ahonen, T. (1994). Clumsiness in adolescence: Educational, motor and social outcomes of motor delay detected at 5 years. *Adapted Physical Activity Quarterly, 11*(2), 115–129.

Capute, A., & Accardo, P. (1996). *Developmental Disabilities in Infant and Child: Neurodevelopmental Diagnosis and Treatment. Section III: Fundamentals of Pediatric Developmental Assessment* (pp. 263–424). Baltimore: Paul H. Brookes.

Cashin, G. (1975). *The Cashin Test of Motor Development.* Unpublished master's thesis, Bowling Green State University.

Cratty, B. J. (1970). *Perceptual and motor development in infants and young children.* New York: Macmillan.

Cratty, B. J. (1972). *Physical expressions of intelligence.* Englewood Cliffs, NJ: Prentice-Hall.

Denckla, M. (1984). Developmental dyspraxia. The clumsy child. In M. D. Levine, & P. Satz (Eds.), *Middle childhood: Development and dysfunction.* Boston: University Park Press.

DeOreo, K., & Keogh, J. (1980). Performance of fundamental motor tasks. In C. Corbin (Ed.), *A Textbook of Motor Development.* (pp. 76–91). Dubuque, IA: W. C. Brown.

Espenschade, A., & Eckert, H. (1980). *Motor development.* Columbus, OH: Merrill.

Flinchum, B. (1975). *Motor development in early childhood: A guide for movement education with ages 2 to 6.* St. Louis: Mosby.

Folio, M., & Fewell, R. (1983). *Peabody Developmental Motor Scales and Activity Cards.* Allen, TX: Developmental Learning Materials Teaching Resources.

Frankenburg, W. K., & Dodds, J. B. (1967). The Denver Developmental Screening Test. *Journal of Pediatrics, 71,* 181.

Frankenburg, W., Dodds, J., Archer, P., Bresnick, B., & Shapiro, H. (1990). *The Denver II: Revision and restandardization of the DDST.* Denver: Denver Developmental Materials.

Gallahue, D., & Ozmun, J. (1998). *Understanding motor development: Infants, children, adolescents, adults.* Boston: McGraw-Hill.

Gesell, A. (1973). *The first five years of life: A guide to the study of the preschool child.* New York: Harper & Row.

Geuze, R., & Borger, H. (1993). Children who are clumsy: Five years later. *Adapted Physical Activity Quarterly, 10,* 10–21.

Gubbay, S. (1975). *The clumsy child—A study of developmental apraxic and agnosid ataxia.* London: W. B. Saunders.

Henderson, S., Knight, E., Losse, A., & Jongmans, M. (1990). The clumsy child in school—are we doing enough? *British Journal of Physical Education, 22*(2) (Suppl 9),2–8.

Henderson, S., & Sudgen, D. (1992). *Movement Assessment Battery for Children.* London: Psychological Corporation.

Illingworth, R. S. (1975). *The development of the infant and young child: Normal and abnormal.* Edinburgh: Livingstone.

Keogh, J. F. (1975). Consistency and constancy in preschool motor development. In H. J. Muller, R. Decker, & F. Schilling (Eds.), *Motor behavior of preschool children.* Schomdorff: Hofman.

Keogh, J., & Sudgen, D. (1991). *Problems of movement skill development.* Columbia: University of South Carolina Press.

Lane, S., Attanasio, C., & Huselid, R. (1994). Prediction of preschool sensory and motor performance by 18-month neurologic scores among children born prematurely. *American Journal of Occupational Therapy, 48*(5), 391–396.

Losse, A., Henderson, S., Elliman, D., Hall, D., Knight, E., & Jongmans, M. (1991). Clumsiness in children—do they grow out of it? A 10-year follow-up study. *Developmental Medicine and Child Neurology, 33,* 55–68.

Lyytinen, H., & Ahonen, N. T. (1989). Motor precursors of learning disabilities. In D. J. Bakker & D. J. Vander Vlugt (Eds.), *Learning disabilities: Vol 1, Neuropsychological correlates* (pp. 35–43). Amsterdam: Swets & Zeitlinger.

Mardell-Czudnowski, C., & Goldenberg, D. (1983). *Development Indicators for the Assessment of Learning—Revised.* Edison, NJ: Childcraft Education.

McCarthy, D. (1972). *McCarthy Scales of Children's Abilities.* New York: Psychological Corporation.

Miller, L. (1988). *Miller Assessment for Preschoolers: Manual Revision.* San Antonio, TX: Harcourt Brace Jovanovich.

Newborg, J., Stock, J., Wnek, L., Guidubaldi, J., & Svinicki, J. (1984). *Batelle Developmental Inventory.* Allen, TX: DLM Teaching Resources.

Paine, R. S., & Oppe, T. E. (1966). *Neurological examination of children.* Philadelphia: Lippincott.

Piaget, J. (1963). *The origins of intelligence in children.* New York: Norton.

Precht, H. (1977). Assessment and significance of behavioral states. In S. R. Berenberg (Ed.). *Brain-fetal and infant-current research on normal and abnormal development* (pp. 79–90). The Hague: Nijoff.

Precht, H., & Beintema, D. (1964). *The neurological examination of the full term newborn infant.* London: Heinemann.

Riggs, M. (Ed.). (1980). *Movement education for preschool children.* Reston, VA: Association of the American Alliance for Health, Physical Education, Recreation and Dance.

Roberton, M., & Halverson, L. (1984). *Developing children: Their changing movements.* Philadelphia: Lea & Febiger.

Roberton, M., & Langendorfer, S. (1980). Testing motor development sequences across 9–14 years. In N. C. Nadeau, et al. (Eds.). *Psychology of motor behavior and sport* (pp. 269–279). Urbana, IL: Human Kinetic Press.

Spelke, E. (1990). Origins of visual knowledge. In D. N. Osherson, S. M. Kosslyln, & J. M. Hollerback (Eds.), *Visual cognition and action* (Vol. 2, pp. 99–127). Cambridge, MA: MIT Press.

Sporns, O., & Edelman, G. (1993). Solving Bernstein's problem: A proposal for the development of coordinated movement by selection. *Child Development, 64,* 960–981.

Stott, L. H., & Ball, R. S. (1965). Infant and preschool mental tests: Review and evaluation. *Monographs of the Society for Research in Child Development, 101,* 30.

Touwen, B. (1976). *Neurological development in infancy.* Philadelphia: J. B. Lippincott Co.

Ulrich, D. (1985). *Test of Gross Motor Development.* Austin, TX: Pro-Ed.

Vulpe, S. G. (1982). *Vulpe Assessment Battery.* Toronto, Canada: National Institute on Mental Retardation.

Wessel, J. (1980). *I CAN Pre-Primary Motor and Play Skills.* East Lansing, MI: Field Service Unit in Physical Education and Recreation for the Handicapped.

Wickstrom, R. (1977). *Fundamental motor patterns.* Philadelphia: Lea & Febiger.

Wild, M. (1938). The behavior pattern of throwing and some observations concerning the course of development in children. *Research Quarterly, 9,* 20–24.

Williams, H. (1983). *Perceptual and motor development in young children.* Englewood Cliffs, NJ: Prentice-Hall.

Williams, H. (1995). *Williams' Preschool Motor Development Checklist.* In H. Williams, *The Perceptual-Motor Development Laboratory Protocols.* Columbia: University of South Carolina.

Williams, H., & Breihan, S. (1979). *Motor control tasks for young children.* Unpublished paper, University of Toledo.

Williams, H., & Breihan, S. (1995). *Motor Control Tasks for Young Children.* In H. Williams, *The Perceptual-Motor Development Laboratory Protocols.* Columbia: University of South Carolina.

Zittel, L. (1994). Gross motor assessment of preschool children with special needs: Instrument selection considerations. *Adapted Physical Activity Quarterly, 11,* 245–260.

CHAPTER 12

ASSESSMENT OF
VISUAL FUNCTIONING

REBECCA R. FEWELL

The world and how it is experienced is significantly different for persons without sight than it is for those who are sighted. The impact of blindness extends beyond the person who is blind: Those who are in both the immediate and the extended world of persons who are blind are also affected. Gowman (1957) considered blindness the most severe of all disabilities and noted the negative stereotype blindness evokes by arousing feelings of pity, threat, and fundamental impotence. Scott (1969) pointed out that blindness could have a variety of effects on social behavior. The severity of difficulty experienced by a person with visual loss is influenced by the cause of the impairments, degree of correction, reactions of others to the loss, and the individual's strengths, weaknesses, and attitudes. One's ability to acquire knowledge through seeing impacts the development of competence in all of life. Without question, a child's visual abilities must be known and considered before an examiner selects tests or procedures for use in any aspect of a full assessment of the child.

As we examine visual functioning in children, it is important that we acknowledge two separate but related challenges. The first is the actual assessment of visual ability and the second is how we make decisions based on that information. Psychologists and diagnostic personnel must make choices as to how to assess children whose visual functioning is limited. Furthermore, if the examiner's role is to make concrete intervention recommendations, then the amount of visual functioning and how a child uses their vision becomes critical in that task. Given that visual functioning impacts so many aspects of one's life, assessment of visual impairment must be broad based. It would include the physical attributes as well as the needs, resources, and expectations of the person who is visually impaired and his or her family. This chapter will review briefly the prevalence and major types of visual impairments in young children, comment

on the early development of vision and the role of vision in other developmental domains, and then describe the most common ways of screening visual functioning. The chapter closes with suggested strategies assessment personnel may want to consider as they undertake assessment responsibilities for children with serious visual problems.

PREVALENCE OF VISUAL IMPAIRMENTS

Fortunately, very few people are totally blind. Jan, Skyanda, and Groenveld (1990) reported that blindness from birth (i.e., congenital blindness) occurs in four of every 10,000 births. Deitz and Ferrell (1993) found that one in every 3,000 newborns was born with some kind of a visual disability. Of children with visual impairments, about 25 percent are legally blind. Many other children may have visual problems and may be under the care of vision specialists, but it is also likely that others will have problems that have gone undetected. The alert examiner will always be on the lookout for signs of vision problems.

CLASSIFICATION OF VISUAL IMPAIRMENTS

Vision is assessed by measuring acuity or sharpness of an image that one can detect at a specific distance and the physical space or field that can be seen without shifting gaze (Langley, 1996). A visual acuity of 20/20 is considered *normal vision*. The numerator indicates the distance at which acuity is measured and the denominator is the size the visual stimulus must be in order to be seen. It is derived from the size a stimulus must be for a person with normal vision to be able to identify the stimulus at a distance of 20 feet. The larger the denominator the larger the stimulus must be in order to be seen. When visual acuity is determined to be 20/200 or worse in the better eye with correction, one is considered *legally blind*. In terms of the efficiency of one's vision, a person who is 20/200 has about 20 percent visual efficiency. One is considered *partially sighted* if vision is determined to be 20/70 or worse in the better eye with correction. However, these definitions can be deceiving, especially in young children. Deitz and Ferrell (1993) point out that the classifications do not reflect fluctuations in visual abilities that are seen in some children, for example, those with transient and permanent cortical visual impairments. At any given time, environmental factors are known to impact acuity in some settings as well as personal proclivities such as neuromotor integrity or organizational behavior (Langley, 1996).

Common visual problems in young children can be classified into four groups: (1) structural abnormalities and disease (e.g., cataracts, conjunctivitis), (2) impaired acuity (e.g., nearsightedness, farsightedness), (3) impaired ocular movements (e.g., nystagmus, strabismus), and (4) impaired awareness due to constricted visual fields or cortical impairment (Jan, Skyanda, Groenveld, & Holt, 1987; Langley, 1996).

The most common cause of visual loss in preschool children is amblyopia or "lazy eye." A child's visual pathways are normal, but the binocular input to the eyes is different, therefore, the images are different. To resolve this visual confusion the child simply stops using the vision in the weaker eye and the stronger eye becomes dominant. If diagnosed early (prior to age 4), amblyopia is easily treatable (France, 1989). The common treatment regime is to patch the stronger eye in order strengthen the use of the weak eye.

DEVELOPMENTAL ASPECTS OF VISION

The normal newborn has a well-developed visual system that is immediately used to gain information about the environment. In the early months following birth visual acuity accommodation and ocular control improve rapidly, giving the normal child a visual acuity of approximately 20/100 (Fantz, Ordy, & Udelf, 1962). A steady increase in spatial abilities occurs between 1 and 6 months of age (Dobson & Teller, 1978). Using various techniques for measurement, visual acuities have been recorded at birth, 6, and 12 months of age as 20/60, 20/50, and 20/20 (Hoyt, Nickel, & Billson, 1982).

Early functional behaviors require the use of vision in hand–mouth, mouth–eye, and hand–eye skills. These skills enable infants to visually locate and suck their fingers, bottles, rattles, and so forth and prepare them to act on their environment by using their hands to grasp spoons and feed themselves, bat mobiles, and eventually direct their own play activities. Increased precision in reaching, placing, and tracking objects leads to the development of visual competence. By 2 years, many of the tasks used to determine cognitive competence depend on vision as the major source of stimulus input (e.g., block building, puzzles, matching tasks, etc.).

IMPACT OF VISUAL IMPAIRMENTS ON DEVELOPMENT

Visual impairments have very serious interactive effects on a child's skill development in all areas. This section briefly describes the major developmental problems associated with visual impairment that could impact assessment.

Motor Development

Without vision, or with very limited vision, children experience the world differently than do children who are sighted. As a consequence, selected motor behaviors develop more slowly or less efficiently than behaviors in children who are sighted. It is also known that some motor skills are never developed in children who are blind (DuBose, 1979). Troster and Brambring (1993) compared the early motor behavior of infants who were blind to infants who were sighted and found significant lags in those who were blind. By 9 months, when most infants who were sighted could sit and play with toys, no infants who were blind could do this. Likewise, at this same age, when all infants who were sighted could crawl, only two of the five infants who were blind tried to move forward with vigorous body movements. Previously Adelson and Fraiberg (1974) found children who were blind lagged 7.15 months behind children who were sighted in walking alone. However, there is far more to the impact of lack of sight than just the achievement of the motor milestones. The quality of movement is significantly less efficient among children who are visually impaired. When walking, the child who is blind will not only be delayed in initiation but is likely to retain a wide lateral gait, walk with toes outward, engage in less cross-lateral rotation, and walk with his or her head held in a downward position. Although little research has been conducted on young preschool children who are visually impaired, even fewer studies have focused on the motor skill development among older preschool children with visual impairments. Folio (1974) examined a sample of children with multiple impairments, including vision, and found them to be delayed in the advanced projectile skills of running, hopping, jumping, and skipping. These delays are not unexpected given that the earlier skills upon which these more advanced skills must build are delayed. Interestingly, Troster and Brambring (1993) found evidence that suggests some infants who are blind apparently learn to walk without having gone through a crawling phase. This may be responsible for the lack of coordination, balance problems, and reduced motor efficiency that are frequently observed in children who are blind.

Fine motor coordination was also found by Troster and Brambring (1993) to be delayed. By 9 months all infants who were sighted could reach and grasp sound toys but no child who was blind did this. Norris, Spaulding, and Brodie (1957) found that preschool children who were blind lagged behind children who were sighted in grasping and using scissors, placing pegs in holes, and scribbling. When delays in basic motor skills are observed at these young ages, it is not surprising that they have long-lasting effects.

Language Development

Several investigators have studied how early language develops in children who are blind. It is well known that in children who are sighted the meaning of words is often first learned through gesture, for example, the gesture of waving "bye-bye." Children who are blind do not have visual access to these gestures. Recently, Iverson and Goldin-Meadow (1997) explored the communication function of gestures in children who are blind and found that these children do produce gestures that resembled those of children who are sighted in both form and content, however, not always in the same context. They concluded that gestures serve a function for the speaker that is independent of its impact on the listener. This may be the basis for some of the communicative differences observed later in life.

As might be expected, first spoken words are different between children who are blind and those who are sighted. For example, ball appears early in the life of a child who is sighted because it is a favorite toy that follows a trajectory that babies like to track. This is not the case in the child without sight, perhaps a reflection of the phrase, "out-of-sight, out-of-mind." However, by 4 or 5 years of age the vocabularies of children who are blind and sighted are quite similar (Warren, 1977).

Several problems in the communication of children who are blind have been noted. Children who are blind sometimes use explosive sounds such as lip smacking, popping, or clicking their tongues as a means of orienting themselves in the physical world. These activities and others can become habit forming and are known as "blindisms." This can lead to expressive language characterized by repetitions of stored facts or of statements previously heard or made, behaviors referred to as "verbalisms" or "parroting" (Harley, 1963).

Verbal comprehension problems can be seen in the difficulty some children who are blind have in following two- and three-stage commands and in making sequenced discriminations among objects (e.g., "before you touch the little circle, give me the large triangle"). The use of personal pronouns illustrates further difficulties for children who are blind. Children who are sighted begin to use the personal pronouns *me* and *I* at about 2½ years of age, whereas children who are blind do not use them until 3 to 4½ years. This might be related to how the child who is blind has an identity of himself or herself as others refer to him or her rather than as an individual capable of acting on the environment. If differences in the rate of language development between children who are sighted and those who are visually impaired continue after the children are 4 to 5 years old, the differences might be related to delayed cognitive or emotional development.

Cognitive Development

Warren (1977) indicated that children who are blind and those who are sighted differ in several areas of cognitive development. Fortunately, many of the deficiencies in children who are blind can be remediated through intervention. Many sensorimotor schemas are delayed in young children who are blind (DuBose, 1976; Piaget & Inhelder, 1969). For example, there is delayed understanding of object concept because objects must be brought to the child who is blind for tactile exploration. Object permanence typically is delayed by one to three years in children who are blind because they are unable to readily follow and note the appearances or disappearance of objects. The child who is sighted can construct and visually compare structures, thus learning about spatial constructions; such simultaneous comparisons are not a part of the experiences of the young child who is blind. Therefore, concepts related to such sensorimotor schemata are delayed in children who are blind relative to their sighted peers. Cause–effect relations also are less likely to be perceived by young children who are blind because they cannot view the consequences of their actions. Likewise, when children who are blind are deprived of opportunities to observe events and their antecedents, they are less able to acquire methods to reach desired ends and understand means–end schemes. As a result, children who are blind have fewer and somewhat fractionated experiences in developing a repertoire of problem-solving skills.

Higgins (1973) examined classification skills among children who are who are blind between the ages of 5 and 11 years and found no evidence of a general developmental classificatory lag. However, the children who are blind did not perform as well on abstract concepts as they did on concrete concepts. Blindness can result in a delay in the acquisition of relational concepts, such as *in front of, behind, beside, between,* and so forth. Additionally, as concepts are used to describe different settings and conditions, they can become increasingly difficult to generalize. Similarly, concepts involving conservation are frequently delayed in the child who is blind. Educators might facilitate the development of conservation in the child who is blind by availing information to the child's nonimpaired senses so that adequate information is available from which to perceive relationships, draw inferences, and make conclusions.

Because most intelligence tests require vision of the examinee, it is difficult to make comparisons between the measured intelligence of children who are both blind and sighted. Smits and Mommers (1976) and Tillman and Bashaw (1968) examined subscale performance on the Wechsler Intelligence Scale for Children (Wechsler, 1949; 1967) and found superior numerical memory performance by children who were blind on the Digit Span subtest, whereas children who were sighted performed significantly higher on the abstract verbal subtest of Similarities. Crucial to the education and general functioning of children who are blind are their abilities to adapt to new situations. Until ability tests are developed to assess the performance of children who are blind on variables crucial to adaptation in a sighted world, we continue to fall far short in the assessment of intelligence among children who are blind.

Perceptual Development

The tactile discrimination abilities of children who are blind and sighted have been compared in several studies. Cutaneous localization (Jones, 1972), form discrimination (Schwartz, 1972), and weight discrimination (Block, 1972) were all found to be developed to a slightly better degree among the children who were blind; however, these differences were small. When more complex or crossmodal perceptual skills (e.g., form identification, spatial relationship, perceptual-motor integration) were examined, children who were blind tended to lag behind their peers who were sighted. However, most of these perceptual studies used subjects over 6 years of age, and the age of onset of blindness appeared to be a crucial variable. Far more research is needed on younger children and on children who are totally without sight if we are to fully understand the impact of blindness on perceptual development.

Social Development

Considerable evidence suggests delayed and aberrant social skills among children who are blind. Vision plays a major role in facilitating the process of human bonding that enables the human infant and his or her parents to develop a special attachment for one another. Without vision, the process is more difficult and complex. The attachment between the infant who is blind and his or her parents emerges at a slower pace and expresses itself through interaction patterns that involve touching and vocal play. For example, the author observed a mother and her infant who was blind engage in repeated dyadic exchanges during a series of tactile games involving their arms and hands.

The play of children who are blind is characterized by delayed expressions of symbolic representation and of the self in play. With fewer opportunities to observe naturally occurring environmental events, it is understandable why play using deferred imitations is both delayed and impoverished among children who are blind. Play enables children to practice the social behaviors that they are expected to use with proficiency at later ages. The inability to observe and interpret the context or situation in which interactions occur makes the learning of nonverbal social skills particularly difficult, resulting in delayed social maturity and interpersonal behavior.

Hallenbeck (1954) studied residential students who were blind and found that a crucial correlate of emotional adjustment was whether the child had experienced a positive relationship with another person before entering school. Other studies have demonstrated the importance of supportive, early emotional relationships to the healthy development of children who are visually impaired. The ways in which parents relate to their young child who is blind invariably affect the child's developing self-concept.

Blindisms or aberrant stereotypic mannerisms such as rocking, hand flicking, eye-poking, and echolalia are common problems with some children who are blind. If these behavioral peculiarities persist, they cause increased negative attention to the child and serve to distance others from the child.

Self-Care Development

Independence and self-care are essential for the healthy development of children who are visually impaired or blind. Without visual models to imitate, children who are blind must learn eating, dressing, bathing, toileting, and grooming skills through more concrete activities and through verbal instruction with physical prompting. Easier nonconventional routes to the desired behavior might be more appropriate than the conventional approach. For example, a child who is blind can learn to apply toothpaste to teeth instead of to a brush. Toileting problems are reported more frequently with children who are blind than with children who are sighted; however, this appears to be related to the lack of visual images and unclear expectations rather than to physical delay. In all areas of self-care, training can be modified for easier task completion. The child who is blind might be slower in achieving independence, but can eventually achieve the same degree of proficiency experienced by individuals who are sighted.

General Observation of Visual Problems

Observations of children performing routine classroom, home, or play activities provide important information concerning a child's functional vision. A parent might wonder why a child sits so close to the television; a playmate might observe that a friend always reaches too far to the left when trying to catch a ball; or a teacher might notice that a child tilts his or her head to one side when reading. If these behaviors are observed in conjunction with other signs of visual impairment, an eye specialist should see the child. Common indications of eye problems are listed in Table 12.1.

ASSESSMENT OF VISION

Ellingham, Silva, Buckfield, and Clarkson (1976) reported four possible factors that identify a child as being at risk for developing a visual impairment: (1) prematurity, (2) family history of a visual defect, (3) infection during pregnancy, and (4) difficult labor. Appropriate vision screening is an important early step in pediatric health care because visual stimulation is critical to normal development; early detection and correction of

TABLE 12.1   Observable Signs of Visual Problems

Eyes turning in or out at any time
Red or watery eyes
Encrusted eyelids
Swollen eyes
Frequent head adjustment when looking at
    distant objects
Focusing difficulties
Tracking difficulties
Rubbing eyes frequently
Complaints of itchy, scratchy, or stinging eyes
Avoidance of close work
Frequent blinking, frowning, or scowling
Tilting or turning of head to focus on objects
Tiring after visual tasks
Movement of head rather than eyes while looking
    at a page
Frequent confusion of similarly shaped letters,
    numbers, and words
Covering of one eye to sight with other eye
Unusual clumsiness or awkwardness
Poor eye–hand coordination
Headaches or nausea after close visual tasks

Source: Reprinted from *Educating Young Handicapped Children* by S. Gray Garwood, 1979, with permission.

problems can prevent serious vision impairment or blindness. Among the problems that can be ameliorated if identified and treated early are strabismus, amblyopia, ocular disease, and refractive errors (Crouch & Kennedy, 1993b).

Visual screening takes place in many different ways and by persons with different levels of training. Some children are screened by pediatricians, others in preschool settings, some in day care centers. Some are not screened until first grade and others are not screened at all. Crouch and Kennedy (1993b) indicate children should be examined for eye problems at four ages: (1) newborn while in the nursery, (2) 6 months during a physical, (3) age 3½ years; and, (4) 5 years and older.

SCREENING TESTS AND ASSESSMENT OF VISUAL FUNCTIONING

Visual screening tests focus on the identification of visual disorders that might be caused by refractive errors or extraocular muscle imbalances. Visual screening is a very inexpensive procedure that requires minimal time and in some cases minimal examiner training. Once characteristics that indicate the presence of refractive errors or physical anomalies have been identified, diagnostic and treatment services can be initiated. If vision screening reveals a possible problem, no further assessment of the child's other skills should occur until the vision problem has been corrected. A number of screening tests have been developed to assist examiners in assessing the vision of young and difficult-to-test children. As new tests are developed that can be completed in a more rapid, accurate, uniform manner, they need to replace those currently available and used by team personnel for screening. Few school systems are equipped with the newer procedures or tests. What follows are tests and procedures that are likely to be available to assessment personnel.

Formal assessment of children who are severely impaired or developmentally disabled requires a comprehensive assessment of the child's functional use of vision. Jose, Smith, and Shane (1980) suggested that evaluation of visual functioning should include sensation, visual-motor, and visual-perceptual skills. Langley (1980a; 1980b) and Langley and DuBose (1976) described batteries of collected activities that can be used to evaluate each of the three areas. The tests include pupillary reactions to light, muscle balance or binocular coordination, blink reflex, eye preferences, use of central and peripheral visual fields, tracking and scanning skills, reaching for lights or for visually presented objects, and shifting attention between visual targets.

Preschool Vision Test

In this test (Allen, 1957) familiar pictures printed on individual cards are used instead of the row of symbols traditionally used when testing older children. The pictures include a birthday cake, a telephone, a man driving a jeep, a bear, a house, a man on a horse, and a Christmas tree. A distance of 15 feet is used for testing because young children have been shown not to attempt deciphering tasks at the usual distance of 20 feet. The test has been used successfully to screen acuity in each eye separately to detect amblyopia. For children three years of age, the Preschool Vision Test makes testing easier than the Snellen Illiterate E Test or other symbol tests.

The Letter Chart for Twenty Feet—Snellen Scale

This chart (National Society to Prevent Blindness, 1974a) is commonly used to measure acuity in older children and adults who are able to read letters. For in-

dividuals lacking these skills, an adaptation of the letter chart can be used that displays the arms of the letter E pointing in different directions and is known as the Symbol Chart for Twenty Feet—Snellen Scale (National Society to Present Blindness, 1974b). The child is taught to point in the same direction as the arms of the E. The child is tested on several rows, each decreasing in size, while standing at a distance of 20 feet. The symbol and letter charts also are available for 10 feet. The Snellen Scale has been used successfully for testing children as young as 3 years. However, in some studies, young children experienced difficulty copying the arms of the E. Sheridan (1960) found that children below the age of 4 frequently made letter-reversal errors; an incorrect response to letter positions might represent a problem with directionality rather than vision problems. Furthermore, the letter E itself might not be a sufficiently interesting stimulus to encourage full participation in the young child.

Screening Tests for Young Children and Retardates (STY-CAR)

This commercially available test battery developed for screening vision in young children (Sheridan, 1973) is comprehensive, easy to administer, and can be given to children as young as 6 months of age. A set of miniature models of toys and graduated sizes of styrofoam balls is used to estimate acuity, visual fields, and processing (Langley, 1996). As soon as the child can match letters, a set of letters is used. Children at the youngest ages are shown only those shapes that they are able to copy; older children are taught to copy letters in midair with their fingers. A more easily interpretable response, used successfully to test children under 5 years of age, is for children to view a letter on the wall chart and then point to the letter on a table in front of them. Testing is most easily performed at a distance of 10 feet because rapport with young children frequently is lost at greater distances. The examiner stands near the chart, points to each of the stimulus letters, and asks the child to point to the same letter on the response board. Each eye can be tested separately by using eye patches alternately. The young child is presented individually blocked letters, one at a time, instead of being presented with the entire chart. Several letters can be effectively used with 4-year-olds, whereas 3-year-olds use only five simple letter shapes (T, H, O, V, X). The STY-CAR test has been used successfully with children as young as 2 years, 2 months and with young children with special needs. This test format also can be used to assess near vision.

Parsons Visual Acuity Test

Spellman, DeBriere, and Cress (1979) worked with children with severe mental retardation and other serious impairments to design a visual acuity assessment procedure based on the theory of errorless learning. This test requires children to discriminate among pictures of a bird, a hand, and a cake, all presented together in a series of mixed cards. Children can respond by pointing, blinking their eyes, or verbalizing a yes/no response to indicate the correct picture. In addition, special training using an intensity-fading program can be used with children who have difficulty discriminating forms. This additional training makes the test particularly useful for children with moderate to severe impairments. Both far- and near-point testing have been accomplished using these procedures. This test can also be used effectively with older children whose mental development is below 2 years of age (Cress, 1987).

Individualized, Systematic Assessment of Visual Efficiency (ISAVE)

This test (ISAVE; Langley, 1997) provides both a detailed assessment process and a screening tool for assessing visual behavior in children with severe disabilities. It was designed for use with children from birth to 5 years of age. The examiner can select all or part of the three components (response to light, fixation, and following). According to the author, there are several unique features in this test: (1) It is an ecological assessment of visual behaviors; (2) it includes a component that addresses postural, movement, and transitional behaviors that support and contribute to the development of specific visual skills; and (3) it includes a component that ascertains whether the child displays the hallmark characteristics associated with cortical visual impairment.

Preferential Looking Models

Over three decades ago Fantz, Ordy, and Udelf (1962) found that infants consistently preferred to look at patterned targets to plain targets. They began using preferential looking to test visual acuity using black and white grating or striped targets of various sizes. The task required the use of resolution acuity as opposed to the typical test of recognition acuity. In the resolution task, a far less sophisticated response is needed; thus, younger children with more serious limitations can be assessed using this technique (Cress, 1987).

A number of researchers have used preferential looking acuity test procedures for persons with disabilities (Duckman & Selenow, 1983; Fagan & Singer, 1983). These researchers report successful testing of children with Down syndrome, cerebral palsy, and multiple impairments. Cress (1987) studied 500 children, of whom 80 percent were developmentally disabled, using a simplified, five-minute preferential looking test. The procedure involved presenting acuity cards in front of the child at distances of 38 cm or 84 cm (depending on the child's age), and having an observer, blind to the placement of the card, determine whether the target is seen by the child. Cress reported on the testing of binocular and monocular acuities in 59 children ranging in age from 10 days to 6 years. The procedure yielded useful thresholds on all children who are developmentally disabled in the study and demonstrated the procedure's usefulness for the early detection of visual impairment.

Stereoscopic Vision Testing

Children with normal visual functions fuse input from both eyes to achieve stereopsis. When stereopsis is not present, problems such as amblyopia, strabismus, and severe refractive error differences between the two eyes can occur. Stereoscopic testing has been conducted successfully in large-scale visual screening programs (Ehrlich, Reinecke, & Simons, 1983). Stereoscopic tests such as the Random-Dot E are inexpensive, accurate, and simple to use (Crouch & Kennedy, 1993a). The terms *visual evoked potential* (VEP), *visual evoked response* (VER), and *visual evoked cortical potential* (VECP) all refer to electrical potentials recorded from the scalp overlying the visual cortex when produced in response to a visual stimulus. Patterned stimuli produce the most reliable VERs and the most common pattern is the checkerboard pattern on a television monitor (Creel, 1993).

Photoscreeners and Videographic Techniques

These procedures require trained technicians and are not likely to be available to traditional school personnel. However, they offer some advantages when screening young or nonverbal children (Cibis & Luke, 1993; Crouch & Kennedy, 1993a). These techniques involve taking pictures of the pupil movement and allowing examiners to compare the qualities of the "red reflex" from the two eyes. From what is seen early in life, some of the signs of possible future problems can be detected and treated, thus diminishing the severity of the problem.

CONSIDERATIONS OF VISUAL ABILITIES IN COGNITIVE ASSESSMENT

At times it is impossible to separate a child's response to a visual stimulus from the cognitive or attitudinal component of the response. Awareness that vision and cognition are related is important in determining why a child performs as he or she does and what, if anything, should be done to intervene. The examiner must be aware that limited visual development and responses to formal and informal assessment might be due to the child's cognitive level and attitudes (Langley, 1980b). Informally, examiners might find it useful to observe a child's performance on cognitive assessment tasks that require visual skills. Table 12.2 lists several visual-oriented tasks found on typical developmental schedules. If it appears that a child's difficulties are visual in nature, it might be helpful to assess downward to determine the developmental age at which the child is

TABLE 12.2 Developmental Sequence of Skills Involving Vision

AGE	VISUAL-ORIENTED TASK
2 to 2½ years	Copies two vertical strokes in imitation; identifies objects in a group pictured; might look at pictures upside down
2½ to 3 years	Copies circle; matches colored blocks; engages in domestic make-believe play
3 to 3½ years	Copies cross; points to forms that are like a model; discriminates between three- and four-object arrays
3½ to 4 years	Traces around diamond; writes letters of first name; identifies colors correctly
4½ to 5 years	Copies rectangle; copies star; reads five sight words
5 to 5½ years	Reads eight words, draws line from dot to dot inches apart; identifies numerals through ten
5½ to 6 years	Copies rectangle with intersecting diagonal lines; reads at a preprimer level; identifies 12 of 26 uppercase letters

successful at using vision to complete fine motor and cognitive tasks.

Listed here are some cognitive skills that can be affected by visual impairments and clues as to whether a visual problem might be interfering with the child's cognitive responses:

1. *Accuracy of approach to objects.* When the child works with nesting toys, Peg-Boards, or pounding benches, note whether the child's approach to the object is on target. Note the direction of the child's movement when it is off-center (i.e., is it consistently in one direction or is it random in nature?). Also note whether the child relies on tactile cues to perform the activity.

2. *Matching.* It is important to note if the child matches objects by shape or color and which attribute is preferred. It is also useful to note the distance at which the child matches common objects of varying sizes.

3. *Following moving objects.* Observe whether the child follows the trajectory of objects spilling from a container or moving through an arc.

4. *Imitation.* Observe the child's ability to imitate both gross and fine motor activities. Determine whether the child can perform the skills without a model.

5. *Recognition.* Observe the child's response to pictures or printed material. Some pictures might elicit attention and recognition, although others do not; note the picture characteristics that distinguish these behaviors.

6. *Object permanence.* Visual memory can be observed in simple situations in which objects are viewed and then removed; note whether the child demonstrates awareness of the unseen object and where it is located.

7. *Reactivation.* Activate an object as the child observes. Give the object to the child to reactivate. Observe visual memory and the child's ability to sequence the operation of the object.

In addition to testing how clearly a child perceives objects at specified distances, it also is important to determine whether both eyes operate in tandem. Patching one eye and observing the child's activities is one way to determine eye preference and assess the strength of each eye separately. A child's negative reaction to being patched might indicate that the covered eye is the child's better one; however, the child might be reacting negatively to the presence of the patch itself and the examiner must discern the difference.

CONSIDERATIONS IN THE ASSESSMENT OF VISUAL PERCEPTION AND INTEGRATION

Visual perception is the detection of a form from an image. If the form is labeled or described, the perception becomes a concept as some degree of cognition and memory is used. In very young infants, visual perception is observed through the duration of the child's attention to stimuli. However, by the time a child is able to label forms or recognize similarities and differences, visual perception usually implies interpretation of what is seen.

Although many educators have developed programs to teach visual perception, this skill obviously cannot be taught to the totally blind child. However, as Barraga (1964) demonstrated, it can be taught to many children with some degree of usable sight. The visual skills described in this section should be assessed whenever visual competence is questioned. These five skills were described by Buktenica (1968); although overlapping, they are nonetheless useful as guidelines for assessment and training:

1. *Visual discrimination.* Visual discrimination is the recognition of similarities and differences. It begins in the very young child when responses to one stimulus differ from responses to other stimuli. For example, newborns discriminate different levels of brightness and prefer to look at patterned stimuli more than stimuli without patterns. Visual discrimination can be examined through the presentation of very similar pictures that differ in one small way. The child can be asked if the pictures are different or the same. Once the child correctly indicates that the pictures are different, the examiner can expand questioning to include the nature of the differences. It is important to determine first whether the child understands the concepts *same* and *different.*

2. *Visual-motor development.* An early form of visual-motor development is tracking or scanning, in which the child follows the movement of an object across his or her field of vision. The integration of visual and motor skills is the basis for many other skills (e.g., caring for self, playing, reaching, aiming, positioning), and it is difficult to identify many tasks that are completely free of this important behavior.

3. *Figure–ground perception.* The ability to see a figure separate from its background is a crucial visual skill. It can be assessed informally with picture books by asking the child to locate objects among groups of objects or by asking the child to select a key element from a visual array.

4. *Spatial relationships.* This aspect of vision includes the ability to orient oneself in space. It can be evaluated by observing the child's ability to orient to *left, right, up,* or *down,* and to arrange and space objects on a page.

5. *Perceptual constancy.* Visual imagery and visual memory are involved in perceptual constancy. The child must recognize an image even though it might vary slightly when seen in a different context. Variations can include changes in size, shape, color, position, design, or placement. Perceptual constancy requires the four previously described skills of perception and can be assessed through tasks that require children to recognize slight variations in objects or identify whole objects when only a portion is viewed.

The five forms of visual perception overlap and performance and training in one area affect performance and training in another. These visual skills are a part of everyday life; they enable one to receive, process, integrate, and synthesize more information. However, one cannot assume that by training a child to use these visual skills more effectively the child will necessarily perform better on academic tasks such as reading and spelling. The best way to improve reading and spelling performance is to teach reading and spelling. Visual training does, however, encourage the child to be more visually sensitive to what is present. For some children, heightened sensitivity can open the way to changes in the use of vision as it is applied in reading, writing, and other academic skills.

Informal tests of visual perception can be developed by the preschool teacher or examiner by gathering materials traditionally encountered in the classroom and observing the child's interactions with the stimulus materials. Formal assessments of visual perception are useful to assess the rate of development over time. A few tests that measure aspects of visual perception are the Developmental Test of Visual Motor Integration (Beery & Buktenica, 1967), Illinois Test of Psycholinguistic Abilities (Kirk, McCarthy, & Kirk, 1968), Developmental Test of Visual Perception (Frostig, Maslow, Lefever, & Whittlesey, 1964), and the Visual Efficiency Scale (Barraga, 1970).

The integration of sensory processes is essential to the development of many other skills. Assessors need to examine the specific visual processing abilities and this is key to the instructional strategies that might be advised. The Test of Sensory Function in Infants (DeGangi & Greenspan, 1989), a test for 4- to 18-month-old infants, assesses skills in five subdomains: reactions to tactile deep pressure, adaptive motor functions, visual tactile integration, ocular motor control, and reactivity to vestibular stimulation.

Visual integration information is also available if one does an item analysis of many of the developmental measures frequently used to assess preschool aged children. Langley (1996) lists several examples, including the Miller Assessment for Preschoolers (Miller, 1982), Hawaii Early Learning Profile for Special Preschoolers (Furuno, O'Reilly, Hosaka, Inatsuka, Zeisloft-Falbey, & Allman, 1988), the Preschool Developmental Profile (Brown, D'Eugenio, Drews, Haskin, Whiteside-Lynch, Moersch, & Rogers, 1981), and the Bayley Scales of Infant Development II (Bayley, 1993).

CONSIDERATIONS AND ADAPTATIONS OF PHYSICAL ENVIRONMENTS FOR ASSESSMENT

The visual environment can have a significant impact on the child's testing performance. For example, if the materials are placed outside of the child's visual field, or the contrasts between the stimulus and the background are not apparent to the child, responses might be recorded as errors when in fact the child did not have sufficient information to make an informed response. For this reason, informal assessment should include observations of the child's responses to stimuli similar to those used in the test and to those under modified environments. Once optimal testing conditions have been determined, formal assessment using the desired measures can begin under those conditions. Harley and Lawrence (1977) described five elements affecting visual performance: brightness, contrast, time, distance, and image size. Regardless of the particular assessment setting, these factors always need to be considered when one selects the materials and conditions to be used when assessing children who are visually impaired:

1. *Brightness.* Most children who are visually impaired benefit from bright illumination; however, children should be positioned so that they do not face the glare of a window or work in the darkness of their own shadow. Optimally, the light source should come from behind the opposite shoulder of the writing hand. Protec-

tion from glare can be controlled through blinds and shades and by redirecting the light source, the visual task, or the child, so that reflections are not directed into the child's line of vision. Optimum uniform lighting is produced indirectly through luminous ceilings or walls, and fluorescent lighting that distributes light in equal amounts from all angles is preferred.

2. *Contrast.* Visual efficiency is improved when contrast is heightened. Harley and Lawrence (1977) reported that black on white or white print on black paper offers the needed contrast for visually impaired children, but black print on buff-colored paper is preferred because buff paper reduces glare. Color combinations that are best for displaying pictures or objects include yellow on black, blue, green, or purple; black-ink, felt-tipped pens are best for writing on light-colored papers.

3. *Time.* Visually impaired children might have a difficult time identifying and attending to events. Informal testing permits the examiner to determine how quickly and efficiently visually impaired children respond to timed, visually demanding test items. It might be deemed necessary to eliminate or substantially adapt tests with timed items if they create an unfair disadvantage.

4. *Distance.* If assessment involves viewing material from a distance, the older preschool child can determine and suggest to the examiner the best viewing distance. For young children, the examiner should experiment with the materials and systematically change the distances until an optimal distance is found. Some children with particularly low vision might need to be as close as 1 to 2 inches from the material, and in such cases easels, bookstands, or adjustable desktops can facilitate visibility.

5. *Size of Image.* The size of pictures, letters, and forms is an important factor to consider in the assessment of the visually impaired. Although many low-vision children can read small print at very close distances, this is very tiring and slow. Some tests are available in large print and others might need to be retyped in large print to facilitate testing low-vision children. Relettering or retyping is more likely to be needed with school-age children than with preschoolers because few preschool tests require the child to examine materials with small print.

6. *Setting.* Whenever possible, the setting for assessing visually impaired children should be the same as that for other children. The importance of the assessment milieu has been documented by several investigators (Barker, 1968; Bortner & Birch, 1970; DuBose, Langley, & Stagg, 1978), and they stress the impact that environmental circumstances have on test performance. The appropriateness of the environment for the skills being assessed can be determined by observing the child in various settings. For example, if expressive language is to be examined through a language sample procedure, the spontaneous language gathered by taking the sample on the playground might be far richer than that taken in the traditional sterile testing room. When children are free to be themselves, select the activities they wish to pursue, and interact with their favorite peers, they are more motivated to communicate than when they are with a strange adult and surrounded by a few selected toys. Observation of the child in the environment in which assessment is to take place can provide valuable information on how the child uses the surroundings. By observing how the child positions himself or herself relative to the lighting, or observing if the child uses his or her fingers to produce changes in the light, one can learn much about the meaning of light for the child. The child's movement in the environment indicates how responsive he or she is to objects and their spatial relationships. These observations can be used to identify the way to position the child for testing and optimal positions for material placement.

7. *Materials.* Informal visual assessment using a variety of materials can yield crucial data for both the examiners who will formally assess the child and teachers who will plan instructional programs. Many commercially available tests are inadequate for the assessment of visually impaired children because items lack optimal stimulus value. It is well known that appealing and stimulating materials attract and motivate children. One of the few tests that provide instructions for adapting items and instructions for visually impaired children is the Developmental Activities Screening Inventory-II (Fewell & Langley, 1984). It is possible to improve materials by adapting them; however, one must clearly indicate how materials were adapted and realize that one is violating test standardization.

The testing materials should be as appropriate for the tasks as possible. Some adaptations that would do this are increasing item size, heightening contrast, substituting three-dimensional materials for standard materials, projecting items onto a television or movie screen, increasing space between items by decreasing the number of items on a page, and outlining items with a heavy black line or a raised line. It is critical that the adaptations do not change the nature of the concept being assessed. To determine the effects various materials have on a particular visual behavior, observe the child's per-

formance using a number of different items. For example, to examine visual pursuit, the following brightly colored objects serve well:

- Very bright lemon yellow, hot pink, or chartreuse yarn ball
- Two-tone slinky toy
- Flashlights with colored disks
- Halloween toys that sparkle, spin, or move in some way
- Lollipops
- Spinning toys
- Pinwheels
- Weebles
- Brightly colored pop beads
- Rolling toys (trucks, balls, etc.) in bright colors

8. *Special Aids.* Optical aids such as magnifying lenses and large-print material are available to render assessment and instruction easier for both the child and the examiner or teacher. The child's instructors probably will be able to suggest a number of useful aids to the examiner. In some cases, formal tests can be presented through the use of these aids, thus expanding the range of tests that can be used with the visually limited child. These facilitative aids become even more valuable when the child enters elementary school and receives assisted instruction. Informal assessment can include observations of the child's reaction to auditory aids such as audio cassette recorders, talking books, talking calculators, abacuses, closed-circuit television, reading machines, and special low-vision activities.

CONSIDERATIONS FOR SPECIAL INSTRUCTIONS

The adaptations that have been discussed are as important for instruction as they are for assessment. The teacher must recognize daily variations in actions in the vision of some children and make the necessary adaptations if needed. For the child who is developmentally young or severely impaired, assessment results might suggest more attention to the training of vision as an end in itself rather than to the training of a skill that is accomplished through vision. Barraga (1964) demonstrated that children who are visually impaired can improve the efficiency of their vision through training, although they might not change their visual acuity. This finding suggests that any child who responds to light and consequently reacts to the stimulus can benefit from visual training activities. Training programs should be conducted throughout the day and not just at a specified time set aside for visual training. The use of visual skills must be integrated into daily routines and made a continuous part of the child's life to become incorporated into the child's behavioral repertoire. Practice in using one's visual skills should take place in a variety of settings. Langley (1980a) suggested the use of multisensory materials for added cues when working with children who are more severely impaired. Initially, when a specific visual skill is being trained, the visual response should be paired with a different sensory stimulus. For example, to train a child to focus on an object, a bell could be attached to the visual stimulus (if the child uses the sense of hearing consistently). Initially, the auditory and visual stimuli are paired; then the auditory stimulus is gradually faded until the child responds to the visual stimulus alone.

Other suggestions for training include the use of simple and manipulative materials. Color is an important attribute to consider when choosing objects with which to work. Red, yellow, and orange are considered the most visually stimulating colors, and black and yellow provide the greatest contrast. It is necessary to have a high contrast between the visual materials and the working surface at all times.

Proper illumination of materials is essential, as is the use of nonglare materials. When the children are working on discrimination tasks, teachers should begin by emphasizing the greatest differences (e.g., size, color, brightness) and then reduce the differences until the child can perform the task without cues. Illumination can be altered if the angle of the material is changed. Some children use their vision more efficiently if class work is placed on a table easel rather than flat on a table or desk. When the teacher observes a child cocking his or her head to one side, it suggests visual field preferences that might influence the placement of materials for optimum visibility.

It is important to remember that visual training on such tasks as tracking, closure, discrimination, and memory might not affect academic performance. Such training might indeed improve visual perception but will probably have little if any direct effect on reading. A far more consequential plan involves task analysis, in which the content or tasks to be learned form the basis for the assessment; analysis of errors indicates what the child knows and does not know and identifies misconceptions and strategy errors.

SUMMARY

This chapter has provided assessment personnel with some basic information on visual development in children and how assessment procedures and tests might be selected that are less likely to penalize children with impaired vision. Initially reviewed were developmental aspects of vision and the impact of visual impairments on motor, language, cognitive, perceptual, social, and self-care development. Readers were provided a list of observable signs of possible visual problems that might be noted during a testing experience. Several tests to screen vision or assess functional vision were described with procedures included for two tests should readers want to use these with children. Special attention was given to the role of vision in cognitive and perceptual assessment because it is important to examiners to separate, to the extent possible, a child's cognitive competence from competence that is dependent on intact and highly functioning visual abilities. Suggestions and considerations are provided for the assessment and instruction of visually impaired children.

REFERENCES

Adelson, E., & Fraiberg, S. (1975). Gross motor development in infants blind from birth. *Child Development, 45,* 114–126.

Allen, H. F. (1957). A new picture series for preschool vision testing. *American Journal of Ophthalmology, 44,* 38–41.

Barker, R. (1968). *Ecological psychology: Concepts and methods for studying the environment of human development.* Stanford, CA: Stanford University Press.

Barraga, N. (1964). *Increased visual behavior in low vision children.* Research Series, American Foundation for the Blind, No. 13.

Barraga, N. (1970). *Visual efficiency scale.* Louisville, KY: American Printing House for the Blind.

Bayley, N. (1993). *Bayley Scales of Infant Development* (2nd ed.). San Antonio, TX: Psychological Corporation.

Beery, K., & Buktenica, N. A. (1967). *Developmental Test of Visual-Motor Integration.* Chicago: Follet.

Block, C. (1972). *Developmental study of tactile-kinesthetic discrimination in blind, deaf, and normal children.* Unpublished doctoral dissertation, Boston University.

Bortner, J., & Birch, H. (1970). Cognitive capacity and cognitive competency. *American Journal of Mental Deficiency, 74,* 735–744.

Brown, S. L., D'Eugenio, D. B., Drews, J. E., Haskin, B. S., Whiteside-Lynch, E., Moersch, M. S., & Rogers, S. J. (1981). *Preschool developmental profile.* Ann Arbor: University of Michigan Press.

Buktenica, N. (1968). *Visual learning.* San Rafael, CA: Dimensions.

Cibis, G. W., & Luke, T. P. (1993). Video vision development assessment. In G. W. Cibis, A. C. Tongue, & M. L. Stass-Isern (Eds.), *Decision making in pediatric ophthalmology* (pp. 202–203). St. Louis, MO: Mosby-Year Book.

Creel, D. J. (1993). Visual evoked response. In G. W. Cibis, A. C. Tongue, & M. L. Stass-Isern (Eds.), *Decision making in pediatric ophthalmology* (pp. 296–297). St. Louis, MO: Mosby-Year Book.

Cress, P. J. (1987). Visual assessment. In M. Bullis (Ed.), *Communication development in young children with deaf-blindness: Literature review III.* Monmouth, OR: Teaching Research Division of Oregon State System of Higher Education.

Crouch, E. R., & Kennedy, R. A. (1993a). Pediatric vision screening techniques. In G. W. Cibis, A. C. Tongue, & M. L. Stass-Isern (Eds.), *Decision making in pediatric ophthalmology* (pp.198–201). St. Louis, MO: Mosby-Year Book.

Crouch, E. R., & Kennedy, R. A. (1993b). Vision screening guidelines. In G. W. Cibis, A. C. Tongue, & M. L. Stass-Isern (Eds.), *Decision making in pediatric ophthalmology* (pp. 196–197). St. Louis, MO: Mosby-Year Book.

DeGangi, G. A., & Greenspan, S. I. (1989). *Test of Sensory Function in Infants.* Los Angeles, CA: Western Psychological Services.

Deitz, S. J., & Ferrell, K. A. (1993). Early services for young children with visual impairment: From diagnosis to comprehensive services. *Infants and Young Children: An Interdisciplinary Journal of Special Care Practice, 6*(1), 68–76.

Dobson, V., & Teller, D. (1978). Visual acuity in human infants: A view and comparison of behavioral and electrophysiological studies. *Vision Research, 18*(11), 1469–1493.

DuBose, R. F. (1976). Developmental needs of blind infants. *New Outlook for the Blind, 2,* 49–52.

DuBose, R. F. (1979). Working with sensorily impaired children (Part I): Visual impairments. In S. G. Garwood (Ed.), *Educating Young Handicapped Children* (pp. 323–359). Germantown, MD: Aspen Systems.

DuBose, R. R., Langley, M. B., & Stagg, V. (1978). Assessing severely handicapped children. *Focus on Exceptional Children, 9,* 1–13.

Duckman, R. H., & Selenow, A. (1983). Use of forced preferential looking for measurement of visual acuity in a population of neurologically impaired children. *American Journal of Optometry & Physiological Optics, 60*(10), 817–821.

Ehrlich, M. I., Reinecke, R. D., & Simons, K. (1983). Preschool vision screening for amblyopia and strabismus programs, methods, guidelines. *Survey of Ophthalmology, 28*(3), 149–163.

Ellingham, T. R., Silva, P. A., Buckfield, P. M., & Clarkson, J. E. (1976). Neonatal at-risk factors, visual defects and the preschool child: A report from the Queen Mary Hospital multidisciplinary child development study. *New Zealand Medical Journal, 83,* 74–77.

Fagan, J. F. III, & Singer, L. T. (1983). Infant recognition memory as a measure of intelligence. *Advances in Infancy Research, II,* 31–78.

Fantz, R., Ordy, J., & Udelf, M. (1962). Maturation of pattern vision in infants during the first six months. *Journal of Comparative and Physiological Psychology, 55,* 907–917.

Fewell, R. R., & Langley, M. B. (1984). *Developmental Activities Screening Inventory-II* (Rev. ed). Austin, TX: Pro-Ed.

Folio, M. R. (1974). *Assessing motor development in multiply handicapped children.* Paper presented at the annual meeting of the Council on Exceptional Children, New York.

France, T. D. (1989). Amblyopia. In S. J. Isenberg (Ed.), *The eye in infancy* (pp. 100–109). Chicago: Year Book Medical Publisher.

Frostig, M., Maslow, P., Lefever, D. W., & Whittlesey, J. R. B. (1964). *The Marianne Frostig Developmental Test of Visual Perception.* Palo Alto, CA: Consulting Psychologists Press.

Furuno, S., O'Reilly, K. A., Hosaka, C. M., Inatsuka, T. T., Zeisloft-Falbey, B., & Allman, T. (1988). *Hawaii Early Learning Profile (HELP).* Palo Alto, CA: VORT Corporation.

Gowman, A. (1957). *The war blind in American social structure.* New York: American Foundation for the Blind.

Hallenbeck, J. (1954). Two essential factors in the development of young blind children. *New Outlook for the Blind, 48,* 308–315.

Harley, R. K. (1963). *Verbalism among blind children.* Research Series, American Foundation for the Blind, No. 10.

Harley, R. K., & Lawrence, A. (1977). *Visual impairments in the schools.* Springfield, IL: Thomas.

Higgins, L. C., (1973). *Classification in congenitally blind children.* Research Series, American Foundation for the Blind, No. 25.

Hoyt, C., Nickel, B., & Billson, F. (1982). Ophthalmological examination of the infant development aspects. *Society of Ophthalmology, 26*(4), 177–185.

Iverson, J. M., & Goldin-Meadow, S. (1997). What's communication got to do with it? Gesture in children blind from birth. *Developmental Psychology, 33* (3) 453–467.

Jan, J. E., Skyanda, A., & Groenveld, M. (1990). Habilitation and rehabilitation of visually impaired and blind children. *Pediatrician, 17,* 202–207.

Jan, J. E., Skyanda, A., Groenveld, M., & Hoyt, C. S. (1987). Behavioral characteristics of children with permanent cortical visual impairment. *Developmental Medicine and Child Neurology, 29,* 571–576.

Jones, B. (1972). Development of cutaneous and kinesthetic localization by blind and sighted children. *Developmental Psychology, 6,* 349–352.

Jose, R. T., Smith, A. J., & Shane, K. G. (1980). Evaluating and stimulating vision in the multiply impaired. *Journal of Visual Impairment and Blindness, 74,* 2–8.

Kirk, S. A., McCarthy, J. J., & Kirk, W. D. (1968). *Examiner's Manual: Illinois Test of Psycholinguistic Abilities* (Rev. ed.). Urbana: University of Illinois Press.

Langley, B., & DuBose, R. F. (1976). Functional vision screening for severely handicapped children. *New Outlook for the Blind, 70,* 346–350.

Langley, M. B. (1996). Screening and assessment of sensory functions. In M. McLean, D. B. Bailey, Jr., & M. Wolery (Eds.), *Assessing infants and preschoolers with special needs* (pp. 123–164). Columbus, OH: Prentice Hall.

Langley, M. B. (1997). *Individualized, Systematic Assessment of Visual Efficiency (ISAVE).* Louisville, KY: American Printing House for the Blind.

Langley, M. B. (1980a). *Assessment of multihandicapped, visually impaired children.* Chicago: Stoelting.

Langley, M. B. (1980b). *Functional vision inventory for the multiply and severely handicapped.* Chicago: Stoelting.

Miller, L. J. (1982). *Assessment for Preschoolers.* Littleton, CO: Foundation for Knowledge in Development.

National Society to Prevent Blindness. (1974a,b). *The Letter Chart for Twenty Feet—Snellen Scale.* New York: Author.

Norris, M., Spaulding, P. J., & Brodie, F. H. (1957). *Blindness in children.* Chicago: University of Chicago Press.

Piaget, J., & Inhelder, B. (1969). *The psychology of the child.* New York: Basic Books.

Schwartz, A. (1972). *A comparison of congenitally blind and sighted elementary school children on intelligence, tactile discrimination, abstract reasoning, perceived physical health, perceived personality adjustment and parent–teacher perceptions of intellectual performance.* Unpublished doctoral dissertation, University of Maryland.

Scott, R. A. (1969). The socialization of blind children. In D. S. Goslin (Ed.), *Handbook of socialization theory and research.* Chicago: Rand McNally.

Sheridan, M. (1973). *The STY-CAR Test of Vision for Retardates.* Windsor, Berks, England: NFER Publishing Co., Ltd.

Sheridan, M. (1973). The STY-CAR Test of Vision for Retardates. Windsor, England: NFER.

Sheridan, M. D. (1960). Vision screening of very young or handicapped children. *British Medical Journal, 51,* 453–456.

Smits, B., & Mommers, M. J. C. (1976). Differences between blind and sighted children on WISC verbal subtests. *New Outlook for the Blind, 70,* 240–246.

Spellman, C. R., DeBriere, T. J., & Cress, P. J. (1979). *Final report from the project for research and development of subjective visual acuity assessment procedures for severely handicapped persons.* Bureau of Education for the Handicapped Grant No. G00-76-02592.

Tillman, M. H., & Bashaw, W. L. (1968). Multivariate analysis of the WISC scales for blind and sighted children. *Psychological Reports, 23,* 523–526.

Troster, H., & Brambring, M. (1993). Early motor development in blind infants. *Journal of Applied Developmental Psychology, 14,* 83–106.

Warren, D. H. (1977). *Blindness and early childhood development.* New York: American Foundation for the Blind.

Wechsler, D. (1949). *Wechsler Intelligence Scale for Children.* New York: Psychological Corporation.

Wechsler, D. (1967). *Manual for the Wechsler Preschool and Primary Scale of Intelligence.* New York: Psychological Corporation.

CHAPTER 13

ASSESSMENT OF AUDITORY FUNCTIONING

CHANDRAKANT P. SHAH
BONNIE J. BLISS

There is increasing evidence that hearing impairment in infancy and early childhood adversely affects the acquisition of speech and language as well as cognitive, emotional, and social development. Although profound hearing impairment in preschool children has always been relatively easily recognized, lesser degrees of hearing impairment have not. A child with undiagnosed hearing loss may be thought to exhibit a behavioral disorder, hyperactivity, autism, or developmental delay. As a result of recent advances in assessment techniques, remarkably accurate diagnoses of hearing impairment can now be made during the first few months of life and appropriate habilitation procedures can be started early.

Because the time from identification of hearing loss until intervention is initiated averages one year (Strong, Clark, & Walden, 1994), it is imperative that the diagnosis of hearing impairment be made as early as possible. No child is too young for the assessment of auditory function.

IMPORTANCE OF EARLY ASSESSMENT

Language Acquisition

One of the most important aspects of children's development is their acquisition of language, which enables them to communicate and relate to the environment. The satisfactory development of two-way spoken communication depends on an intact auditory system (Matkin, 1986) because it provides the primary sensory input. Today many theorists believe that language is innate and all that is needed to trigger language development is an appropriate environment, or that there is some interplay between innate and environmental factors (Bench, 1992). It also is postulated that the brain is in an optimal condition for acquiring language in early childhood; if

deprived of sensory input, only very limited language abilities are expected (Bench, 1992). Superficially, hearing-impaired children appear similar to children with normal hearing up to 6 months of age. As they continue to grow older, though, the differences marking children as hearing impaired develop exponentially.

Mental and Social Development

Hearing impairment can adversely affect children's mental and social development. They might have to deal with denial, rejection, isolation, or overprotective parental attitudes. Depending on the degree of impairment, they might be unable to communicate with or relate to their parents and peers during the early years that are so important for the development of a healthy personality. The frustrations encountered in the educational system by children with even mild or fluctuating hearing loss can be great because the problem may go undiagnosed. Mild to moderate hearing impairment often is mistaken for a behavioral problem or developmental delay even though the range of intelligence is the same in hearing-impaired children as in those with normal hearing.

CLASSIFICATION AND EPIDEMIOLOGY OF HEARING LOSS

Classification

Hearing impairment is a general term that is applied to all degrees of hearing loss and includes the previously used terms *deaf* and *hard of hearing*. Deaf is used to describe the person in whom the auditory sense is nonfunctional for use in communication, even with a hearing aid. Hard of hearing, on the other hand, describes a person in whom the auditory sense remains the primary method of language acquisition and communication even though a hearing aid usually is required. Categories of hearing impairment in the literature vary depending on the author but can be generally defined by levels of decibels (dB) as follows: mild, 20–40 dB; moderate, 41–55 dB; moderately severe, 56–70 dB; severe, 71–90 dB; and profound, over 90 dB. In addition, hearing losses can be classified as conductive, sensorineural, mixed, or central.

Conductive losses result from a breakdown in the normal physical transmission of sound from the external ear to the cochlea because of such factors as congenital abnormalities of the external canal (e.g., atresia), middle ear disease (particularly chronic otitis media), ossicular discontinuity, or otosclerosis. Conductive losses cannot exceed approximately 70 dB because at this level sound is conducted to the cochlea via the cranial bones. Pure conductive losses are characterized by normal bone conduction thresholds and reduced air conduction thresholds, which produce an air-bone gap. Many conductive losses can be medically or surgically corrected.

Sensorineural hearing losses occur because of cochlear or auditory nerve damage and often are the result of genetic factors, viral infections, ototoxic drugs, or overexposure to noise. Bone and air conduction thresholds are similar but reduced and the loss is usually irreversible. An additional problem is that, because the sensory end organ is damaged, the child has difficulty distinguishing speech sounds even in the presence of amplification.

Mixed hearing losses occur when both conductive and sensorineural components are present. The air-bone gap is equivalent to the conductive portion of the loss, but both air and bone threshold levels are lower than normal. English, Northern, and Fria (1973) studied the charts of 404 adult patients with a history of chronic otitis media. They found that a significant proportion had sensorineural deficits in addition to their conductive hearing losses, the degree of sensorineural impairment being directly proportional to the duration of and complications resulting from the otitis media. Middle ear disease can be superimposed on sensorineural loss and it is particularly important to watch for this in children to avoid compromising the residual hearing in a child with a sensorineural impairment.

Central deafness is the result of a problem arising between the auditory end organ and the interpretive or cortical areas of the brain. A delay in speech or language development or difficulty in interpreting speech can occur in the presence of normal hearing thresholds.

It is assumed that all readers of this chapter are familiar with details of the pure-tone audiogram available in any standard audiology text and, therefore, they are not discussed here. Unless otherwise indicated, levels are reported in this chapter in terms of either the 1964 International Organization for Standardization (ISO) or the 1969 American National Standards Institute (ANSI) Specifications for Audiometers which, for all practical purposes, are equivalent.

Epidemiology

Clearly, the definition of hearing impairment determines its apparent incidence and prevalence. The National Association of the Deaf defined the prevocationally deaf as those members of the population who cannot hear and understand speech and who have lost, or never had, that ability before 19 years of age (Schein & Elk, 1974). This population formed the basis of the 1971 National Census of the Deaf Population. In this census, the prevalence of prevocational deafness (in a noninstitutionalized population) was estimated at 2/1,000 in the general population. Of the prevocationally deaf sample, more than 50 percent had lost their hearing before 1 year of age and about 75 percent had lost their hearing before 3 years (Schein & Elk, 1974). If congenital deafness is defined as deafness "present at or existing from the time of birth," its prevalence in Canada is approximately 1/1,500 in the general population (Stewart, 1977). A study in the United Kingdom included only those who had been fitted with a hearing aid and found a prevalence of 1.8 per 1,000 in the Nottingham District Health Authority (Davis & Wood, 1992).

What constitutes significant hearing impairment? On the 1988 National Health Interview Survey—Child Health Supplement in the United States, 3.5 percent of children aged 0 to 17 years were reported by their parents to have deafness or trouble hearing in at least one ear (Boyle, Decoufle, & Yeargin-Allsopp, 1994). Northern and Downs (1991) cited a Health Examination Survey completed by the U.S. Department of Health, Education, and Welfare from 1963 to 1965 that studied children 6 to 11 years of age. Similar to the 1988 survey, this earlier survey showed that 4 percent were judged by their parents as having "trouble hearing." However, less than 1 percent were objectively considered to be hearing impaired according to the criterion that hearing begins with an average 26-dB loss in the frequencies 500–2000 Hz. Kessner, Snow, and Singer (1974) examined 1,639 children 4 to 11 years of age utilizing a failure criterion of only 15 dB in the speech and high frequencies. They found that 2.2 percent of these children had a bilateral loss and 4.5 percent had a unilateral loss in the speech frequencies. Among 4- to 5-year-olds, 4.1 percent had significant bilateral loss in the speech frequencies and the vast majority of these losses were conductive (Kessner et al., 1974). The similarity between this figure and that obtained from parents' questionnaires in the surveys mentioned previously is obvious. Hearing loss was found to be greatest for serous otitis media; the difference in threshold values in the speech frequencies between normal ears and those with clinical serous otitis media was only 7.4 dB. The prevalence of ear pathology reached a peak at 2 years of age, when 30 percent of the ears studied were abnormal (Kessner et al., 1974). Of concern was that the residual hearing loss found in the speech frequencies of children 8 to 11 years old in whom the prevalence of ear pathology had significantly declined.

Comparing prevalence rates across studies is difficult due to the multitude of data collection methods and criteria for hearing loss used (Davidson, Hyde, & Alberti, 1988). Herrgard, Martikainen, and Heinonen (1995) demonstrated the need for standardized criteria in their study of hearing loss among children born preterm. Of the 54 children examined, the number of children classified as being hearing impaired by World Health Organization criteria was 2, by Clark's criterion was 8, and by frequency specific criteria was 28. The Centre for Disease Control's Metropolitan Atlanta Developmental Disabilities Study of 10-year-old children used the criteria of hearing impairment of 40 dB or worse in the better ear at 0.5, 1, or 2 kHz. The prevalence rate was found to be 1.1 per 1,000, which is much lower than the rate described by Northern and Downs in 1991. Interestingly, several studies have noted that the prevalence of hearing impairment is higher among males than females. This observation was confirmed by Cremers, van Rijn, and Huygen (1994) who found that among 162 deaf children in the Netherlands, 54 percent were male and 46 percent were female. The reason for male predominance remains unknown.

ETIOLOGY OF HEARING IMPAIRMENT

The causes of hearing impairment in childhood are classified as prenatal, perinatal, and postnatal factors to avoid the sometimes misleading terms of *congenital* versus *acquired* (Davidson et al., 1988). Congenital refers to a condition existing at or before birth and can include both genetic and nongenetic factors. Some genetic syndromes might not be manifested until after birth and, therefore,

are not congenital. Sometimes the cause of hearing impairment cannot be discerned. The etiology may be unknown in 32 percent to 64 percent of cases in research studies (Todd, 1994). Most prenatal and perinatal hearing impairment becomes evident in early infancy, but usually later than the 6 months recommended by the Joint Committee on Infant Hearing. Mace (1991) found that hearing impairment was discovered in children ranging from age 7 weeks to 10 years, while the median age of identification was 2.1 years. Similarly, a review of the literature by Wong and Shah (1979) revealed that one-fifth to one-third of cases are not discovered until the age of 2 years.

Prenatal Factors

Genetic. Hereditary deafness is estimated to account for about 35 percent to 50 percent of profound childhood deafness (Konigsmark & Gorlin, 1976). In Denmark, the percentage of severe childhood hearing impairment attributed to genetic factors increased from 29 percent (1953) to 33 percent (1983) to 43 percent (1993) (Parving & Hauch, 1994). The mechanisms of genetic transmission can be derived from any standard genetics text and are not discussed here. Konigsmark and Gorlin (1976) identified approximately 150 types of hereditary deafness syndromes, which they classified into eight groups depending on the nature of the associated anomalies. In the following syndromes deafness characteristically develops during the age period under consideration:

- *Cockayne syndrome (autosomal recessive).* Dwarfism senile appearance, mental retardation, and retinal degeneration characterize this syndrome. Hearing usually is normal at birth but progresses to a moderate to severe sensorineural loss during childhood.
- *Crouzon's disease (autosomal dominant).* Crouzon's disease is associated with a conductive hearing loss in approximately one-third of patients. It is characterized by craniofacial dysostosis.
- *Waardenburg syndrome (autosomal dominant with varying expressivity).* Widely spaced medial canthi, flat nasal root, and confluent eyebrows characterize this syndrome. Approximately 20 percent of patients have sensorineural deafness ranging from mild to severe unilateral or bilateral deafness. This syndrome is estimated to account for 2 percent of cases of congenital deafness.
- *Lemieux-Neemeh syndrome.* Progressive distal muscular atrophy, nephropathy, and progressive sensorineural hearing loss beginning in childhood characterize this syndrome.

• *Macrothrombocytopathlia, nephritis, and senso-rineural deafness.* Moderate to severe deafness begins between the ages of 3 to 10 years.

• *Richards-Rundie syndrome (autosomal dominant).* This syndrome is characterized by ataxia, hypogo-nadism, mental retardation, and progressive sensorineu-ral hearing loss first noted around the age of 2 years.

• *Pendred syndrome (autosomal recessive).* This syn-drome involves goiter and profound sensorineural hear-ing loss in more than 50 percent of cases. The deafness usually is diagnosed at 2 years of age and progresses slightly through childhood. This syndrome accounts for about 10 percent of cases of congenital deafness.

• *Turner syndrome.* This syndrome is characterized by short stature, sexual infantilism, various other physi-cal stigmata, and abnormalities of the sex chromatin pat-tern. This syndrome is associated with an increased incidence of otitis media and sensorineural loss with re-cruitment in about 65 percent of cases. Severe deafness, however, is noted in only about 10 percent of cases.

• *Down's syndrome.* This syndrome is caused by tri-somy of chromosome 21, which leads to mental retar-dation and physical abnormalities. In Canada, birth prevalence was 7.8 per 10,000 birth from 1989–1991. Prevalence of hearing loss in this group varies from 38 percent to 78 percent, depending on criteria used. The prevalence among 3½-year-olds attending a Downs' syndrome clinic in Chicago was 28 percent unilaterally and 38 percent bilaterally (Roizen, Wolters, Nicol, & Blondis, 1993).

• *Alport's syndrome (autosomal dominant).* This syndrome is characterized by glomerulonephritis and deafness. About 40 to 60 percent of cases develop sen-sorineural hearing impairment (Northern & Downs, 1991).

Nongenetic. Congenital infections account for 9 per-cent to 14 percent of cases of hearing impairment (Todd, 1994). Parving and Hauch (1994) noted a statistically significant increase in cases caused by prenatal infections in a Danish school for the deaf from 1953 to 1983, which may be in part due to increased knowledge about rubella as a cause of deafness. A 6 percent decrease from 1983 to 1993 was observed. The most common congenital viral infections are Toxoplasmosis, Rubella, Cytomegalovi-rus, and Herpes, which are often referred to as TORCH.

• *Rubella.* Rubella was recognized as a common pre-natal cause of childhood hearing impairment as well as eye defects, congenital heart defects, congenital heart disease, and mental retardation during the mid-1960s. Infection by rubella virus can lead to the inhibition of mitosis, death of infected cell populations, ischemic damage, and chromosomal abnormalities. The probabil-ity of a fetus having congenital defects as a result of ma-ternal infection is directly related to the time of onset of the disease; about 50 percent are affected if the disease occurs during the first month of pregnancy and the inci-dence falls steadily thereafter (Bergstrom, 1977). The prevalence of sensorineural hearing loss caused by ru-bella varies from 5 to 22 per 100,000, depending on the criteria used to define deafness. This translates into 4.5 percent to 32.0 percent of all cases (Davidson et al., 1988). As the immunization of susceptible children in-creases, rubella should become a less frequent etiologi-cal factor.

• *Cytomegalovirus.* Cytomegalovirus has been re-ported to infect ten times as many infants as rubella (Bergstrom, 1977). It produces clinical syndromes in the infant ranging from no symptoms to a picture similar to rubella. Dahle, McCollister, Stagno, Reynolds, and Hoffman (1979) reported progressive hearing loss in four of twelve children with sensorineural hearing im-pairment. Hicks, Fowler, Richardson, Dahle, Adams, and Pass (1993) reported the birth prevalence of congen-ital cytomegalovirus as 1.1 per 1,000 live births. Among those born with an infection, 10.4 percent developed hearing loss >50 dB. Thus, the prevalence of hearing loss due to cytomegalovirus was 0.6 per 1,000. Children with known congenital cytomegalovirus require close monitoring to ensure prompt detection of delayed or progressive hearing loss.

• *Herpes Simplex Virus.* Herpes is a sexually transmit-ted disease that is usually acquired by the neonate while moving through the birth canal. Sometimes it is passed to the fetus via the placenta. Approximately 50 percent of infected neonates die, while only 4 percent suffer no last-ing consequences (Northern & Downs, 1991).

• *Toxoplasmosis.* Toxoplasmosis is a parasite that in-fects 2 to 7 per 1,000 pregnant women in the United States and 30 percent to 40 percent of these women transmit it to the fetus (Northern & Downs, 1991). Infec-tion during the first trimester is most damaging, espe-cially to the eyes and the central nervous system. Sensorineural hearing loss has previously been noted in 14 to 26 percent of infected newborns. However, an on-going collaborative study based in Chicago following in-fected infants prospectively has not yet detected any evidence of hearing loss. All infants were treated with pyrimethamine and sulfonamides before the age of 2.5

months and for a duration of at least 12 months (Stein & Boyer, 1994).

• *Ototoxic drugs.* Many drugs can cause hearing impairment if ingested during pregnancy. Those most commonly implicated in prenatal deafness are streptomycin, quinine, and chloroquine phosphate. The most severe damage to the fetus occurs when the drugs are ingested during the first trimester of pregnancy, particularly in the sixth and seventh weeks. Potential auditory apparatus injury includes damage to the hair cells, middle ear anomalies, absence of the seventh and eighth nerves, and dysplasia of the organ of Corti (Northern & Downs, 1991).

• *Fetal alcohol syndrome.* Excessive drinking during pregnancy has been associated with fetal alcohol syndrome. It is estimated that the birth prevalence of fetal alcohol syndrome in industrialized countries is 1 to 3 per 1,000 live births. Many of these children have developmental delay and physical and behavioral effects including severe learning disabilities. It has been estimated that approximately 40 percent of these children may have hearing impairment.

Perinatal Factors

Perinatal factors account for approximately 13 percent of hearing impairment in children (Davidson et al., 1988). Parving & Hauch (1994) found that the percentage of cases attributed to perinatal factors remained relatively constant from 1953 to 1993 in Denmark.

Prematurity. Prematurity is a commonly mentioned perinatal cause of hearing impairment. In 1990, 5.5 percent and 7.0 percent of all live births were considered low birth weight (less than 2,500 grams) in Canada and the United States respectively. In Canada the percentage of single births weighing less than 1,500 grams was constant at 0.7 percent from 1971 to 1989 (Millar et al., 1991; Ng & Wilkins, 1994). The incidence of hearing loss because of prematurity ranges from 3.3 percent to about 10 percent (Catlin, 1978). The pathogenesis has been attributed to intrapartum hemorrhage into the inner ear.

Hypoxia. Some degree of hypoxia is reported to be present in 5 percent to 10 percent of all births and produces hearing loss in 0.9 percent to 10 percent of infants (Catlin, 1978). Hypoxia can have a toxic effect on the cochlear nuclei and can result in other neurological damage such as cerebral palsy or mental retardation.

Birth Trauma. As with prematurity the hearing impairment because of birth trauma is thought to result from hemorrhage into the inner ear that produces irreversible damage to the organ of Corti from the toxic effects of extravagated blood.

Kernicterus. Kernicterus usually is caused by maternal isoimmunization (because of Rh incompatibility) but also can result from such diverse causes as congenital hemolytic anemia, certain drugs (e.g., vitamin K, sulfonaimides), and hypoxia (Catlin, 1978). Hearing loss ranges from mild to profound, is usually sensorineural, and is commonly bilateral. It is thought to be the result of toxic damage to the cochlear nuclei and/or central auditory pathways. Kernicterus is a good example of how prenatal, perinatal, and postnatal causes of deafness can be related. It has been shown, for example, that the incidence of kernicterus can be increased by such factors as low birth weight, prematurity, birth asphyxia, and certain drugs. Because it is not always possible to separate the contribution made by the various factors to the development of hearing impairment, a high-risk register for neonates that includes the following (Joint Committee on Infant Hearing, 1995) has been developed:

• Family history of severe hearing loss in early childhood
• Significant viral illness during the mother's pregnancy
• Congenital anomaly of the skull, face, ear, nose, or throat
• Prematurity with a birth weight of less than 1,500 g
• Ototoxic medications including, but not limited to, aminoglycosides, used in multiple courses or in combination with loop diuretics
• Bacterial meningitis
• Mechanical ventilation lasting five days or longer
• Hyperbilirubinemia at a serum level requiring exchange transfusion
• Apgar scores of 0 to 4 at 1 minute or 0 to 6 at 5 minutes
• Stigmata or other findings associated with a syndrome known to include a sensorineural and/or conductive hearing loss

There is a separate list of criteria defining infants 29 days to 2 years old at high risk of developing hearing impairment (Joint Committee on Infant Hearing, 1995):

• Parent/caregiver concern regarding hearing, speech, language, and/or developmental delay
• Bacterial meningitis
• Neonatal risk factors that may be associated with progressive sensorineural hearing loss

- Head trauma associated with loss of consciousness or skull fracture
- Stigmas or other findings associated with syndromes known to include sensorineural hearing loss and/or conductive loss
- Ototoxic medications including, but not limited to, aminoglycosides, used in multiple courses or in combination with loop diuretics
- Recurrent or persistent otits media with effusion for at least three months

Postnatal Factors

Studies have attributed 5 percent to 40 percent of childhood hearing impairment to postnatal factors, although, in general, these factors play a less significant role than prenatal and perinatal factors (Davidson et al., 1988).

Otitis Media. Otitis media usually is divided into acute, chronic, and secretory types. The last is not a distinct entity but a phase preceding or following the acute phase and possibly giving rise to chronic middle ear disease. Secretory otitis media is the most common cause of conductive hearing impairment among preschool children; it is particularly common among children with allergies and cleft palate (Eliachar, 1978).

Klein, Teele, and Pelton (1992) reported that by age 1 year, 62 percent of children in greater Boston had at least one episode of acute otitis media and one in six had three or more episodes. They also found that by 3 years of age, 83 percent of the children had at least one episode of acute otitis media and a majority had had three or more episodes. The higher recurrence of otitis media (i.e., three or more episodes) tended to be related to the following factors: male gender, history of ear infection in sibling, occurrence of first episode of otitis media at an early age, and attendance at day care. Parving and Hauch (1994) found a significant decrease in deafness due to otitis media from 1953 to 1993 in deaf children in Denmark.

The prevalence of otitis media is higher among North American Indians and Inuit, although the reasons for this have not been determined. In a survey of 1,109 Native Indian children in British Columbia, Roberts (1976) found that 22.5 percent of those under 2-years of age and 17.5 percent of those 2 to 4 years of age had middle ear disease requiring treatment. Baxter and Ling (1974) examined 3,770 Inuit in the Baffin Zone and found acute otitis media in 6 percent and serous otitis media in about 12 percent of children under 3 years of age. About 20 percent of the population under 20 years of age had scarring of the tympanic membrane, indicat-

ing a history of either suppurative or serous otitis media. The authors found no evidence that Inuit had any unique characteristics of the external canal that could contribute to the high prevalence of middle ear disease; however, the authors did suggest that socioeconomic conditions, specifically lower hygiene standards, might have contributed to the increased prevalence.

In a study of children in Washington, DC, who were between 6 months and 11 years of age, Kessner, Snow, and Singer (1974) found a prevalence of middle ear pathology in 35.6 percent of whites and only 19 percent of blacks.

Otitis media is common among children with cleft palate. Bess, Schwartz, and Redfield (1986) examined 34 children with cleft palates and found the incidence of hearing loss and associated middle ear disease varied from 57 percent to 68 percent depending on the detection procedure used. A Danish study of 44 children with cleft palate found that 32 percent were treated for serous otitis media, compared to 10 to 15 percent in a similar population without cleft palate. The difference in the percentage of children who suffered six or more attacks of acute otitis media was not as great: 11 percent in the children with cleft palate versus 8 percent without (Rynnel-Dagoo, Linberg, Bagger-Sjöbäck, & Larson, 1992). Bluestone (1978) reviewed the pertinent literature and confirmed that about 50 percent of children with cleft palate have associated impairment. The hearing impairment is generally conductive and usually bilateral. The pathogenesis of middle ear disease in children with cleft palate usually is attributed to eustachian tube dysfunction.

Meningitis. Meningitis is the most common cause of severe postnatal sensorineural hearing impairment (Wong & Shah, 1979). In a review of 301 cases of bacterial meningitis from two hospitals in Nottingham, England, Fortnum & Davis (1992) found that 13 percent occurred in infants less than 28 days old, 40.9 percent in infants 1 to 11 months old, 34.6 percent in children age 12 to 59 months, and the remainder (11.6 percent) in children aged 5 to 16 years. The most common causative organism was *Neissera meningitidis,* followed by *Haemophilus influenzae,* then *Streptococcus pneumoniae.* Of those who survived and were located for follow-up testing, 7.4 percent developed sensorineural hearing impairment greater than 20 dB in the worst ear. The presence of hydrocephalus and admission from October to March increased the child's risk of developing any type of hearing impairment. Children aged less than 1 month and greater than 5 years had the most risk of developing bilateral hearing loss, regardless of other factors.

The incidence of bacterial meningitis caused by *Haemophilus influenzae* has been declining in recent years due to the introduction of the Hib vaccine in 1985 aimed at this organism. Stein and Boyer (1994) report three studies that have found an 82 percent to 92 percent decrease in incidence of infection. Assuming that the Hib immunization campaign is completely effective, Stein and Boyer predict a reduction of 1,200 to 1,800 cases of sensorineural hearing loss in infants annually in the United States.

Nadol (1978), who examined 547 cases of meningitis at the Massachusetts General Hospital, reported on hearing loss in nonbacterial forms of meningitis. He found that three of seven patients with fungal meningitis suffered hearing impairment, whereas none of the 304 patients with aseptic or viral meningitis was found to have hearing loss. A diagnosis of bacterial meningitis should always alert the physician to the need for careful follow-up so that any hearing impairment is detected as quickly as possible.

Viral Infections. Common viral diseases that have been implicated in the etiology of childhood hearing impairment include measles, mumps, chicken pox, influenza, and infectious mononucleosis. The measles virus can enter the inner ear directly via the bloodstream or the central nervous system, or it can result in purulent otitis media with subsequent suppurative labyrinthitis and inner ear destruction. Mumps is one of the leading causes of unilateral sensorineural hearing loss in children. Deafness associated with viral diseases usually results from inner ear damage because of direct infiltration of the virus through the internal auditory meatus and generally is of the mild to profound sensorineural type (Northern & Downs, 1991).

Ototoxic Drugs. A number of drugs can injure or destroy the cochlear hair cells in children, thereby causing profound sensorineural deafness. Kanamycin and neomycin are the worst offenders; other drugs include certain antibiotics (particularly dihydrostreptomycin) and antimalarial medication. The hearing loss is usually bilateral and can be of varying degree, because of individual susceptibility to the toxic effects of the drug.

Noise. Noise-induced hearing loss usually is considered an occupational health hazard of the older patient; however, children also can be exposed to noise of sufficient intensity to produce the characteristic sensorineural dip at 4000 Hz. Sources of noise include model aircraft engines, firecrackers, toy caps, toy firearms, and rock music. The incubator with its ambient noise level of 66 to 75 dB has been suspected but not conclusively proven to contribute to hearing impairment in premature infants.

SPEECH AND LANGUAGE DEVELOPMENT

Normal Skills

Knowledge of the landmarks of normal speech and language development is important in conducting an audiological assessment. The material presented in this section is derived from various sources (Berry, 1969; Lillywhite, 1958; Reich, 1986; Sheridan, 1968).

Ages 6–12 months. Children aged 6 months to approximately 1 year are in the babbling stage, producing consonant-vowel pairs and reduplicating them; at 10–12 months they may babble in "sentences," utilizing intonation patterns of adult speech. Few consonant clusters are produced, more middle than initial consonants, and few final consonants. Front vowels, such as *ee* emerge prior to back vowels such as *oo*.

Ages 2–3 years. Children 2 to 3 years old use all vowels and the consonants *m, b, p, f, k, g, w, h, n, t,* and *d.* They tend to omit most final consonants. The intelligibility of their words when heard in context improves from about 65 percent at 2 years of age to about 70 percent to 80 percent by age 3. This is the period of most rapid vocabulary growth; it has been estimated that children's vocabularies double between 2½ and 3 years of age, from approximately 450 to 900 words. Throughout the stages of language development, children's ability to understand words exceeds their expressive vocabulary. They experiment grammatically, putting two or more words together. They enjoy talking to themselves continually while playing, and echolalia is common. They are able to join in nursery rhymes and enjoy listening to simple stories read from picture books. They ask questions beginning with *what* and *where* and use the pronouns *I, me,* and *you.*

Ages 3–4 years. Children's use of the consonants *b, t, d, k,* and *g* improves and they attempt *v, th, s,* and *z* as well as such combinations as *tr, bl, pr, gr,* and *dr.* They might, however, have difficulty with *r* and *l,* and might substitute *w* for these letters or omit them. Speech is approximately 90 percent to 100 percent intelligible provided it is heard in context. Children's vocabulary comprehension increases to about 1,500 words at age 4 and they regularly use 600 to 1,000 words. Their sentences consist of three to four words and they ask questions beginning with *who* and *why*. They are able to use plurals and personal pronouns, carry on simple conversations, and enjoy listening to their favorite stories. They develop standard subject–predicate sentences and attempt to form the past tense.

Ages 4–5 years. Children 4 to 5 years of age consistently use *f* and *v* together with a number of consonant combinations. They might still have problems with *r, l, s, z, sh, ch, j,* and *th,* but there are few if any omissions of initial and final consonants. Speech usually is intelligible in context. Children can comprehend 1,500 to 2,000 words and use 1,100 to 1,600 words. The complexity of words increases to three to four syllables and sentences can be up to six words long. They ask questions beginning with *when* and *how* and use more adjectives, adverbs, prepositions, and conjunctions. Use of pronouns in place of proper nouns increases and they are able to carry out two- or three-stage commands. At this age, children enjoy both listening to and telling long stories. Their voices are better modulated and they tend to copy adult intonation and rhythmic patterns.

Ages 5–6 years. Children who are 5 to 6 years old have mastered the use of *r, l,* and *th* as well as such combinations as *tl, gr, bl, br,* and *pr.* They might still have difficulty with *thr, sk, st,* and *shr* and might continue to distort *s, z, sh, ch,* and *j.* General intelligibility is good and usable expressive vocabularies have increased to 1,500 to 2,100 words and receptive vocabulary to 2,500 to 2,800 words. Syntax is almost normal and they use five- to six-word compound or complex sentences. They experiment orally with various verb forms representing tense, number, or person; they can distinguish among types of nouns and use negation freely in their sentences. They ask the meaning of abstract words, enjoy listening to all types of stories, and might act them out in detail. By the age of 6, they might be able to read simple stories aloud.

It goes without saying that there is wide individual variation and considerable overlap among the various stages described here, which are, after all, only arbitrary divisions. Children's progress depends not only on the quality of their auditory system and mental capacity but also on the stimulation they receive from the environment.

Hearing-Impaired Children

Language development can be impeded whether or not hearing loss is profound. Holm and Kunze (1969) found children who had fluctuating losses and episodes of oti-tis media to be significantly delayed in language perception and production compared with normal hearing peers. Kaplan, Fleshman, Bender, Baum, and Clark (1973), in a study of 489 Inuit children, found that those with a history of otitis media before 2 years of age and a hearing loss of 26 dBHL or greater had a statistically significant loss of verbal ability and were behind normal children in reading, mathematics, and language. In a study of 40 children between the ages of 6 and 11, Zinkus, Gottlief, and Schapiro (1978) found that those with a history of chronic and severe otitis media during the first three years of life had significantly delayed speech and language development, deficits in specific verbal tasks involving auditory processing, difficulty performing tasks requiring the integration of visual and auditory processing skills, reading disorders, and poor spelling.

The impact of hearing impairment on speech development ranges from significant delay in language acquisition and faulty articulation, inflection, and pitch patterns in profoundly hearing-impaired children, to articulation problems (particularly with respect to high-frequency sounds, word endings, and some initial consonants) in those with less severe hearing impairment. Speech sounds vary in their frequency distribution and the ability of a hearing-impaired child to detect them varies similarly. For example, the frequencies of vowels range from 250 to 3300 Hz and their sound is of relatively longer duration ($\geq$100 ms) and more intense than that of consonants. Fricative consonants such as *z* and *s* ("zoo, sun") have higher frequencies (3500 to 8000 Hz), whereas *zh* and *sh* ("measure, shop") have frequencies of 2500 to 4500 Hz; these consonants are more intense and longer than other fricatives such as *h, f,* and the unvoiced *th* (thin), which are especially difficult for children with hearing losses to identify (Skinner, 1978).

Average sound pressure levels (SPL) for speech range from 45 to 60 dB (Skinner, 1988). For children with mild low-frequency hearing loss, many speech cues below 500 Hz are inaudible and consonants are more easily heard than vowels. With a moderate high-frequency hearing loss, on the other hand, vowels, with their greater intensity, are heard more easily than consonants. Short words such as *if, it,* or *the,* which are unstressed and therefore of low intensity, are especially difficult to hear, as are unvoiced stops (*p, t, k*) and fricative consonants (*f, h, s, th*).

Children with a severe loss can hear speech only if it is spoken at close range, whereas children with a profound loss cannot hear speech at all, even their own vocalizations, except with suitable amplification. Obviously, particular problems depend not only on the magnitude of hearing loss but also on the threshold configuration. For example, a child with hearing loss only in the high frequencies might successfully detect most speech sounds and, consequently, the hearing, in the absence of adequate audiological assessment, may be assumed to be grossly normal. The presence of the hearing deficit might not be identified until the child is brought to a speech-language pathologist for misarticulation or lack of discrimination of such high-frequency sounds as *f, s,* and *th* and is subsequently referred to an audiologist for evaluation.

A child with a conductive hearing loss can still discriminate between two sounds of different frequencies, whereas a child with a sensorineural loss cannot unless the frequencies are widely separated; the extent of separation required is directly proportional to the magnitude of hearing loss. A child with sensorineural loss has particular difficulty distinguishing sounds such as *t/k, r/w,* and *ch/sh,* even with a hearing aid (Skinner, 1978). Children with either conductive or sensorineural loss cannot hear sounds below threshold levels. Sounds above threshold, however, may seem abnormally loud to a child with cochlear hearing loss because of the process known as recruitment.

In conclusion, it should be noted that speech is rarely heard against a silent background; it has been estimated that background noise averages 35 to 68 dB (Skinner, 1988), only 10 to 15 dB below speech level. For normal adults, this situation presents no problem because knowledge of the language assists them in deducing sounds from the message context. Because children who are still learning the language lack the knowledge base needed to supply missing acoustic clues, a hearing loss of only 15 dBHL can be highly significant.

PRESENTING PROBLEMS

Delay in identification of hearing impairment in preschool children is quite common (Shah, Dale, & Chandler, 1977). Shah and his colleagues identified stages of delay after parents or others suspected hearing loss and before the child received proper help. The average age of suspicion in young children is 16 months. From suspicion of hearing loss to receiving appropriate diagnostic tests takes from 3 to 66 months. Hence, it is imperative for individuals working with preschool children to be knowledgeable of manifestations of hearing impairment in young children. Table 13.1 shows manifestations of

deafness reported by parents of affected children (Shah et al., 1977). A hearing loss of any degree will cause speech and language delay. How well a child develops communication skills depends in no small part on the degree of hearing loss and early intervention. Even a mild hearing loss is educationally significant. Whether a hearing-impaired child will need speech and language therapy or a complete auditory training program will depend upon the degree of hearing loss (Table 13.2).

Clinical indications of hearing loss in infants and young children can include lack of response to ordinary speech, startling noises, or persons or noises outside the visual field. The hearing-impaired child may exhibit no startle response to loud sounds, slow speech development or poor articulation, behavioral disorders, hyperactivity, and chronic ear infections. Children can be referred for hearing assessment for any of these reasons, because they have been placed on a neonatal high-risk register, or as part of routine follow-up after a viral or bacterial infection such as meningitis or encephalitis. The audiological problem might be only one aspect of other disorders, such as cerebral palsy, autism, and mental retardation.

It is important to note that because hearing loss may be only one part of a larger disease entity and can significantly influence other aspects of the child's development, a child identified as hearing impaired should be closely evaluated. At the Hospital for Sick Children in Toronto, a complete assessment for newly identified hearing-impaired infants and young children involves an extensive team effort. The primary team includes an otologist, audiologist, speech pathologist, pediatrician, neuroradiologist, opthalmologist, social worker, teacher of the hearing impaired, and a representative from the local school authority. In addition, a neurologist, geneticist, psychologist, and psychiatrist can be consulted (Wong & Shah, 1979).

ASSESSMENT PROCEDURES

Though a number of specific tests are described in this section, they do not in themselves constitute a complete audiological assessment because the results obtained must be viewed within the framework of the case history, otological and general medical findings, related educational, social, and psychological information, and receptive and expressive communication data (Lloyd & Cox, 1975). As well, one must be cautious in the interpretation of any one test in isolation; a test-battery approach should be employed. By utilizing middle ear

TABLE 13.1   Manifestations of Deafness Reported by the Parents of 200 Affected Children

MENTIONED BY PARENTS (% OF CASES)	AREA OF DIFFICULTY MANIFESTATIONS
	Hearing
43%	No response to ordinary speech/soft sound/calling name
37%	No response to startling noises/loud sounds/ringing and honking
30%	No response to noises or persons outside visual fields
27%	My child is deaf/has a hearing problem
11%	Wants to see your face when you talk/watches mouths
6%	Listens for and responds to vibration (by placing ear against the stereo or washing machine)
5%	Doesn't play with noisemaking or musical toys
	Talking
39%	Slow to talk/poor speech/no speech
8%	No babbling/doesn't babble like he or she used to
8%	A quiet baby/slept well (through noise)
	Behavior
14%	Doesn't pay attention/doesn't understand/irregular disobedience/hard to handle/have to raise voice often and repeat things
9%	Hyperactive/pulls and points a lot (excessive use of gestures)/ frequently bites/won't play some games with others
7%	Frequent and unusually loud screaming and crying
	Other Ear Problems
23%	Chronic ear infections
6%	Balance problems (slow to sit up and walk)
2%	Fingering the ears frequently (at age 6 to 12 months)

Source: The challenge of hearing impairment in children, by C. P. Shah, M. A. Dale, and D. Chandler, 1977, *Canadian Family Physicians, 23,* pp. 175–183. Reprinted with permission of the authors and the journal.

measures, speech audiometry, and possibly electrophysiological tests in addition to pure-tone audiometry, errors in interpretation may be avoided. Children may for various reasons be nonresponsive to certain stimuli; cross-checking results from more than one test helps ensure greater accuracy in diagnosis.

During the initial period of establishing rapport with the parent and child and obtaining a clinical history, the audiologist can, through simple observation, obtain valuable information about the child's developmental level, voice quality, articulation, extent of vocabulary, and the presence or absence of other physical disabilities or congenital abnormalities. The information gained at this time will assist the audiologist in selecting the appropriate test protocol. A brief inspection of the child's external ear canal can be done at this time to rule out the presence of congenital abnormalities (e.g., atresia), foreign bodies, or impacted cerumen, though with younger or apprehensive children it is often wise to do otoscopy at the end of the test session. Audiological evaluation of the 3- to 6-year-old child normally consists of measuring pure-tone air and bone conduction thresholds, the speech reception threshold, speech discrimination, and impedance/immittance audiometry. Children under 3 are most commonly assessed via behavioral observation or visual reinforcement audiometry, depending on the developmental level. Where indicated, otoacoustic emissions testing and auditory brainstem response audiometry also can be employed. It is most important that assessment of

TABLE 13.2 Degrees of Hearing Impairment

CATEGORY	HANDICAP	SPECIAL NEEDS
Normal (0–15 dB)	None	None
Mild/Slight (16–40 dB)	Educationally significant. Faint or distant speech might be difficult to understand, especially in the presence of background noise.	Monitor condition. Preferential classroom seating is needed. Mild gain amplification might help this child.
Moderate (41–55 dB)	Vocabulary might be limited. Articulation problems can occur; language, reading, and writing skills can be affected.	Might need speech and language intervention. Amplification usually will help. Preferential seating desirable.
Moderate/Severe (56–70 dB)	Speech and language are delayed. Group discussion will be very difficult to follow.	Might need special assistance in classroom. Might require tutor and speech and language help. Amplification is a must.
Severe (71–90 dB)	Speech and language will be distorted and might not develop spontaneously.	Amplification necessary. Needs speech and language remediation and auditory training. Might need special education.
Profound (90+ dB)	Might be more aware of vibrations than tonal sounds. Speech and language are defective and will not develop spontaneously. Hearing does not serve as the primary means for the acquisition of spoken language or for the monitoring of speech.	Usually requires special classes. Might benefit from amplification to monitor own voice and for gross discrimination of sounds.

preschool children be undertaken by audiologists with extensive experience in testing children.

Audiological evaluation of the infant to 2-year-old is not as sensitive in obtaining hearing threshold levels as it is with older children. Age-appropriate norms are established though, which indicate expected auditory behaviors and the intensity of sound to which the child should respond for different age ranges. Routine assessment techniques for this population include behavioral observation audiometry (BOA) and visual response audiometry (VRA). It is sometimes necessary to utilize more objective measures of auditory function in order that more accurate information on auditory threshold may be obtained. Physiological measures, such as auditory brainstem response (ABR), provide a precise measure of the peripheral auditory system from the auditory nerve to the auditory brainstem pathways. Otoacoustic emissions allow assessment of cochlear function, and are also gaining popularity in the clinical setting, particularly in hearing screening.

The audiometric procedures used to assess the hearing of infants and children are classified as subjective (observation of responses to controlled auditory stimuli) and objective (physiological) assessments. Behavioral assessments, such as behavioral observation audiometry, visual response audiometry, and play audiometry, are subjective in nature. The most quantitative of these procedures is play audiometry, which cannot be used successfully until the child is 2½ or 3 years of age. Objective measurements include impedance audiometry and electrophysiological measurements of the auditory system. It is important to remember though, that objective tests are still subject to interpretation, which may vary among examiners.

Subjective Audiometry

Subjective audiometry is useful in children because it allows the audiologist to evaluate the overall development of the child as well as the functional relationship between the child and his or her environment. Appropriate test selection will be determined by the functional capabilities of the child because responses are contingent upon the level of cognitive development. Northern and Downs (1991) developed an Auditory Behavior Index that correlates an infant's developmental level to his or her ability to respond to auditory stimuli. Normal development is as follows:

- *6 weeks to 4 months:* eye widening, eye-shift, and/or cessation of activity to auditory stimuli presented at levels of 70 dBHL for warble-tones and 40–60 dBHL for speech stimuli
- *4 to 7 months:* turning of the head toward the auditory stimuli. Intensity of the auditory stimuli to elicit a head turn is 50 dBHL for warble-tones and 20 dBHL for speech stimuli
- *7 to 9 months:* direct localization of sound to the side and indirectly below ear level to 45 dBHL warble-tones and 15 dBHL speech
- *9 to 13 months:* direct localization of sound to the side, below, and indirectly above ear level to 38 dBHL warble-tones and 10 dBHL speech
- *13 to 16 months:* direct location of sound to the side, above, and below ear level at levels of 30 dBHL for warble-tones, 5 dBHL speech

Children over 16 months of age are expected to respond at levels essentially within the normal range of hearing for both speech and warble-tones.

The meaningfulness of sound to the child also is significant in obtaining a response. Speech is most likely to elicit the lowest minimal response level because it is the most familiar auditory stimulus to the infant and it covers a broad frequency range (acoustic energy from 500 to 3000 H) (Lloyd & Cox, 1975). However, normal hearing should not be assumed only on the basis of a response to such a broad-frequency stimulus as speech, because it is possible a child has a high-frequency hearing loss and is responding only to the lower-frequency components of the speech stimulus. Neither should a failure to respond to warble tones at speech threshold levels be assumed to indicate hearing loss. It is expected that the infant will respond to speech at lower intensity levels than warble-tones. In the sound field environment, the recorded response to all stimuli reflects the sensitivity of the better-hearing ear. In the absence of ear-specific testing under headphones, statements regarding individual ear sensitivity cannot be made, even if speakers are utilized to both the left and the right side. Behavioral assessment of an infant's auditory sensitivity can be

differentiated by whether or not reinforcement is used. Behavioral observation audiometry (BOA) utilizes no reinforcement, whereas visual reinforcement audiometry (VRA) has emerged as a successful assessment tool for ages 6 months through 2 years (Wilson & Thompson, 1984).

Behavioral Observation Audiometry

BOA involves observing the infant's response to a variety of sound stimuli such as voice, warbled pure-tones, and narrow-band noise. The infant should be tested in a double-booth, sound-treated suite with two pediatric audiologists observing the infant's responses. One audiologist is in the sound room with the infant while the other is located in the adjacent room at the audiometer. Both observe the infant's reaction to the stimuli, the one operating the audiometer observing through a two-way mirror. The use of an audiometer allows for control of the stimuli, both in frequency (pitch) and intensity (loudness). The most common stimuli used are warbled pure-tones at 500, 2000, and 4000 Hz and a speech signal (the infant's name, for example, or the repetition of *babababa*). Warble-tones are preferred because they are frequency specific, though if a child is nonresponsive, narrow-band noise (NBN) may be used with some loss of frequency specificity. A speech signal is included because it is familiar to the infant and contains a wide range of frequencies; infants generally respond to speech at a lower intensity than warble-tones. The three frequencies presented are selected for their appropriateness in eliciting information about hearing sensitivity in the frequency range important for hearing and understanding speech.

Bone conduction results are often not reliably obtained from infants, though when loss is detected, an attempt should be made to put the bone conductor on the child. Studying the configuration of the infant's response to the various frequencies more often aids in determining the type of hearing loss. If the child responds age appropriately for the low-frequency stimulus but not for the high-frequency range, a high-frequency sensorineural hearing loss is suspected. Conversely, a poor response to the low-frequency stimulation improving in the high-frequency range might be indicative of a conductive hearing loss, especially if results obtained from impedance measurements are abnormal. The intensity of the auditory signal that will result in an obvious change in the less than 4-month-old infant's behavior is significant, in the range of 70 dB. Therefore, it is difficult to determine a hearing loss of less than a severe to profound degree. Whether the infant being tested is sleeping, crying, or awake and happy will determine how successful the test will be. An infant's responses are reflexive in nature and can include increasing or decreasing activity, change in breathing, eye widening, or cessation of babbling. It is difficult to observe these subtle responses to the auditory stimuli unless the infant is quiet.

A typical response recorded in a normal-hearing 6-week-old infant is recorded in Figure 13.1. The speech awareness threshold of 60 dBHL hearing level is better than the results obtained with the narrow-band noise at the three frequencies tested, which is expected in this age group.

Behavioral observation audiometry is, at best, a method to screen severe-to-profound hearing loss in very young infants. It will not result in information discrete enough to adequately describe auditory function and the need for habilitation in the very young infant.

Nevertheless, valuable information is obtained about the child's general development and his or her ability to interact with the environment and whether further assessment utilizing objective techniques might be required. Although BOA is generally used for testing infants less than 6 months of age, it also might be necessary to use this method of assessment with older infants who are developmentally delayed.

Visual Reinforcement Audiometry

VRA is successful in determining the auditory response of infants and children from 6 months to 2 years of age. As the infant begins to localize to interesting or unusual sounds, he or she can be reinforced with a visual stimulus, the most popular being a lighted, animated toy mounted above the loudspeakers in the test suite. Visual stimuli are used because they are particularly interesting

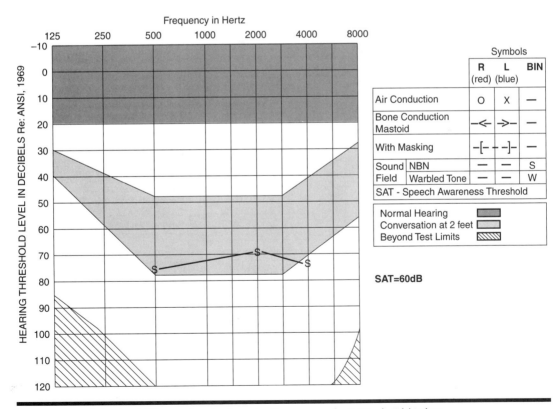

FIGURE 13.1 Behavioral Observation Audiometry Responses of a 6-Week-Old Infant

Source: Information provided with permission from The Hospital for Sick Children, Toronto, Canada.

to this age group and provide an excellent reinforcing function for auditory responses obtained in a formal testing situation (Wilson & Thompson, 1984). This type of audiometry can be performed either in a sound field environment or, with older infants who will tolerate them, under headphones. Two examiners are necessary to complete the assessment; one to occupy the child and one to operate the audiometer. As in BOA, stimuli used are speech and the frequencies 500, 2000, and 4000 Hz. If the child is old enough to allow the use of headphones, pure-tone stimuli are used. Whenever any type of alerting response occurs, such as turning in the direction of the auditory signal, visual reinforcement is presented. If a child does not localize spontaneously, a conditioning procedure may be employed to elicit the appropriate response. With older infants, toys such as puppets, puzzles, or brightly colored pegs are added to the test situation to distract him from continued observation of

the animated toys between presentations of the acoustic stimuli. If the child's attention is not distracted from the visual reinforcer, false positive responses will result. If the distractive toys are too interesting or complex for the child, he or she will become so involved in the task before him or her that he or she will fail to respond when the stimuli are presented.

Visual reinforcement audiometry, because it is done when a child is a bit older and has progressed in auditory development, can produce responses at sound levels lower than those obtained through behavioral observation audiometry. This results in more definitive information about the infant's hearing sensitivity, though the test may still not be sensitive enough to identify a mild hearing loss, especially in the 6- to 8-month-old child (Figure 13.2). As with other forms of testing, minimal response levels improve as the child gets older. Should a child respond consistently to the preceding

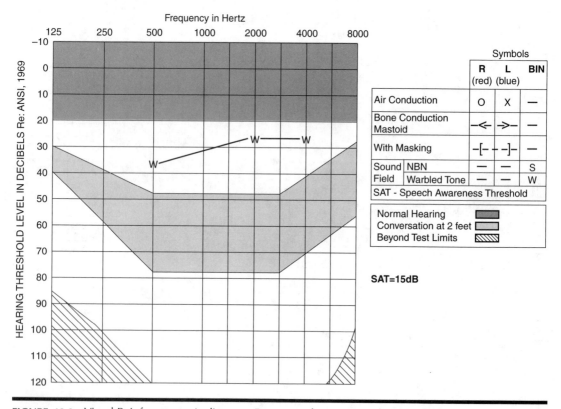

FIGURE 13.2 Visual Reinforcement Audiometry Responses for an 8-Month-Old Infant

Source: Information provided with permission from The Hospital for Sick Children, Toronto, Canada.

stimuli, additional frequencies should be assessed to provide more detail regarding hearing sensitivity.

Play Audiometry

In play audiometry children are taught a response to a stimulus, such as stacking rings on a peg, stacking blocks, or dropping them into a box (Hodgson, 1978). This procedure has been advocated for use with children as young as 2 years, though the probability of successful evaluation increases as the child approaches 3 years of age. Preferably, testing is conducted under headphones, though this technique may also be used in the sound field situation.

The audiologist can utilize the initial moments of the testing session to establish rapport with the child, observe reaction to gross sounds to form some idea of the response threshold, and to introduce the idea of responding to sound in a play setting. A major hurdle to overcome is persuading the child to accept the earphones. This can be facilitated if the examiner wears the headset for a few moments or provides the child with the opportunity to watch another cooperative child being tested. If the child has a marked hearing loss, verbal instructions might be inappropriate and the audiologist might have to utilize pantomime and demonstration to convey the expected response to the child.

Once the child has accepted the earphones, the audiologist must work quickly to complete the testing of essential frequencies before the child becomes tired of the game. Rather than attempting to complete an entire audiogram in one ear, 500, 2000, and 4000 Hz should be tested in each ear, followed, if possible, by testing at 1000 and 250 Hz. The audiologist always must be alert to signs of boredom or restlessness; changing the method of response might be sufficient to get the child to complete the test session. The game should not be so interesting that the child becomes absorbed in it to the exclusion of responding to the stimuli. Other distractions must be avoided and the child kept ready to respond as soon as the auditory signal is presented.

Play audiometry is a well-proven and popular method of testing the auditory sensitivity of preschoolers. If a 3-year-old child cannot respond to play audiometry, some problems other than just hearing impairment should be suspected. Although play audiometry might be useful to the age of 6, most children 5 to 6 years of age are capable of responding via conventional hand-raising techniques. The method that is appropriate to the

child's level of maturation and cooperation should be utilized.

Conventional Audiometry

Children 4 years of age and older with no developmental delay may be able to participate in the test procedures used with adults. Children are taught either to raise a hand, push a button, or clap their hands whenever they hear a sound through headphones. They should be encouraged to respond to the smallest sound that they think they hear. For clinical purposes, the threshold is defined as the faintest pure-tone that can be heard 50 percent of the time and can be approached by a descending-ascending technique. Thresholds are obtained in the ascending mode (i.e., progressing from silence to sound).

Northern and Downs (1991) recommended that the first frequency to be tested should be 2000 Hz because it is the most important indicator of sensorineural hearing loss, followed by 500 Hz, which is significant in determining conductive hearing loss. If children continue to cooperate, these two frequencies can be followed by testing at 1000, 4000, 250, and 8000 Hz in that order. At the conclusion of the air conduction tests, the pure-tone procedure should be repeated, using the bone conduction oscillator. Because the skull is a good conductor of sound, it is possible to by-pass the middle ear structures and obtain a response directly from the inner ear (cochlea) by placing the bone conduction receiver on the mastoid process. A conductive hearing loss is present if the bone conduction results are within the normal range of hearing and the air conduction results are elevated (Figure 13.3). A sensorineural hearing loss is recorded when the air conduction and bone conduction test results are within 10 dB of each other and both are abnormal (Figure 13.4). A mixed hearing loss occurs when both air conduction and bone conduction test results are abnormal, but the bone conduction results are better than the air conduction results (Figure 13.5).

Masking should be used in bone conduction testing whenever the bone conduction threshold is better than the air conduction threshold by greater than 10 dB. In air conduction tests, masking is recommended when the air conduction threshold in the ear being tested exceeds the bone conduction threshold in the other ear by 40 dB or more (Price, 1978). Masking must be employed to ensure the test signal is not crossing over to the nontest ear, resulting in inaccurate threshold determination. To mask, narrow-band noise is presented to the nontest ear

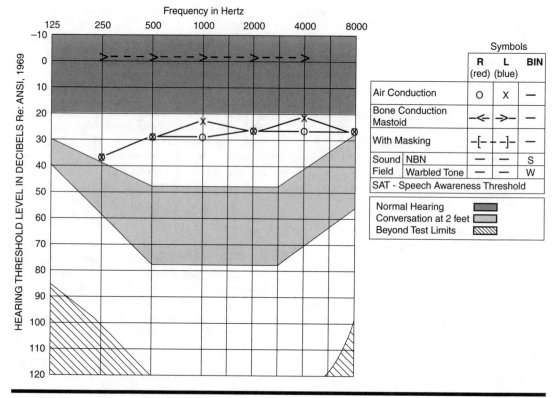

FIGURE 13.3 Conductive Hearing Loss

Source: Information provided with permission from The Hospital for Sick Children, Toronto, Canada.

to prevent the child from perceiving the test stimuli on that side.

Middle ear pathology producing conductive losses can result in fluctuating audiograms from one test period to another. Impedance audiometry plays an important role in clarifying these situations.

Speech Audiometry

The use of pure-tones provides an accurate description of a child's auditory sensitivity. Equally important, however, is the use of speech stimuli to determine a child's recognition and discrimination of speech. In speech audiometry, the *extent* of hearing loss measured by pure-tones 500–2000 Hz generally equals the speech detection or speech reception threshold. The extent and nature (conductive versus sensorineural) of the hearing loss determine the child's ability to understand speech at a comfortable loudness level. This is measured using

speech discrimination tests. The audiologist must use words that are within the child's language experience and must not provide visual cues to the child during the test procedures.

Speech Awareness Threshold

The speech awareness (or detection) threshold (SAT) is the most basic measurement of speech awareness and can be used effectively with infants or children who haven't the language skills necessary to obtain a speech reception threshold. This threshold is the decibel level at which the child just detects the presence of a speech stimulus; comprehension of the stimulus is not required. Any behavioral response is acceptable and various reinforcements might be required. The speech stimulus can be "running speech," calling the child's name, nonsense syllables, or familiar words, such as "bye-bye." In younger or developmentally delayed children, SATs can often be obtained

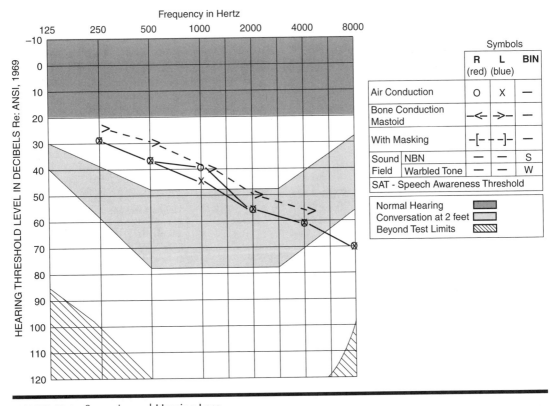

FIGURE 13.4 Sensorineural Hearing Loss

Source: Information provided with permission from The Hospital for Sick Children, Toronto, Canada.

when pure-tone thresholds cannot. The pure-tone audiogram can predict the SAT reasonably well but the reverse is not true. The broad-band range of the speech signal may elicit a response in the presence of a significant higher-frequency hearing loss. For example, normal SATs might be obtained in children who have a total loss of hearing above 1000 Hz (Shepherd, 1978). The SAT is a measure only of the child's ability to detect the presence or absence of speech; the child can do so effectively when only one or two of the major speech frequencies are within the normal hearing range.

Speech Reception Threshold

The speech reception threshold (SRT) is the level at which a child can either correctly repeat or otherwise identify 50 percent of a group of test words. It has been shown to agree closely with the pure-tone average for the speech frequencies (i.e., 500, 1000, and 2000 Hz)

and provides a useful check on the consistency of test results and a baseline value for determining the level for speech discrimination testing (Epstein, 1978).

The speech reception threshold is obtained using spondaic (two-syllable) words that are familiar to the child. Words especially applicable for children include *airplane, baseball, birthday, cowboy,* and *hot dog.* Children first should be familiarized with the test words and encouraged to respond to all words, even if they must "guess." The use of headphones is preferable; however, a sound field environment is acceptable if a child will not wear the headphones. When live voice is used, care must be taken to ensure that each syllable of the test word is given equal emphasis. If no significant hearing problem is apparent, a starting level of 40 dBnHL hearing level is recommended; this can be increased by 15 to 20 dB increments if the child is not responding appropriately. The SRT threshold is reached by decreasing the intensity of presentation in 10 dB steps until the child is unable to

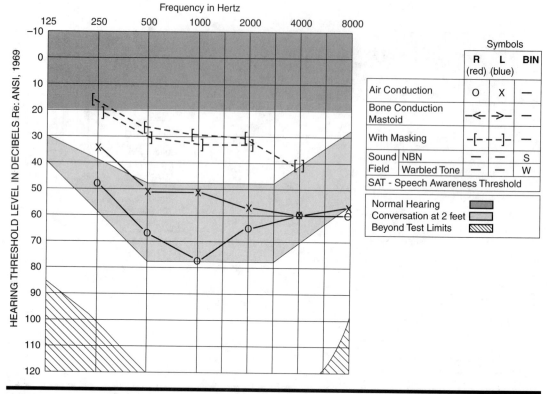

FIGURE 13.5 Mixed Hearing Loss

Source: Information provided with permission from The Hospital for Sick Children, Toronto, Canada.

recognize the words, and then increasing the intensity in 5 dB increments until three of six words are correctly identified.

The relationship between SRT and pure-tone averages of 500, 1000, and 2000 Hz obtained with children 4 years of age and older is as strong as that with adults (Shepherd, 1978). However, certain test modifications might be required, especially with younger children. If the child refuses to talk, the child can be asked to point to the appropriate picture, toy, object, or body part. When there is a marked discrepancy between the SRT and pure-tone thresholds, particularly in the direction of better SRTs, the possibility of a functional (exaggerated) hearing loss must be considered (Epstein, 1978).

Speech Discrimination

The purpose of speech discrimination tests is to discover how well children can understand a speech signal once it

has been made loud enough to be heard comfortably (Epstein, 1978). It must be preceded by determination of the SRT. Speech discrimination is determined by repetition of monosyllabic (one-syllable) words presented at a quiet conversational level; usually 30 dB above the child's SRT or at a normal conversational level of 50 dBHL. Each word list is phonetically balanced with each phoneme occurring in the word list in accordance with its use in the English language. The word lists are presented with no visual or contextual cues to assist in identification of the individual words. Interpreting speech discrimination tests can be difficult because children with hearing loss are likely to have delayed speech and language development. Even if the child hears the word correctly, the examiner might have trouble understanding the response. A written response cannot be expected in this age group. Consequently, a number of picture identification tests have been developed, the most popular being the Word Intelligibility by Picture Identification (WIPI) test developed by Ross and Lerman (1970). The child is required to select the correct picture from a group of six pictures displayed, thereby decreasing the likelihood of selecting the correct picture through chance alone. This test is suitable for 4- to 6-year-olds.

Discrimination is reported in terms of percentage of correct responses at a given dB level. Children with conductive hearing loss usually have a raised SRT but normal speech discrimination. Children with sensorineural hearing loss can have an elevated SRT and poor speech discrimination. Care must be taken in interpreting results of discrimination tests in children with delayed language development. A poor discrimination score will reflect the language delay and, unless some pure-tone threshold information is obtained, can lead to the erroneous assumption of hearing loss. Conversely, normal discrimination scores in the presence of an apparent significant hearing loss might suggest a nonorganic loss. In a person of any age, there might be little or no correlation between speech discrimination scores and ability to function in ordinary conversation with the additional cues of context and vision available. A discrimination score of less than 50 percent, for example, does not necessarily mean the person understands less than one-half of a contextual message (Epstein, 1978). There are problems in accurately assessing speech discrimination, especially in children, and there is a need for the further development of speech discrimination tests for use with this age group.

Objective Audiometry

Impedance/Immittance Audiometry. Otitis media is the most common cause of hearing impairment in preschool and school-age children. Chronic middle ear disease can be painless but nevertheless can adversely affect the child's hearing and his or her language development, especially during the crucial first three years. Otitis media often results in a conductive hearing loss ranging from 15 to 35 dBnHL, although it also can be superimposed on a sensorineural hearing loss. Unfortunately, it is during the early years when detection of a mild or fluctuating hearing loss is most crucial that behavioral audiometry is most unreliable. Consequently, mild hearing loss often escapes detection.

The development of impedance audiometry by Metz in 1946 and its use in North America since 1970 has significantly advanced the assessment of conductive hearing loss in all age groups, but especially in infants and small children (Northern & Downs, 1991). It is ob-

jective, relatively acceptable to young children, and quick and easy to administer. The use of impedance audiometry in the pediatric population can provide objective information on the status of the middle ear. An impedance system consists of a probe tip that is inserted in the test ear, forming an airtight seal. The probe tip contains three tubes: One delivers a probe-tone; the second connects to a microphone to monitor the SPL of the probe-tone in the closed cavity between the probe tip and the tympanic membrane; and the third, which is connected to an air pump, varies the air pressure in the same closed cavity. An earphone for use in the opposite ear for acoustic reflex assessment is also included. Test results are typically displayed graphically. Equipment with multiple choices of probe-tones is currently available and can assist in further delineating middle ear function. Higher-frequency probe-tones, for example, can assist in detecting acoustic reflexes in the neonatal population (Berlin, 1987).

The proper placement of the probe tip will determine if the assessment of the infant's middle ear function is accurate. The infant's ear canal is cartilaginous and curved. If the probe tube is not placed correctly, erroneous measurements from the ear canal wall rather than the eardrum might be obtained.

An impedance measurement is based on the ability of the middle ear to act as a mechanical transducer by posing a certain resistance to vibratory motion in response to acoustic stimuli. The resistance is the algebraic sum of the mass, friction, and elasticity of the system (Sanders, 1975). When sound is presented at the tympanic membrane, some of it is transmitted and some reflected back into the external ear canal. The ratio of acceptance to rejection of sound depends on the total resistance of the middle ear. Stiffness, mass, or flaccidity in the middle ear system results in changes in impedance or, conversely, the compliance of the system. Classically, the impedance audiometry battery consists of three tests: tympanometry, static compliance, and acoustic reflex.

Tympanometry. Tympanometry is a measurement of the relative change in the compliance (mobility) of the middle ear system as air pressure is varied in the external ear canal. The tympanogram is the graphic display of the measurement and generally is classified in terms of depth, shape, and the middle ear pressure yielding greatest compliance. It is assumed that compliance is maximal when the air pressure in the external canal equals that in the middle ear. To obtain a tympanogram, the tympanic membrane is put into a position of known poor mobility, with an air pressure of +200 mm H_2O pumped into the external canal. As the positive air pressure is reduced gradually, and moves to –200 mm H_2O, changes in the compliance of the tympanic membrane are measured. More sound energy is transmitted into the middle ear as the compliance increases, resulting in a fall in the SPL of the external ear canal cavity. It is this fall in SPL that actually is measured by the electracoustic meter (Northern & Downs, 1991).

Jerger (1970) originally described three basic tympanogram types (Figure 13.6). Type A curves show a relatively sharp maximum at or near a middle ear pressure of 0 mm H_2O and are found in normal ears.

There is still some controversy about the range of normal middle ear pressures, but a value of +100 mm H_2O usually is considered within normal limits, as 95 percent of children with normal acoustic reflexes had pressures between 0 and 170 mm H_2O, with no evidence of any other abnormality (Brooks, 1978b; Hopkinson & Schramm, 1979; Sanders, 1975). Deciding on the normal limits depends largely on the actual clinical presentation and whether the test is being used for screening purposes, when lower values might be acceptable to avoid unnecessary medical referrals.

Two subtypes of Type A tympanogram have been identified (Northern & Downs, 1991). The first, Type A_S, is characterized by limited compliance with normal middle ear pressures. This type of tympanogram is seen routinely in infants and might also be seen in otosclerosis, thickened or scarred tympanic membranes, and

tympanosclerosis. The other extreme, Type A_D, demonstrates large changes in compliance with relatively small changes in middle ear pressure. This indicates an unusually flaccid tympanic membrane or disarticulation of the ossicular chain.

A Type B tympanogram is a relatively flat curve showing little change in compliance with changes in air pressure. Usually no point of maximum compliance can be demonstrated. Type B curves are seen in children with serous and adhesive otitis media as well as those with perforations of the tympanic membrane, ventilation tubes, or ear canals occluded with cerumen.

In Type C tympanograms, a relatively normal compliance is demonstrated but at a middle ear pressure of –200 mm H_2O or lower. The tympanic membrane is still mobile though there may be fluid in the middle ear. A Type C tympanogram typically is seen with poor eustachian tube function. The pathological significance of the Type C tympanogram, particularly in children, and its relation to the presence or absence of fluid in the middle ear has been questioned.

The probe-tone frequency utilized can influence results obtained. A 220 Hz tone, for example, which is most commonly used, can produce double-peaked tympanograms in infants (Berlin & Hood, 1987) whereas a 660 Hz tone elicits a single peak.

Static Compliance (Acoustic Impedance).   Static compliance, measured in cubic centimeters, represents a measurement of the compliance of the middle ear system in its resting state. It is the difference between the volume of the external canal space with the eardrum clamped at +200 mm H_2O pressure and that with the eardrum in its most compliant air pressure condition (Northern & Downs, 1991). The measurement of volume is based on the inverse relation of SPL to cavity volume size.

The static compliance values in adults are typically 0.4 to 1.3 cc, though infants may exhibit lower values, down to 0.2 cc. Although the test has limited diagnostic value when viewed in isolation, it can contribute to the diagnostic picture when considered in conjunction with the other impedance tests. It can also be quite useful when performed on different dates because serial measures could help in determining presence or absence of middle ear effusion. An offshoot of the static compliance is the physical volume test, which measures the volume from the probe tip to the eardrum. This is especially important in assessing whether surgically inserted ventilating tubes are patent (open) or if the eardrum is perforated. A small volume in the presence of ventilat-

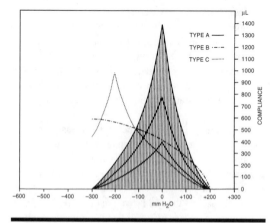

FIGURE 13.6   Classification of Tympanograms

Source: Information provided with permission from The Hospital for Sick Children, Toronto, Canada.

ing tubes would indicate blockage from malfunction of the ventilating tubes. A large volume in the presence of ventilating tubes indicates the tubes are patent and effective. A large volume in the absence of ventilating tubes can indicate a perforated eardrum.

Acoustic Reflex. Loud sound results in a bilateral and reflexive contraction of the stapedius muscle, thereby tightening the ossicular chain and temporarily increasing the impedance of the middle ear (Sanders, 1975). The acoustic reflex threshold is the lowest signal level capable of eliciting the reflex in the stimulated ear and ranges from 70 to 100 dBnHL for pure-tone signals (measured at 500, 1000, 2000, and 4000 Hz) and approximately 65 dBnHL for white noise (Northern & Downs, 1991). It is absent in the presence of middle ear fluid. In a study in which impedance audiometry was performed immediately before myringotomy for suspected serous otitis media, a single reflex measurement at 500, 1000, or 2000 Hz appeared to be as accurate an indicator of middle ear effusion as measurements at all test frequencies (Orchik, Morff, & Dunn, 1978). The reflex can be absent at 4000 Hz even when there is no objective evidence of any abnormality. Because the acoustic reflex is bilateral, both ipsilateral and contralateral reflexes can be recorded. Typically, the ipsilateral reflex is elicited and recorded in the same ear as the impedance probe. For measurement of the contralateral reflex a headphone delivers the signal to the opposite ear while the reflex is measured by the probe (Hayes & Jerger, 1978). The recording of this reflex can lead to confusion in terminology, and Jerger (1972) suggested that the test ear be defined as the ear to which sound is being delivered.

The stapedial reflex threshold has two major contributions to the assessment of hearing status in the pediatric population: the identification of a conductive hearing loss and the evaluation of a sensorineural hearing loss. The acoustic reflex is absent bilaterally in all conductive hearing losses greater than 30 dBnHL (Northern & Downs, 1991). For example, with a left-sided conductive loss greater than 30 dBnHL, when sound is introduced to the left ear, the conductive loss attenuates the signal loudness to such a degree that the ipsilateral reflex cannot be triggered. When the sound is presented conrtralaterally to the normal right ear, the probe tip in the left ear will not detect the contraction due to the inherent middle ear pathology (Jerger, 1970). Ipsilateral reflexes will be present in the normal ear. Acoustic reflex testing is important for children who cannot be tested behaviorally because some indication of the presence or absence of hearing is obtained. A general rule is that the presence of a reflex response normally means a hearing level of 80 dBnHL or better (Jerger, 1970). The absence of the stapedial reflex in the presence of otherwise normal middle ear measurements does not confirm the presence of a sensorineural hearing loss and must be considered in relation to all information obtained. For example, the excess activity of an infant during testing can mask the stapedial muscle contraction.

Each of the three tests in the impedance battery has its limitations, but when they are considered together various diagnostic information is obtained (Table 13.3). It should be remembered that impedance audiometry cannot evaluate sensorineural deficits in the presence of conductive hearing losses and must be used in combination with subjective hearing tests that are appropriate for

TABLE 13.3   Impedance Autometry in Clinical Evaluation

TYMPANOMETRY	IMPEDANCE	ACOUSTIC REFLEX	CONFIRMS BEHAVIORAL AUDIOMETRIC IMPRESSION OF
A in both ears	Normal in both ears	Normal bilaterally	Bilateral normal hearing Bilateral mild to moderate Sensorineural loss, or unilateral mild to moderate sensorineural loss
A in both ears	Normal in both ears	Absent bilaterally	Severe bilateral sensorineural loss
A in one ear, B or C in other ear	Normal in both ears B or C ear	Absent bilaterally	Unilateral conductive loss
B or C in both ears	High in both ears	Absent bilaterally	Bilateral conductive loss

the age of the child. Despite its limitations, impedance audiometry is now firmly established as an essential tool in assessing hearing impairment in infants and children.

Electrophysiological Measures

In the cooperative child, behavioral audiometry and impedance audiometry provide the most accurate assessment of hearing sensitivity, type of hearing impairment, and ability to understand speech. Unfortunately, in the younger child (birth to 2 years of age) behavioral and even impedance audiometry can be difficult or impossible to perform and results can be confusing or inconclusive. This is particularly true for multiply disabled, developmentally delayed, or autistic children. Consequently, the development of objective physiological measures to assess auditory function in otherwise difficult-to-test patients has filled an important diagnostic need (Riko, Hyde, & Alberti, 1985). Auditory evoked potentials were identified in the human electroencephalogram by Davis in 1939 (Glasscock, Jackson, & Josey, 1981). The development of averaging computer technology has enabled this procedure to be adapted for clinical use. Responses generally are divided, based on their latencies, into three groups: slow cortical responses (50 to 60 msec), middle responses (12 to 50 msec), and early responses (occurring within the first 10 msec). The early responses from the cochlea and brainstem pathways are most appropriate in the clinical assessment of infants and difficult-to-test children. These early responses, measured through electrocochleography and brainstem evoked response audiometry, are the most reliable in the pediatric population because they are the least affected by sedation (Jacobson, 1985).

Electrocochleography

Electrocochleography (Ecog.) is the measurement of the compound action potential from the auditory nerve. The best recordings are measured from the promontory in the middle ear using a small-gauge needle passed through the patient's eardrum. General anesthesia is necessary to complete this assessment in a pediatric population. Recordings can be obtained with the electrode attached to the wall of the external auditory canal but the results are not as easy to determine. Electrode placement is crucial and can be disturbed easily if the stimulator (headphone) is not carefully placed.

Test stimuli typically consist of clicks, and elicit a series of three waves (N1-N3), the largest being N1.

The response is typically from the basal end of the cochlea (Northern & Downs, 1991), and threshold of detectability usually approaches the behavioral threshold at or above 2000 Hz, whereas at 1000 Hz the threshold is 10 to 15 dBnHL above the behavioral threshold (Figure 13.7). A conductive hearing loss will result in elevation of the cochlear response but not alter the shape of the electrocochleogram. Sensorineural hearing loss will elicit changes in the electrocochleogram depending upon severity of the hearing loss. The more severe the hearing loss the greater the latency and the smaller the amplitude of the response. The advantages of electrocochleography are (1) information is obtained from each ear, (2) it is not affected by abnormalities in the auditory brainstem of the patient because the response is recorded from the auditory nerve, and (3) it is not affected by sedation or anesthesia. Disadvantages of electrocochleography which have limited its use as a clinical procedure, are (1) the invasive nature of this procedure (needle placement through the eardrum), (2) the need for general anesthesia in the pediatric population, and (3) the lack of information provided in frequencies below 1000 Hz. The advances in the auditory brainstem response procedure have addressed some of the disadvantages of electrocochleography, and ABR has largely supplanted use of electrocochleography.

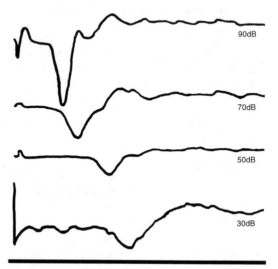

FIGURE 13.7 Electrocochleography Response at 90 dB to Threshold in a 6-Month-Old Infant

Source: Information provided with permission from The Hospital for Sick Children, Toronto, Canada.

Auditory Brainstem Response Audiometry

ABR assessment is a most useful electrophysiological response assessment for infants and young children (Alberti, Hyde, Riko, Corbin, & Abramovich, 1983). It can be performed noninvasively (electrodes are attached to the patient's vertex and mastoids, or ear lobes) and it is not affected by sedation or anesthesia. This is particularly important in assessing the difficult-to-test child who must be sedated to obtain information regarding his or her hearing. In many infants up to 8 months of age, ABR can be obtained with the infant in natural sleep, eliminating the need for sedation or anesthesia.

The auditory brainstem response (ABR) is the early evoked response with a latency between 1 and 10 msec. Stimuli used can include air-conduction and bone-conduction clicks, as well as more frequency-specific tone-bursts. An infant's brainstem response differs from the adult recording in morphology with three major waves typically represented, rather than the six or seven recorded in the adult population. Wave I has been accepted as representing the eighth nerve action potential. The subsequent waves are assumed to represent the combined electrical input of many centers along the auditory pathway, through the inferior colliculus in the upper auditory brainstem. The infant ABR varies from the adult recording in latency as well. Waveform latency is prolonged in children under 18 months but approximates adult values in children over this age. The latency of each of the three major waves and the interpeak latencies (I-III, III-V, I-V) in the ABR are useful diagnostically, but the presence of wave V is most useful for threshold determination. At loud intensities (70 to 90 dBnHL) the three waves are clearly recorded in the normal-hearing infant. Wave V usually occurs 6 to 9 msec following stimulus presentation and is the most consistent and reproducible response, remaining visible as the stimulus intensity is decreased to threshold (Figure 13.8). As threshold is approached, the waveform becomes smaller, and latency increases. When using tone-burst stimuli, the usual distinct waves are not observed, but rather broader, less distinct peaks are evident. Testing typically involves presenting stimuli initially at high levels, and decreasing the intensity until wave V is not visible.

The type of hearing loss, whether conductive or sensorineural, can be defined using ABR. A conductive hearing loss will delay the latencies of waves I, III, and V equally across the tracing. The interpeak latencies (I-III, I-V, III-V) will not change. A sensorineural hearing loss often results in normal latencies at higher intensities, which

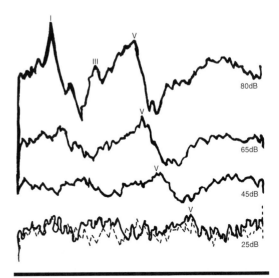

FIGURE 13.8 Brainstem Evoked Response Audiometry Response at 80 dB to Threshold in a 7-Month-Old Infant

Source: Information provided with permission from The Hospital for Sick Children, Toronto, Canada.

may increase as the intensity of the stimulus decreases. It is important to realize that neurological disorders affecting the brainstem and disrupting neural synchrony might result in a grossly abnormal or absent ABR recording in the presence of a normal-hearing ear. Thus, as with other auditory assessment techniques, ABR should be performed as part of a test battery and not in isolation.

Normal-hearing infants produce a brainstem evoked response to clicks 10 to 15 dB above their behavioral threshold in the 1500–4000 Hz range. Early clinical use of the ABR in assessing hearing utilized only a click stimulus for threshold definition because a rapid-onset stimulus is necessary to elicit the response. Hearing-impaired infants, though, can have hearing in the low-frequency range that will be undetected if only the mid- to high-frequency region is tested. The development of frequency-specific stimuli (filtered clicks and tone pips) has resulted in ABR information that can more closely quantify the pure-tone audiometric contour (Hyde, Riko, Corbin, Moroso, & Alberti, 1984). Other techniques such as brief tones in ipsilateral notched noise can also be employed (Stapells, 1994). Bone-conduction clicks can assist in determining the presence of a conductive element to a hearing loss.

An objective neurophysiological test cannot replace information obtained from standard pure-tone and speech tests. These subjective measures are the most reliable indicators of what the child "hears." The ABR monitors the functional integrity of the peripheral auditory system from the ear up to and including the brainstem auditory centers. How well the child is able to make use of the auditory information at higher processing centers and integrate this information in developing language is not evaluated with this test.

Otoacoustic Emissions

Since otoacoustic emissions were first described by Kemp (1978), their use in the assessment of hearing has been the focus of much research. Indeed, the National Institutes of Health Consensus Statement on Early Identification of Hearing Impairment in Infants and Young Children (1993) proposed screening infants via the use of evoked otoacoustic emissions, and research projects are underway to evaluate this technique for universal hearing screening (Bergman et al., 1995; White, Vohr, & Behrens, 1993). Otoacoustic emissions are low-intensity sounds, measurable in the external ear canal, which are generated by normal physiological activity in the cochlea. Produced by the outer hair cells, they are propagated outward through the middle ear and into the ear canal. A number of devices to measure these emissions are currently available and incorporate a sound delivery system, sensitive microphone to detect the emissions, and sophisticated signal processing system. The stimulus delivery and detection portion of the device is contained within a probe, which is introduced into the external auditory canal, similar to the probe utilized in impedance measurements.

There are several categories of otoacoustic emissions, which are classified by the type of stimuli, if any, used to elicit the response. Spontaneous otoacoustic emissions, as suggested by the name, require no stimulus and are present in about 40 percent of normal-hearing ears (Glattke & Kujawa, 1991). They are not commonly used for diagnostic purposes. Most common in the 1000–3000 Hz frequency range, they are present in all age groups, though this declines with ageing. They are not present when hearing loss exceeds 40 dBHL. Evoked otoacoustic emissions are of several types, with transient evoked and distortion-product emissions being of greatest interest clinically due to their usefulness in assessing cochlear function and, by inference, hearing sensitivity. Stimulus frequency emissions, which occur in response to long-duration pure-tones at the stimulus frequency, have not gained clinical popularity at this time.

Transient evoked otoacoustic emissions (Figure 13.9) were first described by Kemp (1978) and are elicited by a brief click stimulus. Time-averaging and amplification are used to record the cochlear response, which occurs over a wide frequency band, as does the stimulus. The emissions are present in virtually all normal-hearing ears but are absent for a particular frequency region when peripheral hearing loss in that area exceeds 35 dBHL (Gorga et. al., 1993). The procedure typically takes only a few minutes and is highly stable and noninvasive. The greatest challenge to the clinician is to keep the child quiet and still for the measurement. The magnitude of the emission is small, and clinical criteria for response typically involve a certain amplitude of response above the background noise floor. Transient evoked otoacoustic emissions are quite reproducible and effective at separating normal from impaired ears in the 2000–4000 Hz range and less so at 1000 Hz (Prieve et. al., 1993).

Distortion product otoacoustic emissions (Figure 13.10) also utilize the inherent nonlinearity of the cochlea in eliciting otoacoustic emissions. Rather than a click stimulus, two tones of similar but different frequencies (F1 and F2) are introduced into the ear canal simultaneously. The measured emission from the cochlea is at neither F1 nor F2 but rather a third frequency that is mathematically related to F1 and F2. The most commonly used frequency is at 2F1-F2, the geometric mean. Typically, a series of tone pairs is presented across a wide range of frequencies, so outer hair cell function can be assessed across the frequency range. The spectrum of a point of a distortion product emission is shown in Figure 13.11. The optimal intensity of F1 and F2 as well as the criteria for acceptable response intensity varies among clinics and is still under investigation (Hall, Baer, Chase, & Schwaber, 1994). Commonly used values are 3 or 6 dB above the noise floor, rather than absolute amplitude (Gorga et al., 1993). It appears that low-level stimuli in the 50–60 dB range are most useful for audiological evaluation (Bonfils & Avan, 1992) as responses to higher stimuli might reflect something other than outer hair cell function. Presence of distortion product otoacoustic emissions to low-level stimuli suggest, as do transient evoked otoacoustic emissions, good outer hair cell function, and by inference good hearing sensitivity. A hearing loss of greater than 35 dBHL can be ruled out by their presence.

A limitation of all forms of otoacoustic emissions testing is that a normally functioning middle ear is required for their detection. The low-intensity emissions

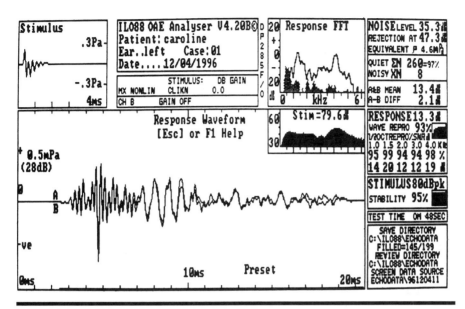

FIGURE 13.9 Normal Transient Evoked Otoacoustic Emission Recorded with IL088 System

Top left panel: Stimulus waveform. *Right side panels:* User settings for various parameters, information regarding response reproducibility and stimulus stability. *Large panel:* Response waveform. *Response FFT panel:* Shaded area represents noise; blank area under the line represents the otoacoustic emission, which is large relative to noise, especially in higher frequencies.

Source: Information provided with permission from The Hospital for Sick Children, Toronto, Canada.

are obliterated by middle ear effusion (Glattke & Kujawa, 1991). As well, movement or vocalizing on the part of the child will make recording the emissions impossible. Both distortion product and transient otoacoustic emissions do poorly at identifying low-frequency hearing loss at 500 Hz, transients better at 1000 Hz; both do well at 2000 Hz, and distortion product emissions are better than transients at 4000 Hz (Gorga et. al., 1993; Gorga et. al., 1993). Otoacoustic emissions are a very promising screening tool for hearing loss. Potential uses include neonatal screening, assessment of nonorganic hearing loss, monitoring of ototoxic drug effects, or assessing cochlear function in patients with abnormal brainstem response (Baldwin & Watkin, 1992). Though threshold determination is not yet possible with these measures, presence or absence of significant hearing loss can be assessed.

Central Auditory Dysfunction

The authors have been concerned, to this point, with assessing the integrity of the peripheral auditory appara-

tus, that is, from the outer ear to the termination of the acoustic nerve in the cochlear nucleus of the brainstem. For auditory stimuli to be meaningful, however, a complex auditory perceptual system to transmit, process, store, and retrieve the information provided by the peripheral mechanism is required. This perceptual system involves, as presented by Northern and Downs (1991), auditory discrimination (recognizing similarities or differences in sound), auditory association (relating an environmental sound to its source), auditory closure (filling in the missing parts of a message), auditory memory (recalling a sequence of auditory information), blending (forming words from separate sounds), binaural synthesis (combining auditory information from the two ears), binaural separation (ignoring input to one ear while listening with the other), and auditory figure–ground perception (discriminating relevant signals from background noise). The child with an auditory perceptual problem has difficulties organizing the auditory events in the environment so that they are meaningful.

Initially, it might be difficult to distinguish the child with central dysfunction who presents with delayed

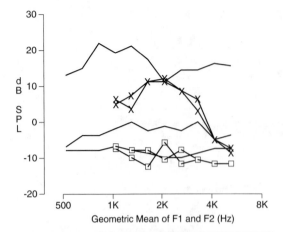

FIGURE 13.10   Normal Distortion Product Otoacoustic Emission Recorded with GSI60 System

Boxes represent the noise floor, and the solid lines are ± 2 SD of The Hospital for Sick Children clinical norms for adults. Xs indicate amplitude of emissions recorded from left ear across frequencies.

Source: Information provided with permission from The Hospital for Sick Children, Toronto, Canada.

demonstrates normal pure-tone thresholds but reduced discrimination scores, difficulty localizing sound, problems hearing in background noise or when several people are talking, inconsistent hearing, or difficulty in remembering and following directions (Flexer, 1994; Northern & Downs, 1991).

A detailed discussion of the tests currently available to assess central auditory dysfunction is beyond the scope of this chapter; however, the types of tests currently in use attempt to assess the various areas described previously. Many are heavily language based and, therefore, inappropriate for use with very young children, those with limited language and reading abilities, or those for whom English is not the first language. Strong maturational factors are also in play, so adequate normative data for different age groups must be provided. Determining the presence of central processing problems in the preschool population is difficult due to these language and normative issues; the Pediatric Speech Intelligibility Test (Jerger & Jerger, 1984) was formulated for use in this population, and electrophysiological tests at levels higher than the brainstem (middle and cortical responses) are under investigation as well. Preschool children show much variability in their performance on many central tests, making assessment difficult (Musiek & Chermak, 1994).

Central auditory dysfunction in the school-age child might be one aspect of a larger learning disability or behavioral disorder. Early detection and differentiation from a peripheral hearing loss and other language-learning problems is essential for appropriate habilitation and suitable placement in the classroom. Accurate diagnosis presents a considerable challenge in such a

language acquisition, poor oral expression, difficulty in responding to or remembering the sequence of oral instructions, or difficulty with sound localization from the child with a peripheral hearing deficit. Also, the problems are often attributed to immaturity, hyperactivity, behavioral disorders, or developmental delay. One should suspect central dysfunction in the child who

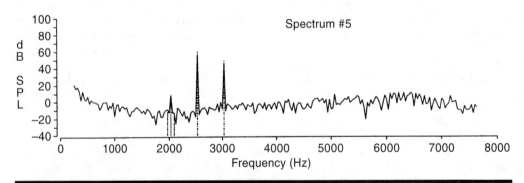

FIGURE 13.11   Spectrum of a Point of the Distortion Product Otoacoustic Emission

F1 (2531 Hz) and F2 (3031 Hz) are the two tallest vertical lines, whereas the distortion product otoacoustic emission occurs at 2031 Hz and is of lower amplitude above the noise floor.

Source: Information provided with permission from The Hospital for Sick Children, Toronto, Canada.

multifaceted condition and continues to be an area of considerable investigation. Speech-language and psycho-educational assessment is a crucial aspect in assessment of this population.

DIFFICULT-TO-TEST CHILDREN

The type of test used and the level of response expected depend on the child's cognitive development and the presence of other physical problems; nowhere is this more true than in evaluating the difficult-to-test child. With recent advances in audiological assessment, the definition of "difficult-to-test" has changed; what was difficult 30 years ago (i.e., any child under the age of 5 years) is now, as we have seen, routine. Uncomplicated peripheral hearing losses might be detected readily within the first few months of life, but accurate diagnosis of hearing impairment in the child with multiple disabilities might be significantly delayed because it is difficult to assess the contribution of each factor to the communication disorder.

Developmental Delay

An especially challenging population for the pediatric audiologist is assessment of children with developmental delay. This in itself does not decrease auditory acuity but children might seem to be hearing impaired because of the delay. The most important principle to remember in dealing with this group of children is that if developmental delay is the only problem, auditory behaviors exhibited will be commensurate with the developmental age. For example, the delayed 2-year-old may show the localizing responses of a 15-month-old and respond to warble-tones at 30 dBHL. If other developmental milestones are in the 15-month range, the audiogram is likely to reflect an age-appropriate response. If results from developmental assessments are not available, the audiologist must make an estimate based on observation and information supplied by the parent.

Children with Down syndrome have a high incidence of conductive hearing loss due to middle ear dysfunction (Kile, 1996). The use of impedance audiometry with this group, though crucial, can be misleading due to the stenotic ear canals often associated with this syndrome. Small ear canal volume readings can make determination of the presence of ventilating tubes or middle ear effusion problematic, though serial measures can assist in interpretation of test results. In sound field behavioral tests, care should be taken to allow the child adequate time to respond to the test stimuli. Due to glo-

bal delay, perception of the test stimulus and formulation of a response might require a longer time than for a normally functioning child.

Children with severe developmental delay can show a complete lack of response to the environment. With these children, a good startle response to 65 dB might be all that can be hoped for from subjective audiological assessment, though behavioral observation and impedance measures might also be most helpful. Children might also respond to recorded music, and although frequency-specific thresholds cannot be obtained in this manner, at least awareness of sound can be documented.

Cerebral Palsy

The difficulty of audiological testing in children with cerebral palsy is largely related to the extent of their physical impairment. Varying degrees of spasticity might prevent the child from performing the physical responses commonly associated with behavioral audiometry, such as turning to localize sound. Furthermore, the involuntary movements associated with athetosis can increase the difficulty of judging an actual response. The noise generated by excessive movement can easily be louder than some of the auditory stimuli.

Clinical assessment also can be complicated by visual abnormalities and/or developmental delay. The audiologist must take time at the beginning of the test period to determine the best way for the child to respond and then condition the response. Physical stress can influence the hearing threshold; when the stress is decreased (e.g., lying rather than sitting), hearing thresholds might improve. Ample time for response must be allowed in the testing procedure. Various forms of behavioral audiometry can be adapted for use with these children, and impedance and possibly electrophysiological response audiometry also can be used.

CNS Disorders

Prenatal or postnatal brain damage can result in disorders of auditory function that are accompanied by decreased threshold sensitivity. Northern and Downs (1991) made two basic assumptions in testing brain-damaged children: First, any reduction in auditory acuity is because of lesions peripheral to the cochlear nuclei; and, second, only in the child with the most severe CNS damage will all four basic auditory reflexes (startle, head-turn, eye-blink, and arousal from sleep) be completely absent. The child's level of behavior must be determined before attempting any formal testing. Tests of central auditory dysfunction already have been discussed; the concern here is with auditory thresholds in the presence of CNS damage.

Inconsistency of response is common in children with CNS damage. In dealing with these children, the audiologist must be adaptable and constantly ready to change the approach or test. If formal testing techniques cannot be used, the examiner must start at the lowest level of response, for the infant under 4 months. Even the demonstration of an unequivocal startle response to 65 dB provides useful clinical information. With severely brain-damaged children, cortical and brainstem evoked response audiometry might help in threshold determination; however, test results must be viewed with caution. Any disorder resulting in neural dysynchrony might yield abnormal ABR results in the presence of normal cochlear function. In these cases screening with otoacoustic emissions might prove most helpful in assessing peripheral auditory function because otoacoustic emissions are preneural in nature.

Blind-Deaf Children

Blind children attempt to localize sound normally at first; however, because of the lack of association and reinforcement, they might eventually stop turning toward the source of sounds and give the appearance of deafness. If they do, in fact, have significant auditory impairment, they might never develop natural orientation responses. Nevertheless, their remaining auditory reflexes can be utilized to advantage. When there is no language development, testing as recommended for infants should be completed. Even if a hearing loss appears unilateral, Northern and Downs (1991) firmly recommended a trial of binaural amplification to provide blind children with every possible binaural clue to enrich their auditory environment.

Emotionally Disturbed/Functionally Hearing Impaired

Hearing loss can coexist with conditions such as childhood schizophrenia, autism, and pervasive developmental delay. On the other hand, it is not uncommon for hearing loss itself to result in behavioral problems such as aggressiveness or withdrawal from external stimuli.

Autistic children are often completely withdrawn and lacking in communication skills, making conventional behavioral audiometry nonproductive. However, auditory reflexes cannot be suppressed and will be elicited in the presence of peripheral auditory function. In addition, observation of children while at play might provide some clue about their hearing; they might show an interest in some quiet sound while ignoring louder stimuli. Impedance measures, otoacoustic emissions, and evoked response audiometry, as objective measurements, can provide invaluable information about the hearing mechanism.

Though perhaps seen more frequently in the school-age population, young children do present with functional, or nonorganic, hearing loss. The child with a functional hearing loss can show a variety of symptoms such as exaggerated listening behaviors or inconsistent test results (either widely varying pure-tone thresholds, or speech reception thresholds much better than pure-tone average). Discrimination scores might be considerably better than one would expect given the apparent degree of hearing loss, or a child might communicate quite easily with the examiner while walking to the test suite, only to suddenly become "hearing impaired" once the headphones are on. An ascending test technique in measuring pure-tone thresholds can be useful when functional loss is suspected. Impedance measures, otoacoustic emissions, or evoked response audiometry can be utilized to verify clinical impressions. More frequently, accurate results can be obtained by reinstructing the child to respond even when the sounds are soft rather than waiting until they are easy to hear.

IMPLICATIONS OF HEARING IMPAIRMENT

An accurate, timely diagnosis of hearing impairment in the preschool child is essential so that habilitative audiological and educational measures, medical or surgical treatment, and/or genetic counseling can be provided when indicated. It also is extremely important to provide a training program for both child and parents to ensure that the child develops adequate communication skills. Because detailed discussion of treatment and habilitation of the hearing-impaired child is beyond the scope of this chapter, only the general philosophy of management is presented. Clearly, medical or surgical management must first be employed to reduce any conductive losses that might exist alone or in conjunction with a sensorineural impairment.

Educational Considerations

Hearing impairment already has been classified in various degrees from mild to profound based on the pure-tone threshold average of 500, 1000, and 2000 Hz. This classification is related to the child's ability to hear and comprehend speech and, therefore, has significant educational implications.

Children with a mild loss (20 to 40 dBHL) can expect to encounter difficulty hearing distant sounds or hearing in a noisy classroom situation, but their speech discrimination usually is normal. If the hearing loss is prelingual, there can be some delay in speech development. Preferential classroom seating might be required and, as the loss approaches 40 dB, the use of hearing aids and other assistive listening devices might be helpful.

A hearing loss of 40 to 55 dBHL can be classified as moderate. If the loss is prelingual, there are significant delays in speech and language development, usually in association with articulation problems. Special preschool training is necessary. Hearing aids are most beneficial to children in this category because their speech discrimination usually is good when amplification is used. Children with moderately severe losses of 55–70 dBHL also require hearing aids and an intensive preschool program for the development of language.

A severe congenital loss (70 to 90 dBHL) results in only rudimentary speech and language development unless special training is provided. A speech and language training program should be instituted as soon as the loss is identified and hearing aids fitted. However, because there is always a sensorineural component with any loss over 70 dB, diminished auditory discrimination can be expected even with hearing aids. Children with profound loss (>90 dBHL) do not develop speech and language without extensive special training. Hearing aids should be used but their value is often very limited, particularly in the child with no residual hearing above 1000 Hz, because of the extremely poor auditory discrimination (Hodgson, 1978; Kemker, 1975). An important consideration is that the hearing aids will provide awareness to acoustic signals in the child's environment, which can be important for safety reasons as well as the recognition that communicative events are occurring. Cochlear implants, which can provide more auditory input, are now frequently considered for this population, though other issues in addition to profound hearing impairment are considerations for candidacy for this device.

Northern and Downs (1991) list four goals for educating the deaf child: adequate language skills, sound mental health, intelligible speech, and the ability to communicate easily with peers. The main methods used to teach spoken communication to hearing-impaired children are auditory/verbal, auditory/oral, and total communication (Johnson, Benson, & Seaton, 1997).

The auditory/verbal method is unisensory, forcing the child to use only auditory clues. Intensive training by specialized teachers and parental involvement are essential. This method relies on the child's functional residual hearing as well as the benefit received from use of a hearing aid or cochlear implant.

The auditory/oral method relies on making the most of residual hearing as well but also stresses speechreading (lipreading) to assist the child in developing speech and language. Ability to speech-read varies widely, however, and many English sounds appear the same when articulated. As with the auditory/verbal method, a high degree of parental involvement is required.

Total communication utilizes all available means of communication: residual hearing, sign language, finger spelling, lipreading, facial expressions, and body language are all employed. The philosophy encourages communication via whatever avenues work, and parents are expected to learn the sign language being utilized so they are involved in the program as well.

A nonverbal language, American Sign Language (ASL) is another option deserving mention. ASL is distinct from English and is extensively used in the deaf community; indeed, it is viewed within the community as the natural language of the deaf. It requires that children have access to signing adults and that their family members learn sign as well. The philosophy is to ensure the child has a primary language available; English may be taught as a second language.

Each method has advantages and disadvantages and slavish adherence to any one is not recommended. Parents of hearing-impaired children are well advised to search out all available options, visit schools, and speak to other parents so they can make an informed decision on educational options. It is important that no matter what option is chosen, parents must reevaluate their child's progress periodically and make changes if adequate progress is not observed. There is no good way to determine which program will provide a child the greatest chance of success.

It must be remembered that the presence of a deaf child in the home can arouse feelings of rejection, guilt, or denial in the parents and places a significant strain on parents and siblings. Consequently, the parents should receive counseling, guidance, and teaching that are designed to increase their ability to provide their child with the necessary auditory and linguistic stimulation in the environment (Flexer, 1994).

Hearing-impaired children can receive their education in a normal classroom setting, in part- or full-time special classes for the hearing impaired in normal schools, or in a residential school for the deaf. The choice of educational facility depends on such obvious factors as the degree of hearing impairment, the age of onset, the language skills already developed, the type of previous communication training, the presence of other physical or mental disabilities, and the available resources. The educational goals of hearing-impaired children are not necessarily met by integrating them into an educational setting for which they are ill-equipped or ill-prepared. Every effort must be made to individualize training programs according to strengths and abilities.

Screening Programs

The establishment of a screening program for a given disorder must be based on the following criteria (Mauk & Behrens, 1993): The disease is serious and prevalent with accepted criteria for diagnosis, there are effective treatments available to ameliorate effects of the disorder, and there are demonstrated advantages to early intervention. There is no single acceptable method for routine screening of neonates. However, in recent years great emphasis has been placed on early identification of children at risk who might develop hearing impairment, screening programs for high-risk groups, and universal screening.

The Joint Committee on Infant Hearing was comprised of representatives from the fields of audiology, otolaryngology, pediatrics, and directors of state health and welfare agencies. The committee endorsed the concept of universal infant hearing screening in its 1994 position statement. Although recognizing the usefulness of high-risk factors, committee members recognized that their utilization resulted in detection of only 50 percent of children with hearing loss; other children with hearing loss were being diagnosed at unacceptably late ages. Detection of hearing loss by 3 months of age was recommended, and both ABR and otoacoustic emissions were endorsed as physiologic measures more sensitive than behavioral tests for very young infants. High-risk factors identified by the Joint Committee on Infant Hearing included, for neonates <29 days, positive family history for childhood sensorineural hearing loss, in utero infections associated with hearing loss, craniofacial anomalies, birth weight <1,500 g, hyperbilirubinemia requiring exchange transfusion, ototoxic medications, bacterial meningitis, Apgar scores <5 at one minute or <7 at five minutes, mechanical ventilation lasting five or more days, and stigmata associated with a syndrome known to involve hearing loss. Infants 29 days through 3 years who require monitoring of hearing include those with a positive family history of delayed onset sensorineural loss, in utero infections, neurofibromatosis type II or neurodegenerative disorders, recurrent otitis media with effusion, or disorders or anomalies affecting eustachian tube function. Other factors for infants and children 29 days through 3 years include caregiver concern regarding hearing, speech, language, or development; bacterial meningitis; head trauma; ototoxic medications; recurrent otitis media; and stigmata of syndromes associated with hearing loss.

SUMMARY

Childhood hearing impairment can cause delayed speech and language acquisition and academic difficulties, and problems in emotional and social adjustment. With improved health care and reduced infant mortality, the proportion of cases of congenital (and, therefore, prelingual) hearing impairment can be expected to increase. Hearing thresholds can be assessed through behavioral audiometry in children as young as 2 years of age and otoacoustic emissions and ABR provide objective means of identifying hearing impairment in children within the first few months of life. Screening programs should be undertaken for high-risk infants and indeed, considering the devastating effect of hearing loss, considerable attention is now given to universal screening for hearing impairment. Physicians and parents must remain alert to problems that suggest hearing loss. A delay in diagnosis until the child enters school cannot be justified and can have profound adverse effects. No child is too young for audiological assessment to begin, and assessment should be arranged when any suspicions exist regarding hearing loss.

REFERENCES

Alberti, P. A., Hyde, M. L., Riko, K., Corbin, H., & Abramovich, S. (1983). An evaluation of BERA for hearing screening in high-risk neonates. *Laryngoscope 93*, 1115–1121.

Baldwin, M., & Watkin, P. (1992). The clinical application of oto-acoustic emissions in paediatric audiological assessment. *Journal of Laryngology and Otology, 106*, 301–306.

Baxter, J. D., & Ling, D. (1974). Ear disease and hearing loss among the Eskimo population of the Baffin Zone. *Canadian Journal of Otolaryngologia 3,* 110–122.

Bench, R. J. (1992). *Communication skills in hearing impaired children.* San Diego, CA: Singular Publishing Group.

Bergman, B., Gorga, M., Neely, S., Kaminski, J., Beauchaine, K., & Peters, J. (1995). Preliminary descriptions of transient-evoked and distortion-product otoacoustic emissions from graduates of an intensive care nursery. *Journal of the American Academy of Audiology, 6,* 150–162.

Bergstrom, L. (1977). Viruses that deafen. In F. H. Bess (Ed.), *Childhood deafness: Causation, assessment and management* (pp. 53–68). New York: Grune & Stratton.

Berlin, C. I., & Hood, L. J. (1987). Auditory brainstem response and middle ear assessment in children. In F. N. Martin (Ed.), *Hearing disorders in children.* (pp. 151–184). Austin, TX: Pro-Ed.

Berry, M. F. (1969). *Language disorders of children: The bases and diagnoses.* New York: Appleton-Century-Crofts.

Bess, F. H., Schwartz, D. M., & Redfield, N. P. (1986). Audiometric impedance, and otoscopic findings in children with cleft palates. *Archives of Otolaryngology, 102,* 465–469.

Bluestone, C. D. (1978). Prevalence and pathogenesis of the ear disease and hearing loss. In M. D. Graham (Ed.), *Cleft palate middle disease and hearing loss* (pp. 27–55). Springfield, IL: Thomas.

Bonfils, P., & Avan, P. (1992). Distortion-product otoacoustic emissions: Values for clinical use. *Archives of Otolaryngology, Head and Neck Surgery, 118,* 1069–1076.

Boyle, C. A., Decoufle, P., & Yeargin-Allsop, M. (1994). Prevalence and health impact of developmental disabilities in U.S. children. *Pediatrics, 93,* 399–403.

Brooks, D. N. (1978a). Evaluation of "hard-to-test" children and adults. In S. Singh & J. Lynch (Eds), *Diagnostic procedures in hearing, language and speech* (pp. 105–137). Baltimore: University Park Press.

Brooks, D. N. (1978b). Impedance screening for school children: State of the art. In E. R. Harford, F. H. Bess, & C. D. Bluestone (Eds.), Impedance Screening for Middle Ear Disease in Children, Proceedings of a Symposium held in Nashville, Tennessee, June 20–22, (pp. 172–180). New York: Grune & Stratton.

Catlin, F. I. (1978). Etiology and pathology of hearing loss in children. In F. N. Martin (Ed.), *Pediatric Audiology* (pp. 3–34). Englewood Cliffs, NJ: Prentice-Hall.

Cremers, C. W. R. J., van Rijn, P. M., & Huygen, P. L. M. (1994). The sex-ratio in childhood deafness, an analysis of the male predominance. *International Journal of Pediatrica Otorhinolaryngology, 30,* 105–110.

Dahle, A. J., McCollister, F. P., Stagno, S., Reynolds, D. W., & Hoffman, H. E. (1979). Progressive hearing impairment in children with congenital cytomegalovirus infection. *Journal of Speech and Hearing Disorders, 44,* 220–229.

Davidson, J., Hyde, M. L., & Alberti, P. W. (1988). Epidemiology of hearing impairment in childhood. *Scandinavian Audiology Supplementum, 30,* 13–20.

Davis, A., & Wood, S. (1992). The epidemiology of childhood hearing impairment: Factors relevant to planning of services. *British Journal of Audiology, 26,* 77–90.

Eliachar, L. (1978). Audiologic manifestations in otitis media. *Otolaryngologic Clinics of North America, 11,* 769–776.

English, G. M., Northern, J. L., & Fria, T. J. (1973). Chronic otitis media as a cause of sensorineural hearing loss. *Archives of Otolaryngology, 98,* 18–22.

Epstein, A. (1978). Speech audiometry. *Otolaryngologic Clinics of North America, 11,* 667–676.

Flexer, C. A. (1994). *Facilitating hearing and listening in young children.* San Diego, CA: Singular Publishing Group.

Fortnum, H., & Davis, A. (1993). Hearing impairment in children after bacterial meningitis: Incidence and resource implications. *British Journal of Audiology, 27,* 43–52.

Glasscock, M., Jackson, C. G., & Josey, A. (1981). *Brainstem electric response audiometry.* New York: Thieme-Stratton.

Glattke, T. J., & Kujawa, S. G. (1991). Otoacoustic emissions. *American Journal of Audiology, 1,* 29–40.

Gorga, M. P., Neely, S. T., Bergman, B. M., Beauchaine, K. L., Kaminski, J. R., Peters, J., Schulte, L., & Jesteadt, W. (1993). A comparison of transient-evoked and distortion-product otoacoustic emissions in normal-hearing and hearing-impaired subjects. *Journal of the Acoustical Society of America, 94,* 2639–2648.

Gorga, M. P., Neely, S. T., Bergman, B. M., Beauchaine, K. L., Kaminski, J. R., Peters, J., & Jesteadt, W. (1993). Otoacoustic emissions from normal-hearing and hearing-impaired subjects: Distortion product responses. *Journal of the Acoustical Society of America, 94,* 2050–2060.

Hall, J. W., Baer, J. E., Chase, P. A., & Schwaber, M. K. (1994). Clinical application of otoacoustic emissions: What do we know about factors influencing measurement and analysis? *Otolaryngology—Head and Neck Surgery, 110,* 22–38.

Hayes, D., & Jerger, J. (1978). Impedance audiometry in otologic diagnosis. *Otolaryngologic Clinics of North America, 11,* 759–767.

Herrgard, E., Martikainen, A., & Heinonen, K. (1995). Hearing loss at the age of 5 years of children born preterm—a matter of definition. *Acta Paediatrica, 84,* 1160–1164.

Hicks, T., Fowler, K., Richardson, M., Dahle, A., Adams, L., & Pass, R. (1993). Congenital cytomegalovirus infection and neonatal auditory screening. *Journal of Pediatrics, 123,* 779–782.

Hodgson, W. R. (1978). Disorders of hearing. In P. H. Skinner & R. L. Shelton (Eds.), *Speech, language, and hearing: Normal processes and disorders* (pp. 316–349). Reading, MA: Addison-Wesley.

Holm, V. A., & Kunze, L. H. (1969). Effect of chronic otitis media on language and speech development. *Pediatrics, 43,* 833–839.

Hopkinson, N. T., & Schramm, V. L. (1979). Preschool otolagic and audiologic screening. *Otolaryngology and Head and Neck Surgery, 87,* 246–257.

Hyde, M. L., Riko, K., Corbin, H., Moroso, M., & Alberti, P. W. (1984). A neonatal hearing screening research program using brainstem electric response audiometry. *Otolaryngology, 13,* 49–54.

Jacobson, J. T. (1985). An overview of the auditory brainstem response. In J. T. Jacobson (Ed.), *The auditory brainstem response.* San Diego, CA: College-Hill Press.

Jerger, J. (1970). Clinical experience with impedance audiometry. *Archives of Otolaryngology, 92,* 311–324.

Jerger, J. F. (1972). Suggested nomenclature for impedance audiometry. *Archives of Otolaryngology, 96,* 1–3.

Jerger, S., & Jerger, J. (1984). *Pediatric speech intelligibility test: Manual for administration.* St. Louis, MO: Auditech.

Johnson, C. D., Benson, P. V., & Seaton, J. B. (1997). *Educational audiology handbook.* San Diego, CA: Singular Publishing Group.

Joint Committee on Infant Hearing. (1995). American Academy of Pediatrics: Joint Committee on Infant Hearing 1994 Position Statement. *Pediatrics, 95,* 152–156.

Kaplan, G. J., Fleshman, J. K., Bender, T. R., Baum, C., & Clark, P. S. (1973). Long-term effects of otitis media: A ten-year cohort study of Alaskan Eskimo children. *Pediatrics, 62,* 577–585.

Kemker, F. J. (1975). Classifications of auditory impairment. *Otolaryngologic Clinics of North America, 8,* 3–17.

Kemp, D. T. (1978). Stimulated acoustic emissions from within the human auditory system. *Journal of the Acoustical Society of America, 64,* 1386–1391.

Kessner, D. M., Snow, C. K., & Singer, J. (1974). *Assessment of medical care for children: Contrasts in health status.* Vol. 3. Washington, DC: Institute of Medicine, National Academy of Sciences.

Kile, J. E. (1996). Audiologic assessment of children with Down syndrome. *American Journal of Audiology, 5,* 44–52.

Klein, J. O., Teele, D. W., & Pelton, S. I. (1992). New concepts in otitis media: Results of investigations of the Greater Boston Otitis Media study group. *Advances in Pediatrics, 39,* 127–156.

Konigsmark, B. W., & Gorlin, R. J. (1976). *Genetic and metabolic deafness.* Philadelphia: Saunders.

Lillywhite, H. (1958). Doctor's manual of speech disorders. *Journal of the American Medical Association, 167,* 850–858.

Lloyd. L. L.. & Cox, B. P. (1975). Behavioral audiometry with children. *Otolaryngologic Clinics of North America, 8,* 89–107.

Mace, A. L., Wallace, K-L., Whan, M. Q., & Steimachowicz, P. G. (1991). Relevant factors in the identification of hearing loss. *Ear and Hearing, 12*(4), 287–293.

Matkin, N. D. (1986). In J. F. Kavanagh (Ed.), *Otitis media and child development* (pp. 3–11). Parkton, MD: York Press.

Mauk, G. W., & Behrens, T. R. (1993). Historical, political, and technological context associated with early identification of hearing loss. *Seminars in Hearing, 14,* 1–17.

Millar, W. J., Stachan, J., & Wadhera, S. (1991). Trends in low birth weight in Canada 1971 to 1989. *Health Reports, 3–4,* 311–325.

Musiek, F. E., & Chermak, G. D. (1994). Three commonly asked questions about central auditory processing disorders: Assessment. *American Journal of Audiology, 3,* 23–27.

Nadol, J. B., Jr. (1978). Hearing loss as a sequela of meningitis. *Laryngoscope, 88,* 739–755.

National Institutes of Health. (1993). Early identification of hearing impairment in infants and young children: Consensus development conference on early identification of hearing impairment in infants and young children.

Ng, E., & Wilkins, R. (1994). Maternal demographic characteristics and rates of low birth weight in Canada, 1961–1990. *Health Reports, 6,* 241–252.

Northern, J. L., & Downs, M. P. (1991). *Hearing in children* (4th ed.). Baltimore: Williams & Wilkins.

Orchik, D. J., Morff, R., & Dunn, J. W. (1978). Impedance audiometry in serous otitis media. *Archives of Otolaryngology, 104,* 409–412.

Parving, A., & Hauch, A. (1994). The causes of profound hearing impairment in a school for the deaf—A longitudinal study. *British Journal of Audiology, 28,* 63–69.

Price, L. L. (1978). Pure tone audiometry. In D. E. Rose (Ed.), *Audiological assessment* (2nd ed., pp. 189–226). Englewood Cliffs, NJ: Prentice-Hall.

Prieve, B. A., Gorga, M. P., Schmidt, A., Neely, S., Peters, J., Schultes, L., & Jestead, W. (1993). Analysis of transient-evoked otoacoustic emissions in normal hearing and hearing impaired ears. *Journal of the Acoustical Society of America, 93,* 3308–3319.

Reich, P. A. (1986). *Language development.* Englewood Cliffs, NJ: Prentice-Hall.

Riko, K., Hyde, M. L., & Alberti, P. W. (1985). Hearing assessment in early infancy: Incidence, detection and assessment. *Laryngoscope, 95,* 135–144.

Roberts, M. E. (1976). Comparative study of pure-tone, impedance, and otoscopic hearing screening methods: A survey of native Indian children in British Columbia. *Archives of Otolaryngology, 102,* 690–694.

Ross, M., & Lerman, J. (1970). A picture identification test for hearing-impaired children. *Journal of Speech and Hearing Research, 13,* 44–53.

Roizen, N. J., Wolters, C., Nicol, T. & Blondis, T. A. (1993). Hearing loss in children with Down syndrome. *Journal of Pediatrics, 123,* S9–S12.

Rynnel-Dagoo, B., Linberg, K., Bagger-Sjöbäck, D., & Larson, O. (1992). Middle ear disease in cleft palate children at three years of age. *International Journal of Pediatric Otorhinolaryngology, 23,* 201–209.

Sanders, J. W. (1975). Impedance measurement. *Otolaryngologic Clinics of North America, 8,* 109–124.

Schein, J. D., & Elk, M. T., Jr., (1974). *The deaf population of the United States.* Silver Spring, MD: National Association of the Deaf.

Shah, C. P., Dale, M. A., & Chandler, D. (1977). The challenge of hearing impairments in children. *Canadian Family Physicians, 23,* 175–183.

Shepherd, D. C. (1978). Pediatric audiology. In D. E. Rose (Ed.), *Audiological assessment* (2nd ed., pp. 261–300). Englewood Cliffs, NJ: Prentice-Hall.

Sheridan, M. D. (1968). *The developmental process of infants and young children* (2nd ed.). London: Her Majesty's Stationery Office.

Skinner, M. W. (1978). The hearing of speech during language acquisition. *Otolaryngologic Clinics of North America, 11,* 631–650.

Skinner, M. W. (1988). *Hearing aid evaluation.* Englewood Cliffs, NJ: Prentice-Hall.

Stapells, D. R. (1994). Low-frequency hearing and the auditory brainstem response. *American Journal of Audiology, 3,* 11–13.

Stein, L. J., & Boyer, K. M. (1994). Progress in the prevention of hearing loss in infants. *Ear and Hearing, 15,* 116–125.

Stewart, I. F. (1977). Newborn infant hearing screening—A five-year pilot project. *Journal of Otolaryngology, 6,* 477–481.

Strong, C. J., Clark, T. C., & Walden, B. F. (1994). The relationship between hearing loss severity to demographic, age, treatment and intervention effectiveness variables. *Ear and Hearing, 15,* 126–137.

Todd, N. W. (1994). At-risk populations for hearing impairment in infants and young children. *International Journal of Pediatric Otorhinolaryngology 29,* 11–21.

White, K. R., Vohr, B. R., & Behrens, T. R. (1993). Universal newborn hearing screening using transient evoked otoacoustic emissions: Results of the Rhode Island hearing assessment project. *Seminars in Hearing, 14,* 18–29.

Wilson, W. R., & Thompson, G. (1984). Behavior audiometry. In J. Jerger (Ed.), *Pediatric audiology* (pp. 1–44). San Diego, CA: College-Hill Press.

Wong, D., & Shah, C. P. (1979). Identification of impaired hearing in early childhood. *Canadian Medical Association Journal, 121,* 529–546.

Zinkus, P. W., Gottlief, M. I., & Schapiro, M. (1978). Development and psychoeducational chronic otitis media. *American Journal of Diseases of Children, 132,* 1100–1104.

CHAPTER 14

ASSESSING MULTICULTURAL PRESCHOOL CHILDREN

ANDRÉS BARONA
MARYANN SANTOS DE BARONA

The need for appropriate evaluation of culturally different preschool children continues to increase. This need is a result of two major developments in the United States. The first development was federal involvement in education in the 1960s and 1970s that resulted in legislation affecting preschool and school-age children. The 1964 Maternal Child Health and Mental Retardation Act and the 1964 Educational Opportunity Act required that educational and social opportunities be provided for all children, while Public Law 94-142 mandated that a free and appropriate education be provided to children with disabilities from the age of 3 (Kelley & Surbeck, 1983). Later legislation in the form of Public Law 94-457 and the Individuals with Disabilities Act (IDEA; P.L. 102-119) further authorized special education and related services to eligible preschool children. Federally funded educational programs designed to implement the terms of these acts were required to implement performance-based evaluations to demonstrate that participating children improve in the areas of achievement, intelligence, or other measurable dimensions (Kelley & Surbeck, 1983). Appropriate preschool assessment instruments, therefore, became necessary not only to determine eligibility but also to measure and demonstrate gains in the specified areas.

The second development that creates an increased need for assessment of culturally different preschoolers is the population shift occurring in the United States. The rate of growth in the number of children has increased since 1990, and in 1996 children under age 18 constituted almost 24 percent of the total U.S. population (Federal Interagency Forum on Child and Family Services [FIFCFS], 1997). This proportion of young children in the population is expected to increase steadily over the next 25 years. Currently, approximately 66 percent of the U.S. population can be considered to be white and non-

Hispanic and it is projected that this percentage will be reduced to 55 percent by the year 2020 (FIFCFS, 1997). Thus, it can be seen that the number of persons from minority cultures in this country is sizable and growing. The increase in the minority population is perhaps most evident when examining the statistics of school-age and younger children: Whereas only about 7.9 percent of the total U.S. population is under 5 years of age, for Hispanics the percentage is 11.8 (U.S. Census, 1994).

By definition, a culturally different child is one who comes "from an ethnic group having sociocultural patterns that differ from those of the predominant society. These groups include Blacks, Hispanic-Americans, American Indians, and Asian-Americans" (Sattler, 1992, p. 592). A child of preschool age who is a member of a culturally different family might share few common experiences with age peers of the dominant American culture. For this young age group, it is expected that the family will be the primary socializing influence because preschool programs reach only about 34 percent of the total population (U.S. Census, 1997), with white children enrolled in nursery schools at a rate twice that of Hispanic children (U.S. Department of Commerce and Management Planning Research Associates, Inc., 1992; cited in Prince & Lawrence, 1993).

The values, behaviors, experiences, and attitudes of these culturally different families vary significantly from those of the typical acculturated middle-class family. These differences can be highlighted by contrasting two cultures' perceptions of giftedness. In mainstream America, a gifted middle-class child is commonly thought to demonstrate high achievement or potential in general intellectual ability, or academic, creative, or psychomotor aptitude (EAC West, 1996; Marland, 1972). In American subcultures, this perspective can vary dramatically. The results of at least one study (Bernal,

1974) indicate that the traits of obedience, common sense, responsibility, respectfulness, independence, self-reliance, and the ability to influence others were emphasized as much as the trait of intelligence when Mexican Americans identified gifted children. From this example, it can be seen that not only do experiences differ for preschool children of different cultures but that certain abilities and characteristics not commonly recognized by U.S. society as reflective of outstanding talent are likely to be selectively reinforced among U.S. minority cultures. In support of this, Hartley (1991, cited in EAC West, 1996) suggests that Navajo traits such as not being competitive or assertive and not asking questions or challenging incorrect statements make identification of gifted and talented Navajo children difficult.

Similarly, cultural differences can affect the way learning occurs as well as what information is learned. Evidence suggests that individuals of different cultures will recall and understand those aspects of a lesson that are most relevant to their own culture. In a cross-cultural study of reading comprehension (Steffensen, Joag-Dev, & Anderson, 1979), American and Indian students read passages describing weddings in both cultures. Members of each culture recalled more information related to the wedding within their own culture. In addition, each culture focused on different aspects of the passages: Americans emphasized the romantic, whereas Indians highlighted the monetary exchange between families. Results of these studies suggest that culturally different students might need assistance in learning information with which they have had little or no prior experience (Fradd, 1987b).

Many individuals from culturally different groups often come from linguistically different backgrounds, specifically non-English-language backgrounds. Approximately 14 percent of children in the United States between 5 and 17 years old speak a language other than English at home, and it is estimated that this proportion may be higher for children younger than 5 years because school may be their first formal encounter with English (Prince & Lawrence, 1993). Although the majority of non-English speakers (i.e., 54 percent) speak Spanish as their primary language, many other languages also are represented (U.S. Census, 1990).

Young children who speak a language other than English as their primary language have the potential to develop academic problems if placed in monolingual English classes upon school entry. Their lack of exposure to the English language greatly increases the probability that they will not understand much of the information that is being communicated to them. Unable to process information provided in English and unaware of what is being said to them, Limited English Proficient (LEP) children can easily become inattentive and distractible. Such behaviors may lead school personnel to conclude that these young children lack school readiness because they do not demonstrate the type of attention span, motivation, or maturity desired and expected in mainstream U.S. school settings. These children can be considered to be at risk for learning academic content such as reading, writing, and arithmetic, as well as for knowing what behaviors are expected in their new, unfamiliar, and structured environment (Bryen & Gallagher, 1983).

It also is suggested that LEP preschool children might experience additional difficulties with the way in which information is conveyed in group situations. Whereas parents of young children often use repetition, emphasis, and the context of the physical environment to assist the child in learning new words, classroom teachers often interact with the entire group and are unable to use repetitive and context-based clues (Bryen & Gallagher, 1983). Information also can be conveyed in more abstract forms. Unfortunately, preschoolers of limited English proficiency are largely unable to benefit fully from these approaches until their English skills are better developed. Instead, they often must rely on the aid of the physical context or the actions of their peers to understand and produce language. Without these aids, learning and possibly behavior problems will occur.

As one might imagine, defining normal development and behavior, as well as being able to identify mild learning problems in young children, is a difficult task given the rapid and variable rate of development among preschool children. For some children, the acquisition rate of cognitive and motor skills is sudden: One moment the skill is not observable while the next it is clearly present. For other children, skill acquisition is a gradual process. Definition of normal development and behavior is even more difficult when a culturally different or LEP preschool child is involved; school personnel often are unaware that aspects of school readiness may be strongly influenced by culture (Prince & Lawrence, 1993), with different ethnicities varying in their rates of development in or emphasis on specific areas (Prince, 1992).

THE PURPOSES OF ASSESSMENT

Assessment of the preschool child serves several purposes. First, assessment can be used to screen children for potential learning problems by a normative comparison to same-age peers. This technique quantifies differences between individuals by describing the child's performance in light of the average performance of a relevant comparison group. Second, it can be diagnostically useful to determine if deficiencies exist in any one of a number of areas. Preschool assessment can measure competencies in either developmental areas or readiness skills (McLoughlin & Lewis, 1986; Paget & Nagle, 1986). Criterion-referenced measures also can be included here, with scores on such measures interpreted relative to an established standard of performance. Finally, assessment can be used to monitor progress that is the result of an intervention (Garber & Slater, 1983). Generally, assessment can be viewed as a means of confirming or denying the presence of a problem for an individual. During the assessment process, information is obtained that specifies the individual's level of functioning and identifies areas of strength and weakness. This information then is used to make intervention decisions to facilitate the development of that individual.

THE PROBLEMS OF ASSESSMENT

Problems Related to the Preschool Child

Obtaining the appropriate information with which to make decisions to assist in further development is likely to be a challenge when preschool children are tested. Generally, preschoolers' social behaviors are not conducive to psychoeducational assessments: Preschool children often follow their own impulses and may be unaccepting of the constraints of the testing situation (Bagnato & Neisworth, 1991; Bondurant-Utz & Luciano, 1994; Gelman, 1979; Ulrey, 1981). Young children often express their feelings easily and can be quite uninterested in their own performance. In addition, test performance can be affected by biological drives such as the need to nap or rest, and behavior can vary significantly over short periods of time. Thus, the examiner needs special skills and understanding to work with the preschooler. Patience and creativity are essential and it is necessary to be both positive and confident in interactions with the child. Finally, the examiner must be able to modify the assessment to accommodate any changes in a child's behavior. These requirements generally represent a departure from the more traditional methods followed for school-age children (Bagnato & Neisworth, 1991; Paget, 1983; Romero, 1992).

Problems Related to Differences in Culture

In the most ideal circumstances, assessment is a complicated process. It is made even more complex when the in-

dividual to be evaluated is from a culturally diverse or limited English-speaking background (Barona & Santos de Barona, 1987). When the unique age-related problems inherent to testing preschool children are added, it becomes crucial to conduct an assessment with even greater care given to both accuracy and an awareness of those social, cultural, and linguistic factors that can influence test performance because "unrecognized diversity...can generate behaviors that interfere with learning and mimic those generated by disabilities" (Barrera, 1995, p. 54).

The culturally different preschooler can differ from a mainstream American peer on a number of important dimensions. If from an economically disadvantaged environment, the minority child might be less attentive and less persistent on tasks because of differences in the demand characteristics between home and school (Garber & Slater, 1983) and, therefore, less likely to do well on tasks with an academic orientation. Solutions to social intervention problems can be both more limited in variety and more aggressive (Spivack & Shure, 1976). It should be noted, however, that when provided with learning environments that reinforced more appropriate learning styles, improvements in reflection and in problem-solving strategies were noted (Garber, 1977; Slater & Heber, 1979; Spivack & Shure, 1976).

Expressive skills and style of interaction with an adult also can differ among culturally different preschoolers (McLaughlin, Gesi Blanchard, & Osanai, 1995). Vocabulary for preschoolers revolves around their experiences. To the extent that a culturally different child has experienced significantly different events from either the mainstream American child or from what the assessment materials cover, that child might be unable to respond in the same manner as his or her peers who have had more exposure with the general subject matter.

Even more significant are the differences in styles of interaction that exist among children of varying cultures. Early social development for Asian Americans and Native Americans differs from the mainstream (Prince, 1992). Furthermore, in some cultures it is considered impolite and even challenging for eye contact to be maintained between a child and an adult, for a child to contradict an adult or to express an opinion that might differ, or to speak to an adult unless spoken to directly. A well-mannered Vietnamese child, for instance, will speak only when spoken to. As a result, voluntary responses in a classroom might be interpreted as showing off or even rude. Respect is shown by sitting quietly and listening attentively. Much can be communicated non-verbally: Thankfulness or apology can be conveyed with silence or a smile. Indeed, within the Vietnamese culture, a verbal expression of thanks would reflect a lack of modesty (Huynh, 1987). In a similar vein, preschool Chinese children frequently are passive participants in a classroom setting and do not compete with other children (Garber & Slater, 1983). After completing a task, they rarely proceed automatically to other work (Tikunoff, 1987). A teacher or evaluator unfamiliar with such cultural characteristics might, unfortunately, conclude that a child who demonstrates any of the preceding characteristics is dull, sullen, unmotivated, or even developmentally delayed.

In still another culture, eye contact has very different connotations than in U.S. society. Unlike American parents and teachers, who when scolding a child might say, "Look at me when I speak to you," Hispanic adults would interpret sustained direct eye contact as an act of defiance. This cultural characteristic holds throughout life. Prolonged eye contact between adolescent or even adult males in the Hispanic culture can lead to fighting because it is read as a challenge. An often-used phrase among adolescent Mexican males is "soy o me paresco?" or "is it me—or do I look like him?" with the implication being "is it me that you are looking for (to fight) or do I just look like him?"

Related to this issue is an important point: Individuals must not be lumped together because of apparent physical similarities. For example, it must be recognized that great diversity in cultural patterns and values exists among Asian cultures. Whereas the parameters of social situations are carefully defined within Cambodian society (Chhim, 1987), Lao adults avoid overt guidance. Rather, Lao children learn through observation and modeling (Khamchong, 1987). A lack of awareness of such variations between cultures, that to many Americans appear strikingly similar because of physical similarities, again can result in erroneous conclusions about the culturally different child.

In the preschool assessment situation in particular these differences may require special intervention or the selection of alternative assessment procedures to maximize the usefulness of the obtained information. Such procedures may supplement or if necessary replace more formal or traditional approaches. The process of assessment of multicultural preschool children has the potential for error or problems in a number of arenas and requires considerable skill, sensitivity, and collaboration. We briefly discuss specific areas that may be problematic and of which evaluators should make special note.

Test Administration Style/Examiner Approach.   It has been suggested that when a culturally different child is assessed, the examiner might need to initiate conversation or even prod the child to respond (Cummins, 1980). Strategies such as the alternation of test items (Zigler & Butterfield, 1968) or the location of the assessment (Silverman, 1971) have had significant and positive effects on test performance. It also is possible that the style and tempo of the examination might need to be modified. The examiner might need to adopt a more facilitative style. As the situation demands, the examiner might need to become more nurturing, affectionate, soft-spoken, directive, "laid back," or reserved. Thus, it is extremely important that the examiner be both aware of basic styles of interaction considered appropriate to the specific child's background and be equipped with a variety of strategies to get the child to demonstrate skill and knowledge.

Language.   Assessing language development issues in a nondiscriminatory manner may pose particular difficulty in light of the scarcity of bilingual professionals qualified to perform assessments and the lack of appropriate assessment tools for both established and less well-established minority populations (Hernandez, 1994). In particular, it is necessary to determine if a child's communication difficulties are due to limited English skills, the process of second language acquisition, or a communication disorder that requires special education intervention (Hernandez, 1994). Young children with linguistic differences are at risk of communication, social, and academic problems (Leung, 1990). Limited proficiency only in English is not sufficient cause for a referral to special education. Age-appropriate skills in the home language indicates that language learning abilities are not compromised. With the exception of stuttering, a language disorder will not be specific to only one language but will be present across languages (Barrera, 1995). Thus, language skills must be evaluated in both English and the child's native language (Dodd, Nelson & Spint, 1995; Hernandez, 1994), and it cannot be assumed that limited proficiency in English means that the child is proficient in the native home language. Limited comprehension in both English and the child's home language may indicate true communication disorder, especially if the confounding effects of chronic poverty or trauma are ruled out (Barrera, 1995).

Making this determination, however, may be a difficult task. First, those involved in the evaluation process should be skilled in the child's primary language and also should be aware of language development milestones and patterns. Second, although it may be relatively easy to identify language problems in monolingual preschool children (Dodd, Nelson, & Spint, 1995), the task becomes increasingly complex when there are skills in both languages. Language development is in a continuous state of flux and is highly dependent on the continuity and richness of a child's language environment. Children developing bilingually may lag four to five months behind children developing monolingually because of the increased complexity of the learning process (Swain, 1972). In addition, the rate of second language acquisition "can vary considerably, depending on factors such as age, strength of native language skills, amount of exposure to the second language, attitude, and language aptitude (Prince & Lawrence, 1993, p. 8). Complicating this issue is the possibility that very young children who are learning English as a second language may lose the ability to speak and understand their home language (Wong-Fillmore, 1992).

Knowledge of social, linguistic, and cultural differences is vital for the appropriate interpretation of test results. Knowledge of such differences alone, however, will not ensure a valid assessment. It is necessary to be aware of the limitations of many of the commonly used assessment instruments as well as the issues and controversies surrounding assessment (Bracken, 1987).

Problems Related to Traditional Assessment Methods and Instruments

As is widely known, much criticism has been leveled at the area of the use of traditional assessment instruments with minority populations. One criticism has been that traditional methods of assessment have made little allowance for cultural differences. Methods that incorporate standardized administration procedures limit the amount and nature of interaction between child and examiner. These methods also permit only a narrow repertoire of acceptable responses, many of which can be completely unknown to a child of a U.S. subculture. Because such a child might respond to an examiner or to the testing situation in a nontraditional way, information related to the child's knowledge base and/or ability level might not be adequately demonstrated. Much of the material in traditional standardized tests is geared primarily toward white, middle-class homes and values (Reynolds & Clark, 1983). Indeed, it is quite likely that an examiner in a nontraditional standardized assessment situation would make erroneous conclusions about a culturally different child's level of functioning and cognitive or educational strengths and weaknesses, when in reality a lack of exposure to pertinent stimuli might be the reason for poor performance.

Although in the past many traditional assessment instruments included standardization samples in which many culturally different groups were underrepresented, this problem largely has been eliminated in recent tests. A review of new and recently revised intelligence tests for preschool children (Flanagan & Alfonso, 1995) indicated that the standardization samples of five frequently used norm-referenced tests, namely Wechsler Preschool and Primary Scales of Intelligence—Revised (WPPSI-R; Wechsler, 1989), Differential Ability Scales (DAS; Elliott, 1990), Stanford-Binet: Fourth Edition (S-B:IV; Thorndike, Hagen, & Sattler, 1986), Woodcock-Johnson Tests of Cognitive Ability—Revised (WJ-R; Woodcock & Mather, 1989, 1990), and Bayley Scales of Infant Development-II (BSID-II; Bayley, 1993), all closely matched population estimates based on U.S. census data and were rated as adequate or good.

Traditional assessment methods also have been plagued with an inability to uniformly predict outcomes for children from diverse backgrounds. Traditional measures typically are most accurate in prediction when white, middle-class children are involved, but are generally unacceptable in their level of predictive ability for minority children (Reynolds & Clark, 1983). Thus, diagnosis and long-range planning are hampered when children from U.S. subcultures are involved.

The tests might not measure the same underlying constructs for all children (Bracken, Barona, Bauermeister, Howell, Poggioli, & Puente, 1990). As an example, the factor structure of one popular test of intelligence for school-age children was found to differ for white, black, and Hispanic children (Santos de Barona, 1981) and it has been hypothesized that using intelligence tests with minorities might measure only the degree of acculturation (Mercer, 1979) rather than level of ability. Similarly, constructs can be measured differently at different ages within the same instrument (Bracken, 1985), thus further limiting the ability to validly interpret test results.

One of the major criticisms aimed at the assessment of *all* preschool children involves limitations in the reliability and validity of the available assessment instruments (Ulrey, 1981), particularly the ability of these measures to satisfactorily evaluate, diagnose, and classify children between the ages of 3 and 5 years. These concerns continue for most of the new and recently revised instruments (Flanagan & Alfonso, 1995) despite the fact that the technical adequacy of these measures has improved and they are superior to "preschool measures that measure language, behavior, and social-emotional functioning" (Flanagan & Alfonso, 1995, p. 86). Indeed, evaluators of preschool children reported that early intelligence tests did not successfully determine eligibility for services 43 percent of the time (Bagnato & Neisworth, 1994). Some differences have been noted, however, by the targeted ages of the instruments and by the level of ability of the young child. Infant assessment instruments such as the original Bayley Scales of Infant Development (Bayley, 1969) or the Apgar Scale (Apgar, 1953) are poor predictors of intelligence and neurological dysfunction, respectively (Thurman & Widerstrom, 1985). Such infant scales are considered to be limited in their ability to estimate future levels of functioning. An exception to this, however, is when low-functioning children are assessed for intelligence; in this case, measured IQs tend to remain relatively stable (Brooks-Gunn & Lewis, 1983; Goodman & Cameron, 1978; Keogh, 1970; Lewis, 1976; McCall, Appelbaum, & Hogarty, 1973; Sattler, 1992; Share, Koch, Webb, & Graliker, 1964).

Preschool tests appear to fare better in their ability to predict future outcomes than do infant tests. The increased predictive accuracy of the preschool tests appears in part to be a function of item content; whereas infant tests are limited largely to perceptual-motor tasks, preschool measures contain items better able to tap the cognitive domain (Sattler, 1992). However, stability of test scores and prediction of future academic performance also appear related to the age at which the initial assessment occurs (Bayley, 1969; McCall, Hogarty, & Hurlburt, 1972; Sattler, 1992). IQs obtained before age 5 must be interpreted cautiously (McCall et al., 1973) because "many of the indicators of later learning difficulties and behavior problems simply are not measurable before the age of 6" (Ulrey, 1981, p. 486).

Although numerous screening, diagnostic, and prescriptive measures that target the preschool population exist, many are unacceptable because of their poor psychometric characteristics (Arffa, Rider, & Cummings, 1984; Bracken, 1987; Rubin, Balow, Dorle, & Rosen, 1978). Test results might lack utility for numerous reasons. First, instruments that utilize norms for comparison purposes might be unacceptable because standardization samples are inadequate in overall size or are unrepresentative of the population for which they are used. For example, many developmental scales developed before 1986 were normed on white, middle-class populations (Garber & Slater, 1983) and, therefore, provide little valid data for interpretation among diverse populations. At the very least, the standardization sample should include a sampling of variables such as age, sex, ethnicity, SES, and geographic region in adequate numbers so that interpretation of test results can occur along these dimensions.

Second, the test might not be able to predict equally well for individuals of all ethnic, socioeconomic, or ability groups. The content of test items might favor a particular group or groups through disproportionate representation of a group, stereotyping, or the use of concepts or materials that are more familiar to some groups than others (Wiersma & Jurs, 1985).

Third, insufficient technical information might be provided, making it difficult to determine a test's utility and soundness; moreover, reliability and validity studies might not have been conducted or might be limited in scope. Reliability refers to consistency of measurement and might take several forms. Test-retest reliability studies, which examine the consistency of measurement or stability of a construct across time (Wiersma & Jurs, 1985), might be difficult to conduct given the rapid rate of development that occurs at the preschool level. Such studies would need to determine a retest period that would reduce the probability of practice effects as well as the likelihood that any change in scores really is because of the child's acquisition of knowledge and skills (Goldman, L'Engle Stein, & Guerry, 1983). Indeed, Flanagan and Alfonso (1995) point out that some test manuals report test-retest information for individuals who were not preschoolers or provide interpretive information useful only to older preschoolers. Equivalence reliability, which involves the consistency of measurement across parallel test forms and can involve a measure of internal consistency (Wiersma & Jurs, 1985), can be obtained in an easier manner (see Bracken, 1987 for suggested technical standards).

A fourth criticism is the fact that many assessment measures fail to provide enough specificity to enable useful decision making regarding service delivery or educational programming. As a result, areas of deficit might not receive adequate prescriptive attention. These limitations have resulted in some reluctance to refer children for formal evaluation to avoid problems caused by premature labeling or possible misclassification. Because labeling or classification can create a negative and lasting stigma, many professionals have avoided assessment at early ages to avoid the negative consequences that occur as a result of this process. This concern has been tempered somewhat by Public Law 99-457, which permits young children with special needs to be served with the general classification of *developmental delay*. In addition, federal guidelines also permit an *at-risk* classification, although it is unclear how many states actually use this option.

Finally, early intelligence tests have been criticized for failing to accommodate a child's response limitations and requiring that specific responses to narrowly defined tasks be demonstrated in an unfamiliar setting (Bagnato & Neisworth, 1994).

A PROCESS FOR THE ASSESSMENT OF CULTURALLY DIFFERENT PRESCHOOL CHILDREN

The complexity involved in the assessment of culturally different children makes it necessary to devote a great deal of time to the assessment process. Traditionally, evaluation has taken a client-centered approach in which data are collected through the use of standardized instruments and observations made in the testing situation. Although the rationale for this approach is valid and ample evidence supports this notion of testing, the approach has a number of shortcomings when culturally different preschool children are involved. A number of areas require close attention and monitoring to ensure that a clear understanding of the child emerges; these areas generally extend the limits of the traditional assessment.

When traditional standardized instruments are used in isolation for culturally different preschoolers, the possibility for confounding test results is great. The unique characteristics of the preschool period, which often is marked by uneven development and growth spurts, combined with the effects of cultural variations in style of interaction, language issues, and problems associated with the assessment instruments create significant difficulties when interpreting rest results. This development-culture-instrument interaction in preschool assessment makes it difficult to determine if test findings are attributable to cultural, language, environmental, developmental, or measurement factors.

What is needed, therefore, are additional methods to obtain valid information about the culturally different preschooler. These methods should provide the opportunity to systematically assess areas of strength and deficit without fear of immediate classification. Thus, the assessment of the culturally different preschooler must allow for sufficient interaction with the child so that conclusions regarding the child's capacity to learn are arrived at with confidence. This strategy should allow for adequate time to identify the relevant factors in the child's learning style as well as effective teaching strategies for that child.

In recent years considerable attention has been given to alternative methods of assessing preschool children. In particular, it has been widely acknowledged that no one assessment method or instrument is appropriate for every child (Bracken, 1994). Rather, it is necessary to identify the unique concerns related to the child and then determine the information that is necessary to address these concerns. Once this information is specified, there should be an awareness of the limitations of the information to be obtained along with how the information can be used to plan appropriate interventions (Gyurke, 1994).

Evaluation of the culturally different preschooler should utilize a team approach that includes *at least one member knowledgeable about the child's language and culture*. Parents and family members should be involved from the outset and the model used in evaluation should permit maximum input from them as well as from a variety of assessment professionals. Both the interdisciplinary model, which involves parents as partners on the team yet utilizes separate assessment by team members, and the transdisciplinary model, in which team members and parents work actively together with the child in arena-style assessments (Bagnato & Neisworth, 1991; Bondurant-Utz & Luciano, 1994) are appropriate.

What follows is a suggested process for the assessment of culturally different preschool children. This method uses a number of strategies to obtain comprehensive information about the child.

Preassessment Data

Information obtained prior to the actual assessment is extremely important. Federal guidelines mandate parental involvement in the evaluation and prescriptive process. Parental input is particularly critical for the culturally different preschooler because the child's experiences often occur almost exclusively within the family environment. Thus, it is important for the parents not only to communicate basic birth, medical, and developmental information but also to provide their perspective on their child's functioning within the family milieu. More specifically, parents should be asked to provide impressions on how the child's skills and behavior compare to other children in the family and community.

Although it is possible to obtain this information through written questionnaires, parent interviews are preferred for the following reasons. First, written communication may be difficult in English or the home language and, therefore, information provided may be minimal. Relatedly, the formality of responding on paper may be threatening and overwhelming for a parent with minimal education or poor writing skills. Second, the interview provides an opportunity to begin to build a relationship of trust between parents and team members, to orient the parents and family members to the evaluation process and their critical role within it, and to empower them to become participants in the process. Finally, contact with the parents provides the evaluator(s)/team with critical information regarding parental awareness of their child's functioning, skill in navigating the frequently complex assessment and referral system, degree of financial/economic risk, available support system, degree of acculturation, and other resources. Such information can assist the evaluating team in determining the family's ability to participate in aspects of their child's intervention as well as the degree of assistance the family will need in such activities; indeed, the selection of particular intervention strategies may depend on the types of information obtained through the interview.

The interview should explore in depth the reasons for referring the child for evaluation. Parental concerns about the child, the evaluation process, and its potential consequences regarding further education should be discussed and clarified. Other referral agents, if applicable, also should be contacted for information. Information gathered during this phase should be comprehensive and include language, motor, and social developmental histories. Medical information and data from day care or preschool settings, if available, also are important. In addition, information related to the family composition, status within the community, and level of acculturation can add significantly to a more complete understanding of the culturally different child.

This information should be compiled to develop an evaluation plan that will identify the types of data to be collected, the individual(s) responsible for obtaining data, and the settings in which the various assessment components will take place. The assessment should be planned to be developmentally and culturally appropriate and consider "the unique cultural aspects that affect how children learn and relate to other people" (McLaughlin et al., 1995, p. 6). Although it is expected that norm-referenced measures may be administered, the degree to which such measures can be validly administered and the results determined to be useful will vary according to the child's language and other skills. Generally, the less acculturated and English proficient, the less valuable information from norm-referenced measures will be. Rather, it is probable that evaluation will be ecological and will identify critical environmental settings and performance expectations as well as the child's ability to function according to expectations within those settings (Lowenthal, 1991). Indeed, the value of ecological assessments for preschool children is being increasingly recognized (Bagnato & Neisworth, 1994).

Language Assessment

Language assessment must be a major focus in the evaluation of culturally different children. Potential or ongoing problems related to limited English proficiency must be separated from either language disorders or slow development, so that appropriate planning and intervention can occur. This can be difficult unless the evaluator is both skilled in the assessment of language and a proficient speaker of the relevant language.

The purpose of this language assessment "is not merely to determine whether the child can communicate well enough to be tested in English but rather to determine the actual levels of skill and fluency in each language spoken and the role that language may play in potential learning problems" (Barona & Santos de Barona, 1987, p. 194). Bilingual development is a complex process that is dependent on the degree to which a child is exposed to and has the opportunity and motivation to use a second language. A child who hears both languages from birth will develop language skills differently from a child who learns a second language after the first has been established. A child learning two languages simultaneously will proceed linguistically in a developmental pattern similar to monolingual speakers, although there may be a slower rate of vocabulary development. A child who establishes skills in one language and then proceeds to learn a second will progress through four distinct developmental stages that include a nonverbal period in which the child begins to crack the code of the second language (McLaughlin et al., 1995). "Because developmentally children may be losing aspects of their first language as the second language is acquired, their performance on tests of language proficiency may be misleading...even though a bilingual child's performance in either language may lag behind that of monolingual speakers of the language in some point of development, the child may actually possess a total vocabulary and total linguistic repertory that is quite similar to that of monolingual speakers" (McLaughlin et al., 1995, p. 5). Because vocabulary often is used as an indicator of cognitive functioning (Lidz & Peña, 1996), it is important to recognize varying language development patterns and avoid erroneous interpretation.

In addition to determining home language and the degree, if any, to which the child has been exposed to English, it is necessary to assess language structure and the child's ability to make functional use of language (Barona & Santos de Barona, 1987). Vocabulary, comprehension, and syntax should be examined within both receptive and expressive aspects of language, and children should be given the opportunity to demonstrate their language skills if necessary in a nonstandardized manner (McLaughlin et al., 1995). Rather than use a formal language instrument, an alternative technique such as the California Early Language Assessment Process may be appropriate because of its emphasis on ongoing observations and data collection. This process emphasizes exploring how children use language over pronunciation, grammar, and vocabulary. Specifically, assessing the child's ability to use language to express feelings and ideas, ask for help, provide information, solve problems, and gain attention will provide valuable insight into the level of language skills as well as direction for future development.

Language assessment should enable a decision regarding the language or languages with which to conduct the remainder of the assessment. Generally, clear dominance in one language would lead to assessment in that language. However, frequently dominance is not clearly established and in these instances evaluation in both English and the home language is recommended to ensure that an adequate sampling of abilities is obtained (Barona & Santos de Barona, 1987).

When concerns about language skills exist, it may be advisable to select a cognitive assessment instrument that will permit nonverbal assessment. Such instruments include the Leiter International Performance Scale [LEITER-R (Roid & Miller, 1997)] and the Universal Nonverbal Intelligence Test (Bracken & McCallum, 1998); in addition, the K-ABC (Kaufman & Kaufman, 1983) and the DAS (Elliott, 1990) contain nonverbal scales.

In the event that a child cannot be evaluated in English, a number of important questions must be addressed. First, a decision must be made as to whether the child should be evaluated only in the home language or if a combination of English and the home language should be used. Often, a monolingual evaluation, even if it is in the home language, is not appropriate because the language familiar to the child is actually a combination of the home language and English. Second, it must be determined if a translated version of the test is available in the child's language. If so, technical information related to the translation should be examined and a determination of the adequacy of its psychometric properties should be made. In particular, attention should be paid to whether norms exist for the translated version as well as to the specific composition of the standardization sample. In addition, some attention should be paid to whether the test is a direct translation of English and if it allows for dialectical differences. Exact equivalents of English concepts might not exist and the difficulty level of both concepts and test items can change in the translation. Also, within the same language, it is possible that multiple acceptable answers can exist depending on the child's region of origin (Barona & Santos de Barona, 1987; Bracken et al., 1990; Bracken & Fouad, 1987; Wilen & Sweeting, 1986).

If a formal translation of the desired test is not available, it might be necessary to create one for the local area. Such a translation should be developed carefully prior to the actual testing session. Standardized procedures should be established for use by all evaluation personnel. Both the translation and the procedures should be reviewed by several proficient speakers of the language to ensure the most accurate translation possible (Bracken & Fouad, 1987; Wilen & Sweeting, 1986).

In the event that a bilingual evaluator is not available, it might be necessary to use an interpreter not related to the child who is fluent in standard English and the home language, and who has had some formal education. This interpreter should receive training in such general aspects of the assessment process as establishing rapport, using standardized test administration procedures, objective observation, and the precise recording of verbal and nonverbal behaviors during the assessment process (Wilen & Sweeting, 1986).

Finally, it should be clearly understood that the primary goal is the collection of useful information for decision making and planning. Thus, flexibility and creativity are essential regardless of the techniques used.

The Traditional Assessment

A number of reviews of various standardized instruments already have been written (Bracken, 1985; McLoughlin & Lewis, 1986; Schakel, 1986) and that information will not be reiterated here. Rather, the purpose of this section is to provide some guidelines for using information derived from such instruments.

Although to this point only the problems associated with standardized assessment instruments have been dealt with as they pertain to culturally different individuals, it must be recognized that standardized instruments do have a useful function. Standardized instruments provide a systematic way to collect data about the child in various domains. Even though the value of specific test items might not be equivalent because of the problems of representation and exposure that have been discussed earlier, the fact that the test was administered under relatively uniform conditions creates some basis for comparison as well as a means with which to judge interactive styles.

When a culturally different child is involved, results of standardized intelligence tests should *not* be used as an absolute index of cognitive functioning. Rather, such results should be viewed as a general estimate of the child's *current level of measurable functioning* in which information has been obtained about the level and types of skills and knowledge that the child has demonstrated relative to other children. As such, it should serve as a marker from which to begin to build for further assessment, if needed, or for making educational recommendations. Depending on the child's unique characteristics, it is possible that a standardized test administration will not be appropriate.

The results of assessment with standardized instruments should provide crucial information regarding the culturally different preschooler. Based on the assessment, the examiner should determine the *relative level of functioning* and whether either overall test performance or specific responses might be related to factors other than ability or achievement. The examiner should have a sense of the validity of test results by evaluating the degree to which the child invested energy and effort in the evaluation tasks. The examiner also should determine how well the child appeared to understand the language in which the assessment was conducted and whether language appeared to affect test results as well as the ability to perform specific tasks.

During this phase, the examiner must bring together all data gathered in earlier stages and evaluate test findings with those data in mind. For example, if a child appeared to attend more when test items were communicated in the home language than in English, the examiner might conclude that the distractibility was primarily because of a language factor. Similarly, a newly immigrated Vietnamese child would not be expected to engage in elaborate or animated verbal interactions in any language. An examiner who encountered such a child would need to conduct an additional investigation to determine why the child was not behaving in the manner expected. Thus, the traditional assessment phase should serve as a forum in which information about the child is integrated, hypotheses are generated and explored, and strategies for either educational recommendation or further assessment are developed.

Diagnostic Placement

Following assessment with traditional standardized instruments and alternative procedures, a decision might be made that insufficient information exists with which to make recommendations about the child. There might be several possible reasons for this realization. First, language, developmental, or cultural factors can appear to have influenced the standardized test results. As noted earlier, normal preschool behavior, such as distractibility, easy fatigue, shyness, and difficulties in separating from mother, lack of familiarity with or inability to successfully work with a specific cultural interaction style, or concern over language involvement can raise questions as to the reliability of test findings. Second, the examiner might feel that the assessment procedures just did not provide an adequate arena in which to sample the child's repertoire of skills and knowledge. It also is possible that more information is needed concerning the way in which the child learns to get clearer ideas regarding future planning for the child.

To avoid the constraints and pitfalls of both cultural and developmental variables and yet obtain useful information, it is necessary that culturally different children be sufficiently acclimated to and comfortable within the assessment setting. To accomplish this goal, it is suggested that the child first undergo a diagnostic placement, particularly if the child has not been enrolled in a preschool program. This consists of an already established preschool enrichment program in which children of various ethnic and cultural backgrounds are cared for on a daily basis and in which bilingual/bicultural personnel are available to assist children with communication needs. This setting ideally should serve a high proportion of children with apparently normal development who can facilitate socialization and model appropriate behavior, as well as provide an informal means of comparison. Such a program can provide, within a nurturing atmosphere, age-appropriate activities geared toward facilitating the child's growth in motor, social, and cognitive areas. As part of its curriculum, mediated learning experiences (Feuerstein, 1979) can be incorporated in which emphasis is on encouraging children to explore a variety of ways to obtain information and solve problems in all dimensions of development and in which the child's progress in accomplishing these tasks can be monitored and measured. Such procedures have been found to provide insight into learning and language functioning for non-English dominant preschoolers and preschoolers with disabilities (Lidz & Peña, 1996; Missiuna & Samuels, 1989).

It is expected that the child's involvement in a diagnostic placement setting will last for an extended period, ranging from three to six months. During this time, the child should be encouraged to participate in activities, and opportunities for appropriate social interactions should be provided.

This diagnostic placement can serve several purposes. For those children who demonstrated difficulty in separation from a significant adult, the routine of daily attendance will accustom the child to interaction with a number of adults. Assessments, when performed, will be less emotionally charged and will occur in an environment with which the child is familiar, resulting in increased responsiveness and attention to task.

While in attendance, the child will come to view learning activities and the presentation of new information as a regular part of the daily routine. The actual measurement of skills, learning styles, and progress often can be accomplished either unobtrusively or with minimal fanfare.

Participation in an ongoing diagnostic setting has a number of advantages. It provides personnel with the opportunity to observe the child in group situations and to assess preferential language and learning styles as well as effective teaching strategies over time. In addition, social adjustment can be monitored because preschool teacher–pupil ratios are relatively small and it is possible to have a greater awareness of the child's overall personality and needs.

Diagnostic placement also permits an assessment of the effects of culture because in many cases an enrichment facility will have children in attendance of both same and different cultures as well as some personnel with similar language skills. The rate with which the child acquires new skills and concepts can be measured and monitored throughout the child's attendance and personnel can identify effective reinforcing conditions to provide the child. Diagnostic placement assessment also will permit a judgment as to the amount of effort that will be needed to work successfully with one child, relative to other children in the center.

Several methods of assessment can be used in this setting to obtain other useful information. These include observations, criterion-referenced tests, and dynamic assessment techniques. *Observations* of the child can assist in assessing social skills and in describing patterns of behavior and styles of interaction in both individual and group settings. Knowledge of information that can facilitate the culturally different child's attending to tasks and responding is extremely useful in the design of effective teaching strategies. For example, if an examiner in the traditional phase of assessment had difficulty getting a culturally different child to invest in the evaluation, one goal of observation might be to determine if the preschooler interacts differently with the adults in the diagnostic setting. If interaction is limited only to adults of similar culture, or if the child has established rapport with some other subset of adults, then goals can be set to broaden the child's interaction patterns. Similarly, it also would be useful to observe the child's interactions with other children and to determine those conditions under which such interactions occur: information related to whether the child interacts only with a particular child or group of children, whether most interactions occur during free play or in structured activities, how the child communicated with others in the diagnostic placement setting, and the nature of the interactions that do occur are all helpful in identifying relevant factors in instructional programming.

Criterion-referenced testing measures "the performance levels of examinees in relation to a set of well-defined objective competencies" (Hambleton, 1982, p. 352). Whereas norm-referenced measures generally allow comparisons among examinees, criterion-referenced measures do not make comparisons among examinees or groups as a primary purpose. Rather, criterion-referenced tests describe what a child specifically knows or can do and, therefore, are useful when planning additional instructional activities.

For example, an examiner might have noted in the standardized assessment that a preschooler had difficulty following directions communicated in either the home language or in English and as a result performed poorly on a number of tasks. During the diagnostic placement, a criterion-referenced measure focusing on basic readiness skills indicated that the child was deficient in demonstrating knowledge of directional concepts such as *through, beside, beneath, right, left,* and so on, and in addition had difficulty remembering and executing directions consisting of more than two parts. Remedial planning for this child, therefore, would involve two components. First, the child would receive direct training in directional concepts. Second, a number of strategies could be interspersed throughout the day in a variety of formal and informal situations to facilitate the child's memory, ability to follow directions, and use of the newly acquired directional concepts.

Dynamic assessment (Feuerstein, 1979) modifies traditional assessment practice in three ways. First, the nature of the interaction between examiner and examinee is shifted from one in which the examiner is neutral and adheres to a standardized script to one in which the examiner assumes the role of teacher and provides mediated learning experiences. In this role, the examiner-turned-teacher intervenes, provides advance organizers and explanations for problems and activities, summarizes experiences, and interjects insightful and clarifying remarks whenever and wherever necessary. Second, training is considered an important part of the assessment and the child is provided not only the principles, skills, and techniques to accomplish a task but also the opportunity to apply these functions to novel tasks. Finally, dynamic assessment results are not interpreted within a product modality in which emphasis is on *what* is known, but rather the results are viewed from a process orientation in which *how* learning occurs is considered important. In this final phase, both unique responses and strategies toward learning are examined to provide direction for both remediation and further education.

Using a test-train-retest paradigm (Sattler, 1992), the child's ability to perform specific tasks and/or solve particular problems first is measured with unfamiliar stimuli. After the initial testing is conducted, the child is taught to solve the task through a variety of methods aimed at helping the child develop appropriate problem-solving strategies. Upon completion of the training phase, the child is again tested on either the original task or on one of its alternate forms.

Contrary to traditional assessment in which the goal is to determine how much and what is known, the dynamic assessment or process-oriented approach seeks to determine the degree to which cognitive structures can be modified, the amount and type of teaching effort that is needed to bring about such modification, the areas of functioning that require intervention to produce the desired effects, as well as identify the child's preferential

learning strategies. Thus, in the course of the total assessment, data related to the rate of acquisition of strategies, skills, and concepts, as well as the generalizability of these strategies, are obtained through interaction with the child and systematic observation (Feuerstein, 1979; Feuerstein, Rand, Haywood, Hoffman, & Jensen, undated; Sattler, 1992).

Although process-oriented techniques for preschool children are in a relatively early stage of development, they "offer the potential of more accurate and less discriminatory diagnostic information, more relevant to an educational or treatment setting than norm-referenced assessment" (Lidz, 1983, p. 60). Although there does not yet exist a well-developed or widely accepted standardized dynamic preschool measure (Lidz, 1983), at least one technique (Brown & Ferrara, 1985) has been suggested to be useful for children from a variety of cultures. This technique involves giving children "a set of increasingly explicit hints toward solution of a problem until they are able to solve it" (Schakel, 1986, p. 109). Furthermore, the use of mediated learning experiences also shows promise with language-minority children (Lidz & Peña, 1996).

Diagnostic assessment placement should continue until assessment and program personnel conclude that sufficient information has been obtained with which to make a set of educational recommendations about the child. At that time, a meeting should be convened of all program personnel who have been involved in aspects of assessment, including the parents and appropriate school and/or agency representatives. During this meeting, all data obtained throughout the assessment process should be thoroughly reviewed and recommendations for the most appropriate way to meet the child's educational needs should be generated. For those children for whom an ongoing education placement is suggested, an individualized education plan specifying those areas requiring remediation should be developed. In addition, the placement setting should be specified. It should be noted that it is entirely possible that a placement recommendation would be to continue participation in the preschool enrichment program in which the diagnostic placement occurred. In such cases, emphasis would shift from assessment to teaching.

SUMMARY

The process of assessing culturally different preschool children is complex. The problems associated with working with young children including: relatively little exposure to U.S. culture, vastly different ways of interacting with adults, and measurement instruments with a limited degree of psychometric soundness cause considerable concern regarding the degree of confidence with which test results can be interpreted, as well as the implications for instructional planning. Assessment of the culturally different preschooler, therefore, must be approached with a great deal of care and with sufficient opportunity to obtain accurate and relevant information.

A suggested procedure for assessment expands the standard assessment process. First, *preassessment data* should go beyond the typical social, medical, and developmental data generally obtained and should include relevant information from all significant individuals involved with the child. Information regarding the family's assimilation into U.S. society is crucial. Second, in-depth investigation of the child's communicative competence must occur. This should include determining the language or combination of languages that the child uses as well as the level of skill and fluency demonstrated in each. *Traditional assessment* with stan-

dardized measures should take place to enable a general estimate of the current level of measurable functioning and to determine a relative level of performance compared to age-equivalent peers. During this phase of the assessment, the examiner should develop a sense for the potential effects of cultural factors in the testing process and should determine the degree of validity of test results. *Alternative assessment procedures* should be incorporated to ensure that children have been given every opportunity to demonstrate their abilities. *Diagnostic placement* in an established preschool enrichment program should be conducted if questions arise concerning the validity of test results or if it is believed that additional information is needed to make educational decisions. A variety of techniques is appropriate for this phase of assessment. Finally, parents, assessment personnel, and appropriate school and agency representatives should review all assessment data in a *review meeting* and together develop educational recommendations for the child.

REFERENCES

Apgar, V. (1953). A proposal for a new method of evaluation of the newborn infant. *Anesthesia and Analgesia, 32,* 260–267.

Arffa, S., Rider, L. H., & Cummings, J. A. (1984). A validity study of the Woodcock-Johnson Psychoeducational Battery and the Stanford-Binet with black preschool children. *Journal of Psychoeducational Assessment, 2,* 73–77.

Bagnato, S. J., & Neisworth, J. T. (1991). *Assessment for early intervention: Best practices for professionals.* New York: Guilford.

Bagnato, S. J., & Neisworth, J. T. (1994). A national study of the social and treatment "invalidity" of intelligence testing for early intervention. *School Psychology Quarterly, 9,* 81–102.

Barona, A., & Santos de Barona, M. (1987). A model for the assessment of limited English proficient students referred for special education services. In S. H. Fradd & W. J. Tikunoff (Eds.), *Bilingual education and bilingual special education: A guide for administrators* (pp. 183–210). Boston: College Hill Press.

Barrera, I. (1995). To refer or not to refer: Untangling the web of diversity, "deficit," and disability. *New York State Association for Bilingual Education Journal, 10,* 54–66.

Bayley, N. (1969). *Bayley Scales of Infant Development.* New York: Psychological Corporation.

Bayley, N. (1993). *Bayley Scales of Infant Development-II.* San Antonio, TX: Psychological Corporation.

Bernal, E. M. (1974). Gifted Mexican-American children: An ethnoscientific perspective. *California Journal of Educational Research, 25,* 261–273.

Bondurant-Utz, J. A., & Luciano, L. B. (1994). *A practical guide to infant and preschool assessment in special education.* Boston: Allyn and Bacon.

Bracken, B. A. (1985). A critical review of the Kaufman Assessment Battery for Children (K-ABC). *School Psychology Review, 14,* 21–36.

Bracken, B. A. (1987). Limitations of preschool instruments and standards for minimal levels of technical adequacy. *Journal of Psychoeductional Assessment, 5,* 313–326.

Bracken, B. A. (1994). Advocating for effective preschool assessment practices: A comment on Bagnato & Neisworth. *School Psychology Quarterly, 9,* 103–108.

Bracken, B. A., & Fouad, N. A. (1987). Spanish translation and validation of the Bracken Basic Concept Scale. *School Psychology Review, 16,* 94–102.

Bracken, B. A., & McCallum, R. S. (1998). *Universal nonverbal intelligence test examiner's manual.* Itasca, IL: Riverside.

Bracken, B. A., Barona, A., Bauermeister, J., Howell, K. K., Poggioli, L., & Puente, A. (1990). Multinational validation of the Spanish Bracken Basic Concept Scale for Cross-Cultural Assessments. *Journal of School Psychology, 28*(4), 325–341.

Brooks-Gunn, J., & Lewis, M. (1983). Screening and diagnosing handicapped infants. *Topics in Early Childhood Special Education, 3,* 14–28.

Brown, A. L., & Ferrara, R. A. (1985). Diagnosing zones of proximal development. In J. Wertsch (Ed.), *Culture, communication, and cognition—Vygotskian perspectives.* London: Cambridge University Press.

Bryen, D. N., & Gallagher, D. (1983). Assessment of language and communication. In K. D. Paget & B. A. Bracken (Eds.), *The psychoeducational assessment of preschool children* (pp. 81–144). New York: Grune & Stratton.

Chhim, S. (1987). *Introduction to Cambodian culture.* San Diego, CA: Multifunctional Resource Center, San Diego State University.

Cummins, J. (1980). Psychological assessment of minority language students. Unpublished manuscript of Ontario Institute for Studies in Education, Toronto, pp. 1–91.

Dodd, J. M., Nelson, J. R., & Spint, W. (1995). Prereferral activities: One way to avoid biased testing procedures and possible inappropriate special education placement for American Indian students. *The Journal of Educational Issues for Language Minority Students, 15,* http://ncbe.gwu.edu/miscpubs/jeilms/vol15/prereferra.html, accessed July 8, 1997.

EAC West, New Mexico State Highlands University. (1996). Evaluation and assessment for Title VII projects—handouts, http://www.ncbe.gwu/edu/miscpubs/eacwest/handouts/gifted/backgrhd.html, accessed July 8, 1997.

Elliott, C. D. (1990). *Differential ability scales: Introductory and technical handbook.* San Antonio, TX: Psychological Corporation.

Federal Interagency Forum on Child and Family Statistics [FIFCFS]. (1997). America's children: Key national indicators of well-being. Washington, DC: U.S. Government Printing Office.

Feuerstein, R. (1979). *The dynamic assessment of retarded performers: The learning potential assessment device theory instruments and techniques.* Baltimore: University Park Press.

Feuerstein, R., Rand, Y., Haywood, H. C., Hoffman, M. B., & Jensen, M. R. (n.d.). L.P.A.D. Learning Potential Assessment Device manual experimental version. Jerusalem: Hadassah-Wizo-Canada Research Institute.

Flanagan, D. P., & Alfonso, V. C. (1995). A critical review of the technical characteristics of new and recently revised intelligence tests for preschool children. *Journal of Psychoeducational Assessment, 13,* 66–90.

Fradd, S. H. (1987). Accommodating the needs of limited English proficient students in regular classrooms. In S. H. Fradd & W. J. Tikunoff (Eds.), *Bilingual education and bilingual special education—A guide for administrators* (pp. 133–182). Boston: College Hill Press.

Garber, H. (1977). Preventing mental retardation through family rehabilitation. In S. Caldwell & J. Stedman (Eds.), *Infant education: A guide for helping handicapped children in the first three years.* New York: Walker and Company.

Garber, H. L., & Slater, M. (1983). Assessment of the culturally different preschooler. In K. D. Paget & B. A. Bracken (Eds.), *The psychoeducational assessment of preschool children* (pp. 443–471). New York: Grune & Stratton.

Gelman, R. (1979). Preschool thought. *American Psychologist, 34,* 900–905.

Goldman, J., L'Engle Stein, C., & Guerry, S. (1983). *Psychological methods of child assessment.* New York: Bruner/Mazel.

Goodman, J. F., & Cameron, J. (1978). The meaning of IQ constancy in young retarded children. *The Journal of Genetic Psychology, 132,* 109–119.

Gyurke, J. S. (1994). A reply to Bagnato and Neisworth: Intelligent versus intelligence testing of preschoolers. *School Psychology Quarterly, 9,* 109–112.

Hambleton, R. K. (1982). Advances in criterion-referenced testing technology. In C. R. Reynolds & T. B. Gutkin (Eds.), *The handbook of school psychology* (pp. 351–379). New York: John Wiley Sons.

Hernandez, R. D. (1994). Reducing bias in the assessment of culturally and linguistically diverse populations. *The Journal of Educational Issues of Language Minority Students, 14,* 269–300.

Hohenshil, T. H., & Hames, C. W. (1988). Preschool assessment: Implications for counselors. *Journal of Counseling and Development, 66,* 251–252.

Huynh, D. T. (1987). *Introduction to Vietnamese culture.* San Diego, CA: Multifunctional Resource Center, San Diego State University.

Kaufman, A. S., & Kaufman, N. L. (1983). *Kaufman Assessment Battery for Children.* New York: Grune & Stratton.

Kelley, M. F., & Surbeck, E. (1983). History of preschool assessment. In K. D. Paget & B. A. Bracken (Eds.), *The psychoeducational assessment of preschool children* (pp. 1–16). New York: Grune & Stratton.

Keogh, S. V. (Ed.). (1970). Early identification of children with potential learning problems. *Journal of Special Education, 4,* 307–363.

Khamchong, L. (1987). *Laos culturally speaking: Introduction to the Lao culture.* San Diego, CA: Multifunctional Resource Center, San Diego State University.

Leung, E. K. (1990). Early risks: Transition from culturally/linguistically diverse homes to formal schooling. *Journal of Education Issues of Language Minority Students, 7,* 35–51.

Lewis, M. (1976). Infant intelligence tests: Their use and misuse. *Human Development, 16,* 108.

Lidz, C. S. (1983). Dynamic assessment and the preschool child. *Journal of Psychoeducational Assessment, 1,* 59–72.

Lidz, C. S., & Peña, E. D. (1996). Dynamic assessment: The model, its relevance as a nonbiased approach, and its application to Latino American preschool children. *Language, Speech, and Hearing Services in Schools, 27,* 367–372.

Lowenthal, B. (1991). Ecological assessment: Adding a new dimension for preschool children. *Intervention in School and Clinic, 26,* 148–162.

Marland, S. (1972). *Education of the gifted and talented: Report to the Congress of the United States by the U.S. Commissioner of Education.* Washington, DC: U.S. Government Printing Office.

McCall, R. B., Appelbaum, M., & Hogarty, P. S. (1973). Developmental changes in mental performance. *Monographs of the Society for Research in Child Development, 38* (3, Serial No. 150).

McCall, R. B., Hogarty, P. S., & Hurlburt, N. (1972). Transitions in infant sensorimotor development and the prediction of childhood IQ. *American Psychologist, 27,* 728–748.

McLaughlin, B., Gesi Blanchard, A., & Osanai, Y. (1995). Assessing language development in bilingual preschool children. *NCBE Program Information Guide Series,* No. 22, www.ncbe.gwu.ncbepubs/pigs/pig22.html, accessed July 8, 1997.

McLoughlin, J. A., & Lewis, R. B. (1986). *Assessing special students* (2nd ed.). Columbus, OH: Merrill.

Mercer, J. (1979). *Technical manual: SOMPA: System of Multicultural Pluralistic Assessment.* New York: Psychological Corporation.

Missiuna, C., & Samuels, M. T. (1989). Dynamic assessment of preschool children with special needs: Comparison of mediation and instruction. *Remedial and Special Education, 10,* 53–62.

Paget, K. D. (1983). The individual examining situation: Basic considerations for preschool children. In K. D. Paget & B. A. Bracken (Eds.), *The psychoeducational assessment of preschool children* (pp. 51–61). New York: Grune & Stratton.

Paget, K. D., & Nagle, R. J. (1986). A conceptual model of preschool assessment. *School Psychology Review, 15,* 154–165.

Prince, C. D. (1992, March 27). Reactions to the Goal 1 Technical Planning Subgroup report on school readiness: Report to the National Education Goals Panel (Tech. Rept. No. 92-03). Washington, DC: National Education Goals Panel.

Prince, C. D., & Lawrence, L. A. (1993). School readiness and language minority students: Implications of the first national education goal. *NCBE FOCUS: Occasional Papers in Bilingual Education,* No. 7, http://www.ncbe.gwu/ncbepubs/focus/focus7.html, accessed July 8, 1997.

Reynolds, C. R., & Clark, J. (1983). Assessment of cognitive abilities. In K. D. Paget & B. A. Bracken (Eds.), *The psychoeducational assessment of preschool children* (pp. 163–190). New York: Grune & Stratton.

Roid, G., & Miller, L. (1997). *Leiter International Performance Scale—Revised.* Wood Dale, IL: Stoelting.

Romero, I. (1992). Individual assessment procedures with preschool children. In E. Vasquez-Nuttall, I. Romero, & J. Kalesnik (Eds.), *Assessing and screening preschoolers* (pp. 55–66). Boston: Allyn and Bacon.

Rubin, R. A., Balow, B., Dorle, J., & Rosen, M. (1978). Preschool prediction of low achievement in basic school skills. *Journal of Learning Disabilities, 11,* 62–64.

Santos de Barona, M. (1981). A study of distractibility utilizing the WISC-R factors of intelligence and Bender error categories in a referred population. *Dissertation Abstracts International, 42,* 4775a.

Sattler, J. M. (1992). *Assessment of Children* (3rd revised and updated ed.). San Diego, CA: Author.

Schakel, J. (1986). Cognitive assessment of preschool children. *School Psychology Review, 15,* 200–215.

Share, J., Koch, R., Webb, A., & Graliker, B. (1964). The longitudinal development of infants and young children with Down's syndrome. *American Journal of Mental Deficiency, 68,* 689–692.

Silverman, E. (1971). Situational variability of pre-schoolers' dysfluency: Preliminary study. *Perceptual and Motor Skills, 33,* 4021–4022.

Slater, M. A., & Heber, F. R. (1979, November). *Final performance report modification of mother-child interaction processes in families at risk for mental retardation.* Washington, DC: Bureau of Education for the Handicapped, Grant 780012.

Spivack, G., & Shure, M. B. (1976). *Social adjustment of young children.* San Francisco: Jossey-Bass.

Steffensen, M. S., Joag-Dev, C., & Anderson, R. C. (1979). A cross-cultural perspective on reading comprehension. *Reading Research Quarterly, 15,* 10–29.

Swain, M. (1972). Bilingualism as a first language. In J. Damico (1991), *Limiting bias in the assessment of bilingual students.* Austin, TX: Pro-Ed.

Thorndike, R. L., Hagen, E. P., & Sattler, J. M. (1986). *Stanford-Binet Intelligence Scale, Fourth Edition.* Chicago: Riverside.

Thurman, S. K., & Widerstrom A. H. (1985). *Young children with special needs.* Boston: Allyn & Bacon.

Tikunoff, W. J. (1987). Mediation of instruction to obtain equality of effectiveness. In S. H. Fradd & W. J. Tikunoff (Eds.), *Bilingual education and bilingual special education: A guide for administrators* (pp. 99–132). Boston: College Hill Press.

Ulrey, G. (1981). The challenge of providing psychological services for young handicapped children. *Professional Psychology, 12,* 483–491.

U.S. Census. (1990). Table 5. Detailed language spoken at home and ability to speak English for persons 5 years and over—50 languages ranked by total number of speakers, U.S. 1990, http://www.census.gov/population/socdemo/language/table5.txt, accessed July 17, 1997.

U.S. Census data. (1994). Table 1. Selected social characteristics of all persons and Hispanic persons by type of origin: March 1994, http://www.census.gov/population/socdemo/language/table1.txt, accessed July 17, 1997.

U.S. Census Bureau. (1997). Highlights of population profile, http://www.census.gov/population/www/pop-profile/highlght.html, accessed July 9, 1997.

Wechsler, D. (1989). Manual for the Wechsler preschool and primary scale of intelligence (WPPSI). San Antonio, TX: Psychological Corporation.

Wiersma, W., & Jurs, S. G. (1985). *Educational measurement and testing.* Boston: Allyn & Bacon.

Wilen, D. K., & Sweeting, C. M. (1986). Assessment of limited English proficient Hispanic students. *School Psychology Review, 15*(1), 59–75.

Wong-Fillmore, L. (1992). When learning a second language means losing the first. *Early Childhood Research Quarterly, 6,* 323–346.

Woodcock, R. W., & Mather, N. (1989, 1990). Woodcock-Johnson revised tests of cognitive ability—standard and supplemental batteries: Examiner's manual. In R. W. Woodcock & M. B. Johnson, *Woodcock-Johnson Psychoeducational Battery—Revised.* Chicago: Riverside.

Zigler, E., & Butterfield, E. (1968). Motivational aspects of changes in IQ test performance and culturally deprived nursery school children. *Child Development, 39,* 1–14.

CHAPTER 15

ASSESSMENT OF PRESCHOOL CHILDREN WITH SEVERE DISABILITIES

KATHRYN CLARK GERKEN

Both the popular press (Riccitello & Adler, 1997) and the professional literature (Anastasiow & Harel, 1993; Steinberg, 1993) make it clear that in spite of or because of our great advances in genetic science and embryology, the rate of birth defects in neonates has not decreased. Riccitiello and Adler report that three out of every 100 newborns have birth defects and Steinberg reports that 1 percent of the premature infants and 1.5 percent of the full-term infants have severe disabilities. Ethical issues such as moral rights, the value of life versus quality of life, and scarcity of resources influence medical and educational interventions for preschoolers with severe disabilities. For over four decades, developmental psychologists have provided evidence from animal and human research indicating that early experience and early intervention have positive outcomes. That early research was the basis for Project Headstart in 1964 and other early intervention services. The authorization of the Handicapped Children's Early Education Program (HCEEP) in 1968 was just the beginning of 30 years of legislation that emphasized early identification and intervention of preschool children with disabilities. During that 30-year time period, there have been numerous studies conducted on the effects of early intervention. Guralnick (1997) provides a review of the research on the effectiveness of early intervention for a wide variety of infants and preschoolers in terms of prenatal, natal, and postnatal risks. Although there is variation in the degree, extensiveness, and duration of effects, Ramey and Ramey (1998) report remarkable consistency in the major research findings. They summarize the history of early intervention and provide a conceptual framework for understanding the effects of early intervention. Ramey and Ramey (1998, pp. 115–118) also discuss the major findings under six principles:

1. Developmental timing—interventions that begin earlier in development and continue longer usually have greater benefits.

2. Program intensity—more intensive programs with children and parents who actively participate produce greater positive effects.

3. Direct provision of learning experiences—direct educational experiences for children versus parental training only result in greater and longer-lasting benefits.

4. Program breadth and flexibility—comprehensive services through many approaches produce greater positive effects.

5. Individual differences—different programs may be needed to produce similar outcomes in children with different risk factors.

6. Ecological domain—adequate environmental supports are needed to maintain positive outcomes.

Although cultural congruence was not included as a principle, Ramey and Ramey (1998) emphasize that interventions provided for children and families must recognize and build on cultural beliefs, traditions, and practices.

The Individuals with Disabilities Education Act Amendments of 1997 (IDEA, P.L. 105-17, 1997) focuses on the changing population in the schools and the necessity for being responsive to an increasingly diverse public school population. As a group, minority children comprise a very large percentage of the school-age population, with a few large city school populations being over 80 percent racially or ethnically diverse (e.g., Baltimore, Chicago, Houston, Los Angeles, Miami) (P.L. 105-17). It is reported in P.L. 105-17 that between 1980 and 1990, the rate of increase for the U.S. population was 53 percent for Hispanics, 13 percent for African Americans, and 107.8 percent for Asians whereas the rate was only 6 percent for whites. The rate of increase for racial and ethnic minority children is higher at the preschool and primary levels than the middle and high school levels. Thus, even in states such as Iowa, with a limited minority population, culturally and/or linguistically diverse (CLD) children make up 40 to 50 percent of some school districts' preschool and primary populations (e.g., Cotter, Columbus Junction, West Liberty). Sinclair (1993) examined the clinical profiles of Headstart children with disabilities who were evaluated by a UCLA/Headstart team in order to look at prevalence rates of certain disorders. The prevalence rates for learning disabilities and serious emotional disturbance (26% and 29%) in this study were considerably higher than the 4 percent rates often touted in official reports. However, even more noticeable was the racial/ethnic makeup of the children identified as having disabilities; 65 percent were identified as Hispanic, 30 percent as African American, and 5 percent as other. These changes in the racial/ethnic profile of the U.S. population necessitate changes in the assessment procedures used to identify children in need of special services. There must be even more emphasis on training psychologists and other school and mental health professionals to conduct interdisciplinary and transdisciplinary assessment. Partnerships in the field of developmental disabilities are necessary to create new knowledge, improve the quality of life for preschoolers with disabilities and their families, and to prevent the mislabeling that too often takes place with CLD children. Some children are viewed as having disabilities when they do not and others who have disabilities and need special services do not receive them.

The last decade has seen assessment being touted as both the bane and salvation of education. In some areas, there has been an increase in high-stakes testing whereas in others, there is a ban or limit on the use of standardized, norm-referenced tests. No longer are assessment specialists arguing over the usefulness of norm-referenced versus criterion-referenced assessment instruments; instead they are arguing over the usefulness of alternative versus traditional assessment in linking assessment to intervention. A new assessment vocabulary has appeared (Appendix A), but those of us who have provided services to children with disabilities for over 20 years know that the words may be new, but the concepts are not. The terms used to discuss the effectiveness of assessment and intervention are also new to the public and to some professionals, but the underlying concepts should not be. Does the assessment technique have social validity and does the intervention have treatment integrity or validity? We have always known that parents should be included in the assessment and intervention procedures for children with disabilities, but P.L. 99-457 in 1986 and Part C of the Reauthorization of IDEA, June 4, 1997 mandate such

inclusion. Multidisciplinary team decisions were mandated in 1975, but it has only been in the last five years that we have touted interdisciplinary and transdisciplinary approaches to assessment and intervention. In spite of these new approaches, we are still making mistakes and overidentifying some children while underidentifying others. The purpose of this chapter is to put all of the parts together to provide guidelines for assessments that are appropriate for all preschoolers with disabilities—those who are CLD and those who are not.

ASSESSMENT ISSUES

During the last two decades, progress in the medical field has led to an increased survival rate of infants with congenital and neonatal complications and increased awareness of the needs of children with more severe and chronic disabilities. Many of these infants will continue to need special services as they grow up. Thus, the difficulties that were discussed by Simeonsson, Huntington, & Parse in 1979, by Simeonsson in 1986 and 1994, by McLean and McCormick in 1993, and by McLean in 1996 regarding the assessment of very young children who have severe disabilities are still present as we approach the twenty-first century. Those difficulties are definitions, family priorities, limitations of the child, limitations of the examiner, limitations of the instruments, measurement errors, and setting errors. Simeonsson's 1986 "Inventory of Assessment Variables" remains a very useful tool to help the examiner eliminate or at least recognize many of the problems in assessment. Table 15.1 presents some of the problems and suggested solutions.

General Definitions

Who are the preschoolers with severe disabilities?

> Sec. 602. DEFINITIONS (P.L. 105-17, 1997)
>
> (A) In General—The term "child with a disability" means a child with mental retardation, hearing impairments (including deafness), speech or language impairments, visual impairments, (including blindness), serious emotional disturbance (hereinafter referred to as emotional disturbance), orthopedic impairments, autism, traumatic brain injury, other health impairments, or specific learning difficulties; and who, by reason thereof, needs special education and related services.
>
> Child Aged 3 Through 9—The term "child with a disability" for a child aged 3 through 9 may, at the

TABLE 15.1 Problems and Solutions in the Assessment of Special Children

PROBLEMS	SOLUTIONS
Definitional Issues	
Lack of agreement on definitions of basic terms	Reduce inconsistency
Need designations that will reflect both presence of disability and degree of impairment	Consider alternative ways in which to define children and designate severity of their disability (functional or educational needs)
Child	
Impaired functioning in more than one area	Consider other limitations
Performance and functioning affected by medication and state	Assess the child's state
Presence of idiosyncratic behaviors	Determine child's modality preference (how can child best receive information and how can
Variability in rate of development across areas	child best respond)
Family	
Lack of knowledge/experience with children with severe disabilities	Provide appropriate training
Personal biases and expectations	Training will require knowledge and skill acquisition
Invalid assumptions concerning effects of the disability	Work with the family to determine their concerns, priorities, and resources
Difficulty interpreting information from professionals	Give the parent the opportunity to observe assessment and intervention activities and have
Focused on long-term goals and predicting the future versus concentrating on the child's current assets	supervised practice with these activities
Lack of special communication skills (e.g., signing skills)	Assist the family in finding additional services Help the family members learn how to communicate with the preschooler
Examiner	
Lack of knowledge/experience with children with severe disabilities	Provide the examiner with opportunities to observe and ask questions
Personal bias and expectations	The examiner should monitor his or her own biases, values, and belief system
Invalid assumptions concerning effects of the disability	Training will require knowledge and skill acquisition and supervised field experiences
Focused on long-term goals and predicting the future versus concentrating on the child's current assets	

discretion of the State and the local educational agency, include a child experiencing developmental delays, as defined by the State, and as measured by appropriate diagnostic instruments and procedures, in one or more of the following areas: physical development, cognitive development, communication development, social or emotional development, or adaptive development; and who, by reason thereof, needs special education and related services.

Sec. 632. DEFINITIONS (P.L. 105-17, 1997)

At-risk INFANT OR TODDLER—an individual under three years of age who would be at-risk of developing a substantial developmental delay if early intervention services were not provided to the individual.

(5) "Infant or toddler with a disability"—

(B) means an individual under three years of age who needs early intervention services because the individual—

(i) is experiencing developmental delays, as measured by appropriate diagnostic instruments and procedures in one or more of the areas of cognitive development, physical development, communication development, social or emotional development, and adaptive development; or

(ii) has a diagnosed physical or mental condition which has a high probability of resulting in developmental delay; and at-risk infants and toddlers. (P.L. 105-17, Section 632, 1997)

As defined by the Developmental Disabilities Assistance and Bill of Rights Act of 1994, the term *developmental disability* means a severe, chronic disability of an individual 5 years of age or older that:

1. is attributable to a mental or physical impairment or combination of mental and physical impairments;
2. is manifested before the individual attains age 22;
3. is likely to continue indefinitely;
4. results in substantial functional limitations in three or more of the following areas of major life activity: self-care, receptive and expressive language, learning, mobility, self-direction, capacity for independent living, and economic self-sufficiency; and reflects the individual's need for a combination and sequence of special, interdisciplinary, or generic services, supports, or other assistance that is of lifelong or extended duration and is individually planned and coordinated, except that such a term, when applied to infants and young children, means individuals from birth to age 5, inclusive, who have substantial developmental delay or specific congenital or acquired conditions with a high probability of resulting in developmental disabilities if services are not provided.

As defined by the Personal Responsibility and Work Opportunity Reconciliation Act of 1996, the term *disability:*

1. requires a child to have a physical or mental condition or conditions that can be medically proven and that result in "marked and severe" functional limitations;
2. requires that the medically proven physical or mental condition or conditions must last or be expected to last at least 12 months, or be expected to result in death;

3. says that a child may not be considered disabled if he or she is working at a job that we consider to be substantial work. However, the law did not change the rules that allow certain children already on the rolls to continue to receive SSI even though they are working.

The National Information Center for Children and Youth with Disabilities defines *severe disabilities and/or multiple disabilities* to apply to people with severe disabilities who traditionally have been labeled as having severe to profound mental retardation. These people require ongoing, extensive support in more than one major life activity in order to participate in integrated community settings and enjoy the quality of life available to people with fewer or no disabilities. Support may be required for life activities such as mobility, communication, self-care, and learning, as necessary for independent living, employment, and self-sufficiency. They frequently have additional disabilities, including movement difficulties, sensory losses, and behavior problems.

Categorical Definitions

Categorical definitions are present in the *Diagnostic and Statistical Manual of Mental Disorders, Fourth Edition (DSM-IV,* 1994). The *DSM-IV* contains a separate section for "Disorders Usually First Diagnosed in Infancy, Childhood, or Adolescence." The disorders in this section that are usually thought of as resulting in severe disabilities are the severe and profound mental retardation categories described under "Mental Retardation" and all the disorders listed under "Pervasive Developmental Disorders." The most widely accepted definitions of mental retardation have been those adopted by the American Association on Mental Retardation (AAMR). However, the ninth edition of the AAMR manual on the definition of mental retardation (Luckasson et al., 1992) increased the psychometrically eligible proportion of the general population (MacMillan, Gresham, & Siperstein, 1993) and excluded the categories or degrees of retardation. Concerns have been raised about this definition and its implications for practice (Belmont & Borkowski, 1994; Jacobson & Mullick, 1992, 1994; Kutik, 1994; MacMillan, Gresham, & Siperstein, 1993, 1995). There are differences in the etiologies, characteristics, and functional needs of persons who have mild mental retardation and those who have severe or profound mental retardation.

According to Luckasson et al. (1992), *mental retardation* refers to substantial limitations in present functioning. It is characterized by significantly subaverage intellectual functioning, existing concurrently with related limitations in two or more of the following applicable adaptive skill areas: communication, self-care, home living, social skills, community use, self-direction, health and safety, functional academics, leisure, and work. Mental retardation manifests before age 18.

The following four assumptions are essential to the application of the definition:

1. Valid assessment considers cultural and linguistic diversity as well as differences in communication and behavioral factors.
2. The existence of limitations in adaptive skills occurs within the context of community environments typical of the individual's age peers and is indexed to the person's individualized needs for supports.
3. Specific adaptive limitations often coexist with strengths in other adaptive skills or other personal capabilities.
4. With appropriate supports over a sustained period, the life functioning of the person with mental retardation will generally improve (Luckasson et al., 1992).

Mental Retardation. *DSM-IV* definitions (*DSM-IV,* 1992) state:

Diagnostic criteria for Mental Retardation

1. Significantly subaverage intellectual functioning: an IQ of approximately 70 or below on an individually administered IQ test (for infants, a clinical judgment of significantly subaverage intellectual functioning).
2. Concurrent deficits or impairments in present adapting functioning (i.e., the person's effectiveness in meeting the standards expected for his or her age by his or her cultural group) in at least two of the following areas: communication, self-care, home living, social/interpersonal skills, use of community resources, self-direction, functional academic skills, work, leisure, health, and safety.
3. The onset is before age 18 years.

Code based on degree of severity reflecting level of intellectual impairment:

317 Mild Mental Retardation: IQ level 50–55 to approximately 70

318.0 Moderate Mental Retardation: IQ level 35–40 to 50–55

318.1 Severe Mental Retardation: IQ level 20–25 to 35–40

318.2 Profound Mental Retardation: IQ level below 20–25

319 Mental Retardation, Severity Unspecified: when there is strong presumption of Mental Retardation but the person's intelligence is untestable by standard tests (p. 46)

Pervasive Developmental Disorders. According to *DSM-IV* (1992), "Pervasive Developmental Disorders are characterized by severe and pervasive impairment in several areas of development: reciprocal social interaction skills, communication skills, or the presence of stereotyped behavior, interests, and activities. The qualitative impairments that define these conditions are distinctly deviate relative to the individual's developmental level or mental age" (p. 65).

Autistic Disorder. According to *DSM-IV* (1992),

Diagnostic criteria for 299.00 Autistic Disorder

A. A total of six (or more) items from (1), (2), and (3), with at least two from (1), and one each from (2) and (3):
   (1) qualitative impairment in social interaction, as manifested by at least two of the following:
      (a) marked impairment in the use of multiple nonverbal behaviors such as eye-to-eye gaze, facial expression, body postures, and gestures to regulate social interaction
      (b) failure to develop peer relationships appropriate to developmental level
      (c) a lack of spontaneous seeking to share enjoyment, interests, or achievements with other people (e.g., by a lack of showing, bringing, or pointing out objects of interest)
      (d) lack of social or emotional reciprocity
   (2) qualitative impairments in communication as manifested by at least one of the following:
      (a) delay in, or total lack of, the development of spoken language (not accompanied by an attempt to compensate through alternative modes of communication such as gesture or mime)
      (b) in individuals with adequate speech, marked impairment in the ability to

initiate or sustain a conversation with others

   (c) stereotyped and repetitive use of language or idiosyncratic language

   (d) lack of varied, spontaneous make-believe play or social imitative play appropriate to developmental level

(3) restricted repetitive and stereotyped patterns of behavior, interests, and activities, as manifested by at least one of the following:

   (a) encompassing preoccupation with one or more stereotyped and restricted patterns of interest that is abnormal either in intensity or focus

   (b) apparently inflexible adherence to specific, nonfunctional routines or rituals

   (c) stereotyped and repetitive motor mannerisms (e.g., hand or finger flapping or twisting, or complex whole-body movements)

   (d) persistent preoccupation with parts of objects

B. Delays or abnormal functioning in at least one of the following areas, with onset prior to age 3 years: (1) social interaction, (2) language as used in social communication, (3) symbolic or imaginative play.

C. The disturbance is not better accounted for by Rett's Disorder or Childhood Disintegrative Disorder.

Diagnostic criteria for 299.80 Rett's Disorder

A. All of the following:

   (1) apparently normal prenatal and perinatal development

   (2) apparently normal psychomotor development through the first 5 months after birth

   (3) normal head circumference after birth

B. Onset of all of the following after the period of normal development:

   (1) deceleration of head growth between ages 5 and 48 months

   (2) loss of previously acquired purposeful hand skills between ages 5 and 30 months with the subsequent development of stereotyped hand movements (e.g., hand-wringing or hand washing)

   (3) loss of social engagement early in the course (although often social interaction develops later)

   (4) appearance of poorly coordinated gait or trunk movements

   (5) severely impaired expressive and receptive language development with severe psychomotor retardation

Diagnostic criteria for 299.10 Childhood Disintegrative Disorder

A. Apparently normal development manifested for at least the first 2 years after birth as manifested by the presence of age-appropriate verbal and non-verbal communication, social relationships, play, and adaptive behavior.

B. Clinically significant loss of previously acquired skills (before age 10 years) in at least two of the following areas:

   (1) expressive or receptive language

   (2) social skills or adaptive behavior

   (3) bowel or bladder control

   (4) play

   (5) motor skills

C. Abnormalities of functioning in at least two of the following areas:

   (1) qualitative impairment in social interaction (e.g., impairment in nonverbal behaviors, failure to develop peer relationships, lack of social or emotional reciprocity)

   (2) qualitative impairments in communication (e.g., delay or lack of spoken language, inability to initiate or sustain a conversation, stereotyped or repetitive use of language, lack of varied make-believe play)

   (3) restricted, repetitive, and stereotyped patterns of behavior, interests, and activities, including motor stereotypes and mannerisms

D. The disturbance is not better accounted for by another specific Pervasive Developmental Disorder or by Schizophrenia.

Diagnostic criteria for 299.80 Asperger's Disorder

A. Qualitative impairment in social interaction, as manifested by at least two of the following:

   (1) marked impairment in the use of multiple nonverbal behaviors such as eye-to-eye gaze, facial expression, body postures, and gestures to regulate social interaction

   (2) failure to develop peer relationships appropriate to developmental level

(3) a lack of spontaneous seeking to share enjoyment, interests, or achievements with other people (e.g., by a lack of showing, bringing, or pointing out objects of interest to other people)

(4) lack of social or emotional reciprocity

B. Restricted repetitive and stereotyped patterns of behavior, interests, and activities, as manifested by at least one of the following:

(1) encompassing preoccupation with one or more stereotyped and restricted patterns of interest that is abnormal either in intensity or focus

(2) apparently inflexible adherence to specific, nonfunctional routines or rituals

(3) stereotyped and repetitive motor mannerisms (e.g., hand or finger flapping or twisting, or complex whole-body movements)

(4) persistent preoccupation with parts of objects

C. The disturbance causes clinically significant impairment in social, occupational, or other important areas of functioning.

D. There is no clinically significant general delay in language (e.g., single words used by age 2 years, communicative phrases used by age 3 years).

E. There is no clinically significant delay in cognitive development or in the development of age-appropriate self-help skills, adaptive behavior (other than in social interaction), and curiosity about the environment in childhood.

F. Criteria are not met for another specific Pervasive Developmental Disorder or Schizophrenia. (pp. 70–72)

Functional Definitions

The federal definition of developmental disabilities (DD) is a functional definition because emphasis is placed on the functional limitations the person with DD exhibits rather than limitations exhibited on standardized measures of ability. Those who support functional definitions believe that the primary basis for a diagnosis of exceptionality varies as a function of the nature of the condition and that there is no uniform criterion or dimension suitable to define all conditions (Simeonsson, 1986). A functional definition emphasizes the basic skills children need to live and play in their natural environment. A child who cannot feed himself or herself or accomplish any of the basic self-help skills would be limited in independent

functioning and would need ongoing support in several major life areas. Sailor and Guess's (1983) functional definition of *severely handicapped* remains timely except for their use of the word *handicap* rather than *disability*.

Children who are severely handicapped are significantly delayed in their development relative to their nonhandicapped peers. They learn, under the most ideal conditions, at a significantly slower rate than nonhandicapped students or students in remedial special education programs. Their learning impairment is usually associated with significant delay in several critical aspects of development (p. 12).

The emphasis in this chapter is on those preschoolers who, because of the breadth, intensity, or duration of physical, mental, or social/emotional disabilities, or the combination of two or more seriously disabling conditions, need services beyond those ordinarily offered in regular education programs.

INCIDENCE/PREVALENCE

Between 1976 and 1996, the number of students who participated in federal programs for children with disabilities increased by 51 percent. In 1987, Snell estimated that .05 percent of the U.S. population had a severe disability. However, it is difficult to accurately indicate how many children from birth through 5 years old have disabilities that require special services because of the problems that still exist regarding definitions and the confusion regarding incidence and prevalence figures. *Incidence* means extent or range of occurrence of a condition whereas *prevalence* is the measure of how many people have the condition at a particular time. Information from the National Information Center for Children and Youth with Disabilities (NICHCY, 1997) indicates that 89,646 students with multiple disabilities were served during the 1994–1995 school year.

How many of those were preschool-age children? According to the U.S. Department of Education (NCES, 1994), 100,000 to 150,000 infants with major birth defects are born annually. Approximately 8,000 of them die during infancy, but the others survive and are in need of special services. During the 1991–1992 fiscal year, 2.2 percent of children from birth to 3 years old were diagnosed as having a disability and .4 percent of those were labeled as having a severe disability. For 3- to 5-year-olds, 5.2 percent were identified as having a disability with .7 percent of those disabilities considered severe. In December 1991, 21.2 percent of children less than 6 years of age (91,950 children) were receiving SSI. The Seventeenth Annual Report to Congress (U.S. Department of

Education, 1995) indicated that 154,065 children 0 to 2 years old were receiving services because of identified disabilities. This was a change in the total number being served of +7.4 percent. The number of 3- to 5-year-olds who were identified as having a disability was 493,425, which was 4.2 percent of the population. The numbers of preschoolers being served is reported differently in various sources. The *Digest of Educational Statistics,* (NCES, 1997) reported that from 1990 to 1991, there were 440,661 children from birth to 5 years old identified as in need of special services and that from 1996 to 1997, there were 544,436 identified. According to *DSM-IV,* persons with severe or profound mental retardation make up 4 to 6 percent of the total population of persons diagnosed as having mental retardation. *DSM-IV* lists four specific disorders under Pervasive Developmental Disorders: Autism, two to five cases per 10,000 individuals; Rett's Disorder, reported occurring only in females and data limited to case studies; Childhood Disintegrative Disorder, limited epidemiological data, very rare occurrence, more common among males; and Asperger's Disorder, limited information on prevalence, more common in males. Trohanis (1995) reports that since the 1992–1993 school year, all states and jurisdictions have been ensuring a free appropriate public education (FAPE) to all eligible 3- to 5-year-olds and since September 30, 1994, all eligible states and jurisdictions have been providing an entitlement to early intervention services for children from birth through 2 years of age. This led to dramatic growth in the number of children served. For over 10 years, there has been an increase in the numbers of preschoolers who are in need of special services. The reasons for this continuous increase are multifaceted. Children with severe birth defects are now surviving past infancy; psychosocial risks are viewed as potent as biological risks and both are often present in a child (Blackman, 1996; Bricker, 1996). Gerken (1991) noted improvements in our identification procedures and instruments and such improvements have continued throughout the 1990s. There have also been increased federal and state incentives to identify and provide services to infants and toddlers with disabilities.

Some states have included at-risk infants and toddlers in their services rather than just infants and toddlers with known disabilities. The changes in IDEA (P.L. 105-17, Part C, 1997) that increase funding, allow and encourage the identification of at-risk infants and toddlers, and the provision of services to 3- to 9-year-olds who are experiencing developmental delays should result in continuous increases in the number of preschoolers receiving special services.

APPROACH TO ASSESSMENT

Appropriate assessment is the framework for appropriate intervention. The 1990s have brought about important changes in the assessment process for all children. Techniques have been borrowed from other disciplines and some that were more often used to assess children with severe disabilities are now being used for all children. We are no longer attempting to fit the severely disabled preschooler into a dated and ineffectual assessment model. New trends in the assessment of preschoolers have come about because of the aforementioned legislation, research in child development, and discoveries made by program staff regarding what works in the applied setting. A shift from product-oriented assessment to process-oriented assessment has occurred along with naturalistic formats. Fewell (1991) described the following types of assessment that emerged from applied settings: adaptive assessment, arena assessment, ecological inventories, interactive assessment, and judgment-based assessment. Appendix 1 contains a glossary of the assessment vocabulary of the 1990s. In many instances new words have been used to describe assessment techniques that were already being used by conscientious psychologists and other preschool specialists. We have made good progress, but much remains to be done. The *Principles and Recommendations for Early Childhood Assessment* submitted to the National Education Goals Panel (1998) are necessary and admirable but not sufficient for culturally competent assessment:

1. Assessments should bring about benefits for children.
2. Assessments should be tailored to a specific purpose and should be reliable, valid, and fair for that purpose.
3. Assessment policies should be designed recognizing that reliability and validity of assessments increase with children's age.
4. Assessments should be age appropriate in both content and the method of data collection.
5. Assessments should be linguistically appropriate, recognizing that to some extent all assessments are measures of language.
6. Parents should be a valued source of assessment information, as well as an audience for assessment results.

More attention must be paid to the diversity present in preschoolers, beyond linguistic differences, and the parents or guardians of the preschoolers must be an integral part of the assessment process from beginning to end, not passive sources of information or audience members for assessment results. Current books on the assessment of young children (Bagnato & Neisworth, 1991, 1994; Cohen & Spenciner, 1994, 1998; McLean, Bailey, & Wolery, 1996; Nuttall, Romero, & Kalesnik, 1992; Wortham, 1995) emphasize the changes that have occurred in assessment in the 1990s: the family's role in the assessment process, the importance of understanding and being responsive to diversity, observation in the natural environment, assessing play, using alternative assessment instruments, conducting program evaluations, and linking the interpretation and reporting of assessment information to intervention. Another major change in the assessment process for preschoolers is the emphasis on transdiciplinary team approaches versus unidisciplinary, multidisciplinary or interdisciplinary team approaches (Bagnato & Neisworth, 1991, 1994; Benner, 1992; Bergen, 1994; Brown, Thurman, & Pearl, 1993; Cohen & Spenciner, 1994; Gibbs & Teti, 1990; Rainforth, York, & MacDonald, 1992; Rokusek, 1995; Stoneman & Malone, 1995). Although definitions of these team approaches vary across authors, Table 15.2 describes the basic differences.

There is more than one definition of the transdisciplinary approach. In some instances, it is only thought of in the context of arena assessment in which individuals representing various disciplines watch one or two persons work with the child. However, a much broader definition simply implies that the persons from many disciplines and the family members are working together to conduct the most appropriate assessment and that discipline lines are often crossed. Gibbs and Teti (1990) believe that the transdisciplinary team approach requires role expansion, arena evaluation, and role release. For a transdisciplinary approach to be effective educational, conceptual, and administrative adjustments are needed. However, it is believed that the efforts to make these adjustments will result in more effective assessments and interventions. Bergen (1994) believes that an ideal transdisciplinary model includes professionals from many disciplines who work as an interactive team with direct guidance from family members in order to develop an integrated IFSP. She also believes that there are four basic assumptions underlying the model: (1) The family must be closely involved with the assessment process; (2) the model can result in a cost-effective, accurate, and educationally sound assessment, which will result in a developmentally appropriate intervention; (3) the services will be respectful and supportive of families; and (4) collaborative approaches can be demonstrated by a

TABLE 15.2 Assessment Teams

UNIDISCIPLINARY	MULTIDISCIPLINARY	INTERDISCIPLINARY	TRANSDISCIPLINARY
Assessment by one person who represents one discipline.	Separate assessments by team members—each person represents a discipline and conducts the assessment designated for his or her discipline.	Separate assessments by team members—each person represents a discipline and conducts the assessment designated for his or her discipline.	Assessments are conducted by team and family members who are best prepared to conduct the particular assessment. There is a crossing of discipline lines and role release.
Individual is responsible for conducting all of the assessment.	Each team member is responsible for conducting assessment appropriate for his or her discipline.	Team members are responsible for sharing information with other team members.	Team members (including family members) have planned the assessment together and may conduct the assessment together. They share all information and work to implement a unified service plan.

wide range of professionals. Bergen believes that when an effective transdisciplinary approach is in place, there will be the following benefits to the families, the children, and the team:

Family
1. Integral team members
2. Decrease in redundant questions from professionals
3. Participation in problem-solving experiences

Preschooler
1. Assessment information gathered at one time
2. Strengths and weaknesses assessed in a natural setting
3. Increased access to services that are consistent, integrated, and comprehensive

Team
1. More integrated assessment
2. Knowledge level of team members expanded as they share and receive information
3. More comprehensive and effective interventions

Across the state of Iowa, I have observed many different versions of these four assessment team approaches as services are provided to preschoolers with disabilities. The transdisciplinary team approach appears to be more prevalent in the rural areas of Iowa where much role release already occurs. The choices of who will actually present tasks to the child, who will gather developmental information from parents, and who will conduct direct observations in the home and preschool settings are made because of the context of the situations, the knowledge and skill levels of the participants, and the availability of the various team members. In the larger towns or cities in Iowa, the approach still appears to be an interdisciplinary one in which the members of the team collaborate, but each person has set tasks to perform. In some areas, the psychologist is not an early childhood team member until the children are placed in center-based programs. The school psychologist may not see an infant unless the infant is brought to a diagnostic clinic. In other areas, the school psychologist is involved in providing in-home services to all infants and toddlers who are not receiving center-based services. The composition of early childhood teams varies across the state according to the age of the preschooler and/or the philosophy of the administrator of early childhood services.

Although there has been limited evaluation of any of the team approaches, during the last five years, families and professionals have been asked to give their opinions on the transdisciplinary approach. McWilliam, Lang, Vandiviere, Angell, Collins, & Underdown (1995) reported that overall family members felt very positive about the professionals' willingness to listen and to respect family opinions. Family members also reported that services were available and the team members seemed to work well together. There was a direct relationship between the families' perceptions of having a good experience and the personal characteristics of individual team members and the benefits the children received. When a family reported having a bad experience, it was related to poor professional attitudes or difficulties in finding out about, getting, and monitoring services.

Bergen (1994) also reports on the common concerns professionals have about the transdisciplinary process. There is often a lack of training and guidance in the team process, team meetings lack meaningful discussions, participation in the team process varies across disciplines, and sometimes the team members are unable to work together as an integrated team. To be successful, the team members need training in team communication techniques, team-building activities, and conflict resolution skills. This type of training should occur at the preservice and in-service levels and must provide content and practice in order to develop effective teams. Continuous evaluation of the transdisciplinary team approach should occur.

Not only is there variation in the type of team used to provide services, there is also variation in the assessment model used to gather information. Many of the infants and toddlers with severe disabilities are identified at birth, but knowledge that there is a disability and that medical intervention may be needed is not sufficient for developing an individualized family service plan (IFSP). Professionals who work with infants and preschoolers who have severe disabilities agree that early identification and intervention are necessary, that all children can make progress when appropriate assessment and intervention occur, and that the assessment must be a continuous process. This requires an interdisciplinary or transdiciplinary team approach that includes the family in each step of the process. What they do not agree on is the actual model of assessment that should be used. It has been over 20 years since public school services to preschoolers with severe disabilities were mandated and the same two basic models of assessment have been used with persons with severe or profound disabilities: the developmental model and the behavioral model. Although we continue to add variations of these models in our quest to find the best model, what should be clear to the person who works with preschoolers with severe disabilities is that there is no one best model. These preschoolers are a diverse group in terms of their disabilities, their strengths, and their needs and each will need an individualized assessment plan. The professional needs to learn how to use many different models and how to choose the model or combination of models most appropriate for an individual child. Table 15.3 provides a brief overview of the basic developmental and behavioral models plus selected variations. Browder (1991) provides a thorough review of these models and promotes using some features from each model in the assessment process.

PROFESSIONAL PREPARATION

The 1990s have brought about changes in the assessment process and in intervention practices. Many children with severe disabilities are being included in regular classroom settings with some assistance for some children. Bailey, Simeonsson, Yoder, and Huntington (1990) surveyed program chairpersons and faculty members from nursing, nutrition, occupational therapy, physical therapy, psychology, social work, special education, and speech-language pathology to determine the core curriculum for early intervention personnel in these eight disciplines. There was a great deal of variability both within and across disciplines in the amount and kind of instructional and clinical experiences students in these disciplines received for working with preschoolers with disabilities and their families. However, the overall conclusion was that the students received minimal preparation to work with preschoolers who were disabled and their families. Wolery et al. (1994) surveyed general early childhood educators to determine if there were representatives from various disciplines working in these early childhood education programs. The major finding was that the presence or absence of other disciplines was directly related to whether inclusion of disabled preschoolers was occurring, but the public kindergartens had employed the highest percentage of various disciplines (78.2 percent). Only 11.3 percent of the community early childhood programs that had integrated a special needs child into the program included other disciplines in their team meetings. Of the 483 questionnaires returned, 326.5 indicated they had more than one discipline working with their program.

Sexton et al. (1996) investigated in-service training strategies. Their survey of 242 early service providers revealed that the majority reported receiving more passive types of in-service strategies versus active ones and few of the respondents reported receiving support following training. The respondents reported that the passive, didactic training procedures were less likely to result in actual practice changes than more dynamic strategies such as direct observation, modeling, and practice. The authors believe that training that focuses on specific skills allows participants to observe and actively practice the desired behaviors. Gallagher, Malone, Cleghorne, and Helms (1997) surveyed 115 early intervention personnel, representing 11 disciplines, to find out their perceived current need for training and various training preferences. The results indicate that relative to traditional competencies, assessment was the top priority need for 70 percent of the sample and 50 percent of the respondents wanted more information about family systems and family involvement. For contemporary competencies, technology was viewed by 70 percent of the respondents as a top training need. When asked to indicate their top three current training needs, 43 percent of the respondents rated typical/atypical development as their number-one current training need. Training preferences and motivational factors were also examined. The preferences were for training to occur in the fall, on a weekday morning, through the use of conferences and workshops. More than half the respondents wanted the training to occur during their contractual time. In the 23 years since P.L. 94-142 was passed, progress has been made in training early childhood special educators, but we have not done as well with support personnel or regular educators who encounter the preschooler with severe disabilities in the regular education classroom. McDonnell, Brownell, and Wolery (1997) found in a national survey of preschool teachers ($n = 500$) that the majority of the teachers were not certified in either early childhood education or early childhood special education and only 25 percent of them worked with a special educator concerning special needs children who were in their classrooms.

Buysse, Wesley, Keyes, and Bailey (1996) used two methods to assess the attitudes of 52 early childhood teachers about serving children with disabilities and about inclusion. These findings were similar to findings in the 1970s regarding mainstreaming children with disabilities. Teachers were more comfortable serving children with mild versus severe disabilities. Teachers were concerned about the lack of training regular early childhood teachers had to work with preschoolers with disabilities and the lack of opportunities the disabled child would have to receive special services. Since the passage of P.L. 99-457 in 1986, all persons who provide services to preschoolers with disabilities have been concerned

TABLE 15.3 Assessment Models for Severely Disabled Preschoolers

NAME	DESCRIPTION	ADVANTAGES	DISADVANTAGES	EXAMPLES OF INSTRUMENTS	REFERENCES
Developmental Perspective					
Psychometric	The foundation is a maturational theory of child development. Judgment is based on performance on a norm-referenced device assessing basic developmental skills.	Shows how a child compares to others in a normative group relative to basic developmental skills.	Does not show what functional skills a child has or needs. There is no link between assessment and intervention. Relies heavily on motor performance. High incidence of false positives and false negatives.	Bayley Scales of Infant Development II, 1993	Bagnato and Neisworth, 1991; Benner, 1992; Browder, 1991; Cohen and Spenciner, 1994, 1998
Cognitive Stages Perspective	Judgment is based on performance of the cognitive stages of development (such as Piagetian stages).	Enhances understanding of observed behavior. Compares progress of child with developmental age rather than chronological age peer. Emphasizes a process-based approach.	Performance depends on motor skills and cooperation of infant. Does not show what functional skills a child needs. Does not show if skills of severely disabled follow same sequence. Intervention program based on this might waste instructional time.	Ordinal scales of psychological development Infant psychological development scales	Brenner, 1992; Cohen & Spenciner, 1994, 1998
Developmental Diagnostic-Prescriptive Model	Judgment is based on performance on norm-referenced and criterion-referenced devices.	Separates child from the norm plus provides a detailed profile of skills and deficit.	Comprehensive assessment but episodic. No systematic review of learners' progress and adaptations based on this review.	Perceptions of developmental skills	Bagnato and Neisworth, 1991

(continued)

TABLE 15.3 Continued

NAME	DESCRIPTION	ADVANTAGES	DISADVANTAGES	EXAMPLES OF INSTRUMENTS	REFERENCES
Developmental Perspective					
Ecological	Judgment is based on natural unobtrusive observation of child.	Can observe the influence of environment on behavior and development of child. Comprehensive.	Might have problems with objectivity, reliability of observers. Does not consider developmental level or make peer comparisons.	Specimen records, chronology of events Ecological inventory	Benner, 1992; Browder, 1991
Neurobiological Approach	Focus is on the physical state of the child and should involve assessment of neurological integrity, behavioral organization and needs, temperament, and state of consciousness.	Can be used across cultures.	Needs to look at other aspects of development.	Neonatal Behavioral Assessment Scale (Brazleton, 1984)	Benner, 1992; Cohen and Spenciner, 1994, 1998; Salvia and Ysseldyke, 1995
Behavioral Models					
Functional Analysis	Judgment is based on systematic observation in the natural environment and analysis of behavior and situational variables influencing behavior.	Age-irrelevant assessment strategies, criterion-referenced, pinpoints behaviors of concern.	Does not document progress compared to peers. Does not consider developmental level.	Checklists, rating scales	Benner, 1992; Browder, 1991

NAME	DESCRIPTION	ADVANTAGES	DISADVANTAGES	EXAMPLES OF INSTRUMENTS	REFERENCES
Behavioral Models					
Task Analysis	Judgment based on observation of a child completing a task.	Specifies the subcomponents necessary to complete a task, identifies specific steps for assessment and instruction.	Different steps or behaviors might have different levels of difficulty, often there is no time-based measure; thus, an accomplished task might have limited functional utility if performed slowly.	Checklists	Browder, 1991
Ecological Inventory	Environment (not infant/child) is assessed; judgment is based on the characteristics of the infant/child's current and future environment. The infant/child is then assessed to see if he or she has the skills needed in the environment.	Helps generate or adapt individualized curriculum.	Can lead to an unmanageable list of skill needs. Setting priorities can be difficult. Must use other procedures to assess infant/child's performance of selected skills.	Checklists, inventories SPECS 1990 B&N	Browder, 1991
Precision Teaching	Judgment is based on observation of a child's performing a response repetitiously or performing a chain of responses without teacher interruption.	Assessment is direct and frequent. Provides systematic data.	Model does not specify how skills should be selected. Age relevance and environmental relevance may be ignored.		Browder, 1991

(continued)

TABLE 15.3 Continued

NAME	DESCRIPTION	ADVANTAGES	DISADVANTAGES	EXAMPLES OF INSTRUMENTS	REFERENCES
Behavioral Models					
Adaptive-Transactive Perspective	Judgment is based on interactions and transactions between a child and external stimuli.	Evaluates child behavior in context of environment in which it occurs or in relationship to the interactions surrounding its occurrence.	Does not document progress compared to peers, does not consider developmental level.	Home, infant questionnaire	Benner, 1992
Massed Trial Assessment	Presentation of repeated opportunities to respond to a test or teaching situation.	Multiple opportunities for input/child to respond correctly.	Response may not generalize to natural situations.		Browder, 1991
Individualized Curriculum Sequencing Model	Skill clusters developed and presented.	Acquisition and generalization checked concurrently.	Response claims may not be comprehensive enough.		Browder, 1991

about adequate training of teachers and support personnel. As the federal laws (IDEA, 1990, 1991, 1997; Americans with Disabilities Act [ADA], 1990) mandated that there be a range of options, including enrollment in regular early childhood programs, available for preschool children with disabilities and developmental delays, it was apparent that there was a need for additional trained personnel. Current practice finds many preschoolers with disabilities attending private and public preschools with their nondisabled peers. Pervasive system changes make it imperative that teachers and support personnel receive the training necessary to provide appropriate assessment, accommodations, and interventions. There has been a push from parents, educators, and professional organizations (Association of Teacher Educators, Division for Early Childhood of the Council for Exceptional Children, National Association for the Education of Young Children) to ensure that the persons working with the children would have adequate training (P. S. Miller, 1992a, 1992b; Stayton & Miller, 1993). Ethical concerns were raised about placing preschoolers with disabilities into classrooms or programs in which the teachers did not have knowledge or skills for working with the disabled preschooler. In 1994, 15 states had proposed or already had separate licensure for early childhood and early childhood special education. Some of these are separate endorsements but are required. In 1994, the State of Iowa began discussing licensing changes so that all teachers working with young children would have adequate knowledge and skills to work with young children with or without disabilities. The Iowa State Board of Educational Examiners sought input from educational practitioners and professional colleagues across the state in the fall of 1994. The board sent out 100 mailings, asking for input, and then followed these up with several meetings across the state. The end result was a Unified Early Childhood Endorsement for Early Childhood and Early Childhood Special Education (birth through age 8) and an Endorsement for Early Childhood Strategist. Even after four years of input, there are still changes being made in the unified endorsement and it will not go into effect until 2002. Ethical concerns have been expressed about placing preschoolers with disabilities into classrooms with untrained teachers.

The person who receives a unified licensure would not be licensed to teach a preschooler with a hearing impairment or teach children who are in a special class with integration or who have been identified as autistic. Thus, it would appear that the early childhood educator would be prepared to work with children with mild or moderate disabilities versus severe or profound disabilities.

The content for this endorsement and most of the endorsements for teachers of early childhood education are based on the NAEYC (1991) guidelines for preparation of early childhood professionals, as discussed next.

Associate and Bachelor's Level.   Personnel should demonstrate knowledge and application of:

1. child development and learning
2. curriculum development and implementation
3. family and community relationships
4. assessment and evaluation
5. professionalism
6. field experience-observation, participation, and supervision (at least 300 clock hours)

Advanced Degrees.   Master's degree personnel should demonstrate that they have met all of the foregoing requirements and another eight guidelines that focus on enhancing competence, working collaboratively with persons from other disciplines, serving as mentor/supervisor of others, and exhibit an awareness of sociocultural, historical, and political forces that influence diverse delivery systems.

Doctoral degree personnel should meet all of the foregoing requirements plus an additional five areas of competency focusing on leadership, the understanding, conducting, and translating of research findings, and the understanding of the diversity of delivery systems.

The preservice and in-service needs for personnel vary across the severity of children's disabilities. Interestingly, one of the areas still not settled regarding the unified endorsement in Iowa is whether the person with the unified endorsement is prepared to work with severely disabled preschoolers as well as preschoolers with mild or moderate disabilities. Gerken's (1991) discussion of professional training needs is still timely. Current books such as Wyley's (1995) book on premature infants and their families, Anastasiow and Harel's (1993) book on at-risk infants and disabilities and Brown, Thurman, and Pearl's (1993) book on interventions make it all too clear that there is information that must be acquired by the professional who works with infants and children with severe disabilities. Bricker and Widerstrom (1996) have written a book that focuses on preparation of personnel from many disciplines.

The following list is a compilation of information from many sources regarding personnel preparation and direct observation of inadequate or insufficient training. At a minimum training should include the following:

1. *Thorough knowledge of development in typical and atypical infants and children.* For example, the professionals who work with preschoolers must recognize when observed overactivity and distractibility, negativism and oppositional behavior, and perseveration are within the normal parameters for infants and young children. Current textbooks on child development will have tables of "normal" development and there are many excellent and recent resources containing research results and tables of normal and abnormal development (Damon, 1998; Newman & Newman, 1997). Johnson-Powell's (1997) chapter on cultural assessment contains such a table and reminds the reader that such tables are based on Western nosological considerations and may not be appropriate for persons who are not fully acculturated. Knowledge of those factors that enhance and deter development singly or in combination with other factors is a neccessity. Books such as those by Sternberg (1994), Browder (1991), and Snell (1987, 1993) provide valuable information about the needs of persons with profound disabilities.

2. *Thorough knowledge of common medical and health terms, and of the health, emotional and educational needs of infants and preschoolers who have chronic illnesses and medical disorders that require specialized care.* An understanding of the long-term effects of these health problems is needed; including knowledge of the effects of the death of an infant or preschooler on other children, parents, teachers, and support personnel. The early childhood specialist must receive information about chronic illnesses and medical disorders, the symptoms exhibited, and the type of care needed. Brown and Brown (1994) list some of the established medical conditions and disorders that the early childhood specialist must understand: chromosomal anomalies and genetic disorders, neurological disorders, congenital malformations, inborn errors of metabolism, sensory disorders, severe atypical developmental disorders, and toxic exposure. This is not an all-inclusive list. Many preschoolers with severe disabilities have health problems that require long-term care and some of the health conditions are terminal. Early childhood specialists must also be given information about the grieving process so they can help others and themselves when a death of a preschooler occurs.

3. *Thorough understanding of assessment and measurement.* During the 1980s and 1990s many new terms were introduced in assessment. Although not all are re-ally new, they have left some consumers confused about what is really appropriate. Many consumers of assessment techniques have forgotten the basic measurement tenants. A new technique that is considered more authentic because it is a direct observation of a child in a natural setting is no more useful than a standardized instrument administered in a clinic if it does not result in reliable and valid results. A very simple definition of *reliability* is the extent to which an assessment instrument is consistent in measuring whatever it does measure. All persons who assess children must remember that reliability is a necessary but insufficient characteristic of an assessment instrument. The instrument must also be valid. Is the assessment measure doing the job for which it is used? Gibbs and Teti (1990) believe that assessment instruments must be reliable, valid, objective, free from bias, and efficient. Many new instruments are created each year. The professional must know when an instrument is technically adequate, when it is appropriate for the preschooler as is, or when adaptations are necessary, and when the administration of an assessment technique will be helpful in planning interventions.

4. *The ability to apply this knowledge when conducting assessment and intervention with preschoolers with severe disabilities and their families.* The early childhood specialist must know how to work with a family to determine what is really needed by a child and his and her family and whether a program of intervention is working. Two measurement terms that appeared in the professional literature in the 1980s but have been more thoroughly discussed in the 1990s are *social validity* and *treatment integrity.* "Social validation generally refers to establishing the extent to which the goals of intervention practices, the procedures used to pursue these goals, and the outcomes of our efforts to reach these goals are acceptable to the community of people concerned with individuals whom the procedures are intended to help" (Lloyd & Heubusch, 1996, p. 8). Social validity is most often assessed by an interventionist or researcher who may subjectively evaluate outcomes after intervention or at best asks for consumer opinions. There can be problems with this just as there are with other techniques for evaluating outcomes via third-party informants (Lloyd & Heubusch, 1996). Determining the acceptability of behavioral and other types of intervention by consumers is very important. It is the consumer, not the professional, who must usually conduct the treatment. If a treatment is not viewed as an acceptable intervention by the person who will conduct it, it may not be conducted at all or may be conducted without integrity. Finding out what is acceptable may help the professionals work more closely with families to set up a more effective intervention plan.

Most of the investigations of treatment acceptability in the 1980s were analog studies asking persons (not necessarily the actual consumer of services) to rate treatment applied to case studies or simulations rather than real cases. The results of those studies identified several variables that were related to treatment acceptability: amount of time needed to implement the procedure, the side effects of treatment, the type of treatment (positive or negative approach), severity of the problem and the perceived effectiveness of the treatment. Thus, Reimers, Wacker, Cooper, and De Raad (1992) decided to examine analog and naturalistic ratings of acceptability by asking 40 parents to rate the acceptability of treatments in case studies before their own child was evaluated at the Behavioral Pediatrics Clinic. After the evaluation of their own child, they were asked to rate the acceptability of his or her plan. The researchers were also able to investigate the relationship between acceptability of the treatment and compliance in carrying it out over time. There were similar findings across the analog and clinical data relative to the use of positive reinforcement procedures, but in contrast to other studies, behavioral treatments were not necessarily favored for severe behavior problems. The relationship between acceptability and compliance with the treatment procedures increased over time. Gresham, Gansle, and Noell (1993) reviewed all behavior analysis studies that appeared in the *Journal of Applied Behavior Analysis (JABA)* between 1980 and 1990 and found that the accuracy of treatment implementation (treatment integrity) was investigated in only 16 percent of the studies. They also found that in two-thirds of the studies, the components of the treatment were not operationally defined. Several recommendations were made to improve confidence in research findings and to make sure clients receive the prescribed treatment. They can be summarized as follows:

a. Provide clear definitions of all independent variables (treatment).
b. Determine criteria for accuracy of implementation of treatment.
c. Determine levels of treatment integrity.
d. Gather sufficient samples of treatment integrity.
e. Check for reactivity to an observer's presence.
f. Check periodically for the accuracy of the interventionist's procedures.

Reimers, Wacker, Derby, and Cooper (1995) added an additional component to the studies of treatment ac-

ceptability by also investigating whether the parents' beliefs regarding the cause of their child's behavior would be related to the acceptability of treatment. They found that if parents attributed their children's problems to physical reasons, they were less likely to rate behavioral treatments as acceptable.

5. *Training in consultation skills that are associated with successful clinical outcomes.* Far too often information is shared with parents and team members in a way that is not beneficial. Sanders and Lawton (1993) provide a guided participation model of information transfer, which involves a series of communicative tasks, with provisions for parents to process, react to, and challenge the professionals' views. Although this model seems to be professional centered versus family centered, the steps in the session could be put into place in a family-centered model as well. These "common-sense" suggestions that are supported by the research literature are too often ignored.

a. Prepare for all sessions—have stated goals, determine what information is needed, and how long it will take to share the information.
b. Establish an agenda.
c. Summarize the presenting problem.
d. Present descriptive information regarding the problem and check for accuracy of descriptions and understanding by all participants.
e. Review possible causes of the problem.
f. Discuss all the options for future actions.
g. Have knowledge of family systems, family-focused interventions, and social policies.

There is a wide array of family systems and professionals who must understand these and be flexible in their judgment about what constitutes a healthy family. Powell, Batsche, Ferro, Fox, and Dunlap (1997) discuss six principles that are associated with strength-based approaches to family support: a philosophy based on family strength; a partnership approach to service provision; a family-centered, family-driven agenda; an individualized response to family needs and capacities; a broad-based, comprehensive view of family development; and an assessment of outcomes based on family functioning and the quality of life of family members. Harbin (1993) discusses the need for professionals to understand the priorities and concerns of the family and the stages that family members are going through. The professional needs to be knowledgeable about the effects of early childhood disabilities on family functioning and how families cope with disabilities.

6. *Supervised practica experiences.* Because of the shortage of licensed and/or trained persons to work with preschoolers with disabilities, many teachers, psychologists, social workers, and others began providing services to the preschoolers and their families without having adequate training and supervision. Many mistakes were made and many persons were alienated by ineffectual services. For teachers of early childhood special education, many states allow a minimum of 300 clock hours of practica with preschoolers with disabilities. That is the equivalent of about 37 days of experience. At least twice that many clock hours are required for student teaching in a regular elementary or secondary classroom. I believe that the challenges one faces when working with preschoolers with disabilities require additional supervised experience. Being allowed to work in the classroom as a teacher or a support person, without any supervision, because of a shortage of trained personnel is a disservice to the professional, the child being served, and his or her parents.

7. *Training in cultural competence, aware of own biases, demonstration of sensitivity to the particular cultural orientation of the family.* The National Council for Accreditation of Teacher Education and the Council for Exceptional Children approved standards and guidelines mandating that teacher education programs in special education provide multicultural education throughout their curricula. In 1998, most state departments of education required the same curricula infusion in regular education programs. Foster and Iannaccone (1994) analyzed the content of 16 textbooks that were frequently used in a survey course on exceptionality. Some multicultural information was found in all of the books; five had considerably more information than others. What is important to find out is if such requirements have resulted in more awareness and respect for the differences in others. The reality in one large midwestern university is that the required course in human relations has had a very limited effect on changes in attitudes toward persons who are different from the majority culture. The practitioner in early childhood special education must be aware of his or her own values and beliefs and how these might interfere when working with families with different values and beliefs. The professional should take the time and effort to gather appropriate information about the family's values and attempt to provide services within appropriate cultural and ethnic contexts for the child and his or her family. Rogers, Ponterotto, Conoley, and Wiese (1992) surveyed 121 directors of doctoral and nondoctoral school psychology programs to determine to what extent the programs integrated multicultural themes into core courses, offered minority related courses, exposed students to culturally diverse students during practica and internships, provided minority issues research opportunities, and had culturally diverse persons among faculty and students. Despite verbal commitment to multicultural training, the majority of the programs were not spending much time on multicultural training. Rounds, Weil, and Bishop (1994) discuss the following principals of culturally competent practice: acknowledging and valuing diversity, conducting a cultural self-assessment, recognizing and understanding the dynamics of difference, acquiring cultural knowledge, and adapting to diversity. They believe that services that are truly family centered will emphasize respect for family diversity and focus on family strengths and priorities. Self-assessment should be part of the training to be a culturally competent service provider. McWilliam and Bailey (1993) report that the field of early intervention has just recently begun to understand the impact of interventionists' personal beliefs and values on the effectiveness of services. Ethnographic interviewing, participant observation, and role-plays are strategies that can be used effectively to implement culturally competent practice.

8. *Training in a variety of intervention strategies for a variety of needs.* The "one size fits all" approach will not work for preschoolers with severe disabilities and their families (Telzrow, 1993; Thurman, 1993). The ideal combination of coursework and field experiences is one in which all knowledge and skills learned in the classroom are applied in an environment that fosters collaboration in assessment and intervention. The preschoolers and families may have multiple service needs. Supervision and feedback should be provided to the trainee to ensure that the trainee understands when intervention activities might target many goals across settings and when site-specific activities may be needed to target other goals. Miller (1992a) found that few early childhood specialists knew anything about the theoretical underpinnings of curriculum implementation. Wolery and McWilliam (1998) and Wolery and Schuster (1997) provide good suggestions about classroom-based interventions. The foundation for intervention needs to be the knowledge and application of developmental and learning theories to curriculum implementation.

9. *Training in needs assessment and program evaluation.* Over 25 years have passed since psychologists and other professionals who conduct assessment were mandated to conduct more thorough assessments that could be linked to intervention (P.L. 94-142, 1975). Yet, far too often, the assessment process stops with the evaluation of the child. The early intervention specialists need to be trained to use assessment to determine the needs of families and school personnel as well as the children and be able to assess the outcomes of intervention for children, families, and school personnel. Bergen (1994) has samples of forms for conducting family needs assessments. Benner's (1992) chapter on determining program effectiveness provides guidelines for six models of evaluation: goal-attainment evaluation, input-based judgmental evaluation, output-based judgmental evaluation, decision-facilitation evaluation, and naturalistic evaluation. She points out the need to look at child outcome, parent satisfaction, and employee morale. She has many suggestions for measuring child outcomes. Cohen and Spenciner (1994) provide guidelines for individual and program evaluations. Simeonsson, Bailey, Huntington, and Brandon (1991) provide a simple goal attainment scale to be used with families. Bailey, McWilliam, Darkes, et al. (1998) believe that there has not been enough attention paid to identifying and assessing family outcomes. They present a framework for assessing family outcomes that includes eight questions about the family's view of the special service system and the impact the early intervention has on the various domains of family life. Nagle (1995) discusses the importance of needs assessment and presents the assets and limitations of different needs assessment methodologies.

10. *Training in the ethical and legal issues that surround working with preschoolers with disabilities and their families.* The early childhood specialists must be knowledgeable about the education and civil rights laws that are directly related to the services they provide (ADA, 1990; Family Educational Rights and Privacy Act [FERPA], 1974; IDEA, 1997; Section 504 of the Rehabilitation Act of 1973) as well as the ethical codes that pertain to their specific disciplines. Reviewing case studies and participating in role-plays are helpful techniques for application of the knowledge. Hayes, Hayes, Moore, and Ghezzi (1994) cover many of the ethical issues that occur when working with developmentally disabled children and families.

11. *Training that is interdisciplinary and transdisciplinary at both the preservice and in-service levels.* All of the early childhood intervention professionals need to communicate during their training across disciplines. Bergen (1994) believes that for a transdisciplinary model to be fully implemented with infants and preschoolers, collaborative cross-disciplinary experiences

in assessing infants and toddlers should be a requirement in personnel preparation programs. Facts and values regarding inclusion, normalization, and integrated practice need to be discussed and decision-making models be used to develop the most appropriate interventions for infants and children. Orelove and Sobsey's (1996) and Hanson and Carta's (1995) books emphasize the need to use a transdisciplinary approach when working with children with multiple disabilities. McWilliam and Bailey (1994) found significant differences in the perceptions and beliefs of occupational and physical therapists, special educators, and speech and language pathologists, with the special educators being more likely to use and favor integrated services. These professionals deliver their services in different ways and they need to be aware of and understand the various models for service delivery. There must be recognition of the time and effort it takes to work together to develop priorities for preschoolers with disabilities. Not all professionals have been exposed to transdisciplinary models and have difficulty with role release. If knowledge and awareness of transdisciplinary approaches are introduced at the preservice level, fewer "turf" problems should occur at the professional level.

12. *Evaluation of training.* Changes in training to meet the needs of consumers will only occur if the effectiveness of the training is assessed. Kaiser and McWhorter's (1990) book focuses on general topics in the preparation of personnel to work with persons with disabilities and provides individual chapters for very specific needs. They also provide six chapters on personnel preparation models that have supportive evidence that they work. Too often the evaluation of preservice and in-service training focuses only on participant satisfaction. Fredericks and Templeman (1990) suggested that at least five levels of training evaluation should take place:

a. Trainee satisfaction
b. Trainee skills or knowledge acquired
c. Trainee implementation of knowledge or skills acquired
d. Child behavior changes as a result of knowledge or skills acquired by the trainee
e. Program changes

In evaluating the progress of graduate students and trainees, we often forget to do those simple steps we know are necessary to effect change:

a. Identify trainees' needs by asking the trainees what they need and observing them doing their work.

b. Identify training competencies.

c. Design training objectives.

d. Design training activities.

The Teaching Research Infant and Child Center in Monmouth, Oregon, has been conducting in-service training for over 25 years and has found that providing the training in a neutral site, providing practica-based training, and using multiple presentation formats are effective components in ensuring success of the training.

13. *Training in qualitative and quantitative research design.* The training needs to be at a level sufficient enough to either design prospective, longitudinal studies with adequate comparison groups and/or integrate empirical findings into training, service delivery, and policy decisions (Paget, 1992).

ASSESSMENT WITHIN THE CONTEXT OF THE FAMILY

Harbin (1993) believes that the child interventionists' views of the family have changed dramatically since the 1950s when the focus of intervention for severely disabled preschoolers would have been institutionalization with parents relinquishing all decision making to the institution versus the 1990s when the focus of intervention is on the individualization of programs and families are involved in all steps of the assessment and intervention process. In the decade since P.L. 99-457 mandated the collaborative development of individualized family service plans (IFSP), there has been increased emphasis on assessment and intervention for preschoolers with disabilities being conducted within the context of the family. However, there have been important changes in our models of collaboration. We have moved from professional-centered models to family-allied models, family-focused models, and family-centered models. New instruments were developed to assess family needs and concerns. Sexton, Burrell, and Thompson (1992) investigated the measurement integrity of the *Family Needs Survey* (FNS) (Bailey & Simeonsson, 1990), which was created to both identify family needs and prescribe interventions. Mothers completed this 35-item scale by indicating for each item whether the family had a need, did not have a need, or was uncertain about the need. Sexton et al. report adequate support for the internal consistency, reliability, and factor structure of the FNS for a sample of 53 mothers of young children with disabilities. The areas the mothers were most concerned about were the present and future services for their children, information about how to teach their children, and information

about the child's condition or disability. A need for social support was also a need for over 50 percent of the mothers. Assessment must take place within each family and, although this might be a helpful instrument in assessing individual family needs, the FNS should not be thought of as a normative instrument from which one could make generalizations about family needs. King, Rosenbaum, and King (1996) describe the development of the *Measure of Processes of Care* (MPOC-56), which is a 56-item questionnaire used to determine how parents and guardians of children with chronic health problems evaluate the services they and their children receive and how these services are related to child outcome. Good internal consistency and test-retest reliability were reported for a sample of 653 parents and factor analysis supported the MPOC-56 as a multidimensional instrument. Parents were able to differentiate among five aspects of care for children across different types of programs of care. The authors believe that the MPOC-56 is widely applicable. Limitations were that only parents in the Ontario area, who had children with neurodevelopmental disabilities, were surveyed. However, this instrument could be modified to be part of the evaluation of programs for children with any type of disability.

The focus in early intervention has moved from the child to providing support for the family and from a deficit model to a strength-based approach. The final version of P.L. 99-457 has mandated a family-centered approach in which family members must determine their priorities, concerns, and resources. It is much easier to provide services from a deficit model with a focus on the deficits present in a child and his or her family rather than attempt to help families identify their strengths and build on these strengths to accomplish goals and to promote the well-being of all family members. Beckman and Boyes (1993) provide a very practical guide for families of young children with disabilities. Bernheimer, Gallimore, and Kaufman (1993) make very good suggestions about how to get families involved in the assessment, intervention, and decision-making processes necessary to effect positive changes.

Bailey, Buysee, Edmondson, and Smith (1992) surveyed 237 professionals who were working in early intervention programs in four different states, to determine if family-centered services were being provided. There were significant discrepancies between typical and ideal roles for parents. The professionals were generally unwilling to assume responsibility for the barriers preventing such services (15 percent) and placed most of the blame on parent barriers. Wesley, Buysse, and Tyndall

(1997) conducted focus groups to explore parents' and professionals' experiences and perspectives about inclusion and early intervention. There were discrepancies in parents' and professionals' views of current situations and their ability to envision ideal services. Filer and Mahoney (1996) found the same discrepancies in their views of ideal services. However, Ableboone, Goodwin, Sandall, Gordon, and Martin (1992) found parents and professionals sharing some of the same concerns regarding access to services and the development and coordination of services. Wyly (1995) discusses some of the barriers to family-centered care and intervention such as training priorities, critical care approaches, attitudes of the professionals, equipment and technology, communication, and insufficient staff to train parents who might need training to carry out an intervention in the home. McWilliam, Ferguson, Harbin, Porter, Munn, and Vandiviere (1998) studied 100 IFSPs to determine whether they were family centered versus child centered and found they were overwhelmingly focusing on child-related goals versus family-related goals. In spite of the 10 years that have passed since federal laws mandated IFSPs, the plans look very much like the child-centered plans from the past.

Thus, in spite of our mandates to work collaboratively with families, much of our evaluation of such work demonstrates we have a long way to go. Turnbull and Ruef (1997) interviewed 17 families of children, youth, and adults with disabilities and found that the families themselves have had to be the catalysts in attaining inclusive lifestyle supports for the person with disabilities. Many had no regular or convenient access to state-of-the-art or practical information needed to help the family with home and community routines. The collaborative linkage between families, friends, school personnel, other mental health professionals, and community members was missing.

Trivette, Dunst, Boyd, and Hamby (1995) report that although the term *family-centered* is used extensively in the literature on early intervention, there is a great deal of diversity in definitions and applications of the term. Therefore, to determine whether a program actually operated in the way the model of the program was described, 150 parents of preschoolers with disabilities who were from North Carolina and 130 parents of preschoolers with disabilities from Pennsylvania were asked to complete the *Helpgiving Practices Scale* and the *Personal Control Appraisal Scale* and asked how often a target help-giver worked with a parent each month, on the average, during the last six months. Trivette et al. found

that the sources of variations in parents' assessments of help-giving practices were related to differences in program models and not parent or family characteristics. The authors also reported that the differences in parents' perceptions of personal control in receiving help from a help-giver were almost entirely attributable to the combination of program characteristics and help-giving practices. More positive assessments of help-giving practices were given for those programs that were family centered and had more frequent contact with the parents. This kind of study supports the belief that program policies and practices are potent factors in attitudes toward help and empowerment of parents. Trivette, Dunst, and Hamby (1996) investigated the relationships between human services program models and help-giving practices, and between both program models and help-giving practices and help-seekers' perceptions of their control of a situation. Their respondents were mothers from 107 low socioeconomic families. Although there are a number of limitations in this study, the implications for practice are that the most effective help-giving practices are those that involve the help-seeker and result in the help-seeker becoming more competent. Further research will need to focus on child and family outcomes, beyond being satisfied with services.

CULTURALLY COMPETENT ASSESSMENT PRACTICES

Barrera (1993) recommended that when assessing a culturally and/or linguistically diverse (CLD) child, the following variables be considered:

1. The child's level of acculturation.
2. The home and community environments.
3. The child's preferred learning and interactive behaviors.
4. The child's and family's linguistic and sociocultural experiences and resources.
5. The child's language history and usage patterns.
6. The child's linguistic and metalinguistic proficiency.

Johnson-Powell's (1997) chapter on the "Culturologic Interview" contains four very helpful tables indicating what needs to be done to shape the content, context, and purpose of the interview, what needs to be included in an interview, a guide to diagnostic assessment of children that includes normal landmarks in development and signs of psychological disturbance from birth through adolescence, and the items that should be present in a clinical case review. Anderson and Goldberg

(1991), Dana (1993), Lynch and Hanson (1992, 1993, 1996), Suzuki, Meller, and Ponteretto (1996), Garcia and Malkin (1993), and Salend (1997) all provide guidelines for conducting appropriate assessments and intervention with CLD children. Sexton, Lobman, Constans, Snyder, and Ernest (1997) administered the Early Intervention Multicultural Practices Survey to 170 early intervention-ists who were attending a statewide training session on multicultural issues and practices. Overall these interven-tionists were more positive about their interactions with African American families than they were about the level of administrative support for their multicultural practices. The authors concluded that it would be very important to include program administrators in multicultural training activities. A qualitative research design that included di-rect observations at inclusive preschool sites and face-to-face interviews with parents, classroom personnel, and program administrators was used to examine the relation-ships among language, culture, and disability (Hanson, Gutierrez, Morgan, Brennan, & Zercher, 1997). A total of 112 children were observed in 16 early childhood programs. The findings of the study demonstrated the complexity and interrelatedness between contexts and systems. Culture and language did influence how much a child with a disability participated in the activities in the regular preschool program. The social and learning op-portunities for children with disabilities, who did not speak English, were limited.

THE ASSESSMENT PROCESS

Before the assessment process begins, we need assur-ance that we have an examiner who is skilled in building and maintaining a positive relationship with the infant or young child with severe disabilities. The examiner must also be skilled in selecting, administering, and interpret-ing appropriate assessment techniques in a culturally competent manner. We have discovered that effective procedures for assessing young children with disabilities is very different from what might be considered tradi-tional assessment with older children (McLean et al., 1996). The characteristics of infants and toddlers, with or without disabilities, do not make them good candi-dates for being assessed by unfamiliar adults in unfamil-iar settings. Too often we have continued to rely on procedures used with older children when assessing pre-schoolers. Many errors in assessment occur under those conditions. The presence of a disability will make the task of conducting an appropriate assessment even more challenging. The same comprehensive sequence of as-

sessment procedures should be used with preschoolers who have severe disabilities as are used with other chil-dren: case finding/identification, tracking, screening, diagnosis, functional assessment, performance monitor-ing, and program evaluation. Case finding/identification and screening are often combined into one step of the process for preschoolers with severe disabilities because the children are often identified at birth or shortly there-after. The sequence and purpose of these procedures are presented in Table 15.4.

Child Find/Case Finding

P.L. 105-17 (1997) lists the requirements for a statewide system of services for infants and toddlers. The require-ments include a comprehensive child-finding system, a public awareness program focusing on early identifica-tion, and a central directory of services, resources, and experts available in the state. Child finding or case find-ing is the comprehensive search for the children who need to be screened. It is usually done by public an-nouncements via brochures, press, radio, and posters of the early intervention activities taking place within the geographic area covered. Systems of referral can be es-tablished in many locations: medical centers, education agencies, day care/preschools, and social service agen-cies as well as any other health care providers. It is hoped that some of the public awareness activities that take place under Child Find may lead to primary prevention activities as persons become more knowledgeable about risk factors. Although there is not universal agreement on what risk factors or combination of risk factors are most highly related to later disabilities, everyone does agree that the presence of multiple risk factors is related to a higher probability of delay or disability. Dunst (1993) has summarized a list of risk and opportunity factors that in-fluence human development. Bricker (1996) stated that if prevention and early detection are our goals for child finding and screening, then the emphasis should be shifted from examining predictor variables to systematic monitoring of children's developmental progress.

Tracking

At-risk registers have been in existence in the United Kingdom for over 25 years and are now in place in many other parts of the world. In many instances, they are now called tracking or monitoring systems, but their purpose remains the same. They were established to follow the progress of infants and young children who are consid-

TABLE 15.4 Sequence of Assessment Procedures

SEQUENCE	PURPOSE	TARGET POPULATION
Case finding/identification	To increase public awareness of services available for disabled preschoolers To find infants and preschoolers likely to have a disability	General public Parents Medical personnel Infants and preschoolers
Screening	To identify children who are not within the normal range of development and need further evaluation	At-risk or disabled infants and preschoolers Parents and guardians
Diagnoses	Pinpointing the nature and degree of a problem	Disabled infants and preschoolers
Educational assessment	Pinpointing specific skills and learning needs of infants and preschoolers	Disabled infants and preschoolers
Performance monitoring	Continuous and ongoing evaluation of children's performance	Disabled infants and preschoolers
Program evaluation	Evaluate overall effectiveness of intervention program	Disabled infants and preschoolers Parents and guardians Teachers and therapists

Source: Benner, 1992; Cohen & Spenciner, 1994, 1998; Gerken, 1991; McLean, 1996.

ered to be at risk because of biological or environmental factors. Bricker (1996) believes that current models of screening and tracking are problematic because assessment is often infrequent and does not include familiar caregivers in the process. She proposes a three-step model for prevention and early detection: screening, determining eligibility, and intervention. Step 1 includes semiannual well-baby checks. Parents and guardians are asked to assess their child's progress by completing questionnaires or checklists every three to four months. If any problems are detected, the child is referred to Step 2 for a professional evaluation that is conducted with parent/guardian input. If no problems were found during Step 1 or Step 2, continued monitoring will occur under Step 1. Children with documented problems in Step 2 are referred to Step 3. McLean (1996) reports that the Ages and Stages Questionnaire (ASQ) (Bricker, Squires, Mounts, Potter, Nickel, & Farrell, 1995) was developed specifically for monitoring child development at a distance. Parents are asked to complete 11 questionnaires about their child's behavior over a four-year period (ages 4 months through 48 months). The ASQ could also be administered as an interview via the phone or in person. O'Brien,

Rice, and Roy (1996) have created criteria for providing early intervention in neonatal intensive care units.

Identification/Screening

There is overlap in the instruments that are used in tracking, identifying, and screening children. The same instrument could be used to track, identify, and screen infants and preschoolers who are sufficiently delayed in one or more domains and need further assessment. The Committee on Children with Disabilities (1994) of the American Academy of Pediatrics lists the following as essential components of the screening process:

1. *Sensitive attention to parent concerns*
2. *Thoughtful inquiry about parental observations*
3. *Observation of a wide variety of the child's behavior*
4. *Examination of specific developmental attainments*
5. *Use of all encounters for observing and recording developmental status*

6. *Screening of vision and hearing to rule out sensory impairment as a cause of the delay*
7. *Observation of parent–child interaction (p. 864)*

Benner (1992), McLean (1996), Cohen and Spenciner (1994, 1998), and Salvia and Ysseldyke (1995, 1998) provide reviews of screening instruments. Although some screening instruments have been revised since 1990, there were relatively few new instruments developed in the last five years. Also many instruments that were intended for screening instruments have also been used to determine a diagnosis.

Two instruments frequently used in the hospital setting are the Apgar Score (1953) and the Neonatal Behavioral Assessment Scale (NBAS) (Brazelton, 1978, 1984). The Apgar is a rating of five physical signs one minute and five minutes after birth. The NBAS is an interactive assessment, which measures behavioral and neural organization using 28 behavioral items and 20 reflexive items. Gerken's (1991) brief review of scales that summarize prenatal and perinatal risk factors is still of value even though most of the instruments were developed at least 20 years ago.

Instruments used outside of the hospital setting and frequently sited in the professional literature were the AGS Early Screening Profiles (Harrison et al., 1990), the Batelle Developmental Screening Test (1984), the Brigance Early Preschool Screen (1990) and Brigance Preschool Screen (1985), the Denver II (Frankenburg & Dodds, 1990), the DASI II (Fewell & Langley, 1984). DIAL-R (Mardell-Czudnowski & Goldenberg, 1990), First STEP (Miller, 1993), and Early Screening Inventory (ESI). Only the AGS, the ESI, and the FirstSTEP report adequate reliability and validity for use as screening instruments.

Salvia and Ysseldyke (1995) reviewed the Infant Mullen Scales of Early Learning (IMSEL) (Mullen, 1989) and the Mullen Scales of Early Learning (MSEC) (Mullen, 1995). These instruments were designed to be diagnostic tests of mental and motor ability in infants (birth to 36 months) and preschoolers (21 months to 63 months). Interscorer reliability is excellent for both instruments, but internal consistency reliability is suitable only for screening purposes.

It is clear that continued research is needed to identify the responses of typical and atypical infants and the variables that result in neurological and/or developmental disabilities. Although not universally supported, there is a need to proceed with services based on identi-fied risks and needs rather than wait for a final diagnosis. This view is represented in the changes in IDEA that occurred in P.L. 105-17 (1997). It is also clear that appropriate screening requires the integrated efforts of parents, medical professionals, educators, other support personnel, and the community.

Diagnosis/Educational Planning

Once an infant or preschooler has been identified as a child who is developmentally delayed, the next step is to determine exactly what the child and his or her family needs to function effectively. The purpose of diagnosis and educational planning is to pinpoint the strengths and areas of need present in the severely disabled preschooler as well as the concerns, priorities, and resources present in the family. Services to preschoolers with disabilities were advocated over 30 years ago (HCEEP, 1968) and criteria for appropriate assessment were established as part of P.L. 94-142 (1975). Why is inappropriate assessment of infants and preschoolers with severe disabilities still occurring over 20 years later? Perhaps because some persons still believe that a standardized, norm-referenced index of ability is needed in order to meet the criteria for services. What is most important is that comprehensive, culturally sensitive, reliable, and valid assessments be conducted (IDEA, 1997).

It is apparent that appropriate assessment for preschoolers is different than for school-age children and that there is no one assessment instrument that will provide sufficient information to either diagnose or help plan for a child. There is a continuum of options in assessment that goes beyond how will the team function (who does what) and what model of assessment should be used. Some instruments or techniques assess one specific area or skill whereas others assess multiple skills or areas of development. A few instruments have been developed specifically for infants and preschoolers with disabilities, but many have not. Many standardized instruments are not appropriate for severely disabled children because there are not a sufficient number of items that can be used to assess an infant or preschooler with limited communication or motor skills. The content for instruments used for children under 2 years of age consists of simple, readily observable motor actions, whereas the assessment instruments for 2- to 6-year-olds measure communication, motor, cognitive, self-help, and preacademic skills. Table 15.5 is a matrix of many of the possible choices a team (this includes family members) must make. The team must consider what they

TABLE 15.5   Matrix of Assessment Options

	1	2	3	4	5	6	7	8	9	10	11	12	13	14	15	16
1		X	X	X	X	X	X	X	X	X	X	X	X	X	X	X
2			X	X	X	X	X	X	X	X	X	X	X	X	X	X
3				X	X	X	X	X	X	X	X	X	X	X	X	X
4					X	X	X	X	X	X	X	X	X	X	X	X
5						X	X	X	X	X	X	X	X	X	X	X
6							X	X	X	X	X	X	X	X	X	X
7								X	X	X	X	X	X	X	X	X
8									X	X	X	X	X	X	X	X
9										X	X	X	X	X	X	X
10											X	X	X	X	X	X
11												X	X	X	X	X
12													X	X	X	X
13														X	X	X
14															X	X
15																X
16																

1 = Adaptive
2 = Analog
3 = Criterion-referenced
4 = Curriculum-referenced
5 = Direct
6 = Indirect
7 = Informal
8 = Formal

9 = Naturalistic
10 = Norm-referenced
11 = Performance
12 = Play-based
13 = Portfolio
14 = Process-oriented
15 = Product-oriented
16 = Transdisciplinary play-based

know about each individual child and about these various techniques and choose those that are most efficient and effective.

In 1998 there were legislative and professional mandates to provide family-centered assessment that is direct, continuous, and linked to life skill objectives.

ASSESSMENT: HOW DO YOU GET WHERE YOU NEED TO GO?

Assistive Technology and Adaptive Assessment

Infants and preschoolers with severe or profound disabilities may never develop functional speech or have control of their motor responses. Thus, the professional who works with this population must have the skills to conduct appropriate assessment using assistive technology and/or know how to assess the child who uses assisted augumentative communication systems (Technology Re-

lated Assistance for Individuals Act, 1988). The June 4, 1997 amendments to IDEA reinforced the need to use assistive technology if it will improve the day-to-day functioning of disabled persons. Thus, the professional and popular literature has much more information available about such devices. Dorman (1998) has provided a list of devices that can be used to help disabled students function more effectively as well as a list of distributors. Parette, Dunn, and Hoge (1995) also provide information about low-cost devices that can be used at home. Beukelman and Mirenda's (1992) book focuses on augmentative and alternative communication. Adapted switch toys and microcomputer software have been used in conducting assessment and intervention (Kinsley & Langone, 1995). The purpose of the Preschool Technology Training Project (1995) was to help early childhood personnel and families understand the value of assistive technology and be able to use it to help preschoolers become active participants in their own assessment and intervention process. The training focused on assistive technology policy, adaptive play, augmented and alternative communication, computer use, and funding. Gestures and signing may be used by some preschoolers with disabilities whereas others may use language boards, switches, and computers to communicate. What one may discover in the assessment process is that an infant or precholer not using such devises would benefit from the use of assistive technology. Only a few of the books that focus on the assessment of infants and preschoolers cover the assistive technology available (Benner, 1992; McLean et al., 1996). However, Parette has written several articles regarding the use of assistive devices in the home and in the educational setting (Parette, 1994, 1997; Parette & Angelo, 1996; Parette & Brotherson, 1996; Parette & Marr, 1997). Table 15.6 contains strategies and adaptations needed for assessing the severely disabled.

Informal Assessment

The matrix of assessment options (Table 15.6) and the glossary in Appendix 1 illustrate the plethora of available assessment techniques. It is apparent that a technique could fit under more than one descriptive category. However, the majority of the "popular" techniques that have been written about in the 1980s and 1990s fit under the umbrella of informal techniques because they do not have norms and standard instructions to follow. However, a few of these techniques have been used in empirically based studies. They have standard instructions and provide important idiographic information about one or more children. They have also been labeled alternate or authentic assessment. Pett (1990) states that authentic assessments are performance based, realistic, and instructionally appropriate. For example, curriculum-based assessment (CBA) has been touted as an alternative, authentic assessment technique that has many models. Depending on the model and the definition that are used, CBA could be a norm-referenced or criterion-referenced, formal or informal, standardized or nonstandardized, direct or indirect, process-oriented or product-oriented technique that is presented in an arena or in a one-to-one session. What the early interventionist must keep in mind is that an instrument is not automatically better because it is called an authentic instrument or a curriculum-referenced instrument. It must have validity and reliability. If decisions are being made about an infant or preschooler's life, then those assessment techniques must have content and predictive validity at a minimum along with social validity and treatment integrity.

Some of the assessment techniques receiving considerable press in the 1990s are techniques that are most readily used with preschoolers who are in a center-based program in which multiple samples of behavior can be gathered. They also appear more appropriate for 2- to 5-year-olds versus birth to 2-year-olds. However, careful planning will result in parents as well as teachers and other early childhood specialists being able to use the techniques effectively to help determine a treatment plan and monitor progress.

Interviews

Structured and unstructured interviews have been used as assessment tools since the time of Plato and Socrates. Freud certainly conducted interviews with adults in the 1800s. According to Edelbrock and Costello (1990), the use of the interview as an assessment tool for children developed along diagnostic and descriptive lines. The diagnostic line paralleled the emergence of more differentiated taxonomies of childhood disorders, which occurred in the 1960s, and the descriptive line was being used in the 1950s. Their value in the assessment of preschoolers is dependent on the purpose of the interview, what is asked, how it is asked, where and when it is asked, and by whom it is asked. The reliability and the validity of an interview are enhanced when a structured interview with specific questions is used. The interview is often part of other assessment techniques or assessment systems. Sattler's (1998) book on interviewing children and families is a very important addition to the assessment area. He has devoted over 1,000 pages to discussing the skills needed to be an effective interviewer, providing guidelines for observing infants and children and for conducting a variety of interviews, providing models for interviewing, and giving many examples of semistructured interviews. He has covered areas that are often difficult to deal with because many of us lack the knowledge and skills to conduct interviews in such cases as terminal illness or child abuse. Appendix A in Bergen's (1994) book contains excellent examples of interviews and observation instruments that can be used when working with preschoolers with disabilities. Katz (1994) presented an observational guide for parents to look at their children's development. This guide could be easily converted into a developmental interview during which the parent is asked to respond to questions about his or her referred infant or preschooler's behavior. The 10 areas presented were sleeping habits, eating habits, toilet habits, range of emotions, friendships (if old enough to play with others), variations in play,

TABLE 15.6 Strategies/Adaptations Needed for Assessing the Severely Disabled

DISABLING CONDITION	EXAMINER REQUIREMENTS	INSTRUMENT/ TECHNIQUE SELECTION	STRATEGIES AND ADAPTATIONS
Severe communication deficit	Awareness of child's limitations. Knowledge and experience with alternative communication systems.	Use instruments with limited or no language demands. Select instruments designed for communication-disabled children.	Modify verbal instructions, alternate verbal and nonverbal instructions. Use gestures, signs, pictures, and visual cues to present tasks and allow the same technique for responses. Provide communication boards, rigid head pointers, bliss symbols, electronic voice synthesizers, and adapted switch toys.
Motor impairment	Awareness of child's limitations, medical management issues, positioning. Consultation with appropriate medical personnel; knowledge and experience with motor-impaired children. Be able to informally evaluate the child's vision, hearing, speech, sitting balance, arm-hand use, ability to indicate yes or no verbally or nonverbally.	Use tests requiring limited or no motor demands. Select tests designed for motor-impaired population.	Modify instructions and allow modification of response, such as choice-pointing, multiple-choice format, stabilizing the child's hand, enlarging objects (blocks, beads, etc.). Allow enough time for child to respond. Provide rest periods.
Deficits in social interactions	Awareness of child's limitations. Experience with children with such deficits.	Use techniques requiring minimal social interaction.	Keep social interactions simple, low demands for child.
Deficits in attention, organization	Awareness of child's limitations. Experience with children with such deficits.	Choose simple techniques with clear guidelines.	Simple presentations of materials, short work periods.
Deficits in motivation	Awareness of child's sources of motivation.		Use wide variety of reinforcers. Provide success experiences.

Source: Browder, 1991; Dorman, 1998; Gerken, 1991; Parette, 1997; Parette, Dunn, & Hoge, 1995.

curiosity, interest, spontaneous affection, and enjoyment of the "good things of life." The guide could also be adapted as a handout for parents. Katz also makes suggestions for intervention. An interview that can be conducted in a nonthreatening way and provide valuable information is the "Describe a typical day" interview. The parent or guardian is asked to describe a typical day with the infant or preschooler, from wake-up time in the morning until the child is asleep at night. The interviewer should obtain consent to tape the interview or keep a running record of the information.

Developmental Scales and Checklists

Many nonstandardized instruments that assess the development and progress of infants and preschoolers were developed or revised during the 1980s and 1990s. The Brigance Diagnostic Inventory—Revised (Brigance, 1991), The Early Intervention Developmental Profile (Rogers et al., 1981), the Hawaii Early Learning Profile (Furuno et al., 1988), the Learning Accomplishment Profile (Sanford & Zelman, 1981), the Minnesota Infant Development Inventory (Ireton, 1992), the Assessment Log and Developmental Progress Chart—Infants, 2nd Edition (1991), and the Assessment Log and Developmental Progress Chart—Preschoolers (1990) are all criterion-referenced instruments that are intended to provide useful information for program planning and progress monitoring. The latter two are part of the widely used Carolina Curriculum for Infants and Toddlers with Special Needs (Johnson-Martin, Jens, Attermeier, & Hacker, 1991) and the Carolina Curriculum for Preschoolers with Special Needs (Johnson-Martin, Attermeier, & Hacker, 1990). Each of these instruments has strengths and weaknesses and, because they do not have norms, reliability and validity are highly dependent on the examiners' skills in the assessment and interpretation of infants' and preschoolers' developmental status. The developers of some of these instruments intended for them to be administered by a multidisciplinary team in the child's natural setting.

Curriculum-Based Assessment

Four current CBA models that are frequently used in early childhood education are the generic CBA, curriculum-based developmental assessment (CBDA), curriculum-embedded assessment (CEA), and curriculum-referenced assessment (CRA). A generic CBA assessment could include many different techniques to assess a child in his

or her own curriculum (observations, portfolios, informal checklists, and interviews). *Curriculum-based developmental assessment* is a term that Bagnato and Neisworth (1991) used to describe what they consider the best approach to assessing young children. CBDA assesses the child using developmental landmarks or expectancies to determine the goals and objectives for intervention. They believe that developmental CBA can be used to identify program entry points for a child, aid in program planning, track child progress, and evaluate the program. They also believe that it encourages interdisciplinary collaboration and provides an indirect form of norm-based assessment. Choosing a developmental curriculum is one of the most important program decisions that must be made and child, setting, and curriculum characteristics must be considered. Bagnato and Neisworth (1991) believe that CEA and CRA are types of developmental CBAs. CRA is based on a generic curriculum rather than the specific one a child is using. The Brigance Diagnostic Inventory of Early Development (BDIED) would be considered a CRA.

CEA uses the child's current program curriculum to conduct the assessment and intervention. The child is assessed in his or her own curriculum. Bagnato and Neisworth (1991) use the Hawaii Early Learning Profile (HELP) and HELP for Special Preschoolers (HELP-SP) as examples of CEA. Meisels (1995) has created the "Work Sampling System," which he describes as a curriculum-embedded assessment. His system has three complimentary components: developmental guidelines and checklists, portfolios, and summary reports.

Portfolio Assessment

A portfolio is a record of a child's work. Various definitions have been given for portfolio assessment, but all have the record of work as a basic component. The components of a portfolio can also include the many informal assessments that have been used with the preschooler (observations, checklists, rating scales, and screening tests). For many years, teachers and support personnel have recognized the importance of keeping samples of a child's work in order to pinpoint areas of difficulty and strengths. The reliability and validity of a portfolio approach to assessment are dependent on the purpose of the portfolio, the content of the portfolio, and the representativeness of the content. Grace (1992) believes that the material in a portfolio should be organized by chronological order and category. Fogarty (1996) has edited a collection of articles that offer practical, well-researched answers to a variety of questions about portfolios. Meisels and Steele (1991) present guidelines for collecting portfolios.

Observation

Observation is often a component of other assessment techniques and sometimes is not given recognition as a separate assessment technique. It can be as simple as watching an infant or preschooler for a period of time and writing down everything that the infant or preschooler does during that time period, or as complex as a rigorous naturalistic observation system that requires the pinpointing of behaviors to be observed, and reliability and validity checks. Genishi (1992) uses teachers' stories to illustrate ways to assess children in their everyday classroom life through informal observation and documentation of behavior. Martin (1996) also emphasizes the importance of observation in evaluating young children and has stressed the importance of conducting developmentally appropriate evaluation (DAE) in order to conduct developmentally appropriate practice (DAP). Observation can be either systematic or nonsystematic, norm or criterion referenced, in a natural setting or a clinic setting. Conducting systematic observation in a natural setting has been considered the most reliable and valid method of observation, especially when compared to such techniques as anecdotal records, running records, checklists, and rating scales. However, at least two relatively new approaches to assessment have observation as their base. Those are play-based assessment and functional analysis.

Play-Based Assessment (PBA)

At a very informal level, play-based assessment is simply observing a child at play. Systematic observation could be used or an anecdotal report of child behavior. One advantage of the very informal approach is that the child is being observed in the natural environment where the child must function each day. Often, when a person is talking about play-based assessment with infants and preschoolers, he or she is talking about observing a child complete tasks presented by a professional and/or a parent in an arena setting. The arena setting is simply a circle with the target child and one or two adults in the middle with observers sitting around them. This setting could be the child's home, but many families do not have homes that are equipped to have several professionals sitting in a circle observing, and many professionals do

not provide services outside of their professional setting. PBA allows or even requires flexibility on the part of the examiners, it is intended to include parents in the assessment process, and it is a natural, holistic approach that is appropriate for infants and preschoolers at all ability levels. Observer bias is one of the many major disadvantages. If one observes a variety of early childhood special programs, one will see very different approaches being labeled as PBA. The structure may be nonexistent and the observer may not have appropriate training to conduct reliable and valid observations.

An approach to PBA that deals with some of the disadvantages of unstructured observation of an infant or preschooler at play is Linder's Transdisciplinary Play-Based Assessment (TPBA) (1993a) and Transdisciplinary Play-Based Intervention (TPBI) (1993b). She describes TPBA as follows: "TPBA involves the child in structured and unstructured play situations with at varying times, a facilitating adult, the parent(s), and another child or children" (Linder, 1993a, p. 1). Linder has designed TPBA for children whose cognitive functioning level is between infancy and age 6. There are some similarities between this approach and Bagnato and Neisworth's curriculum-based developmental assessment. The assessment consists of observing the infant or preschooler responding to developmental tasks in the cognitive, social-emotional, communication and language, and sensory-motor domains. It is considered a dynamic approach to assessment that ends in a written report and program plan. Linder (1993a, 1993b) has two manuals that contain the information needed to conduct TPBA and TPBI and a manual device to develop the curriculum (Linder, 1993c). There are many good examples in the manual. The content of the assessment, the team members involved, the structure of the situation, and the questions asked or tasks presented vary in order to meet individual child needs. PBA and TPBA are both idiographic approaches to assessment. At a minimum, TPBA will include the child, a parent, a professional who serves as a facilitator, observers, and a video camera operator. Guidelines for presenting tasks and assessing the infant or child in the four domains reported earlier are provided in the manual. Worksheets are also provided to help the team write qualitative statements about the observed strengths and needs of the infant or preschooler. Once tasks and an examiner have been chosen, the tasks are presented to the infant or preschooler while the team members observe. The session is videotaped so team members can review it. After the observation, a postsession meeting is conducted, the videotape is analyzed, the guidelines and worksheets are correlated, preliminary transdisciplinary recommendations are made, a program-planning meeting is convened, and a formal report is written.

TPBA can be used to identify needs, develop an intervention plan, and evaluate progress. Linder (1993a) believes that TPBA can lead to role release, extension, expansion, exchange, and support. She has also noted some limitations, as there are few reliability and validity studies, a limited look at parent–child interactions, and philosophical and professional differences that occur within and outside the team. Myers, McBride, and Peterson (1996) conducted one of the few validity studies of TPBA. Data on consumer perceptions, time factors, functional utility, and parent–staff congruence on judgment-based ratings were compared for children who had been randomly assigned to either a multidisciplinary, standardized, or play-based assessment. The particular transdiciplinary, play-based procedures used were based on methods from Child Development Resources (1992). The authors reported evidence for the social validity of the transdisciplinary, play-based assessment model in citing higher scores in the areas of mothers' ratings, professional staff ratings, time efficiency, two undergraduate students' ratings of the functional utility of reports, and the congruence of professionals' and mothers' ratings of the children on the same judgment-based developmental profile. Limitations of this study were noted by the authors as small sample size, the same team members conducted both types of assessment, and the mothers completed the judgment-based developmental profile for both types of assessment. Other concerns about the limitations of this study beyond those noted by the authors are that the authors made their own subjective beliefs about the two assessment approaches evident at the beginning and conclusion of their article. The following quote in Myers et al. (1996) possibly reveals a limited awareness of what appropriate standardized assessment should include or the authors' observations of very inappropriate standardized assessment.

> By definition, standardized assessments do not include involvement of parents. Transdisciplinary methods, however, typically provide opportunities for parents to facilitate the child's performance by physically supporting the child, actually eliciting behaviors or providing information about the child's behavior in normative situations. (p. 104)

Additional statements implying that parents are not given opportunities for input when standardized assessment instruments are used are insulting to those who

were providing services to preschoolers with disabilities and involving the families in every step of the assessment process long before P.L. 92-142 or P.L. 99-457 required parent consent and involvement. In fact, assessment of infants is almost impossible without assistance and input from parents.

Functional Analysis/Assessment

Functional assessment became one of the many new assessment terms to appear in the 1980s. It has been used to describe any assessment that was conducted in a child's natural environment, but the origin of the term is from the behavioral assessment literature. Iwata, Dorsey, Slifer, Bauman, and Richman (1982) are credited with presenting the first comprehensive and standardized methodology for conducting functional analysis when they analyzed the function of self-injurious behavior. The methodology was adapted to analyze the function of a wide variety of behaviors. Sometimes the terms *functional analysis, functional assessment,* and even *ecobehavioral assessment* are used interchangeably. Wolery, Bailey, and Sugai (1988) defined functional assessment as the process of determining the relationship between a child's behavior and the environmental factors that may cause or maintain it. Strain, McConnell, Carta, Fowler, Neisworth, and Wolery (1992) define ecobehavioral assessment as the process of determining functional relationships between environmental events and children's behavior. They believe that it attempts to study broader contextual or setting events that may affect behavior. Gable (1996) believes that functional analysis is a more rigorous application of functional assessment because it involves the experimental manipulation of person–environment events that are thought to influence the target behavior and the systematic documentation of changes in that behavior. Neef and Iwata's (1994) overview of current research on functional analysis makes it very clear that most of the research has focused on a variety of maladaptive behaviors and has attempted to answer two questions: "(a) What types of assessment methodologies provide reliable and valid data about behavioral function, and how can they be adapted for use in a particular situation? and (b) How might the results from such assessments improve the design and selection of treatment procedures?" (Neef & Iwata, 1994, p. 211). Mace (1994) reports that there are three main types of functional analysis methodologies that have been used: (a) indirect methods such as rating scales completed by a caretaker, (b) descriptive methods that use direct observations to formulate hypotheses about the functions of behavior, and (c) experimental methods that attempt to isolate and control the contingencies that may maintain the maladaptive behavior. Each of these methodologies has assets and limitations. One of the early limitations of all methodologies was that most of the early studies were analogue studies conducted in a clinic setting. The external validity of the analogue studies has been questioned because it is not known how much can be generalized to the home, school, and playground. During the 1990s several brief functional analysis studies were conducted that support the use of this methodology in outpatient clinics as well as inpatient clinics (Cooper et al., 1992; Northrup, Wacker, Berg, Kelly, Sasso, & DeRaad, 1994; Reimers et al., 1993; Umbreit & Blair, 1997). However, questions persist regarding the usefulness of functional analyses (Iwata, 1994). It is clear that the process of determining the function of one or more behaviors is not as simple as it first appeared to be. Gable believes that there has been a lack of precise information communicated across researchers and practitioners; the research is scattered and incomplete, a reliable database is needed in which multiple functions of a target behavior are investigated, the interactive effects of a variety of both antecedent and consequent variables need to be identified and evaluated (Stephens, 1998), and even more studies should be conducted in the child's natural setting. Direct and systematic replication of studies across settings and with a broad range of behaviors needs to be conducted. The control conditions and demand situations need to be standardized so that there is confidence in what has been introduced into the research. It is clear that multiple antecedent and consequential behaviors must be studied. Variables must be well defined because the behaviors that may be classified as noncompliant, aggressive, and so on may mean very different things for different children. These behaviors might be the result of the interaction of multiple potential variables. A major goal in any assessment process is to increase the external validity of the approach. It is clear that individualized approaches to treatment need to continue (Brown & Seklemian, 1993) because aggressive and noncompliant behaviors have been shown to occur for very different reasons across children, settings, and situations.

Informal Analysis Techniques

Whether standardized assessment or nonstandardized assessment is conducted, error pattern analysis and task analysis are invaluable techniques that can be used to pinpoint the pattern of errors the infant or preschooler might make or to determine which behaviors the child cannot perform. These techniques can be used to analyze performance on cognitive, language, social-emotional, and sensory-motor tasks. Both have been used in assessment and intervention for preschoolers with disabilities.

Summary

Each of the foregoing techniques can be useful in obtaining information about infants and preschoolers. However, each is just one part of the assessment process. At a minimum intrarater and interrater reliability and/or test-retest reliability data must be gathered and outcome data must be evaluated. Bracken's (1994) cautions about the promotion of alternate assessment practices in early childhood education over traditional assessment practices must be heeded.

Formal Assessment

The professional literature in the 1980s and 1990s has contained numerous articles dealing with the limitations of standardized testing for all children and especially for preschoolers with disabilities (Bagnato & Neisworth, 1994; Bracken, 1987, 1991; Salvia & Ysseldyke, 1998). The limitations are evident in many instances, but some limitations are stated as facts, without having empirical support.

Auditory and Visual Assessment. Screening of vision and hearing must precede other assessment in order to rule out that delays are a result of impaired sensory systems, and also because the earlier any sensory impairments are identified and managed, the less likely they will interfere with development in other areas.

Neurobehavioral Assessment. O'Donnell (1996) stated that the neurobehavioral assessment of infants was introduced to the field of child development over 20 years ago and that the constructs of concern and the assessment strategies originated in developmental neurology, behavioral pediatrics, and developmental psychology. The developmental exam of infants is an important part of training in the fields of neurology and pediatrics. The exams are usually conducted by physicians and/or nurse practitioners rather than psychologists and educators. Yet, all early childhood specialists need to understand such assessment and its link to intervention. Some of the standardized instruments that were developed or revised in the 1980s and 1990s are the Neurological Assessment of the Preterm and Full-Term Newborn Infant (Dubowitz & Dubowitz, 1981), the

NBAS (Brazelton, 1984), the Assessment of Preterm Infants (Als, Lester, Tronick, & Brazelton, 1982), and Neurobehavioral Maturity Assessment (Korner et al., 1987). These instruments are used for assessing neurological integrity, behavioral organization and needs, temperament, and state of consciousness. Extensive knowledge in brain–behavior relationships, motor development, biomedical risk conditions, and extensive training and experience with infants are necessary to be an effective examiner. Current approaches to newborn assessment recognize the need to assess the infant's physical and social context and the interactions between the infant and his or her environment. It is also clear that examiners need to provide sufficient information to the consumers (parent or guardian, other caretakers, and interventionists) so that the assessment results can be used effectively to determine an intervention plan.

Intelligence/Cognition. In the past, measures of intellectual or cognitive ability were used with infants and preschoolers without considering all of the psychometric and practical limitations of the instruments. Most of the major individual tests of cognition or intelligence that are used with infants and preschoolers were revised during the 1980s and 1990s. Test authors carefully selected and revised items and attempted to find representative standardization samples. For example, one of the best, but outdated, measures of infant ability, the Bayley Scales of Infant Development, was revised in 1993. The BSID-II (Bayley, 1993) was normed with 1-month-old to 42-month-old children, old items were deleted or revised, and new items were added. Yet, there is limited evidence of criterion-related and construct validity. The internal consistency reliability of the Mental, Motor, and Behavior Rating Scales varies across ages, and interscorer agreement appears adequate only for the Mental Scale. The Battelle Developmental Inventory (Newborg et al., 1984) and the Developmental Profile II (Alpern, Boll, & Shearer, 1986) are examples of standardized instruments for infants and preschoolers that lack adequate information about reliability and validity (Snyder, Lawson, Thompson, Stricklin, & Sexton, 1993). Other measures of cognitive development that were developed to be used with preschool-age children (ages 2 to 5) such as the DAS (Elliott, 1990), K-ABC (Kaufman & Kaufman, 1983), SB-IV (Thorndike, Hagen, & Sattler, 1986), and WPPSI-R (Wechsler, 1989) all have difficulties with long administration time and limited floors. They are not appropriate to use with preschoolers who have severe disabilities because they would provide a very small sample of the preschoolers' behaviors. Age discontinuities within scales have also been a problem for many of the preschool instruments. Appendix 2 contains resources for reviews of many of the standardized instruments for infants and preschoolers and other chapters in this book provide information about some of the instruments that are often used to assess infants and preschoolers.

Motor Skills

Physical and occupational therapists, nurses, pediatricians, psychologists, and early childhood special educators have conducted assessment of motor skills. They have used formal and informal techniques to predict motor performance, identify children with current motor delays, and evaluate changes in motor performance. Juelsgaard (1996) has an activity book of motor skills that could be used for both assessment and intervention. Harris and McEwen (1996) emphasize the importance of identifying functional motor skills or activities rather than assessing components of movement and developmental milestones. They believe that this approach to assessment will lead to interventions that are immediately meaningful to children and their families, enable the children to be more independent and be able to function in a less restrictive environment, and make it easier for the family to care for the child. The Movement Assessment of Infants (Chandler, Andrews, & Swanson, 1980) is a widely used instrument for predicting future motor problems. A newer tool used to predict motor outcomes is the Test of Infant Motor Performance (Campbell, 1993). A tool used to identify already existing motor delays is the Alberta Infant Motor Scale (Piper & Darrah, 1993). The Peabody Developmental Motor Scale (Folio & Fewell, 1983) is an older, but widely used norm-referenced and criterion-referenced instrument that evaluates gross and fine motor performance. The techniques used to assess changes in motor functioning may consist of either criterion-referenced or judgment-based evaluations or the monitoring of the accomplishment of behavioral objectives, goal-attainment scaling, and single-subject research methodologies. None of the norm-referenced motor assessment instruments appear sensitive enough to detect changes in motor skills.

Communication Skills

Crais and Roberts (1996) review over 30 standardized and nonstandardized speech and language assessment instruments. Communication skills are usually assessed in the multiple-skill instruments that have been developed for infants and preschoolers. Although the language of infants is limited to sounds and motor activities, by the time children are 2 years old, they have already began to use and understand language. The four dimensions of language that need to be assessed are:

1. The articulation and mastery of the sound system—*phonology.*
2. The understanding and use of grammatical structure—*syntax.*
3. The understanding and use of words and concepts—*semantics.*
4. The functional and interpersonal understanding and use of language—*pragmatics.*

There are formal and informal assessment techniques that have been developed to assess these four dimensions of language. However, currently there are no comprehensive language assessment instruments that measure all dimensions sufficiently and are technically adequate. A comprehensive language assessment instrument would need to meet the following criteria:

1. The instrument must be based on a well-constructed model or theory of language development.
2. It must thoroughly assess the comprehension and production of all four dimensions of language.
3. The instrument must be developmental in nature—taking into account the qualitative differences that occur.
4. The instrument must recognize and consider the variations in dialect that occur at the phonologic, syntactical, semantic, and pragmatic levels.
5. The norm sample must be representative of the population that will be assessed with the instrument.
6. Internal consistency reliability and test-retest reliability must be high enough (.90+) so that the instrument can be used with confidence when making intervention plans for a preschooler.
7. Content, construct, and predictive criterion-related validity must be demonstrated with appropriate representatives that will be assessed with the instrument.

Until the 1991 amendments to IDEA allowed noncategorical reporting of preschoolers' disabilities, 70 percent of the 3- to 5-year-olds served under IDEA were labeled as having a communication disorder. A very important part of communication behavior is knowing the purpose or reason for using language, thus *pragmatics* are of paramount importance when developing intervention plans. Many of the preschoolers who have severe communication disabilities as their primary or secondary disability can form words and even learn the rules for putting the words together. For example, the echoic behavior of some preschoolers with autism is amazing as they repeat an hour-long conversation they heard. There are no phonological or syntactical errors in their monologues, yet they are not interpreting and using language appropriately in social, cognitive, or linguistic contexts. Often they cannot let someone else know what they want, or tell someone about an event, describe an activity, or demonstrate awareness of another person's presence.

Most of the standardized measures of language are for children who are at least 3 years old because it is difficult to develop instruments that take into consideration the types of structures and operations that children have acquired before age 3 (or even later). Many of the standardized instruments assess only one or two of the dimensions of language via tests of articulation, auditory discrimination, grammar rules, grammar redundancy, vocabulary, and basic concepts. Some specialists in language believe that samples of spontaneous and elicited language are most helpful in assessing for possible language disabilities. However, as with any informal assessment tool, the sample will only be as reliable and valid as the examiner's skills in accounting for the setting, the task the child is engaged in, the topic, and characteristics of the listener that might interfere with language production or comprehension. The listener characteristics that may either hinder or enhance children's language production (race/ethnicity, dominant language, gender, and voice quality) vary across children.

Adaptive Behavior. The construct called adaptive behavior is not new (Harrison, 1991; Harrison & Robinson, 1995; Reschly, 1990). Edgar Doll discussed the functional ability of persons to demonstrate personal independence and social responsibility in the 1950s and Rick Heber's 1959 AAMD definition of mental retardation included the construct. Over 50 years later, personal independence and social responsibility remain the key components of measures of adaptive behavior. Since the 1991 amendments to IDEA (P.L. 102-119), *adaptive development* is the term used to describe the self-help skills of infants and toddlers. Early childhood specialists need to be knowledgeable about the measurement of adaptive behavior/development because it is used for identifying preschoolers as developmentally delayed and for program planning. Controversy regarding the overlap in measures of cognition and adaptive development remains today and many of the instruments already discussed are also considered measures of adaptive behavior. Horn and Childre (1996) list the multidomain instruments that include the adaptive behavior domain as well as specific measures of adaptive behavior. Their review of adaptive behavior measures, along with the reviews of Cohen and Spenciner (1994, 1998) and Salvia and Ysseldyke (1995), list only one new test developed in the 1990s and two tests that were revised in the 1990s. The new instrument, Checklist of Adaptive Living Skills, is a criterion-referenced checklist that has limited evidence of reliability and validity. The AAMR Adaptive Behavior Scale—School was revised in the 1990s. It is a norm-referenced instrument designed for children between ages 3 and 18. It is more reliable for children with mental retardation than for other children. The Scales of Independent Behavior were revised in 1996 (SIB-R). These scales are norm-referenced scales that are to be individually administered to measure the adaptive and problem behavior of infants to adults. They appear to have adequate reliability, validity, and standardization population and can be used for identification, placement, program planning, and progress monitoring. With all areas of assessment, early childhood specialists must proceed with caution when using these instruments and not rely on them for all assessment information. They can be valuable tools to use when assessing a preschooler with severe disabilities, but their value is dependent on appropriate assessment in the preschoolers' natural environments and appropriate interpretation. The assessment of adaptive development needs to be a continuous process in which information is gathered from caretakers and the child is directly observed in daily family, child, and center activities.

Social Development.   Many of the techniques used to assess the social development and social interactions of preschoolers have already been discussed as interviews, observations across multiple settings, play-based assessment, curriculum-based assessment, criterion-referenced and norm-referenced instruments, and functional assessment. McClellan and Katz (1993) developed a simple checklist of social skills. Odom and Munson (1996) provide descriptions and examples of many types of techniques that were developed in the 1980s and 1990s to assess the social behavior and interactions of infants and preschoolers. They also provide examples of the many types of techniques. As in all other areas of preschool assessment, the setting, task, participants, and observers can substantially affect the infant or preschooler's social performance. Standardized instruments revised or developed in the 1990s that are appropriate for 2- to 5-year-

olds include the Autism Screening Instrument for Educational Planning, Second Edition (Krug, Arick, & Almond, 1993); the Child Behavior Checklist for Ages 4–18 (Achenbach, 1988, 1991a, 1991b) and the Child Behavior Checklist for Ages 2–3 (Achenbach, 1988, 1991a, 1991b); the Early Childhood Behavior Scale (McCarney, 1992); the Behavior Assessment System for Children; and the Preschool and Kindergarten Behavior Scales (PKBS) (Merrell, 1994). Each of these instruments has strengths that put it ahead of the earlier developed instruments, but none of them should be used alone. Those that are part of a system such as the CBCl and BASC are more comprehensive in that they provide an opportunity to gather information from more than one person in more than one way.

Environmental Assessment.   The number of environments that the preschooler with severe disabilities encounters may be limited because of a need for accommodations. This is one of the major reasons environmental assessment should be conducted, to determine if adaptations are needed in order for the child to function at his or her best. Are there accommodations that need to be made in the home, in the preschool, the medical clinic, and any other setting where the child needs to be for part of his or her day? Assessment of the preschooler's environments is necessary to determine whether they are safe, warm, comfortable places that are adequately supervised. The assessment of a school or center environment must include the physical space, equipment and materials, teacher–child ratios, scheduling of activities, and the peer environment. National, state, and local guidelines have been published regarding standards for preschool settings. Many of the same factors must be assessed in the home and medical center. The actual assessment techniques include observation, drawing schematics, checklists, rating scales, and ecobehavioral inventories. Cohen and Spenciner (1994) and Karp (1996) describe commercially available environmental assessment instruments for the home and school settings. Many of these instruments are criterion-referenced instruments.

Assessment Systems

Assessment or diagnostic systems were designed to provide comprehensive assessment in many domains and to link assessment to intervention and monitoring of progress. There are several systems for school-age children that include measures of cognitive ability and academic readiness or achievement but are not necessarily linked to intervention and progress monitoring. In the field of early childhood, the systems are different in content and format, but all include the assessment and identification of needs, the development of an intervention plan and the evaluation of progress. The ABILITIES Index (Simeonsson & Bailey, 1989) the Assessment, Evaluation, and Programming System (AEPS), Volumes 1 and 2, Measurement for Birth to Three Years (Bricker, 1993) and Curriculum for Birth to Three Years (Cripe, Slentz & Bricker, 1992), the Carolina Curriculum for Infants and Toddlers with Special Needs (CCITSN) (Johnson-Martin, Jens, Attermeier, & Hacker, 1991), the System to Plan Early Childhood Services (SPECS) (Bagnato & Neisworth, 1990), Transdisciplinary Play-Based Assessment (TPBA) (Linder, 1993a), and Transdisciplinary Play-Based Intervention (TPBI) (Linder, 1993b) are examples of such systems for infants and toddlers. The ABILITIES Index is included here even though it was developed before 1990 because there have been several evaluations of it during the 1990s. The ABILITIES Index was developed as a way to describe the functional abilities and limitations of young children across nine domains. The instrument was not designed to replace standardized assessments of children but as an efficient way for many different persons to rate a child's functional abilities, come to a consensus, and develop an appropriate intervention plan. Bailey, Simeonsson, Buysse, and Smith (1993) assessed the reliability of the ABILITIES Index with parents of young children who had disabilities and with professionals who provided services for these children. They found that across all raters, 86 percent of the ratings of one rater were within one point of those of a second rater. The correlations between raters were low to moderate across individual items and several items consistently accounted for lower levels of agreement across all three groups (parents, teachers, specialists). Stability of ratings based on 40 teachers rating the same child on two occasions was higher than interrater reliability. Buysse, Smith, Bailey, and Simeonsson (1993) investigated the consumer validity of the ABILITIES Index by asking parents, teachers, therapists, and Developmental Evaluation Center specialists to evaluate the ABILITIES Index. In general, it was rated positively across a number of dimensions. However, there were important group differences on four of the dimensions. Parents were consistently more positive than teachers, therapists, and specialists in their evaluation of the ABILITIES Index. Bailey, Buysse, Simeonsson, Smith, and Keyes (1995) studied the level

of agreement of professionals' judgments about children's limitations, the factors that influenced agreement, and the outcomes achieved when the team was asked to develop a consensus rating. There was 67 percent exact agreement on a child's general level of functioning.

Volume 1 of the Assessment, Evaluation and Programming System for Infants and Children (AEPS) (Bricker, 1993a) contains the tests and data recording forms, the family report, the child progress record, and the family interest surveys that can be used for birth to 3 years whereas Volume 2 (Bricker, 1993b) contains the curriculum that can be used separately or in conjunction with the AEPS test and can be used at home or in an early education setting. There are cross-references between the test and the curriculum. The AEPS test is criterion referenced but has support for adequate interobserver and test-retest reliability and content and concurrent validity. The CCITSN (Johnson-Martin et al., 1991) test instrument is called the Assessment Log. It assesses 24 areas of development for birth through 24 months. The manual includes directions for using the Assessment Log, making adaptations, and incorporating intervention activities into routine care or playtime. Insufficient information is provided about the technical adequacy of the system.

SPECS is a five-step system developed by Bagnato and Neisworth (1990) for 2- to 6-year-olds. It has three interrelated components: Developmental Specs (D-Specs); Team Specs (T-Specs); and Program Specs (P-Specs). Parents and practitioners who rate the child's developmental and behavioral status in 19 areas of functioning carry out the first step (D-Specs). The ratings are based on observation, interviews, or direct testing. Then the team of parents and practitioners completes a plan for service delivery (T-Specs). The P-Specs detail the scope and intensity of a child's program and can be used to monitor progress. Structured clinical judgment ratings are used to assess the functional competencies of the children. The five steps of the process are:

1. Have all team members contribute to the assessment.
2. Determine team consensus.
3. Establish the level of service needed.
4. Determine the needed program intensity.
5. Repeat SPECS to monitor progress.

Cohen and Spenciner's 1994 review of SPECS is positive but also includes important cautions. The rating scale assumes that the rater has strong knowledge of typical early childhood development and the directions for rating the items are not always clear. This may be why the test-retest reliability coefficients are in the .60s to .70s versus the desired .90s. Relative to validity, correct classifications ranged from 66 percent to 90 percent depending on the discipline of raters.

TPBA (Linder, 1993a) is not only an a transdiciplinary model for assessing play but has guidelines for assessing cognitive, social-emotional, communication/language, and sensori-motor development. It is considered a process assessment that was specifically designed to link assessment to intervention and TPBI (Linder, 1993b). Outcomes of the TPBA are used to determine which developmental processes and functional skills should be strengthened or increased. The TPBI manual is used to relate domains and integrate intervention strategies into an inclusive curriculum. This system has many assets because the assessment and intervention components are flexible, holistic, process oriented, and involve parents and children. There are also limitations to the system. There may not be a large enough sample of parent–child behavior and there is little information available regarding the reliability and validity of the system.

INTERVENTIONS

Does early intervention improve a child's current functioning level and will it make any difference over time? Both the popular and professional press have reported positive results (Guralnick 1997a, 1997b; Ramey & Ramey 1998). Longitudinal studies of preschoolers with disabilities have found that the results are most positive when there are protective factors within the child, the family environment, and the larger social environment. It is very clear as we begin the twenty-first century that we need to focus on the strengths and protective factors present in preschoolers with disabilities and in their families. Intervention needs to be solution focused and result in positive changes for the child and his or her family. Shonkoff (1993) suggested that there were three significant challenges confronting early childhood intervention in the 1990s: the need to rethink disciplinary boundaries, refine intervention goals, and redefine family–professional relationships. Those challenges remain and we need to broaden our view of families and their role in the assessment and intervention process. Intervention still needs to be specific, realistic, and individualized. Resources need to be matched to specific child and family service objectives rather than to categories of children and families. The 1990s brought major changes in the

field of the severely and profoundly disabled (Anastasiow & Harel, 1993). One of those changes was a move away from rigid behavioral or developmental approaches to a functional approach that will help individuals discover that they are a person who has needs, there are other persons who can help them meet their needs, and they can meet some of their needs themselves. They may never attain symbolic functioning, but they can learn to request help for needs they cannot meet by themselves and can do it in a positive way. Their ability to work and play in the future is linked to their early childhood environment. The professionals in early childhood assessment and intervention must recognize the differences that are in each infant and preschooler because of families and other environmental variables. Attention must focus on child development and family adaptation and on the resilience and protective factors that are present.

McWilliam and Bailey (1993) discusses six barriers to achieving quality services in early childhood education. They are:

1. The collision of principles.
2. The structure of communities.
3. The support of others.
4. Early interventionist's job requirements.
5. Professional skills and knowledge.
6. Personal values and beliefs.

The early childhood specialist must be aware of these barriers and have a plan to deal with each one. The collision of principles can occur between the wide array of professionals who provide services to preschoolers with disabilities or between parents and guardians and the professionals. Community structure can significantly influence the actual delivery of services to preschoolers and their family members in terms of the financial and human resources available to the families in the community and the service delivery model that is used. It is much more difficult to deliver quality services when few options are available or services are fragmented. Support from others may not be present because various team members (including parents and guardians) may hold different values and be working on different goals. The job requirements of early interventionists can also interfere with the delivery of effective services whether it is because of limited time or limitations within the work setting. A lack of professional skills and knowledge can definitely interfere with the provision of quality. McWilliam and Bailey (1993) points out that interventionists' personal beliefs and values about the needs of children and families may prevent them from understanding what families really want. The need for more child collaboration as well as increased parent–professional collaboration is emphasized (Anastasiow & Harel, 1993; Goodman, 1994; Fox, Hanline, Vail & Galant, 1994). Developmentally appropriate practice (DAP) is another catch phrase that appeared in the 1990s, but it simply emphasizes providing the same kind of learning opportunities to the preschooler with disabilities as are presented to the preschooler who does not have any disabilities (Fox & Hanline, 1993; Fox et al., 1994; Wolery & McWilliam, 1998). DAP involves inclusion for most young children who have disabilities.

Inclusion of preschoolers with disabilities into integrated preschool programs has legal, rational, moral, and empirical bases (Bailey, McWilliam, Buysse, & Wesley, 1998). However, it is not always possible to find appropriate integrated programs (Bailey et al., 1998; McCormick, Noonan, & Heck, 1998). Bailey et al. (1998) believe that the desired combination of high-quality programs with specialized services and family-centered practices is difficult to achieve. McCormick et al. (1998) found that within-class variables accounted for most of the variance in disabled preschoolers' social interactions in integrated preschool programs. Hundert, Mahoney, Mundy, and Vernon (1998) are among the few researchers who have attempted to investigate the developmental and social gains of severely disabled preschoolers in segregated versus integrated preschool programs. They found that the segregated programs for preschoolers with severe disabilities had lower adult–child ratios and, therefore, more adult enrichment, but the preschoolers in the segregated programs made fewer developmental gains than the severely disabled preschoolers who were in integrated programs. None of the severely disabled preschoolers made much progress in social skills over the academic year. Social competence is an area that has been of concern and McCollum (1995) found a lack in the quality and quantity of IEP goals dealing with social competency. Lowenthal (1996) outlines seven effective practices for teaching social skills to preschoolers who have a disability. What must be kept in mind is that these guidelines of systematic arrangement of classroom environment, peer imitation, teacher prompts, group affection activities, positive reinforcement by teachers, peer-mediated interventions, and correspondence training must be individualized for each child.

Kauffman (1996) summarizes some of the concerns regarding the limited effect research has had on our practice in the classrooms. He believes that researchers need

to be trained to do better research and policy makers trained to make better choices. Far too often, what is popular and being used lacks empirical support. Kauffman believes that research-based procedures should:

1. Involve minimal risk for harm.
2. Be practical and sustainable.
3. Be believable and socially valid.
4. Be implemented with a high degree of fidelity.
5. Be accompanied by systematic training programs.
6. Be accurately described and based on acceptable tenants.

Carnine (1993, 1997) believes research must be trustworthy, usable, and accessible to be of value in the schools. How can we help provide empirically validated treatments to infants and preschoolers? Wyly (1995) believes that we have made progress in our assessment and intervention of premature infants. Individualized assessments of the infant's maturational level, tolerance of stimulation, and response to stimuli are used to plan appropriate developmental interventions that are conducted during caregiving activities.

Fewell (1996) reports that we have made great strides in caring for the physical needs of young children, but that our efforts to care for their educational health lag far behind.

> *To cast the net of early intervention to all young children who need it will require a vocal, active, and committed cadre of believers, willing to convince others that this goal is not only appropriate and achievable but a wise investment. (p. 362)*

Rosenbaum (1997) presents the limitations and benefits of parents and professionals working as equal partners, but his conclusion is that if we are sharing the responsibilities of decision making with families, we are also sharing the responsibility for outcomes. Although Simeonsson's book on risk, resilience, and prevention is about children and adolescents, many of his points are appropriate for early childhood education. Simeonsson (1994) focuses on a primary prevention agenda, yet recognizes that secondary and tertiary prevention will also be necessary. The goals for a primary prevention agenda are:

1. *promote the development of children*
2. *reduce the need for diagnostic, curative, and therapeutic services*
3. *reduce the need for rehabilitative, corrective, remedial and other intensive programs (p. 6)*

REFERENCES

Ableboone, H., Goodwin, L. D., Sandall, S. R., Gordon, N., & Martin, D. G. (1992). Consumer based early intervention services. *Journal of Early Intervention, 16,* 201–209.

Achenbach, T. M. (1988). *Child behavior checklist/2-3.* Burlington, VT: Center for Children, Youth, and Families.

Achenbach, T. M. (1991a). *Child behavior checklist/4–18.* Burlington, VT: Center for Children, Youth, and Families.

Achenbach, T. M. (1991b). *Teacher's report form.* Burlington, VT: Center for Children, Youth, and Families.

Alpern, G. G., Boll, T. J., & Shearer, M. S. (1986). *Development Profile II,* Los Angeles: Western Psychological Services.

Als, H., Lester, B. M., Tronick, E. Z., & Brazelton, T. B. (1982). Toward a research instrument of the assessment of preterm infants' behavior (APIB). In H. Fitzgerald, B. M. Lester, & M. W. Yogman (Eds.), *Theory and research in behavioral pediatrics* (Vol. 1, pp. 35–132). New York: Plenum.

American Psychiatric Association. (1994). *Diagnostic and statistical manual of mental disorders* (4th ed.). Washington, DC: Author.

Anastasiow, N. J., & Harel, S. (Eds.). (1993). *At-risk infants: Intervention, families and research.* Baltimore: Paul H. Brookes.

Anderson, M., & Goldberg, P. F. (1991). *Cultural competence in screening and assessment: Implications for services to young children with special needs ages birth through five.* College Park, MD: U.S. Department of Education, ERIC Clearinghouse on Assessment and Evaluation. (ERIC Document Reproduction Service No. ED 370 313)

Bagnato, S. J., & Neisworth, J. T. (1990). *System to plan early childhood services (SPECS).* Circle Pines, MN: American Guidance Service.

Bagnato, S. J., & Neisworth, J. T. (1991). *Assessment for early intervention: Best practices for professionals.* London: Guilford Press.

Bagnato, S. J., & Neisworth, J. T. (1994). *Assessment for early intervention: Best practices for professionals.* New York: Guilford Press.

Bailey, D. B. (1988). Assessing needs of families with handicapped infants. *Journal of Special Education, 22,* 117–127.

Bailey, D. B., & Simeonsson, R. (1988). *The family needs survey.* (Report No. CB 8180). Chapel Hill: University of North Carolina, Frank Porter Graham Child Development Center.

Bailey, D. B., Jr. (1996). Assessing family resources, priorities, and concerns. In M. McLean, D. B. Bailey, Jr., & M. Wolery, *Assessing infants and preschoolers with special needs* (2nd ed., pp. 202–233). Columbus, OH: Merrill.

Bailey, D. B., Jr., Buysse, V., Edmondson, R., & Smith, T. M. (1992). Creating family-centered services in early intervention: Perceptions of professionals in four states. *Exceptional Children, 58,* 298–309.

Bailey, D. B., Jr., Buysse, V., Simeonsson, R. J., Smith, T., & Keyes, L. (1995). Individual and team consensus ratings of child functioning. *Developmental Medicine and Child Neurology, 37,* 246–259.

Bailey, D. B., Jr., McWilliam, R. A., Buysse, V., & Wesley, P. W. (1998). Inclusion in the context of competing values in early childhood education. *Early Childhood Research Quarterly, 13,* 27–47.

Bailey, D. B., Jr., McWilliam, R. A., Darkes, L. A., Hebbeler, K., Simeonsson, R. J., Spiker, D., & Wagner, M. (1998). Family outcomes in early intervention: A framework for program evaluation and efficacy research. *Exceptional Children, 64,* 313–328.

Bailey, D. B., Jr., & Simeonsson, R. J. (Eds.). (1988). *Family assessment in early intervention.* Columbus, OH: Merrill.

Bailey, D. B., Jr., & Simeonsson, R. J. (1990). *Family Needs Survey Revised.* Chapel Hill: University of North Carolina, Frank Porter Graham Child Development Center.

Bailey, D. B., Jr., Simeonsson, R. J., Buysse, V., & Smith, T. (1993). Reliability of an index of child characteristics. *Developmental Medicine and Child Neurology, 35,* 806–815.

Bailey, D. B., Jr., Simeonsson, R. J., Yoder, D. E., & Huntington, G. S. (1990). Preparing professionals to serve infants and toddlers with handicaps and their families: An integrative analysis across eight disciplines. *Exceptional Children, 57,* 26–35.

Barrera, I. (1993). Effective and appropriate instruction for all children: The challenge of cultural/linguistic diversity and young children with special needs. *Topics in Early Childhood Special Education, 13,* 461–587.

Bayley, N. (1993). *Bayley scales of infant development* (2nd ed.). San Antonio, TX: Psychological Corporation.

Beckman, P. J., & Boyes, G. B. (1993). *Deciphering the system: A guide for families of young children with disabilities.* Cambridge, MA: Brookline Books.

Belmont, J. M., & Borkowski, J. G. (1994). Prudence, indeed, will dictate… Review of *Mental retardation: Definition, classification, and systems of supports* (9th ed.). *Contemporary Psychology, 39,* 495–496.

Benner, S. M. (1992). *Assessing young children with special needs: An ecological perspective.* New York: Longman.

Bergen, D. (1994). *Assessment methods for infants and toddlers: Transdisciplinary team approaches.* New York: Teachers College Press.

Bergen, D., & Everington, C. (1994). Assessment perspectives for young children with severe disabilities or environmental trauma. In D. Bergen (Ed.), *Assessment methods for infants and toddlers: Transdisciplinary team approaches* (pp. 216–233). New York: Teacher College. Press.

Bernheimer, L. P., Gallimore, R., & Kaufman, S. Z. (1993). Clinical child assessment in a family context: A four-group typology of family experiences with young children with developmental delays. *Journal of Early Intervention, 17*(3), 253–269.

Beukelman, D., & Mirenda, P. (1992). *Augmentative and alternative communication: Management of severe communication disorders in children and youth.* Baltimore: Paul H. Brookes.

Blackman, J. A. (1996). Social policy solutions to social problems. *Journal of Early Intervention, 20*(4), 296–298.

Bondurant-Utz, J. A., & Luciano, L. B. (1994). *A practical guide to infant and preschool assessment in special education.* College Park, MD: U.S. Department of Education, ERIC Clearinghouse on Assessment and Evaluation. (ERIC Document Reproduction Service No. ED 371 525)

Bracken, B. A. (1987). Limitations of preschool instruments and standards for minimal levels of technical adequacy. *Journal of Psychoeducational Assessment, 5,* 313–326.

Bracken, B. A. (Ed.). (1991). *The psychoeducational assessment of preschool children* (2nd ed.). Boston: Allyn and Bacon.

Bracken, B. A. (1994). Advocating for effective preschool assessment practices: A comment on Bag-

nato and Neisworth. *School Psychology Quarterly, 9,* 103–108.

Brazelton, T. B. (1978). Introduction. In A. Sameroff (Ed.), Organization and stability of newborn behavior: The Brazelton neonatal behavioral assessment scale. *Monographs of the Society for Research in Child Development, 43*(5-6), 1–14.

Brazelton, T. B. (1984). *Neonatal behavioral assessment scale* (2nd ed.). (Clinics in Developmental Medicine, No. 88). Philadelphia: Lippincott.

Bricker, D. (Ed.). (1993a). *Assessment, evaluation, and programming system for infants and children, Volume 1, AEPS measurement for birth to three years.* Baltimore: Paul H. Brookes.

Bricker, D. (Ed.). (1993b). *Assessment, evaluation and programming system for infants and children, Volume 2, AEPS curriculum for birth to three years.* Baltimore: Paul H. Brookes.

Bricker, D. (1996). The goal: Prediction or prevention? *Journal of Early Intervention, 20*(4), 294–296.

Bricker, D., Squires, J., Mounts, L., Potter, L., Nickel, B., & Farrell, J. (1995). *Ages and Stages Questionnaires.* Baltimore: Paul H. Brookes.

Bricker, D., & Widerstrom, A. (Eds.). (1996). *Preparing personnel to work with infants and young children and their families: A team approach.* Baltimore: Paul H. Brookes.

Brigance, A. H. (1990). *Brigance Early Preschool Screen for Two-Year-Old and Two-and-One-Half-Year-Old Children.* North Billerica, MA: Curriculum Associates.

Brigance, A. H. (1991). *Brigance© Diagnostic Inventory of Early Development—Revised.* North Billerica, MA: Curriculum Associates.

Browder, D. M. (1991). *Assessment of individuals with severe disabilities: An applied behavior approach to life skills assessment.* Baltimore: Paul H. Brookes.

Brown, C. W., & Seklemian, P. (1993). The individualized functional assessment process for young children with disabilities: Lessons from the Zebley Decision. *Journal of Early Intervention, 17*(3), 239–252.

Brown, W., & Brown, C. W. (1994). Defining eligibility for early intervention. In W. Brown, S. K. Thurman, & L. F. Pearl (Eds.), *Family centered early intervention with infants and toddlers: Innovative cross-disciplinary approaches.* Baltimore: Paul H. Brookes.

Brown, W., Thurman, S. K., & Pearl, L. F. (Eds.). (1993). *Family centered early intervention with infants and toddlers: Innovative cross-disciplinary approaches.* Baltimore: Paul H. Brookes.

Buysse, V., Smith, T. M., Bailey, D. B., Jr., & Simeonsson, R. J. (1993). Consumer validation of an index characterizing the functional abilities of young children with disabilities. *Journal of Early Intervention, 17*(3), 224–238.

Buysse, V., Wesley, P., Keyes, L., & Bailey, D. B., Jr. (1996). Assessing the comfort zone of child care teachers in serving young children with disabilities. *Journal of Early Intervention, 20*(3), 189–203.

Campbell, S. K. (1993). Future directions for physical therapy assessment in infancy. In I. J. Wilhelm (Ed.), *Physical therapy assessment in infancy* (pp. 293–308). New York: Churchill Livingstone.

Carnine, D. (1993, December 8). Facts, not fads. *Education Week,* 40.

Carnine, D. (1997). Bridging the research-to-practice gap. *Exceptional Children, 63,* 513–521.

Chandler, L. S., Andrews, M. S., & Swanson, M. W. (1980). *Movement assessment of infants: A manual.* Rolling Bay, WA: Infant Movement Research.

Child Development Resources. (1992). *Transdisciplinary area assessment process viewing guide.* Lightfoot, VA: Child Development Resources Training Center.

Cohen, L. G., & Spenciner, L. J. (1994). *Assessment of young children.* New York: Longman.

Cohen, L. G., & Spenciner, L. J. (1998). *Assessment of children and youth.* New York: Longman.

Committee on Children with Disabilities. (1994). Screening infants and young children for developmental disabilities. *Pediatrics, 93*(5), 863–865.

Cooper, L. J., Wacker, D. P., Thursby, D., Plagmann, L. A., Harding, J., Millard, T., & Derby, M. (1992). A functional analysis of the role of task preferences, task demands, and adult attention on child behavior: Application to an outpatient and classroom setting. *Journal of Applied Behavior Analysis, 25,* 823–840.

Crais, E. R., & Roberts, J. E. (1996). In M. McLean, D. B. Bailey, Jr., & M. Wolery (Eds.), *Assessing infants and preschoolers with special needs* (2nd ed., pp. 334–397). Columbus, OH: Merrill.

Cripe, J., Slentz, K., & Bricker, D. (1992). *AEPS curriculum for birth to three years* (Vol. 2). Baltimore: Paul H. Brookes.

Damon, W. (1998). *Handbook of child psychology* (5th ed.). New York: John Wiley & Sons.

Dana, R. H. (1993). *Multicultural assessment perspectives for professional psychology.* Boston: Allyn and Bacon.

DEC Task Force on Recommended Practices. (1993). *DEC recommended practices: Indicators of quality in programs for infants and young children with special needs and their families.* Reston, VA: Council for Exceptional Children.

Dorman, S. M. (1998). Assistive technology: Benefits for students with disabilities. *Journal of School Health* [On-line], *68,* 120–123. Available: http://web7.searchbank.com/infotrac/session/720/807/2258854w5/89!xrn_3

Dubowitz, L. M. S., & Dubowitz, V. (1981). *The neurological assessment of the preterm and full-term newborn infant.* Philadelphia: Lippincott.

Dunst, C. J. (1993). Implications of risk and opportunity factors for assessment and intervention practices. *Topics in Early Childhood Special Education, 13* (2), 143–153.

Edelbrock, C., & Costello, A. J. (1990). Stuctured interviews for children and adolescents. In G. Goldstein & M. Hersen (Eds.), *Handbook of psychological assessment* (2nd ed., pp. 308–323). Elmsford, NY: Pergamon Press.

Education for All Handicapped Children Act of 1975, P.L. 94-142, 20 U.S.C. §1400 et seq.

Education of the Handicapped Act Amendments of 1986, P.L. 99-457, 20 U.S.C. §1400 et seq.

Elliott, C. (1990). *Differential Ability Scales.* San Antonio, TX: Psychological Corporation.

Fewell, R. R. (1991). Trends in the assessment of infants and toddlers with disabilities. *Exceptional Children, 58*(2), 166–173.

Fewell, R. R. (1996). Expanding future directors in our second decade of services. *Journal of Early Intervention, 20*(4), 356–363.

Fewell, R. R., & Langley, M. B. (1984). *Developmental activities screening inventory (DASI-II).* Austin, TX: Pro-Ed.

Filer, J. D., & Mahoney, G. J. (1996). Collaboration between families and early intervention service providers. *Infants and Young Children, 9,* 22–30.

Fleischer, K. H., Belgredan, J. H., Bagnato, S. J., & Ogonosky, A. B. (1990). An overview of judgment-based assessment. *Topics in Early Childhood Special Education, 10,* 13–23.

Fogarty, R. (Ed.). (1996). *Student portfolios: A collection of articles.* Palatine, IL: IRI/Skylight Training and Publishing.

Folio, R. M., & Fewell, R. (1983). *Peabody Developmental Motor Scales.* Allen, TX: DLM Teaching Resources.

Foster, H. L., & Iannaccone, C. J. (1994). Multicultural content in special education introductory textbooks. *Journal of Special Education, 28,* 77–92.

Fox, L., & Hanline, M. F. (1993). A preliminary evaluation of learning within developmentally appropriate early childhood settings. *Topics in Early Childhood Education, 13,* 308–327.

Fox, L., Hanline, M. F., Vail, C. O., & Galant, K. R. (1994). Developmentally appropriate practice: Applications for young children with disabilities. *Journal of Early Intervention, 18,* 243–257.

Frankenburg, W. K., & Dodds, J. B. (1990). *Denver II screening manual.* Denver, CO: Denver Developmental Materials.

Fredericks, H. D., & Templeman, T. P. (1990). A generic in-service training model. In A. P. Kaiser & C. M. McWhorter (Eds.), *Preparing personnel to work with persons with severe disabilities* (pp. 301–317). Baltimore: Paul H. Brookes.

Furuno, S., O'Reilly, K. A., Hosaka, C. M., Inatuska, T. T., Zeisloft-Faley, B., & Allman, T. (1988). *Hawaii Early Learning Profile* (HELP). Palo Alto, CA: VORT.

Gable, R. A. (1996). A critical analysis of functional assessment: Issues for researchers and practioners. *Behavioral Disorders, 22*(1), 36–40.

Gallagher, P., Malone, D. M., Cleghorne, M., & Helms, K. A. (1997). Preceived inservice training needs for early intervention personnel. *Exceptional Children, 64,* 19–30.

Garcia, S. B., & Malkin, D. H. (1993). Toward defining programs and services for culturally and linguistically diverse learners in special education. *Teaching Exceptional Children, 26*(1), 52–58.

Genishi, C. (Ed.). (1992). *Ways of assessing children and curriculum: Stories of early childhood practice.* New York: Teachers College Press.

Gerken, K. C. (1991). Assessment of preschool children with severe handicaps. In B. A. Bracken (Ed.), *The psychoeducational assessment of preschool children* (2nd ed.). Boston: Allyn and Bacon.

Gibbs, E. D., & Teti, D. M. (Eds.). (1990). *Interdisciplinary assessment of infants: A guide for early intervention specialists.* Baltimore: Paul H. Brookes.

Goodman, J. F. (1994). Early intervention for preschoolers with developmental delays: The case for increased child collaboration. *Psychological Reports, 75,* 479–496.

Grace, C. (1992). *The portfolio and its use: Developmentally appropriate assessment of young children.* Urbana, IL: ERIC Clearinghouse on Elementary and Early Childhood Education. (ERIC Document Reproduction Service No. ED 351 150)

Greenspan, S. I., & Meisels, S. (1994). Toward a new vision for developmental assessment of infants and young children. *Zero to Three, 14,* 1–8.

Gresham, F. M., Gansle, K. A., & Noell, G. H. (1993). Treatment integrity in applied behavior analysis with children. *Journal of Applied Behavior Analysis, 26*(2), 257–263.

Guralnick, M. J. (Ed.). (1997a). *The effectiveness of early intervention.* Baltimore: Paul H. Brookes. (ERIC Document Reproduction Service No. ED 414 694)

Guralnick, M. J. (1997b). Second-generation research in the field of early intervention. In M. J. Guralnick (Ed.), *The effectiveness of early intervention* (pp. 3–20). Baltimore: Paul H. Brookes.

Handicapped Children's Early Education Act of 1968, P.L. 90-538, 20 U.S.C. § 621 et seq.

Hanson, M. J., & Carta, J. J. (1995). Addressing the challenges of families with multiple risks. *Exceptional Children, 62,* 201–212.

Hanson, M. J., Gutierrez, S., Morgan, M., Brennan, E. L., & Zercher, C. (1997). Language, culture, and disability: Interacting influences on preschool inclusion. *Topics in Early Childhood Special Education, 17*(3), 307–336.

Harbin, G. L. (1993). Family issues of children with disabilities: How research and theory have modified practice in intervention. In N. J. Anastasiow & S. Harel (Eds.), *At-risk infants: Intervention, families and research* (pp. 101–114). Baltimore: Paul H. Brookes.

Harris, S. R., & McEwen, I. R. (1996). Assessing motor skills. In M. McLean, D. B. Bailey, Jr., & M. Wolery, *Assessing infants and preschoolers with special needs* (2nd ed., pp. 305–333). Columbus, OH: Merrill.

Harrison, P. L. (1991). Assessment of adaptive behavior. In B. A. Bracken (Ed.), *The psychoeducational assessment of preschool children* (2nd ed., pp. 168–186). Boston: Allyn and Bacon.

Harrison, P. L., & Kaufman, A. S., Kaufman, N. L., Bruininks, P. H., Rynders, J., Ilmer, S., Sparrow, S. S., & Cicchetti, D. V. (1990). *AGS early screening profiles.* Circle Pines, MN: American Guidance Service.

Harrison, P. L., & Robinson, B. (1995). Assessment of adaptive behavior. In A. Thomas & J. Grimes (Eds.), *Best practices in school psychology-III.*

Washington, DC: National Association of School Psychologists.

Harry, B. (1992). *Cultural diversity, families, and the special education system: Communication and empowerment.* New York: Teachers College Press.

Hayes, L. J., Hayes, G. J., Moore, S. C., & Ghezzi, P. M. (Eds.). (1994). *Ethical issues in developmental disabilities.* Reno, NV: Context Press.

Horn, E. M., & Childre, A. (1996). Assessing adaptive behavior. In M. McLean, D. B. Bailey, Jr., & M. Wolery, *Assessing infants and preschoolers with special needs* (2nd ed., pp. 462–490). Columbus, OH: Merrill.

Hundert, J., Mahoney, B., Mundy, F., & Vernon, M. L. (1998). A descriptive analysis of developmental and social gains of children with severe disabilities in segregated and inclusive preschools in southern Ontario. *Early Childhood Research Quarterly, 13,* 49–65.

Individuals with Disabilities Education Act Amendments of 1997. P.L. No. 105-17, 105 Stat. (1997).

Ireton, H. (1992). *Child Development Inventories* (formerly Minnesota Child Development Inventories). Minneapolis, MN: Behavior Science Systems.

Iwata, B. A. (1994). Functional analysis methodology: Some closing comments. *Journal of Applied Behavior Analysis, 27*(2), 413–418.

Iwata, B. A., Dorsey, M., Slifer, K., Bauman, K., & Richman, G. (1982). Toward a functional analysis of self-injury. *Analysis and Intervention in Developmental Disabilities, 2,* 3–20.

Jacobson, J. W., & Mullick, J. A. (1992). A new definition of mentally retarded or a new definition of practice. *Psychology in Mental Retardation and Developmental Disabilities, 18*(2), 9–14.

Jacobson, J. W., & Mullick, J. A. (1994). The power of positive stereotyping or…Have you changed the way you think yet? *Psychology in Mental Retardation and Developmental Disabilities, 19*(3), 8–16.

Johnson-Martin, N. M., Attermeier, S. M., & Hacker, B. J. (1990). *The Carolina curriculum for preschoolers with special needs* (2nd ed.). Baltimore: Paul H. Brookes.

Johnson-Martin, N. M., Jens, K. G., Attermeier, S. M., & Hacker, B. J. (1991). *The Carolina curriculum for infants and toddlers with special needs* (2nd ed.). Baltimore: Paul H. Brookes.

Johnson-Powell, G. (1997). The culturologic interview: Cultural, social, and linguistic issues in the assessment and treatment of children. In G. Johnson-Powell & J. Yamamoto (Eds.), *Transcultural child development: Psychological assessment and treatment* (pp. 349–364). New York: John Wiley & Sons.

Juelsgaard, C. (1996). Early childhood motor skills information packet. Des Moines: Iowa State Department of Education. (ERIC Document Reproduction Service No. ED 403 077)

Kaiser, A. P., & McWhorter, C. M. (1990). *Preparing personnel to work with persons with severe disabilities.* Baltimore: Paul H. Brookes.

Karp, J. M. (1996). Assessing environments. In M. McLean, D. B. Bailey, Jr., & M. Wolery (Eds.), *Assessing infants and preschoolers with special needs* (2nd ed., pp. 234–267). Columbus, OH: Merrill.

Katz, L. G. (1994). *Assessing the development of preschoolers: ERIC digest.* College Park, MD: U.S. Department of Education, ERIC Clearinghouse on Assessment and Evaluation. (ERIC Document Reproduction Service No. ED 372 875)

Kauffman, J. M. (1996). Research to practice issues. *Behavioral Disorders, 22*(1), 55–60.

Kaufman, A., & Kaufman, N. (1983). *Kaufman Assessment Battery for Children, interpretive manual.* Circle Pines, MN: American Guidance Service.

King, S. M., Rosenbaum, P. L., & King, G. A. (1996). *Developmental Medicine and Child Neurology, 38,* 757–772.

Kinsley, T. C., & Langone, J. (1995). Applications of technology for infants, toddlers, and preschoolers with disabilities. *Journal of Special Education Technology, 12,* 312–324.

Korner, A. F., Kraemer, H. C., Reade, E. P., Forest, T., Dimiceli, S., & Thom, V. (1987). A methodological approach to developing procedures for testing the neurobehavioral maturity of preterm infants. *Child Development, 58,* 1479–1487.

Krug, D. A., Arick, J. R., & Almond, P. J. (1993). *Autism screening instrument for educational planning second edition.* Austin, TX: Pro-Ed.

Kutik, E. (1994). Region II survey results. *News II, 3,* 2.

Linder, T. W. (1993a). *Transdisciplinary play-based assessment: A functional approach to working with young children* (Rev. ed.). Baltimore: Paul H. Brookes.

Linder, T. W. (1993b). *Transdisciplinary play-based assessment and intervention: Child and program summary forms.* Baltimore: Paul H. Brookes.

Linder, T. W. (1993c). *Transdisciplinary play-based intervention: Guidelines for developing a meaningful curriculum for young children.* Baltimore: Paul H. Brookes.

Lloyd, J. W., & Heubusch, J. D. (1996). Issues of social validation in research on serving individuals with emotional or behavioral disorders. *Behavioral Disorders, 22*(1), 8–14.

Lowenthal, B. (1996). Teaching social skills to preschoolers with special needs. *Childhood Education, 72,* 137–140.

Luckasson, R., Coulter, D. L., Polloway, E. A., Reiss, S., Snell, M. E., Spitalnik, D. M., & Stark, J. A. (1992). *Mental retardation: Definition, classification, and systems of supports.* Washington, DC: American Association on Mental Retardation.

Lynch, E. W. (1992). Developing cross-cultural competence. In E. W. Lynch & M. J. Hanson (Eds.), *Developing cross-cultural competence: A guide for working with young children and their families* (pp. 35–59). Baltimore: Paul H. Brookes.

Lynch, E. W. (1993, June). *Cross-cultural competence: From surprise to sensitivity to success.* Paper presented at the 28th Annual Meeting of the Association for the Care of Children's Health, Chicago.

Lynch, E. W., & Hanson, M. J. (Eds.). (1992). *Developing cross-cultural competence: A guide for working with young children and their families.* Baltimore: Paul H. Brookes.

Lynch, E. W., & Hanson, M. J. (1993). Changing demographics: Implications for training in early intervention. *Infants and Young Children, 6*(1), 50–55.

Lynch, E. W., & Hanson, M. J. (1996). Ensuring cultural competence in assessment. In M. McLean, D. B. Bailey, Jr., & M. Wolery, *Assessing infants and preschoolers with special needs* (2nd ed., pp. 69–96). Columbus, OH: Merrill.

Mace, F. C. (1994). The significance and future of functional analysis methodologies. *Journal of Applied Behavior Analysis, 27*(2), 385–392.

MacEachron, A. E., & Gustavsson, N. S. (1997). Reframing practitioner research [essay]. *Families in Society: The Journal of Contemporary Human Services, 78,* 651–656.

MacMillan, D. L., Gresham, F. M., & Siperstein, G. N. (1993). Conceptual and psychometric concerns about the 1992 AAMR definition of mental retardation. *American Journal on Mental Retardation, 98,* 325–335.

MacMillan, D. L., Gresham, F. M., & Siperstein, G. N. (1995). Heightened concerns over the 1992 AAMR definition: Advocacy versus precision. *American Journal on Mental Retardation, 100,* 87–97.

Mardell-Czudnowski, C., & Goldenberg, D. (1990). *Developmental Indicators for the Assessment of Learning—Revised.* Circle Pines, MN: American Guidance Service.

Martin, S. (1996, April). *Developmentally appropriate evaluation: Convincing students and teachers of the importance of observation as appropriate evaluation of children.* Paper presented at the Association for Childhood Education International Conference, Minneapolis, MN.

McCarney, S. (1992). *Preschool Evaluation Scale.* Columbia, MO: Hawthorne.

McClellan, D. E., & Katz, L. G. (1993). *Young children's social development: A checklist. ERIC digest.* College Park, MD: U.S. Department of Education, ERIC Clearinghouse on Assessment and Evaluation. (ERIC Document Reproduction Service No. 356 100)

McCollum, J. (1995). Social competence and IEP objectives: Where's the match? *Journal of Early Intervention, 19,* 283–285.

McCormick, K. (1996). Assessing cognitive development. In M. McLean, D. B. Bailey, Jr., & M. Wolery (Eds.), *Assessing infants and preschoolers with special needs* (2nd ed., pp. 268–304). Columbus, OH: Merrill.

McCormick, L., Noonan, M. J., & Heck, R. (1998). Variables affecting engagement in inclusive preschool classrooms. *Journal of Early Intervention, 21,* 160–176.

McDonnell, A. P., Brownell, K., & Wolery, M. (1997). Teaching experience and specialist support: A survey of preschool teachers employed by programs accredited by NAEVC. *Topics in Early Childhood Special Education, 17*(3), 263–285.

McLean, M. (1996). Assessment and its importance in early intervention/early childhood special education. In M. McLean, D. B. Bailey, Jr., & M. Wolery (Eds.), *Assessing infants and preschoolers with special needs* (2nd ed., pp. 1–22). Columbus, OH: Merrill.

McLean, M., Bailey, D. B., Jr., & Wolery, M. (1996). *Assessing infants and preschoolers with special needs* (2nd ed.). Columbus, OH: Merrill.

McLean, M., & McCormick, K. (1993). Assessment and evaluation in early intervention. In W. Brown, S. K. Thurman, & L. F. Pearl (Eds.), *Family-centered early intervention with infants and toddlers: Innovative cross-disciplinary approaches* (pp. 43–81). Baltimore: Paul H. Brookes.

McQuaide, S., & Ehrenreich, J. H. (1997). Assessing client strengths [article]. *Families in Society: The Journal of Contemporary Human Services, 78,* 201–212.

McWilliam, P. J., & Bailey, D. B., Jr. (Eds.). (1993). *Working together with children and families.* Baltimore: Paul H. Brookes.

McWilliam, R. A., & Bailey, D. B. (1994). Predictors of service-delivery models in center-based early intervention. *Exceptional Children, 61*(1), 56–71.

McWilliam, R. A., Ferguson, A., Harbin, G. L., Porter, P., Munn, D., & Vandiviere, P. (1998). The family-centeredness of individualized family service plans. *Topics in Early Childhood Special Education, 18,* 69–82.

McWilliam, R. A., Lang, L., Vandiviere, P., Angell, R., Collins, L., & Underdown, G. (1995). Satisfaction and struggles: Family perceptions of early intervention services. *Journal of Early Intervention, 19,* 43–60.

Meisels, S. J. (1995). *Performance assessment in early childhood education: The work sampling system: ERIC digest* (Report No. EDO-PS-95–6). Urbana, IL: U.S. Department of Education. (ERIC Document Reproduction Service No. ED 382 407)

Meisels, S. J., & Steele, D. (1991). *The early childhood portfolio collection process.* Ann Arbor: University of Michigan Center for Human Growth and Development.

Meisels, S. J., & Wiske, M. S. (1988). *Early Screening Inventory.* New York: Teachers College Press.

Merrell, K. W. (1994). *Preschool and kindergarten behavior scales: Test manual.* Brandon, VT: Clinical Psychology.

Miller, L. J. (1993). *FirstSTEP Screening Test for Evaluating Preschoolers.* San Antonio, TX: Psychological Corporation.

Miller, P. S. (1992a). Linking theory to intervention practices with preschoolers and their families: Building program integrity. *Journal of Early Intervention, 15,* 315–325.

Miller, P. S. (1992b). Segregated programs of teacher education in early childhood: Immoral and inefficient practice. *Topics in Early Childhood Special Education, 11,* 39–52.

Mullen, E. M. (1989). Identifying specific learning profiles in young developmentally delayed (DD) children: Infant Mullen Scales of Early Learning (IMSEL). *Pediatric Research, 25,* A16.

Mullen, E. M. (1995). *Mullen Scales of Early Learning.* Circle Pines, MN: American Guidance Service.

Myers, C. L., McBride, S. L., & Peterson, C. A. (1996). Transdisciplinary, play-based assessment in early childhood special education: An examination of social validity. *Topics in Early Childhood Special Education, 16,* 102–126.

Nagle, R. J. (1995). Conducting needs assessments. In A. Thomas & J. Grimes (Eds.), *Best practices in school psychology-III* (pp. 421–430). Washington, DC: The National Association of School Psychologists.

National Association for the Education of Young Children. (1991). *Guide to accreditation by the National Academy of Early Childhood Programs* (Rev. ed.). Washington, DC: Author.

National Center for Education Statistics. (1994). *Digest of education statistics: Guide to sources.* Washington, DC: U.S. Department of Education.

National Center for Education Statistics. (1997). *Digest of education statistics* (NCES 98-015). Washington, DC: U.S. Department of Education.

National Education Goals Panel. (1998). *Principles and recommendations for early childhood assessments.* Washington, DC: U.S. Government Printing Office.

National Information Center for Children and Youth with Disabilities. (1997). *General information about severe and/or multiple disabilities* (Fact Sheet Number 10) [On-line]. Available: http://hichey.org/pubs/factshe/fs10txt.htm

Neef, N. A., & Iwata, B. A. (1994). Current research on functional analysis methodologies: An introduction. *Journal of Applied Behavior Analysis, 27*(2), 211–214.

Newborg, J., Stock, J. R., Wnek, L., Guidubaldi, J., & Svinicki, J. (1984). *The Battelle Developmental Inventory.* Allen, TX: DLM Teaching Resources.

Newman, P. R., & Newman, B. M. (1997). *Childhood and adolescence.* Pacific Grove, CA: Brooks/Cole.

Northrup, J., Wacker, D. P., Berg, W. K., Kelly, L., Sasso, G., & DeRaad, A. (1994). The treatment of severe behavior problems in school settings using a technical assistance model. *Journal of Applied Behavior Analysis, 27*(1), 33–47.

Nuttall, E. V., Romero, I., & Kalesnik, J. (Eds.). (1992). *Assessing and screening preschoolers: Psychological and educational dimensions.* Boston: Allyn and Bacon.

O'Brien, M., Rice, M., & Roy, C. (1996). Defining eligibility criteria for preventive early intervention in an NICU population. *Journal of Early Intervention, 20*(4), 283–293.

Odom, S. L., & Munson, L. J. (1996). Assessing social performance. In M. McLean, D. B. Bailey, Jr., & M.

Wolery, *Assessing infants and preschoolers with special needs* (2nd ed., pp. 398–434). Columbus, OH: Merrill.

O'Donnell, K. J. (1996). Neurobehavioral assessment of the newborn infant. In M. McLean, D. B. Bailey, Jr., & M. Wolery (Eds.), *Assessing infants and preschoolers with special needs* (2nd ed., pp. 165–201). Columbus, OH: Merrill.

Orelove, F., & Sobsey, D. (1996). *Educating children with multiple disabilities: A transdisciplinary approach* (2nd ed.). Baltimore: Paul H. Brookes.

Paget, K. D. (1992). Parent involvement in early childhood services. In M. Gettinger, S. N. Elliott, & T. R. Kratochwill (Eds.), *Preschool and early childhood treatment directions* (pp. 89–112). Hillsdale, NJ: Lawrence Erlbaum.

Parette, H. P. (1994). Assessing the influence of augmentative and alternative communication devices on families of young children with disabilities. *Perceptual and Motor Skills, 78,* 1361–1362.

Parette, H. P. (1997). Assistive technology devices and services. *Education and Training in Mental Retardation and Developmental Disabilities, 32,* 267–280.

Parette, H. P., & Angelo, D. H. (1996). Augmentative and alternative communication impact of families: Trends and future directions. *Journal of Special Education, 30,* 77–98.

Parette, H. P., & Brotherson, M. J. (1996). Family participation in assistive technology assessment for young children with mental retardation and developmental disabilities. *Education and Training in Mental Retardation and Developmental Disabilities, 31,* 29–43.

Parette, H. P., Dunn, N. S., & Hoge, D. R. (1995). Low-cost communication devices for children with disabilities and their family members. *Young Children, 50,* 75–81.

Parette, H. P., & Marr, D. D. (1997). Assisting children and families who use augmentative and alternative communication (AAC) devices: Best practices for school psychologists. *Psychology in the Schools, 34,* 337–346.

Pett, J. (1990). What is authentic evaluation? Common questions and answers. *Fair Test Examiner, 4,* 8–9.

Piper, M. C., & Darrah, J. (1993). *Motor assessment of the developing infant.* Philadelphia: W. B. Saunders.

Powell, D. S., Batsche, C. J., Ferro, J., Fox, L., & Dunlap, G. (1997). A strength-based approach in support of multi-risk families: Principles and issues.

Topics in Early Childhood Special Education, 17(1), 1–26.

Preator, K. K., & McAllister, J. R. (1995). Assessing infants and toddlers. In A. Thomas & J. Grimes, *Best practices in school psychology-III.* Washington, DC: National Association of School Psychologists.

Preschool Technology Training Team Project. (1995). *Assistive technology for preschoolers with disabilities: Collected resources.* Tallmadge, OH: Family Child Learning Center. (ERIC Document Reproduction Service No. ED 415 015)

Rainforth, B., York, J., & MacDonald, C. (1992). *Collaborative teams for students with severe disabilities: Integrating therapy and educational services.* Baltimore: Paul H. Brookes.

Ramey, C. T., & Ramey, S. L. (1998). Early intervention and early experience. *American Psychologist, 53,* 102–120.

Reimers, T. M., Wacker, D. P., Cooper, L. J., & DeRaad, A. O. (1992). Acceptability of behavioral treatments for children: Analog and naturalistic evaluations by parents. *School Psychology Review, 21,* 628–643.

Reimers, T. M., Wacker, D. P., Cooper, L. J., Sasso, G. M., Berg, W. K., & Steege, M. W. (1993). Assessing the functional properties of noncompliant behavior in an outpatient setting. *Child and Family Behavior Therapy, 15*(3), 1–15.

Reimers, T. M., Wacker, D. P., Derby, K. M., & Cooper, L. J. (1995). Relation between parental attributions and the acceptability of behavioral treatments for their child's behavior problems. *Behavioral Disorders, 20*(3), 171–178.

Reschly, D. J. (1990). Best practices in adaptive behavior. In A. Thomas & J. Grimes (Eds.), *Best practices in school psychology—II* (pp. 29–42). Washington, DC: National Association of School Psychologists.

Reynolds, C., & Kamphaus, R. (1992). *Behavior Assessment System for Children.* Circle Pines, MN: American Guidance Service.

Riccitello, R., & Adler, J. (1997, Spring/Summer Special Edition). Your baby has a problem. *Newsweek,* 46–50.

Rogers, M. R., Ponterotto, J. G., Conoley, J. C., & Wiese, M. J. (1992). Multicultural training in school psychology: A national survey. *School Psychology Review, 21,* 603–616.

Rogers, S. J., Donovan, C. M., D'Eugenio, D. B., Brown, S. L., Lynch, E. W., Moersch, M. S., &

Schafer, D. S. (1981). *Early intervention developmental profile*. Ann Arbor: University of Michigan Press.

Rokusek, C. (1995). Introduction to the concept of interdisciplinary practice. In B. A. Thyer & N. P. Kropf (Eds.), *Developmental disabilities: A handbook of interdisciplinary practice* (pp. 1–12). Cambridge, MA: Brookline Books.

Rosenbaum, P. L. (1997). Partnerships: Challenges and rewards. *Developmental Medicine & Child Neurology, 39,* 573.

Rounds, K. A., Weil, M., & Bishop, K. K. (1994). Practice with culturally diverse families of young children with disabilities. *Families in Society: The Journal of Contemporary Human Services* [CEU article no. 38], 3–15.

Sailor, W., & Guess, D. (1983). *Severely handicapped students—An instrumental design*. Boston: Houghton Mifflin.

Salend, S. J. (1997). What about our schools, our languages. *Teaching Exceptional Children, 29*(4), 38–41.

Salvia, J., & Ysseldyke, J. E. (1995). *Assessment* (6th ed.). Boston: Houghton Mifflin.

Salvia, J., & Ysseldyke, J. E. (1998). *Assessment* (7th ed.). Boston: Houghton Mifflin.

Sanders, M. R., & Lawton, J. M. (1993). Discussing assessment findings with families: A guided participation model of information transfer. *Child and Family Behavior Therapy, 15*(2), 5–35.

Sanford, A. R., & Zelman, J. G. (1981). *The Learning Accomplishment Profile*. Winston-Salem, NC: Kaplan.

Sattler, J. M. (1988). *Assessment of children* (3rd ed.). San Diego, CA: Author.

Sattler, J. M. (1998). *Clinical and forensic interviewing of children and families: Guidelines for the mental health, education, pediatric, and child maltreatment fields*. San Diego, CA: Author.

Sexton, D., Burrell, B., & Thompson, B. (1992). Measurement integrity of the family needs survey. *Journal of Early Intervention, 16,* 343–352.

Sexton, D., Lobman, M., Constans, T., Snyder, P., & Ernest, J. (1997). Early interventionists' perspectives of multicultural practices with African-American families. *Exceptional Children, 63,* 313–328.

Sexton, D., Snyder, P., Wolfe, B., Lobman, M., Stricklin, S., & Akers, P. (1996). Early intervention in-service training strategies: Perceptions and

suggestions from the field. *Exceptional Children, 62,* 485–495.

Shonkoff, J. P. (1993). Developmental vulnerability: New challenges for research and service delivery. In N. J. Anastasiow & S. Harel (Eds.), *At-risk infants: Interventions, families and research* (pp. 47–54). Baltimore: Paul H. Brookes.

Simeonsson, R. J. (1986). *Psychological and developmental assessment of special children*. Boston: Allyn and Bacon.

Simeonsson, R. J. (1990). *Psychological and developmental assessment of special children* (2nd ed.). Boston: Allyn and Bacon.

Simeonsson, R. J. (Ed.). (1994). *Risk resilience and prevention*. Baltimore: Paul H. Brookes.

Simeonsson, R. J., & Bailey, D. (1989). *The Abilities Index* (Rev. ed.). Chapel Hill: The University of North Carolina, Frank Porter Graham Child Development Center.

Simeonsson, R. J., Bailey, D. B., Jr., Huntington, G. S., & Brandon, L. (1991). Scaling and attainment of goals in family-focused early intervention [brief report]. *Community Mental Health Journal, 27*(1), 77–83.

Simeonsson, R. J., Huntington, G. S., & Parse, S. A. (1979). *Assessment of children with severe handicaps: Multiple problems, multivariate goals*. Chapel Hill: The University of North Carolina, Frank Porter Graham Child Development Center, Carolina Institute for Research on Early Education of the Handicapped.

Sinclair, E. (1993). Early identification of preschoolers with special needs in Headstart. *Topics in Early Childhood Special Education, 13*(2), 184–201.

Snell, M. E. (Ed.). (1987). *Systematic instruction of persons with severe handicaps* (3rd ed.). Columbus, OH: Charles E. Merrill.

Snell, M. E. (Ed.). (1993). *Systematic instruction of persons with severe disabilities* (4th ed.). Columbus, OH: Charles E. Merrill.

Snyder, P., Lawson, S., Thompson, B., Stricklin, S., & Sexton, D. (1993). Evaluating the psychometric integrity of instruments used in early intervention research: The Battelle Developmental Inventory. *Topics in Early Childhood Special Education, 13* (2), 216–232.

Squires, J., Bricker, D., & Potter, L. (1993). *Infant/child monitoring questionnaires: Procedures manual*. Eugene: University of Oregon Center on Human Development.

Stayton, V. D., & Miller, P. S. (1993). Combining general and special early-childhood education standards in personnel preparation programs: Experiences from 2 states. *Topics in Early Childhood Special Education, 13,* 372–387.

Steinberg, A. (1993). Ethical issues in early intervention. In N. J. Anastasiow & S. Harel (Eds.), *At-risk infants: Intervention, families and research* (pp. 13–17). Baltimore: Paul H. Brookes.

Stephens, T. J. (1998). *The use of antecedent and consequence manipulations to assess and treat noncompliance in young children.* Unpublished doctoral dissertation, The University of Iowa, Iowa City.

Sternberg, L. (Ed.). (1994). *Individuals with profound disabilities: Instructional and assistive strategies* (3rd ed.). College Park, MD: U.S. Department of Education, ERIC Clearinghouse on Assessment and Evaluation. (ERIC Document Reproduction Service No. ED 388 008)

Stoneman, Z., & Malone, D. M. (1995). The changing nature of interdisciplinary practice. In B. A. Thyer & N. P. Kropf (Eds.), *Developmental disabilities: A handbook for interdisciplinary practice* (pp. 234–247). Cambridge, MA: Brookline Books.

Strain, P. S., McConnell, S. R., Carta, J. J., Fowler, S. A., Neisworth, J. T., & Wolery, M. (1992). *Topics in Early Childhood Special Education, 12*(1), 121–141.

Suzuki, L. A., Meller, J. P., & Ponteretto, J. G. (Eds.). (1996). *Handbook of multicultural assessment: Clinical, psychological, and educational applications.* San Francisco, CA: Jossey-Bass.

Technology Related Assistance Act of 1988, Pub. L. No. 100–407 (S2561), Stat. 1044 (1988).

Telzrow, C. F. (1993). Commentary on comparative evaluation of early intervention alternatives. Special issues: Comparative evaluations of early intervention alternatives. *Early Education and Development, 4,* 359–365.

Thorndike, R. L., Hagen, E., & Sattler, J. (1986). *Technical manual, The Stanford-Binet Intelligence Scale: Fourth edition.* Chicago: Riverside.

Thurman, K. (1993). Some perspectives on the continuing challenges in early intervention. In W. Brown, S. K. Thurman, & L. F. Pearl (Eds.), *Family centered early intervention with infants and toddlers: Innovative cross-disciplinary approaches* (pp. 303–316). Baltimore: Paul H. Brookes.

Thyer, B. A., & Kropf, N. P. (Eds.). (1995). *Developmental disabilities: A handbook for interdisciplinary practice.* Cambridge, MA: Brookline Books.

Trivette, C. M., Dunst, C. J., Boyd, K., & Hamby, D. W. (1995). Family-oriented program models, helpgiving practices, and parental control appraisals. *Exceptional Children, 62*(3), 237–248.

Trivette, C. M., Dunst, C. J., & Hamby, D. (1996). Characteristics and consequences of help-giving practices in contrasting human services programs. *American Journal of Community Psychology, 24*(2), 273–293.

Trohanis, P. L. (1995). *Progress in providing services to young children with special needs and their families: An overview and update on implementing The Individuals With Disabilities Education Act (IDEA)* (NEC*TAS Notes No. 7) [On-line]. Available: http://www.nectas.unc.edu/idea/nnotes7.htm

Turbiville, V., Lee, I., Turnbull, A., & Murphy, D. (1993). *Handbook for the development of a family-friendly individualized family service plan (IFSP).* Lawrence: University of Kansas, Beach Center on Families and Disabilities.

Turnbull, A. P., & Ruef, M. (1997). Family perspectives on inclusive lifestyle issues for people with problem behavior. *Exceptional Children, 63,* 211–227.

Umbreit, J., & Blair, K.-S. (1997). Using structural analysis to facilitate treatment of aggression and noncompliance in a young child at-risk for behavioral disorders. *Behavioral Disorders, 22*(2), 75–86.

U.S. Congress (1994, January 25). Developmental Disabilities Assistance and Bill of Rights Act Amendments of 1994. Senate Report 1284. Washington, DC: Author.

U.S. Congress (1993, August). Technology-Related Assistance for Individuals with Disabilities Amendments of 1993. H. R. 2339 (Report No. 103-208). Washington DC: Author.

U.S. Department of Education. (1995). *Seventeenth annual report to Congress on the implementation of the Individuals with Disabilities Education Act.* Washington, DC: Author.

U.S. Department of Education (1997). *Nineteenth annual report to Congress on the. implementation of the Individuals with Disabilities Education Act.* Washington, DC: Author.

U.S. Department of Education. (1998). *The condition of education 1998: School years ending 1977–1966.* Washington, DC: Author.

Wechsler, D. (1989). *WPPSI-R manual.* San Antonio, TX: Psychological Corporation.

Wesley, P. W., Buysse, V., & Tyndall, S. (1997). Family and professional perspectives on early intervention: An exploration using focus groups. *Topics in Early Childhood Special Education, 17,* 435–456.

Witt, J. C., Elliott, S. N., Daly, E. J., III, Gresham, F. M., & Kramer, J. J. (1998). *Assessment of at-risk and special needs children* (2nd ed.). Boston: McGraw-Hill.

Wolery, M. (1996). Monitoring child progress. In M. McLean, D. B. Bailey, Jr., & M. Wolery (Eds.), *Assessing infants and preschoolers with special needs* (2nd ed., pp. 519–560). Columbus, OH: Merrill.

Wolery, M., Bailey, D. B., & Sugai, G. M. (1988). *Effective teaching: Principles and procedures of applied behavior analysis with exceptional students.* Boston: Allyn and Bacon.

Wolery, M., & McWilliam, R. A. (1998). Classroom-based practices for preschoolers with disabilities. *Intervention in School and Clinic, 34,* 95+.

Wolery, M., & Schuster, J. W. (1997). Instructional methods with students who have significant disabilities. *Journal of Special Education, 31,* 61–79.

Wolery, M., Venn, M. L., Holcombe, A., Brookfield, J., Martin, C. G., Huffman, K., Schroeder, C., & Fleming, L. A. (1994). Employment of related service personnel in preschool programs: A survey of general early educators. *Exceptional Children, 61,* 25–39.

Wortham, S. C. (1995). *Measurement and evaluation in early childhood education* (2nd ed.). Englewood Cliffs, NJ: Prentice Hall.

Wyly, M. V. (1995). *Premature infants and their families: Developmental interventions.* San Diego, CA: Singular.

APPENDIX 1

PRESCHOOL ASSESSMENT VOCABULARY FOR THE 1990s

Adaptive assessment   Changing the format or content of the assessment technique to fit the specific needs of the infant or child.

Adaptive-transactive assessment   Assessment of the interaction of the infant or child with his or her social and physical environment.

Alternative assessment   Assessing an individual using techniques other than norm-referenced standardized tests, requires observation of the infant's or child's response to a task.

Arena assessment   A child is presented with various activities to complete by a facilitator who is familiar with the child. Parents and/or other professionals observe and record their observations using a running record.

Assessment system   The combination of multiple assessment techniques and/or areas in order to provide comprehensive information. The system could include formal and informal techniques used by one or more assessors.

Augmentative assessment   Assessment of the infant or child using the communication or locomotion devices that are needed for "appropriate" assessment (communication boards, synthesized speech systems, etc.).

Authentic assessment   Assessment that occurs in a real-life situation and is based on standards present in that context.

Benchmark assessment   The use of a detailed description of specific levels of infant or child performance against which to judge the performance of another infant or child.

Criterion-referenced assessment   Judgments regarding performance are based on a set of well-defined objectives and/or competencies.

Culturally competent assessment   Assessment that is sensitive and responsive to cultural differences. The assessor is aware of his or her own cultural values and limitations, has acquired cultural-specific information, recognizes the integrity of all cultures, and applies this knowledge when assessing members of diverse groups.

Curriculum-based assessment (CBA)   A variety of techniques used to directly assess a child's functioning in his or her own curriculum.

Curriculum-based measurement (CBM)   A model of CBA in which there are standard directions and norms used to evaluate performance.

Curriculum-embedded assessment   A model of CBA in which an infant or child's specific program curriculum is used for testing and teaching.

Curriculum-referenced assessment   A model of CBA in which an infant or child is assessed using developmental tasks from a generic curriculum.

Direct assessment versus indirect assessment   Assessment of specific skills versus global or inferential assessment.

Dynamic assessment   The assessment process actively involves the infant or child in learning. It is often referred to as a test-teach-test model.

Ecological assessment   Assessment of all aspects of all of the environments of an infant or child.

Family-directed or family-centered assessment   Family members are an integral part of the assessment process. They select which information to share with others regarding their resources, priorities, and concerns.

Family-focused assessment   The assessment process will include assessment of family needs but may be directed by professionals' assessment of family functioning versus self-assessment.

Formal/informal assessment   Formal assessment usually means the use of standardized assessment techniques to gather information whereas informal assessment can be the use of many different techniques to gather information. The informal techniques include reviewing records, conducting observations, and presenting tasks to the infant or child. The informal techniques are not standardized and do not have norms.

Functional analysis/functional assessment   These two terms are often used very differently, but both should mean using assessment to determine the function of a behavior exhibited by an infant or child. The assessor wants to know what is maintaining a behavior.

Interview-based assessment (IBA)   This is a new term, not a new assessment technique. It is the use of an interview to gather information.

Judgment-based assessment (JBA)   This is another new term, not a new technique. It simply means collecting the judgments or perceptions of various persons regarding the infant's or child's behavior. This could include the use of rating scales.

Performance-based assessment   Assessment based on direct demonstration of knowledge, skill, or behavior.

Play-based assessment   Observation of a child during play activities. This could be structured or unstructured and could be recorded through systematic observation of a running record.

Portfolio assessment   Collection of the products of a child's play or work that demonstrates what he or she can do.

Progress monitoring   Continuous assessment and recording of a child's knowledge, skills, or behaviors.

Reinforcer assessment   Identification of the consequences to a behavior that will result in the behavior increasing.

Structural assessment   Observation and manipulation of the environment to determine the effects of the structural or context variables on the behavior.

Transdisciplinary play-based assessment (TPBA)   Linder's (1993a) model of observations of infants and young children in structured and unstructured play situations. There may be one or more adults present and one or more other children depending on the purpose of the observation. Specific questionnaires have been developed for assessment of specific domains in specific play situations.

APPENDIX 2

RESOURCES FOR ASSESSMENT

Assessment Guidelines for Infants and Preschoolers with Disabilities

Bagnato and Neisworth, 1991; Beckman and Boyes, 1993; Benner, 1992; Bergen, 1994; Bondurant-Utz and Luciano, 1994; Bricker, 1993; Cohen and Spenciner, 1994, 1998; Committee on Children with Disabilities, 1994; Dunst, 1993; Fewell, 1991; Fleisher et al. 1990; Fox et al. 1994; Genishi, 1992; Gerken, 1991; Gibbs and Teti, 1990; Harris and McEwen, 1996; Katz, 1994; Linder, 1993; McLean, Bailey, and Wolery, 1996; Nuttall, Romero, and Kalesnik, 1992; Preator and McAllister, 1995; Simeonsson, 1986, 1990; U.S. Department of Education, 1988; Wolery, 1996; Wortham, 1995

Assessment Guidelines for Individuals with Severe Disabilities

Bergen, 1994; Bergen and Everington, 1994; Browder, 1991; Sattler, 1988; Snell, 1987, 1993; Sternberg, 1994; Thyer and Kropf, 1995

General Evaluation of Assessment Instruments

Salvia and Ysseldyke, 1995, 1998; Sattler, 1988; Witt, Elliot, Daly, Gresham and Kramer, 1998

Descriptions and Evaluations of Instruments for Infants and Preschoolers with Disabilities

Bagnato and Neisworth, 1991; Benner, 1992; Bergen, 1994; Brown, Thurman, and Pearl, 1993; Cohen and Spenciner, 1994, 1998; Gibbs and Teti, 1990; McLean, Bailey, and Wolery, 1996; Squires, Bricker, and Potter, 1993; Wortham, 1995

Descriptions and Evaluations of Instruments for Infants and Preschoolers with Severe Disabilities

Bagnato and Neisworth, 1991, 1994; Bergen, 1994; Browder, 1991; Brown, Thurman, and Pearl, 1993; Cohen and Spenciner, 1994, 1998; Dorman, 1998

Descriptions and Evaluations of Instruments for Assessing Family Needs and Concerns

Bailey, 1996; Bailey et al., 1998a, b, 1990, 1998; Bricker et al., 1995; McLean, Bailey, and Wolery, 1996; McQuaide and Ehrenreich, 1997; Turbiville et al., 1993; Turnbull and Rueff, 1997

Guidelines for Assessment with Culturally and/or Linguistically Diverse Families

Barrera, 1993; Benner, 1992; Bergen, 1994; Cohen and Spenciner, 1994, 1998; Dana, 1993; Harry, 1992; Johnson-Powell, 1997; Lynch, 1992, 1993; Lynch and Hanson, 1996; McLean, Bailey, and Wolery, 1996; Nuttall, Romero, and Kalesnik, 1992; Rounds, Weil, and Bishop, 1994; Salvia and Ysseldyke, 1998; Sattler, 1988; Suzuki, Meller, and Ponteretto, 1996

CHAPTER 16

PRESCHOOL CREATIVITY

E. PAUL TORRANCE

Although there has been increasing interest in assessing the creativity of older individuals in recent years, there has not been much interest in assessing the creativity of preschool children.

Genuine skepticism among psychologists, educators, and the general public has hindered progress in assessing the creativity of preschool children. Most people have believed that preschool children are incapable of creative thinking and have attached little importance to what a few psychologists have called "creative" in young children. However, poets, artists, and even scientists have continued to assure us that young children are indeed creative and that this creativity is important.

There are many authorities who maintain that a child's creativity is set by the age of 3 and that kindergarten (age 5) may be too late to give stimulation (Ibuka, 1985). However, the research evidence seems to indicate that individual differences in creativity are due to training, whereas intelligence seems to have a significant hereditary component. This will be discussed later.

Elizabeth G. Andrews was one of the few psychologists who studied the creativity of preschool children (Andrews, 1930). From her work in the 1920s, she concluded that creative imagination exists in varying degrees in all normal children. Andrews also observed wide individual differences in the extent and types of creative imagination in preschool children, She believed that the kinds of creative imagination that she studied were important. She urged that preschool children be allowed to develop their prevailing interests. She also felt young children benefited from encouragement for every creative act, even when their actions did not conform to adult standards.

WHY TEST THE CREATIVITY OF PRESCHOOL CHILDREN?

There are many excellent reasons for testing the creativity of preschool children. Elizabeth Andrews saw it as a part of vocational guidance for every child. She believed that vocational guidance should be initiated in the nursery—not by forcing on the child a vocation selected by the teacher or parent, but by allowing the child to develop along the lines of his or her greatest strengths and interests. She recognized that people are most greatly motivated to do the things that they can do best. It should certainly be the goal of gifted/talented education to become aware of these special abilities and to provide opportunities for their fullest development.

Since the days of Alfred Binet and Sigmund Freud, psychologists have known of the great importance of early learned behavior. Binet, for example, urged that teachers build upon the learning skills that children have already acquired by the time they enter school. For the most part, these are creative skills, such as imagining, questioning, singing, dancing, and storytelling. Usually these skills are ignored and unused, creating a serious discontinuity between preschool learning and school learning.

It is reasonable to expect that education would endeavor to keep alive and further develop promising creative talent among young children. However, the reverse seems to be true. Anyone who observes the behavior of infants from birth will note enormous individual differences in their curiosity, experimentation, and creative learning. Children who most strongly display these creative behaviors are often punished by parents

---

This chapter contains material adapted from the manual for Thinking Creatively in Action and Movement, published by Scholastic Testing Service, Inc. Used by permission.

and teachers who find creative behavior inconvenient and difficult to manage. However, children who fail to manifest curiosity and other creative learning behaviors are stimulated to display such behaviors and are rewarded accordingly. Thus, the way that society treats the creativity of preschool children seems to wipe out individual hereditary differences. Therefore, it is not surprising that classical twin studies of the heritability of creative abilities show practically no heritability for these abilities (Pezullo, Thorsen, & Madaus, 1972; Torrance, 1979).

Professionals in the field of gifted/talented education should be concerned with identifying and developing all strengths that can be used to facilitate important kinds of intellectual, academic, psychomotor, artistic, and empathic growth. Children's creative abilities are indisputably important in facilitating all of these kinds of growth. A consistent finding among all of those who have studied outstanding creative achievements is that a common characteristic of people who have achieved important breakthroughs in every field is their creativity. Thus, creativity should be considered in any evaluation associated with efforts to encourage excellence.

Professionals in gifted/talented education should also be concerned about discovering and creating the conditions that facilitate creative development among young children. Scientifically developed information is needed. As always, such scientific findings must rely upon measurement. Many important questions about creating conditions to facilitate creative development cannot be answered without instruments for testing the creativity of preschool children.

PROBLEMS OF TESTING CREATIVITY IN PRESCHOOLERS

A basic problem in assessing any behavior among preschool children is in eliciting the kind of behavior the tester desires. Even among first grade children, some skilled teachers are unable to elicit verbal responses from certain children. Many of the demands made by psychometrists of preschool children have always seemed unreasonable to me. Thus, in designing instruments and procedures for testing the creativity of preschool children, the following guidelines are important:

1. The tasks in tests of creativity should permit preschool children to respond to modalities appropriate to their developmental characteristics. Most of the early tests of creativity for young children re-

lied heavily on verbal responses at a time when children are developmentally in the sensorimotor stage (Piaget, 1973). (It should also be noted that Piaget speaks of the sensorimotor stage as one of intellectual development.) Thus, the kinesthetic modality is the most appropriate modality for eliciting the creativity of most preschool children because skills in this modality are most practiced at the preschool age.

2. Tasks should contain procedures for warm-up and motivation. These warm-up and motivational procedures should be common to the experiences of 3- to 8-year old children.

3. Tests should sample the kinds of creativity that are important in the lives of such children. Otherwise, preschool children will not be motivated to think or create. The test should make sense to them.

4. Tests should be easy to administer and score. The warm-up and test exercises themselves should be as natural to the experiences of preschool children as possible, yet challenging and capable of eliciting behaviors never before displayed by them. The test tasks should be neither long nor hurried. It takes time to warm up and motivate children, yet they fatigue easily and are unable to maintain a high level of performance over a long period of time.

THE HISTORY OF TESTING THE CREATIVITY OF PRESCHOOL CHILDREN

Prior to the work of Elizabeth G. Andrews, there seem to have been few attempts to test the creativity of preschool children. McCarty had used drawings and Abramson had used inkblots to test the creativity of children within this range (Abramson, 1927; McCarty, 1924). However, drawings are not appropriate for this purpose until a child has had enough practice with some kind of marking tool. Many children in the 3- to 5-year age range have had little or no experience in drawing or using a marking tool. Because the inkblots require verbal responses, many children in this age range are unable to respond adequately. They may have in mind a rich image but are unable to label it.

While attempting to study several types of imaginative and creative activity, Andrews used a variety of methods and observations. Three of her tests were presented tachistoscopically with the task of forming new products (transformations). The following kinds of observations were made of the imaginative play of children from 2 to 6: imitation, experimentation, transformation of objects, transformation of animals, acts of sympathy, dramatizations, imaginary playmates, fanciful explanations, fantastic stories, new uses of stories, constructions, new games, extensions of language, appropriate quotations, leadership with plan, and aesthetic appreciation.

Andrews was also more systematic and thoroughgoing than earlier investigators had been in tracing the development of creative imagination during the preschool years. She discovered that total creative imagination scores were highest between the ages of 4 years, and 4 years 6 months, with a sudden drop at about age 5 when the child enters kindergarten. The ability to redefine, restructure, or recombine reached a peak between the ages of 3 and 4 years. These abilities decreased after age 4. Analogy reached a height during the fourth year and declined during the fifth. "Don't know" responses decreased steadily with chronological age up to 4 years and then slightly increased. The more creative types of imagination reached a high point between ages 3 years, 6 months and 4 years, 6 months, with their lowest ebb during the fifth year. Andrews also found low and insignificant correlations between IQ and imagination and mental age and imagination. She reported that teachers' judgments were unreliable as criteria for measuring creative imagination.

As in the author's studies with older children in the 1950s and 1960s, Andrews found that all children of high intelligence did not necessarily have a high degree of creative imagination (Torrance, 1962). However, she also found that there were numerous instances in which children were both highly intelligent and creative. She believed that these were the really gifted children who might become creative scientists and artists if the school did not smother their creative imagination by its zeal to turn all fantasy into fact, and destroy at its conception that power of mind that combines experience and new ideas.

The present author initiated efforts in 1958 to develop tests of creative thinking that would extend downward to 5-year-olds. These tests were finally integrated into the *Torrance Tests of Creative Thinking* (Torrance, 1966, 1974). These tests proved to be only marginally successful even with 5-year-olds and were unsuitable with 3- and 4-year-olds. It was not until 1966 at the University of Georgia that the author made serious efforts to test the creativity of preschool children. Initial efforts included a Mother Goose Problems Test; a Construction Test (involving Legos blocks); an Originality Test calling for unusual images associated with different shaped wooden blocks; a Question Asking Test calling for questioning responses to Mother Goose prints, stories, and

poems; and a Just Suppose Test based on original drawings of unlikely situations (Torrance, 1968, 1970). Most of these procedures relied heavily on verbal responses and were generally disappointing in their results. However, it was out of these disappointments that the idea for *Thinking Creatively in Action and Movement* emerged. In day care centers and in other programs for preschool children, the author set out to observe the ways in which preschool children expressed their creative thinking. It was on the basis of these experiences that the procedures described herein were developed.

Before turning to the development and use of *Thinking Creatively in Action and Movement,* it seems fitting to acknowledge the important role of Elizabeth K. Starkweather in the history of testing the creativity of preschool children. Before her untimely death, Starkweather had invested heavily in the development of a set of promising instruments for assessing the creativity of preschool children (Starkweather, 1968, 1976). The most promising of these are listed here:

1. *The Starkweather Form Boards Test* to assess conformity–nonconformity. Four form boards pictured scenes familiar to most children in the United States (a tree, a house, a playground, and a barnyard). The boards and pictures are colored, and an opportunity to conform is provided by black-and-white line drawings placed behind each form board.
2. *The Starkweather Target Game,* designed to measure young children's willingness to try difficult tasks, and to accept the challenge of a calculated risk. It consists of a box-shaped target that responds like a jack-in-the-box. When a bull's-eye at the front of the target is hit, the lid opens and a surprise picture appears. The ability of each child is pretested to determine what is difficult for each child. On each trial the child must make a choice between an easy task and a difficult one.
3. *The Starkweather Originality Test,* to assess originality of thinking. It consists of a pretest or warm-up session, in which the examiner encourages the child to think of a variety of responses, and the test proper, in which the child's responses to additional shapes are accepted without question. The pretest consists of eight plastic foam pieces, and the test proper consists of 40 pieces, four from each of ten different shapes.

Starkweather had plans for having the testing materials manufactured commercially, but this was never accomplished. She did provide a number of people with instructions for producing the materials and administering and scoring tests.

PRESCHOOL CREATIVITY

Creative ability stands as a unique and distinctive aspect within the realm of giftedness. Perhaps the most important aspect of creativity is the fact that creative behavior is potentially available to everyone (Guilford, 1968, 1986; Parnes, 1981; Taylor, 1964; Torrance, 1962, 1972a, 1972b) and often some degree is evident at some point in almost everyone's experiences. Elements of creative behavior can be elicited, supported, and trained through a variety of methods and procedures (Amabile, 1987; Parnes, 1987). This fact has been clearly demonstrated for more than three decades (Binet, 1909; Guilford, 1956, 1960; Parnes & Meadow, 1960).

In view of current evidence concerning human functioning, it would seem unthinkable for psychologists and educators to continue ignoring children's creative functioning in the assessment of preschool children (Torrance, 1962, 1963, 1965, 1972, 1981a, 1931b; Torrance & Wu, 1981).

Definition

Some degree of creativity is required whenever a person is faced with a problem for which he or she has no learned or practiced response. Because preschool children are constantly facing such situations, they are constantly using and practicing their creative thinking abilities.

Torrance has offered a more formal, process definition of creativity (1969, p. vii):

> *Creative behavior occurs in the process of becoming sensitive to or aware of problems, deficiencies, gaps in knowledge, missing elements, disharmonies, and so on; bringing together in new relationships available information: defining the difficulty of identifying the missing elements; searching for solutions, making guesses, or formulating hypotheses about the problems or deficiencies; testing and retesting them; perfecting them; and finally communicating the results.*

This is a natural, healthy human process common among almost all children. Strong human motivations are at work at each stage.

The degree of creativity will depend on the extent to which the result (1) shows novelty and value (either for the child or for the culture), (2) is unconventional in the sense that it diverges from previously accepted visions, (3) is true, generalizable, and surprising in the light of what the child knew at the time, and (4) requires persistence in going beyond previous performances.

The creative behavior of preschool children is characterized by wonder and magic. Most healthy young children have the spirit, unless they have been victims of neglect, harshness, lack of love, or severe deprivation. Because of the sense of wonder and magic, children learn from experience, manipulating objects, rearranging things and combining them in different ways, singing, dancing, storytelling, and the like.

Creative Ways of Learning

Preschool children are experts in creative learning because by the age of 2 to 3 years they have acquired considerable experience in learning by questioning, inquiring, searching, manipulating, experimenting, and playing to find out in their own way the truth about things. If they sense that something is wrong or missing, that something is out of place, they are uncomfortable until they do something to find out about it: They start exploring, testing, questioning, and searching through whatever modalities are available to them. Whenever they discover something new, they want to tell or show it to somebody. At times, creative thinking is lightning quick. At other times, we must wait patiently, and then it may come lightning quick. The following characteristics of young children help them learn creatively (Torrance, 1969):

1. long attention span
2. capacity for organization
3. seeing things from a different perspective
4. exploring before formal instruction
5. using silence and hesitation
6. taking a "closer look" at things
7. using fantasy to solve developmental problems
8. storytelling and song making

Tentative Hierarchy of Creative Thinking Skills

There has been little serious attempt to identify the hierarchy of creative thinking skills and establish a developmental timetable for preschool children. The expression of creative thinking skills depends on the modalities accessible to the children. There are enormous individual differences among young children in the development of speech. Until a child develops speech skills, we cannot expect much verbal creativity. However, most preschool children seem to develop the following skills by the time they are ready for school (Torrance, 1970):

1. The child will be able to produce new combinations through manipulation.
2. The child will be able to see and produce many possible combinations or new relationships.
3. The child will be able to identify missing elements in pictures and shapes, letters, and so on at a very gross level.
4. The child will be able to produce increasingly more complex combinations through manipulation and move to deliberate experimentation.
5. The child will be able to see and produce increasingly larger numbers of possibilities in combining symbols, objects, numerals, people, places, and so on.
6. The child will increase verbal fluency by naming new combinations of shapes, sounds, animals, and so on at a simple level.
7. The child will be able to make syntheses by giving titles or labels to pictures, stories, songs, and poems.
8. The child will have improved skills in asking questions about missing elements in objects, pictures, stories, situations, and so on.

It is not possible to specify the precise ages at which each of these, characteristics and skills emerges. Much depends on the development of various sensory skills and verbal development.

SOURCES OF INFORMATION ABOUT POTENTIAL CREATIVITY

Information about potential creativity can be derived from a rich assortment of sources. All are potentially applicable to a preschool population, though several particular sources are more appropriate and informative for this age group than the others. The combined effects of a child's age and prior experiences support the use of sets of indicators for specific children at different times.

Ehrlich (1980) lists the following techniques useful in the identification of creativity among the very young (3 to 7 years of age). This list includes the following possibilities:

1. biographical data
2. checklists and rating scales
3. objective testing: achievement in specific areas
4. observations: formal and informal
5. parent nominations
6. peer nominations
7. performance tests (work and behavior samples)
8. personal interview
9. professional nominations and judgments

Ehrlich also included group and individual intelligence tests. She might have included group and individual creativity tests, as will be shown later in this chapter.

The traditional method includes what are often considered to be the formal sources of information, such as group objective screens, possibly followed by individual screening. Typically, this means the use of objective intelligence testing and/or achievement testing for specific areas of achievement. The traditional method has been so called because of its consistent and often exclusive use in the identification of gifted individuals despite the fact that this process can be both time consuming and costly (Renzulli & Smith, 1977). Much of the attraction and use of this method stems from the history of psychological and psychoeducational assessment, from its relative origins with Binet and Simon (1916) in the early part of the nineteenth century through the longitudinal work of Terman and his associates (1925) and Terman and Oden (1947) with highly intellectually gifted individuals.

The twentieth-century trend in objective testing was built on a belief that important information can be gained through the application of these instruments. In fact, many objective intelligence tests have been proven to be both valid and reliable for their particular purposes across a broad range of age groups. These basic requirements of reliability do not always extend down to the range of the very young, though (Bracken, 1987). Test development with the very young is extraordinarily expensive and requires skilled administrators. Young children are quite variable in their performance and are not always motivated to perform their best. Here lies one of the difficulties in using the traditional method with preschoolers, especially to the exclusion of any other source of information. This point leads to another concern over the use of objective tests: Objective testing alone does not adequately address the range of potential giftedness. Multiple indicators are needed, especially with the very young children. A third point of concern over objective measures is that typically only individually administered tests can be used with the very young. Although this has been demonstrated frequently to enhance a child's total score (i.e., they test as more intelligent individually than in group administration), it also accounts for a higher cost in time and money.

Instrument selection should be the result of informed consideration and thorough investigation of the available measurement tools, not a random process or a forced choice, if possible. To aid in this often difficult and confusing process, Ehrlich (1980) suggests a set of 10 criteria for the evaluation and selection of prospective instruments or measurement techniques that could potentially be adopted to an assessment program. These criteria are:

1. objectivity
2. reliability
3. validity
4. historical record of success
5. appropriateness of language
6. cultural appropriateness
7. cost of administration
8. time to administer

Biographical Data

For young children, a well-developed biographical record and subsequent analysis can provide a variety of clues about the child's potential creativity, despite the child's relatively brief life span. Generally, this source can provide important developmental information about a specific child in relation to his or her peers of the same culture. Items worthy of notice include early psychomotor, language, and numerical development; early reading (especially self-taught); and special interests and hobbies (especially if self-initiated and pursued with dedication, enthusiasm, and for long or consistent periods of time). This information depends highly on parents' observations, which form an important component in the early identification process.

Checklists and Rating Scales

These instruments often have strong intuitive appeal but frequently lack the appropriate psychometric properties of validity and reliability. For this reason, in part, they cannot be used as exclusive means of identification. This is not to imply that the process of appropriate psychometer development could not be undertaken; this typically involves much time and money that could be spent elsewhere. Because checklist and rating scales typically are based on the observations of gifted individuals' behaviors, they often have a high content validity. They do, therefore, offer a quick-screening method of the identifi-

cation of gifted individuals from within a heterogeneous group. These instruments also are usually economical in terms of time and money. With proper training and care, the use of these instruments can provide an accurate and inexpensive prescreening component of a broader and more thorough assessment program.

Observations

Observation is the general category under which the various nomination techniques, interviews, questionnaires, and the like all fall. When formally undertaken, with well-designed schedules and trained observers, children's behaviors can be observed and assessed in naturally occurring situations at home or school, during play or work, and while they are alone or interacting with peers or others. Observational techniques can be developed and statistically validated, but the results most likely will not reach the level of objective validity and reliability of standardized instruments. Although these methods can provide a wealth of information, the less formal the process, the less reliable are the results. Informal observations are very subjective and open to observer bias or lack of appropriate observer training, leading to both false-positive and false-negative misidentifications of gifted children. Observations also are costly in time and staff needs, if not in material costs.

Parent Nominations

Parents' observations offer one of the richest sources of information about children's abilities and behaviors. Other relatives should also be considered as data sources. Often grandparents, aunts and uncles, and siblings can provide detailed and additional information beyond the parents' knowledge that can be used as a confirmation of a child's interests and abilities.

Parents tend to underestimate their children's abilities. Careful questioning can elicit appropriate information to be used as the basis of an informed judgment by trained professionals. Interviews and nomination forms must be prepared in such a way as to elicit spontaneous responses, unprompted by the interviewer or nomination format. The goal should be objective reporting of the child's behaviors and abilities, not responses prompted by or intended to please the interviewer. As with other identification methods, parent nominations can provide one source of information in a broader assessment plan but should not be used as a single identification criterion.

Peer Nominations

Peer nominations are perhaps the least useful and reliable of the suggested methods for early identification. Young children's judgments are often subject to a variety of irrelevant factors such as clothing or attractiveness. Often they reflect their teachers' attitudes in school settings. When children have been together as a group for a period of time, their nominations can be a significant indication of an individual child's abilities in specific domains such as leadership, movement, or art.

Professional Judgments

Professional judgments would include those from teachers and other school personnel, health care professionals, and any other individuals with whom the child has had extensive and frequent interactions. Professionals' judgments often are useful as supportive, confirmatory information after initial screening and more objective identifications have been made. These judgments can be used in later assessments for specific program placements. This information must be considered carefully, including the circumstances of the relationship and the context, to be alert to potential biases in either direction. For example, teachers have been shown to be relatively poor identifiers of gifted children, even with in-depth and appropriate training (Ehrlich, 1980). Teachers often seem to be subject to affective biases in their judgments and selections of gifted children. They mistakenly associate socially appropriate behavior as an indicator of giftedness (e.g., maturity) while discounting a variety of accurate indicators that frequently are viewed merely as disruptive and apparent challenges. Teacher judgments can be guided and might provide useful input, as can any professional judgment, but clearly this information cannot be used as a primary determinant in the assessment process.

Performance Tests and Behavior Samples

Performance abilities typically refer to talent in the visual and/or performing arts. Identification in these domains should be based on observation and behavior sampling. Few, if any, standardized instruments appear to be available for performance measurements of children's abilities below the age of 8 (Ehrlich, 1980).

The expression of unusual talent or ability will be evidenced by varying and different behaviors specific to the different talent areas. Talent in visual art will be manifested by a different type of behavior and product from talent in movement or athletics. These manifestations also might express creative ability, but talent in a specific performance or visual art should not be equated with creativity itself, especially in the very young. Many of children's behaviors can be expressive of creative abilities, but very specific types of behaviors, which can form sets relative to a particular talent, are what should be considered as appropriate talent indicators. Knowledgeable individuals or groups should be consulted as judges of behavior or work samples (i.e., people whose expertise in a given area can be relied upon as the criterion of evaluation).

In all situations, physical maturation probably will influence expressed behavior; this must be considered during any evaluation. Another point of concern relates to specific training: Trained behaviors should not be confused with talent because trained behaviors express prior knowledge and experiences as well as a possible talent.

Personal Interviews

Interviews are another unreliable technique for assessing a child's level and range of giftedness, especially when used by themselves. Many factors can influence the course and outcome of an interview, including the child's motivation level, language skills, shyness, difficulties in establishing an open, facilitating rapport between the child and interviewer, other situational factors (e.g., removal from preferred activities leading to a lack of responsiveness or hesitancy), health, and temporary dispositional affects, Interviews rarely have the objectivity and lack of bias needed for a valid assessment of ability.

Interviews can be useful as a vehicle for demonstrating a child's language ability and range of information. They can also serve as supplements to information gathered through other techniques and to probe issues or ideas suggested by testing or one of the other data sources. Information from interviews will best serve assessment needs if interviews follow some type of consistent framework or guidelines and reflect critical points of interest and particular program structures and goals.

ASSESSING CREATIVE GIFTEDNESS

Informal Assessment Techniques

Two types of informal assessment techniques are useful in assessing the creativity of preschool children: indications of precocity (performance of tasks well beyond age expectations), and behavioral indicators of specific creative strengths. Information concerning these informal indicators of creative talent can be reported by parents, teachers, or others who are in a position to observe children in action.

Indications of Precocity

Among the most widely used informal procedures are the Renzulli-Hartman scales. They are based on a survey of the research concerning characteristics of gifted children (Renzulli & Hartman, 1971). Their validity is supported by at least one experimental study with preschool children (Malone & Moonan, 1975). The following are examples that appear to be particularly well suited for assessing the creativity of preschool children:

1. *The child has unusually advanced vocabulary for age level.* Creatively gifted children are particularly characterized by their use of descriptive, feeling, and action words and the way they combine these creatively to express feelings, observations, and problem solutions.

2. *The child possesses a large storehouse of information about a variety of topics.* Intellectually gifted children also possess a large storehouse of information, but creatively gifted children possess a great deal of information learned incidentally, that is, information not deliberately taught to them by anyone.

3. *The child has rapid insight into cause-and-effect relationships.* It is unusual for preschool children to formulate cause-and-effect relationships. Thus, the ability to do so is itself an indicator of giftedness. Creatively gifted children also express alternative cause-and-effect relationships.

4. *The child is a keen and alert observer—usually "sees more" or "gets more" out of a story, picture, film, sightseeing trip, and so on.* A mark of creatively gifted children is the ability to imagine objects from different visual perspectives.

5. *The child becomes absorbed and truly involved in certain topics or problems.* A common sign of creativity is "falling in love" with something, persisting in trying to find out more about it, and solving new problems regarding it.

6. *The child strives toward perfection or excellence— is self-critical.* Most children are satisfied if they are just able to complete or perform tasks satisfactorily. This is not enough for creative children. They have an image of performance excellence and strive for such an attainment.

7. *The child is interested in many "adult" problems such as religion, politics, sex, race, and so on.* Ordinarily, preschool children cannot imagine themselves into the problems of others, especially adults.

8. *The child likes to organize and bring structure to things, people, and situations.* Intellectually gifted children tend to organize things sequentially, whereas gifted children are likely to organize them in such ways as to show new or unusual relationships between them.

9. *The child displays a great deal of curiosity about many things and an intense curiosity about something.* Creative children are interested in almost everything, but when attending to something of intense interest they might ignore other things and resist efforts made to interest them in something else.

10. *The child displays a keen sense of humor and sees humor in situations that might not appear to be humorous to others.* Creative children specialize in seeing and producing perceptual incongruities that at first might appear to be silly or nonsense to the adult.

Behavioral Indicators of Creative Strengths

Torrance (1977) suggested detailed checklists of behavioral indicators of creative strengths. Table 16.1 is an abbreviated list of the indicators that are at least fairly common among preschool children. Most of these behavioral indicators generally are regarded as being beyond the developmental level of preschool children. Thus, children not displaying these behaviors should not be regarded as normal or even as not gifted. However, if these behaviors are displayed with any degree of consistency, such behaviors are regarded as possible indicators of creative talent.

Formal Assessment Techniques

Although there is a variety of procedures for assessing creative thinking abilities, only a few such instruments are suitable for use with preschool children. Most tests call for oral, verbal, or drawing responses, and most preschool children are limited in expressing their creativity in these modalities because the requisite skills are not adequately developed.

Starkweather (1964, 1971) pioneered the development of creativity tests for preschool children. Her test tasks required neither verbal skills nor drawing ability, and were quite promising, but required considerable equipment for their administration and were never

TABLE 16.1   Checklist of Behavioral Indicators of Creative Strengths

Improvisation with commonplace materials
Makes toys from commonplace materials and junk
Makes games from common materials, natural settings, etc.
Uses common objects for unintended uses in the home, school, and on the playground
Makes "inventions" from common objects
Uses common objects to solve problems in creative dramatics, art, etc.

Role playing and storytelling
Becomes deeply involved in role playing, creative dramatics, or storytelling
Produces many fresh ideas in the process of role playing and storytelling
Makes up unusual, surprising solutions in stories and role playing
Produces solutions to collision conflicts for which there seem to be no logical solutions

Visual arts
Just loves to paint, draw, sculpt, etc.
Experiences deep absorption and great joy in drawing, painting, sculpting, etc.
Understands (comprehends) subject matter by "drawing it"
Communicates skillfully and powerfully through drawings, paintings, and other visual media

Creative movement and dance
Just loves creative movement and dance
Becomes intensely absorbed in creative movement and dance
Persists for long periods in creative movement and dance
Can interpret songs, poems, stories, etc. through creative movement and dance
Can elaborate ideas through creative movement and dance
Movement and dance facilitate learning and understanding of events, concepts, and reading/literary materials

Music and rhythm
Writes, draws, works, moves with rhythm
Interprets ideas, events, feelings, and subject matter through music and/or rhythm
Becomes deeply involved and works perserveringly through music and/or rhythm
Is exceptionally responsive to sound stimuli and uses music and rhythm to facilitate the learning of subject matter

Expressive speech
Speech is colorful and picturesque
Speech includes analogies and metaphors
Speech is vivid (i.e., lively, intense, exciting, etc.)
Invents words and combinations of words to express concepts and feelings for which vocabulary is inadequate
Tells stories and recounts happenings as though the thing is happening

Fluency and flexibility in nonverbal modes
Produces many ideas through drawings, manipulation, movement, etc.
Arranges blocks and other play materials in many combinations
Assembles and reassembles complex machines with ease
Produces images in response to music, sounds, movement
Is good at "making things go"

(continued)

TABLE 16.1   Continued

Group skills
Influences other children in projects he or she initiates
Organizes the group and group tasks with skill
Working in groups sparks imagination and facilitates problem solving
Becomes more alive in small groups
Is intensely aware of the feelings and skills of others in small groups
Supports other members of the group and helps just at the right time
Initiates activities in small groups

Responsiveness to the concrete
Produces a large flow of ideas and alternative solutions when concrete objects are involved
Conceptualizes problems in terms of concrete objects
Uses concrete objects to generate new ideas
Works intensely for long periods on concrete puzzles, mechanical problems, etc.

Responsiveness to the kinesthetic
Skillfully communicates ideas through movement
Skillfully interprets the movements of others
Movement is effective as warm-up for creative activities
Displays skillful manipulative movement
Makes quick, decisive movements in mime, creative dramatics
Shows movement in drawings and other visual products
Displays total bodily involvement in interpreting a story, song, etc.

Humor
(Whenever production of humor occurs among preschool children, it should be regarded as a possible indicator of creative giftedness)
Makes people laugh a lot in games
Makes up humorous jokes and stories
Describes personal experiences with humor

Persistence and problem-centeredness
Does not give up easily in solving a problem
Persists in asking questions about a problem or event
Is stimulated by challenging problems
Is hard to distract when absorbed in a problem
Returns to a problem or unfinished task time after time

Source: From Checklist of behavioral indicators of creative strengths by E. P. Torrance, *Discovery and nurturance of giftedness in the culturally different,* 1977, 29–54. Copyright © 1977 by The Council for Exceptional Children. Reprinted with permission.

widely used. Her untimely death apparently halted further development of these instruments. However, they have been described carefully in the literature and provide possible clues for others wishing to extend the development of assessment procedures in this area.

At present, the most widely used formal procedures for assessing creative thinking abilities are those developed by Torrance (1974, 1981a, 1981b, 1985).

The long-range predictive validity of these tests taken during the elementary and high school years has been reported (Torrance, 1972a, 1972b, 1974, 1975, 1981 b), but thus far there has been no study reporting a relationship between the test performances of preschool children and creative achievements in adulthood. The major instruments for use with young children are described next.

Torrance Tests of Creative Thinking

The Torrance Tests of Creative Thinking (Torrance, 1974) consist of alternate forms of two batteries: Thinking Creatively with Words (Verbal Forms A and B) and Thinking Creatively with Pictures (Figural Forms A and B). The figural forms can be administered from 5 years old upward in groups and require 30 minutes of testing time. Standard scoring provides measures of fluency, flexibility, originality, and elaboration. A new alternative scoring system provides norm-referenced measures of fluency, originality, elaboration, resistance to premature closure, and abstract thinking and criterion-referenced measures or indicators of imagery, synthesis, humor, putting things in context, and other indicators of creative thinking in the visual modality.

The verbal forms can be administered to children from kindergarten through grade 3 as an individual test and require 45 minutes for administration. They provide scores for fluency, flexibility, and originality. Some of the verbal tasks are difficult for most preschool children but can identify highly gifted children in the verbal creative modality.

This test was originally developed in 1958 and has been used in over 2,000 published research studies. Scores on these tests show little racial or socioeconomic bias when used with preschool children. The figural tests have been used quite successfully with deaf children, and the verbal tests have proved quite successful with both vision-impaired and hearing-impaired children.

Thinking Creatively in Action and Movement

Thinking Creatively in Action and Movement (Torrance, 1981 a) permits children to respond in movement, in words, or in a combination of both. It is designed to be used with 3- to 8-year-old children. The tasks or activities that comprise this instrument are designed to sample some of the more important kinds of thinking abilities of preschool children. The test can be administered within a reasonable length of time and with equipment readily available in most schools, day care centers, nurseries, kindergartens, and other child care facilities. The test was under development for 6 years and has been used in a number of investigations.

Most tests that have been developed for young children have low test-retest reliability, require elaborate equipment, require verbal or drawing responses, and have low continuity with tests of creative thinking with older children. Thinking Creatively in Action and Movement does not require verbal responses, although verbal responses are accepted. The author believes that this is an advantage because children at these ages (especially 3- and 4-year-olds) have only marginal skills for expressing their ideas in words and drawings. Preschool children express thought through the kinesthetic modality more than the other modalities. The only equipment the test requires is paper cups and a wastebasket.

The responses called for are of the type that have been practiced by American children prior to age 3, regardless of culture, race, or socioeconomic status. However, the content and mode of responding will be influenced by such factors as the child's physical status, special disabilities (deafness, blindness, etc.), exposure to other children, economic status, and parental dominance or restriction. However, these factors themselves do not influence scores significantly. For example, although affluent children produce more verbal responses than poor children, poor children produce more movement and action responses than affluent children. Their mean scores, however, do not differ (Haley, 1978). Similarly, children in isolated rural areas perform as well as city children (Smith & Downey, 1975).

RATIONALE

Because children can behave creatively in an almost infinite number of ways, it is difficult to sample their creative thinking abilities. To solve this problem, four activities that sample some of the most important ways that young children use their creative thinking abilities were selected: How Many Ways?, Can You Move Like?, What Other Ways?, and What Might It Be? Let us examine the rationale for each of the four sets of exercises.

Activity 1 (How Many Ways?)

Almost from birth, children find ways of getting from one place to another. Some children move only in ways in which they are encouraged or taught and do not invent other original ways to travel. Other children entertain themselves or solve ongoing problems in their daily lives by inventing many ingenious ways to get from one place to another. Some even persist in using forbidden ways of movement and then are punished. With some children, it seems that the more that certain ways of moving are discouraged, the more ingenious they become in inventing new ways of moving.

The first activity in Thinking Creatively in Action and Movement is designed primarily to sample children's ability to produce alternate ways of moving. Both verbal and action responses, and combinations of both verbal and action responses, are accepted.

Activity 2 (Can You Move Like?)

The second activity (Can You Move Like?) is designed to sample the child's ability to imagine, empathize, fantasize, and assume unaccustomed roles. Children begin early to imitate the movements of animals and people. In this is the slow beginning of empathy. This activity provides six situations, four of them asking the child to pretend that he or she is an animal or object (tree, rabbit, fish, and snake), and the other two casting the child in roles related to other objects (driving a car and pushing an elephant off a desired object).

Activity 3 (What Other Ways?)

Creative persons must be able to return to the same old tasks or objects repeatedly and see them in new ways. In a task such as putting a paper juice cup in a wastebasket, children try different ways to accomplish this task. Creative children invent many unusual ways of doing a simple task such as this, perhaps largely as an escape from boredom or in search of novelty. It also permits them to test their abilities and the limits of a situation. Less creative children will perform the task only in the ways they are "supposed to" or are taught. Thus, it is reasoned, the ability to produce a large number of alternative or unusual ways to put a paper cup in a wastebasket will be a good indicator of a child's creative thinking potential.

Activity 4 (What Might It Be?)

It is natural for children to improvise with common objects in their environment and use them for other than their intended purposes. Some children can imagine a commonplace object as almost anything they need to support their play, work, and problem solving—at least until they learn too well that they should use objects for "what they are supposed to be for." We teach children that a chair is to sit on rather than to ride on; a table is to eat from instead of a launching pad or a stage; and a cup is to drink from and not to throw like a ball or spin like a top.

Paper juice cups are familiar to almost all children in day care centers, nurseries, kindergartens, and church schools. Although unusual uses of cups are usually discouraged, except of course in an art class, the irrepressible nature of childhood frequently prevails and the young inventor goes on. Children can find a legitimate outlet for this creativity through this test. It is quite similar to the Unusual Uses test used in many tests of creativity for older children and adults and is one of the most predictive test tasks in such batteries.

RELIABILITY AND VALIDITY

Reliability

As with the Torrance Tests of Creative Thinking, interscorer reliability is easily maintained through careful use of the scoring guide at a level in excess of 0.90 (Torrance, 1974). Bolen, using a sample of 30 second graders, obtained a reliability coefficient of 0.96 and no significant differences in means (Bolen, 1976). Against the scoring of one user, the author's research assistant rescored 18 records and obtained reliability coefficients of 0.99 for fluency. With a sample of 50 records, the author and a research assistant obtained reliability coefficients of 0.99 for fluency and 0.98 for originality, and no significant differences in means.

Test-Retest Reliability

A preliminary study of the test-retest reliability yielded satisfactory results. With a sample of 20 children ranging in age from 3 to 5 years who were tested two weeks apart, an overall test-retest reliability coefficient of 0.84 was obtained by two graduate assistants. Reliability coefficients for the separate activities were as follows: Activity 1 = 0.71; Activity 2 = 0.70; Activity 3 = 0.67; and Activity 4 = 0.58. With a test of this type, the overall reliability seems to be the important value because children on different occasions distribute their creative energies differently. For example, a child on a first testing may give few responses on Activity 1 but then warms up and becomes quite productive on Activities 3 and 4. On the second testing, this same child may be highly motivated, give an extraordinarily large number of responses in Activity 1, and expend much energy in Activity 2. This child may then be fatigued and give few responses in Activities 3 and 4. Such a performance would contribute to low test-retest reliability on specific activities in the battery but would not affect overall reliability. For this and other reasons, the use of single activities to obtain a measure of creative potential is strongly discouraged.

Validity Studies

The 1992 *Cumulative Bibliography of Thinking Creatively in Action and Movement* (Torrance & Rose, 1992) lists 53 studies using this test, most of which deal with some aspect of validity. There have thus far been no studies of longitudinal validity because it is extremely difficult to do such studies. Most of the studies of validity have been described in the technical-norms manual (Torrance, 1981a). Studies that have been published since the manual was published have been equally favorable.

This test was favorably reviewed in *The Ninth Mental Measurements Yearbook* by Renzulli (1985) and by Rust (1985). Although this test taps primarily the kinesthetic type of creativity, other types of creativity are even more limited for the reasons already described in this chapter.

IMPLICATIONS FOR THE ASSESSMENT OF PRESCHOOL CHILDREN

The results of both the informal and formal assessment procedures described in this chapter primarily should be used to make parents, teachers, school psychologists, and others aware of the creative strengths of preschool children. However, caution must be used in prediction at the preschool level; many societal conditions influence creative development and opportunities for creative expression and achievement.

It is important that parents, teachers, and school psychologists recognize that creative thinking is a skill that has to be developed by direct attention. This practice must take place in the right environment and with the right tools. Some people believe that creative thinking is so natural a skill that there is no need to make any deliberate effort to develop it; however, without deliberate effort the degree of skill developed is likely to fall far below the child's potential.

REFERENCES

Abramson, I. (1927). Essai d'ètalonnage de deux tests d'imagination et d'observation. *Journal de Psychologie,* 370–379.

Amabile, T. M. (1987). The motivation to be creative. In S. G. Isaksen (Ed.), *Frontiers of Creativity Research,* 223–254.

Andrews, E. G. (1930). The development of imagination in the preschool child. *University of Iowa Studies in Character, 3*(4).

Binet, A. (1909). *Les idees modernes sur les enfants.* Paris: E. Flammarion.

Binet, A., & Simon, T. (1916). *The development of intelligence in children.* (E. S. Kite, Trans.) Baltimore: Williams & Wilkins.

Bolen, L. M. (1976). Effects of race, sex, and kindergarten attendance on the creative thinking of second graders. Unpublished paper. Greenville, NC: Eastern Carolina University.

Bracken, B. A. (1987). Limitations of preschool instruments and standards for minimal levels of technical adequacy. *Journal of Psychoeducational Assessment, 5,* 313–326.

Ehrlich, V. Z. (1980). Identifying giftedness in the early years: From 3 through 7. In Ventura County Superintendent of Schools (Ed.), *Educating the preschool/primary gifted and talented,* 3–22. Los Angeles, CA: N/S LTI on the Gifted and Talented.

Guilford, J. P. (1956). The structure of intellect. *Psychological Bulletin, 53,* 267–293.

Guilford, J. P. (1968). *Intelligence, creativity and their educational implications.* San Diego, CA: Robert A. Knapp.

Guilford, J. P. (1986). *Creative talents: Their nature, use and development.* Buffalo, NY: Bearly Limited.

Haley, G. A. (1978). Training advantaged and disadvantaged black kindergartners in sociodrama: Effects on creativity and free-recall variables of oral language. Doctoral dissertation, University of Georgia. *Dissertation Abstracts International,* 1979, *39A,* 4129. (University Microfilms Order No. 79-01642)

Ibuka, M. (1985). *Kindergarten may be too late!* New York: Simon & Schuster.

Malone, C., & Moonan, W. J. (1975). Behavioral identification of gifted children. *Gifted Child Quarterly, 19,* 301–306.

McCarty, S. A. (1924). *Children's drawings: A study of interest and abilities.* Baltimore: Williams & Wilkins.

Parnes, S. J. (1981). *The magic of your mind.* Buffalo, NY: Bearly Limited.

Parnes, S. J. (1987). The creative studies project. In S. G. Isaksen (Ed.), *Frontiers of creativity research,* 156–188.

Parnes, S. J., & Meadow, A. (1960). Evaluation of persistence of effects produced by a creative problem-solving course. *Psychological Reports, 7,* 357–361.

Pezullo, T. R., Thorsen, E. E., & Madaus, G. F. (1972). The heritability of Jensen's Level I and II and divergent thinking. *American Educational Research Journal, 9,* 539–546.

Renzulli, J. S. (1985). Review of Thinking Creatively in Action and Movement. In J. V. Mitchell, Jr. (Ed.), *The ninth mental measurements yearbook,* Vol. II. Lincoln: University of Nebraska Press, 1619–1621.

Renzulli, J. S., & Hartman, R. K. (1971). Scale for rating behavioral characteristics of superior students. *Exceptional Children, 38,* 243–248.

Renzulli, J. S., & Smith, L. H. (1977). Two approaches to identification of gifted students. *Exceptional Children, 43,* 512–518.

Rust, J. O. (1985). Review of Thinking Creatively in Action and Movement. In J. V. Mitchell, Jr. (Ed.), *The ninth mental measurements yearbook,* Vol. II. Lincoln: University of Nebraska Press, 1621.

Smith, J., & Downey, C. (1975). Competency on comparison of creativity skills of different groups of disadvantaged children. Unpublished paper, Department of Educational Psychology, University of Georgia.

Starkweather, E. K. (1964). Problems in the measurement of creativity in preschool children. *Journal of Educational Measurement, 1,* 109–114.

Starkweather, E. K. (1968). Studies of the creative potential of young children. In F. E. Williams, (Ed.), *Creativity at home and in school.* St. Paul, MN: Macalester Creativity Project, Macalester College.

Starkweather, E. K. (1971). Creativity research instrument designed for use with preschool children. *Journal of Creative Behavior, 5,* 245–255.

Starkweather, E. K. (1976). Creativity research instruments designed for use with preschool children. In A. M. Biondi, & S. J. Parnes, (Eds.), *Assessing creative growth: The tests—Book one.* Buffalo, NY: Creative Education Foundation.

Taylor, C. W. (Ed.) (1964). *Widening horizons in creativity.* New York: John Wiley.

Terman, L. M. (1925). *Genetic studies of genius: Vol. 1—Mental and physical traits of a thousand gifted children.* Stanford, CA: Stanford University Press.

Terman, L. M., & Oden, M. H. (1947). *Genetic studies of genius: Vol. IV—The gifted child grows up: Twenty-five years' follow-up of a superior group.* Stanford, CA: Stanford University Press.

Torrance, E. P. (1962). *Guiding creative talent.* Englewood Cliffs, NJ: Prentice-Hall.

Torrance, E. P. (1963). *Education and the creative potential.* Minneapolis, MN: University of Minnesota Press.

Torrance, E. P. (1965). *Rewarding creative behavior.* Englewood Cliffs, NJ: Prentice-Hall.

Torrance, E. P. (1968). Must pre-primary educational stimulation be incompatible with creative development? In F. E. Williams, (Ed.), *Creativity at home and in school.* St. Paul, MN: Macalester Creativity Project, Macalester College.

Torrance, E. P. (1969). *Dimensions of early learning series: Creativity.* Sioux Falls, SD: Adapt Press.

Torrance, E. P. (1970). *Encouraging creativity in the classroom.* Dubuque, IA: William Brown.

Torrance, E. P. (1972a). Career patterns and peak creative achievements of creative high school students twelve years later. *Gifted Child Quarterly, 16,* 75–88.

Torrance, E. P. (1972b). The predictive validity of the Torrance Tests of Creative Thinking. *Journal of Creative Behavior, 6,* 236–252.

Torrance, E. P. (1974). *Norms-Technical manual: The Torrance Tests of Creative Thinking.* Bensenville, IL: Scholastic Testing Service. (Original research edition published in 1966 by Personnel Press, Princeton, NJ.)

Torrance, E. P. (1977). *Discovery and nurturance of giftedness in the culturally different.* Reston, VA: Council on Exceptional Children.

Torrance, E. P. (1979). Unique needs of the creative child and adult. In A. H. Passow, (Ed.), *The gifted and the talented: Their education and development.* Chicago: National Society for the Study of Education.

Torrance, E. P. (1981a). *Thinking Creatively in Action and Movement.* Bensenville, IL: Scholastic Testing Service.

Torrance, E. P. (1981b). Predicting the creativity of elementary school children (1958–80)—and the teachers who made a difference. *Gifted Child Quarterly, 25,* 55–62.

Torrance, E. P. (1985). A change in concept of intelligence. *Human Intelligence International Newsletter, 6* (23), 9.

Torrance, E. P., & Rose, L. H. (1992). *Cumulative bibliography of Thinking Creatively in Action and Movement.* Athens, GA: Georgia Studies of Creative Behavior.

Torrance, E. P., & Wu, T. H. (1981). A comparative longitudinal of the adult creative achievements of elementary school children identified as highly intelligent and highly creative. *Creative Child and Adult Quarterly, 6,* 71–76.

CHAPTER 17

ASSESSMENT OF SOCIAL AND EMOTIONAL DEVELOPMENT IN PRESCHOOL CHILDREN

LORI K. KEITH
JONATHAN M. CAMPBELL

Increasingly, professionals are called upon to evaluate very young children's cognitive, language, and social-emotional functioning. The focus of this chapter is on the latter area of functioning. The impetus for the increased frequency of early childhood evaluations is the result of several factors. First, entrance into child care programs provides an earlier opportunity to compare a child with peers who serve as a normative group with regard to social development (Martin, 1991). Parents also possess an increasing knowledge of the normal developmental course for children and are more frequently concerned about aspects of their child's progress at younger ages (Martin, 1991). Third, documentation of special needs is often required prior to the provision of early intervention. Furthermore, federal mandates to serve children with special needs beginning at birth generally require such documentation as an indication of eligibility (U.S. Department of Education, 1997). Finally, increasing research into social and emotional development and functioning among preschool children has focused attention on the need for sound assessment procedures and instrumentation in this area. Empirical evidence has highlighted the benefits and efficacy of early intervention, which has led to the need for earlier assessment and diagnosis (Bradley, Whiteside, Mundfrom, Casey, Kelleher, & Pope, 1994; White, 1986).

This chapter will focus on specific purposes and major influences on social-emotional development that are foundational to conducting assessments. A brief overview of several disorders of social and emotional development often diagnosed in young children will also be presented. Finally, limitations associated with evaluating social and emotional development in preschool children and the primary assessment techniques currently in use will be reviewed.

PRIMARY PURPOSES OF ASSESSMENT

Because assessment can take many forms, the scope of the evaluation will be determined by its purpose. One such purpose is screening, in which a large number of children are briefly evaluated to rule out the need for more extensive assessment procedures. Many preschools, including Headstart centers, conduct annual screenings that target all aspects of development in order to identify and intervene early with children with special needs. The purpose of screening is generally to reverse, ameliorate, or lessen the impact of a predicted negative outcome through early treatment. One vivid example is the widely implemented medical screening for Phenylketonuria (PKU), which, if left untreated in early infancy, often results in severe to profound mental retardation. With dietetic intervention in the first days and years of life, however, mental retardation can be avoided. Because basic social and emotional skills are either not developed or measurable at such early ages, social and emotional developmental screening is not always possible or helpful during infancy (Frankenburg, 1985). One early option during the toddler years is preschool classroom observation. Children who lack age-appropriate social skills that might be remediated and thereby prevent a cycle of peer rejection and its detrimental correlates can be identified through classroom observation (Parker & Asher, 1987; Rubin, Hymel, & Mills, 1989).

A second purpose for assessments is to gather data for the description or diagnosis of specific conditions. A third purpose for assessment follows the second purpose, which is to recommend interventions to ameliorate or minimize the diagnosed condition. Intervention may take place at many levels and may include environmental, medical, parental, or child-focused strategies. For example, a young child diagnosed with Pervasive Developmental Delay may require medication, a child-focused behavior modification plan, a special class placement, and/or parental education and support. A comprehensive evaluation of this child's social and emotional strengths and weaknesses is invaluable in understanding which areas to target for intervention.

Finally, assessment is an important component of research into early childhood social and emotional development, and the prevention and treatment of disorders diagnosed in young children. Appropriate identification is necessary to understand the course of disorders and treatment outcomes. Additionally, a good understanding of early childhood social and emotional development often requires accurate assessment of current levels of functioning.

MAJOR INFLUENCES ON SOCIAL AND EMOTIONAL DEVELOPMENT

Professionals who assess social and emotional functioning in young children must have a fundamental understanding of child development, as well as the influences that bear on social and emotional development. Developmental influences are far-reaching and must be considered as part of any comprehensive assessment of social and emotional functioning. Major influences include characteristics of the child (Garmezy, Masten, & Tellegen, 1984; Umansky, 1983), parental style and parental characteristics (Emde & Easterbrooks, 1985; Umansky, 1983; Werner, 1984), family characteristics (Bowlby, 1988; Umansky, 1983), environmental influences (Bronfenbrenner, 1977; Garmezy, Masten, & Tellegen 1984; Sameroff, 1986), and the various interactions of these factors (Bowlby, 1988; Bronfenbrenner, 1977; Garmezy, Masten, & Tellegen, 1984). Because the development of social and emotional functioning is complex, attention paid to any one influencing factor is somewhat limiting. To fully understand early childhood psychosocial development, it is necessary to appreciate the interaction of all components.

Child Characteristics

That particular influences would play a significant role in child development seems obvious; however, childhood characteristics and their individual influences have long been accepted overwhelmingly as unidirectional (Grusec & Lytton; 1988; Umansky, 1983). Currently, the recipricol role of child characteristics in shaping the envir-

onment and, consequently, in shaping the child's development through environmental response to the child, is well documented (Bell, 1968; Brooks-Gunn, 1985; Cohen & Beckwith, 1979; Lewis & Rosenblum, 1974). Investigations into the relationship between infant behavior and its effects on caregivers and later peer relationships and adjustment are particularly compelling when describing the influence of characteristics of the child on social and emotional development (Easterbrooks & Lamb, 1979; Petit, Dodge, & Brown, 1988; Werner, 1984).

Several characteristics indigenous to the child have been collectively researched and described as temperament. Although many definitions of exist, temperament may be specifically defined as "individual differences in the strength, timing, and regularity of arousal and emotions" (Grusec & Lytton, 1988, p. 120), or the *how* of behavior, rather than the *what* or *why* (Thomas & Chess, 1977, p. 4). Additionally, researchers have operationalized temperament as specific, observable behaviors beginning with the New York Longitudinal Study in which Thomas, Birch, Chess, Hertzig, and Korn (1963) described nine dimensions including *activity level, rhythmicity, approach-withdrawal, adaptability to change, threshold of responsiveness, intensity of reaction, mood, distractibility,* and *attention span.* Though temperament is believed to be moderately stable in general, the dimensions of activity level, distractibility, and fearfulness have been most predictive of later behavior (Martin, Drew, & Gaddis, 1988). Furthermore, Thomas and Chess (1977) grouped the nine descriptions of temperament into three general prototypes. The *easy child* is characterized by positive responsiveness to caregivers, adaptability, and playfulness. In turn, this child will be most likely to receive positive attention from caregivers. The *difficult child* is the recipient of less supportive caregiving based on his or her low degree of responsiveness. For instance, the difficult child is often fussy, cries more than other infants, and is difficult to comfort. The third prototype is that of the *slow-to-warm child* who is described as adapting to change slowly. Such a child elicits varying degrees of attention and support from caregivers, which results in inconsistent opportunities for positive interaction. The likelihood of a tenuous caregiver–child relationship as a result is increased.

Difficult temperament is the most frequently studied behavioral constellation. As defined by Thomas and Chess (1977), difficult temperament refers to "irregularity in biological functions, negative withdrawal responses to new stimuli,... slow adaptability to change, and intense mood expressions which are frequently negative" (p. 23). Subsequent investigations have shown evidence for a link between early difficult temperament and later behavior disorders (Bates, Maslin, & Frankel, 1985; Graham, Rutter, & George, 1973) and difficult temperament and increased risk for child abuse (Gill, 1970). The preponderance of evidence also indicates that attributions of causality are likely from the direction of the child rather than the caregiver where "difficultness" is concerned (Grusec & Lytton, 1988).

Similarly, Hermanns, Cats, and den Ouden (1985) followed very low-birth-weight children (<1,500 grams) without physical complications for two to four years. They hypothesized that characteristics associated with preterm infants would independently influence mother–child interactions. Findings included a separate temperamental profile for very low-birth-weight children from infants described as "difficult." Very low-birth-weight children were found to be extremely physically active, very distractible, and irritable. These children are described as having a "fatiguing" temperament that requires considerable emotional and physical energy from parents to maintain acceptable interactions.

Recent research in the area of developmental psychopathology indicates that certain child characteristics serve as protective factors against stressors. Similar to the results of investigations of temperament, Garmezy (1985) has identified "dispositional" attributes as protective mechanisms. Children who exhibit these characteristics demonstrate higher levels of social and emotional adjustment than children who experience similar stressors and do not possess the identified attributes. Specifically, infants who tolerate environmental change, are easily comforted, and are physiologically regulated are likely to be more resilient than "difficult" children (Block & Block, 1980). Others have described resilient children as those with temperamental attributes that elicit positive responses from others (Rutter, 1978).

In addition to temperament, a child's physical appearance has been shown to contribute to attributions made by caregivers, teachers, and peers. Specifically, Langlois, Ritter, Casey, and Sawin (1995) found that infants' physical attractiveness related to maternal behaviors and attitudes, with more attractive children receiving more affectionate attention. According to Langlois and Downs (1979), the behaviors of physically less attractive preschool children were comparable to more attractive children at age 3. At age 5, however, children rated as unattractive were more aggressive toward peers and more active in general. Finally, a strong positive relationship exists between teacher ratings of social competence and the physical attractiveness of preschool and elementary children (Eagly, Ashmore, Makhijani, & Longo, 1991; Ritts, Patterson, & Tubbs, 1992).

A child's gender is also associated with a differential response from the environment that influences social and emotional development. For proponents of a biological perspective, differences in social behavior of males and females may be explained by physiological differences (Maccoby & Jacklin, 1979; Tieger, 1980). Regardless of etiological issues, however, empirical evidence consistently supports higher levels of aggression and less effective interpersonal skills for boys compared to girls, particularly at younger ages (Berk, 1997; Maccoby, 1990).

Parental Characteristics

In addition to child characteristics, traits of the parents and their approach in relating to their children are major influences on the children's social and emotional development. Factors influencing parental style predate the child's birth. Social learning theory points to the major role of the parents' own childhood experiences in the development of their later parenting practices. Additionally, personal characteristics, norms of society, and religious beliefs all influence parents' child-rearing practices and styles (Grusec & Lytton, 1988).

Parental style has been categorized by Baumrind (1973) as fitting one of three styles: the *authoritarian parent* who emphasizes firm limits and discourages independence, the *authoritative parent* who also firmly enforces rules but encourages independence, and the *permissive parent* who is generally passive and sets few limits. Comparison of preschool children from all three types of families indicated that children from authoritative homes demonstrated higher levels of social responsibility in the form of positive peer interactions, a higher achievement orientation, cooperativeness with adults, and independence in terms of nonconformity and purposefulness (Baumrind, 1973). More recently, Roopnarine (1987) found that children reared by authoritative parents engaged in fewer negative parenting behaviors than those reared with other parenting styles.

The past three decades of research in the area of resilient children who, despite poverty, parental mental illness, and/or family discord, manage to cope successfully with chronic stressors indicate that one close bond with a caregiver during the first years of life is a crucial factor in achieving resilience, as well as a basic sense of trust

(Werner, 1984). Similarly, the positive results of secure early attachment versus the dire consequences of insecure attachment to a primary caregiver have been the subject of much theory and investigation (Bowlby, 1988). Consistent with Baumrind's work, investigators also point to family cohesion and warmth (Luthar & Zigler, 1991), along with reasonable structure and clear rules (Rutter, 1985), as having a positive relationship with children's ability to cope with stressors including poverty, discrimination, and lengthy childhood hospitalizations. Finally, children who are emotionally well adjusted and socially competent despite chronic stressors frequently are provided a sense of meaning, purpose, and opportunity by their families (Antonovsky, 1979).

Environmental Influences

Because families do not exist in isolation, societal influences play a significant role in the social and emotional development of young children. Bronfenbrenner (1986) points to the impingement of external systems on the family and the development of the child. In particular, parental employment systems and social networks, educational systems, judicial systems, and public policy are all factors that affect the child's development, directly or indirectly. In the childhood resilience literature, the availability of external support systems is cited as a protective mechanism against chronic stress (Luthar & Zigler, 1991). For example, Segal (1988) partially accounts for children's resilience as follows: "One factor turns out to be the presence in their lives of a charismatic adult—a person with whom they identify and from whom they gather strength. And in a surprising number of cases, that person turns out to be a teacher" (p. 2). Other supportive relationships in society might be found through extended family, peers, and religious affiliations.

Interaction of Influences

Now that several influences on social and emotional development have been considered independently, the interaction of these factors will be addressed. Clearly, human development is complex and dynamic and occurs under the influence of many factors at various levels at any given point in time. Indeed, bidirectionality and interaction are major themes in developmental theories, indicating that no single influence is alone responsible for outcomes. Bronfenbrenner (1977) outlined one of the most wide-ranging theories of the interaction of factors. He described the *microsystem* as the interaction between the child and direct influences including parents and peers. The *mesosystem* represents the interaction between the microsystem and the *ectosystem,* which includes peripheral influences such as parental social networks. Finally, the *exosystem* is representative of institutions external to the family including governmental entities and policies.

Empirical evidence for the interactional nature of the developmental process is abundant. For example, when measured by parent report, some investigators purport that temperament may be better understood as parental perception rather than as a trait wholly residing in the child (Bates, 1980). This illustrates the bidirectional nature of influences on social and emotional development because it is implied that an infant's behavior is interpreted by the parent as belonging to the child. It is the sum of influential factors and their interaction that produce the end result. Researchers have also focused on the notion of emotional availability, a construct that is congruent with the notion of the interaction of influences on development. Emde and Easterbrooks (1985) define emotional availability as "the degree to which each partner expresses emotions and is responsive to the emotions of the other" (p. 80). As measured through observation of dyadic interaction, the degree of emotional availability between primary caregivers and young children is a salient predictor of later emotional adjustment (Emde & Easterbrooks, 1985). The authors advocate the use of such observation, both formally and informally, as a screening device. Similarly, Sameroff (1975) referred to the transactional view of development, which purports that psychological development is the result of "continual and progressive interplay between the organism and its environment" (p. 281). Most recently, in her introduction to the American Psychologist Special Issue on developmental science, Hetherington (1998) summarized the current state of empirical efforts by stating, "the importance of understanding development by examining interactions and relationships within and among social contexts in families, peer groups, schools, neighborhoods, and workplaces are pervasive themes…" (pp. 93–94).

FREQUENTLY DIAGNOSED DISORDERS IN EARLY CHILDHOOD

One aspect of the framework for considering assessment of social and emotional development is the type of pathology that will no doubt be the focus of some evaluations with young children. A brief overview of frequently diagnosed conditions will hopefully serve as an impetus for further exploration into the broad literature available on each disorder. Until very recently, much more attention was given to the study of psychopathology in adults than in children. The swiftly growing corpus of child psychopathology literature is founded on the understanding that (1) many childhood disorders have lifelong consequences for the child and society; (2) adult dysfunction often has some connection to early childhood; and (3) improved diagnostic systems, intervention programs, and prevention efforts are needed (Mash & Dozois, 1996). Furthermore, the growing understanding of childhood psychopathology has contributed to an increase in the assessment of social and emotional development.

Although several widely used classification systems exist, the *Diagnostic and Statistical Manual of Mental Disorders, Fourth Edition (DSM-IV)* (American Psychiatric Association, 1994) is generally accepted as the standard among psychologists and psychiatrists. The *DSM-IV* describes several developmental disorders as "usually first diagnosed in infancy, childhood, or adolescence." Most of the childhood conditions described in *DSM-IV* and "most problems identified in children are associated with their perception of reality, their interactions with adults, their interactions with other children, and the relationship between their behavior and learning" (Umansky, 1983, p. 427). Six of the most frequently diagnosed conditions in young children with wide-ranging effects on the course of social and emotional development will be reviewed.

Mental Retardation

Mental retardation is defined as "significantly subaverage general intellectual functioning that is accompanied by significant limitations in adaptive functioning..., and is manifested during the developmental period" (APA, 1994, p. 39). Clearly, the social and emotional development of children is not distinct from their cognitive development. Thus, assessment of children with mental retardation generally reveals concomitant deficits in social skills such as perspective-taking and language pragmatics, and disordered emotional development or psychopathology (Reiss, Levitan, & Szyszko, 1982). Additionally, researchers have noted a significantly higher number of infants with difficult temperaments among children with mental retardation (Bridges & Cicchetti, 1982). As with social and emotional development in children without mental retardation, the results of a longitudinal study by Brooks-Gunn and Lewis (1982)

point to the interactional influence of parent and child on decreased vocalization and social smiling in infants with Down syndrome. Specifically, the "infant's capacity in part determines maternal responsiveness to maternal expression. However, the mother's perception of capacity or rate of [the infant's] acquisition also influences her behavior" (p. 185).

Pervasive Developmental Disorders

According to *DSM-IV* (APA, 1994), "Pervasive Developmental Disorders are characterized by severe and pervasive impairment in several areas of development: reciprocal social interaction skills, communication skills, or the presence of stereotyped behavior, interests, and activities" (p. 65). Autism is the most widely recognized of the Pervasive Developmental Disorders, all of which have dysfunctional social interaction as a central and common feature. Specifically, infants and young children with Autistic Disorder appear to be specifically impaired in social abilities such as formation of attachment bonds, shared attention with another person, imitation of others, perspective-taking, and imaginative play (Klinger & Dawson, 1996).

Attention Deficit Disorders

The core feature of Attention Deficit Disorders is "a persistent pattern of inattention and/or hyperactivity—impulsivity that is more frequent and severe than is typically observed in individuals at a comparable level of development" (APA, 1994, p. 78). A child who exhibits such high levels of inattention, impulsivity, and hyperactivity is also at risk for problems with social, cognitive, and emotional adjustment. Furthermore, these children typically experience increasing difficulty compared to their peers in adapting to demands for self-regulation of behavior, affect, and organization of their environment (Barkley, 1996). Parental frustration and negative parent–child interactions may be the earliest indications of a child with an Attention Deficit Disorder.

Attachment Disorders

Attachment to others may be described along a continuum from secure to unattached; thus, it is not an all or nothing proposition. The attachment patterns of most children lie somewhere in the middle of the continuum. Children with Attachment Disorder, however, are found at the negative extreme and are generally considered to form poor attachments as the result of early trauma, particularly in the form of severe abuse or neglect (Magid & McKelvey, 1987). Attachment disorders indicate a central disruption in social and emotional development. Specifically, *DSM-IV* describes Reactive Attachment Disorder of Infancy or Early Childhood as evidenced by "markedly disturbed and developmentally inappropriate social relatedness in most contexts that begins before age five" (APA, 1994, p. 116). Although the underlying features remain constant, one of two clinical presentations is typically dominant. *DSM-IV* describes the *inhibited type* as a child who fails to initiate social interactions or to respond appropriately to overtures by others. Excessive inhibition, hypervigilance, resistance to comfort by caregivers, and an approach–avoidance interaction style are also frequently observed. The *disinhibited type,* on the other hand, is characterized by lack of selectivity in attachments and excessive familiarity with others (APA, 1994). Because some of the behavioral aspects of Attachment Disorders are similar to Attention Deficit Disorders, including impulsivity and poor peer relations, and because pathological care is often difficult or impossible to document, misdiagnosis is common. Treatment and research surrounding these two classes of disorders, however, are vastly different and necessitate close scrutiny in diagnosis (Keith, 1996).

Depressive Disorders

Within the past 20 years, recognition of the existence of depression in children has generated a wealth of theoretical and empirical efforts. As a result, myths such as the belief that childhood depression does not exist; is brief, reactive, and developmentally appropriate; or is expressed only through somatic complaints, school difficulties, or behavioral problems have been refuted (Hammen & Rudolph, 1996). Although separate diagnostic categories for children are not included in *DSM-IV,* special considerations for diagnosing children as opposed to adults are provided. For instance, a diagnosis of Dysthymic Disorder, a milder but more chronic form of depression, in adults requires the presence of symptoms for at least two years, whereas for children, the minimum duration is specified as one year (APA, 1994). With depressive disorders, disruption in development may occur across affective, social, cognitive, and physical domains. Specifically, children with depression frequently exhibit irritability, sadness, aggression, and behavioral problems. Additionally, disturbed appetite

and sleep patterns and deflated academic performance may occur with depression.

Behavior Disorders

Defined primarily by cultural norms, antisocial behavior is classified by *DSM-IV* into two primary categories of Conduct Disorder and Oppositional Defiant Disorder. Considered by some to be a milder developmental precursor of Conduct Disorder, Oppositional Defiant Disorder is more often diagnosed in childhood (Hinshaw & Anderson, 1996). According to *DSM-IV,* "a recurrent pattern of negativistic, defiant, disobedient, and hostile behavior toward authority figures" is the defining feature (p. 91). In contrast, Conduct Disorder is characterized by more serious destructive and aggressive behavior and is generally not diagnosed in the preschool years. Given that defiance is a developmental norm for preschoolers, careful consideration is required to determine the presence of problematic behavior beyond that typical for peers.

GENERAL LIMITATIONS IN ASSESSING PRESCHOOLERS

At this point, it is important to introduce three predominant problems faced when assessing the social-emotional functioning of preschool children. First, preschoolers are unique in that their cognitive and language abilities are restricted (Bierman & Schwartz, 1986). Second, it is more difficult to reliably describe social-emotional functioning compared to the majority of other characteristics of young children, such as perceptual-motor skills, cognitive functioning, and academic achievement (Martin, 1991). Third, the range of normal developmental variability is broader for preschoolers than older children or adolescents (Wheatcraft & Bracken, in press). The combination of these three general limitations creates special problems in the assessment of social and emotional functioning of preschool children.

Cognitive Limitations of the Preschool Child

Compared to older children and adolescents, preschool children are cognitively limited, thereby influencing assessment practices in a variety of ways. First, most preschoolers cannot read; therefore, a host of useful instruments that require this fundamental skill cannot be used to describe preschoolers' social-emotional functioning (e.g., Martin, 1991). For example, widely used self-report measures of personality or social functioning are eliminated from use with preschool children. Second, preschoolers lack the range of verbal expressivity seen in older children, adolescents, and adults; therefore, they have difficulty describing thoughts, feelings, or relationships with others. Also, preschoolers are usually able to provide only a general idea of what they think and feel through verbal means. Third, preschoolers are usually not aware of the purposes of assessment and often cannot adjust their behavior to meet the demands of the assessment situation, such as controlling behavior or concentrating for extended periods of time. Fourth, preschoolers are typically limited in their understanding of social-emotional concepts (Bierman, 1990), so inquiry about emotions or feelings is often misunderstood. Fifth, preschool children typically engage in rather rigid styles of thinking that are marked by egocentrism and the inability to make meaningful comparisons against others (Bierman, 1990; Martin, 1991). For example, preschoolers may identify themselves as the strongest, fastest, and smartest of their friends or simply may not be able to make such comparisons. In general, the foregoing cognitive limitations create problems for the professional asked to describe preschool children's social and emotional functioning.

Limitations Related to the Content Area

Coupled with preschool children's cognitive limitations is the problem of describing social and emotional characteristics per se. Characteristics outside of the realm of social and emotional functioning are typically described more reliably. For example, physical, cognitive, and academic characteristics are more stable than social and emotional traits (Martin, 1991). A primary reason that social and emotional characteristics are described less reliably is that social and emotional functioning varies across different contexts. For example, a child may demonstrate social anxiety only when meeting new adults and not new peers. Preschoolers, and other persons, typically do not behave as consistently over time on social and emotional dimensions as compared to other characteristics (Martin, 1991).

Increased Variability in Development

A final general limitation affecting the assessment of social-emotional functioning of preschoolers involves the large range of normal developmental progress in preschoolers (Wheatcraft & Bracken, in press). That is, the range of what is considered normal social and emotional development is broader for preschoolers than older children, adolescents, or adults. This creates special problems when attempting to discriminate between preschool children who demonstrate normal social-emotional functioning versus those whose functioning is deficient or disordered (Wheatcraft & Bracken, in press). As will be seen later, each limitation can create measurement problems when assessing social and emotional characteristics of preschool children, especially for traditional assessment procedures.

PRIMARY ASSESSMENT TECHNIQUES

Despite the aforementioned general limitations in the measurement of preschoolers' social-emotional functioning, sound assessment procedures exist. Methods for evaluating the social-emotional functioning of preschoolers include interviewing, direct observation, third-party ratings, projective techniques, and play-based assessment. The purpose of this section is to introduce a broad range of techniques available for assessing preschoolers' social-emotional development; therefore, breadth of coverage is emphasized over depth. The rationale and content of each broad assessment category are introduced briefly and a discussion of advantages and disadvantages associated with each assessment technique follows each introduction.

Interviewing

Interviewing Preschool Children.   Interviewing is a widely used technique to gather information regarding the preschool child's social and emotional functioning (Martin, 1986). As in the case of evaluating older children and adolescents, psychologists often interview both the child and at least one adult caregiver; however, interviewing preschoolers creates special problems associated with the general limitations identified earlier. First, cognitive restrictions produce limited understanding of social and emotional questions and unrealistic "all-or-none" categorizations of self and others (Bierman, 1990). For example, preschoolers typically define others as either good or bad without understanding that persons can exhibit both qualities. Second, formally interviewing children below the age of 6 has been discouraged due to unreliable information that young children typically provide (e.g., Martin, 1986). Third, preschool children are often shy and timid when meeting someone new; therefore, when interviewing a preschool child, traditional formal interviewing methods are often abandoned for alternative techniques, such as free-play sessions (Sattler, 1998).

Despite the limitations mentioned earlier, interviewing preschool children presents two distinct advantages. First, compared to adults, young children are not as self-conscious and often not as inhibited during an interview, which can yield valuable information about the child's perspective and concerns (Bierman & Schwartz, 1986; Martin, 1986). Furthermore, Sattler (1998) asserts that preschoolers often demonstrate the cognitive capacity to respond to *short* probing questions designed to clarify content. Second, the interview provides the means to establish rapport with the preschool child early in the evaluation of social and emotional functioning (Sattler, 1998). Based on the limitations mentioned earlier, Sattler (1992) offered useful suggestions concerning how to encourage preschoolers to talk about themselves. For example, interviewing might take place in a playroom equipped with a variety of creative materials, such as paper, crayons, clay, or paints. Initial interaction with the interviewer might take the form of a game, introducing a novel toy, or some other shared creative activity.

Interviewing Caregivers.   In addition to interviewing the child, preschool assessors typically interview the child's caregivers, such as parents, teachers, or day care workers, for additional information regarding social-emotional functioning. For adults, traditional formal interviews are quite useful. Interviews with significant caregivers constitute a crucially important part of any assessment procedure. Parents tend to be especially knowledgeable about their child's social-emotional functioning and are usually able to relay detailed information to the interviewer. Although parents and other caregivers often provide useful information about the child's social and emotional adjustment, a carefully conducted and thoughtful interview with parents or teachers accomplishes more than information gathering. Initial interviews constitute the first step in building rapport with family members, which will be useful in subsequent intervention efforts, if necessary. Rapport building can be accomplished if family members are actively engaged during the interview and treated as respected and valued members in the assessment process (Sattler, 1998). Sattler provides a host of useful guidelines to follow when interviewing caregivers.

Advantages of Interviewing Caregivers.   The interview holds specific advantages over other assessment

techniques. First, interviews allow for flexible assessment of social-emotional functioning. For example, the interviewer can clarify unclear responses through follow-up questioning, evaluate particular strengths and/or weaknesses in detail, and change the focus of the interview as necessary. Second, interviews allow the assessor to simultaneously evaluate the veracity of report by observing nonverbal cues, such as facial expression, change in tone of voice, or diverted eye contact (Sattler, 1992). For example, when verbal content of an answer and nonverbal cues do not match, this may suggest that the respondent is not answering questions truthfully, or that a truthful response is particularly troubling for the respondent.

Structured Diagnostic Interviews.   Four structured diagnostic interviews exist for use with older preschool children, ages 6 and up, and their parents: (a) the Child Assessment Schedule (CAS; Hodges, Kline, Stern, Cytryn, & McKnew, 1982), (b) the Diagnostic Interview for Children and Adolescents (DICA; Herjanic, Herjanic, Brown, & Wheatt, 1975), (c) the Diagnostic Interview Schedule for Children (DISC; Costello, Edelbrock, Dulcan, Kalas, & Klaric, 1984), and (d) the Schedule for Affective Disorders and Schizophrenia for School Aged Children (K-SADS; Puig-Antich & Chambers, 1978). The structured diagnostic interviews are administered typically by professionals, although the DICA and DISC were specifically designed to be used by lay interviewers. Each interview includes child and parent versions that sample specific diagnostic symptoms and yield common DSM diagnoses, including ADHD, Depression, Anxiety, Separation Anxiety, Phobias, and Obsessive-Compulsive Disorder. Reliability studies that have sampled children as young as age 6 have yielded kappa statistics that range from .21 to .83, with kappas equal to or below .40 considered poor agreement (Hodges, 1993). Test-retest and interrater correlations range from .38 to .89. In general, validity data on these scales are quite limited, especially when utilized with children as young as 6 years of age (Hodges, 1993). Studies examining mother–child concordance for the CAS with both psychiatric and non-referred children have found (a) moderate to low agreement for conduct/behavioral problems (range = .63 to .26), (b) moderate to nonsignificant agreement for affective symptoms (range = .46 to –.05), and, (c) low to nonsignificant agreement for symptoms of anxiety (range = .26 to .05) (Hodges, Gordon, & Lennon, 1990; Thompson, Merritt, Keith, Murphy, & Johndrow, 1993). The moderate to nonsignificant correlations point to the importance of using multiple respondents when assessing affective and behavioral problems, especially with younger children.

Limitations of Interviewing Caregivers.   As with any assessment method, interviews suffer from weaknesses. First, interviewees may respond inaccurately to interview questions. Inaccurate responding may result for a variety of reasons, such as intentional malingering, problems with remembering specific details about the child's past social and emotional functioning, or simply a parent's tendency to view his or her child in a positive manner. Second, estimates of reliability and validity of unstructured interviews are virtually impossible to establish (Sattler, 1992, 1998), and reliability and validity estimates for structured interviews can be quite low. Third, the interviewer can unwittingly facilitate inaccurate responding with use of subtle verbal and nonverbal cues, such as nodding in anticipation of a positive response to an interview question.

Observation Methods

A second major technique used in the assessment of the preschool child's social-emotional functioning involves the direct observation of the child. Direct observation of the preschool child can take place in varied contexts. Within naturalistic environments, the assessor can observe the child at home, school, or day care setting. The assessor may also observe the child in more structured conditions, such as a standardized intellectual assessment or free-play session in an office. The structure required in behavioral observation can vary as well. Formal observation methods may be quite structured, as in the case of interval sampling of behaviors in which one records the presence or absence of a particular behavior during a prespecified interval of time. Other formal observation methods may require less structure by only requiring the observer to create general impressions of the child or environment. For example, the Home Observation for Measurement of the Environment (HOME; Caldwell & Bradley, 1984) requires the observer to record the presence or absence of certain behaviors or environmental characteristics, such as the presence of books or play materials at home and affective aspects of the child–parent relationship. Informal observation methods are those that occur during other interactions with the child, such as behavior observed as the child separates from parents in a clinic waiting room or during a cognitive assessment. Each type of observation is important in the evaluation of preschool children's social-emotional functioning. It is most important to observe the child across different contexts and settings, as behavior observed in one setting may not generalize to other settings (e.g., Bracken, 1991; Martin, 1986). If behavioral observation is not possible outside the standardized assessment setting, the assessor should note that behavior observed in an office setting may not generalize well to other contexts (Bracken, 1991).

Advantages of Observing Preschool Children.   Generally, observations of preschool children enjoy improved reliability when contrasted with interviews, especially when standardized observation methods are used. For example, interobserver agreement for the HOME inventory averages approximately 90 percent (Bradley & Caldwell, 1988). In addition, observational methods of assessment do not require preschool children to describe their affective states or behavior because the examiner views these firsthand; therefore, observations tend to circumvent some of the cognitive and language limitations outlined earlier. Third, compared to older children, young children tend to act naturally while being observed, perhaps due to lower levels of self-consciousness than older children and adolescents (Martin, 1986). Finally, observations may take place simultaneously within the context of other assessment activities, such as during a cognitive test administration.

Limitations to Observing Preschool Children.   The overwhelming drawback to observation is the high cost in terms of time. As noted previously, contextual factors influence behavior, such as physical setting and persons present. Therefore, behavior observation should take place over varied contexts, which requires additional time. In addition to these factors, mastering coding systems can also be time-consuming (Martin, 1986). Similar to informal interview methods, the psychometric properties of informal observations are not known; therefore, reliability and validity estimates are unavailable for independent scrutiny. Furthermore, the presence of an observer can change the nature of the observation setting and introduce demand characteristics for parents, siblings, and others. This may distort observations in problematic ways. For example, family members may change behavior in response to the child due to a desire to be positively appraised. Finally, the observer may introduce his or her own biases into the observation process by systematically viewing the child in overly positive or negative ways.

Third-Party Rating Instruments

Third-party ratings are also commonly used for assessing social-emotional functioning of preschool children. Martin (1991) identified third-party rating scales as *the* primary assessment tools in evaluating social-emotional functioning of preschool children. Typically, respondents familiar with the preschool child, such as a parent, day care worker, or teacher, respond to a list of items that describes the child across a variety of domains. Items often sample content areas of specific and often problematic behaviors (e.g., "throws things at parents,"), interaction styles ("is shy around adults,"), or affective tendencies (e.g., "is irritable"). Respondents are asked to indicate the presence or absence of a behavior, such as with the Personality Inventory for Children (PIC; Wirt, Lachar, Klinedinst, & Seat, 1984) or frequency of behavior, such as with the Child Behavior Checklist (CBCL; Achenbach, 1991, 1992).

Rating scales vary according to breadth of coverage with some designed to yield a rather comprehensive profile of the preschool child's social-emotional functioning, such as the Behavior Assessment System for Children (BASC; Reynolds & Kamphaus, 1992), and others measuring fewer aspects of adjustment, such as the Attention Deficit Disorders Evaluation Scale (ADDES; McCarney, 1995). Several rating scales consist of "systems" of assessment by offering multiple rating checklists for multiple respondents that yield scores across similar clusters of behaviors that can be compared. For example, the Social Skills Rating System (SSRS; Gresham & Elliott, 1990) includes both parent and teacher rating forms that yield summary scores for similar behavioral clusters. Table 17.1 presents a representative but incomplete list of third-party rating instruments that are available for the assessment of social-emotional functioning in preschoolers.

Advantages of Third-Party Ratings. Third-party rating instruments offer two distinct advantages. Efficiency constitutes the first clear advantage. Ratings are typically completed by respondents in fewer than 20 minutes and yield a host of information about the social-emotional functioning of the preschool child. Additionally, rating forms are inexpensive, simple to administer and complete, and are usually easy to score. A second advantage of third-party ratings is that respondents are typically persons who have observed the child over long periods of time and constitute part of the child's natural environment. Also, parents and other caretakers of the preschool child are usually highly motivated to observe the child's behavior (Martin, Hooper, & Snow, 1986). The use of parents and teachers as respondents is particularly important because these persons often initiate referrals for children's mental health services (Achenbach, McConaughy, & Howell, 1987).

Limitations of Third-Party Rating Instruments. Third-party rating instruments suffer from two major disadvantages: (a) undesired variability in ratings, which is common to all third-party ratings instruments, and (b) questionable technical qualities, which can be unique to preschool versions of social-emotional rating instruments (e.g., Campbell, in press). Martin (1986, 1991) and colleagues (e.g., Martin et al., 1986) have identified four sources of "unwanted" variance produced by third-party rating instruments: rater variance, setting variance, temporal variance, and instrument variance. Rater variance is attributed to raters who view the preschool child in the same setting, such as a preschool classroom, but rate the child differently. Rater variance is common among systems of social-emotional ratings scales in which low to moderate interrater agreement exists between respondents (e.g., Achenbach et al., 1987; Walker & Bracken, 1996). Bracken, Keith, and Walker (1994) investigated the psychometric qualities of 13 preschool third-party measures of social-emotional functioning and found that interrater reliability between parents typically fell within a range of .38 to .74 whereas agreement between teachers ranged from .34 to .87. Similar to reliability estimates of structured interview techniques, interrater agreement between third-party raters appears to vary according to the type of behavior being rated, with ratings of externalizing symptoms (e.g., aggression) achieving higher levels of agreement than internalizing symptoms (e.g., withdrawal). Interrater disagreement in third-party scales is unavoidable. Indeed, even under ideal rating circumstances, when two biological, cohabiting parents rated their own children, median interrater correlations were observed to be .60 (Walker & Bracken, 1996).

Setting variance refers to variability in the child's behavior according to context. Raters familiar with the child's behavior at home may not see problematic behavior in other contexts, such as at preschool or day care. Evidence for setting variance exists by contrasting interrater reliabilities for informants across different settings. For example, interrater agreement between teachers is consistently higher than interrater agreement between teachers and parents for the Preschool and Kindergarten Behavior Scales (PKBS; Merrell, 1994).

TABLE 17.1 Brief Description of Third-Party Reports Assessing the Social-Emotional Functioning of Preschool Children

SCALE	AGE LEVEL	SAMPLE OF SCALE CONTENT	AVERAGE MEDIAN SUBTEST RELIABILITY[a]	AVERAGE TOTAL TEST RELIABILITY[a]	AVERAGE INTERRATER RELIABILITY
BASC					
Parent	4–18 yr		.76	.89	.58
Teacher	4–18 yr		.83	.93	.71
Burks's	3–4 yr; Grade K	Self-blame, anxiety, withdrawal, anger control, aggression, dependency	NR	No total test score	.74
CBCL					
Competence	2–18 yr	Social withdrawal, depression, anxiety, aggression, somatic problems, immaturity	.56	.60	.78
Problem	2–18 yr		.77	.96	.76
CRS					
Parent 48	3–17 yr	Conduct problems, anxiety, impulsive behavior, learning problems, inattention	NR	No total test score	.41[b]
Teacher 28	3–17 yr		NR	No total test score	
Parent 93	6–14 yr		NR	No total test score	.85
Teacher 39	4–12 yr		.84	No total test score	
Devereux					
Eyberg					
ECBI	2–12 yr	Conduct problems, intensity	.98	No total test score	.83
SESBI	Preschool		.97	No total test score	.86
Louisville	4–6 yr	Aggression, hyperactivity, fear, somatic problems	.84	No total test score	NR
PBQ	3–6 yr		NR	NR	NR

SCALE	AGE LEVEL	SAMPLE OF SCALE CONTENT	AVERAGE MEDIAN SUBTEST RELIABILITY[a]	AVERAGE TOTAL TEST RELIABILITY[a]	AVERAGE INTERRATER RELIABILITY
PIC	3–16 yr	Depression, social skills, withdrawal, anxiety, hyperactivity, delinquency	.81	No total test score	.73
PKBS	3–6 yr	Social skills, problem behaviors	.92	.97	.40
SSRS					
Parent	Preschool–Grade 12	Social skills, problem behaviors	.72	.82	.25[c]
Teacher	Preschool–Grade 12		.85	.88	
TABC					
Parent	3–7 yr	Emotional intensity, distractibility, activity	.67	No total test score	.45
Teacher	3–7 yr		.85	No total test score	.34
VABS	0–18 yr, 11 mo	Socialization, daily living skills, communication	.77	.96	.74
Walker	2 yr–Grade 3		NR	.98	.81

Note: BASC = Behavior Assessment System for Children, Burks's = Burks's Behavior Rating Scale, CBCL = Child Behavior Checklist, CRS = Conners's Rating Scale, Devereux = Devereux Rating Scales for Children, Eyberg = Eyberg Child Behavior Checklist, Louisville = Louisville Behavior Checklist, PBQ = Preschool Behavior Questionnaire, PIC = Personality Inventory for Children, PKBS = Preschool and Kindergarten Behavior Scales, SSRS = Social Skills Rating System, TABC = Temperament Assessment Battery for Children, VABS = Vineland Adaptive Behavior Scales, Walker = Walker Problem Behavior Identification Checklist

[a]Internal consistency reliability

[b]Parent Form 48 with Teacher Form 28

[c]Parent and Teacher Agreement

NR = Not reported

Temporal variance refers to the observation that preschool children's behavior changes over time, thus yielding differences in an identical respondent's ratings over some interval of time. Temporal variance may be particularly problematic in the assessment of preschool social-emotional functioning due to rapid developmental changes that young children experience.

Instrument variance refers to observed variability that occurs when two rating instruments designed to measure similar constructs yield different results (Martin et al., 1986). Interpretation is hindered when psychometrically equal scales yield different results because the examiner cannot be sure which rating scale to interpret with confidence.

To address the problem of variability in third-party rating instruments, Martin et al. (1986) described an assessment strategy designed to help the assessor identify each source of variance. Ideally, evaluation of a preschool child's social-emotional functioning would consist of gathering third-party ratings in a multisetting, multisource, and multi-instrument design (Martin et al., 1986). In this assessment model, the preschool child's behavior is rated across at least two settings (e.g., home and school), by at least two raters for each setting (e.g., mother and father), and with at least two instruments for each rater (e.g., CBCL and SSRS). It is easy to see how the number of ratings increases as each source of variance is accounted for in the assessment model. If one were to also account for time variance in the assessment model, a total of 16 third-party ratings would be collected in the end. Data can be aggregated over all rating scales and the subsequent value is deemed to be more reliable than any individual rating. Determining sources of rating disagreements can help to isolate situationally specific aspects of problematic social-emotional functioning. Martin and colleagues identify their assessment model as an ideal, and correctly point out that as third-party assessments deviate from the ideal, conclusions regarding the child's social-emotional functioning are weakened.

In addition to problems associated with unwanted variance in measurement, third-party preschool rating instruments can be technically weak. Bracken et al. (1994) evaluated 13 third-party rating instruments according to Bracken's (1987) minimum standards of technical adequacy for preschool assessment instruments. The review pointed to limitations in third-party instrumentation such as small, regional standardization samples, subscale reliabilities less than the .80 criterion, and global scale reliabilities less than the .90 criterion. No third-party rating instrument met all specified psychometric criteria; however, many measures fell short on only one or two standards. In terms of psychometric soundness, social-emotional third-party rating instruments performed comparably to preschool cognitive tests and seemed to fare somewhat better than speech and language tests (Bracken et al., 1994). In addition, the authors observed that newer third-party rating instruments, such as the PKBS or BASC, generally demonstrated the best technical characteristics and should probably replace older rating scales, such as the Preschool Behavior Questionnaire (PBQ; Behar & Stringfield, 1974).

Projective Assessment

Projective assessment has a long history of use in the assessment of children's emotional functioning and personality (e.g., Rabin & Haworth, 1960). Projective techniques are the least structured of the aforementioned assessment methods and typically require free expression through verbal, graphic, or written means. All projective assessment techniques share the core theoretical assumption that the respondent externalizes covert aspects of personality during his or her response (Rabin & Haworth, 1960). Of course, different assessment techniques assume that different aspects of personality are being externalized. For example, Human Figure Drawing (HFD) representations may be assumed to tap one's body image or self-concept as well as other unconscious attitudes, beliefs, and feelings (Jones, 1992). Traditional projective assessment techniques include drawings, word associations, apperception tests, and Rorschach.

Advantages of Projective Techniques. Projective assessment tasks are typically enjoyable for young children. In addition, activities such as drawing, telling stories, and playing are familiar to most children and they usually participate energetically in them. Therefore, projective techniques can be used to build rapport with young children by allowing familiar and comfortable modes of interaction with an unfamiliar adult. Projective methods can also produce a good "match" with preschool children's communication styles. For example, those who employ HFDs in the social-emotional assessment of young children have argued that drawings are the natural medium for children's communication (Koppitz, 1968).

Limitations of Projective Techniques. Again, developmental limitations associated with preschool children also restrict the use of projective techniques in assessment of social-emotional functioning. Limitations are associated primarily with disparities between the preschool child's verbal, cognitive, and motor skills and task demands required in projective assessment. Apperception tasks, such as the Children's Apperception Test (CAT; Bellack & Bellack, 1949) or Roberts Apperception Test for Children (RATC; McArthur & Roberts, 1982), require the respondent to tell stories about pictorial stimuli. Children younger than 6 often name components of the cards or offer simple descriptions about the contents of the card. This observation probably relates to the concrete style of thinking described previously and certainly limits meaningful interpretation.

Projective drawing techniques, such as the HFD, are typically unusable with children below the age of 4 or 5 because the child's drawings are limited to single lines, circles, crosses, and squares (Chandler & Johnson, 1991; Jones, 1992; Martin, 1991). The "scribbles" are viewed as having no representational quality and are, therefore, not interpreted. Children ages 4 to 7 begin to show signs of symbolic representation by drawing "tadpole people" (Chandler & Johnson, 1991). In her work on HFDs, Koppitz (1968) included children as young as 5 years old in her normative sample of 1,856 children and, subsequently, asserted that indicators of emotional problems (e.g., unusual omissions, shading, or added detail) could be seen in HFDs of children as young as 5. In general, critics of projective assessment have attacked the tests' psychometric properties, claiming that projective techniques lack adequate temporal and interrater reliability and demonstrate poor validity (Obrzut & Boliek, 1986).

Play-Based Assessment

Assessing young children's social and emotional development within the context of play has a long history (e.g., Berk, 1997). This is understandable given young children's spontaneous, zealous, and often quite dramatic play activities as well as the reality that children spend much of their time engaged in play. Play is what young children will do if given the chance; it is "what they do best and most attentively" (Reynolds & Jones, 1997, p. 3). In terms of assessing children's social-emotional development, play has meant many things to many people. For some assessors, play offers the opportunity to sample a child's behavior within a more naturalistic context than an office. For others, children's play is representational, whereby children communicate about their inner experience by transforming abstract experience into concrete terms. In terms of structuring social-emotional as-

sessment, play-based assessment can occur within the context of a larger assessment strategy, or play-based assessment may constitute the single modality for assessing a wide range of preschool children's abilities.

Play-Based Assessment Coupled with Traditional Techniques. Within the context of a traditional assessment strategy, play-based assessment offers a unique opportunity for social-emotional evaluation, allowing for simultaneous observation of behavior and its interpretation. Sattler (1998) outlines useful guidelines when observing young children at play, including noting how the child enters the playroom (e.g., cautious, excited), the child's energy level during play (e.g., lethargic, energetic), the child's affect and tone during play activities (e.g., aggressive, defiant, cooperative), and the child's attitude toward adults in play (e.g., responsive, compliant). Careful observations during play offer the clinician a unique opportunity to assess affect, behavior, and interpersonal style in a relatively natural setting.

In addition, many professionals working with children have asserted that children represent their thoughts, feelings, and experiences through play (e.g., Reynolds & Jones, 1997). Thematic interpretation of play may occur at several levels. For example, young children's play may be interpreted (a) at a general level of organization, which may reflect the child's perception of his or her environment (e.g., organized, scattered); (b) in terms of actual content during play (e.g., a doll described as being mad); and/or (c) in terms of overriding themes noted in play (e.g., heroic, destructive). Themes may then be interpreted as reflecting how the child views his or her world and self as well as general expectations about how the two interact.

Comprehensive and standardized coding manuals exist for certain play-based assessment activities. For example, the MacArthur Story-Stem Battery (MSSB; Bretherton, Oppenheim, & Prentiss, unpublished) uses a play narrative strategy for assessment. Here, children are presented with problematic interpersonal situations using plastic dolls and are required to complete the story. The MSSB allows for systematic coding of content themes (e.g., aggression), parental themes (e.g., protection), and affective expression during play (e.g., anger or joy) (Robinson, Mantz-Simmons, & MacFie, 1997). Interrater reliability has been reported to range from $r = .80$ to $r = .96$ for components of this coding system (Warren, Oppenheim, & Emde, 1996). Level of affective distress experienced by the child or by a character in the story has related significantly to mother-, father-, and teacher-rated externalizing problems on the CBCL (Warren et al., 1996).

Transdisciplinary Play-Based Assessment. Linder (1993) outlines a comprehensive assessment system on play-based behaviors, Transdisciplinary Play-Based Assessment (TPBA). Within this assessment model, traditional evaluation techniques outlined earlier are abandoned and *all* aspects of the preschool child's abilities are assessed through careful observation of play activities. The child's abilities are assessed through a combination of structured and unstructured activities with "facilitators," parents, and another child. Cognitive, social-emotional, language, and sensorimotor development is evaluated within the context of a playroom environment. In the particular case of social-emotional assessment using TPBA, facilitators observe and rate the following: (a) characteristics of the child's temperament; (b) aspects of mastery motivation; (c) social interactions with the examiner, parents, and a peer; (d) emotional characteristics of the child's play; and (e) awareness of social conventions. For example, when evaluating the child's awareness of social conventions, TPBA observers rate the child's use of appropriate greetings, sharing behavior, and respect for adult authority (Linder, 1993).

Advantages of Play-Based Assessment Techniques. Observing children at play is often useful because children are likely to feel more comfortable at play and behave in a more naturalistic manner than during structured assessment activities. Children usually engage in play activities attentively and with enthusiasm; therefore, the assessor can observe the child at his or her best. In the specific instance of TPBA, Linder (1993) asserted that TPBA holds numerous advantages over traditional assessment techniques, including (a) evaluations that occur within a natural environment, (b) easier rapport building, (c) flexible testing procedures, (d) active participation by the parents in the assessment, and (e) more information made available about qualitative aspects of the child's abilities that are useful in guiding intervention.

Limitations of Play-Based Assessment Techniques. Play-based assessment relies primarily on observational methods; therefore, play-based techniques and TPBA share shortcomings associated with the observational assessment methods identified earlier. In addition to these general limitations, two specific restrictions are associated with TPBA. First, TPBA observations do not yield standardized scores that may be necessary to accurately describe current levels of functioning and to secure intervention services for young preschool children (Linder, 1993). Second, TPBA evaluates a broad range of abilities over a relatively short period of time (i.e., 60 to 90 minutes); thus, comprehensive assessment of social-emotional functioning is unlikely and follow-up evaluations are probably necessary.

RECOMMENDATION FOR ASSESSMENT DESIGN

Although primary assessment techniques differ in content and method, similar recommendations guide their practical use. Despite theoretical and practical differences, consensus appears to have been reached regarding the best approach to preschool social-emotional assessment. Most authors agree that the best assessment strategy is a multidimensional one that involves evaluating preschool functioning with multiple methods, via multiple sources, across multiple settings, and over multiple occasions (e.g., Bagnato & Neisworth, 1991; Bracken, 1996; Martin et al., 1986; Umansky, 1983; Wheatcraft & Bracken, in press). Thus, a multidimensional assessment strategy incorporates the various techniques introduced earlier with the goal of minimizing limitations associated with any single technique. Each assessment technique yields unique information and should be selected for use based on the purpose of the assessment. For example, norm-referenced tests are most helpful when comparing the child's social-emotional adjustment against a normative criterion; other methods, such as TPBA and observation, are perhaps more useful in designing interventions (Wheatcraft & Bracken, in press).

CHAPTER SUMMARY AND CONCLUSIONS

Increasingly, clinicians are called on to assess preschool children's social and emotional functioning for screening, diagnosis, and intervention planning. Currently, theoretical and empirical work supports the notion that a host of factors operates in complex ways to influence young children's social and emotional development. This reality causes problems for practitioners assigned the task of describing social and emotional characteristics of a preschool child at a single point in time. In addition to limited understanding of the complex interrelationships that seem to exist between causal factors, assessments are also hindered by preschoolers' cognitive functioning and the variable nature of social and emotional characteristics per se. Current assessment technologies hold unique strengths and weaknesses; therefore, the use of a single assessment technique for description, diagnosis, or treatment planning is not recommended. Ideally, the best assessment efforts designed to accomplish these purposes are those that (a) sample a variety of behaviors; (b) use varied assessment techniques, informants, settings, and instrumentation; and (c) incorporate the findings into a meaningful whole.

REFERENCES

Achenbach, T. M. (1991). *Manual for the Child Behavior Checklist/4-18 and 1991 profile.* Burlington: University of Vermont, Department of Psychiatry.

Achenbach, T. M. (1992). *Manual for the Child Behavior Checklist/2–3 and 1992 profile.* Burlington: University of Vermont, Department of Psychiatry.

Achenbach, T. M., McConaghy, S. H., & Howell, C. T. (1987). Child/adolescent behavioral and emotional problems: Implications of cross-informant correlations for situational specificity. *Psychological Bulletin, 101,* 213–232.

American Psychiatric Association. (1994). *Diagnostic and statistical manual of mental disorders* (4th ed.). Washington, DC: Author.

Antonovsky, A. (1979). *Health, stress, and coping: New perspectives on mental and physical well-being.* San Francisco: Jossey-Bass.

Bagnato, S. J., & Neisworth, J. T. (1991). *Assessment for early intervention: Best practices for professionals.* New York: Guilford Press.

Barkley, R. A. (1996). Attention-deficit/hyperactivity disorder. In E. J. Mash, & R. A. Barkley (Eds.), *Child Psychopathology.* New York: Guilford Press.

Bates, J. E. (1980). The concept of difficult temperament. *Merrill-Palmer Quarterly, 26,* 299–319.

Bates, J. E., Maslin, C. A., & Frankel, K. A. (1985). Attachment security, mother–child interaction, and temperament as predictors of behavior-problem ratings at age three years. In I. Bretherton & E. Waters (Eds.), Growing points of attachment theory and research. *Monographs of the Society for Research in Child Development, 50* (1-2, Serial No. 209).

Baumrind, D. (1973). The development of instrumental competence through socialization. In A. Pick (Ed.), *Minnesota Symposia on Child Psychology* (Vol. 7, pp. 3–46). Minneapolis: University of Minnesota Press.

Behar, L., & Stringfield, S. (1974). *Manual for the Preschool Behavior Questionnaire.* Durham, NC: Author.

Bell, R. Q. (1968). A reinterpretation of the direction of effects in studies of socialization. *Psychological Review, 75,* 81–85.

Bellack, L., & Bellack, S. S. (1949). *The Children's Apperception Test.* New York: C. P. S. Company.

Berk, L. (1997). *Child Development* (3rd ed.). Boston: Allyn & Bacon.

Bierman, K. L. (1990). Using the clinical interview to assess children's interpersonal reasoning and emotional understanding. In C. R. Reynolds & R. W. Kamphaus (Eds.), *Handbook of psychological and educational assessment of children: Personality, behavior, and context* (pp. 204–219). New York: Guilford Press.

Bierman, K. L., & Schwartz, L. A. (1986). Clinical child interviews: Approaches and developmental considerations. *Journal of Child and Adolescent Psychotherapy, 3,* 267–278.

Block, J. H., & Block, J. (1980). The role of ego-control and ego-resiliency in the organization of behavior. In W. A. Collins (Ed.), *Development of cognition, affect, and social relations: The Minnesota Symposia on Child Psychology, Vol. 13* (pp. 39–101). Hillsdale, NJ: Lawrence Erlbaum.

Bowlby, J. (1988). *A secure base: Parent–child attachment and healthy human development.* New York: Basic Books.

Bracken, B. A. (1987). Limitations of preschool assessment and standards for minimal levels of technical adequacy. *Journal of Psychoeducational Assessment, 5,* 313–326.

Bracken, B. A. (1991). The clinical observation of preschool assessment behavior. In B. A. Bracken (Ed.), *The psychoeducational assessment of preschool children* (pp. 40–52). Boston: Allyn & Bacon.

Bracken, B. A. (1996). Clinical applications of a context-dependent, multidimensional model of self-concept. In B. A. Bracken (Ed.), *Handbook of self-concept: Developmental, social, and clinical considerations* (pp. 463–504). New York: John Wiley and Sons.

Bracken, B. A., Keith, L. K., & Walker, K. C. (1994). Assessment of preschool behavior and social-emotional functioning: A review of thirteen third-party instruments. *Assessment in Rehabilitation and Exceptionality, 1,* 331–346.

Bradley, R. H., & Caldwell, B. M. (1988). Using the HOME inventory to assess the family environment. *Pediatric Nursing, 14,* 97–102.

Bradley, R., Whiteside, L., Mundfrom, D., Casey, P., Kelleher, K., & Pope, S. (1994). Contribution of early intervention and early caregiving experiences to resilience in low-birthweight, premature children living in poverty. *Journal of Clinical Child Psychology, 23,* 425–434.

Bretherton, I., Oppenheim, D., Prentiss, C. (n.d.) *The MacArthur Story-Stem Battery.* Unpublished manuscript.

Bridges, F., & Cicchetti, D. (1982). Mother's ratings of the temperament characteristics of Down syndrome infants. *Developmental Psychology, 18,* 238–244.

Bronfenbrenner, U. (1977). Toward an experimental ecology of human development. *American Psychologist, 32,* 513–531.

Bronfenbrenner, U. (1986). Ecology of the family as a context for human development: Research perspectives. *Developmental Psychology, 22,* 723–742.

Brooks-Gunn, J. (1985). Dyadic interchanges in families with at-risk children. In W. K. Frankenburg, R. N. Emde, & J. W. Sullivan, (Eds.), *Early identification of children at risk: An international perspective.* New York: Plenum Press.

Brooks-Gunn, J., & Lewis, M. (1982). Affective exchanges between normal infants and handicapped infants and their mothers. In T. Field & A. Fogel (Eds.), *Emotion and early interaction.* Hillsdale, NJ: Erlbaum.

Caldwell, B. M., & Bradley, R. H. (1984). *Home observation for measurement of the environment.* Little Rock: University of Arkansas.

Campbell, J. M. (in press). [Review of the Social Skills Rating System, Preschool Version]. *Journal of Psychoeducational Assessment.*

Chandler, L., & Johnson, V. (1991). *Using projective techniques with children: A guide to clinical assessment.* Springfield, IL: Charles C. Thomas.

Cohen, S. C., & Beckwith, L. (1979). Preterm infant interaction with the caregiver in the first year of life and competence at age two. *Child Development, 50,* 767–776.

Costello, A. J., Edelbrock, L. S., Dulcan, M. K., Kalas, R., & Klaric, S. H. (1984). *Report on the NIMH Diagnostic Interview Schedule for Children (DISC).* Washington, DC: National Institute of Mental Health.

Eagly, A. H., Ashmore, R. D., Makhijani, M. G., & Longo, L. C. (1991). What is beautiful is good, but...: A meta-analytic review of research on the physical attractiveness stereotype. *Psychological Bulletin, 110,* 109–128.

Easterbrooks, M. A., & Lamb, M. E. (1979). The relationship between quality of infant–mother attachment and infant competence in initial encounters with peers. *Child Development, 50,* 380–387.

Emde, R. N., & Easterbrooks, M. A. (1985). In W. K. Frankenburg, R. N. Emde, & J. W. Sullivan (Eds.), *Early identification of children at risk: An international perspective.* New York: Plenum Press.

Frankenburg, W. K. (1985). The concept of screening revisited. In W. K. Frankenburg, R. N. Emde, & J. W. Sullivan (Eds.), *Early identification of children at risk: An international perspective.* New York: Plenum Press.

Garmezy, N. (1985). Stress-resistant children: The search for protective factors. In J. E. Stevenson (Ed.), *Recent research in developmental psychopathology* (pp. 213–233). Oxford: Pergamon Press.

Garmezy, N., Masten, A. S., & Tellegen, A. (1984). The study of stress and competence in children: A building block for developmental psychopathology. *Child Development, 55,* 97–111.

Gill, D. G. (1970). *Violence against children.* Cambridge, MA: Harvard University Press.

Graham, P., Rutter, M., & George, S. (1973). Temperamental characteristics as predictors of behavior disorders in children. *American Journal of Orthopsychiatry, 43,* 328–339.

Gresham, F. M., & Elliott, S. N. (1990). *Social Skills Rating System.* Circle Pines, MN: American Guidance Service.

Grusec, J. E., & Lytton, H. (1988). *Social development: History, theory, and research.* New York: Springer-Verlag.

Hammen, C., & Rudolph, K. D. (1996). Childhood depression. In E. J. Mash, & R. A. Barkley (Eds.), *Child psychopathology.* New York: Guilford Press.

Herjanic, B., Herjanic, M., Brown, F., & Wheatt, T. (1975). Are children reliable reporters? *Journal of Abnormal Child Psychology, 3,* 41–48.

Hermanns, J., Cats, B., & den Ouden, L. (1985). The development of temperament in very low birth weight children. In W. K. Frankenburg, R. N. Emde, & J. W. Sullivan (Eds.), *Early identification of children at risk: An international perspective.* New York: Plenum Press.

Hetherington, E. M. (1998). Relevant issues in developmental science: Introduction to the special issue. *American Psychologist, 53*(2), 93–94.

Hinshaw, S. P., & Anderson, C. A. (1996). Conduct and oppositional defiant disorders. In E. J. Mash & R. A. Barkley (Eds.), *Child psychopathology.* New York: Guilford Press.

Hodges, K. (1993). Structured interviews for assessing children. *Journal of Child Psychology and Psychiatry and Allied Disciplines, 34,* 49–68.

Hodges, K., Gordon, Y., & Lennon, M. P. (1990). Parent–child agreement on symptoms assessed via a clinical research interview for children: The Child Assessment Schedule (CAS). *Journal of Child Psychology and Psychiatry and Allied Disciplines, 31,* 427–436.

Hodges, K., Kline, J., Stern, L., Cytryn, L., & McKnew, D. (1982). The development of a child assessment interview for research and clinical use. *Journal of Abnormal Child Psychology, 10,* 173–189.

Jones, C. J. (1992). *Human figure drawings of mildly handicapped students.* Springfield, IL: Charles C. Thomas.

Keith, R. (1996). Children at risk for reactive attachment disorder: Assessment, diagnosis and treatment. *Progress: Family Systems Research and Therapy, 5,* 83–98.

Klinger, L. G., & Dawson, G. (1996). Autistic Disorder. In E. J. Mash, & R. A. Barkley (Eds.), *Child psychopathology.* New York: Guilford Press.

Koppitz, E. M. (1968). *Psychological evaluation of children's human figure drawings.* Yorktown Heights, NY: The Psychological Corporation—Harcourt Brace Jovanovich.

Langlois, J. H., & Downs, C. A. (1979). Peer relations as a function of physical attractiveness: The eye of the beholder or behavioral reality? *Child Development, 50,* 409–418.

Langlois, J. H., Ritter, J. M., Casey, R. H., & Sawin, D. B. (1995). Infant attractiveness predicts maternal behaviors and attitudes. *Developmental Psychology, 31,* 464–472.

Lewis, M., & Rosenblum, L. A. (1974). *The effect of the infant on its caregiver.* New York: Wiley.

Linder, T. W. (1993). *Transdisciplinary play-based assessment: A functional approach to working with young children* (Rev. ed.). Baltimore: Paul H. Brookes.

Luthar, S. S., & Zigler, E. (1991). Vulnerability and competence: A review of research on resilience in childhood. *American Journal of Orthopsychiatry, 61,* 6–22.

Maccoby, E. E. (1990). Gender and relationships: A developmental account. *American Psychologist, 45,* 513–520.

Macoby, E., & Jacklin, C. (1979). Concentrations of sex hormones in umbilical-cord blood: Their relation to sex and birth order of infants. *Child Development, 50,* 632–642.

Magid, K., & McKelvey, C. A. (1987). *High risk: Children without a conscience.* Golden, CO: M & M Press.

Martin, R. P. (1986). Assessment of the social and emotional functioning of preschool children. *School Psychology Review, 15,* 216–232.

Martin, R. P. (1991). Assessment of social and emotional behavior. In B. A. Bracken (Ed.), *The psychoeducational assessment of preschool children* (2nd ed., pp. 450–464). Boston: Allyn & Bacon.

Martin, R. P., Drew, D., & Gaddis, L. (1988). Prediction of elementary school achievement from preschool temperament: Three studies. *School Psychology Review, 17,* 125–137.

Martin, R. P., Hooper, S., & Snow, J. (1986). Behavior rating scale approaches to personality assessment in children and adolescents. In H. M. Knoff (Ed.), *The assessment of child and adolescent personality* (pp. 309–351). New York: Guilford Press.

Mash, E. J., & Dozois, D. J. A. (1996). Child psychology: A developmental-systems perspective. In E. J. Mash & R. A. Barkley (Eds.), *Child Psychopathology* (pp. 3–60). New York: Guilford Press.

McArthur, D. S., & Roberts, G. E. (1982). *Roberts Apperception Test for Children: Manual.* Los Angeles: Western Psychological Services.

McCarney, S. B. (1995). *Attention Deficit Disorders Evaluation Scale.* Columbia, MO: Hawthorne Educational Services.

Merrell, K. W. (1994). *Preschool and Kindergarten Behavior Scales.* Brandon, VT: Clinical Psychology Publishing.

Obrzut, J. E., & Boliek, C. A. (1986). Thematic approaches to personality assessment with children and adolescents. In H. M. Knoff (Ed.), *The assessment of child and adolescent personality* (pp. 173–198). New York: Guilford Press.

Parker, J. G., & Asher, S. R. (1987). Peer relations and later personal adjustment: Are low-accepted children at risk? *Psychological Bulletin, 102,* 357–389.

Petit, G. S., Dodge, K. A., & Brown, M. M. (1988). Early family experience, social problem solving patterns, and children's social competence. *Child Development, 59,* 107–120.

Puig-Antich, J., & Chambers, W. (1978). *The Schedule for Affective Disorders and Schizophrenia for*

School-Age Children (Kiddie-SADS). New York: New York State Psychiatric Institute.

Rabin, A. I., & Haworth, M. R. (1960). *Projective techniques with children*. New York: Grune and Stratton.

Reiss, S., Levitan, G. W., & Szyszko, J. (1982). Emotional disturbance and mental retardation: Diagnostic overshadowing. *American Journal of Mental Deficiency, 86,* 567–574.

Reynolds, C. R., & Kamphaus, R. W. (1992). *Behavior Assessment System for Children*. Circle Pines, MN: American Guidance Service.

Reynolds, G., & Jones, E. (1997). *Master players: Learning from children at play*. New York: Teachers College Press.

Ritts, V., Patterson, M. L., & Tubbs, M. E. (1992). Expectations, impressions, and judgments of physically attractive students: A review. *Review of Educational Research, 62,* 413–426.

Robinson, J., Mantz-Simmons, L., & MacFie, J. (1997). *Memphis narrative coding manual*. Unpublished manuscript.

Roopnarine, J. L. (1987). Social interaction in the peer group: Relationship to perceptions of parenting and to children's interpersonal awareness and problem-solving ability. *Journal of Applied Developmental Psychology, 8,* 351–362.

Rubin, K. H., Hymel, S., & Mills, R. S. (1989). Sociability and social withdrawal in childhood: Stability and outcomes. *Journal of Personality, 57,* 237–255.

Rutter, M. (1978). Early sources of security and competence. In J. Bruner, & A. Garton (Eds.), *Human growth and development*. New York: Oxford University Press.

Rutter, M. (1985). Resilience in the face of adversity: Protective factors and resistance to psychiatric disorder. *British Journal of Psychiatry, 147,* 598–611.

Sameroff, A. J. (1975). Early influences on development: Fact or fancy? *Merrill-Palmer Quarterly, 21,* 267–294.

Sameroff, A. J. (1986). Environmental context of child development. *The Journal of Pediatrics, 109,* 192–200.

Sattler, J. M. (1992). *Assessment of children* (3rd ed.). San Diego, CA: Author.

Sattler, J. M. (1998). *Clinical and forensic interviewing of children and families*. San Diego, CA: Author.

Segal, J. (1988). Teachers have enormous power in affecting a child's self-esteem. *Brown University Child Behavior and Development Newsletter, 4,* 1–4.

Thomas, A., Birch, H. G., Chess, S., Hertzig, C., & Korn, S. (1963). *Behavioral individuality in early childhood*. New York: New York University Press.

Thomas, A., & Chess, S. (1977). *Temperament and development*. New York: Brunner/Mazel.

Thompson, R. J., Merritt, K. A., Keith, B. R., Murphy, L. B., & Johndrow, D. A. (1993). Mother–child agreement on the Child Assessment Schedule with nonreferred children: A research note. *Journal of Child Psychology and Psychiatry and Allied Disciplines, 34,* 813–820.

Tieger, T. (1980). On the biological basis of sex differences in aggression. *Child Development, 51,* 943–963.

Umansky, W. (1983). Assessment of social and emotional development. In K. D. Paget and B. A. Bracken (Eds.), *The psychoeducational assessment of preschool children* (pp. 417–441). Orlando, FL: Grune and Stratton.

U.S. Department of Education, Office of Special Education and Rehabilitative Services (1997). Individuals with Disabilities Education Act Amendments of 1997. Washington, DC.

Walker, H. M. (1983). *Walker Problem Behavior Identification Checklist*. Los Angeles: Western Psychological Services.

Walker, K. C., & Bracken, B. A. (1996). Inter-parent agreement on four preschool behavior rating scales: Effects of parent and child gender. *Psychology in the Schools, 33,* 273–283.

Warren, S. L., Oppenheim, D., & Emde, R. N. (1996). Can emotions and themes in children's play predict behavior problems? *Journal of the American Academy of Child and Adolescent Psychiatry, 10,* 1331–1337.

Werner, E. E. (1984). Resilient children. *Young Children,* 68–72.

Wheatcraft, T. K., & Bracken, B. A. (in press). Early identification and intervention of psychosocial and behavioral effects of exceptionality. In D. H. Saklofske & V. L. Schwean (Eds.), *Handbook of psychosocial characteristics of exceptional children*. New York: Plenum.

White, K. R. (1985–86). Efficacy of early intervention. *The Journal of Special Education, 4,* 401–416.

Wirt, R. D., Lachar, D., Klinedinst, J. K., & Seat, P. D. (1984). *Multidimensional description of child personality: A manual for the Personality Inventory for Children*. Los Angeles: Western Psychological Services.

CHAPTER 18

NEUROPSYCHOLOGICAL ASSESSMENT OF THE PRESCHOOL CHILD

STEPHEN R. HOOPER

The examination of brain–behavior relationships in the preschool child is a fledgling area; moreover, the assessment of these relationships is quite challenging to the psychologist working with this population. These concerns were raised previously (Hooper, 1991), and they continue to remain accurate to the present. Despite these overriding concerns, exciting advances have slowly trickled forth within the domain of the neuropsychological assessment of the preschool child (e.g., Aylward, 1997; Korkman, Kirk, & Kemp, 1998). These advances have included the emergence of more varied tools to measure aspects of cognitive functioning and the development of a contemporary formal battery to assess neurocognitive functioning.

Legislative mandates also have fueled these advances. Primary among these mandates has been the passage of Public Law 99-457 in 1986 explicitly focusing on the needs of preschool children with special needs, and the 1991 reauthorization of funds for special education programs with the Individuals with Disabilities Education Act (IDEA). This revision of the original law made services for the 3- to 5-year-old population mandatory for states rather than optional, and the 1997 amendments to IDEA (Public Law 105-117) further extended the funding of preschool services (Umansky & Hooper, 1998), with an effort to address ages birth to 5. These mandates are in concert with Public Law 94-142 and the position of the National Joint Committee on Learning Disabilities (NJCLD, 1986) on the needs of the preschool child with a learning disability.

The increased focus on the needs of preschool children with exceptionalities also has served to encourage research examining neurocognitive mechanisms of preschool children with a variety of developmental needs. This is no accident because children with a wide array of acquired and neurodevelopmental problems are now populating preschool classes and are requiring special preschool services across the country. In part, improvements in medical care have contributed to lessening the mortality among sick or injured infants and toddlers; however, we are learning that the decrease in mortality likely has contributed to an increase in morbidity. It is this latter supposition that has contributed to increased research and clinical efforts addressing the assessment and treatment needs of preschool children with exceptionalities. For example, such efforts have examined the neurocognitive functioning of low-birth-weight preschoolers (Sommerfelt, Markestad, & Ellertsen, 1998), the effects of various drugs on preschool development (Walsh, Kastner, & Harmon, 1996), traumatic brain injury outcomes during the preschool years (Wrightson, McGinn, & Gronwall, 1995), attention problems (Ashley & Barkley, in press), and assessment–treatment linkages for learning (Korkman & Peltomaa, 1993). Furthermore, the need to develop appropriate educational programs highlights the concurrent need for detailed profiles of abilities, and neuropsychological assessment strategies can provide one vehicle for addressing this need. Needless to say, the growth and interest in this assessment domain continue to expand and become more important to the assessment, diagnosis, and treatment planning of young children with special needs.

Given the steady growth of interest in this assessment domain as applied to preschool children, this chapter presents the current status of the neuropsychological assessment of the preschool child. The discussions for this chapter will focus largely on the preschool years proper, that is, the ages 3 through 5 years. The utility of neuropsychological testing for this population is elucidated and, subsequently, followed by a discussion of the various neuropsychological assessment strategies available to psychologists and neuropsychologists. The discussion spans formal batteries as well as eclectic, informal batteries. Some screening tools also are mentioned. The chapter concludes with a brief discussion of some broader issues associated with neuropsychological testing of preschool children.

UTILITY OF A NEUROPSYCHOLOGICAL APPROACH

There are numerous complexities related to the neuropsychological assessment of children (Teeter & Semrud-Clikeman, 1997; Tramontana & Hooper, 1988a). Some of these complexities include test selection, interpretation issues, assessment–treatment linkages, and crucial developmental factors that also contribute to behavior and learning. These concerns are magnified further when a neuropsychological perspective is applied to children below the age of 6 years. Aylward (1988) has described this latter area as a "no man's land" with respect to its current level of development.

Despite these concerns, a number of investigators have asserted the utility of employing a neuropsychological approach with preschoolers (Aylward, 1988; Deysach, 1986; Hartlage & Telzrow, 1982, 1986; Hooper, 1988; Korkman et al., 1998; Molfese, 1992; Wilson, 1992)—even from a preventative perspective (Korkman & Peltomaa, 1993). Consistent with the use of neuropsychological methods with school-age children and adults, a neuropsychological approach for the preschool child can yield a wealth of information pertaining to diagnostic profile description, prognosis, and various treatment factors. More generally, a neuropsychological perspective should serve to advance the understanding of brain–behavior relationships in the preschool population.

Diagnostic Profile Description

Historically, the primary role of a neuropsychological approach in diagnosis was to determine the presence of neurological deficits or dysfunction. Assessment procedures were designed to detect and localize brain lesions that would contribute to the discrimination between typically developing children and those with brain impairment. Prior to the mid-1970s, neuropsychological assessment strategies were appealing because of their noninvasive nature. Although the separation of children with and without brain impairment could be achieved, a review of various attempts at lesion localization in children concluded that there currently is minimal support for this practice (Chadwick & Rutter, 1983). Furthermore, given the recent advances of other neurodiagnostic methods, such as Magnetic Resonance Imaging

(MRI), quantitative electroencephalography (EEG), and Functional Magnetic Resonance Imaging, the need to diagnose brain impairment solely with neuropsychological methods has been lessened. Difficulties with neuropsychological diagnosis have been compounded by the lack of an adequate nosology for various kinds of neurologically based disorders.

Despite these difficulties, neuropsychological diagnosis has not been abandoned completely, but it has shifted roles with respect to its emphasis. In this regard, about two decades ago Behr and Gallagher (1981) proposed for professionals to use a more flexible definition of what constitutes special needs in the preschool population. They suggested that the definition should describe not only the *extent* of developmental variation but also the *type* of variation. Consistent with this, neuropsychological diagnosis is concerned with the detailed and comprehensive description of a child's profile of strengths and weaknesses. This profile may provide clues reflecting the effects of a brain lesion or neurodevelopmental anomaly on subsequent learning and behavior. It also may lend much needed information to increasing our understanding of brain-behavior relationships during this developmental period. Furthermore, the emphasis on profile description has forced clinicians to address the ecological validity of a set of neuropsychological findings (i.e., what is being affected in the child's day-to-day life and what might be affected later). In this regard, clinicians have begun to apply their findings to the preschool classroom setting, the preschooler's adaptive behavior and learning needs, and parent–child and teacher–child interactions. This latter application is critical in that it can help to bring the family into the treatment equation as required by federal law.

Neuropsychological testing also offers a unique diagnostic complement to other educational and neurological procedures by providing specific descriptions of the neurocognitive manifestation of brain impairment (Tramontana & Hooper, 1988b). This will apply to preschool children with acquired brain injuries and related neurological disorders, systemic illnesses, psychiatric disorders, or neurodevelopmental disorders, and requires a keen understanding of the particular environmental demands on a child over time (e.g., the shifting school requirements for learning). For example, one of the most common neurosurgical interventions in childhood involves the insertion of a shunt for the treatment of hydrocephalus. Children who have been treated—even successfully—for hydrocephalus by shunt insertion have demonstrated cognitive deficits ranging from inattention and impulsivity to more specific problems with memory and visual-motor skills (Landry, Jordan, & Fletcher, 1994). The neuropsychological assessment of a preschool child with a shunt requires not only a comprehensive appraisal of a wide range of abilities but also careful and systematic monitoring of the child's developing skills, particularly as the child moves from the demands of preschool to those of more formal schooling.

The diagnostic utility of preschool neuropsychological assessment also is relevant to children in the nonmedical domain in that approximately 10 percent of preschool children are estimated to experience learning and behavioral difficulties secondary to minor neurological disorders (Kalverboer, 1971). Neurobehavioral connections also might be more clear with preschoolers because of the relatively minimal influences of factors such as feelings of failure, labeling, expectancy artifacts, and social-emotional concerns (Ellison, 1983). Although these factors can manifest in preschool children, in older children these psychosocial variables typically play a larger role in a child's overall functioning, thus blurring possible neurobehavioral linkages. A comprehensive neuropsychological assessment will contribute to obtaining a detailed description of a child's specific strengths and weaknesses and, consequently, to the early identification and treatment of neurocognitive difficulties. It also might begin to elucidate risk factors associated with certain developmental outcomes.

Prognosis

Obtaining a detailed description of a child's neurocognitive functioning is only part of the process for understanding a preschooler's difficulties. Unless the child is inflicted with a degenerative neurological process that is progressing rapidly, it is extremely difficult to predict a particular behavioral outcome. Some longitudinal efforts have been conducted in the areas of learning disability (Satz, Taylor, Friel, & Fletcher, 1978; Spreen & Haaf, 1986; Stevenson & Newman, 1986), language disorders (Molfese & Molfese, 1997), infant hemispherectomy (Dennis, 1985a, 1985b), and traumatic brain injury (Ewing-Cobbs, 1997), and these efforts have begun to provide some clues as to prognostic issues during the preschool years.

An important role for preschool neuropsychological assessment is the monitoring of a child's acquisition and/or reacquisition of function after brain injury. There is a complex array of factors that interact to influence the recovery patterns and developmental progress of chil-

dren who experience early brain insults (Chelune & Edwards, 1981) and knowledge with respect to the impact of specific neuropathological processes on a young child's prognosis is only beginning to surface (Ewing-Cobbs et al., 1997). Furthermore, deficits involving "silent" brain regions might not become apparent until challenged at later developmental stages (Hooper, 1988; Rourke, Bakker, Fisk, & Strang, 1983), thus making the need for detailed, comprehensive, and ongoing systematic neuropsychological assessment crucial to issues of prognosis. For example, Ewing-Cobbs et al. (1997) suggest that long-term neuropsychological follow-up should be ongoing for 10 to 20 years to fully understand the impact of an early brain injury on later-developing abilities such as executive functions.

To illustrate these concerns, over two decades ago Satz, Taylor, Friel, and Fletcher (1978) demonstrated an overall correct classification rate of 84 percent in predicting second grade reading skills. Although the prediction rate was lowered to about 76 percent when examining fifth grade outcomes, Satz and colleagues were able to identify a different set of predictors that proved useful in the early prediction of learning disabilities. When these data were examined more closely, however, a high rate of false negatives (i.e., children initially estimated to be functioning at a satisfactory level in kindergarten) was noted. In fact, more than a quarter of the "normal" functioning kindergarten children later showed significant reading problems during the fifth grade.

The neuropsychological screening procedures employed by Satz and colleagues did prove useful in accurately predicting the extreme ends of the reading recognition continuum, and the model did suggest possible neurobehavioral prognostic indicators of future learning problems. Since that time other prognostic indicators of learning problems have been asserted. For example, using meta-analysis Horn and Packard (1985) found behavioral measures, language tasks, and IQ to be the best single predictors of reading achievement in grades 1 and 3. Tramontana, Hooper, and Selzer (1988) found effective predictors to span cognitive, verbal, and perceptual/perceptual-motor areas of functioning. These investigators also noted the complexities involved in accurately identifying specific predictor-criterion relationships. They also called for more detailed questions in describing prognostic relationships in the learning patterns of preschool children. Korkman and Peltomaa (1993) provided a nice operationalization of this by identifying phonological processing deficits in preschool children and intervening successfully during that time period to minimize the impact of these deficits once children reached formal schooling.

Treatment Issues

The neuropsychological assessment of the preschool child perhaps has its greatest potential impact in contributing to the development of treatment programs, the monitoring of the intervention process and suggesting adjustments based on follow-up findings, and the minimizing of educational and emotional difficulties associated with brain impairment and dysfunction. These contributions are particularly relevant for the preschooler who has the benefit of participating in early intervention programs under current federal and state mandates. Neuropsychological assessment can play a formative role in developing a treatment program tailored to the needs of a child with a particular exceptionality. The detailed strengths and weaknesses generated via a neuropsychological assessment can provide the foundation for an aggressive treatment program. Although little is known about actual assessment–treatment linkages for the preschool child, treatment options tend to be guided by theoretical orientation, clinical experiences, and the availability of therapeutic resources. More generally, however, evidence does exist to support the benefits of early intervention for children at environmental risk (Ramey & Ramey, 1994) and at biological risk (Blair, Ramey, & Hardin, 1995), and a comprehensive neuropsychological assessment could aid in guiding this process.

Once an individualized treatment program is established, it becomes important for the progress of the child to be monitored closely. This is important not only from charting progress rates, but also from the standpoint of providing needed adjustments in the treatment program. The monitoring of a child's progress is crucial to determining the effectiveness of the neurosurgical, pharmacological, educational, and/or cognitive-behavioral intervention strategies. Craft, Shaw, and Cartlidge (1972) have shown the importance of monitoring developmental progress with respect to treatment planning by documenting that even mildly brain-injured infants who were described as "fully recovered" continued to manifest cognitive, behavioral, and sensorimotor deficits several years following their injuries. Similarly, Aylward, Gustafson, Verhulst, and Colliver (1987) noted that diagnoses of motor functioning in infants were more stable over time whereas cognitive functioning status was more likely to change. Bagnato and Dickerson-Mayes (1986)

also demonstrated the importance of monitoring developmental progress with respect to treatment planning in brain-injured infants and preschoolers following approximately a 3½-month inpatient rehabilitation. These gains were noted to occur across all developmental domains, with gains ranging from 77 percent in gross motor functions to 93 percent in cognitive functions.

Given their knowledge of brain–behavior relationships, child neuropsychologists have become more involved in the actual treatment components of adults and school-age children. Particular efforts have spanned the cognitive, educational, behavioral, and affective rehabilitation domains (Boll & Barth, 1981; Incagnoli & Newman, 1985). These efforts only have begun to be asserted with respect to preschool children. As brain–behavior relationships in the preschool population are better understood, the direct involvement of the neuropsychologist undoubtedly will increase for this population.

NEUROPSYCHOLOGICAL ASSESSMENT PROCEDURES

Despite its fledgling status, preschool neuropsychological assessment procedures are beginning to emerge. Most of the procedures parallel assessment models utilized with adults and school-age children and, generally, tend to cover a broad array of cognitive and motor functions. This section discusses the neuropsychological assessment strategies available for the preschool child. At present, there are two formal batteries available for use with preschool children, one of which has recently been introduced in the United States. The discussion of these formal batteries is followed by a presentation of informal approaches. The informal approaches typically are driven by a specific set of constructs, either clinically or empirically derived, and are operationalized by specific available tools tapping these domains. Included here is a discussion of how some of the available intellectual test batteries can facilitate the development of these batteries. Finally, neuropsychological screening procedures are mentioned.

Formal Neuropsychological Batteries

Given the dearth of appropriate neuropsychological batteries for the preschool child, neuropsychologists have had to depend on their knowledge of brain–behavior relationships and neurodevelopmental theory in constructing assessment methodologies. Previously there was only one formal neuropsychological battery that could be applied to the preschool population. In addition to this battery, there now are other recognized formal neuropsychological batteries that have some application to preschool children. These include the Reitan-Indiana Neuropsychological Battery (Reitan, 1969) and the NEPSY (Korkman et al., 1998). Several other formal batteries exist that may have significant importance for neuropsychological testing (e.g., Woodcock-Johnson Cognitive Battery—Revised, Cognitive Assessment System), but their application appears appropriate for children ages 5 and older; moreover, their application to preschool populations remains unclear at present.

Reitan-Indiana Neuropsychological Battery. This battery is a downward extension of the Halstead-Reitan Neuropsychological Battery for Children and was designed for children ages 5 through 8 years. The tasks and accompanying directions were simplified and shortened in an effort to adjust for the developmental differences suspected between the older and younger children. As with the version of the battery used for older children, these tasks typically are administered in conjunction with intellectual, academic/preacademic, lateral dominance, and social-behavioral measures. Traditional components of the Reitan-Indiana Battery include modified versions of the Category Test, Tactual Performance Test, and Finger Tapping Test (Electric). The allied procedures of Strength of Grip, Sensory-Perceptual Examination, and Tactile Form Recognition also typically are administered. The Aphasia Screening Test and Finger-Tip Number Writing of the Sensory-Perceptual Examination were modified slightly for the younger population. In addition, several new tests were developed for inclusion in the battery. These included the Marching Test, Color Form Test, Progressive Figures Test, Matching Pictures Test, Target Test, and the Individual Performance Tests (i.e., Matching Figures, Matching Vs, Concentric Square, and Star). Collectively, these newer tasks attempt to assess gross motor coordination, selective attention, cognitive flexibility, visual perception, visual memory, fine-motor speed, and abstract reasoning.

Taken together, the Reitan-Indiana tasks purport to assess a broad range of functions including gross and fine-motor skills, sensory-perceptual abilities across visual, auditory, and tactile modalities, abstract thinking and problem solving, language, cognitive flexibility, and memory. Findings are interpreted in terms of four methods of inference that include level of performance, pattern of performance, pathognomonic signs, and left-right differences on sensory and motor tasks (Selz & Re-

itan, 1979). These four levels of inference are important in that they contribute to distinguishing neuropsychological procedures from more traditional psychological and developmental assessment approaches, particularly with the preschool-age band.

Level of performance refers to the comparison of a child's scores to an appropriate reference group. Findings from this method will indicate whether a child's performance is normal or abnormal. *Pattern of performance* provides insights into the child's relative strengths and weaknesses across various functions. This method of inference also might provide clues with respect to intervention strategies for a particular child. *Pathognomonic signs* refer to symptoms or behaviors that are distinctively characteristic of a particular disease or disorder (e.g., brain impairment/dysfunction). The investigation of neuropsychological data for pathognomonic signs is especially relevant to the preschool child because their significance depends on the developmental appropriateness of a particular behavior for a given age. For example, visual-spatial reversals in a 3- or 4-year-old child's written output would not be pathognomonic, but their appearance in an 11- or 12-year-old suggests pathology. Obviously, knowledge of normal developmental parameters is necessary for employing this method of inference with preschool children. The final method of inference regarding brain functioning is *left-right differences*. With this inference, performance differentials in the sensory and motor domains on the two sides of the body are examined. Although slight left-right differences are expected, with the dominant side typically being stronger, more efficient, better coordinated, and accurate, lateralized sensory and/or motor deficits are considered to be among the most significant indicators of brain involvement in adults and children (Rourke, 1983).

Despite the relative popularity of the Reitan procedures, the Reitan-Indiana was designed only to address the latter stages of the preschool years. Although the same could be stated for this battery as was noted earlier for some other batteries with normative data beginning at age 5 years (e.g., Woodcock-Johnson Test of Cognitive Abilities—Revised, Cognitive Assessment System), there has been some application of the tasks to kindergarten children (Satz et al., 1978; Teeter, 1985; Townes, Turpin, Martin, & Goldstein, 1980), as well to preschoolers ages 2, 3, and 4 (Reitan & Davison, 1974). The application of the assessment procedures and the four methods of inference to children younger than age 5 years, however, will require continued study.

NEPSY: A Developmental Neuropsychological Assessment. The NEPSY (*NE* for neuro, *PSY* for psychology) arguably represents one of the first well-normed and well-standardized neuropsychological battery for children ages 3-0 through age 12 (Korkman et al., 1998). Across this age range, the NEPSY permits a closer examination of abilities tapping five major domains: Attention/Executive Functions, Language, Sensorimotor Functions, Visuospatial Processing, and Memory and Learning. Within each of these domains there is a variety of subtests that can be examined via quantitative as well as qualitative strategies. There is great flexibility in administration wherein the entire battery can be administered, a core set of tasks can be administered, or a specific domain and/or subtests can be tapped. It is important to recognize that these domains are not true factors but, rather, conceptually constructed domains of neuropsychological functioning that are interrelated. Standard scores are generated for the subtests and domains, and qualitative analyses allow for more idiosyncratic examination of a child's performance on the NEPSY. The NEPSY is grounded in neurodevelopmental theory as presented by Luria (1980) and, as such, allows for evaluation of simple as well as complex functions within each domain. In addition, the NEPSY was developed on children with neurodevelopmental disorders (e.g., learning disabilities) and children with acquired disorders (e.g., traumatic brain injuries) and, thus, may prove more useful in delineating profiles of abilities in both groups of disorders. Published versions of the NEPSY also have been produced in Finland and Sweden, and it has been adapted for use in Israel.

For the preschool child ages 3 to 4, the NEPSY provides a core number of subtests as well as an expanded version. Within the Attention/Executive Function Domain there are two core subtests, Visual Attention and Statue, which tap selective visual attention and motor persistence. In the Language Domain there are three core subtests, Body Part Naming, Phonological Processing, and Comprehension of Instructions. These subtests tap expressive and receptive capabilities, with a particular focus on developmentally emergent phonological processing abilities. Two additional subtests can be administered within the language domain, Verbal Fluency and Oromotor Sequences, which tap verbal speed and oral-motor coordination. Within the Sensorimotor Domain there are two core subtests, Imitating Hand Positions and Visuomotor Precision. These subtests measure motor praxis and dexterity. One additional subtest can be administered to this age group, Manual Motor Sequences,

which taps motor planning and motor sequencing. The Visuospatial Domain is comprised of two subtests for preschoolers, Design Copying and Block Construction, subtests that measure visuoconstructive abilities and visual-spatial functioning. Finally, the Memory and Learning Domain allows for two subtests for this age range, Narrative Memory and Sentence Repetition, both tapping short-term verbal recall. Examiners can administer the core subtests and, if any type of problem or concern is raised, then the additional subtests can be administered. Qualitative observations also can be recorded on each subtest (e.g., motor tremors, motor overflow, perseverations, misarticulations, etc.), and compared to the normative group with respect to the pathognomonic aspects of the behavior. The entire 14 subtests can be administered in about one hour, depending on the status of the preschooler, whereas the core battery can be completed in less than one hour.

In addition to providing a well-standardized, well-normed set of procedures, the NEPSY demonstrated adequate reliability estimates, although the Attention/Executive Functions Domain was somewhat lower (r = .70). The validity of the tasks also appears to be satisfactory. In fact, the NEPSY compares favorably to many intellectual and achievement tasks, and its application to children with a variety of disorders appears promising. Its application to preschool children with a variety of disorders remains to be seen, however, and the field will await findings from investigators using the NEPSY with these populations.

Intellectual Batteries. Pending the availability and ultimate usefulness of the formal neuropsychological assessment batteries for preschoolers, child psychologists and neuropsychologists have depended on many of the more traditional intellectual test batteries as the core of an assessment strategy. In fact, many of these batteries are presented in more detail in this text; however, given their importance to the construction of a neuropsychological battery for preschool children, an overview is provided here with a particular focus on their utility in preschool neuropsychological testing.

The Wechsler Preschool and Primary Scales of Intelligence—Revised (WPPSI-R), for example, is useful for preschoolers down to about age 3 years. As with the older-age versions of the Wechsler scales, the WPPSI-R provides measures of verbal and nonverbal abilities. Specific subtests purportedly assess the retrieval and application of previously learned material as well as the acquisition of new information. Generally, the tasks included on the WPPSI-R provide for a solid foundation from which to organize additional neuropsychological assessment methods and/or to develop neurocognitive hypotheses. Whereas the older-age versions of the Wechsler scales have been shown to be quite sensitive to brain impairment in children and adolescents (Reitan, 1974; Sattler, 1994), the WPPSI-R has not been explored as extensively in this regard.

The McCarthy Scales of Children's Abilities (MSCA) is now a bit dated with respect to its normative base, but its overall structure continues to have relevance for preschool neuropsychological testing. Bracken (1991) noted that the MSCA maintains a number of weaknesses and is long overdue for a revision, but that it also can be complementary to other measures in developing a detailed profile of cognitive strengths and weaknesses. It can be used with children as young as 30 months and provides an adequate sampling of language, perceptual, motor, and memory abilities. In fact, Teeter (1985) found the MSCA to be roughly equivalent to the Reitan-Indiana in predicting later academic achievement in kindergarten children.

The Kaufman Assessment Battery for Children (K-ABC) is another instrument that can be used with preschoolers down to about 30 months of age. The K-ABC is unique in its attempt to separate problem-solving or fluid abilities, as defined by simultaneous and sequential processing, from learned or crystallized functions (i.e., achievement). Although the K-ABC was not designed to serve as a single neuropsychological assessment battery, its theoretical underpinnings and its distinction between problem-solving abilities and learned skills makes it an interesting test to consider for the core of a larger neuropsychological battery for preschoolers. Despite this assertion and the work that has been conducted to date exploring the K-ABC from a neuropsychological perspective (Majovski, 1984; Reynolds, Kamphaus, Rosenthal, & Hiemenz, 1997), there has been precious little work conducted with preschoolers; however, its utility continues to be promising with this population.

The Differential Abilities Scales (DAS) represent a battery of tasks tapping cognitive abilities and achievement skills in children from 30 months through 17 years. The Cognitive Battery includes 17 subtests divided into two broad age domains: Preschool Level and School-Age Level. For the Preschool Level, there are two further age subdivisions. For children ages 30 months through 41 months there are four core subtests for administration. These include Block Building, Verbal Comprehension, Picture Similarities, and Naming Vocabulary, and

generate a single overall factor called General Conceptual Ability (GCA). The Recall of Digits and Recall of Objects subtests can be administered to children ages 36 to 41 months as supplemental diagnostic procedures. Children ages 3 years, 6 months through 5 years, 11 months take six core subtests: Verbal Comprehension, Picture Similarities, Naming Vocabulary, Early Number Concepts, Copying, and Pattern Construction. These subtests combine to form the GCA as well as the Verbal Ability and Nonverbal Ability clusters. Keith (1990) critiqued the DAS and noted that it provided a good measure of overall level of functioning, and that it provided good measures of verbal and nonverbal abilities—even for preschoolers. Keith also reported that the factors of the DAS seemed to be stable across the age range of the test. As with most of the intellectual batteries, the DAS seems to hold great promise for inclusion in a larger preschool neuropsychological battery but, to date, few studies have examined its utility in this regard.

The Stanford-Binet Intelligence Scale-Fourth Edition (SB-IV) requires little in the way of introduction, and its use with preschool children has been well described (McCallum, 1991). As the Stanford-Binet begins its fifth revision (Wasserman, personal communication, January 29, 1998), it remains one of the major tools available to assess the intelligence of preschool children. In addition to its ability to tap overall level of functioning, the SB-IV attempted to provide estimates of separate domains of functioning. These included Verbal Reasoning, Quantitative Reasoning, Abstract/Visual Reasoning, and Short-Term Memory, and held potential to provide nice core components of a preschool neuropsychological battery. McCallum (1991) noted, however, that the technical adequacy of the SB-IV was less than impressive for preschoolers, although many of the core technical standards were satisfied. Furthermore, the four factors were not identified for the preschool portions of the battery, with two broader factors being recognized: verbal and nonverbal abilities (Thorndike, 1990). These difficulties with the factor structure seriously challenged the multidimensionality of the SB-IV at the preschool level, and probably has served to limit its use in neuropsychological testing with this population. The planned revision for the Stanford-Binet, however, currently will be based on contemporary factor analytic models of cognition (Carroll, 1993), and should hold great promise for inclusion in preschool neuropsychological testing procedures.

One last battery that will be mentioned with respect to its potential utility in preschool neuropsychological testing is the recent revision of the Leiter International Performance Scale (Leiter-R). The Leiter has been around since the early 1930s and has provided clinicians and researchers with a nonverbal measure of cognitive abilities. The current revision of the Leiter continues in that mode, being applicable to individuals ages 2 through 20 years, but the test is now based on item-response theory, factor analysis, and Rasch scaling. The Leiter-R consists of 20 subtests organized into four domains: reasoning, visualization, memory, and attention. Included within these domains are subtests tapping visual figure–ground, visual discrimination, visual sequencing, short-term and delayed visual memory and learning, nonverbal working memory, visual recognition memory, and sustained attention. Standard scores are provided along with age and grade equivalents that are directly tied to developmental growth curves. Reliability and validity of the test are satisfactory, and its application to children with a wide range of developmental disabilities and acquired problems appears promising. The factors of this battery appear to remain intact for preschool-age children, and they should assist in providing detailed cognitive descriptions of preschool children having a wide range of exceptionalities and levels of function. The Leiter-R also should prove useful in efforts to identify brain–behavior relationships in the preschool population.

Multidimensional Developmental Scales.   In addition to the standard measures of intelligence that are available, there are a number of multidimensional developmental scales that can be used quite nicely with a preschool population. The multidimensional nature of these scales make them possible candidates for inclusion in a neuropsychological appraisal of a preschool child. For example, the Battelle Developmental Inventory (BDI; Newborg, Stock, Wnek, Guidubaldi, & Svinicki, 1984) is a 341-item battery that can be used for children from birth up through age 8 years. The items are distributed across five domains and 22 subdomains: Personal Social (Adult Interaction, Expression of Feelings/Affect, Self-Concept, Peer Interactions, Copying, and Social Role), Adaptive (Attention, Eating, Dressing, Personal Responsibility, and Toileting), Motor (Muscle Control, Body Coordination, Locomotion, Fine Muscle, and Perceptual Motor), Communication (Receptive and Expressive), and Cognitive (Perceptual Discrimination, Memory, Reasoning and Academic Skills, and Conceptual Development). The BDI has a solid normative base and provides both developmental age and developmental quotients in the results. Further-

more, it has been used with preschool children with a variety of disorders (e.g., Fragile X Syndrome). Its utility in terms of brain–behavior relationships remains to be determined, but its multidimensionality should assist in developing a comprehensive neuropsychological appraisal for preschoolers.

Another such battery is the Mullen Scales of Early Learning (Mullen, 1995). The Mullen is a multidimensional test designed for infants and preschool children from birth through 68 months of age. It taps a child's functioning across five domains: Gross Motor (only for birth through 33 months), Visual Reception, Fine-Motor, Receptive Language, and Expressive Language. The Mullen yields normative scores (i.e., T-scores) for each of these domains, as well as an overall developmental score called the Early Learning Composite from the four cognitive scales. Those familiar with the Bayley Scales of Infant Development will see some similarities with the Mullen Scales, but the Mullen should lend itself to better assessment–treatment linkages and it seems to provide more details with respect to tracking developmental progress and/or recovery of function. This test clearly holds some merit for inclusion in a neuropsychological battery for preschoolers with exceptionalities.

Informal Neuropsychological Batteries

Despite these recent advances in neuropsychological, psychological, and developmental test procedures for preschool children, the greatest amount of work devoted to the preschool years has focused on the development of informal batteries. Lezak (1995) offered recommendations for the construction of informal test batteries. Lezak suggested that the construction of an informal battery should provide for the examination of a broad range of input and output functions. The actual procedures selected for inclusion should be developmentally appropriate, have satisfactorily normative data, and serve to provide for a certain degree of redundancy. The battery also should be practical in relation to the fundamental purpose(s) of the neuropsychological examination. Informal batteries also should have the capacity to address the qualitative (i.e., *how* a child performs or approaches a task) and quantitative (i.e., level and pattern of performance) aspects of a child's functioning, depending on the specific referral questions or general orientation of the examiner. With these guidelines in mind, several clinical and empirical preschool neuropsychological assessment models have emerged over the past several years that have described specific constructs important to this developmental time period. These models are listed in Table 18.1.

As can be seen from the models presented in Table 18.1, there is considerable overlap between the clinical models with respect to the neuropsychological constructs tested. Generally, these models attempt to assess language, motor skills, sensory-perceptual abilities, memory, higher-order problem solving, and preacademic skills, thus providing a comprehensive examination of a broad array of functions. The clinical models presented by Deysach (1986) and Wilson (1986, 1992) are noteworthy in their attempts to provide a systematic examination of a broad range of functions in a hierarchical fashion (i.e., systematically measuring simple to more complex functions). Deysach (1986) stated that it is useful to assess simple as well as more complex functions across both input and output modalities. Similarly,

Wilson (1986, 1992) presented a flexible, hypothesis-testing model utilizing a branching technique. Using her model, an initial assessment strategy is employed to assess higher-order, more complex cognitive processes. Depending on how the child performs on this initial testing procedure, additional assessment strategies are selected based on identified areas of weakness or concern in an effort to examine the child's difficulties in a more comprehensive manner. This "branching" or hypothesis-testing approach requires the examiner to be a keen observer and to be sensitive to qualitative and quantitative aspects of a child's performance.

In contrast to the clinical models, empirical models hold great potential for delineating specific neuropsychological constructs relevant to the preschool child. Utilizing a battery of neurocognitive tasks, Jansky (1970) provided one of the first studies uncovering specific

TABLE 18.1 Clinical and Empirical Models Proposing Neuropsychological Assessment Constructs for the Preschool Child

MODEL	NEUROPSYCHOLOGICAL CONSTRUCTS	MODEL	NEUROPSYCHOLOGICAL CONSTRUCTS
Clinical Models Aylward (1988)	Basic neurological functions Receptive functions Expressive functions Processing Mental activity		Auditory short-term memory Retrieval Visual Visual-spatial Visual cognition Visual short-term memory Motor Fine-motor Gross motor
Deysach (1986)	Gross motor Fine motor Sensory-perceptual Verbal Short-term memory Abstraction/concept formation	*Empirical Models* Jansky (1970)	Visual-motor Oral language Pattern matching Pattern memory
Hartlage & Telzrow (1986)	Cognitive ability Basic language Preacademic Motor Sensory Social Adaptive	Silver & Hagin (1972)	Auditory association Visual-neurological Psychiatric impairment Chronological age General intelligence
Wilson (1986)	Language Auditory integration Auditory cognition	Satz et al. (1978)	Socioeconomic status Conceptual-verbal Sensorimotor-perceptual

underlying neuropsychological constructs of the preschooler. In her factor analysis of these tasks, Jansky found factors encompassing oral language, memory, visual-motor abilities, and abstract thinking. All of these factors, particularly oral language, were found to be significantly predictive of second grade reading skills.

Silver and Hagin (1972) found five factors in their preschool assessment battery. These factors were slightly different than those obtained by Jansky (1970) and included factors measuring auditory association, visual-neurological functioning, higher-order problem solving, and interestingly, chronological age and psychiatric impairment. These factors accounted for approximately 61 percent of the entire battery, with the auditory association and visual-neurological factors being most predictive of later reading problems.

The final empirical study generating neuropsychological constructs relevant to the preschool child was conducted by Satz and colleagues (1978), who conducted a factor analysis of 16 variables obtained from a large kindergarten population that resulted in three factors accounting for approximately 68 percent of the variance. These factors spanned sensorimotor-perceptual skills, verbal conceptual abilities, and verbal-cultural variables. These investigators found their factors, especially the sensorimotor-perceptual factor, to be predictive of later reading problems. They also found the predictive relationship to vary according to developmental parameters, thus placing differential importance on different factors for particular developmental periods.

It should be noted that the development of the neuropsychological constructs associated with the empirical models emanated from examination of a specific population of children (i.e., children at risk for learning disabilities). Consequently, their generalizability to neuropsychological assessment of other neurologically impaired populations (e.g., preschool traumatic brain injury) remains to be seen. In general, the models provide evidence for constructs tapping motor, sensory, language, visual processing, memory, and abstract thinking/concept formation. An examination of these models reveals that only two of them (Deysach, 1986; Wilson, 1992) attempt to examine functions in a hierarchical fashion (i.e., simple to more complex), only one of the models addressed some aspect of executive functions (i.e., Deysach, 1986), and none of them specifically described attentional components. The importance of these latter domains highlights the need for a more comprehensive examination of underlying constructs within the preschool years (e.g., Gnys & Willis, 1991; Welsh, Pennington, & Grossier, 1991), particularly with

respect to developmental continuity into the school-age years and their overall utility with respect to diagnosis and treatment. Nonetheless, the clinical and empirical models provide the conceptual foundation for developing an informal neuropsychological assessment battery for the preschool child.

The specific constructs employed should be selected in an effort to obtain a broad-based assessment of abilities. The test selection will be limited only by their availability and the knowledge of the examiner. In this regard, Table 18.2 provides a set of proposed constructs, based on the models presented to date, and representative procedures that could be used in constructing an informal preschool neuropsychological battery. In general, it is suggested that the psychologist employ one of the major intellectual batteries (e.g., WPPSI-R, K-ABC, DAS) as the core of the neuropsychological assessment in tandem with measures of preacademic and social-behavioral functioning as needed. Depending on the psychometric qualities of the instrument selected, specific components of this tool could be used to address measurement within a specific construct. Additional neuropsychological procedures should be selected according to (1) the needs of the child, (2) the specific referral questions, and (3) the general philosophical approach of the examiner (e.g., is a branching assessment strategy being employed?). Furthermore, it will be important for the examiner to focus on observing the qualitative aspects of a child's spared and impaired abilities and, if appropriate, to gain information that will facilitate interpretation of the data using Reitan's four levels of inference. A hierarchical progression of tasks within a construct, ranging from simple to complex, will assist in identifying specific areas of concern. It also may be important, depending on the needs of the examiner, for the instruments selected to have adequate normative data for the preschool child so that all scores can be converted into a common metric for comparative purposes (e.g., T-scores). This also could facilitate developmental surveillance and related tracking of behavioral changes.

Informal batteries will require the child psychologist and neuropsychologist to have a good foundation in child development, a solid background in neurodevelopmental theory and related issues, and an extensive knowledge of relevant tools to use in conjunction with a particular set of constructs. With this in mind, however, the examiner employing an informal assessment approach should be keenly aware of the potential psychometric and interpretive difficulties posed by using multiple instruments having different normative bases. Furthermore, when using subtests from larger batteries, the examiner should be aware of the psychometric prop-

TABLE 18.2   A Sample of Selected Procedures for Key Neuropsychological Constructs in an Informal Battery

NEUROPSYCHOLOGICAL CONSTRUCT	REPRESENTATIVE MEASURES
Motor	Finger Oscillation (Electric)
	Purdue Pegboard
	Developmental Test of Visual-Motor Integration—Third Edition
Tactile-Perceptual	Finger Localization
	Tactile Form Recognition
Attention	Gordon Diagnostic System
	Goldman-Fristoe-Woodcock Auditory Selective Attention Test
Language	Expressive One Word Picture Vocabulary Test
	Peabody Picture Vocabulary Test—Third Edition
	Bracken Basic Concept Scale
Visual Processing	FKSB Recognition-Discrimination
	Test of Visual-Perceptual Skills
Memory	Goldman-Fristoe-Woodcock Auditory Memory Test
	K-ABC Face Recognition
Executive Functions	WPPSI-R Mazes Subtest
	Reitan-Indiana Progressive Figures Test
	Reitan-Indiana Color Form Test

erties of those tasks (e.g., subtest specificities) in order to understand the limits of their interpretability.

Screening Approaches

Neuropsychological screening approaches attempt to identify those children with suspected central nervous system involvement and differentiate them from their typically developing peers. Screening procedures should not be designed to be definitive with respect to their diagnostic capabilities, but they should have significant sensitivity to the problem in question. It is unlikely that a single test could serve as an adequate neuropsychological screening tool. In fact, Lezak (1995) recommended the use of a multiple-test approach in structuring a screening battery. Lezak suggested that some tests should be sensitive to generalized neurological dysfunction and others should be selected because of their sensi-

tivity to specific functional domains. It also might prove fruitful to include instruments that encompass Reitan's four methods of inference in an effort to broaden the interpretive base of a screening battery. Tupper (1986) stated that a good neuropsychological screening battery should be age/developmentally appropriate, acceptable to the professionals who will be following the child, and easy to administer and interpret. It also should have satisfactory reliability and validity, demonstrate acceptable sensitivity (i.e., identify true problems) and specificity (i.e., identify true normals), and be cost-effective.

There are numerous psychological screening procedures available for preschool children (Lichtenstein & Ireton, 1991), most of which have been designed to identify children who are at risk for later learning impediments. Some of the more prominent preschool screening batteries include the Florida Kindergarten Screening Battery (FKSB; Satz & Fletcher, 1982), the McCarthy

Screening Test (MST; McCarthy, 1978), the Quick Neurological Screening Test (QNST; Mutti, Sterling, & Spalding, 1978), the Neurological Dysfunctions of Children (NDOC; Kuhns, 1979), and the Pediatric Extended Examination at Three (PEET; Blackman, Levine, & Markowitz, 1986).

The FKSB and MST were both designed to predict later academic difficulties when given during the preschool years. In particular, the FKSB was developed from a larger battery of neuropsychological measures with the final tasks being selected based on their combined predictive accuracy. It requires approximately one hour for administration and includes four tasks: Recognition-Discrimination, Finger Localization, Peabody Picture Vocabulary Test—Revised, and the Developmental Test of Visual-Motor Integration. These latter tests have been revised in the past several years and it remains unclear how the revised versions of these tests will impact on the overall predictive accuracy of this battery. Alphabet Recitation is an optional fifth test. Although the FKSB has been criticized (Gates, 1984), it still represents one of the first screening batteries developed from a neuropsychological perspective.

The MST was designed as an abbreviated version of the MSCA. Employed for children ages 4½ to 6, it contains 6 of the 18 parent scale's subtests and classifies children as "at risk" or "not at risk." Specific subtests were included because of their simplicity in administration, ease of scoring, and their minimal time requirements. These included Right-Left Orientation, Verbal Memory, Draw-A-Design, Numerical Memory, Conceptual Grouping, and Leg Coordination. The MST requires about 20 to 30 minutes to administer. There has been little work examining the neuropsychological utility of this screening tool and, given the relatively dated nature of the normative base in tandem with emergent assessment technology, the future of this tool is uncertain.

The NDOC and QNST are somewhat different in their conceptualization and largely attempt to assess soft neurological signs. Neither of these procedures provides much data to support their screening capabilities, but Tupper (1986) noted that these procedures do seem to have face validity. The NDOC is an 18-item examination that is scored in a dichotomous "yes–no" fashion. It can be used for children as young as age 3 years and interpretation is aided by 13 different item clusters.

The QNST similarly contains 15 items measuring a variety of soft signs (e.g., repetitive hand movements, tandem walking). Although a numerical score is obtained for each item, a large portion of the interpretation is qualitative in nature and focuses on *how* a child per-

forms a particular task. Based on the scores obtained, the QNST classifies children into High, Suspicious, and Normal categories, with the first two classifications suggesting possible central nervous system dysfunction.

A final screening instrument to be discussed is the PEET. The PEET is a neurodevelopmental assessment system constructed to contribute to the early identification and understanding of learning, attentional, and behavior problems in children ages 3 to 4. The PEET provides tasks assessing gross and fine-motor skills, language, visual-motor, memory, and intersensory integration. These tasks are structured around three major input-output channels including Auditory-Verbal Communication, Visually Directed Manipulation, and Spatial-Somatic Integration. Within each channel a hierarchy of increasingly complex functions is represented that provides a unique interpretive asset for individuals using this screening tool. A child's behavior during the examination also can be rated in a systematic fashion. Although the multidimensionality of this screening battery is intriguing, and generally more comprehensive than its competitors, very little information has been generated with respect to its reliability and validity, particularly with respect to its stated purposes (Blackman, Levine, Markowitz, & Aufseeser, 1983).

ISSUES IN PRESCHOOL NEUROPSYCHOLOGICAL ASSESSMENT

Unlike assessment with adults and older children, testing with preschool children tends to present a unique set of potential problems and issues that can influence neuropsychological results. First and foremost is the young age of the child. Preschoolers have precious little stamina for sitting still and concentrating for prolonged periods of time. In fact, these developmental concerns likely will be exacerbated in a child manifesting neurological or neurodevelopmental problems. Consequently, subjecting a preschool child to a long testing regimen actually could prove counterproductive. The clinician should attempt to modify the assessment battery to address the referral questions thoroughly, but efficiently, and to fit the needs of the child (e.g., perhaps employing multiple sessions).

Second, and related to the age of the child, is the issue of testing protocol. Just because you tell youngsters to work quickly, or as fast as they can, does not mean that they will. Concepts related to speed, following directions, and waiting for the next instruction are just coming into the awareness of preschool children, and these "test savvy" behaviors actually may be nonexistent in children who have not attended some kind of preschool setting. Temperamental issues may be present as well, and these issues need to be addressed by the examiner. Although these issues may seem trite to the experienced examiner, they can be devastating to obtaining reliable neuropsychological test data.

The reliability of a preschooler's responses also is a constant issue. In this regard, and in tandem with Lezak's (1995) suggestions for developing an informal battery, it will be critical for a certain amount of redundancy and task repetition to be built into a neuropsychological battery in an effort to account for these "normal" response inconsistencies. This becomes particularly important in profile interpretation and in the planning of intervention strategies. These response inconsistencies of the preschool child also may contribute to lowering the magnitude of predictor-criterion relationships in this population which, in turn, will interfere with prognostic implications.

Finally, the brain–behavior relationships in this population need to continue to receive investigation. Little is known about these relationships at present, although the interjection of a neurodevelopmental framework will provide a vehicle for increasing the understanding of these relationships. The interaction and possible synergistic effects between biological and psychosocial factors in a child's (neuro)development also need to be incorporated into any neuropsychological assessment paradigm that might be utilized. In fact, the psychologist or neuropsychologist providing neuropsychological assessment to the preschool child should have a strong foundation in central nervous system development and neurodevelopmental theory, and it should be this foundation that guides test selection and interpretation for any particular preschool child. Although a discussion of these issues is beyond the scope of this chapter, comprehensive presentations can be obtained elsewhere (Kolb & Fantie, 1997; Teeter & Semrud-Clikeman, 1997).

CONCLUSIONS

This chapter has provided an overview of neuropsychological assessment procedures for the preschool child. In addition to discussing relevant issues supporting the use of a neuropsychological perspective with preschool children, a variety of assessment procedures was presented. Noteworthy among these procedures is the recent publication of a comprehensive neuropsychological battery for children that has a downward extension into the preschool years. Although the clinical and research utility of the NEPSY with preschool children remains to be determined, its neurodevelopmental theoretical foundation and good psychometric properties make it a strong candidate to advance the field of child neuropsychology with preschoolers. At the very least, the NEPSY does seem to offer the field an assessment alternative that has never been available previously.

Although the recent assessment technology is a welcomed addition to the field of child neuropsychology, the informal battery approach to preschool neuropsychological assessment remains highly utilized. Several models are available for formulation of broad-band constructs; however, more work is needed here with respect to providing a comprehensive array of constructs for the preschool years. These models require the examiner to be familiar with a wide variety of assessment tasks, and the interpretation of the informal battery demands knowledge of normal and abnormal brain development and the application of neurodevelopmental theory. In this regard, several intellectual measures have been published that also hold promise for inclusion in the neuropsychological assessment of preschool children. Noteworthy among these batteries is the Differential Ability Scales and the Leiter International Performance Scale—Revised. Their breadth of coverage and strong technical properties should strengthen any informal assessment battery in which they may be utilized.

Finally, it is important to recognize that a preschool neuropsychological assessment should go beyond what might be obtained from more traditional psychological assessments at this age level, and it has the potential to address the specific needs of a preschooler with exceptionalities in a comprehensive fashion. With the development of neuropsychological tasks sensitive to the various aspects of brain development, and the increased understanding of the impact of various neuropathological processes during these critical years, the development of preschool neuropsychological assessment also will continue to move forward. It will be exciting to see what advances have emerged in the neuropsychological assessment of preschool children during the next decade.

REFERENCES

Aylward, G. P. (1988). Infant and early childhood assessment. In M. G. Tramontana & S. R. Hooper (Eds.), *Assessment issues in child neuropsychology* (pp. 225–248). New York: Plenum.

Aylward, G. P. (1997). *Infant and early childhood neuropsychology.* New York: Guilford Press.

Aylward, G. P., Gustafson, N., Verhulst, S. J., & Colliver, J. A. (1987). Consistency in the diagnosis of cognitive, motor, and neurologic function over the first three years. *Journal of Pediatric Psychology, 12,* 77–98.

Bagnato, S. J., & Dickerson-Mayes, S. (1986). Patterns of developmental and behavioral progress for young brain-injured children during interdisciplinary intervention. *Developmental Neuropsychology, 2,* 213–240.

Behr, S., & Gallagher, J. J. (1981). Alternative administrative strategies for young handicapped children. A policy analysis. *Journal of the Division for Early-Childhood, 2,* 113–122.

Blackman, J. A., Levine, M. D., & Markowitz, M. (1986). *Pediatric Extended Examination at Three.* Cambridge, MA: Educators Publishing Service.

Blackman, J. A., Levine, M. D., Markowitz, M. T., & Aufseeser, C. L. (1983). The pediatric extended examination at three. A system for diagnostic clarification of problematic three-year-olds. *Developmental and Behavioral Pediatrics, 4,* 143–150.

Blair, C., Ramey, C. T., & Hardin, J. M. (1995). Early intervention for low birth weight, premature infants: Participation and intellectual development. *American Journal on Mental Retardation, 99,* 542–554.

Boll, T. J., & Barth, J. T. (1981). Neuropsychology of brain damage in children. In S. B. Filskov & T. J. Boll (Eds.), *Handbook of clinical neuropsychology* (pp. 418–452). New York: John Wiley and Sons.

Bracken, B. A. (1991). The assessment of preschool children with the McCarthy Scales of Children's Abilities. In B. A. Bracken (Ed.), *The psychoeducational assessment of preschool children* (2nd ed., pp. 53–85). Boston: Allyn & Bacon.

Carroll, J. B. (1993). *Human cognitive abilities: A survey of factor-analytic studies.* New York: Cambridge University Press.

Chadwick, O., & Rutter, M. (1983). Neuropsychological assessment. In M. Rutter (Ed.), *Developmental neuropsychiatry* (pp. 181–212). New York: Guilford Press.

Chelune, G. J., & Edwards, P. (1981). Early brain lesions. Ontogenetic-environmental considerations. *Journal of Consulting and Clinical Psychology, 49,* 777–790.

Craft, A., Shaw, D., & Cartlidge, N. (1972). Head injuries in children. *British Medical Journal, 4,* 200–203.

Dennis, M. (1985a). Intelligence after early brain injury. I. Predicting IQ scores from medical variables. *Journal of Clinical and Experimental Neuropsychology, 7,* 526–554.

Dennis, M. (1985b). Intelligence after early brain injury. II. IQ scores of subjects classified on the basis of medical history variables. *Journal of Clinical and Experimental Neuropsychology, 7,* 555–576.

Deysach, R. E. (1986). The role of neuropsychological assessment in the comprehensive evaluation of preschool-age children. *School Psychology Review, 15,* 233–244.

Ellison, P. H. (1983). The relationship of motor and cognitive function in infancy, preschool and early school years. *Journal of Clinical Child Psychology, 12,* 81–90.

Ewing-Cobbs, L., Fletcher, J. M., Levin, H. S., Francis, D. J., Davidson, K., & Miner, M. E. (1997). Longitudinal neuropsychological outcome in infants and preschoolers with traumatic brain injury. *Journal of the International Neuropsychological Society, 3,* 581–591.

Gates, R. D. (1984). Florida Kindergarten Screening Battery (Test Review). *Journal of Clinical Neuropsychology, 6,* 459–465.

Gnys, J. A., & Willis, W. G. (1991). Validation of executive function tasks with young children. *Developmental Neuropsychology, 7,* 487–501.

Hartlage, L. C., & Telzrow, C. F. (1982). Neuropsychological assessment. In K. Paget & B. A. Bracken (Eds.), *Psychoeducational assessment of preschool children* (pp. 295–320). New York: Grune and Stratton.

Hartlage, L. C., & Telzrow, C. F. (1986). *Neuropsychological assessment and intervention with children and adolescents.* Sarasota, FL: Professional Resource Exchange.

Hooper, S. R. (1988). The prediction of learning disabilities in the preschool child: A neuropsychological perspective. In M. G. Tramontana & S. R. Hooper (Eds.), *Assessment issues in child neuropsychology* (pp. 313–335). New York: Plenum.

Hooper, S. R. (1991). Neuropsychological assessment of the preschool child: Issues and procedures. In B. A. Bracken (Ed.), *The psychoeducational assessment of preschool children* (2nd ed., pp. 465–485). Boston: Allyn and Bacon.

Horn, W. G., & Packard, T. (1985). Early identification of learning problems. A meta-analysis. *Journal of Educational Psychology, 77,* 597–607.

Incagnoli, T., & Newman, B. (1985). Cognitive and behavioral interventions. *International Journal of Clinical Neuropsychology, 7,* 173–182.

Jansky, J. J. (1970). *The contribution of certain kindergarten abilities to second grade reading and spell-*

ing achievement. Unpublished doctoral dissertation, Columbia University, New York.

Kalverboer, A. F. (1971). Free-field behavior in preschool boys and girls. In G. B. Stoelinga & J. J. Van der Werff Tem Bosch (Eds.), *Normal and abnormal development of brain and behavior* (pp. 187–203). The Netherlands: Leiden University Press.

Keith, T. Z. (1990). Confirmatory and hierarchical confirmatory analysis of the Differential Ability Scales. *Journal of Psychoeducational Assessment, 8,* 391–405.

Kolb, B., & Fantie, B. (1997). Development of the child's brain and behavior. In C. R. Reynolds & E. Fletcher-Janzen (Eds.), *Handbook of clinical child neuropsychology* (2nd ed., pp. 17–41). New York: Plenum Press.

Korkman, M., Kirk, U., & Kemp, S. (1998). *NEPSY. A Developmental Neuropsychological Assessment.* San Antonio, TX: Psychological Corporation.

Korkman, M., & Peltomaa, A. K. (1993). Preventive treatment of dyslexia by a preschool training program for children with language impairments. *Journal of Clinical Child Psychology, 22,* 277–287.

Kuhns, J. W. (1979). *Neurological dysfunctions of children.* Monterey, CA: Publishers Test Service.

Landry, S. H., Jordan, T., & Fletcher, J. M. (1994). Developmental outcomes for children with spina bifida and hydrocephalus. In M. G. Tramontana & S. R. Hooper (Eds.), *Advances in child neuropsychology* (Vol. 2, pp. 85–118). New York: Springer-Verlag.

Lezak, M. D. (1995). *Neuropsychological assessment* (4th ed.). New York: Oxford University Press.

Lichtenstein, R., & Ireton, H. (1991). Preschool screening for developmental and educational problems. In B. A. Bracken (Ed.), *The psychoeducational assessment of preschool children* (2nd ed., pp. 486–513). Boston: Allyn and Bacon.

Luria, A. R. (1980). *The working brain.* New York: Basic Books.

Majovski, L. V. (1984). The K-ABC. Theory and applications for child neuropsychological assessment and research. *Journal of Special Education, 18,* 257–268.

Mariani, M. I., & Barkley, R. A. (1997). Neuropsychological and academic functioning of preschool boys with Attention Deficit Hyperactivity Disorder. *Developmental Neuropsychology, 13,* 111–129.

McCallum, R. S. (1991). The assessment of preschool children with the Stanford-Binet Intelligence Scale: Fourth Edition. In B. A. Bracken (Ed.), *The psycho-*

educational assessment of preschool children (2nd ed., pp. 107–132). Boston: Allyn and Bacon.

McCarthy, D. (1978). *Manual for the McCarthy Screening Test.* New York: Psychological Corporation.

Molfese, D. L., & Molfese, V. J. (1997). Discrimination of language skills at five years of age using event-related potentials recorded at birth. *Developmental Neuropsychology, 13,* 135–156.

Molfese, V. J. (1992). Neuropsychological assessment in infancy. In F. Boller & J. Grafman (Series Eds.), I. Rapin & S. J. Segalowitz (Section Eds.), *Handbook of neuropsychology: Volume 6. Child neuropsychology* (pp. 353–376). Amsterdam: Elsevier.

Mullen, E. M. (1995). *Mullen Scales of Early Learning.* Circle Pines, MN: American Guidance Service.

Mutti, M., Sterling, H. M., & Spalding, N. V. (1978). *QNST: Quick Neurological Screening Test* (rev. ed.). Novato, CA: Academic Therapy Publications.

National Joint Committee on Learning Disabilities (NJ-CLD). (1986). *A position paper of the National Joint Committee on Learning Disabilities.* Baltimore: Orton Dyslexia Society.

Newborg, J., Stock, J. R., Wnek, L., Guidubaldi, J., & Svinicki, J. (1984). *Battelle Developmental Inventory.* Allen, TX: DLM Teaching Resources.

Ramey, C. T., & Ramey, L. R. (1994). Which children benefit the most from early intervention? *Pediatrics, 94,* 1064–1066.

Reitan, R. M. (1969). *Manual for administration of neuropsychological test batteries for adults and children.* Indianapolis, IN: Author.

Reitan, R. M. (1974). Psychological effects of cerebral lesions in children of early school age. In R. M. Reitan & L. A. Davison (Eds.), *Clinical neuropsychology: Current status and applications* (pp. 53–90). New York: John Wiley and Sons.

Reitan, R. M., & Davison, L. A. (Eds.) (1974). *Clinical neuropsychology: Current status and applications.* New York: John Wiley and Sons.

Reynolds, C. R, Kamphaus, R. W., Rosenthal, B. L. & Hiemenz, J. R. (1997). Applications of the Kaufman Assessment Battery for Children (K-ABC) in neuropsychological assessment. In C. R. Reynolds & E. Fletcher-Janzen (Eds.), *Handbook of clinical child neuropsychology* (2nd ed., pp. 252–269). New York: Plenum.

Rourke, B. P. (1983). Outstanding issues in research on learning disabilities. In M. Rutter (Ed.), *Developmental neuropsychiatry* (pp. 564–574). New York: Guilford Press.

Rourke, B. P., Bakker, D. J., Fisk, J. L., & Strang, J. D. (1983). *Child neuropsychology.* New York: Guilford Press.

Sattler, J. (1994). *Assessment of children.* San Diego, CA: Author.

Satz, P., & Fletcher, J. M. (1982*). Florida Kindergarten Screening Battery.* Odessa, FL: Psychological Assessment Resources.

Satz, P., Taylor, H. G., Friel, J., & Fletcher., J. M. (1978). Some developmental and predictive precursors of reading disabilities. A six-year follow-up. In A. L. Benton & D. Pearl (Eds.), *Dyslexia: an appraisal of current knowledge* (pp. 315–347). New York: Oxford University Press.

Selz, M., & Reitan, R. M. (1979). Rules for neuropsychological diagnosis and classification of brain function in older children. *Journal of Consulting and Clinical Psychology, 47,* 258–264.

Silver, A. A., & Hagin, R. A. (1972). Profile of a first grade. A basis for preventive psychiatry. *Journal of the American Academy of Child Psychiatry, 11,* 645–674.

Sommerfelt, K., Markestad, T., & Ellertsen, B. (1998). Neuropsychological performance in low birth weight preschoolers: A population-based, controlled study. *European Journal of Pediatrics, 157,* 53–58.

Spreen, O., & Haaf, R. G. (1986). Empirically derived learning disability subtypes. A replication attempt and longitudinal patterns over 15 years. *Journal of Learning Disabilities, 19,* 170–180.

Stevenson, H. W., & Newman, R. S. (1986). Long-term prediction of achievement and attitudes in mathematics and reading. *Child Development, 57,* 646–659.

Teeter, P. A. (1985). Neurodevelopmental investigation of academic achievement. A report of years 1 and 2 of a longitudinal study. *Journal of Consulting and Clinical Psychology, 53,* 709–717.

Teeter, P. A., & Semrud-Clikeman, M. (1997). *Child neuropsychology. Assessment and interventions for neurodevelopmental disorders.* Boston: Allyn and Bacon.

Thorndike, R. M. (1990). Would the real factors of the Stanford-Binet Fourth Edition please come forward? *Journal of Psychoeducational Assessment, 8,* 412–435.

Townes, B. D., Turpin, E. W., Martin, D.C., & Goldstein, D. (1980). Neuropsychological correlates of academic success among elementary school children. *Journal of Consulting and Clinical Psychology, 6,* 675–684.

Tramontana, M. G., & Hooper, S. R. (Eds.) (1988a). *Assessment issues in child neuropsychology.* New York: Plenum.

Tramontana, M. G., & Hooper, S. R. (1988b). Child neuropsychological assessment. Overview of current status. In M. G. Tramontana & S. R. Hooper (Eds.), *Assessment issues in child neuropsychology* (pp. 1–38). New York: Plenum.

Tramontana, M. G., Hooper, S. R., & Selzer, S. C. (1988). Research on the preschool prediction of later academic achievement. *Developmental Review, 8,* 89–147.

Tupper, D. E. (1986). Neuropsychological screening and soft signs. In J. E. Obrzut & G. W. Hynd (Eds.), *Child neuropsychology, Vol. 2: Clinical practice* (pp. 139–186). New York: Academic Press.

Umansky, W., & Hooper, S. R. (Eds.) (1998). *Young children with special needs* (3rd ed.). Upper Saddle River, NJ: Prentice Hall.

Walsh, K. K., Kastner, T. A., & Harmon, R. F. (1996). Crack cocaine exposure in preschool children: Focusing on the relevant issues [comment]. *Journal of Developmental and Behavioral Pediatrics, 16,* 418–424.

Welsh, M. C., Pennington, B. F., & Grossier, D. B. (1991). A normative-developmental study of executive functions: A window on prefrontal function in children. *Developmental Neuropsychology, 7,* 131–149.

Wilson, B. C. (1986). An approach to the neuropsychological assessment of the preschool child with developmental deficits. In S. B. Filskov & T. J. Boll (Eds.), *Handbook of clinical neuropsychology, Vol. 2* (pp. 121–171). New York: Wiley.

Wilson, B. C. (1992). The neuropsychological assessment of the preschool child: A branching model. In F. Boller & J. Grafman (Series Eds.), I. Rapin & S. J. Segalowitz (Section Eds.), *Handbook of neuropsychology: Vol. 6. Child neuropsychology* (pp. 377–394). Amsterdam: Elsevier.

Wrightson, P., McGinn, B., & Gronwall, D. (1995). Mild head injury in preschool children: Evidence that it can be associated with a persisting cognitive defect. *Journal of Neurology, Neurosurgery, and Psychiatry, 59,* 375–380.

CHAPTER 19

EARLY CHILDHOOD SCREENING FOR DEVELOPMENTAL AND EDUCATIONAL PROBLEMS

GILBERT R. GREDLER

The stated purpose for early childhood screening is to identify those children who may have difficulty in learning as they enter school. School personnel then plan and implement appropriate interventions for these children.

This chapter will address a number of issues involved in screening children aged 3 to 6: difficulties in making predictions about possible developmental and learning problems, methods of determining the adequacy of the screening measures, and suggestions about ways to improve early identification procedures.

The current practice of early screening of children was derived from the practice of early medical screening (Potton, 1983). The purpose of medical screening is to detect disorders that can be certified by additional tests and appropriate treatment then instituted. Such early assessment and treatment actions obviously can produce major benefits for the child. One such benefit is that which results from screening newborns for PKU. Prior to legislation that mandated such testing, this condition typically was not diagnosed until children were 4 years of age. However, when treatment for PKU is not begun in the early weeks of life, mental retardation soon becomes evident. Thus, early screening and treatment have effectively reduced the problem (Frankenburg, 1985).

Assumptions of psychological and educational screening at an early age reflect the functioning of the medical model. They are as follows:

1. "early identification can accurately pinpoint the child's difficulties and a program can then be tailored to help ameliorate these difficulties";
2. if early detection is not undertaken, the child is likely to remain behind during most of his or her school years;
3. preschool screening will, in some cases, lead to "total or near total remediation of...problems prior to the beginning of first grade." (Reynolds, 1979, p. 277).

These assumptions imply that (1) psychological and educational screening is the primary mechanism of identifying problems, and (2) accurate predictions about subsequent developmental and learning problems can be made about young children.

Potton (1983) noted that psychologists and educators often attempt to identify children at an early age who are likely to have reading problems due to a delay in language or speech development or because of emotional problems or cognitive deficits. However, he indicated that such personnel are speculating that the child will be vulnerable to learning problems as a result of these specific factors. According to Potton, the process should be labeled "speculative screening" because the poor performance has not yet appeared and it is not certain that the child will indeed experience learning problems.

Dworkin (1989) also noted that screening is not the only process by which developmental problems are detected. Conditions such as cerebral palsy, muscular dystrophy, moderate and severe mental retardation, Down syndrome, and autism are detected by other methods. These additional methods include (1) suspicions on the part of the parents, (2) abnormalities found from a pediatric examination, (3) a family history of a handicap, or (4) problems resulting from an accident or illness (p. 1002).

The result is that the goal of a screening program in the school will probably be aimed more at subtle impairments in development such as language delays, possible learning disabilities, mild retardation and problematic motor skills (Adelman, 1982; Dworkin, 1985; Keogh & Bernheimer, 1996).

DIFFICULTIES IN PREDICTING LEARNING PROBLEMS

Several issues must be considered when screening for possible learning problems in young children. The first issue is related to identifying learning disabilities. Keogh & Bernheimer (1996) state that if learning disability is defined within an educational framework such a definition "almost precludes identification in the early years" (p. 21). They also point out that language problems, delays in neurodevelopment, as well as behavioral problems, may not be signs of learning disabilities. Instead, they may be reflective of problems that are present in children with mild retardation or maladjustment (p. 27).

Other screening issues are related to instability of young children's behavior, determining the meaning of the "at-risk" label, and the use of inappropriate screening measures. This latter issue can be divided into two parts: (1) historical attempts by the school to screen for learning and behavioral problems, and (2) psychometric issues in the use of tests and observational and behavioral checklists.

The following sections will consider each of these topics. First a discussion of traditional screening approaches used by schools is presented.

TRADITIONAL APPROACHES TO SCHOOL SCREENING

American schools have been involved for over 50 years in screening young children who were believed to be at risk for academic failure. Described next are the most common screening methods used in the schools.

Raising the Entrance Age

Quite popular as a screening device is the belief that children can be effectively screened for possible learning problems by insisting on a high chronological age before entry to school. That this belief has strong support can be seen by the steady rise in the age required for school entrance over the past 40 years. Where most schools once allowed children to enter school if they attained a chronological age of 5 by December 1 or December 31, the prevailing entrance age cutoff date today is September 1.

Maturational psychologists and educators insist that with a higher entrance age most behavioral and learning problems of young children will lessen if not disappear. However, as long ago as 1959, Clark recog-

nized the extensive variability in mental age present in any age group within a chronological age range of 12 months. He stated that "changing the chronological entrance age for boys and girls is an inefficient way of meeting the problem (of ability to learn) and will create as many problems as it will solve" (p. 70).

Placement in Special Programs

Another historical approach to reduce possible learning problems has been to inaugurate special programs. For the "unready" preschool child, a prekindergarten program was offered. For the unready kindergarten child, a two-year kindergarten program might be suggested; for an unready child, eligible for first grade, a pre–first grade or transition program would be suggested. The purpose of many school screening programs was to simply find the unready child and then offer the parents one of the foregoing options.

Retention

The most common method used by schools for children with learning problems has been retention. Although retention is used at all grade levels, this device is particularly popular when dealing with kindergarten and first grade children. For instance, from 1988 to 1989 California schools retained 57,000 students. Of this number, 23,000 or 40 percent repeated kindergarten and almost 18,000 or 32 percent repeated first grade. Thus, 72 percent of all elementary school retentions in California for that year occurred in kindergarten and first grade. In Greenville, South Carolina, 997 students were retained during the school year from 1995 to 1996. Of that number 40 percent or about 400 students were failed in first grade.

A major problem with the use of retention is that the specific learning problems of the child do not receive needed attention. Another issue that must be addressed is the instability of the child's behavior.

Instability of Behavior

Silva and Ross (1980) investigated the motor development of children at age 3 and again at age 5; their results indicate the ephemeral nature of these deficits. Of 800 children tested, 31 demonstrated poor motor performance at age 3. However, at age 5, only 10 of the 31 children continued to exhibit poor motor performance. The other 21 children did not differ from the total sample on motor ability, language, or assessed intelligence.

The 10 children who continued to perform poorly on motor tests at age 5 also were deficient in language and intellictual level at that age. However, the other 21 children who performed poorly at age 3 had caught up by age 5. Had the results of the tests of the 3-year-olds been used to identify potential learning problems, two out of three children would have been misclassified.

The results of the Silva and Ross study indicate that motor delays observed in many children at age 3 tend to be unstable and often may not be associated with other areas of the child's development. The researchers concluded that "these results do not suggest that delayed motor development, at least at the preschool level, deserves identification and intervention efforts" (Silva & Ross, 1980, p. 224).

McGuire and Richman (1987) investigated the persistence of behavior problems in children aged 2 to 4 years. In a sample of 300 children attending regular school, 91 percent who originally had shown no problem behaviors had the same status 20 months later. Of the children rated as having problems, 90 percent showed improvement in behavior without any special intervention. In a group of 109 children attending day care facilities, 86 percent of the children who originally were judged as showing no problem behavior continued in that classification. However, only 42 percent of the problem children showed improvement. McGuire and Richman suggest that, in this latter case, high parental unemployment, low SES status, and family stress were influential in explaining the differences in outcome between the two groups of children.

Of importance is that 58 percent of the "problem" children with adverse family backgrounds demonstrated definite improvement in behavior 20 months later without any special intervention efforts.

Lindsay (1984) also made pertinent comments about the variability in behavior: "Children not only develop at different rates, they change position relative to each other on different dimensions, and also their own profiles of abilities over time" (p. 175). Also, for early identification to make sense, there must be sufficient consistency over time between a child's early functioning and what is educationally significant for the child in later years (Lichtenstein & Ireton, 1984, p. 65).

Lindsay (1984) also stated: "A child's status at any time is seen to be a result of the interaction between intrinsic and extrinsic strength and weaknesses. In addi-

tion, there is a third dimension of time: the pattern may change from month to month, or even more quickly" (p. 176). Lindsay continued by mentioning that children at the extremes (of a distribution) are more predictable, but this evidence applies to groups of children. The performance of individuals within these groups may be quite variable; however, the performance of the majority of children who are not at the extremes and who are not subject to extensive influences may also be quite variable (Lindsay, 1984, p. 176).

Use of Inappropriate Measures

Instruments used to identify or predict problems in learning and/or behavior must undergo stringent development procedures to ensure accuracy. As discussed in a later section of this chapter, error rates of these measures are much higher than commonly believed. In order to rely on the score obtained from a screening test, the test must have adequate validity and reliability. The concept of validity refers to the degree to which the test actually measures the behavior in which we are interested (Aylward, 1994). The concept of reliability refers to the degree that the results of our measurement will be consistent. In other words, repeating the measurement should yield similar results (Aylward, 1994).

Defining the At-Risk Population

The educational concept of "at risk" is of an abstract nature, is composed of complicated concepts, and is difficult to explain by a single score from a screening test (Potton, 1983).

Difficulty in reaching agreement about which child is truly at risk for later learning problems is widespread. Estimates of those who are likely to have learning problems later in school have varied from 7 percent to 50 percent of the school population (Leach, 1980). Often the definition of a potential learning problem is derived from the particular philosophy of the school. For example, schools that expect a high level of reading readiness skills or knowledge of words and letters in those children entering first grade will define learning problems differently from schools that do not hold these expectations for the children.

Because schools define success in school in different ways, the concept of who is at risk will, therefore, also vary. For example, an analysis of the schools in Boulder, Colorado, indicated that kindergarten retention rates varied from 0 to 25 percent. The children who were labeled as failures in one school (and who were retained) had counterparts of similar kindergarten performance in another school who were promoted to first grade and succeeded (Shepard & Smith, 1985).

Different expectations for entering abilities and different definitions of success, therefore, constitute one problem in defining the at-risk population. Another problem is that no screening instrument can assess the quality of teaching that the child will receive. In other words, accurately defining who is at risk requires an analysis of the subsequent teaching environment.

These concerns and problems lead us to ask how an appropriate screening program can be devised. Brown (1996), a professor of pediatrics, is quite adamant about the attempt to identify preschool-age children as being at risk for learning disabilities. He stated that "unfortunately, a reliable method for identifying children with learning disabilities at an early age (before first grade, and usually not until beginning second grade) does not yet exist" (p. 38).

In the sections that follow desired characteristics of screening measures and the types of screening measures in use will be discussed. Then suggestions for organizing a screening program will be outlined.

Developmental Screening Tests and School Readiness Measures

Two types of instruments are commonly used to screen young children: developmental screening measures and readiness measures. Developmental screening measures are designed to assess the developmental level of the child's potential to acquire skills rather than the degree to which a specific skill has been acquired (Meisels, 1994). Such screening tests typically examine motor coordination, memory of visual sequences, verbal expression, language comprehension, and social-emotional status (Lichenstein & Ireton, 1991; Meisels, 1994).

Readiness tests tend to assess skills believed to be related to school learning tasks and to be predictive of school success. Areas included on readiness tests are cognitive skills, language, motor skills, copying shapes, concept development, and perceptual processes (Lichenstein & Ireton, 1991).

Although these descriptions indicate differences between developmental screening tests and school readiness tests, Lichenstein and Ireton (1991) note that "it is difficult to make clear content distinctions between developmental and school readiness measures" (p. 493). Shepard and

Graue (1993) also state that developmental screening measures are like mini-IQ tests; an analysis of content overlap between particular developmental screening measures and IQ tests indicates that these measures contain 60 percent to 90 percent similar items (p. 297).

CALCULATING PREDICTIVE VALIDITY OF SCREENING MEASURES

Regardless of whether a developmental screening test, readiness measure, or a teacher rating scale is used, the intent is to predict future performance or behavior. Therefore, to determine if a child has developmental deficits the psychometric properties of such measures must be analyzed first.

The child's score on a test or rating scale functions as a prediction score. That is, if placed in the regular kindergarten or first grade, the child is predicted to experience problems in learning.

A test or screening measure that identifies those children with potential learning problems and does not misclassify other children is said to have predictive validity. Determining the predictive validity of an instrument requires two sets of data. One is the children's scores on the screening measure. Then, one or more years later, data are collected again on the children to determine which children actually developed problems. Typically, some type of achievement measure or behavioral rating scale is used at that time. This assessment is referred to as the criterion measure.

Two types of information are determined from the scores on the screening measure. They are the number of children identified as at risk and the number identified as not at risk. Two types of information also are determined from the scores on the criterion measure. They are the number of children who developed learning problems or behavioral problems and the number who did not (as indicated by adequate school performance).

In other words, the data from administration of the screening test and the criterion measure yield four possible outcomes. Organization of the data into a 2×2 matrix provides a basis for the analysis of the screening measure (see Table 19.1).

In the matrix, the numbers of children accurately identified by the screening measure are represented by Cells *a* and *d*. That is, the number of children predicted to have learning problems and who subsequently performed poorly are found in Cell *a*. This group is referred to as the valid positives. Cell *d* reflects the number who were identified as not at risk and who later performed

TABLE 19.1 Possible Outcomes of Screening

SUBSEQUENT PERFORMANCE ON THE CRITERION MEASURE	DECISION ON THE SCREENING OR DIAGNOSTIC TEST	
	At Risk	*Not at Risk*
Poor performance	(*a*) Number identified as at risk and there is a poor outcome; valid positive (VP)	(*b*) Number identified as not at risk who later perform poorly; false negative (FN)
Adequate performance	(*c*) Number identified as at risk but there is a "good" outcome; i.e., child performs adequately; false positive (FP)	(*d*) Number identified as not at risk and subsequent performance is adequate; valid negative (VN)

adequately. They are the valid negatives. These two groups then are the number of children identified accurately by the screening measure.

In contrast, Cells *b* and *c* reflect the numbers of children who have not been identified correctly. The number indicated by the screening measure as not at risk and who subsequently perform inadequately are the false negatives (Cell *b*). The false positive group (Cell *c*) is the number of children identified originally as at risk who later demonstrated adequate performance on the criterion.

Table 19.2 illustrates a hypothetical data set of 215 children who were administered a readiness test at the beginning of kindergarten and then a standardized reading test at the end of first grade. For this data set, the number of valid positives is 30 and the number of valid negatives is 160. The former number reflects the accurate identification of children said to be at risk. The latter number reflects the accurate identification of children

predicted to be not at risk. However, 40 children who were predicted to perform poorly were later found to be successful in first grade reading (false positives) and 15 children predicted to be not at risk performed poorly on the criterion reading test (false negatives).

The data obtained from such a prediction matrix may then be used to compare screening instruments in various ways. One comparison is the overall effectiveness of the instrument, which is the percentage of the total group correctly identified by the instrument. In other words, the valid positives (Cell *a*) plus the valid negatives (Cell *d*) are what percentage of the total class? The formula for computing this index is $(a + d) (a + b + c + d)$. For the hypothetical data set ($N = 245$), the overall effectiveness is .78. (See Tables 19.3 and 19.4).

The total ratio, however, often is a misrepresentation of the true effectiveness of a screening instrument. The reason is that Cell *d* (the valid negatives) usually contains a large number. That is, the instrument identifies

TABLE 19.2 Relationship between Readiness Level and First Grade Reading: A Hypothetical Case

PERFORMANCE ON THE CRITERION MEASURE (1ST GRADE READING TEST)	PERFORMANCE ON THE SCREENING MEASURE (DEVELOPMENTAL SCREENING MEASURE OR READINESS TEST)		
	Poor Performance (At Risk)	*Good Performance (Not at Risk)*	*Totals N*
Poor performance	(*a*) 30 (VP)	(*b*) 15 (FN)	45
Good performance	(*c*) 40 (FP)	(*d*) 160 (VN)	200
Totals	70	175	245

TABLE 19.3 Indices of Predictability for a Screening Measure

INDEX	COMPONENTS	FORMULA
Overall effectiveness	Number of successes and failures correctly identified / Total class	$\dfrac{a+d}{a+b+c+d}$
Index of sensitivity (percentage of poor performers correctly identified by the screening test)	Number of poor performers correctly identified originally by the screening test / Total number of poor performers at criterion	$\dfrac{a}{a+b}$
Index of specificity (percentage of adequate performers correctly identified originally by the screening test)	Number of adequate performers correctly identified originally by the screening test / Total number of adequate performers at criterion	$\dfrac{d}{c+d}$
Percentage of children identified as at risk who later failed	Number of at-risk identifications who later performed poorly / Total number originally identified as at risk	$\dfrac{a}{a+c}$
Percentage of children identified as not at risk who later performed adequately	Number of not-at-risk identifications who later performed poorly / Total number originally identified as at risk	$\dfrac{d}{b+d}$

a large number of children who will not be at risk and who later do perform adequately in school. Thus, a high effectiveness ratio reported for an instrument frequently reflects the ability of the screening instrument to predict (accurately) the academic performance of the children who were considered originally not to be at risk (Leach, 1980). In the hypothetical example given (e.g., Tables 19.2 and 19.4), 175 students were predicted to perform

TABLE 19.4 Indices of Predictability for a Hypothetical Screening Instrument

INDEX	FORMULA	VALUES	PERCENTAGE/ RATIO
(a) Overall effectiveness	$\dfrac{a+d}{a+b+c+d}$	$\dfrac{190}{245}$	.78
(b) Index of sensitivity	$\dfrac{a}{a+b}$	$\dfrac{30}{45}$	.67
(c) Index of specificity	$\dfrac{d}{c+d}$	$\dfrac{160}{200}$	.80
(d) Percentage of children identified as at risk who later failed (positive predictive value)	$\dfrac{a}{a+c}$	$\dfrac{30}{70}$	.43
(e) Percentage of children identified as not at risk who later performed adequately	$\dfrac{d}{b+d}$	$\dfrac{160}{175}$	.91

adequately on academic tasks and 160 or 91 percent did in fact do so. Thus the effectiveness ratio of .78 neglects to make manifest the very poor ability of the screening measure to predict the subsequent performance of those stated to be at risk.

The Interpretation of Matrix Data

Once the ratios as outlined in Tables 19.3 and 19.4 have been calculated, the obvious question is what should be the minimum level of accuracy for a screening measure to be acceptable for use by educators and psychologists. To answer this question, the conceptual framework that Kingslake (1983) proposes is important in interpreting a screening measure.

First, Kingslake indicates that portraying the four types of outcomes in a 2×2 matrix is essential. Then the matrix data should be examined from a *retrospective* point of view. This means the question to be considered is: Of all the children who actually perform poorly, what percentage was originally identified as being at risk by the screening measure? The reader should refer to the data in Table 19.4 for an answer to this question. As illustrated, 67 percent of all children who actually performed poorly in reading were originally designated as at risk on the screening measure $(a/a + b)$. Thus, 33 percent of all children who actually became poor readers were missed by the readiness test. How acceptable is the miss rate of 33 percent? Kingslake (1983) states that at least 75 percent of the failing population should be originally identified by a screening measure. Because the screening only identified 67 percent of the group of children who failed, the screening measure "fails" on this standard.

Kingslake states that the second question to be addressed involves a *prospective* judgment about the accuracy of the original label of "at risk." Do all the children designated as being at risk by the readiness test actually perform poorly in reading? The results from Table 19.4 indicate quite definitely that a large percentage of the children labeled as at risk in fact did *not* perform poorly in reading at the end of the first grade $(a/a + c)$. The predictive accuracy of the at-risk classification indicates that only 43 percent of the children originally labeled as being possible learning problems actually did perform poorly in reading at the end of first grade. Once again the screening measure fails to meet Jansky's (1978) and Kingslake's (1983) criterion that the accuracy of detection should be 75 percent or higher. (See Table 19.4.)

In the example given it should be noted that 57 percent of the children who had performed poorly on the screening measure would not need an intervention program. Including these children would have given the impression that intervention was effective when in fact the majority of children were good readers at the end of first grade despite their at-risk status on the screening measure.

Both retrospective and prospective judgments are interrelated and the accuracy of both must be considered in any analysis of the value of a screening measure. More emphasis has been placed in this chapter on the prospective use of predictive data because school personnel make program and placement decisions based mainly on the fact that the child has been labeled as "at risk" or "immature."

A Comparison of Several Current Readiness Tests

Table 19.5 illustrates the predictability indices computed from data reported by different researchers on a number of readiness tests. In the table, the author of the particular study for the test is listed first, followed by the test name. Column 1 is the percentage of correct predictions made by the test or the overall effectiveness for the reported data. Column 2 is the index of sensitivity, that is, the percentage of poor performers on the criterion measure who were correctly identified *earlier* by the screening test. Column 3 indicates the percentage of adequate performers who were correctly identified by the screening test *originally* (the index of specificity). Column 4 indicates the percentage of children identified as at risk who later failed to meet the criterion set (the positive predictive value), and column 5 indicates the percentage of children identified as not at risk who later succeeded. Finally, column 6 reports the percentage of the total number of children who actually are failing (the prevalence rate of poor performance occurring in the population).

DEVELOPMENTAL AREAS OF ASSESSMENT

A number of areas should be considered in screening the child's developmental status. They are cognitive status, language status, fine and gross motor skills, and information about parental concerns.

Cognitive Status

A number of abilities comprise the cognitive state of the child. These abilities include concept development (i.e., relationship of objects to each other such as *under, over, next to, behind,* etc. and shapes, colors, letters, and numbers), word knowledge, and memory.

TABLE 19.5 Reanalysis of a Sample of Screening Procedures

Author(s) of Research Study	Predictor of At-Risk Status	Criterion Measure	**1** % of Total Group Correctly Identified (Hit Rate) $\dfrac{a+d}{a+b+c+d}$	**2** Index of Sensitivity $\dfrac{a}{a+b}$	**3** Index of Specificity $\dfrac{a}{c+d}$	**4** % of Children Identified as At Risk Who Performed Poorly Later $\dfrac{a}{a+c}$	**5** % of Children Identified as Not At Risk Who Later Succeeded $\dfrac{d}{b+d}$	**6** % of Children Who are Actually Performing Poorly (i.e., Prevalence Rate) $\dfrac{a+b}{a+b+c+d}$
Badian, 1982	Kindergarten Screening Battery	Good/poor academic achievement at end of 3rd grade	92%	91%	89%	57%	99%	10%
Jansky & deHirsch, 1972	Perceptual Motor & Language Measures	Reading test at end of 2nd grade	77%	77%	66%	58%	82%	38%
Funk, Sturner, & Green, 1986	McCarthy GCI	CTB/McGraw Hill Prescriptive Reading Inventory	80%	77%	81%	46%	94%	18%
Funk, Sturner, & Green, 1986	McCarthy GCI	California Achievement Test (1st grade)	83%	76%	85%	66%	90%	27%
Funk, Sturner, & Green, 1986	McCarthy GCI	California Achievement Test (2nd grade)	79%	80%	91%	50%	91%	27%
Flannigan, 1994	DIAL-R	Iowa Test of Basic Skills	88%	20%	98%	66%	89%	12%

406

Although intelligence and academic achievement are strongly correlated, the correlation of intelligence scores in preschool years with later achievement in elementary schools is only about .50 (Shepard, 1993). Camp, van Doorminck, Frankenburg, & Lampe, (1977) investigated the relationship of preschool IQ scores to later school problems of these children when in elementary school. Children with IQs of 84 and below were predicted to develop learning problems whereas those with IQs higher than 84 were predicted to be normal. However, the results indicated an incorrect prediction in 31 percent of the cases studied (Dworkin, 1985).

In a more recent study, Funk, Sturner, and Green (1986) investigated the relationship of intelligence of the academic performance of kindergarten, first, and second grade students. Children were tested prior to kindergarten entry on the McCarthy Scales of Children's Abilities. The resultant score is called a General Cognitive Index (GCI).

Although investigators obtained adequate indices of sensitivity (range .76 to .80) and specificity (range .81 to .91), the positive predictive value ratios (PPV) were low ranging from .46 for kindergarten children to .66 for first grade children to .50 for second grade children. Matrix analysis for the kindergarten children indicated that many children with lower IQs (i.e., 84 and below) and who were predicted to have had learning problems in fact were performing adequately. The false positive rate of .54 for the kindergarten children is quite high (see Table 19.5).

The sensitivity index of .80 and the specificity index of .91 for second grade students were quite satisfactory. However, the positive predictive value of .50 indicates that half the number of the second grade children with lower IQs were performing adequately. Obviously, other developmental factors were involved in these children's successful performance. The McCarthy scale is a well-constructed and lengthy test; screening measures of cognitive status, however, will be less valid and reliable because of brevity.

Language Status

Language development proceeds rapidly during the preschool period. It is important to the performance of the child entering school because so many of the academic tasks involve effective speech and language functioning.

Educators are particularly concerned with the development of phonological processing, an important part of language competence. Such processing involves the sound patterns of language that are used to communicate (Snowling, 1996). Specifically, screening of pho-

nological awareness would assess the child's ability to rapidly name letters, to select and discriminate among initial consonants as well as final consonants, and being able to recognize the appropriate number of syllables within words (Felton, 1992). It is also important to ascertain if the child can rapidly name objects and be able to perform memory tasks such as repeating strings of words in the order presented.

An investigation of language functioning of kindergarten children ($\overline{X}$ CA = 6-1; range 5-5 to 7-4) was undertaken by Felton (1992). Utilizing a number of tasks that reflect phonological development, Felton compared the results from these measures with the child's reading status in third grade. Reading performance was categorized into four levels: severely disabled, poor, average, and superior reader.

Results indicated both adequate sensitivity and specificity with respective ratios of .81 and .80 for the language screening battery. Thus, 81 percent of very poor readers in the third grade had obtained poor scores on the language screening battery when it was administered prior to kindergarten. Also, 80 percent of the children who were adequate third grade readers had been previously identified in kindergarten as not being at risk. However, the positive predictive value ratio (PPV) was only .31. This meant that 69 percent of kindergarten children who performed poorly on the screening battery were now either average or superior readers in the third grade, contrary to the prediction.

Felton states that "false positive rates must be evaluated in terms of the advantages of early diagnosis and potentially effective early intervention vs. the potential negative impact of labelling" (p. 225). In addition the efficiency and cost of an intervention program must be considered. In this case 55 children earned at-risk status on the language battery; however, only 17 or 31 percent continued in their low status and became poor readers in the third grade. An intervention program for all 55 children would have been a costly as well as an unnecessary undertaking.

These results do not mean that we should ignore low scores on such a battery; rather, these results should be considered along with results of other psychological measures as well as family factors before an intervention program is initiated for the children.

Fine/Gross Motor Skills

Gross and fine motor skills are considered by many school personnel as important to the young child's successful functioning in school. Such abilities would include being able to use crayons and pencils on school tasks, buttoning clothes, tying shoes, combing hair, and so on. However, motor skill development is not considered as important, for example, as language functioning (Glascoe, 1991). And "delayed motor milestones or delayed motor development do not preclude successful learning" (Dworkin, 1989, p. 25).

However, if significant delays were observed at age 5 or 6 and were corroborated by a low score on a screening measure such as the motor scale of the McCarthy, then a full-scale assessment of motor functioning utilizing the Bruininks-Oseretsky might be indicated.

Parental Concerns as a Predictor of Problems

Information from parents about their children's development should also be obtained. The question to ask is if such information can serve as an effective screening technique in identifying children who may be at risk for possible learning problems.

School screening personnel generally use parent interviews to obtain information about the child's development. However, the questions often are inadequately phrased or important data are not requested. An example from a current parent interview form in one school is as follows: "Was your child born prematurely?" No other questions in this area were asked. Most important would be to ascertain whether the premature child was of low birth weight.

In a recent study, Glascoe (1997) obtained information from the parents of 408 children between 21 and 84 months of age. The sample reflected socioeconomic and demographic characteristics similar to data from the 1900 U.S. Census.

A standardized parent report measure, the Child Development Inventory (CDI), a 300-item measure, was used to obtain developmental information on the children. The inventory is comprised of items for the following areas: language, self-help, social, motor, health, and preacademic and academic skills.

Parents' beliefs that there was a problem were compared to the children's performance on a battery of diagnostic tests. Ninety-six percent of parents who stated they had few or no concerns about their children's development were in agreement with the results of the diagnostic battery (i.e., specificity). In other words, of the 267 parents who stated they had no concerns, 255 made judgments that were in accordance with the results of the diagnostic battery. In actual practice, children of these parents could be excused from further screening. How-

ever, of the 141 parents who stated they had definite concerns, only 44 or 31 percent of their children actually performed poorly on the diagnostic battery. The false positive rate of 69 percent is quite high and indicates that parental concerns alone could not be utilized as a screening device. However, subsequent observation of these children by the kindergarten teacher as well as the school psychologist could be an effective means of detecting which children might need further screening and/or assessment.

SUGGESTIONS FOR A SCHOOL SCREENING PROGRAM

Rafoth (1997) has outlined in detail the steps necessary to develop appropriate screening procedures. Her guidelines include choosing appropriate goals, providing specific interventions for children identified as being at risk, coordinating the child's educational and behavioral needs with curriculum plans of the teacher, using valid and reliable measures, and incorporating results of research studies into school practices. The most important question to answer is: Do the implemented screening measures reflect important developmental factors that are in turn related to adequate school performance?

Children enter school when they attain a specific chronological age as set by the state in which they live. Screening of children for possible developmental deficits could then be undertaken. Areas that appear to be problematic can be followed up by observation and more in-depth diagnostic procedures if necessary.

The environment within which the child will be functioning must be carefully considered. Environment is defined as including a number of important factors: skill of the teacher, type of curriculum in the classroom, and attitudes the teacher brings to the classroom. Rist (1970) has dramatically shown how teachers' attitudes negatively affected their interactions with kindergarten children and the children's subsequent opportunities for learning in the classroom. Shepard & Smith (1985) demonstrated that kindergarten teachers' beliefs about children's learning and the role of the school were related to the number of children retained in their kindergarten classes.

Any screening program must also include an appropriate intervention program. Too often a program of early identification is devised only to confirm possible deficit areas with little or no follow-up. Therefore, a worthwhile screening program will provide information on the child's areas of competence and strengths as well as possible deficit areas (Dworkin, 1989).

The purposes of any screening program must be fully explained to the parents of the children. Parents have become quite concerned about the emphasis on screening and testing programs in the school. These concerns have led to increased litigation; a topic discussed in the following section.

LEGAL ISSUES IN SCREENING AND PLACEMENT OF YOUNG CHILDREN

A number of legal issues concerning screening and placement options have arisen within the past several years. These issues involve determining when children should be screened for possible learning problems, parental rights, and types of placements for children deemed to be at risk. All of these problems are noted in the following case.

Children in a northern New York State school district were required to take the Gesell Readiness Test in June prior to entrance to kindergarten in September. A mother objected to the fact that her daughter was assigned to a "developmental" kindergarten because the child was not considered "ready" for a regular kindergarten program. Because the mother felt her concerns were not adequately addressed by school personnel, legal action was brought and resulted in the following decision:

1. *The child was to be transferred to a regular kindergarten and no kindergarten child henceforth was to be placed in a developmental kindergarten without written consent from the parent;*
2. *The readiness test in use did not meet professional standards of reliability and validity and therefore was inappropriate;*
3. *The school failed to place students in a regular educational environment first, to determine whether the child could satisfactorily function within a regular school setting;*
4. *The school failed to evaluate students individually in order to assess specific areas of educational need;*
5. *The school failed to make use of information from a variety of sources;*
6. *Students suspected of possible problems should have been referred for further diagnostic assessments;*
7. *and it was concluded that the school did not attempt to implement an intervention program before placing the children in a segregated*

setting. (State of New York Department of Education, 1987)

SUMMARY AND RECOMMENDATIONS

Several implications concerning early identification and screening programs stem from the previous discussion. Changes will need to be made in order for screening programs to become more effective and helpful for children. Currently many schools collect data in preschool or prekindergarten "roundups." To attempt to make educational judgments from this information before formal schooling begins is difficult at best. Questions can be raised as to the purpose for which these data are to be used:

1. In an analysis of a community screening program, Cadman and associates (1984) concluded that there was little evidence to demonstrate the effectiveness of intervention for developmental and learning problems. Shepard and Graue (1993) state that empirical evidence as to the efficacy of early intervention programs is equivocal and probably stems from the fact that many intervention programs provide only 1 to 3 hours a week of specialized instruction (p. 300).

2. Screening tests and developmental assessments can be of help in the placement of children with moderate and severe disabilities (Shepard & Graue, 1993). However, Dworkin (1989) emphasizes that many of these children have already been identified without having been involved in any screening program.

3. School personnel often make placement decisions based solely on one screening measure. This decision may be to delay school entry for a year, retain the child, or place the child either in a prekindergarten or pre–first grade program. In such situations, the screening measure actually has been substituted for a complete diagnostic assessment.

4. Multiple sources of information about the child should be sought and carefully evaluated. Such an action will help to reduce errors that can result from brief encounters with the child.

5. Another suggestion is for school personnel to rethink the use of the traditional preschool and kindergarten roundups. Delaying most screening procedures until the child is actually enrolled in a kindergarten program may result in a more productive identification process.

Observations of children by the kindergarten teacher over a time span of several weeks, accompanied by the use of appropriate screening and assessment measures and observations by the school psychologist, would help produce more valid cases of children with possible learning and/or behavioral problems. Reassigning a school psychologist to work full-time with a small group of kindergarten and first grade teachers and be available for consultation sessions on an ongoing basis would be an expeditious move.

6. Such a change in screening procedures as described could produce a positive reaction from parents of young children entering school. Parental anxieties and concerns about screening programs have been underestimated by school personnel (Gredler, 1992). Parents will be relieved and appreciative when they learn that judgments they consider monumental (i.e., delayed entry, placement in prekindergarten or pre–first grade programs or learning disabilities) are not being made immediately. Instead their child is being given an opportunity to be a part of the regular classroom program.

7. It also needs to be made explicit that some young children who do not show any signs of developmental delay or learning problems may exhibit deficits in performance as they become older (Glascoe, 1991). However, implementation of a program of "developmental surveillance" as outlined by Dworkin (1989) will help to detect such cases.

As Dworkin (1989) states: "Surveillance encompasses all primary care activities related to the monitoring of the development of children" (p. 620). And he continues that "screening tests are but one strategy whereby the...professional may perform skilled observations of the children" (p. 621).

8. Standardized screening and diagnostic tests are preferable to use of an array of informal measures (e.g., various checklists, use of lists of milestones, or "one-minute probes" of the child's curriculum performance). As Glascoe (1991) states, informal techniques are often used on an inconsistent basis, often containing a poor selection of items and lacking information on how to interpret the results accurately (Glascoe, 1991, p. 2).

9. It can, therefore, be concluded that early identification programs need further evaluation and revision. Monitoring of young children's learning and behavior should be improved and become a continuous process. And as Lindsay (1984) states, appropriate screening and diagnostic measures should also be incorporated into the monitoring systems. Further efforts should be made to coordinate the efforts of teachers, parents, school psychologists, and pediatricians and to integrate the information they offer. These efforts will help lead to further individualization of instruction and effective intervention efforts for children.

REFERENCES

Adelman, H. S. (1982). Identifying learning problems at an early age: A critical appraisal. *Journal of Clinical Child Psychology, 11,* 255–261.

Aylward, G. P. (1994). *Practitioner's guide to developmental and psychological testing.* New York: Plenum.

Badian, N. (1982). The prediction of good and poor reading before kindergarten entry: A 4-year follow-up. *Journal of Special Education, 16,* 309–318.

Brown, F. R. (1996). Neurodevelopmental evaluation (the physician's diagnostic role in learning disabilities). In F. R. Brown, E. H. Aylward, & B. K. Keogh (Eds.), *Diagnosis and management of learning disabilities* (3rd ed., pp. 37–59). San Diego, CA: Singular Publishing Group.

Cadman, D., Chambers, L. W., Walter, S., Feldman, W., Smith, K., & Ferguson, R. (1984). The usefulness of the Denver Developmental Screening Test to predict kindergarten problems in a general community population. *American Journal of Public Health, 74,* 1093–1096.

Camp, B. W., van Doorminck, W. J., Frankenburg, W. K., & Lampe, J. M. (1977). Preschool developmental testing in prediction of school problems. *Clinical Pediatrics, 16,* 257–263.

Clark, W. W. (1959). Boys and girls—are there significant ability and achievement differences? *Phi Delta Kappan, 41,* 73–76.

Dworkin, P. H. (1985). *Learning and behavior problems of school children.* Philadelphia: W. B. Saunders.

Dworkin, P. H. (1989). Developmental screening—expecting the impossible? *Pediatrics, 83,* 619–622.

Felton, R. H. (1992). Early identification of children at risk for reading disabilities. *Topics in Early Childhood Special Education, 12*(2), 212–229.

Flannigan, W. J. (1994). *The DIAL-R as a predictor of subsequent school success.* Unpublished doctoral dissertation. Kansas State University, Manhattan.

Frankenburg, W. K. (1985). The concept of screening revisited. In W. K. Frankenburg, R. W. Ende, & J. W. Sullivan (Eds.), *Early identification of children at risk* (pp. 3–17). New York: Plenum.

Funk, S. G., Sturner, R. A., & Green, J. A. (1986). Preschool prediction of early school performance: Relationship of McCarthy Scales of Children's Abilities prior to school entry to achievement in kindergarten, first, and second grades. *Journal of School Psychology, 24,* 181–194.

Glascoe, F. P. (1991). Developmental screening: Rationale, methods, and application. *Infants and Young Children, 4,* 1–10.

Glascoe, F. P. (1997). Parents' concerns about children's development: Prescreening technique or screening test? *Pediatrics, 99,* 522–528.

Gredler, G. R. (1992). *School readiness: Assessment and educational issues.* Brandon, VT: Clinical Psychology Publishing.

Jansky, J. J. (1978). A critical review of some developmental and predictor precursors of reading disabilities. In A. L. Benton & D. Pearl (Eds.), *Dyslexia: An appraisal of current knowledge* (pp. 331–347). New York: Oxford University Press.

Jansky, J. J., & deHirsch, K. (1972). *Preventing reading and failure.* New York: Harper & Row.

Kingslake, B. J. (1983). The predictive (in) accuracy of on-entry to school screening procedures when used to anticipate learning difficulties. *British Journal of Special Education, 10,* 24–26.

Keogh, B. K., & Bernheimer, L. P. (1996). Learning disabilities in preschool children. In F. R. Brown, E. H. Aylward, & B. K. Keogh (Eds.), *Diagnosis and management of learning disabilities* (3rd ed., pp. 19–36). San Diego, CA: Singular Publishing Group.

Lindsay, G. (Ed.). (1984). *Screening for children with special needs.* Dover, NH: Groom Helm.

Leach, D. J. (1980). Considerations in screening for school learning difficulties: An overview of practice. *Educational Studies, 6,* 181–197.

Lichenstein, R., & Ireton, H. (1984). *Preschool screening.* New York: Grune and Stratton.

Lichenstein, R., & Ireton, H. (1991). Preschool screening for developmental and educational problems. In B. A. Bracken (Ed.), *Psychoeducational assessment of preschool children* (pp. 486–513). Boston: Allyn and Bacon.

McGuire, J., & Richman, N. (1987). Outcome of behavior problems in the preschool setting. *Child Care, Health, and Development, 13,* 403–414.

Meisels, S. J. (1994). *Developmental screening in early childhood: A guide* (4th ed.). Washington, DC: National Association for the Education of Young Children.

Potton, A. (1983). *Screening.* London: MacMillan Education.

Rafoth, M. A. (1997). Guidelines for developing screening programs. In G. R. Gredler (Ed.), *Special Issue: School Readiness, 34,* 129–142.

Reynolds, C. R. (1979). Should we screen preschools? *Contemporary Educational Psychology, 4*(2), 175–181.

Rist, R. C. (1970). Student social class and teacher expectations: The self-fulfilling prophecy in ghetto education. *Harvard Educational Review, 40,* 411–451.

Shepard, L. A., & Graue, M. E. (1993). The morass of school readiness screening: Research on test use and validity. In B. Spodek (Ed.), *Handbook of research on the education of young children* (pp. 293–305). New York: Macmillan.

Shepard, L. A., & Smith, M. L. (1985). Boulder Valley kindergarten study: Retention practices and retention effects. Boulder University of Colorado, Laboratory of Educational Research.

Silva, P. A., & Ross, B. (1980). Gross motor development and delays in development in early childhood: Assessment and significance. *Journal of Human Movement Studies, 6,* 211–226.

Snowling, M. J. (1996). Annotation: Contemporary approaches to the teaching of reading. *Journal of Child Psychiatry and Psychology, 37,* 139–148.

State of New York Department of Education. (1987). Appeal case of Diane and David Liebfred, November 30.

CHAPTER 20

PLAY-BASED APPROACHES TO PRESCHOOL ASSESSMENT

MICHELLE SCHICKE ATHANASIOU

As a major activity of childhood, play has been given considerable attention by professionals concerned with the diagnosis and treatment of young children. Although play was first used as a medium for assessing and treating emotional and behavioral difficulties, more recent attention has focused on the information play can provide about child development. This interest is based on the developmental nature of play and its correspondence to cognitive, social/emotional, language, and motor functioning.

The present chapter is divided into two major sections. In the first section, an overview of play development is presented, along with brief discussions of how play is related to development in other domains. The second section is concerned with play-based assessment. Two play-based instruments are described. Next, informal play observations are discussed, followed by a consideration of the strengths and limitations of this approach to assessment. Finally, the use of play for diagnosing and treating emotional and behavior problems is briefly addressed.

OVERVIEW OF PLAY DEVELOPMENT

Prior to discussing play development, it is important to review the definition of play. A substantial amount of attention has been paid to the issue of defining play. The construct has proven difficult to define because of the breadth of behaviors that can be considered play (Wolery & Bailey, 1989) and the numerous settings and circumstances in which play can occur. What have helped shape accepted definitions of play have been discussions about the characteristics of play. Some commonly accepted play characteristics include the following (Hughes, 1995):

1. *Play is intrinsically motivated.* It is not dependent on rewards or other external motivation. It is engaged in for the sheer pleasure of doing so.

2. *Play is freely chosen.* Any coercion to engage in an activity may preclude it from being considered play.
3. *Play is pleasurable.* It is something enjoyable that usually elicits positive affect.
4. *Play is nonliteral.* It involves an element of pretending or make-believe. It should be noted that some argue that earlier actions with objects that do not involve pretending are also play (Smilansky, 1968).
5. *Play involves active engagement.* During play, children are more attentive to the play than most other stimuli.

In addition to the characteristics of play already discussed, play can be considered a developmental phenomenon that follows a relatively set sequence. The following section contains a brief discussion about typical play development. This discussion includes information about the development of play throughout childhood but focuses primarily on advances made in early childhood. To that end, the following information pertains to how play development relates to advances in cognitive skills and the increasingly social nature of play. Although other aspects of play are certainly important (e.g., competition, object usage), a more comprehensive discussion of play development is beyond the scope of this chapter.

COGNITIVE DIMENSIONS
OF PLAY DEVELOPMENT

Advances in the sophistication of children's play follow concurrent advances in cognitive development. Play begins as a sensorimotor activity, becomes more symbolic as representational abilities develop, and late in the preschool period begins to become more realistic and concrete. Young children's play begins with what Piaget (1962) called "sensorimotor" play. This type of play emerges at approximately 4 months and is characterized by activities that are physical in nature. It involves the accidental discovery of pleasure derived from physical actions; these actions are repeated to prolong or continue the environmental effects of such behaviors. For example, infants bang objects on tables in order to produce an effect (i.e., sound production). Smilansky (1968) referred to this type of play as "functional," in that it produces functional pleasure. Prior to the first 8 to 12 months, infants repeat motor movements, but because the interest is more in the action than the effect, this type of activity is considered the exercise of reflexes as opposed to "play." Throughout the period of sensorimotor play, young children's play behaviors become more complex. Infants begin to experiment with different actions to produce novel effects. Rather than simply banging an object on the table, infants will shake, drop, and bang the object against other objects to experience the effects of these different actions. In doing so, infants learn about the functions and properties of objects. As these experimental sensorimotor actions become more sophisticated, their practice begins to resemble symbolic representational activities (Rubin & Pepler, 1982). Toward the end of Piaget's sensorimotor period, children begin to mentally represent objects and, thus, rely less on the need to physically manipulate objects to attain goals (i.e., infants learn to mentally anticipate the effects of their actions). This development paves the way for subsequent and more mature play forms.

Symbolic play, which appears slowly beginning in the second year of life, requires the use of mental symbols to represent objects (Piaget, 1962). It is during this period that pretend or make-believe play begins. Symbolic play becomes increasingly sophisticated throughout the preoperational period (i.e., 2 to 6 or 7 years). The development of symbolic play can be characterized by advances in at least three areas: decontextualization, decentration, and integration. Decontextualization refers to the extent to which children substitute one object for another. Early in symbolic play (i.e., at approximately 12 to 13 months), children's substitutions are made with objects that are similar to the real object (McCune-Nicholich, 1981). A child may pretend to drink from an empty cup, for example. McCune-Nicholich stated that, at first, drinking from an empty cup demonstrates knowledge of objects' functions, such that an empty cup prompts the scheme of drinking. Shortly thereafter, this object substitution is done at will in a playful manner. Object substitution becomes less dependent on functional or characteristic similarity as children develop. By age 3, children are able to substitute play objects that bear little resemblance to the real object. For example, a child can pre-

tend a long stick is a horse for riding (McCune, 1995; McCune-Nicholich, 1981; Rubin & Pepler, 1982). According to Vygotsky (1966), this shift occurs as the child is able to focus less on the objects themselves and more on the "meanings" ascribed to them.

A related advancement in the development of symbolic play is the degree to which pretend play behaviors are planned in advance. Initially, pretend play sequences appear to be prompted by and dependent on present objects. A child who is playing with a doll and a cup may have the doll drink from the cup, for example. Later, young children begin to plan pretend activities in the absence of environmental props and, subsequently, gather the necessary materials to enact the planned pretend. McCune (1995) referred to this type of symbolic play as "hierarchical pretend." A child might, for example, want to play "going to the store." Realizing objects such as keys and a car are needed, the child retrieves necessary items (McCune-Nicholich, 1981; Rubin & Pepler, 1982).

With regard to decentration, symbolic play initially is self-referenced in that pretend actions are directed toward the self. Children initially pretend to feed themselves, for example. Later, between 15 and 21 months, pretend actions directed toward others are demonstrated, such that the child might pretend to feed a doll (McCune-Nicholich, 1981). Still later, the objects in children's play become actors (Fein, 1981). At this level, a child might have one doll pretend to feed another doll. This last stage requires the child to recognize that something other than the self can perform actions, which signifies a decline in egocentric thought. The child's ability to have objects serve as actors performing increasingly complex roles increases throughout the preoperational period.

Symbolic play also becomes increasingly integrated during this period. In early symbolic play, pretend play is limited to one play behavior at a time (McCune-Nicholich, 1981). By late in children's second year, children become better able to join play behaviors to form multi-scheme combinations (Hughes, 1995). For example, a very young child might pretend to feed a doll. As symbolic play becomes more sophisticated, the child feeds the doll, rocks the doll, and puts the doll to bed. Three-year-olds continue combining play behaviors into increasingly complex play sequences (Hughes, 1995).

By around age 5 or 6, children begin to move toward concrete operational thought. Related changes in cognitive patterns are reflected in play behaviors. For example, children this age want more realistic props or toys to use during pretend play (Hughes, 1995). Unlike the young preoperational child, however, this desire for realistic props is not the result of cognitive limitations; rather it reflects the emergence of reality-based thought.

Emerging concrete operational thought coincides with the next stage of play, "games with rules" play (Piaget, 1962). At this stage, children's thought is more logical and orderly, and play becomes more realistic and rule governed (Hughes, 1995). "Games with rules" play is characterized by games involving competition between two or more players. Although rules do exist in sensorimotor (e.g., peek-a-boo) and symbolic play (e.g., a child may announce he or she is the baby, and later change into the mommy or daddy), these types of play do not require the presence of more than one person, and the rules in these types of play are flexible. In "games with rules" play, the rules are agreed to in advance and are not changed during the course of the play (Rubin & Pepler, 1982).

In general there is research to support the Piagetian scheme of play development (see Fein, 1981; Hughes, 1995). Nevertheless, some researchers have found that some less mature forms of play behaviors do not necessarily decline with age as Piaget posited (Fein, 1981). For example, de Lorimier, Tessier, and Doyle (1995) did not find differences in the quality of pretend play between 4- and 6-year-olds. In addition, even at older ages, children engage in sensorimotor play activities at times (e.g., in novel situations; when playing outdoors) (Fein, 1981). Hughes (1995) wrote that no single study observing children over the entire age span has been conducted, making it difficult to definitively describe the adherence of Piaget's model to children's play.

SOCIAL DIMENSIONS OF PLAY DEVELOPMENT

According to Piaget, play becomes increasing social throughout the preschool period. The ability to play with other children reflects the increasing social maturity of children. Nevertheless, Piaget's interest lay primarily in the cognitive aspects of play development. Mildred Parten (1932), by contrast, provided an early framework for play development specifically as a social entity. By observing the play of nursery school children ages 2 to 5, Parten proposed five stages of social play behaviors that were supposedly related to children's increasing social skills:

1. *Solitary play.* This type of play, according to Parten, involves children playing alone with toys or engaging in activities independent of other children, with no attempts at social interaction.
2. *Onlooker play.* This type of play involves children watching or otherwise showing an interest in the play of nearby children, but no attempts to join the play are made.
3. *Parallel play.* Parallel play occurs when children near each other play with similar toys in similar ways, but mutual play does not occur.
4. *Associative play.* This play includes interaction among children through sharing materials, but the play is loosely organized, and the child's own play is of greater interest than that of others.
5. *Cooperative play.* This play involves group activity that is goal oriented, and children work together to devise or elaborate on a game or play theme.

According to Parten, as children's social skills increase, they display increasingly more of the later types of play and rely less on solitary and parallel play. Therefore, younger children would be expected to play alone or in tandem with other children, but as social interaction skills increase, children would then begin to engage in more associative and cooperative play.

Although widely cited as a useful framework, some writers have questioned Parten's typology. Howes and Matheson (1992) wrote that Parten's stages do not form a developmental sequence that reflects increases in social competence. Instead, they are more likely to appear as sequences in individual play episodes. Children may play alone, and as their social comfort increases in the play environment, they often progress to playing with others close by. Smith (1978) stated that children often rehearse play skills in solitary play before trying them out with others. Therefore, solitary play does not necessarily imply social immaturity. Finally, it has been stated that Parten underestimated the ability of toddlers to play together in a cooperative manner (Hughes, 1995).

Howes and Matheson (1992) also developed and validated a typology for the development of social play skills. Unlike Parten's model, this scheme has more of a focus on pretend play skills with peers. According to this model, peer play begins with *parallel aware play,* which emerges at approximately 12 to 15 months and is defined as parallel play with eye contact (Howes, Unger, & Seidner, 1989). Next, *simple social play* emerges (15–20 months) (Howes et al., 1989). This is defined as playing the same or a similar activity while engaging in social interaction. *Complementary and reciprocal social play* occurs at 13 to 23 months and includes demonstration of action-based role reversals in games (e.g., run and chase). *Cooperative social pretend play* (24–30 months) is the enactment of complementary roles within social pretend play (roles being clear by the actions of the children). Finally, *complex social pretend play* (30–35 months) is described as social pretend play with meta-communication about the pretend aspects of the play (Howes & Matheson, 1992).

According to Howes (1987), the third stage in this model (complementary and reciprocal social play) requires young children to structure social interaction and assume the role of the partner, in that the partners exchange turns and action roles. What differentiates complementary and reciprocal social play from cooperative social pretend play is that in the former the roles that are reversed are action roles (e.g., the one who hides and the one who finds); in the latter pretend roles are reversed (e.g., doctor and patient). Although solitary pretend play is displayed prior to this time, social pretend play is expected to emerge later because of its more complex nature. Specifically, social pretend play requires engaging in coordinated pretend play with a peer (Howes, 1987; Howes et al., 1989). During this stage, children play together in a pretend fashion without verbally communicating about their pretending. Finally, complex social pretend play includes metacommunication about the nonliteral aspects of play. For example, children engaging in complex social pretend play direct each others' pretend play by giving each other instructions (e.g., "You be the mommy and I'll be the baby, and let's say I'm sick."). Because complex social pretend play requires children to communicate about the pretense with a peer who is equal to themselves in terms of communicative sophistication, Howes and Matheson (1992) stated this type of play represents an intersection of cognitive, linguistic, and social aspects of development.

THE IMPORTANCE OF PLAY: RELATION TO OTHER DEVELOPMENTAL DOMAINS

The development of play does not occur in isolation; rather, its progression is related to the development of skills in several domains. The following is a brief synopsis of the relation of play to cognitive, social/emotional, language, and motor development, in terms of how play enhances functioning in these domains and vice versa. For more extensive information, the reader is referred to Hughes (1995), Slade and Wolf (1994), and Yawkey and Pellegrini (1984).

Cognitive Development

Play and its relation to cognitive characteristics has been studied extensively, probably in part because of the role of cognition in the development of play. One aspect of play/cognition relationships that has been given signifi-

cant attention is the effect of play on decentration (ability to consider more than one aspect of a situation or problem at a time) and reversibility (recognition that reversing a process will bring about the original conditions from which the process began). Sutton-Smith (1967) and Golomb and Cornelius (1977) wrote that symbolic play involves children transforming objects and roles while at the same time maintaining their original identity. In that sense, children are demonstrating precursors to all forms of conservation. Several researchers have found, in experimental investigations, that children who receive training in symbolic play (i.e., experimenter engages in pretend episode with child and then prompts the child in a playful manner to state how and why the situation is not real) demonstrate improvements in decentering, conservation, and role reversal (Fink, 1976; Golomb & Cornelius, 1977). In addition, although there are some contradictory findings (Fein, 1981), others have found that symbolic play is related to creativity and problem solving (Athey, 1984). Fink (1976) found that training in imaginative play processes resulted in more displayed imaginativeness during free play as compared to children who did not receive such training. Pepler and Ross (1981) reported that children who were provided with convergent play materials (i.e., formboard pieces) performed better on convergent problem-solving tasks (i.e., tasks for which there are multiple possible solutions) than children provided opportunities to play with divergent play materials (i.e., formboard pieces and formboard). Finally, play appears to promote hypothetical reasoning, spatial concepts, classification, and measurement (Hughes, 1995).

Social/Emotional Development

With regard to social development, it has been found that play with peers is related to advances in social skills. First, in pretend play, children are able to practice playing social roles other than that which in reality limit them. This allows children to develop concepts of different roles and the behaviors associated with such roles (Athey, 1984). Second, play with peers affords young children the opportunity to practice various social skills necessary for functioning in a social world. Hughes (1995) stated that play requires group cooperation; therefore, peer play provides opportunities to practice cooperating. It is important to note, however, that although play and cooperation are related, causal relationships have not been determined (Fein, 1981). Play also has been found to be related to peer acceptance, popularity, and various indices of social competence (Howes & Matheson, 1992). A third aspect of play and social development relates to conflict and negotiation. During peer play, rules are established and followed. Not surprising,ly, conflicts often ensue when one or more parties decide to change or ignore rules. Play provides children with practice at handling these conflicts.

With regard to emotional functioning, play has long been recognized as an avenue for expressing emotional issues; this recognition is seen in the use of play as a therapeutic medium with children (Hughes, 1995). Pretend play makes it possible for children to express feelings and explore possible solutions to problems in a relatively safe atmosphere (Athey, 1984; de Lorimier et al., 1995). This can be seen, for example, when children act out familiar domestic scenes in play. Relatedly, Parker and Gottman (1989) stated that the primary affective task of preschool children is to learn to regulate affect and behavior in arousing situations. During play, children are in a state of arousal. If they are unable to control their affect and behavior, they risk losing play partners. Prolonging play, therefore, serves to motivate children to learn affective regulation.

Language Development

Play is also related to the development of language. Especially as play becomes more social, it provides opportunities to practice and refine language skills. Researchers have found that advances in play and language follow parallel courses, especially at very young ages (Bornstein, Vibbert, Tal, & O'Donnell, 1992; Casby & Corte, 1987; McCune, 1995; McCune-Nicholich, 1981; Ogura, 1991). This parallel is not necessarily seen as causal but rather the result of cognitive advances that allow for use of mental representation in both symbolic play and language (McCune, 1995; McCune-Nicholich, 1981). Language development is also important for structuring social pretend play. For example, Farver (1992) studied the development of linguistic competence as it relates to structuring pretend play sequences with peers. She found that the sophistication of pretend play structuring increased with age, facilitating social pretend maturity. Language skills, therefore, are related to the ability to engage in social pretense.

Motor Development

Play influences motor development primarily through the repetition of motor sequences with objects used in play (Athey, 1984). Early sensory exploration of objects helps develop and refine motor skills to permit later, more functional use of objects in play. Conversely, increases in motor skills permit more refined play with objects. The play of 2-year-olds, for example, mostly involves large muscle play. This is related to the increases in gross motor competence at this age (Hughes, 1995).

In summary, play is a developmental phenomenon that follows a distinct sequence. Play begins as a sensorimotor activity, then becomes more symbolic in nature, and later becomes more orderly and rule based. Socially, children's focus on social play with peers increases with age. These social play episodes also increasingly involve pretending. Play is important for furthering development in other areas, and it is enhanced by increased development in other domains. As a major activity of childhood, the importance of play cannot be overstated. Its significance has led to the recognition that play is an appropriate medium for assessing young children's functioning. In addition to developmental significance, play usually is an enjoyable activity, it has practical value, and it normalizes children's interactions with their environment (Wolery & Bailey, 1989). Vygotsky (1966) stated that "a child's greatest achievements are possible in play" (p. 14), suggesting that assessment during play may elicit children's best efforts.

PLAY-BASED ASSESSMENT

The use of play as medium for assessing and treating children began early in the twentieth century (O'Connor, 1991). At this time, psychoanalysts began interpreting children's play for the information it could provide about emotional functioning. Since that time, play has been used by therapists of many theoretical orientations in therapy with children (Hughes, 1995; Whaley, 1990). Play-based assessment of developmental functioning, by contrast, has a relatively recent history. Begun as a method of gaining information primarily about infants and toddlers, strategies for assessment through observations of play have been in existence since the late 1970s and early 1980s (Lynch, 1996). Play-based assessment has been used across disciplines by those desiring a natural approach to assessing young children. Interest in play-based assessment has increased more recently with the publication of Linder's (1990) transdisciplinary play-based assessment model, which will be discussed in the next section.

MODELS OF PLAY-BASED ASSESSMENT

Play-based assessment is a technique represented by a myriad of different procedures, instruments, and methods that differ on several dimensions. First, some models are primarily used in research related to play development, and at least one is intended for use by developmental specialists for evaluation and program planning for young children (Linder, 1993b). Other differences in the way assessment tools are set up also differentiate them (Fewell & Glick, 1993). For example, methods differ with regard to the amount of structure in the model. Structure refers to the degree to which directions given, toys provided, and so on are used to prompt certain behaviors. Measures also differ on the amount of specificity of coding and scoring play behaviors. Some methods employ scoring based on behaviors seen with specific toys. Others allow more flexibility in the context in which behaviors are observed. Finally, procedures differ in terms of how play behaviors are elicited from a child. Whereas some methods involve simply inviting a child to play, others use prompts to encourage certain behaviors.

The following section describes two methods of play-based assessment that differ on several of the aforementioned dimensions. These two instruments were chosen to present an example of a clinical tool and a research tool that are widely cited in the literature; many other play-based approaches are available. It is important to note that play assessment is often an informal procedure during which play is seen as giving information about various developmental skills. A brief discussion of informal observations of play will follow descriptions of the two play measures.

Transdisciplinary Play-Based Assessment

Transdisciplinary play-based assessment (TPBA; Linder, 1993b) is an observational scale of play development designed for use by early childhood assessment teams. Among the most widely used models of play-based assessment, this system includes the evaluation of several developmental domains, as well as assessment and intervention guidelines for children ages birth to 6 years. TPBA can be conducted for program eligibility decisions, to plan interventions, and to monitor progress toward treatment goals. In this model, children are observed at play, providing professionals information about the child's development in four domains: cognitive, communication, social-emotional, and sensorimotor. Observations of play skills are the basis for decisions about children's strengths and weaknesses and intervention goals.

Team Functioning. Professionals using TPBA function as a transdisciplinary team, which means they see the child together, information is shared across disci-

plines, and members contribute information and ideas to disciplines other than their own. This model is different from a multidisciplinary model in which children are seen by several disciplines independent from one another, and from the interdisciplinary model, in which disciplines see the child separately but then meet to discuss the child's results and program recommendations. The team typically includes a speech-language pathologist, an occupational therapist or physical therapist, and a teacher or psychologist. One member of the team is the play facilitator; this person actually interacts with the child during the assessment. Another member is the parent facilitator. This professional communicates with the parents, obtains information from them, helps to involve them in the assessment, and explains assessment activities to them. Other professionals present observe play behaviors and record their observations. One member may be used to videotape the session.

In the TPBA model, parents are involved throughout the entire process, promoting solid parent–professional teamwork. Prior to the play assessment, parents complete checklists of their child's at-home behaviors. During a portion of the assessment, parents play with their child. Finally, subsequent to the assessment, parents are involved in team discussions and program planning.

Procedures. TPBA can be conducted in any large room, with toys placed in distinct areas (e.g., block area, sand/water table area). A typical early childhood classroom is usually ideal, but assessments can also be conducted in homes, as long as necessary materials are available. Six phases constitute the assessment process. In Phase I the child plays at will, with the play facilitator imitating, modeling, and expanding on the child's play. Phase II involves bringing structure into the play situation in order to elicit play behaviors that the child previously did not spontaneously demonstrate. In Phase III a peer is brought into the play session, so that observations of child–child interaction can be made. Parents are observed playing with the child in both unstructured and structured play situations in Phase IV. In Phases V and VI, respectively, observations of motor play are made, and a snack is given to allow for a screening of oral-motor difficulties.

No specific behaviors are required in this model; rather, observations of various aspects of cognitive, social-emotional, communication, and sensorimotor skills are made in order to describe a child's abilities and set intervention goals. As such, this model provides no scores for a child. For each of the domains, the manual includes observation guidelines that may help to focus professionals. For example, in the cognitive domain, professionals are guided to look at such behaviors/ attributes as attention span, locus of control, symbolic and representational play, problem-solving approaches, and so on. In addition, observation worksheets and summary sheets are available for each domain (Linder, 1993a). These sheets provide space to write down observations for later use in decision making and program planning.

After the assessment is completed, a series of seven steps is followed. First, a postsession meeting is held as soon after the assessment as possible. At the meeting professionals discuss their observations and ideas or hypotheses about the child's functioning. The second step involves analyzing the videotape produced during the session. This allows for investigating hypotheses discussed in the meeting and noting behaviors that were overlooked during the assessment. Third, observations are used to derive qualitative descriptions of the child's level of development, based on developmental guidelines provided in the manual. Next, summary sheets corresponding to each assessed domain are completed, so that information is compiled in a more usable format. Information on this sheet includes the child's strengths, a rating of the child's abilities plus a justification for the rating, and objectives related to the area. Fifth, preliminary transdisciplinary recommendations are formulated. At this stage disagreements are discussed so that team consensus can be reached. Sixth, a program planning meeting (IFSP/IEP) is held to look at assessment information, decide about program eligibility, and plan formal intervention goals. Finally, a formal report is written that addresses the qualitative and quantitative descriptions of the child, interventions, and program goals.

The TPBA model is the most comprehensive model of play-based assessment available. It allows for the assessment of several developmental domains, is based on a team approach to evaluation, and gives specific guidelines for interpretation of child play behaviors. The model has intuitive appeal, due to these factors, as well as the child friendliness of the procedures. Despite these strengths, however, only one study investigating the psychometric properties of the instrument or procedure is available.

Friedli (1994) examined the validity and reliability of TPBA by conducting TPBA evaluations with 20 children between 3½ and 6 years of age (10 with and 10 without identified disabilities). Content validity of the TPBA model was investigated by having 24 early childhood professionals rate the clarity, comprehensiveness,

and relevance of the areas assessed in the domains of cognition, language, social-emotional, and sensorimotor (e.g., attention span, mastery motivation, phonology, mobility in play). The validity of TPBA was lent support, in that professionals viewed all areas assessed by the TPBA model as clear, comprehensive, and relevant (i.e., mean ratings for all areas exceeded 4.6 on a 7-point Likert scale).

Concurrent validity was addressed by administering the Battelle Developmental Inventory to all participants, and comparing the degree to which the professionals reached the same decision about whether the participants would be eligible for special education services based on Battelle and TPBA data. In addition, agreement on conclusions about ipsative strengths and weaknesses of participants based on the two instruments was compared. Chi-square analyses supported similar findings between instruments in terms of eligibility decisions and intraindividual comparisons. One major limitation regarding the first concurrent validity question (i.e., eligibility decision) was that the professionals conducting the assessment were not blind to subjects' disability classifications (identified or nonidentified).

Both test-retest and interrater reliability were examined (Friedli, 1994). Test-retest reliability was examined by comparing test and retest summary sheet ratings for 10 of the subjects. Chi-square analyses on the ratings were statistically significant for all domains, suggesting that ratings remained consistent across a six-week period. With regard to interrater reliability, chi-square analyses comparing summary sheet ratings for two independent observers of 10 taped TPBA administrations were conducted. Again, statistical significance was reached for all domains (i.e., cognitive, language, social-emotional, sensorimotor).

The Friedli (1994) study represents a good first attempt at investigating the psychometric properties of TPBA. Nevertheless, the study had a small sample size. Few, if any, broad conclusions about the efficacy of an assessment procedure can be based on the results of one study, suggesting that more research of this kind is in order.

Play Assessment Scale

The Play Assessment Scale (PAS; Fewell, 1992) is an experimental and observational measure of play development for use with children ages 2 to 36 months. It contains a series of 45 play items, sequenced in terms of developmental skills needed to perform the item. Observations of play skills are used to compute a "play age" for the assessed child.

Procedures. The PAS can be administered by a teacher, parent, experimenter, or other adult familiar with the PAS procedures. Fewell (1992) stated that, because play skills can be based on a behavior seen with numerous toys, examiners need to be very familiar with the skills being targeted and how examples of the skill being targeted might be demonstrated. Eight toy sets corresponding to developmental levels are listed in the scale directions. Examiners choose several toy sets corresponding to the child's chronological age or presumed developmental level.

The assessment, which can be conducted in any comfortable environment that is spacious enough for floor play, consists of two conditions. In the first condition, observations are made of the child's spontaneous play behaviors. Specifically, the child is observed playing with the toys until no novel behaviors are produced (i.e., usually between 2 and 15 minutes). In the second, limits of play development are assessed by prompting the child to perform items. Prompts are gradually increased from verbal to motor to verbal plus motor.

Item Content and Scoring. Items are based on play behaviors with toys that are indications of development. Items on the scale include increasingly sophisticated behaviors ranging from visually tracking toys to simple functional behaviors directed toward the self (e.g., brushing hair) to symbolic pretend behaviors with a doll being the actor. Each item is scored as either occurring during the first condition (spontaneous), the second condition (prompted), or neither. Only those behaviors observed during the spontaneous condition are counted toward the child's computed play age. Play ages are derived by counting numbers of behaviors credited between a basal and ceiling, and converting raw scores to play ages on a conversion chart. Observations of behaviors elicited during the prompted condition are used for qualitative descriptions of child development and emerging skills.

The PAS has several strengths as a play assessment method. First, it is a relatively easy scale to administer, provided the examiner is familiar with behaviors of interest. Second, the PAS has more evidence of validity than other play assessment scales. Studies correlating PAS scores to other developmental instruments have lent some support to the instrument as a measure of development. Eisert and Lamorey (1996) found correlations of

.45., .56, and .56 between the PAS and the fine motor, adaptive behavior, and language subscales of the Gesell Developmental Schedules (Knobloch, Stevens, & Malone, 1987). The PAS has been found to correlate strongly with various nonstandardized measures of communication (.80 to .94), cognition (.85 to .89) and social functioning (.77 to .92) (Fewell & Rich, 1987). Finally, Finn and Fewell (1994) found correlations ranging from .87 to .93 between the PAS and nonstandardized measure of receptive, expressive, and nonverbal communication. Weaknesses of the PAS include play ages not being derived from a standardization sample, little parental involvement in the procedure, a limited age range for the scale (i.e., 2 to 36 months), and no evidence of the scale's reliability.

Informal Observations of Play

In addition to formal play-based assessment measures, assessment based on play can also be conducted through informal or nonstructured play observations. In nonstructured observations, as in formal instruments, clinicians observe children (or children and their parents) at play, and play behaviors form the basis of decisions about developmental level and/or treatment. In addition, developmental level typically is determined by comparing behaviors to prior information about developmental norms. Unlike more formal measures, however, the clinician has more freedom to structure the observation setting in a way that is most comfortable for the family and clinician, and in a manner that is most likely to elicit behaviors of interest (Segal & Webber, 1996).

Several specific aspects of nonstructured play observations can be determined by the clinician. One important decision is where to conduct the observation. Observations may be conducted in a clinical setting, home setting, or child care/classroom setting. Malone, Stoneman, and Langone (1994) found that, particularly for children with disabilities, observations of independent play were superior to observations in a classroom with peers. Specifically, these authors found that the distractions in the classroom made it difficult for children to maintain sustained levels of play. Home settings are more likely to put the child at ease; however, toys may need to be transported to the home if they are not already available.

A related issue is the materials that will be used. Segal and Webber (1996) stated that it is appropriate for the toys used to be determined by parents. If observations are conducted in the home, it is appropriate to use toys already in the home. Using toys familiar to the child may lead more quickly to play. Specifically, in novel situations children's behaviors are at first exploratory in nature. Exploration is differentiated from play in several ways (Hughes, 1995; Johnson, Christie, & Yawkey, 1987). First, exploration involves more stereotypical behaviors; during play, children are more flexible and relaxed. Second, during exploration, children's affective state is thought to be neutral to mildly negative. As previously discussed, play usually is associated with positive affect. In addition, whereas play involves using objects for stimulation, exploration is used to gain information about objects. Finally, exploration involves more intensity and attention than play. Thus, if the intent is to assess play behaviors, it is important to ensure that children are familiar with surroundings and/or materials. This can be done by conducting observations in the home or with the child's toys, or by allowing the child time to explore the environment prior to beginning observations. Time to get comfortable is not only important for nonstructured observations but also for more formal procedures.

Another decision is whether to include parents in the play observations. Gowen, Johnson-Martin, Goldman, and Hussey (1992) found in a study of 40 children (20 with and 20 without identified disabilities) that mothers serving as play partners during play episodes served to increase the level of their children's play. Through suggesting and modeling, mothers encouraged play behaviors that were at or slightly higher than their current levels. In addition, play was facilitated for less mobile children by mothers' bringing toys to and holding toys for their children. These findings applied to both sexes; race was not investigated, because 90 percent of the subjects were Caucasian. If independent or spontaneous play behaviors are the focus of the observation, it would be preferred to exclude parents for the same reasons. Observations of parent and child at play together can also provide important information about parent–child interactions (e.g., parent responsiveness, child compliance).

BENEFITS OF PLAY-BASED ASSESSMENT

Proponents of play-based assessment have discussed in depth the advantages of the approach. Primarily these advantages are related to what are believed by many researchers and professional organizations to constitute the tenets or standards for early childhood assessment. This section contains a discussion of the advantages of

play-based assessment, and how these perceived benefits relate to early childhood assessment standards.

Flexibility

Play-based assessment generally includes a great deal of flexibility in its procedures (Fewell & Rich, 1987; Linder, 1993b). In typical play assessment methods, children are allowed to play while observations are being made. The specific behaviors required often are not predetermined. This flexibility is believed to be less stressful, less threatening, and to result in increased cooperation from young children (Fewell & Kaminski, 1988; Linder, 1993b; Myers, McBride, & Peterson, 1996). Fewell and Rich (1987) found that no child in their study resisted the administration of a play-based procedure. Bagnato and Neisworth (1994) have stated that, in order for early childhood assessment procedures to be developmentally friendly, flexible administration procedures are necessary.

The flexibility in the administration of play-based procedures also means that every child is testable (Linder, 1993b). With play-based assessment, observations of what a child does at play are the basis for decisions and service plans. According to Fewell and Rich (1987), play is related to several domains that are difficult to assess in children with severe impairments. Children with sensory impairments and limited cognitive skills have similar opportunities as typically developing children to display their skills in various developmental domains during play. Flexibility meets federal mandates that children should not be assessed using instruments that penalize them in one area because of a deficit in another (Finn & Fewell, 1994). Conversely, flexibility makes reliability and validity more difficult to investigate.

Links to Intervention

Researchers and professional groups have been adamant that early childhood assessment should provide information that not only provides for noncategorical eligibility determination (Bagnato, Neisworth, & Munson, 1993), but information that is linked directly to intervention planning (Bagnato et al., 1993; Greenspan & Meisels, 1994; Linder, 1993b; NASP, 1991). Assessment is only the first step in the service delivery process. Information obtained from play-based assessments can be directly translated into intervention recommendations and IFSP/IEP goals and objectives, possibly enhancing treatment validity (i.e., extent to which assessment information leads to valid treatments) (Bagnato & Neisworth, 1994; Fewell & Rich, 1987; Linder, 1993b). TPBA, for example, includes summary worksheets on which observed competencies and limitations are directly translated into goals for the child, and a second volume that focuses on transdisciplinary approaches to play-based interventions for young children (Linder, 1993c). Although these methods appear to put intervention planning at the forefront, claims of treatment validity are premature, as no empirical evidence is available to suggest that early childhood professionals in fact implement assessment-derived interventions, or that implementation of these interventions leads to improved functioning.

Relatedly, assessment should be able to be used to monitor child progress once interventions have been implemented (Bagnato et al., 1993; Cichetti & Wagner, 1990). Because play-based assessment provides information that is linked to an intervention curriculum, and because practice effects are less of an issue with this type of assessment (i.e., TPBA has no specific items to remember), progress toward goals can easily be measured by intermittent assessment of this type (Linder, 1993b).

Family Involvement

Another strength of play-based assessment is the ease with which parents can be brought into the assessment/intervention planning process. Both federal mandates and best practices dictate that assessment with young children needs to be family friendly, recognizes the import of involving parents in the entire assessment process, and calls for parent–professional teamwork (Bagnato & Neisworth, 1994; Bagnato et al., 1993). Play-based assessment is set up so that parents are easily made part of the team. TPBA in particular involves the parents at every phase of the assessment process, including having parents play with their child during the assessment, so that important information about parent–child interaction can be obtained.

Ecological Focus

Play-based assessment is ecologically sensitive. Ecological assessments recognize the importance of various contexts in which children operate; play-based assessment can involve observations of children with parents and peers. In addition, assessment can be conducted in a child's home or classroom setting. Because of the flexibility of play-based approaches, ecological factors that might influence child responding (e.g., child–examiner variables, child-setting variables) are recognized and can be modified.

Team Collaboration

Early childhood assessment should be conducted by several disciplines and should involve team collaboration and consensus (Greenspan & Meisels, 1994; NASP, 1991). Play-based assessment easily adheres to these ideals. Fewell and Glick (1993) stated that, because play is not the unique study of any particular discipline, it is a good medium for bringing together members from various areas. In addition, in the TPBA model members of various disciplines gather their information based on the same set of child behaviors, which may lead to better team communication and collaboration (Linder, 1993b).

Social Validity

There is limited evidence of the social validity of play-based assessment. Social validity is the validation of work by consumers of that work (Wolf, 1978), and it provides an index of the acceptability of procedures, usually to professionals and parents, as well as the perceived importance of the information gained. One study to date has examined social validity of play-based assessment. Myers et al. (1996) compared parent and professional perceptions of transdisciplinary play-based assessment and multidisciplinary standardized assessment. The standardized assessments consisted of individual professionals separately administering discipline-specific standardized instruments (e.g., Bayley Scales of Infant Development-II; Receptive-Expressive Emergent Language-III). Results suggested that parents viewed the two types of evaluations equally as favorably. Professionals reported that play-based assessment produced more information about communication, social development, and motor skills than traditional assessment. Information produced about cognitive, sensory, and self-help skills was commensurate across groups. Also, school psychologists and speech-language pathologists viewed play-based assessments as better for ascertaining child strengths and weaknesses. In addition, play-based assessments were completed in a significantly shorter amount of time than standardized assessments for early childhood special education teachers. No significant differences in the amount of time spent in assessment for speech pathologists, school psychologists, occupational therapists, or physical therapists were found. Finally, with regard to utility of written reports, play-based reports were rated significantly higher than standardized reports for ease of obtaining an overview of the child's abilities, areas of concern, developmental areas covered in the report, absence of jargon, integration of cross-discipline information, and objectives being based on the child's strengths and weaknesses.

In summary, professionals viewed transdisciplinary assessment as superior to multidisciplinary standardized assessment for providing information in some areas (i.e., communication, social, motor), as well as utility of written reports. Parents, however, rated the two models equally favorably. The two models took equal amounts of time for most professionals. Some support for social validity is provided in this study, in that the transdisciplinary model was viewed as equal or superior to the multidisciplinary model in all respects. Obviously, much more research is needed to draw broad conclusions about the social validity of the method.

Other Strengths

There are several other strengths of play-based assessment. First, this type of assessment is natural to young children (Linder, 1993b). Because young children spend much of their time at play, conducting assessments using play as the basis of information lessens artificiality in the assessment situation. Second, in play-based assessment, information about development in various domains (e.g., cognition, motor, social, language) is gleaned through play. As such, it is not necessary to compartmentalize development according to domain; some claim this leads to a more holistic view of the child (Linder, 1993b; Wolery & Dyk, 1984). In addition, when play-based assessment is conducted as part of an interdisciplinary or transdisciplinary process, redundancy in testing is limited, such that information related to all disciplines is based on the same behavioral data (Linder, 1993b; Wolery & Dyk, 1984). Finally, Linder (1993b) stated that rapport with children is more easily gained with a transdisciplinary play-based model of assessment. Specifically, only one professional directly interacts with the child in this model, making it easier for the child to feel comfortable. No empirical support for this claim is available, however.

In summary, play-based assessment has several characteristics that make it an attractive assessment approach. It is a flexible approach that elicits information from a naturally occurring behavior in a young child's repertoire. This flexibility allows for modifications so that, regardless of impairment severity, all children can be tested. Play-based assessment easily involves parents and is otherwise ecologically sensitive. Play-based assessment encourages team cooperation and consensus because members from all disciplines can be involved simultaneously in the assessment process. A holistic view of a child's functioning is encouraged by looking at development as an integrated, rather than compartmentalized, phenomenon. Finally, the approach attends to the importance of linking assessment to intervention, although data as to treatment validity are limited at present.

LIMITATIONS OF PLAY-BASED ASSESSMENT

Despite its many strengths and advantages, play-based assessment cannot be considered a panacea for early childhood assessment due to several significant actual and potential limitations. Shortcomings include a dearth of research on the reliability and validity of play-based measures along with unsupported claims about the strengths of the approach, state regulations that may preclude the use of play-based assessment in isolation as a method for determining service eligibility, some limitations to the amount of information that can be derived from play-based measures, and limited information about diversity issues with this type of assessment.

Reliability and Validity

With regard to reliability and validity concerns, it appears that play-based assessment has gained widespread use, despite the lack of information on the psychometric integrity of the method (Eisert & Lamorey, 1996; Myers et al., 1996). Proponents of this and other nontraditional assessment methods have argued that the paucity of research investigating traditional types of reliability and validity (e.g., interrater reliability, concurrent validity) is less important for early childhood developmental testing than for other types of assessment. It is stated that information related to treatment validity and social validity of early childhood assessment measures is more important (Bagnato & Neisworth, 1994).

There are at least two issues that arise in response to claims that social and treatment validity are paramount with regard to play-based assessment. First, although treatment and social validity are undoubtedly important (as they are with any measure), it does not follow that they can be used to the exclusion of other types of reliability and validity. For example, regardless of the number of useful recommendations that are based upon an assessment, it is still important to have at least some certainty that the same findings would have emerged from other professionals who witness the same behavior. Relatedly, it is important to ascertain empirically whether behaviors observed during play-based assessment represent the constructs supposed, and that information obtained from play-based assessment correlates with other measures of development. Finally, it is important to know about the predictive validity of play-based measures. It is suggested that, although indices such as treatment and social validity are imperative, they should be used in conjunction with more traditional reliability and validity measures, not instead of them (Bracken, 1994). As previously discussed, only one study has examined the reliability and validity of the TPBA model. More validity research has been conducted using the PAS; however, this instrument is most widely used as a research tool.

The fact that decisions or judgments are made by professionals in response to behaviors observed during play-based assessment makes it characteristic of judgment-based assessment (Neisworth & Bagnato, 1988). Judgment-based assessment is that in which professional perceptions of many individuals are collected and used to make evaluations of children's functioning (Fleischer, Belgredan, Bagnato, & Ogonosky, 1990). Specifically, these measures involve collecting, structuring, and in some cases quantifying impressions (or judgments) of professionals. Although there are many positive aspects of judgment-based approaches, it is important to consider research on the limitations of human judgment. Reviews of related research suggest that humans are very prone to error in their judgment because of poor judgment habits and cognitive limitations (Faust, 1986; Tversky & Kahneman, 1974). Furthermore, professionals and experts are as prone to these errors in judgment as are nonprofessionals and nonexperts (Faust, 1986). Because mechanical methods of data integration appear to be superior to clinical methods, it seems imperative to incorporate at least some measures that rely on mechanical integration of information (i.e., standardized measures) into an assessment battery for young children.

The second issue with some authors' claims that treatment and social validity can be used in place of other types of validity and reliability information is that, even if it were true that social and treatment validity were all the data needed to support the integrity of this method, we currently do not have sufficient evidence of either. As discussed, only one empirical study addressing the social validity of play-based assessment is available. Although the Myers et al. (1996) study lends partial support for play-based assessment's social validity (i.e., parents were equally favorable of the play-based and multidisciplinary models; professionals preferred the play-based model), the study represents only a very first step in supporting claims of social validity.

Determining Eligibility

A second limitation of play-based assessment is that, depending on the specific measure used, the data produced may not be sufficient for eligibility determination. Linder's TPBA model, for example, produces qualitative data about the presence or absence of developmental skills based on professional observations and judgments. Neither standard scores nor percentage delay indices are derived from the measure. In many states, clinical opinion apart from the quantitative determinants of relative functioning is insufficient for placement in special education, especially in the birth to age 3 population (Schicke & Hankey, 1997).

Scope of Information Obtained

Play-based measures differ from each other in terms of the developmental domains assessed. Obviously, other measures would have to be used to supplement play-based measures when such measures do not cover all domains of interest. Fewell's model, for example, appears to provide information about the areas of expressive language and fine motor skills (Eisert & Lamorey, 1996). Linder (1993b) stated that, although her TPBA model assesses four broad domains of functioning (i.e., cognition, language, sensorimotor, and social-emotional), some information needed may not be gleaned from a play-based assessment alone. She stated, for example, that receptive language skills are difficult to determine with play-based approaches because to give children instructions, responses to which can provide information about receptive language, would be to deviate from the flexibility of the TPBA approach. Therefore, although play-based assessment may produce useful developmental information, other approaches may be needed for a more comprehensive picture of a child's functioning.

Cultural Differences and Disability Influences

Information about cultural, gender, race, ethnicity, and age differences, as well as differences in play behaviors that are related to certain disabilities (e.g., sensory impairments), and how these affect performance on play-based measures is needed in order for professionals to be sensitive to such differences so as not to unfairly penalize children. For example, cultural and socioeconomic differences may exist in the pretend play of children, and these differences may appear as, but not reflect, differences in cognitive functioning or symbolic representational skills (see Hughes, 1995). Differences in sensorimotor and symbolic play that appear to be more related to a disability than developmental level have also been found for various disabilities (Rogers, 1988). Guidelines for interpretation of play-based approaches are needed in order to use these methods to fairly evaluate all children.

Other Limitations

Other potential limitations to play-based assessment were discussed by Segal and Webber (1996). These include expense, logistical concerns, and difficulty of clinicians remaining purely observers. In addition, some parents may find play-based observations intrusive, and sometimes play observations do not yield a sufficient amount of information, particularly if a child perseverates on one play action. Including some structure in the play assessment in the form of prompting for emerging behaviors, for example, may alleviate this concern.

Given the strengths and limitations of play-based assessment, it is suggested that the model can provide important information about practical and functional skills of young children, which can be easily translated into interventions. Nevertheless, research on the reliability and validity of this information is imperative. It is also suggested that these procedures be used in conjunction with more traditional forms of assessment (Linder, 1993b). Combining the two models will account for the strengths and limitations of both and will more likely provide all the information necessary for eligibility determination as well as program planning.

PLAY AND THERAPEUTIC ASSESSMENT

As previously discussed, play has been used as a medium for assessing and treating emotional difficulties since the late 1910s. The use of play for this purpose is based in part on the idea that, because of young children's cognitive and linguistic limitations, many of their feelings, thoughts, experiences, ascriptions, beliefs, and perceptions are communicated through play (Landreth,

1991; O'Connor, 1991). In addition, children's defenses are less pronounced when at play, play has a cathartic effect, and it allows children to practice roles and behaviors in a safe context (Hughes, 1995). Play currently is used by therapists of various theoretical orientations for the assessment and treatment of children with emotional and behavior problems, as well as those who have been traumatized.

One common use of play for the assessment of children is to assess sexual victimization of young children with the use of anatomically detailed dolls. In this method, children are given dolls complete with genitalia to play with, with the supposition that children who have been sexually abused or otherwise inappropriately exposed to sexual content will have the dolls act out sexual behaviors. Although the use of this method is commonplace in many judicial systems, research on the validity of the method is less conclusive than its use suggests (Wolfner, Faust, & Dawes, 1993).

The Erica Method, a modification of Lowenfield's (1950) World Technique is another play diagnosis method that can be used to make decisions about children's emotional states. This method involves presenting the child with 360 miniature toys and a piece of clay. The toys are in a 12-compartment box, with each box representing the theme of the toys inside. The child is also given two boxes of sand—one wet and one dry. The constructions the child produces are analyzed in order to make diagnoses of the child in four areas: developmental, milieu, somatic/psychosomatic, and psychopathological. Information gained from the assessment method can be used in treatment planning for the child.

Other play assessment techniques include but are in no way limited to the use of puppets, whereby children put on puppet shows, and form (e.g., creativity, coherence, intelligibility, impulsivity) and content (e.g., characters, setting, plot, theme) dimensions are evaluated to give information about a child's defenses, coping styles, preoccupations, and conflicts (Irwin, 1993). Also, "feelings faces," which are pictures of faces with expressions indicative of various emotions, have been used to help children identify their emotions (Whaley, 1990), and observations of children and their parents at play have been used to gain information about parent–child relationships (Segal & Webber, 1996).

The preceding examples show how play can be used in psychotherapeutic interactions with children. For more detailed discussions about the therapeutic uses of and interpretation of emotions via play, refer to Axline (1969), Klein (1955), Landreth (1991), O'Connor

(1991), and Schaefer and Cangelosi (1993). The examples presented here highlight the variety of ways play can be used as a medium for diagnosing and treating children with emotional and behavioral issues. In fact, the use of play for these purposes is a precursor and basis for using play to assess developmental functioning of children.

SUMMARY

Given the significance of play, it appears that play-based assessment is a viable means of evaluating infants and preschool children. As a means of communication by young children, play is an appropriate and sensitive medium for diagnosing and treating emotional issues. With regard to assessing developmental functioning, play-based methods have numerous characteristics that are consistent with many federal mandates and best practices statements of several relevant professional organizations. Despite these advantages, play-based assessment is not at the point of replacing more traditional methods of assessment. Much more research related to the reliability and validity of data collected from, as well as interventions based upon, play-based approaches is needed. In addition, more research on cultural, age, ethnic, racial differences, and disability influences on play is also necessary, so that the fairness of this method can be ensured for all children.

REFERENCES

Athey, I. (1984). Contributions of play to development. In T. D. Yawkey & A. D. Pelligrini (Eds.), *Child's play: Developmental and applied* (pp. 9–28). Hillsdale, NJ: Erlbaum.

Axline, V. (1969). *Play therapy* (Rev. ed.). New York: Ballantine Books.

Bagnato, S. J., & Neisworth, J. T. (1994). A national study of the social and treatment "invalidity" of intelligence testing for early intervention. *School Psychology Quarterly, 9,* 81–102.

Bagnato, S. J., Neisworth, J. T., & Munson, S. M. (1993). Sensible strategies for assessment in early intervention. In D. M. Bryant & M. A. Graham (Eds.), *Implementing early intervention: From research to effective practice* (pp. 148–182). New York: Guilford Press.

Bornstein, M. H., Vibbert, M., Tal, J., & O'Donnell, K. (1992). Toddler language and play in the second year: Stability, covariation and influences of parenting. *First Language, 12,* 323–338.

Bracken, B. A. (1994). Advocating for effective preschool assessment practices: A comment on Bagnato and Neisworth. *School Psychology Quarterly, 9,* 103–108.

Casby, M. W., & Corte, M. D. (1987). Symbolic play performance and early language development. *Journal of Psycholinguistic Research, 16,* 31–42.

Cichetti, D., & Wagner, S. (1990). Alternative assessment strategies for the evaluation of infants and toddlers: An organizational perspective. In S. J. Meisels & J. P. Shonkoff (Eds.), *Handbook of early childhood intervention* (pp. 246–277). New York: Cambridge University Press.

de Lorimier, S., Doyle, A. B., & Tessier, O. (1995). Social coordination during pretend play: Comparisons with nonpretend play and effects on expressive content. *Merrill Palmer Quarterly, 41,* 497–516.

Eisert, D., & Lamorey, S. (1996). Play as a window on child development: The relationship between play and other developmental domains. *Early Education and Development, 7,* 221–235.

Farver, J. M. (1992). Communicating shared meaning in social pretend play. *Early Childhood Research Quarterly, 7,* 501–516.

Faust, D. (1986). Research on human judgment and its application to clinical practice. *Professional Psychology: Research and Practice, 17,* 420–430.

Fein, G. G. (1981). Pretend play in childhood: An integrative review. *Child Development, 52,* 1095–1118.

Fewell, R. R. (1992). *Play assessment scale* (5th rev.). Unpublished document. Miami: University of Miami School of Medicine.

Fewell, R. R., & Glick, M. P. (1993). Observing play: An appropriate process for learning and assessment. *Infants and Young Children, 5,* 35–43.

Fewell, R. R., & Kaminski, M. B. (1988). Play skills development and instruction for young children with handicaps. In S. L. Odom & M. B. Karnes (Eds.), *Early intervention for infants and children with handicaps* (pp. 145–157). Baltimore: Paul H. Brookes.

Fewell, R. R., & Rich, J. S. (1987). Play assessment as a procedure for examining cognitive, communication, and social skills in multihandicapped children. *Journal of Psychoeducational Assessment, 2,* 107–118.

Fink, R. S. (1976). Role of imaginative play in cognitive development. *Psychological Reports, 39,* 895–906.

Finn, D. M., & Fewell, R. R. (1994, July–August). The use of play assessment to examine the development of communication skills in children who are deaf-blind. *Journal of Visual Impairment & Blindness,* 349–356.

Fleischer, K. H., Belgredan, J. H., Bagnato, S. J., & Ogonosky, A. B. (1990). An overview of judgment-based assessment. *Topics in Early Childhood Special Education, 10*(3), 13–23.

Friedli, C. R. (1994). *Transdisciplinary play-based assessment: A study of reliability and validity.* Unpublished doctoral dissertation, University of Colorado, Boulder, CO.

Golomb, C., & Cornelius, C. B. (1977). Symbolic play and its cognitive significance. *Developmental Psychology, 13,* 246–252.

Gowen, J. W., Johnson-Martin, N., Goldman, B. D., & Hussey, B. (1992). Object play and exploration in children with and without disabilities: A longitudinal study. *American Journal on Mental Retardation, 97,* 21–38.

Greenspan, S. I., & Meisels, S. (1994). Toward a new vision for the developmental assessment of infants and young children. *Zero to Three, 14*(6), 1–8.

Howes, C. (1987). Social competence with peers in young children: Developmental sequences. *Developmental Review, 7,* 252–272.

Howes, C., & Matheson, C. C. (1992). Sequences in the development of competent play with peers: Social and social pretend play. *Developmental Psychology, 28,* 961–974.

Howes, C., Unger, O., & Seidner, L. B. (1989). Social pretend play in toddlers: Parallels with social play and with solitary pretend. *Child Development, 60,* 77–84.

Hughes, F. P. (1995). *Children, play, and development* (2nd ed.). Boston: Allyn and Bacon.

Irwin, E. C. (1993). Using puppets for assessment. In C. E. Schaefer & D. M. Cangelosi (Eds.), *Play therapy techniques* (pp. 69–81). Northvale, NJ: Jason Aranson.

Johnson, J. E., Christie, J. F., & Yawkey, T. D. (1987). *Play and early childhood development.* Glenview, IL: Scott Foresman.

Klein, M. (1955). The psychoanalytic play technique. *American Journal of Orthopsychiatry, 25,* 223–227.

Knobloch, H., Stevens, F., & Malone, A. (1987). *Manual of developmental diagnosis: The administration and interpretation of the Revised Gesell & Amatruda Developmental and Neurological Examination.* Houston, TX: Developmental Evaluation Materials.

Landreth, G. L. (1991). *Play therapy: The art of the relationship.* Bristol, PA: Accelerated Development.

Linder, T. W. (1990). *Transdisciplinary play-based assessment.* Baltimore: Paul H. Brookes.

Linder, T. W. (1993a). *Transdisciplinary play-based assessment and intervention: Child and program summary forms.* Baltimore: Paul H. Brookes.

Linder, T. W. (1993b). *Transdisciplinary play-based assessment: A functional approach to working with young children* (Rev. ed.). Baltimore: Paul H. Brookes.

Linder, T. W. (1993c). *Transdisciplinary play-based intervention: Guidelines for developing a meaningful curriculum for young children.* Baltimore: Paul H. Brookes.

Lowenfield, M. (1950). The nature and use of the Lowenfield World Technique in work with children. *Journal of Psychology, 30,* 325–331.

Lynch, E. W. (1996). Assessing infants: Child and family issues and approaches. In M. J. Hanson (Ed.), *Atypical infant development* (2nd ed., pp. 115–146). Austin, TX: Pro-Ed.

Malone, D. M., Stoneman, Z., & Langone, J. (1994). Contextual variation of correspondences among measures of play and developmental level of preschool children. *Journal of Early Intervention, 18,* 199–215.

McCune, L. (1995). A normative study of representational play at the transition to language. *Developmental Psychology, 31,* 198–206.

McCune-Nicholich, L. (1981). Toward symbolic functioning: Structure of early pretend games and potential parallels with language. *Child Development, 51,* 785–797.

Myers, C. L., McBride, S. L., & Peterson, C. A. (1996). Transdisciplinary, play-based assessment in early childhood special education: An examination of social validity. *Topics in Early Childhood Special Education, 16,* 102–126.

National Association of School Psychologists (1991). *Position statement on early childhood assessment.* Washington, DC: Author.

Neisworth, J. T., & Bagnato, S. J. (1988). Assessment in early childhood special education. In S. L. Odom & M. B. Karnes (Eds.), *Early intervention for infants and children with handicaps* (pp. 23–49). Baltimore: Paul H. Brookes.

O'Connor, K. J. (1991). *The play therapy primer: An integration of theories and techniques.* New York: John Wiley and Sons.

Ogura, T. (1991). A longitudinal study of the relationship between early language development and play development. *Journal of Child Language, 18,* 273–294.

Parker, J. G., & Gottman, J. M. (1989). Social and emotional development in a relational context. In T. J. Berndt & G. Ladd (Eds.), *Peer relationships in child development.* New York: Wiley.

Parten, M. (1932). Social participation among preschool children. *Journal of Abnormal and Social Psychology, 27,* 243–269.

Pepler, D. J., & Ross, H. S. (1981). The effects of play on convergent and divergent problem solving. *Child Development, 52,* 1202–1210.

Piaget, J. (1962). *Play, dreams and imitation in childhood.* New York: W. W. Norton & Company.

Rogers, S. (1988). Cognitive characteristics of handicapped children's play: A review. *Journal for the Division of Early Childhood, 12,* 161–168.

Rubin, K. H., & Pepler, D. J. (1982). Children's play: Piaget's views reconsidered. *Contemporary Educational Psychology, 7,* 289–299.

Schaefer, C. E., & Cangelosi, D. M. (1993). *Play therapy techniques.* Northvale, NJ: Jason Aranson.

Schicke, M. C., & Hankey, K. J. (1997, December). *Increasing involvement of school psychologists in infant/toddler service delivery.* Paper presented at the meeting of Zero to Three, Nashville, TN.

Segal, M., & Webber, N. T. (1996). Nonstructured play observations: Guidelines, benefits, and caveats. In S. J. Meisels & E. Fenichel (Eds.), *New visions for the developmental assessment of infants and young children* (pp. 207–230). Washington, DC: Zero to Three.

Slade, A., & Wolf, D. P. (1994). *Children at play: Clinical and developmental approaches to meaning and representation.* New York: Oxford University Press.

Smilansky, S. (1968). *The effects of sociodramatic play on disadvantaged preschool children.* New York: Wiley.

Smith, P. K. (1978). A longitudinal study of social participation in preschool children: Solitary and parallel play reexamined. *Developmental Psychology, 14,* 517–523.

Sutton-Smith, B. (1967). The role of play in cognitive development. *Young Children, 22,* 361–370.

Tversky, A., & Kahneman, D. (1974). Judgment under uncertainty: Heuristics and biases. *Science, 185,* 1124–1131.

Vygotsky, L. S. (1966). Play and its role in the mental development of the child. *Soviet Psychology, 12*(6), 62–76.

Whaley, A. L. (1990). A play technique to assess young children's emotional reactions to personal events: A cognitive-developmental approach. *Psychotherapy, 27*(2), 256–260.

Wolery, M., & Bailey, D. B. (1989). Assessing play skills. In D. B. Bailey & M. Wolery (Eds.), *Assessing infants and preschoolers with handicaps* (pp. 428–446). Columbus, OH: Merrill.

Wolery, M., & Dyk, L. (1984). Arena assessment: Description and preliminary social validity data. *Journal for the Association of Persons with Severe Handicaps, 9,* 231–235.

Wolf, M. M. (1978). Social validity: The case for subjective measurement or how applied behavior analysis is finding its heart. *Journal of Applied Behavior Analysis, 11,* 203–214.

Wolfner, G., Faust, D., & Dawes, R. M. (1993). The use of anatomically detailed dolls in sexual abuse evaluations: The state of the science. *Applied and Preventive Psychology, 2,* 1–11.

Yawkey, T. D., & Pellegrini, A. D. (1984). *Child's play: Developmental and applied.* Hillsdale, NJ: Lawrence Erlbaum Associates.

CHAPTER 21

A CONCEPTUAL FRAMEWORK FOR INTERPRETING PRESCHOOL INTELLIGENCE TESTS

DAWN P. FLANAGAN
JENNIFER MASCOLO
JUDY L. GENSHAFT

It will likely come as no surprise to the readers of this text that intelligence tests, like other standardized, norm-referenced measures (e.g., language batteries, behavior rating scales), are limited in their utility with a preschool population (especially preschoolers younger than 4 years in age) (Bagnato & Neisworth, 1994; Bracken, 1987, 1994; Flanagan & Alfonso, 1995; Wilson, 1992). Specifically, preschool intelligence tests generally have been found to fall short of a desired level of technical adequacy (see Alfonso & Flanagan, 1999, and Bracken & Walker, 1997 for a summary). Despite the psychometric limitations of certain preschool intelligence tests at certain ages, they are among the *most* technically adequate of all standardized, norm-referenced preschool tests. When used as part of a well-designed battery that complements the nature of the child, the referral, and other instruments incorporated in the evaluation, these measures can yield important and useful information (Bracken, 1994; Wilson, 1992). It is our contention that the inherent value of the data yielded by any given preschool intelligence test is related directly to the *level of expertise* that the examiner possesses in the test interpretation process.

In order for the value of preschool intelligence tests to be realized, they must be used intelligently (Bracken, 1994). The intelligent use of preschool measures involves developing expertise in test interpretation. In this chapter we propose that expertise in preschool test interpretation represents a complex interaction between *declarative knowledge* (i.e., knowledge about test characteristics, standards, the developing preschool child, etc.) and *procedural knowledge* (i.e., knowledge about how to use tests and make psychometrically and theoretically defensible interpretations of test performance). Examiners must accumulate a large amount of domain-specific knowledge about preschool cognitive ability tests (e.g., knowledge of psychometric test characteristics) or a sufficient declarative knowledge base as well as much experience in solving problems related to test interpretation (e.g., knowing how to solve referral-related problems) or a sufficient procedural knowledge base in order to be effective in interpreting and linking test data to referral concerns. That is, effective test interpretation necessitates access to well-organized, domain-specific knowledge and skill in applying that knowledge appropriately.

This chapter will offer a conceptual framework for interpreting preschool intelligence tests that draws upon (and borrows from) the terminology and concepts inherent in the cognitive psychology and human information processing literature. Specifically, this chapter will describe the declarative knowledge base considered minimally necessary for interpreting preschool intelligence tests and provide an example of how this knowledge can be used (procedurally) to (1) form and test hypotheses related to referral concerns and (2) draw conclusions. It is hoped that the conceptual framework presented in this chapter will provide readers with the information necessary to develop expertise that will allow them to move more quickly and efficiently through the interpretive process and be more reflective as a result of the breadth and depth of their knowledge.

DECLARATIVE KNOWLEDGE NEEDED FOR TEST INTERPRETATION

Declarative knowledge is defined typically as knowledge of facts, definitions, generalizations, and rules, all of which can exist in specific domains (Eggen & Kauchak,

1997). When considering the use of preschool intelligence tests, it appears that several *domain-specific knowledge bases* or foundational sources of information are necessary to interpret test performance. The most salient of these specific domains of knowledge includes (but is not limited to) the following: (1) psychometric characteristics of tests, (2) qualitative characteristics of tests, and (3) theoretical characteristics of tests. Collectively, these domain-specific knowledge bases represent the individual's declarative knowledge base for test interpretation. An examiner's ability to interpret test data depends, in part, on the *amount* of domain-specific knowledge the examiner has at his or her disposal (Bruning, Schraw, & Ronning, 1995). The specific domains of knowledge considered minimally necessary to facilitate the interpretation of preschool intelligence tests are described briefly here.

The Psychometric Knowledge Base

The *psychometric knowledge base* includes information about the psychometric or technical characteristics of tests. For the purpose of this chapter, the psychometric knowledge base is defined by several important technical test characteristics including test reliability, *g* loadings, specificity, floors, and item gradients. One or more of these characteristics are usually necessary to consider prior to selecting tests and/or interpreting test performance. The nature of the referral can guide decisions related to which technical characteristics ought to be considered in the test selection and interpretation process. For example, if a 3-year-old child is referred because of suspected developmental delay, then the *floor* of a test is one important psychometric characteristic to consider before selecting the instrument for use. Tests with poor floors can *overestimate* ability in very young children and in low-functioning children and will not provide much information about a child's capabilities.

Evaluations of the reliability, *g* loading, specificity, floor, and item gradient test characteristics (and the criteria used to make these evaluations) for preschool intelligence tests are reported in Table 21.1. The following preschool intelligence tests were evaluated: Differential Ability Scales (DAS; Elliott, 1990), Kaufman Assessment Battery for Children (K-ABC; Kaufman & Kaufman, 1983), Stanford-Binet Intelligence Scale: Fourth Edition (S-B:IV; Thorndike, Hagen, & Sattler, 1986), Wechsler Preschool and Primary Scale of Intelligence—Revised (WPPSI-R; Wechsler, 1989); and Woodcock-Johnson Psychoeducational Battery—Revised (WJ-R;

Woodcock & Johnson, 1989). These instruments were selected for review because, in the field of intellectual assessment and within the psychometric tradition, they are considered to be the major batteries available for assessing cognitive capabilities in the preschool population (Alfonso & Flanagan, 1999; Bracken & Walker, 1997; Wilson, 1992). Each of the psychometric characteristics mentioned previously will be defined briefly. Space limitations preclude an in-depth discussion of these characteristics. The reader is referred to Alfonso and Flanagan (1999), Bracken (1987, 1991), Bracken & Walker (1997), Flanagan and Alfonso (1995), and McGrew and Flanagan (1998) for extensive coverage of issues related to the technical qualities of (preschool) intelligence tests.

Reliability. The reliability of a particular test is important to consider because it affects interpretation of the test results. Reliability is defined as "the degree to which test scores are free from errors of measurement" (APA, 1985, p. 19). Reliability guides decisions concerning the range of scores (i.e., standard error of measurement) likely to occur as the result of irrelevant chance factors. In its broadest sense, test reliability indicates the extent to which individual differences are attributed to true differences in the characteristics under investigation or chance errors (Anastasi & Urbina, 1997). The degree of confidence one can place in a test score is directly related to the reliability of the instrument. Unreliable test scores can contribute to misdiagnosis and result in inappropriate placement and treatment decisions. Selecting tests that have good reliability can reduce these problems. Tests that have "low" reliability (i.e., coefficients <.80; see Table 21.1) are considered inadequate for making individual judgments about test performance (Salvia & Ysseldyke, 1991). Tests with "medium" reliability coefficients (.80 to .89) are considered appropriate only for making *screening* decisions, whereas tests with "high" coefficients (.90 or greater) are considered appropriate for making educational and diagnostic decisions when supported by additional data sources (see McGrew & Flanagan, 1998 for a more detailed discussion).

g-loadings. *g*-loading characteristics are also important to consider in the test interpretation process. Intelligence tests are interpreted often as reflecting a *general mental ability* called *g* (Anastasi & Urbina, 1997; Bracken & Fagan, 1990; Carroll, 1993a; French & Hale, 1990; Horn, 1988; Jensen, 1984; Kaufman, 1979; Keith, 1997; Sattler, 1992; Thorndike & Lohman, 1990). Despite the numerous theoretical arguments that surround

TABLE 21.1 Evaluation of Psychometric Characteristics of Preschool Intelligence Batteries

BATTERY COMPOSITE SCORES SUBTEST	RELIABILITY[1]	g LOADING	SPECIFICITY	FLOOR	ITEM GRADIENTS
Differential Ability Scales (DAS)					
General Conceptual Ability (GCA)	High			Adequate	
Verbal Ability	Medium			Adequate	
Nonverbal Ability	Medium			Adequate	
Verbal Comprehension	Medium	High at ages 2-0 to 4-0 Medium at age 5-0	Ample	Adequate	Good at ages 2-0 to 3-0 Fair at ages 4-0 to 5-0
Naming Vocabulary	Low	High at ages 2-0 to 3-0 Low at ages 4-0 to 5-0	Ample	Inadequate from ages 2-6 to 2-8	Poor at ages 2-0 and 5-0 Fair at ages 3-0 to 4-0
Picture Similarities	Low	Medium	Ample	Inadequate from ages 3-6 to 3-11	Good at ages 2-0 to 3-0 Fair at ages 4-0 to 5-0
Pattern Construction	Medium	Medium	Ample	Inadequate from ages 3-6 to 3-11	Good
Copying	Medium	Medium	Ample	Inadequate from ages 3-6 to 4-2	Good at age 4-0 Fair at ages 3-0 to 5-0
Early Number Concepts	Medium	High	Ample	Inadequate from ages 3-6 to 3-11	Good at age 4-0 Fair at ages 3-0 and 5-0
Block Building	Low	Medium	Ample	Inadequate from ages 2-6 to 3-2	Poor
Matching Letter-Like Forms	Medium	Medium	Ample	Inadequate from ages 4-6 to 5-5	Fair
Recall of Digits	Medium	Medium at ages 3-0 to 4-0 Low at age 5-0	Ample	Inadequate from ages 3-0 to 3-5	Good
Recall of Objects	Low	Low	Ample	Inadequate from ages 4-0 to 4-2	Good

BATTERY COMPOSITE SCORES SUBTEST	RELIABILITY[1]	g LOADING	SPECIFICITY	FLOOR	ITEM GRADIENTS
Differential Ability Scales (DAS)					
Nonverbal Ability					
Recognition of Pictures	Low	Medium at ages 3-0 to 4-0 Low at age 5-0	Ample	Inadequate from ages 3-0 to 3-11	Poor
Kaufman Assessment Battery for Children (K-ABC)					
Mental Processing Composite (MPC)	Medium			Inadequate from ages 2-6 to 3-3	
Sequential Processing	Medium			Inadequate from ages 2-6 to 4-4	
Simultaneous Processing	Medium			Inadequate from ages 2-6 to 3-4	
Magic Window	Low	High at age 2-0 Medium at ages 3-0 to 4-0	Ample	Inadequate from ages 2-6 to 3-3	Poor
Face Recognition	Low	Medium	Ample	Inadequate from ages 2-6 to 4-3	Good at age 2-0 Fair at age 3-0 Poor at age 4-0
Gestalt Closure	Low	Medium	Ample	Inadequate from ages 2-6 to 4-3	Good at ages 4-0 to 5-0 Fair at ages 2-0 to 3-0
Triangles	High	Medium at age 4-0 High at age 5-0	Ample	Inadequate from ages 4-0 to 7-11	Fair
Matrix Analogies	Medium	Medium at age 5-0	Ample	Inadequate from ages 5-0 to 7-11	Good
Spatial Memory	Low	High at age 5-0	Ample	Inadequate from ages 5-0 to 6-2	Good

(continued)

TABLE 21.1   Continued

BATTERY COMPOSITE SCORES SUBTEST	RELIABILITY[1]	g LOADING	SPECIFICITY	FLOOR	ITEM GRADIENTS
Kaufman Assessment Battery for Children (K-ABC)					
Simultaneous Processing					
Hand Movements	Low	Medium	Ample	Inadequate from ages 2-6 to 5-3	Poor at age 2-0 Fair at age 3-0 Good at age 4-0
Number Recall	Medium	High at ages 2-0 to 3-0 Medium at ages 4-0 to 5-0	Ample	Inadequate from ages 2-6 to 4-3	Fair at ages 2-0 to 3-0 Poor at ages 4-0 to 5-0
Word Order	Medium	High	Ample	Inadequate from ages 4-0 to 5-11	Good at age 5-0 Fair at age 4-0
Stanford-Binet Intelligence Scale: Fourth Edition (SB:IV)					
Test Composite	High			Inadequate from ages 2-3 to 3-3	
Verbal Reasoning	High			Inadequate from ages 2-3 to 3-3	
Abstract Visual Reasoning	Medium to High			Inadequate from ages 2-3 to 3-3	
Quantitative Reasoning	Medium			Inadequate from ages 2-3 to 4-11	
Short-Term Memory	High			Inadequate from ages 2-3 to 3-7	
Vocabulary	Medium	High	Ample at ages 2-0 to 3-0 Adequate at age 4-0 Inadequate at age 5-0	Inadequate from ages 2-0 to 3-3	Good
Absurdities	Medium	High	Ample	Inadequate from ages 2-0 to 4-3	Good at ages 2-0 to 4-0 Fair at age 5-0
Comprehension	Medium	High	Adequate	Inadequate from ages 2-0 to 3-3	Good

BATTERY
COMPOSITE SCORES

SUBTEST	RELIABILITY[1]	g LOADING	SPECIFICITY	FLOOR	ITEM GRADIENTS
Stanford-Binet Intelligence Scale: Fourth Edition (SB:IV)					
Short-Term Memory					
Pattern Analysis	Medium	High at ages 3-0 to 4-0 Medium at ages 2-0 and 5-0	Ample	Inadequate from ages 2-0 to 3-3	Good
Copying	Medium	Medium	Ample	Inadequate from ages 2-0 to 3-11	Good at ages 4-0 to 5-0 Fair at ages 2-0 to 3-0
Quantitative	Medium	Medium at ages 2-0 to 3-0 High at ages 4-0 to 5-0	Ample	Inadequate from ages 2-0 to 4-11	Good at ages 2-0 to 4-0 Fair at age 5-0
Bead Memory	Medium	Low at age 2-0 Medium at ages 3-0 to 5-0	Ample	Inadequate from ages 2-0 to 4-3	Good
Memory for Sentences	Medium	Medium	Ample	Inadequate from ages 2-0 to 3-11	Good
Wechsler Preschool and Primary Scale of Intelligence—Revised (WPPSI-R)					
Full Scale IQ	High			Inadequate from ages 2-11 to 3-2	
Verbal Scale	High			Adequate	
Performance Scale	High			Adequate	
Information	Medium at ages 3-0 to 4-0 Low at age 5-0	High	Ample at age 5-0 Adequate at ages 3-0 to 4-0	Inadequate from ages 2-11 to 3-11	Good at age 3-0 Fair at ages 4-0 to 5-0
Vocabulary	Medium	High	Ample	Inadequate from ages 2-11 to 3-2	Good
Arithmetic	Low at age 3-0 Medium at ages 4-0 to 5-0	High	Ample at ages 3-0 and 5-0 Adequate at age 4-0	Inadequate from ages 2-11 to 3-8	Good

(continued)

TABLE 21.1 Continued

BATTERY COMPOSITE SCORES SUBTEST	RELIABILITY[1]	g LOADING	SPECIFICITY	FLOOR	ITEM GRADIENTS
Wechsler Preschool and Primary Scale of Intelligence—Revised (WPPSI-R)					
Performance Scale					
Comprehension	Medium	High at ages 3-0 to 4-0 Medium at age 5-0	Ample	Inadequate from ages 2-11 to 4-8	Good at ages 3-0 to 4-0 Fair at age 5-0
Similarities	Medium	High	Ample	Inadequate from ages 2-11 to 4-2	Good
Picture Completion	Medium	High at ages 3-0 to 4-0 Medium at age 5-0	Ample	Inadequate from ages 2-11 to 3-11	Good
Block Design	Medium	Medium at age 3-0 High at ages 4-0 to 5-0	Ample	Inadequate from ages 2-11 to 4-5	Good
Object Assembly	Low	Medium	Adequate at age 3-0 Inadequate at ages 4-0 to 5-0	Adequate	Good
Mazes	Medium at age 3-0 Low at ages 4-0 to 5-0	Medium	Ample	Inadequate from ages 2-11 to 3-8	Good
Geometric Design	Medium at ages 3-0 to 4-0 Low at age 5-0	Medium	Ample	Inadequate from ages 2-11 to 3-11	Good
Animal Pegs	Data not available	Medium	Data not available	Inadequate from ages 2-11 to 4-2	Good
Sentences	Medium at ages 3-0 to 4-0 Low at age 5-0	High at ages 3-0 to 4-0 Medium at age 5-0	Ample	Inadequate from ages 2-11 to 3-8	Good
Woodcock-Johnson Psychoeducational Battery—Revised (WJ-R)					
Broad Cognitive Ability Early Development Scale	High			Adequate	

BATTERY COMPOSITE SCORES SUBTEST	RELIABILITY[1]	g LOADING	SPECIFICITY	FLOOR	ITEM GRADIENTS
Woodcock-Johnson Psychoeducational Battery—Revised (WJ-R)					
Memory for Names	Medium	Data not available	Data not available	Inadequate from ages 2-0 to 2-5	Good at age 2-0 Fair at ages 3-0 to 5-0
Memory for Sentences	High	Data not available	Data not available	Adequate	Fair
Incomplete Words	Medium	Data not available	Data not available	Inadequate from ages 2-0 to 4-3 and 90+	Fair at ages 2-0 to 4-0 Poor at age 5-0
Visual Closure	Medium at ages 2-0 to 4-0 Low at age 5-0	Data not available	Data not available	Adequate	Fair at ages 2-0 to 4-0 Poor at age 5-0
Picture Vocabulary	Medium	Data not available	Data not available	Inadequate from ages 2-0 to 2-1	Good at age 2-0 Fair at ages 3-0 to 4-0 Poor at age 5-0

Source: From *The Intelligence Test Desk Reference (ITDR): Gf-Gc Cross-Battery Assessment*, by K. S. McGrew and D. P. Flanagan, 1998, Boston: Allyn & Bacon. Adapted with permission.

Note: Evaluation of reliability coefficients was based on the following criteria: High = .90; Medium = .80 to .89 inclusive; Low = <.80. General factor or *g* loadings were classified as follows: Good = .70 or higher; Fair = .51 to.69; Poor = .50 or lower. Evaluation of specificity was based on the following: Ample = a test's unique reliable variance is equal to or above 25% of the total test variance and it exceeds error variance (1-reliability); Adequate = meets only one of the criteria for ample; Inadequate = meets neither criteria for ample. Evaluation of test floors was based on the following criteria: Adequate = a raw score of 1 is associated with a standard score that is greater than 2 standard deviations below the normative mean of the test; Inadequate = a raw score of 1 is associated with a standard score that is not more than 2 standard deviations below the normative mean of the test (Bracken, 1987). Item gradients were evaluated according to the following criteria: Good = <5% violations; Fair = >5% to ≤ 15% violations; Poor = >15% violations (McGrew & Flanagan, 1998). A violation is defined as a one-unit increase in raw score points that results in a change of more than 1/3 standard deviation in standard score values.

[1] With the exception of speeded tests, all reported reliabilities were estimates of how consistently examinees performed across items or subsets of items in a single test administration (i.e., internal consistency). For speeded tests, reported reliabilities were estimates of how consistently examinees performed on the same set of items at different times (i.e., test-retest or stability reliability) (cf. McGrew & Flanagan, 1998).

the concept and meaningfulness of g, an appreciation of a (sub)test's relationship to a general intelligence factor is considered useful in interpretation (Bracken & Fagan, 1990; Kaufman, 1979, 1990a; Roid & Gyurke, 1991). g loadings provide information that is needed to anticipate those tests within an intelligence battery that are likely to vary from the remainder of the test profile (Kaufman, 1979; Kamphaus, 1993). Tests that are expected to be at a similar level of performance as most of the other tests in the battery (and the global or full scale score) are those that have "high" g factor loadings (see Table 21.1). If these tests vary significantly from the middle of a test profile, then examiners may need to examine noncognitive variables (e.g., level of motivation and interest in the task; Kaufman, 1979; McGrew, 1984; Roid & Gyurke, 1991). In contrast, tests that are expected to vary from the other tests within an intelligence battery, are those that have "low" g factor loadings (see Table 21.1). Thus, a test with a low g factor loading that differs from most other tests in the battery may not represent a diagnostically or clinically significant finding. Knowledge of each test's loading on the general factor (g) within an intelligence battery is important because it can help practitioners identify unusual test variations.

Specificity.   Knowledge of a test's specificity can also inform interpretation. The portion of a test's variance that is reliable and unique to the test is called specificity. According to Reynolds and Kaufman (1990), specificity refers to that part of a test's variance that is "not shared or held in common with other tests of the same scale" (p. 151). Tests with high or medium specificity (i.e., classified as "ample" and "adequate," respectively, in Table 21.1) may be interpreted as measuring an ability unique and specific to that test. The unique variance of tests with low specificity (classified as "inadequate" in Table 21.1) should not be interpreted. Test specificity assists practitioners in determining when it is appropriate to interpret individual tests as measuring distinct abilities within an intelligence battery. However, because a test's specificity usually represents the *smallest* portion of its reliable variance, caution should always be exercised when interpreting the unique variance of any test (for a more detailed discussion of test specificity, see Flanagan, Andrews, & Genshaft, 1997). It is important to note that tests with inadequate specificity (as well as tests with low g factor loadings) may be *valuable* in test interpretation if they are included as part of a composite with other similar tests. Because a test's level of specificity and g loading are related to the breadth or diversity of

tests included in the battery, these test characteristics are relative and somewhat arbitrary (McGrew & Flanagan, 1998; McGrew, Untiedt, & Flanagan, 1996).

Test Floors.   Because test floors have been identified as one of the poorest technical qualities of preschool intelligence tests (Bracken, 1987; Flanagan & Alfonso, 1995), this characteristic ought to be evaluated during the test selection process. Intelligence batteries with "adequate" (or *low*) floors (see Table 21.1) will yield scores that discriminate effectively among several levels of functioning at the lower extreme of the cognitive ability continuum. Tests with "inadequate" (or *high*) floors (see Table 21.1) cannot adequately distinguish between individuals functioning in the low average and borderline ranges of ability or between various levels of mental retardation (i.e., mild, moderate, severe) because they contain an insufficient number of easy items (Bracken, 1987). Intelligence batteries that do not have adequate floors will provide little (if any) information about what a young child *can do*. Therefore, tests with inadequate floors should not be used for diagnostic, classification, or placement decisions, especially with individuals who are suspected of developmental delay (Bracken, 1987; Flanagan & Alfonso, 1995; McGrew & Flanagan, 1998).

Item Gradients.   The information gained from examining the item gradients of a test complements information related to the floor of the test. That is, the extent to which a test effectively differentiates among various ability levels at the low end of the cognitive ability continuum (e.g., low average, borderline, mild mental retardation) can be determined by examining test floors, whereas the extent to which a test effectively differentiates across the entire range of the trait or ability measured can be determined by examining item gradients. In other words, item gradients (sometimes referred to as item density) are sensitive to *fine gradations* in ability across the scale of the test. Item gradient refers to the density of items across a test's latent trait scale. A test with good item gradient characteristics has items that are approximately equally spaced in difficulty along the entire scale of the test, and the distance between items is small enough to allow for reliable discrimination between individuals on the latent trait measured by the test (McGrew & Flanagan, 1998). Item gradient information is concerned with the extent to which changes in a single raw score point on a test result in excessively large changes in ability scores (or standard scores; Bracken, 1987).

Little attention has been paid to item gradients in the mainstream test development and evaluation literature. The first investigator to highlight the importance of item gradients and to present procedures for evaluating this test characteristic was Bracken (1987). Several years later, Flanagan and Alfonso (1995) updated the item gradient information for preschool intelligence tests offered by Bracken (1987) using a slight modification of his procedure. Both procedures, however, defined an *item gradient violation* as a one-unit increase in raw score points that resulted in a change of more than $\frac{1}{3}$ standard deviation in standard score values (cf. Bracken, 1987).

Most recently, McGrew and Flanagan (1998) developed a system for evaluating the item gradients of intelligence tests that differed from previous methods. Briefly, they tallied the number of item gradient violations for eight major intelligence tests and compared these values to the total number of possible item gradient violations for the respective test. For example, if a test had two item gradient violations out of a possible 50 (i.e., 50 possible raw score changes across the entire scale), the test was characterized as having 4 percent (2 of 50) item gradient violations. McGrew and Flanagan calculated the total percentage of item gradient violations for the major intelligence tests at every age level, including preschool (i.e., ages 2 to 5 years).

To establish a system of item gradient evaluation, McGrew and Flanagan (1998) examined the distribution of the percentage of item gradient violations for all subtests across all age levels and across all intelligence batteries included in their investigation. Results indicated that tests showed less than or equal to 5 percent violations approximately 80 percent of the time, 5 percent and 15 percent violations approximately 12 percent of the time, and greater than 15 percent violations approximately 8 percent of the time. When combined with logical considerations, these data were used to categorize tests as having *good* (<5 percent violations), *fair* (>5 percent to 15 percent violations), or *poor* (>15 percent violations) item gradient characteristics at each age level for which the test provided norms. The item gradient evaluations of intelligence tests at the preschool age range are reported in Table 21.1. Tests with poor item gradients will not detect fine gradations in ability and, therefore, should be interpreted with caution.

In summary, having access to the psychometric characteristics of preschool intelligence tests (i.e., a psychometric knowledge base) will provide practitioners with information that allows them to select and interpret tests more appropriately. Knowledge of a test's floor and item gradient characteristics will aid practitioners in choosing an instrument that may be more sensitive to measurement of ability in preschool children at the low end of the cognitive ability continuum. Knowledge of a test's specificity and *g*-loading characteristics will aid practitioners in making more appropriate interpretations of subtest performance and subtest variation, respectively. Finally, knowledge of a test's reliability can aid in both test selection and test interpretation. For example, a test that has an internal consistency reliability coefficient of .85 may be used most effectively as a *screening* instrument and should not be interpreted diagnostically. Although knowledge of the psychometric characteristics of preschool intelligence tests is necessary for proper use and interpretation, it is not sufficient for these purposes. Qualitative test characteristics are also necessary to consider.

The Qualitative Knowledge Base

The *qualitative knowledge base* includes information about tests (generally of a nontechnical nature) that can enrich and inform the test selection and interpretation process. For the purpose of this chapter, the qualitative knowledge base is defined by several important test characteristics or contextual factors that are likely to influence test performance including degree of cultural content inherent in the test, degree of linguistic demand necessary to perform the test, incidence of basic concepts in test directions, background/environmental factors and individual/situational factors, as well as examiner and test-setting variables. As was true of psychometric characteristics, the nature of the referral can guide decisions related to which *qualitative* characteristics ought to be considered in test use and interpretation. For example, if a 4-year-old child, who is learning English as a second language, is referred because of a suspected language delay in his or her primary language, then the examiner must pay careful attention to the extent to which linguistic demands and background/environmental variables (e.g., language stimulation, cultural opportunities, etc.) may influence test performance.

Table 21.2 includes a description of the preschool subtests (i.e., task demands) of the major preschool intelligence batteries. In addition, the degree of cultural content and linguistic demand (i.e., "high," "moderate," or "low") inherent in the individual subtests of these batteries is provided. Table 21.2 also lists the basic concepts that are included in the directions of the subtests of intelligence tests as well as the age at which such concepts typically are attained. Finally, the background/environmental and individual/situational variables that are likely to influence performance on the subtests of the major preschool intelligence batteries are listed in this table. These qualitative characteristics along with examiner and test-setting variables will be defined briefly later. For a more detailed and expansive discussion of these and other qualitative characteristics of intelligence tests, refer to Alfonso and Flanagan (1999), Bracken (1991), Bracken & Walker (1997), McGrew and Flanagan (1998), Paget (1991), and Sattler (1988).

Degree of Cultural Content and Linguistic Demand.
According to Ortiz and Flanagan (1998), assessment of the intellectual capabilities of culturally and linguistically diverse populations is one of the most difficult tasks facing psychologists today. An overrepresentation of individuals from diverse populations in special education and other remedial programs has resulted because of a failure to accurately distinguish normal, culturally based variation in behavior, first and second language acquisition, acculturation, and cognitive development from true disabilities (Cervantes, 1988; Ortiz, Flanagan, & McGrew, 1998). Systematic and appropriate evaluation methods must be incorporated in the assessment of culturally and linguistically diverse populations in order to circumvent the negative effects on learning, social, and psychological development that can result from improper educational placement (Dunn, 1968; Hobbs, 1975; Jones, 1972; cf. Ortiz et al., 1998).

"As much as practitioners, trainers, and scholars subscribe to the philosophy that well-standardized and psychometrically sound instruments can be an important and valuable component of assessment, the changing demographics of the United States mandate that the influences of cultural and linguistic factors on test performance be considered as equally important (Dana, 1993)" (McGrew & Flanagan, 1998, p. 427; see also APA, 1990). In order to address cultural and linguistic influences, Ortiz et al. (1998) constructed a matrix of cognitive ability tests in which the tests were organized according to three important characteristics: (1) degree of cultural content, (2) degree of linguistic demand, and (3) stratum I and stratum II abilities measured according to *Gf-Gc* theory. The latter test characteristic will be discussed in the next section of this chapter. The first two characteristics represent the broad cultural and linguistic considerations inherent in bilingual, cross-cultural, nondiscriminatory assessment. Classification of tests according to degree of cultural and linguistic demand is

discussed briefly here. (Refer to Ortiz et al., 1998 for a more detailed discussion of these important test characteristics.)

All subtests of eight major intelligence batteries (including preschool tests) have been classified according to their "degree of cultural content," or the degree to which they required specific knowledge of and experience with mainstream U.S. culture (see Ortiz et al., 1998, for a discussion). Classification of tests along the cultural dimension was based on logical analyses of task demands following criteria related to process, content, and nature of expected response. Tests that were more process dominant (versus product dominant), included abstract or novel stimuli (versus culture-specific stimuli), and required simple, less culturally bound communicative responding, such as head nods and pointing (see McCallum & Bracken, 1997), were thought to yield scores that are less influenced by an individual's level of exposure to mainstream U.S. culture (Jensen, 1974; Valdés & Figueroa, 1994). Ortiz et al.'s logical classifications of all subtests of the major preschool intelligence tests as either "high," "moderate," or "low" in cultural content are reported in Table 21.2.

Classification of tests along the linguistic dimension was based on factors related to test administration and responding. First, tests were evaluated according to the degree to which they involved expressive and receptive language skills on behalf of the examiner in order to be administered correctly. Some tests have relatively long instructions (e.g., Wechsler Block Design subtest), whereas others can be administered using gestures (e.g., the new Universal Nonverbal Intelligence Test; Bracken & McCallum, 1998) or minimal language (e.g., K-ABC). Second, tests were evaluated on the basis of the level of language proficiency required by the examinee in order to understand the examiner's instructions and offer an appropriate response. Responses for some tests require considerable expressive language skills (e.g., Wechsler Vocabulary and Comprehension subtests) whereas others may be accomplished without uttering a word (e.g., Wechsler Picture Completion). Based on a consideration of a test's language requirements for both the examiner and examinee, Ortiz et al. (1998) classified all subtests of the major preschool intelligence tests as having either "high," "moderate," or "low" linguistic demand (see Table 21.2).

The cultural-linguistic classification system of intelligence tests offered by Ortiz et al. (1998) and presented in McGrew and Flanagan (1998) is grounded in contemporary theory and research. As such, it provides

TABLE 21.2 Qualitative Factors to Be Considered in Preschool Intelligence Test Interpretation

BATTERY	TASK DEMAND	DEGREE OF CULTURAL CONTENT/ LINGUISTIC DEMAND	BASIC CONCEPTS IN TEST DIRECTIONS (AGE OF CONCEPT ATTAINMENT)[1]	BACKGROUND/ ENVIRONMENTAL AND INDIVIDUAL/SITUATIONAL FACTORS THAT INFLUENCE TEST PERFORMANCE
Differential Ability Scales (DAS)				
Subtests for Preschool-Age Children				
Verbal Comprehension	Manipulate objects or identify objects in pictures in response to orally presented instructions	high/high	Verbal conceptual knowledge	Language stimulation, environmental stimulation, educational opportunities/ experiences, cultural opportunities/experiences, attention span, concentration, distractibility, reflectivity/ impulsivity
Naming Vocabulary	Provide a verbal for objects or pictures of objects	high/high	Conceptual knowledge	Language stimulation, environmental stimulation, educational opportunities/ experiences, cultural opportunities/experiences, alertness to the environment, intellectual curiosity
Picture Similarities	Identify one of four stimulus pictures that match a target picture	moderate/low	on (3), under (4), both (4), like (5), four, row	Language stimulation, environmental stimulation, educational opportunities/ experiences, alertness to the environment
Pattern Construction	Manipulate flat squares or blocks to construct a series of designs	low/high	finished (3), in (3), black (4), yellow (4), tops (4), together (4), both (4), different (5), like (5), same (5), side(s) (5), pieces (5), all (5), right (>5), straight	Vision difficulties, environmental stimulation, *visual-motor coordination, reflectivity/ impulsivity, field dependence/ independence, flexibility/ inflexibility, planning, ability to perform under time pressure*

(continued)

TABLE 21.2 Continued

Subtests for Preschool-Age Children

BATTERY	TASK DEMAND	DEGREE OF CULTURAL CONTENT/ LINGUISTIC DEMAND	BASIC CONCEPTS IN TEST DIRECTIONS (AGE OF CONCEPT ATTAINMENT)[1]	BACKGROUND/ ENVIRONMENTAL AND *INDIVIDUAL/SITUATIONAL* FACTORS THAT INFLUENCE TEST PERFORMANCE
Differential Ability Scales (DAS)				
Copying	Reproduce line drawings, letter shapes, or geometric figures	low/low	same (5)	Vision difficulties, environmental stimulation, *visual-motor coordination*
Early Number Concepts	Demonstrate understanding of numerical concepts such as counting, number recognition, size, and basic arithmetic using colored chips or pictures	moderate/moderate	Numerical conceptual knowledge	Language stimulation, environmental stimulation, educational opportunities/ experiences
Block Building	Replicate two- or three-dimensional designs using wooden blocks	low/moderate	big (3), one (4), same (5), like (5), another (5), right (>5)	Environmental stimulation, *visual-motor coordination*
Matching Letter-Like Forms	Locate an identical match of a target letter-like shape	low/low	down (5)	Vision difficulties, educational opportunities/experiences, *reflectivity/impulsivity*
Recall of Digits	Repeat verbatim a series of orally presented digits	low/moderate	after (>5)	Hearing difficulties, attention span, concentration, distractibility, verbal rehearsal, visual elaboration, organization
Recall of Objects	Recall the names of 20 objects presented on a picture card after card is removed from view	moderate/low	same (5), all (5), before (>5), some (>5), more, as many, order	Environmental stimulation, attention span, concentration, distractibility, verbal rehearsal, verbal elaboration
Recognition of Pictures	View pictures of objects and identify those same objects when presented in a second picture that has a larger array of objects	moderate/low	on (3)	Concentration, reflectivity/ impulsivity, verbal elaboration

440

Subtests for Preschool-Age Children

Kaufman Assessment Battery for Children (K-ABC)

BATTERY	TASK DEMAND	DEGREE OF CULTURAL CONTENT/ LINGUISTIC DEMAND	BASIC CONCEPTS IN TEST DIRECTIONS (AGE OF CONCEPT ATTAINMENT)[1]	BACKGROUND/ ENVIRONMENTAL AND INDIVIDUAL/SITUATIONAL FACTORS THAT INFLUENCE TEST PERFORMANCE
Magic Window	Provide a name for pictures that are exposed by moving them past a narrow slit or "window" (making the picture only partially visible throughout the presentation)	moderate/low	None included in test directions	*Environmental stimulation, concentration, reflectivity/ impulsivity, visual elaboration*
Face Recognition	Select one or two faces from a group photograph that had been shown briefly in a preceding photograph	moderate/low	None included in test directions	*Concentration, reflectivity/ impulsivity, verbal elaboration*
Gestalt Closure	Name the object or scene depicted in a partially completed "inkblot" drawing	moderate/low	None included in test directions	*Vision difficulties, environmental stimulation, visual acuity, field dependence/independence*
Triangles	Use two-color triangles to reproduce a series of two-dimensional printed designs	low/low	one (4), together (4)	*Vision difficulties, environmental stimulation, visual-motor coordination, reflectivity/ impulsivity, field dependence/ independence, flexibility/ inflexibility, planning*
Matrix Analogies	Choose the picture or abstract design that best completes a visual analogy	low/low	one (4), right (>5), with	*Vision difficulties, environmental stimulation, reflectivity/ impulsivity, field dependence/ independence, flexibility/ inflexibility, planning*
Spatial Memory	Recall the location of pictures on a page following a 5-second interval exposure	moderate/low	None included in test directions	*Environmental stimulation, concentration, verbal rehearsal*

(continued)

441

TABLE 21.2 Continued

BATTERY	TASK DEMAND	DEGREE OF CULTURAL CONTENT/ LINGUISTIC DEMAND	BASIC CONCEPTS IN TEST DIRECTIONS (AGE OF CONCEPT ATTAINMENT)[1]	BACKGROUND/ ENVIRONMENTAL AND *INDIVIDUAL/SITUATIONAL* FACTORS THAT INFLUENCE TEST PERFORMANCE
Subtests for Preschool-Age Children				
Kaufman Assessment Battery for Children (K-ABC)				
Hand Movements	Imitate a series of hand movements in the same sequence as demonstrated by the examiner	low/low	None included in test directions	Attention span, concentration, distractibility, verbal rehearsal, visual elaboration
Number Recall	Repeat orally presented number sequences verbatim	low/moderate	some (>5)	Hearing difficulties, *attention span, concentration, distractibility, verbal rehearsal, visual elaboration, organization*
Word Order	Touch a series of pictures in the same sequence as they were named by the examiner	moderate/low	some (>5), before (>5)	Hearing difficulties, *attention, concentration, distractibility, verbal rehearsal, visual elaboration*
Stanford-Binet Intelligence Scale: Fourth Edition (SB:IV)				
Vocabulary	Either identify pictures named by the examiner by pointing or (later) orally define words	high/high	on (3), in (3), top (4), different (5), another (5), some (>5), in front, dollar	Language stimulation, environmental stimulation, educational opportunities/ experiences, cultural opportunities/experiences, intellectual curiosity
Comprehension	For items 1 through 6, examine a picture of a child and identify body parts; for items 7 through 42, respond to questions relating to everyday problem situations including survival behavior to civic duties	high/high	some (>5)	Language stimulation, environmental stimulation, educational opportunities/ experiences, cultural opportunities/experiences, alertness to the environment

BATTERY	TASK DEMAND	DEGREE OF CULTURAL CONTENT/ LINGUISTIC DEMAND	BASIC CONCEPTS IN TEST DIRECTIONS (AGE OF CONCEPT ATTAINMENT)[1]	BACKGROUND/ ENVIRONMENTAL AND *INDIVIDUAL/SITUATIONAL* FACTORS THAT INFLUENCE TEST PERFORMANCE
Subtests for Preschool-Age Children				
Stanford-Binet Intelligence Scale: Fourth Edition (SB:IV)				
Absurdities	Point to or describe the absurdity when presented with a situation that is contrary to common sense	high/high	some (>5)	Language stimulation, environmental stimulation, educational opportunities/ experiences, cultural opportunities/experiences, alertness to the environment
Pattern Analysis	For items 1–6 place puzzle pieces into a formboard; in subsequent items, reproduce patterns using blocks; this is a timed test	low/high	finished (3), in (3), top (4), together (4), into (4), different (5), like (5), all (5), another (5)	Vision difficulties, environmental stimulation, *visual-motor coordination, reflectivity/ impulsivity, field dependence/ independence, flexibility/ inflexibility*
Copying	Construct models with monochromatic blocks or use pencil and paper to draw a variety of designs to match a model	low/low	like (5), some (>5), with	Vision difficulties, environmental stimulation, *visual-motor coordination*
Quantitative	Provide solutions for applied mathematics problems and demonstrate knowledge of mathematics concepts	moderate/high	on (3), up (3), in (3), one (4), two (4), top (4), together (4), different (5), like (5), side (5), all (5), next (5), order (5), another (5), some (>5), next to, beside, with	Math difficulties, environmental stimulation, educational opportunities/experiences, concentration, *reflectivity/ impulsivity, flexibility/inflexibility*
Bead Memory	For items 1–10, recall which of one or two beads was exposed; for items 11 through 42, place beads on a stick in the same sequence as shown in a picture (following a 5-second exposure)	low/moderate	on (3), in (3), one (4), two (4), like (5), away (5), over [direction] (>5), some (>5)	Vision difficulties, environmental stimulation, concentration, *reflectivity/impulsivity, field dependence/independence, flexibility/inflexibility, verbal rehearsal*

(continued)

TABLE 21.2 Continued

Subtests for Preschool-Age Children

BATTERY	TASK DEMAND	DEGREE OF CULTURAL CONTENT/ LINGUISTIC DEMAND	BASIC CONCEPTS IN TEST DIRECTIONS (AGE OF CONCEPT ATTAINMENT)[1]	BACKGROUND/ ENVIRONMENTAL AND *INDIVIDUAL/SITUATIONAL* FACTORS THAT INFLUENCE TEST PERFORMANCE
Stanford-Binet Intelligence Scale: Fourth Edition (SB:IV)				
Memory for Sentences	Repeat verbatim orally presented sentences	moderate/high	None included in test directions	Hearing difficulties, language stimulation, *attention span, concentration, distractibility, verbal rehearsal, visual elaboration*
Wechsler Preschool and Primary Scale of Intelligence—Revised (WPPSI-R)				
Information	Respond to a series of orally presented questions that assess knowledge about events, objects, places, and people	high/high	on (3), in (3), two (4), together (4), pieces (5), another (5), before (>5), after (>5), four, night, wood	Environmental stimulation, educational opportunities/ experiences, cultural opportunities/experiences, alertness to environment, intellectual curiosity
Vocabulary	Provide definitions for a series of orally presented words	high/high	some (>5)	Language stimulation, environmental stimulation, educational opportunities/ experiences, cultural opportunities/experiences, alertness to the environment, intellectual curiosity
Arithmetic	Solve and respond orally to a series of orally presented arithmetic problems without paper or pencil	moderate/moderate	on (3), in (4), some (>5)	Math difficulties, educational opportunities/experiences, *attention span, concentration, distractibility, visual elaboration*
Comprehension	Provide an oral response to a series of orally presented questions that focus on everyday problems or understanding of social rules and concepts	high/high	in (3), one (4), another (5), sick, before, hot, cold	Language stimulation, environmental stimulation, educational opportunities/ experiences, cultural opportunities/experiences, alertness to the environment

Subtests for Preschool-Age Children

Wechsler Preschool and Primary Scale of Intelligence—Revised (WPPSI-R)

BATTERY	TASK DEMAND	DEGREE OF CULTURAL CONTENT/ LINGUISTIC DEMAND	BASIC CONCEPTS IN TEST DIRECTIONS (AGE OF CONCEPT ATTAINMENT)[1]	BACKGROUND/ ENVIRONMENTAL AND *INDIVIDUAL/SITUATIONAL* FACTORS THAT INFLUENCE TEST PERFORMANCE
Similarities	Explain the similarity of the common objects or concepts represented by a pair or orally-presented words	high/high	in (3), up (3), together (4), both (4), like/alike (5), all (5), another (5), nickel, penny	Language stimulation, environmental stimulation, educational opportunities/ experiences, cultural opportunities/experiences
Picture Completion	Identify an essential missing part from a set of pictures of common objects and scenes; this is a timed test	moderate/low	in (3), missing (5)	Vision difficulties, alertness to the environment, *visual acuity, field dependence/independence*
Block Design	Replicate a set of modeled or printed two-dimensional geometric patterns using two-color cubes; This is a timed test	low/high	red (3), up (3), on (3), one (4), white (4), together (4), through (4), side (5), like (5), same (5), another (5), some (>5), next to	Color blindness, reflectivity/ impulsivity, field dependence/ independence, flexibility/ inflexibility, planning, ability to work under time pressure
Object Assembly	Assemble a set of puzzles of common objects into meaningful wholes; this is a timed test	moderate/moderate	in (3), big (3), together (4), through (4), fast (4), like (5), pieces (5), all (5), some (>5)	Alertness to the environment, *reflectivity/impulsivity, field dependence/independence, planning, ability to perform under time pressure*
Mazes	Complete, with a pencil, a series of increasingly difficult mazes	low/high	on (3), in (3), up (3), out of (3), boy (3), little (3), finished (3), inside (4), into (4), middle (4), like (5), wrong (5), all (5), another (5), without (>5), over [direction] (>5), over [time]	Vision difficulties, *visual-motor coordination, reflectivity/ impulsivity, field dependence/ independence, planning, ability to perform under time pressure*

(continued)

TABLE 21.2 Continued

BATTERY	TASK DEMAND	DEGREE OF CULTURAL CONTENT/ LINGUISTIC DEMAND	BASIC CONCEPTS IN TEST DIRECTIONS (AGE OF CONCEPT ATTAINMENT)[1]	BACKGROUND/ ENVIRONMENTAL AND *INDIVIDUAL/SITUATIONAL* FACTORS THAT INFLUENCE TEST PERFORMANCE
Subtests for Preschool-Age Children				
Wechsler Preschool and Primary Scale of Intelligence—Revised (WPPSI-R)				
Geometric Design	Examine a simple design, and, with the design in view, point to another design that is exactly like it from an array of four designs; then draw geometric designs from a printed model	low/low	up (3), finished (3), two (4), both (4), like/alike (5)	Vision difficulties, environmental stimulation, *visual-motor coordination*
Animal Pegs	Insert colored pegs into holes on a board according to a key at the top of the board; this is timed test	moderate/high	up (3), in (3), white (4), under (4), top (4), fast (4), black (4), yellow (4), piece (5), different (5), next (5), right (>5), after (>5), blue, row, with	Vision difficulties, attention span, concentration, distractibility, *visual acuity, reflectivity/ impulsivity, verbal elaboration, visual elaboration, planning, visual-motor coordination, ability to perform under time pressure*
Sentences	Repeat verbatim orally presented sentences	moderate/high	same (5), after (>5)	Hearing difficulties, language stimulation, attention span, concentration, distractibility, *verbal rehearsal, visual elaboration*
Woodcock-Johnson Psychoeducational Battery—Revised (WJ-R)				
Memory for Names	Learn associations between novel auditory and visual stimuli (an auditory-visual association task)	low/moderate	more (>5)	Environmental stimulation, concentration, *ability to use feedback to monitor performance, reflectivity/impulsivity, verbal elaboration, visual elaboration*
Memory for Sentences	Remember and repeat verbatim phrases and sentences presented by a tape player or, in certain cases, by an examiner	moderate/high	on (3), two (4), same (5), some (>5), after (>5)	Hearing difficulties, language stimulation, attention span, concentration, distractibility, *verbal rehearsal, visual elaboration*

BATTERY	TASK DEMAND	DEGREE OF CULTURAL CONTENT/ LINGUISTIC DEMAND	BASIC CONCEPTS IN TEST DIRECTIONS (AGE OF CONCEPT ATTAINMENT)[1]	BACKGROUND/ ENVIRONMENTAL AND *INDIVIDUAL/SITUATIONAL* FACTORS THAT INFLUENCE TEST PERFORMANCE
Subtests for Preschool-Age Children				
Woodcock-Johnson Psychoeducational Battery—Revised (WJ-R)				
Incomplete Words	Listen to a recorded word that has one or more phonemes missing, and identify the complete word	moderate/high	on (3), two (4), whole (4), next (5), some (>5), after (>5), woman	Hearing difficulties, reading difficulties, environmental stimulation, educational opportunities/experiences, attention span, concentration, distractibility, hearing acuity, verbal rehearsal
Visual Closure	Identify a drawing or picture that is altered through distortions, missing lines or areas, or a superimposed pattern.	moderate/low	behind (3), in (3), another (5)	Vision difficulties, environmental stimulation, *visual acuity, field dependence/independence*
Picture Vocabulary	Provide a verbal label for familiar and unfamiliar pictured objects.	high/moderate	on (3), another (5)	Language stimulation, environmental stimulation, educational opportunities/ experiences, cultural opportunities/experiences, alertness to the environment, intellectual curiosity

Source: Adapted from *The Intelligence Test Desk Reference (ITDR) Gf-Gc Cross-Battery Assessment,* by K. S. McGrew and D. P. Flanagan, 1998, Boston: Allyn and Bacon. Adapted with permission.

[1]When a basic concept is reported without a parenthetical age reference, the typical age of concept attainment was not available.

practitioners with critical information that can be used to compile a *selective* set of measures that may yield a more empirically defensible assessment of cognitive abilities that is sensitive to the discriminatory aspects of the tests themselves. (See McGrew & Flanagan, 1998, for a step-by-step approach to constructing culturally and linguistically sensitive assessments.) "Carefully reasoned selection and use of tests of cognitive ability that have lower cultural and linguistic demands can serve to reduce the distance between an individual's level of acculturation, proficiency with the English language, and the inherent demands of the test, thereby increasing validity" (Ortiz & Flanagan, 1998, p. 8). When the cultural and linguistic characteristics of tests are considered *in combination with other relevant information,* interpretation of test performance with second language learners or individuals who are not acculturated fully into the U.S. mainstream culture can be made less biased, resulting in a more valid representation of actual ability (Ortiz & Flanagan, 1998; Ortiz et al., 1998).

Ortiz et al. (1998) recognize that their cultural-linguistic classification system is an initial framework and that continued research on the cultural and linguistic parameters of cognitive ability tests is needed. They stated that their classifications are

> *clearly* subjective *and were derived primarily from a combination of recognized issues found in the literature as well as our own judgements and are insufficient, by themselves, to establish a comprehensive basis for assessment of diverse individuals. They are intended only to supplement the assessment process by guiding test selection that may more appropriately meet the needs of culturally and linguistically diverse populations within the context of a broader, defensible system of bilingual, nondiscriminatory, cross-cultural assessment… [t]hey may also serve as a starting point for both researchers and practitioners to begin establishing empirically supportable standards for practice.* (p. 437, emphasis in the original)

Incidence of Basic Concepts in Preschool Test Directions. When intelligence tests are used to assess the cognitive functioning of preschool children, an awareness of the basic concepts that are included in standard test administration procedures and the probability of a young child understanding (or misunderstanding) those concepts is integral to test interpretation. That is, tests that include a high incidence of basic concepts during

standard administration procedures may yield spuriously low scores for preschool children because their linguistic knowledge is limited (Bracken, 1986; Flanagan, Alfonso, Kaminer, & Rader, 1995; Glutting & Kaplan, 1990; Kaufman, 1978, 1990b).

The results of previous studies (e.g., Bracken, 1986) suggest that practitioners should not assume that preschoolers fully comprehend the standard directions of most major intelligence tests. For instance, intelligence test directions that include "difficult" basic concepts (e.g., *without, over, after*), long sentences, and/or the passive voice may not be understood by preschool children (Alfonso & Flanagan, 1999; Boehm, 1991; Bracken, 1986; Flanagan et al., 1995; Kaufman, 1978, 1990b). In the event that a child does not understand test directions due to complex linguistic demands, he or she may not perform optimally. As a result, this child's obtained scores may *underestimate* ability. Furthermore, intelligence tests that require conceptual or linguistic knowledge that is *above age level* may pose a threat to the construct validity of the instrument (Bracken, 1986). It seems most important to examine the incidence of basic concepts in test directions when evaluating the performance of preschoolers and children from economically or socially disadvantaged and/or culturally and linguistically diverse backgrounds (see Alfonso & Flanagan, 1999; Bracken, 1986; Flanagan et al., 1995; Kaufman, 1978). Table 21.2 lists the basic concepts that are included in preschool intelligence tests as well as the age at which these concepts typically are attained (cf. McGrew & Flanagan, 1998).

Background/Environmental and Individual/Situational Variables. Two additional broad categories of variables that are important to consider when interpreting an individual's performance on preschool intelligence tests include background/environmental and individual/situational variables. These two sets of variables (or noncognitive factors) inform the interpretive process by focusing and placing an individual's test performance within an appropriate context. Background/environmental variables (e.g., language stimulation, educational opportunities and experiences) typically have a distal (i.e., far or remote) influence on an examinee's test performance because they do not directly operate during the testing session, but rather, may have contributed to the development of the traits that are measured by a test (McGrew & Flanagan, 1998). For example, the meaning of a very low auditory processing test score would be different for a child with a history of inner ear infections as compared to a child without such a history. In the case of the child with chronic ear infections, a practitioner may reason that such difficulties may have hindered the development of auditory processing abilities. Thus, prior development or certain environmental factors may affect the development of the ability being assessed.

Conversely, individual/situational variables (e.g., attention span, distractibility, concentration) are intrinsic to the examinee and can have a proximal (i.e., near or immediate) influence on test performance (either in a positive or negative direction) during the testing session (McGrew & Flanagan, 1998). For instance, highly distractible behavior during testing may influence performance negatively, leading to spuriously low scores. That is, when a child exhibits highly distractible behavior during the administration of a particular test, the reliable variance associated with the test is reduced, with the result being a tautological increase in error variance. Thus, noncognitive factors (in this case, distractibility) must play a significant role in interpreting test performance.

Knowledge of both the background/environmental and individual/situational variables that may have either distal or proximal influences on an individual's test performance is necessary for appropriate interpretation. Specifically, this knowledge allows a practitioner to make informed judgments about the degree to which the portion of a test's reliable variance (which represents the primary focus of interpretation) is a valid indicator of the ability that is measured by the test (McGrew & Flanagan, 1998).

Table 21.2 lists the background/environmental and individual/situational variables that may influence performance on preschool intelligence tests. Definitions for these variables can be found in Table 21.3. The variables presented in Table 21.3 were derived through an expert consensus process. The interested reader is referred to McGrew and Flanagan (1998) for details.

Examiner and Test-Setting Variables. Additional variables that are likely to have a proximal influence on a preschool child's test performance include those intrinsic to the examiner and to the setting in which the child is evaluated. Examiner variables refer to characteristics of the examiner that can facilitate or inhibit the examinee's performance. For example, examiners who are able to handle materials skillfully, adjust the pace of the assessment, and establish and maintain rapport with the child are likely to be successful in eliciting the child's best effort (or optimal performance) (Paget, 1991). Examiner characteristics such as spontaneity, enthusiasm, and well-timed feedback are also critical because they serve to maintain the preschool child's focus, interest, and motivation throughout the evaluation session (Paget, 1991). Conversely, examiners who are overly formal with a child, use language above the child's level, or are inflexible in their assessment style may inhibit the child's test performance, potentially resulting in an underestimate of functioning (Harrison, 1990; Lidz, 1991; Paget, 1991).

Test-setting variables or the physical characteristics of the test environment also can facilitate or inhibit a preschool child's performance. For example, variables such as appropriate furniture (e.g., a table that the child can easily reach to manipulate test materials, chairs low enough for the child's feet to reach the floor), an engaging room that allows the preschooler to feel comfortable and familiar (i.e., contains a few age appropriate toys), and adequate space for both structured and unstructured interactions among participants in the assessment setting (Harrison, 1990; Paget, 1991; Wilson, 1992) can facilitate test performance. Conversely, test-setting variables that inhibit performance include a distracting environment (e.g., an abundance of toys), an overly formal, "sterile" environment, or one that does not consider the preschooler's physical limitations (Paget, 1991). Although certain test manuals discuss examiner characteristics that are important in engaging a very young child in a task and include guidelines for constructing an appropriate preschool testing environment, it is ultimately the responsibility of examiners to become familiar with these conditions and conduct themselves accordingly.

In summary, having access to the qualitative characteristics of preschool intelligence tests will provide practitioners with important information, above and beyond the psychometric domain, that will enhance their ability to select, and especially interpret, preschool intelligence tests more effectively. Although knowledge of the background/environmental and individual/situational variables is integral to understanding the test performance of any child, knowledge of the degree of cultural content and linguistic demand of cognitive ability tests as well as the conceptual knowledge necessary to comprehend instructions seems particularly relevant for multicultural/multilingual preschool populations. Furthermore, skill and experience in knowing how to test very young children and construct an environment conducive to their special needs will facilitate optimal test performance. Due to the more subjective nature of the qualitative characteristics of tests (as compared to the psychometric characteristics), it is recommended that the information included in this section of the chapter

TABLE 21.3 Definitions of Background/Environmental and Individual/Situational Influences on Preschool Intelligence Test Performance

FACTORS AFFECTING TEST PERFORMANCE	DEFINITION
Background/Environmental Influences	
Hearing difficulties	A past history of significant problems in the perception of auditory stimuli
Vision difficulties	A past history of significant problems in the perception of visual stimuli
Language stimulation	The extent to which an examinee's verbal communication skills have been influenced by frequent interaction with the environment
Cultural opportunities and experiences	The extent to which an examinee has been exposed to a wide array of opportunities and experiences that impart knowledge of a culture
Educational opportunities and experiences	The extent to which an examinee has been exposed to a wide array of formal and informal educational experiences
Environmental stimulation	The extent to which an examinee's environment cultivates exploration and opportunities important for development
Alertness to the environment	The extent to which an examinee is attentive to his or her surroundings
Intellectual curiosity	The extent to which an examinee displays a tendency to explore and seek out knowledge and new learning
Individual/Situational Influences	
Attention span	An examinee's ability to selectively focus on specific stimuli for a relatively brief period of time
Concentration	An examinee's ability to focus on stimuli for a sustained period of time
Distractibility	The tendency of an examinee's attention to be drawn away from stimuli that should be the focus of attention by irrelevant stimuli
Ability to perform under time pressure	The extent to which an examinee is capable of maintaining an optimal level of performance during a specific period of time
Visual-motor coordination	An examinee's ability to coordinate the movement of his or her eyes and hands when holding and/or manipulating objects
Color blindness	A congenital visual defect that results in an examinee's inability to perceive certain colors; the extent to which an examinee can accurately discriminate visual stimuli; the sharpness of the examinee's visual perception
Visual acuity	
Verbal elaboration	The strategy of verbally relating new information to already existing information to facilitate the transfer of the information to the store of acquired knowledge (i.e., long-term memory)
Hearing acuity	The extent to which an examinee can accurately discriminate auditory stimuli; the sharpness of an examinee's auditory perception
Reflectivity versus impulsivity	An examinee's tendency to respond either deliberately (reflectively) or quickly (impulsively) when confronted with problem-solving situations
Field dependence versus independence	The examinee's tendency to be significantly affected (dependent) or not affected (independent) by irrelevant factors or stimuli in a perceptual field

FACTORS AFFECTING TEST PERFORMANCE	DEFINITION
Individual/Situational Influences	
Verbal rehearsal	The strategy of verbally repeating (covertly or overtly) information in short-term memory to facilitate the immediate use of information
Visual elaboration	The strategy of visually relating new information to already existing information to facilitate the transfer of the information to the store of acquired knowledge (i.e., long-term memory)
Organization	The strategy of grouping together several different "chunks" or clusters of information to aid in the retrieval of information
Planning	The process of developing efficient methods or solutions (i.e., plans) to a problem prior to starting the problem
Use of feedback	The ability of the examinee to use feedback to monitor performance

Source: Definitions were reproduced from *The Intelligence Test Desk Reference (ITDR) Gf-Gc Cross-Battery Assessment,* by K. S. McGrew and D. P. Flanagan, 1998, Boston: Allyn and Bacon. Adapted with permission.

and in Table 21.2 be used cautiously. That is, this qualitative information should be used only to *guide* test selection and interpretation.

The Theoretical Knowledge Base

Although both psychometric and qualitative test characteristics aid practitioners in making sound judgments about test use and interpretation, the meaningfulness of such judgments is enhanced greatly when it is grounded in an empirically supported theoretical model of the structure of intelligence. According to Kamphaus (1993), "[k]nowledge of theory is important above and beyond research findings as theory allows the clinician to do a better job of conceptualizing a child's score" (p. 44). Unfortunately, the practice of grounding intelligence test interpretation in a well-researched theoretical model of the structure of cognitive abilities is uncommon (Kamphaus, Petoskey, & Morgan, 1997). The omnipresent Wechsler scale in most psychological assessment batteries, regardless of age of examinee or reason for referral, supports the conclusion that many cognitive ability interpretations are atheoretical or based on outdated or incomplete conceptions of intelligence (Carroll, 1993b; Flanagan & Genshaft, 1997; Flanagan & McGrew, 1997; Genshaft & Gerner, 1998; Harrison, Flanagan, & Genshaft, 1997; Kamphaus, 1993; McGrew & Flanagan, 1998; Naglieri,

1997; Shaw, Swerdlick, & Laurent, 1993; Sternberg, 1993).

McGrew and Flanagan (1998) concluded that "there currently exists a significant 'theory-practice' gap in the field of intellectual assessment due to the dominant use of the Wechsler batteries in practice" (p. 6). In order to narrow this gap, there is a need to understand what intelligence tests measure according to contemporary theory and research and to design assessments in a manner consistent with a well-validated theoretical model of the structure of cognitive abilities. Although many theories of intelligence exist, such as Carroll's Three-Stratum Theory, Gardner's Theory of Multiple Intelligences, the Horn-Cattell *Gf-Gc* Theory, Feuerstein's Theory of Structural Cognitive Modifiability, the Luria-Das Model of Information Processing, and Sternberg's Triarchic Theory of Intelligence (see Flanagan, Genshaft, & Harrison, 1997, for a comprehensive description of these theories), the *Gf-Gc* theoretical model has been identified as the most well researched and empirically supported within the *psychometric tradition* (Carroll, 1993a; Daniel, 1997; Esters, Ittenbach, & Han, 1997; Gustaffson & Undheim, 1996; Horn & Noll, 1997; Kranzler, 1997; Messick, 1992; McGrew & Flanagan, 1998; Roberts, Pallier, & Goff, in press). As such, it represents a viable framework from which to interpret cognitive functioning.

Contemporary Gf-Gc Theory. Briefly, *Gf-Gc* theory is an empirically validated theory of the structure of cognitive abilities that is based on the analyses of several hundred data sets that were not limited to the subtests of a specific intelligence battery. Following from the work of Raymond Cattell (1941), Horn (1991, 1994; Horn & Noll, 1997) conducted a systematic program of *Gf-Gc* research that resulted in the specification of 10 broad cognitive abilities: Fluid Intelligence (*Gf*), Crystallized Intelligence (*Gc*), Short-Term Acquisition and Retrieval (*Gsm*), Visual Intelligence (*Gv*), Auditory Intelligence (*Ga*), Long-Term Storage and Retrieval (*Glr*), Cognitive Processing Speed (*Gs*), Correct Decision Speed (*CDS*), Quantitative Knowledge (*Gq*), and Orthographic Knowledge (*Grw*). A general description of these abilities is provided in Table 21.4.

Horn's *Gf-Gc* research was supported recently by Carroll's (1993a) expansive factor analytic investigation. Carroll (1993a, 1997) conducted a comprehensive review and reanalysis of nearly all of the theoretical and empirical (i.e., factor analytic) human cognitive ability research collected over a period that spanned more than six decades. His work culminated in a hierarchical model called the Three-Stratum Theory of Cognitive Abilities. A *general ability* factor (or *g*) is situated at the top of Carroll's model hierarchy (i.e., stratum III). This general stratum subsumes eight *broad* (or stratum II) abilities, which are quite similar to the *Gf-Gc* abilities in Horn's model (see McGrew & Flanagan, 1998, for a discussion of model similarities and distinctions). Stratum II abilities, in turn, subsume nearly 70 *narrow* (or stratum I) abilities. For example, *g* subsumes the broad ability of Fluid Intelligence (*Gf*), which, in turn, subsumes several narrow abilities (e.g., Inductive Reasoning [I], Quantitative Reasoning [RQ], etc., see Table 21.4 for definitions). The strata differ in degree of generality with the broad (stratum II) abilities representing the "basic constitutional and long standing characteristics that govern or influence a great variety of behaviors in a given domain" (Carroll, 1993a, p. 634). Based on the culmination of Carroll's massive factor analytic review and reanalysis of several hundred cognitive ability data sets, he concluded, "[t]he Cattell-Horn model ...is a true hierarchical model covering all major domains of intellectual functioning...among available models it appears to offer the most well-founded and reasonable approach to an acceptable theory of the structure of cognitive abilities" (p. 62).

Thus, although several theories have much to offer with respect to understanding intelligence, within the psychometric tradition, the *Gf-Gc* models of Horn and Carroll appear to constitute the fundamental structure of this multidimensional psychological construct. As such, *Gf-Gc* theory represents a useful framework for developing and interpreting cognitive ability tests (Carroll, 1997; Esters et al., 1997; Flanagan & McGrew, 1997; Woodcock, 1990; Ysseldyke, 1990) and organizing more comprehensive assessments of intellectual functioning (see Carroll, 1997; Daniel, 1997; Flanagan, McGrew, & Ortiz, in press; McGrew & Flanagan, 1998).

With the exception of the WJ-R, preschool intelligence tests were not developed from the *contemporary Gf-Gc* theoretical model (e.g., Horn, 1991, 1994). Most preschool intelligence tests purport to measure two broad intellectual abilities, namely Verbal and Nonverbal/Spatial. Many preschool intelligence tests also include one or more subtests that purport to measure short-term memory and/or quantitative knowledge. Regardless of the number of abilities that seemingly underlie these preschool measures, results of factor analyses typically support an underlying *dichotomous* model of ability. Among the preschool intelligence tests discussed in this chapter, the DAS and WPPSI-R appear to have the strongest factor analytic support for the configuration of their respective subtests into separate Verbal and Nonverbal or Perceptual Organization scales, respectively, at the preschool ages (e.g., Elliott, 1990; Gyurke, Stone, & Beyer, 1990, Keith, 1990). Weaker evidence was found for the S-B:IV, K-ABC, and WJ-R (Flanagan & Alfonso, 1995).

Little evidence is available to support the division of the S-B:IV subtests into four cognitive domains (i.e., Verbal Reasoning, Abstract/Visual Reasoning, Quantitative Reasoning, Short-Term Memory) (e.g., Kline, 1989). Similarly, although independent factor analyses of the K-ABC demonstrate a dichotomous representation of the abilities measured by this battery, the definition of these abilities has been questioned (e.g., Keith, 1985; McGrew, 1997). Finally, ample evidence is available to support the *Gf-Gc* model that underlies the WJ-R (e.g., Yssledyke, 1990). However, this factor analytic support is strongest for ages 5 through adulthood. Therefore, the WJ-R can be interpreted from the contemporary *Gf-Gc* theoretical model most confidently for individuals at the upper end of the preschool age range (i.e., 5-year-olds not in kindergarten) and beyond (i.e., through 95 years). Thus, the WJ-R is best understood as a measure of general ability for preschoolers. The general lack of *theoretically driven* factor analytic investigations at the preschool age range has serious implications for understanding the constructs that underlie preschool intelligence tests and, therefore, for interpretation.

TABLE 21.4 Definitions of Broad and Narrow *Gf-Gc* Constructs Measured by Preschool Intelligence Tests

GF-GC **BROAD STRATUM II ABILITY** *Narrow Stratum I Name (Code)*	**DEFINITION**
Fluid Intelligence (*Gf*)	Ability to reason, form concepts, and problem solve using novel information and/or procedures
Induction (I)	Ability to discover the underlying characteristic (e.g., rule, concept, process, trend, class membership) that governs a problem or a set of materials
Quantitative Reasoning (RQ)	Ability to inductively and deductively reason with concepts involving mathematical relations and properties
Quantitative Knowledge (*Gq*)	Ability to comprehend quantitative concepts and relationships and to manipulate numerical symbols
Mathematical Knowledge (KM)	Range of general knowledge about mathematics
Mathematical Achievement (A3)	Measured mathematics achievement
Crystallized Intelligence (*Gc*)	Measures an individual's breadth and depth of general knowledge and knowledge of a culture including verbal communication and reasoning using previously learned procedures
Language Development (LD)	General development, or the understanding of words, sentences, and paragraphs (*not* requiring reading), in spoken native language skills
Lexical Knowledge (VL)	Extent of vocabulary that can be understood in terms of correct word meanings
Listening Ability (LS)	Ability to listen and comprehend oral communications
General (Verbal) Information (KO)	Range of general knowledge
Short-Term Memory (*Gsm*)	Ability to temporarily hold information in immediate awareness and then use it within a few seconds
Memory Span (MS)	Ability to attend to and immediately recall temporally ordered elements in the correct order after a single presentation
Visual Memory (MV)[1]	Ability to form and store a mental representation or image of a visual stimulus and then recognize or recall it later
Visual Processing (*Gv*)	Ability to analyze and synthesize visual information
Visualization (VZ)	Ability to mentally manipulate objects or visual patterns and to "see" how they would appear under altered conditions
Spatial Relations (SR)	Ability to rapidly perceive and manipulate visual patterns or to maintain orientation with respect to objects in space
Visual Memory (MV)[1]	Ability to form and store a mental representation or image of a visual stimulus and then recognize or recall it later
Spatial Scanning (SS)	Ability to accurately and quickly survey a spatial field or pattern and identify a path through the visual field or pattern
Serial Perceptual Integration (PI)	Ability to identify a pictorial or visual pattern when parts of the pattern are presented rapidly in order

(continued)

TABLE 21.4   Continued

GF-GC BROAD STRATUM II ABILITY	DEFINITION
Narrow Stratum I Name (Code)	
Closure Speed (CS)	Ability to quickly combine disconnected, vague, or partially obscured visual stimuli or patterns into a meaningful whole, without knowing in advance what the pattern is
Flexibility of Closure (CF)	Ability to identify a visual figure or pattern embedded in a complex visual array, when knowing in advance what the pattern is
Auditory Processing (*Ga*)	Ability to analyze and synthesize auditory information
Phonetic Coding (PC)	Ability to process speech sounds, as in identifying, isolating, and blending sounds; phonological awareness.
Resistance to Auditory Stimulus Distortion (UR)	Ability to understand speech and language that has been distorted or masked in one or more ways.
Long-term Storage and Retrieval (*Glr*)	Ability to store information and retrieve it later through association.
Associative Memory (MA)	Ability to recall one part of a previously learned but unrelated pair of items when the other part is presented (i.e., paired-associative learning).
Free Recall Memory (M6)	Ability to recall as many unrelated items as possible, in any order, after a large collection of items is presented.
Processing Speed (*Gs*)	Ability to fluently perform cognitive tasks automatically, especially when under pressure to maintain focused attention and concentration.
Rate-of-Test-Taking (R9)	Ability to rapidly perform tests which are relatively easy or that require very simple decisions.

Source: Adapted from *The Intelligence Test Desk Reference (ITDR) Gf-Gc Cross-Battery Assessment,* by K. S. McGrew and D. P. Flanagan, 1998, Boston: Allyn and Bacon. Adapted with permission.

Most definitions were derived from Carroll (1993a). This table contains only those narrow abilities found to be measured by preschool intelligence tests. For a complete list of *Gf-Gc* narrow ability definitions, see Carroll (1993a). Two-letter factor codes (e.g., RQ) are from Carroll (1993a).

[1]Results of joint factor analyses have been somewhat inconsistent in that some report measures of visual memory to load on a *Gv* factor whereas others report these measures to load on a *Gsm* factor (see Carroll, 1993 for a review). The most recent analyses support the inclusion of visual memory in the *Gv* domain (see Flanagan et al., in press, for details).

Gf-Gc Constructs Underlying Preschool Intelligence Tests.   In an effort to address the lack of theory-driven analyses of the structure of cognitive abilities at the preschool age range, *Gf-Gc* organized joint factor analyses have been conducted recently with preschool children (e.g., joint WJ-R and DAS factor analyses; Laurie Ford, personal communication, April 7, 1998). Based on the results of these analyses as well as other *Gf-Gc* orga-nized joint factor analyses and logical task analyses (see Flanagan et al., in press; McGrew, 1997; McGrew & Flanagan, 1998; Woodcock, 1990), the abilities underlying all preschool intelligence tests have been classified according to *Gf-Gc* theory. These classifications (cf. McGrew & Flanagan, 1998) along with the constructs purported to underlie each preschool intelligence test according to the test author(s) are provided in Table 21.5.

TABLE 21.5 Description of Theoretical Constructs Measured by Intelligence Batteries with Norms for Preschool-Age Children

SUBTESTS FOR PRESCHOOL-AGE CHILDREN	CONSTRUCT(S) MEASURED ACCORDING TO TEST AUTHOR(S)	BROAD AND (NARROW) GF-GC CONSTRUCTS MEASURED ACCORDING TO RECENT FACTOR ANALYSES[1]	WELL-REPRESENTED GF-GC CONSTRUCTS[2]	UNDER-REPRESENTED GF-GC CONSTRUCTS[2]	GF-GC CONSTRUCTS NOT MEASURED BY THE BATTERY
Differential Ability Scales (DAS)			Gc Gv, Gsm[3]	Gq, Glr, Gf	Ga, Gs
Verbal Comprehension	Verbal Ability	Crystallized Intelligence (Gc) (**Language Development-LD, Listening Ability-LS**)			
Naming Vocabulary	Verbal Ability	Crystallized Intelligence (Gc) (**Language Development-LD, Lexical Knowledge-VL**)			
Picture Similarities	Nonverbal Ability	Fluid Intelligence (Gf) (**Induction-I**)			
Pattern Construction[4]	Nonverbal Ability Spatial Ability	Visual Processing (Gv) (**Spatial Relations-SR,** Visualization-VZ)			
Copying	Nonverbal Ability	Visual Processing (Gv) (Visualization-VZ)			
Early Number Concepts	General Conceptual Ability	Quantitative Knowledge (Gq) (**Math Achievement-A3, Mathematical Knowledge-KM**)			
Block Building	Perceptual–Motor Ability	Visual Processing (Gv) (**Visualization-VZ**)			
Matching Letter-Like Forms	Visual-Perceptual Matching	Visual Processing (Gv) (**Visualization-VZ**)			
Recall of Digits	Short-Term Auditory Memory	Short-Term Memory (Gsm) (**Memory Span-MS**)			

(continued)

TABLE 21.5 Continued

SUBTESTS FOR PRESCHOOL-AGE CHILDREN	CONSTRUCT(S) MEASURED ACCORDING TO TEST AUTHOR(S)	BROAD AND (NARROW) GF-GC CONSTRUCTS MEASURED ACCORDING TO RECENT FACTOR ANALYSES[1]	WELL-REPRESENTED GF-GC CONSTRUCTS[2]	UNDER-REPRESENTED GF-GC CONSTRUCTS[2]	GF-GC CONSTRUCTS NOT MEASURED BY THE BATTERY
Differential Ability Scales (DAS)			*Gc Gv, Gsm*[3]	*Gq, Glr, Gf*	*Ga, Gs*
Recall of Objects	Short- and Intermediate-Term Verbal Memory	Long-Term Storage and Retrieval (*Glr*) (**Free Recall Memory-M6**) Visual Processing (*Gv*) (*Visual Memory-MV*)			
Recognition of Pictures	Short-Term Visual Memory	Visual Processing (*Gv*) (***Visual Memory-MV***)			
Kaufman Assessment Battery for Children (K-ABC)			*Gv, Gsm*[3]	*Gf, Gq*	*Gc*[5], *Ga, Glr, Gs,*
Magic Window	Simultaneous Processing	Visual Processing (*Gv*) (**Serial Perceptual Integration-PI,** *Closure Speed-CS*)			
Face Recognition	Simultaneous Processing	Visual Processing (*Gv*) (***Visual Memory-MV***)			
Gestalt Closure	Simultaneous Processing	**Visual Processing (*Gv*)** (***Closure Speed-CS***)			
Triangles	Simultaneous Processing	**VISUAL PROCESSING (*Gv*)** (***Visualization-VZ, Spatial Relations-SR***)			
Matrix Analogies	Simultaneous Processing	[Fluid Intelligence (*Gf*)] (***Induction-I***) [Visual Processing (*Gv*)] (***Visualization-VZ***)			

456

SUBTESTS FOR PRESCHOOL-AGE CHILDREN	CONSTRUCT(S) MEASURED ACCORDING TO TEST AUTHOR(S)	BROAD AND (NARROW) GF-GC CONSTRUCTS MEASURED ACCORDING TO RECENT FACTOR ANALYSES[1]	WELL-REPRESENTED GF-GC CONSTRUCTS[2]	UNDER-REPRESENTED GF-GC CONSTRUCTS[2]	GF-GC CONSTRUCTS NOT MEASURED BY THE BATTERY
Kaufman Assessment Battery for Children (K-ABC)			*Gv, Gsm*[3]	*Gf, Gq*	*Gc*[5]*, Ga, Glr, Gs,*
Spatial Memory	Simultaneous Processing	[Visual Processing (*Gv*)] (***Visual Memory-MV, Spatial Relations-SR***) [Short-Term Memory (*Gsm*)] (*Memory Span-MS*)			
Hand Movements	Sequential Processing	[Visual Processing (*Gv*)] (***Visual Memory-MV***) [Quantitative Knowledge (*Gq*)] (***Math Achievement-A3***)			
Number Recall	Sequential Processing	**SHORT-TERM MEMORY (*Gsm*)** (***Memory Span-MS***)			
Word Order	Sequential Processing	**SHORT-TERM MEMORY (*Gsm*)** (***Memory Span-MS***)			
Stanford-Binet Intelligence Scale: Fourth Edition (SB:IV)			*Gc, Gv, Gsm*[3]	*Gq*	*Ga, Glr, Gs*
Vocabulary	Crystallized Intelligence (*Gc*) Verbal Reasoning	**CRYSTALLIZED INTELLIGENCE (*Gc*)** (***Language Development-LD, Lexical Knowledge-VL***)			
Comprehension	Crystallized Intelligence (*Gc*) Verbal Reasoning	Crystallized Intelligence (*Gc*) (***Language Development-LD, General Information-KO***)			
Absurdities	Crystallized Intelligence (*Gc*) Verbal Reasoning	Crystallized Intelligence (*Gc*) (***Language Development-LD***, *General Information-KO*)			

(continued)

TABLE 21.5 Continued

SUBTESTS FOR PRESCHOOL-AGE CHILDREN	CONSTRUCT(S) MEASURED ACCORDING TO TEST AUTHOR(S)	BROAD AND (NARROW) GF-GC CONSTRUCTS MEASURED ACCORDING TO RECENT FACTOR ANALYSES[1]	WELL-REPRESENTED GF-GC CONSTRUCTS[2]	UNDER-REPRESENTED GF-GC CONSTRUCTS[2]	GF-GC CONSTRUCTS NOT MEASURED BY THE BATTERY
Stanford-Binet Intelligence Scale: Fourth Edition (SB:IV)			*Gc, Gv, Gsm*[3]	*Gq*	*Ga, Glr, Gs*
Pattern Analysis	Fluid Intelligence (*Gf*) Abstract/Visual Reasoning	**VISUAL PROCESSING (Gv)** (***Visualization-VZ,*** Spatial Relations-SR)			
Copying	Fluid Intelligence (*Gf*) Abstract/Visual Reasoning	[Visual Processing (*Gv*)] (*Visualization-VZ*)			
Quantitative	Crystallized Intelligence (*Gc*) Quantitative Reasoning	**QUANTITATIVE KNOWLEDGE (Gq)** (***Math Achievement-A3***) Fluid Intelligence (*Gf*) (*Quantitative Reasoning-RQ*)			
Bead Memory	Short-Term Memory (*Gsm*)	**Visual Processing (Gv)** (***Visual Memory-MV***)			
Memory for Sentences	Short-Term Memory (*Gsm*)	[Short-Term Memory (*Gsm*)] (***Memory Span-MS***) [Crystallized Intelligence (*Gc*)] (***Language Development-LD***)			
Wechsler Preschool and Primary Scale of Intelligence—Revised (WPPSI-R)			*Gc, Gv,*	*Gsm, Gq, Gs, Gf,*	*Ga, Glr*
Information	Verbal Comprehension	**CRYSTALLIZED INTELLIGENCE (Gc)** (***General Information-KO***)			
Vocabulary	Verbal Comprehension	**CRYSTALLIZED INTELLIGENCE (Gc)** (***Language Development-LD, Lexical Knowledge-VL***)			

SUBTESTS FOR PRESCHOOL-AGE CHILDREN	CONSTRUCT(S) MEASURED ACCORDING TO TEST AUTHOR(S)	BROAD AND (NARROW) GF-GC CONSTRUCTS MEASURED ACCORDING TO RECENT FACTOR ANALYSES[1]	WELL-REPRESENTED GF-GC CONSTRUCTS[2]	UNDER-REPRESENTED GF-GC CONSTRUCTS[2]	GF-GC CONSTRUCTS NOT MEASURED BY THE BATTERY
Wechsler Preschool and Primary Scale of Intelligence—Revised (WPPSI-R)			*Gc, Gv,*	*Gsm, Gq, Gs, Gf,*	*Ga, Glr*
Arithmetic	Verbal Comprehension	**QUANTITATIVE KNOWLEDGE (Gq)** (***Math Achievement-A3***) *Fluid Intelligence (Gf)* (*Quantitative Reasoning-RQ*)			
Comprehension	Verbal Comprehension	**CRYSTALLIZED INTELLIGENCE (Gc)** (***Language Development-LD, General Information-KO***)			
Similarities	Verbal Comprehension	**CRYSTALLIZED INTELLIGENCE (Gc)** (***Language Development-LD,*** *Lexical Knowledge-VL*)			
Picture Completion	Perceptual Organization	[*Visual Processing (Gv)*] (*Flexibility of Closure-CF*) [*Crystallized Intelligence (Gc)*] (*General Information-KO*)			
Block Design	Perceptual Organization	**VISUAL PROCESSING (Gv)** (***Spatial Relations-SR,*** *Visualization-VZ*)			
Object Assembly	Perceptual Organization	**VISUAL PROCESSING (Gv)** (***Closure Speed-CS,*** *Spatial Relations-SR*)			
Mazes	Perceptual Organization	*Visual Processing (Gv)*[6] (***Spatial Scanning-SS***)			
Geometric Design	Perceptual Organizations	*Visual Processing (Gv)* (***Visualization-VZ***)			

(continued)

TABLE 21.5 Continued

SUBTESTS FOR PRESCHOOL-AGE CHILDREN	CONSTRUCT(S) MEASURED ACCORDING TO TEST AUTHOR(S)	BROAD AND (NARROW) GF-GC CONSTRUCTS MEASURED ACCORDING TO RECENT FACTOR ANALYSES[1]	WELL-REPRESENTED GF-GC CONSTRUCTS[2]	UNDER-REPRESENTED GF-GC CONSTRUCTS[2]	GF-GC CONSTRUCTS NOT MEASURED BY THE BATTERY
Wechsler Preschool and Primary Scale of Intelligence—Revised (WPPSI-R)			*Gc, Gv,*	*Gsm, Gq, Gs, Gf,*	*Ga, Glr*
Animal Pegs	Perceptual Organization	Processing Speed (*Gs*) (***Rate-of-test-taking-R9***)			
Sentences	Verbal Comprehension	Short-Term Memory (*Gsm*) (***Memory Span-MS***) Crystallized Intelligence (*Gc*) (***Language Development-LD***)			
Woodcock-Johnson Psychoeducational Battery—Revised (WJ-R)			None	*Glr, Gsm, Gv, Ga, Gc*	*Gs, Gf*
Memory for Names	Long-Term Storage and Retrieval (*Glr*)	**LONG-TERM STORAGE AND RETRIEVAL (*Glr*)** (***Associative Memory-MA***)			
Memory for Sentences	Short-Term Memory (*Gsm*)	[Short-Term Memory (*Gsm*)] (***Memory Span-MS***) [Crystallized Intelligence (*Gc*)] (***Language Development-LD***)			
Incomplete Words	Auditory Processing (*Ga*)	**AUDITORY PROCESSING (*Ga*)** (***Phonetic Coding-PC,*** Resistance to Auditory Stimulus Distortion-UR)			
Visual Closure	Visual Processing (*Gv*)	Visual Processing (*Gv*) (***Closure Speed-CS***)			

SUBTESTS FOR PRESCHOOL-AGE CHILDREN	CONSTRUCT(S) MEASURED ACCORDING TO TEST AUTHOR(S)	BROAD AND (NARROW) GF-GC CONSTRUCTS MEASURED ACCORDING TO RECENT FACTOR ANALYSES[1]	WELL-REPRESENTED GF-GC CONSTRUCTS[2]	UNDER-REPRESENTED GF-GC CONSTRUCTS[2]	GF-GC CONSTRUCTS NOT MEASURED BY THE BATTERY
Woodcock-Johnson Psychoeducational Battery—Revised (WJ-R)					
Picture Vocabulary	Crystallized Intelligence (Gc)	CRYSTALLIZED INTELLIGENCE (Gc) (Lexical Knowledge-VL, General Information-KO, Language Development-LD)	None	Glr, Gsm, Gv, Ga, Gc	Gs, Gf

Source: The *Gf-Gc* classifications reported in this table were reproduced from *The Intelligence Test Desk Reference (ITDR) Gf-Gc Cross-Battery Assessment,* by K. S. McGrew and D. P. Flanagan, 1998, Boston: Allyn and Bacon. Reprinted with permission. Based on the method and criteria used therein.

[1]Broad ability classifications in bold/capital letters are "empirical: strong" measures; broad abilities in bold/lowercase letters are "empirical: moderate" measures; broad abilities in brackets (I) are "empirical: mixed" measures; broad abilities in regular type/lowercase are logically based measures. All narrow abilities are in italics. Narrow abilities in bold/italics are "probable" measures; narrow abilities in regular type/italics are "possible" measures.

[2]A construct is well represented when two or more qualitatively different narrow ability indicators are used to measure it. A construct is considered underrepresented when it is measured by less than two qualitatively different indicators.

[3]There is a lack of agreement in the research literature on whether Visual Memory (MV) is a narrow ability subsumed by *Gsm* or *Gv* (Carroll, 1993a). Therefore, any battery that was found to include both Visual Memory and Memory Span tests were said to have adequate *Gsm* representation. Current research, however, appears to support visual memory as a narrow ability indicator of *Gv* primarily (see Flanagan et al., in press, for details).

[4]Pattern Construction purportedly measures Nonverbal Ability at the younger ages (3–6 to 5–11) and Spatial Ability at the older ages (6–0 to 17–11) (Elliott, 1990).

[5]The K-ABC Achievement Test provides qualitatively different indicators of *Gc* (McGrew & Flanagan, 1998).

[6]The Mazes subtest on the WPPSI-R, is an "empirical: moderate" measure of Visual Processing (*Gv*) (Woodcock, 1990).

An examination of the information presented in Table 21.5 demonstrates that the Verbal scales of most preschool intelligence tests measure mainly aspects of Crystallized Intelligence (*Gc*). Specifically, the narrow abilities in this domain (i.e., *Gc*) that are represented among preschool intelligence tests include Language Development (LD), Lexical Knowledge (VL), Listening Ability (LS), and General Information (KO; see Table 21.4 for definitions of these abilities). Although *Gc* subsumes far more than four narrow abilities (see Carroll, 1993a, 1997), it is this set of abilities that defines *Gc* according to popular preschool intelligence batteries. While the Verbal scales of most preschool intelligence tests yield scores that can be interpreted as estimates of *Gc,* the nonverbal aggregates yielded by these instruments are more difficult to interpret.

Table 21.5 shows that the subsets of most nonverbal scales (i.e., DAS Nonverbal/Spatial, K-ABC Simultaneous Processing, S-B:IV Abstract/Visual Reasoning, and WPPSI-R Perceptual Organization) are comprised mainly of tests of Visual Processing (*Gv*). Specifically, the subtests that make up these nonverbal scales primarily measure narrow abilities subsumed by *Gv*. Collectively, the *Gv* narrow abilities represented across preschool intelligence tests include Visualization (VZ), Spatial Relations (SR), Visual Memory (MV), Spatial Scanning (SS), Serial Perceptual Integration (PI), Closure Speed (CS), and Flexibility of Closure (CF; see Table 21.4 for definitions of these abilities). Because most nonverbal scales are comprised of narrow ability indicators of *Gv,* they may be more appropriately interpreted as estimates of this broad *Gf-Gc* ability rather than as estimates of *nonverbal intelligence*—an elusive term or label that is often misunderstood (see McCallum & Bracken, 1997; McGrew & Flanagan, 1998, for a discussion).

However, some nonverbal scales of preschool intelligence tests include narrow ability indicators (i.e., subtests) of broad *Gf-Gc* abilities other than *Gv*. For example, the DAS Picture Similarities and K-ABC Matrix Analogies subtests appear to measure inductive reasoning (I; a narrow ability subsumed by *Gf*), and the WPPSI-R Animal Pegs subtest appears to measure mainly rate of test taking (R9; a narrow ability subsumed by *Gs*). That is, in addition to narrow ability indicators of *Gv,* the nonverbal scales of the DAS, K-ABC, and WPPSI-R contain a subtest that measures a narrow ability that is *irrelevant to the construct being measured*

(e.g., *Gv*) (Messick, 1995, p. 742). In other words, the nonverbal scales of these instruments represent *mixed* measures of two distinct, broad *Gf-Gc* constructs—a condition that complicates or misinforms interpretation (Briggs & Cheek, 1986; McGrew & Flanagan, 1998; Wilson, 1992).

Invalidity in Assessment. *Construct-irrelevant variance* represents a ubiquitous source of invalidity in assessment. It is often assumed erroneously that a single scale measures a single construct. When one operates under this assumption and interprets composites accordingly, misinformation will likely result. Knowledge of the stratum II *Gf-Gc* classifications of all major preschool batteries (presented in Table 21.5) provides the information necessary to evaluate the abilities that contribute to a particular scale or composite/cluster across the preschool intelligence tests, thus aiding in interpretation (see McGrew & Flanagan, 1998). The purest measures of any composite are those that contain only construct-*relevant* variance (see also Briggs & Cheek, 1986). For example, the S-B:IV Verbal Reasoning composite contains only measures that are associated with *Gc*.

Knowledge of the stratum II abilities that underlie preschool intelligence batteries is necessary but not sufficient in the interpretive process. It is also important to understand the stratum I *Gf-Gc* abilities that underlie preschool intelligence tests. Knowledge of stratum I *Gf-Gc* test classifications guards against *construct underrepresentation,* another ubiquitous source of invalidity in assessment. Construct underrepresentation is present when an assessment "is too narrow and fails to include important dimensions or facets of the construct" (Messick, 1995, p. 742). Before making interpretations regarding an individual's functioning in a broad cognitive domain (e.g., *Gc, Gv, Gs,* etc.), one must ensure that this domain was assessed via at least *two qualitatively different indicators* (i.e., by at least two subtests that measure two *different* narrow abilities subsumed by the broad ability) (Comrey, 1988; Flanagan & McGrew, 1997). For example, the WPPSI-R Perceptual Organization scale (*excluding* the optional Animal Pegs subtest) provides an excellent estimate of *Gv* because it contains several qualitatively different indicators of this broad ability. Specifically, Table 21.5 shows that the narrow abilities that combine to yield the Perceptual Organization IQ (an estimate of *Gv*) on the WPPSI-R include Flexibility of Closure, Spatial Relations, Closure

Speed, Spatial Scanning, and Visualization (see Table 21.4 for definitions).

Conversely, although the WJ-R includes measures of five different broad cognitive abilities at the preschool level (i.e., *Glr, Gsm, Ga, Gv,* and *Gc*), all of these broad abilities are *underrepresented*. That is, each broad ability is measured by only *one* narrow ability indicator (or subtest). Thus, interpreting any WJ-R subtest as a measure of its respective broad ability is inappropriate because there are not enough qualitatively different indicators of the broad abilities included on the WJ-R (Early Development Scale) to represent them adequately. Before making interpretations or generalizations about a preschooler's ability in the broad domains of *Glr, Gsm, Ga, Gv,* and *Gc* on the WJ-R, this instrument must be supplemented with at least one additional, qualitatively different narrow ability indicator in each domain (see Flanagan et al., in press; McGrew & Flanagan, 1998).

Table 21.5 shows that *eight* broad (stratum II) *Gf-Gc* cognitive abilities (i.e., *Gc Gf, Gv, Gq, Glr, Gsm, Ga, Gs*) are represented across five major preschool batteries. However, as can be seen in column 4 of this table, most batteries only represent two to three broad cognitive abilities *well* (e.g., *Gc* and *Gv*). Many *Gf-Gc* abilities are underrepresented (see Table 21.5, column 5) on preschool intelligence tests (i.e., they are represented by only one narrow ability indicator). Caution must be exercised when interpreting underrepresented constructs and the interpretation of these constructs ought to reflect the *narrow ability* that underlies the subtest rather than the broad ability by which it is subsumed. Commonly underrepresented *Gf-Gc* abilities among the preschool instruments include *Gq* and *Gf*. Finally, the last column in Table 21.5 shows that most current preschool instruments *do not measure* many *Gf-Gc* abilities. For example, only one test of *Ga* (i.e., WJ-R Incomplete Words—a measure of phonetic coding) was found among the 45 subtests for preschoolers included in Table 21.5. Because simple phonological awareness has been established as a precursor to reading success (e.g., Chafouleas, Lewandowski, Smith, & Blachman, 1997; Perfetti, Beck, Bell, & Hughes, 1987), measures of this cognitive process (e.g., tests of certain narrow abilities subsumed by *Ga*) should be included on preschool intelligence batteries. Failure to measure certain *Gf-Gc* abilities (such as *Ga*) may have significant implications for remedial or educational program planning (e.g., Mather, 1991).

Toward a More Valid Assessment of Cognitive Abilities. An examination of the *Gf-Gc* stratum I and stratum II classifications of the major preschool intelligence batteries reveals a number of important conclusions. First, when the universe of the major preschool cognitive ability tests is considered (as represented in Table 21.5), it is evident that aspects of *eight* broad cognitive abilities (i.e., essentially, the full range) can be assessed in preschool children. In support of this conclusion, the results of recent *Gf-Gc* organized joint factor analyses provided support for a *multiple* (five-factor) (rather than dichotomous) model of the structure of intelligence in a sample of upper-level preschool children (ages 3 to 6 years) (Laurie Ford, personal communication, April 7, 1998). Second, when one considers that broad abilities are interpreted most confidently when they are represented by two qualitatively different measures, it is possible to represent five broad *Gf-Gc* abilities well (i.e., *Gc, Gf, Gv, Gq, Glr*) using the tests presented in Table 21.5. Third, *in-depth assessment* (i.e., assessment of *three or more* qualitatively different indicators) of a broad cognitive ability is possible only in the areas of *Gc* and *Gv*. That is, *Gc* and *Gv* are the only cognitive constructs that are represented by more than three qualitatively different indicators across preschool intelligence batteries.

In summary, the stratum I and stratum II *Gf-Gc* classifications presented in Table 21.5 represent an important aspect of the *theoretical knowledge base* that is necessary for appropriate preschool intelligence test interpretation. It seems clear that more can be understood about a preschool child's cognitive capabilities than may be gleaned through the administration of a single intelligence battery. As such, McGrew and Flanagan (1998) offered a theoretically and psychometrically defensible means of augmenting any given intelligence test to ensure that a wider range of broad cognitive abilities is assessed. Their approach, called *Gf-Gc cross-battery assessment,* allows for the *selective measurement* of the broad range of *Gf-Gc* abilities in a time-efficient and referral-relevant manner (see Flanagan et al., in press; McGrew & Flanagan, 1998, for details). Cross-battery assessment would be particularly relevant if an "extensive evaluation of cognitive function [is needed] for the purpose of obtaining a baseline set of measures prior to the delivery of early intervention services" (Wilson, 1992, p. 382). More specifically, it would aid practitioners in their attempt to "touch all of the major cognitive areas, with emphasis on those most suspect on the basis of history, observation, and on-going test findings" (Wilson, 1992, p. 382).

THREE DECLARATIVE KNOWLEDGE BASES FOR TEST INTERPRETATION IN PERSPECTIVE

The three knowledge bases (psychometric, qualitative, and theoretical) presented in this chapter can be conceptualized best as consisting of a multitude of distinct ideas or *propositions*. Propositions are defined as the smallest unit of knowledge that can stand as a separate assertion (Bruning et al., 1995). They are akin to separate pieces or bits of information. For example, Table 21.1 shows that the *specificity* for the DAS Verbal Comprehension subtest is *ample,* indicating that this test may be interpreted as measuring a unique ability if it deviates significantly from similar tests in the battery. This bit of information constitutes a proposition. In essence, Tables 21.1 through 21.5 are comprised of hundreds of individual propositions.

Propositions, in and of themselves, are necessary but not sufficient for test interpretation. That is, propositions must be combined into meaningful *networks* in the interpretive process. *Propositional networks* can be conceptualized as sets of interrelated propositions (Gagne, 1985). They contain information that is linked through ideas or characteristics common to a particular element. To demonstrate, a propositional network for the DAS Verbal Comprehension subtest is depicted in Figure 21.1.

Figure 21.1 shows all of the important psychometric, qualitative, and theoretical characteristics associated with this subtest. For instance, the psychometric propositions related to the Verbal Comprehension subtest for 3-year-old children are as follows: reliability, *medium; g*-loading, *high;* specificity, *ample;* test floor, *adequate;* and item gradients, *good.* The qualitative propositions for this subtest demonstrate that it has a high degree of cultural content and linguistic demand and that performance on this test may be influenced by certain background/environmental variables (e.g., language stimulation, environmental stimulation), as well as specific individual/situational variables (e.g., distractibility). With regard to the theoretical propositions, this subtest has been found to measure crystallized intelligence (*Gc*), primarily the narrow abilities of language development and listening ability. Collectively, this information constitutes a necessary foundation from which to interpret performance on the subtest, whether it deviates significantly from the child's averaged test performance or is part of a broader test composite. Because the relationships among the psychometric, qualitative, and theoretical characteristics of tests are crucial to interpretation, it is useful to represent important characteristics of all (sub)tests in propositional networks, such as the one presented in Figure 21.1 (Gagne, 1985).

The forming of propositional networks facilitates access to *well-organized,* domain-specific knowledge and, more importantly, provides the database(s) from which to make informed interpretations. However, because this type of knowledge (i.e., declarative) is relatively *static,* it does not supply the *procedures* necessary to facilitate (or actually make) test interpretations. In order to make interpretations (i.e., perform actions) that are systematic, fluid, and meaningful, a more *dynamic* knowledge base (i.e., a procedural knowledge base) also is required.

PROCEDURAL KNOWLEDGE NEEDED FOR TEST INTERPRETATION

Procedural knowledge is knowledge of *how* to perform tasks or activities and it is inferred from an individual's performance (Eggen and Kauchak, 1997). Unlike declarative knowledge, activation of procedural knowledge results in the *transformation* of information rather than the simple recall of information (Gagne, 1985). For example, knowing that the reliability of a verbal intelligence scale is .80 is a proposition (i.e., a bit of information signifying that something is the case). Knowing how to transform this information into something more meaningful and useful (i.e., this scale has *medium* reliability and, therefore, may be used for screening but not diagnostic purposes) is an example of procedural knowledge. Thus, procedural knowledge is dynamic and operates on declarative (or relatively static) information to transform it.

Procedural knowledge can be conceptualized as *productions*. Productions are defined as condition-action rules (i.e., they program certain actions to take place when specified conditions exist). A production has two clauses, an "if" clause and a "then" clause. The "if" clause specifies conditions that must exist for a given set of actions to take place, whereas the "then" clause lists the actions that take place when the conditions of the "if" clause are met (Eggen and Kauchak, 1997; Gagne, 1985). Evaluating "if" statements involves *thinking,* and taking action prescribed by "then" statements involves *doing.* Thus, procedural knowledge is conceptualized largely as a dynamic thinking-doing process.

The flowchart presented in Figure 21.2 exemplifies that the interpretation of a young child's performance on cognitive ability tests is a dynamic thinking-doing process. Via a series of "if-then" clauses, this flowchart

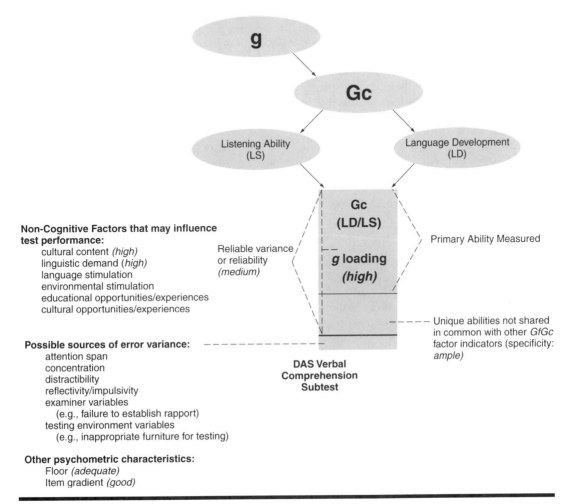

FIGURE 21.1   Example of a Propositional Network Using the DAS Verbal
Comprehension Subtest

Test characteristics listed in this figure were taken from Tables 21.5 and are specific to 3-year-olds.
Evaluations of test characteristics are printed in italics.

Source: From K. S. McGrew and D. P. Flanagan, *The Intelligence Desk Reference (ITDR) Gf-Gc
Cross-Battery Assessment.* Copyright © 1998 by Allyn & Bacon. Adapted by permission.

guides practitioners through the fundamental ("how to")
procedures of test interpretation. As demonstrated in
Figure 21.2, the first step in this process is to examine
test results and determine if there are any normative
subtest/cluster strengths or weaknesses. Upon finding a
normative subtest/cluster weakness, for example, a practitioner should consider the following *production* in order to know how to proceed: *if* the subtest/cluster is

psychometrically sound, *then* move to the next step in
the interpretive process (i.e., determine whether historical, qualitative, or observational factors significantly
influenced test performance); *if* the test is not psychometrically sound, *then* administer a more technically adequate subtest or cluster that purports to measure the
same underlying construct before making interpretations about performance in that particular domain. Thus,

the existence or absence of the condition (in this instance, psychometric soundness of the test) determined the action to be taken (i.e., determine whether noncognitive factors influenced test performance or administer a similar, more psychometrically sound test prior to making interpretations).

As is also evident from the flowchart presented in Figure 21.2, the forming and testing of hypotheses is part of procedural knowledge because it occurs as a consequence of evaluating "if" statements and interpreting the results of actions taken in response to "then" statements. To illustrate, *if* a significant normative weakness is associated with three subtests in a child's profile of test scores, *then* it may be hypothesized that the child has a weakness in the cognitive ability purported to underlie this set of subtests. However, *if* these three subtests required a high level of receptive language for success and *if* the examinee had a history of chronic ear infections, *then* caution would be exercised in test interpretation (as these three subtest scores may be spuriously low) and additional measures of the same cognitive ability—measures that deemphasize or omit receptive language requirements—would need to be administered prior to drawing conclusions about the child's functioning in that domain. If upon administering similar cognitive tests with *low* language requirements, the child's performance falls within the *average* range of ability, then the examiner may conclude that the cognitive ability underlying these measures is within normal limits (i.e., age appropriate). However, it is necessary to determine whether difficulty on cognitive tests with high receptive language demands is the result of a medical condition (related to a history of ear infections) or some sensory, cognitive processing, or language deficit. Thus, the procedural knowledge base facilitates the forming and testing of hypotheses.

In sum, the interpretive flowchart presented in Figure 21.2 consists of a number of productions, and, depending on the existence or absence of the condition specified in the production, different actions are proposed and various hypotheses are formed and tested. The aggregate of these productions constitutes a *procedural knowledge base for test interpretation*.

INTERACTING DECLARATIVE AND PROCEDURAL KNOWLEDGE BASES FOR INTERPRETATION

The conceptual interpretive framework presented in this chapter is represented schematically in Figure 21.3. As may be seen in this figure, the reason for referral represents the *input* or raw data from which to begin organizing a battery of tests designed to provide insight into the nature of the presenting problems of the preschool child. Organization, administration, scoring, and eventual interpretation of a battery of tests (all productions) presuppose a sound declarative knowledge base, as indicated by the shaded area within the figure. The activation of the procedural knowledge base, described therein as "thinking" and "doing," is dependent upon "if" and "then" statements, respectively.

As stated previously, in order to respond to "if-then" clauses, a declarative knowledge base is necessary to evaluate whether the conditions are present or absent (Gagne, 1985). In other words, knowing that a subtest/ cluster must be reliable to proceed in the interpretive process supplies a condition; however, verifying the presence or absence of that condition requires drawing upon a declarative knowledge base. Thus, in the interpretive process, declarative knowledge provides the information needed to evaluate a variety of conditions— conditions necessary to perform interpretive procedures.

Through a variety of thinking and doing activities, hypotheses related to the referral are developed, tested, refined, and either supported or not supported by the assessment data. This process of forming and testing hypotheses through a series of evaluations (of test data) and actions (e.g., conducting more in-depth assessment in a given domain) is depicted by the double sets of arrows in Figure 21.3. Eventually, this process results in conclusions about the child's performance that enable the practitioner to address the referral concerns adequately.

Because learning is a by-product of the interaction between declarative and procedural knowledge (Eggen and Kauchak, 1997), it is likely that, at this stage in the interpretive process, the conclusions that are reached represent new knowledge (Gagne, 1985). Upon drawing conclusions, the new knowledge gained from the interpretive process becomes part of declarative knowledge (as depicted by the arrows that filter back into the declarative knowledge base from the "Reaching Conclusions" box in Figure 21.3).

In sum, declarative and procedural knowledge for test interpretation interacts in a variety of ways to solve problems (i.e., answer referral questions). Competent performance in the use and interpretation of preschool intelligence tests is a function of the level and quality of procedural knowledge, whereas determining what information is necessary to bring to bear in novel situations (i.e., referrals) is dependent upon declarative knowledge (Bruning et al., 1995). Following the analysis of a

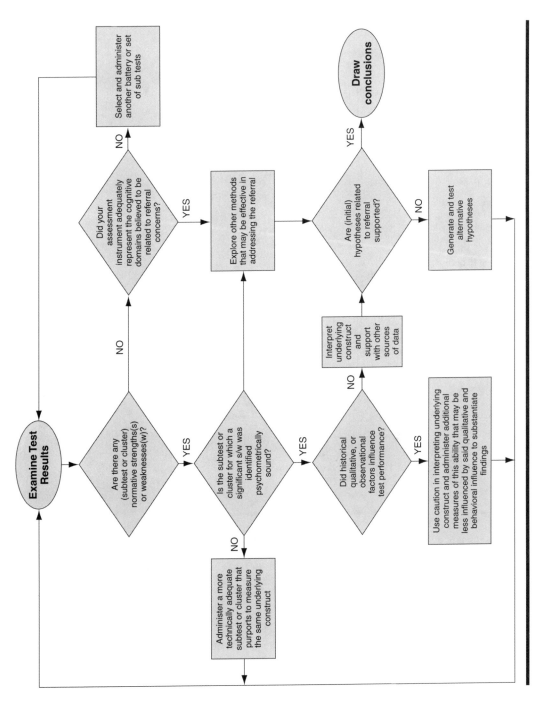

FIGURE 21.2 Interpretive Flowchart for Preschool Intelligence Tests

467

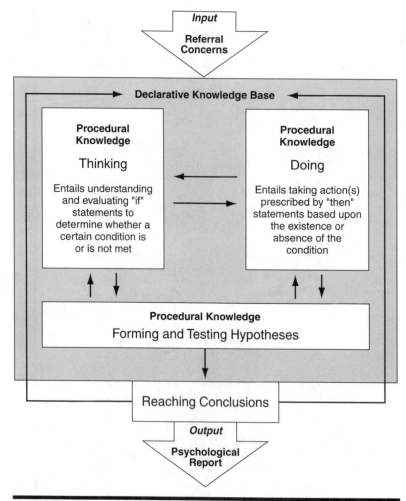

FIGURE 21.3   Schematic Representation of Interacting Declarative and Procedural Knowledge Bases for Test Interpretation

variety of sources of data, hypotheses are formed, tested, and either supported or not supported, conclusions are reached, and the output is the *synthesis* of the assessment data in the form of a written psychological report (see Figure 21.3).

CONCLUSION

The conceptual interpretive framework presented in this chapter was intended to provide information necessary to enable practitioners to develop expertise in analyzing data yielded from preschool intelligence batteries. It was based on the premise that intelligence tests for preschoolers can yield important information about a young child's cognitive capabilities if used intelligently and interpreted within the context of a broader assessment that complements the nature of the child, the referral, and other instruments included in the evaluation. The intelligent use of test results requires practitioners to apply a variety of psychological skills, knowledge, and expertise throughout the assessment process (Bracken, 1994).

Because the interpretation of intelligence test performance is an activity that has significant implications (e.g., diagnostic, treatment, placement) for the children who are evaluated, practitioners engaged in the practice of assessing the cognitive functioning of preschoolers have a responsibility to develop *expertise* in test interpretation. Experts have a significant breadth and depth of knowledge that allows them to approach and solve problems in an efficient and reflective manner (Bruning et al., 1997). They are highly skilled and knowledgeable in a particular area. Because the *level* of expertise in test interpretation possessed by practitioners is related directly to the quality of their interpretations, this chapter highlights important characteristics of preschool intelligence tests as well as the fundamental procedures of test interpretation considered minimally necessary for adequate analysis of intellectual assessment data. This information was conceptualized as declarative and procedural knowledge, respectively.

It was recommended that practitioners develop well-organized, domain-specific knowledge (i.e., declarative knowledge) regarding the psychometric, qualitative, and theoretical characteristics of preschool intelligence batteries. Specifically, we proposed that developing expertise in test interpretation requires one to acquire and accumulate a vast amount of information about the technical and theoretical aspects of cognitive ability tests as well as the noncognitive factors (i.e., background/environmental and individual/situational) that are likely to influence test performance (as reported in McGrew & Flanagan, 1998). Also, because interpretation of intellectual performance involves forming and testing hypotheses based on areas of cognitive strength and weakness, developing expertise involves constructing and following a well-defined set of interpretive actions or procedures, which consists largely of knowing *how* to make sound interpretations and how to support these interpretations with other sources of data. Thus, this chapter demonstrates how declarative knowledge interacts with procedural knowledge in complex ways to solve referral-related problems and, hence, generate new knowledge.

The breadth and depth of declarative and procedural knowledge that are necessary for defensible interpretation of cognitive assessment data are acquired *tacitly* over an extended period of time (Wagner & Sternberg, 1985). Therefore, developing expertise in test interpretation may be conceived of as a daunting task, but it is necessary to optimize the appropriateness of the decisions that are made based on a preschool child's cognitive test performance. Failure to develop expertise in test interpretation will constrain practitioners, resulting in their following the same routine for every assessment due to limited declarative and procedural knowledge for interpreting cognitive assessment data. Novices do not share the same level of flexibility that is afforded to practitioners who have a high level of psychological skills and practices within their professional test interpretation repertoire. Interpretations of cognitive ability test performance that are made by experts will ultimately lead to well-informed decisions about a child's capabilities and, thus, constructive educational or remedial program plans.

Assessment is a process. The quality of information yielded by this process is determined, to a large extent, by the examiner's level of expertise in test interpretation. Tests do not make decisions, rather, they provide information that can contribute to the decision-making process (Bracken, 1994). Due to the critical decisions that are made following the assessment of a preschool child's cognitive functioning, expertise in the interpretive process is necessary to maximize the utility of test data. Experts in intelligence test interpretation can represent problems more effectively, organize their knowledge in more meaningful ways, and make interpretations that are intellectually respectable and that have accountability. It is hoped that the conceptual interpretive framework presented in this chapter provides practitioners with an appropriate foundation from which to begin thinking about and organizing information related to the interpretation of preschool intelligence test performance and from which to develop expertise in the interpretive process.

REFERENCES

Alfonso, V. A., & Flanagan, D. P. (1999). Assessment of cognitive functioning in preschoolers. In E. V. Nutall, I. Romero, & J. Kalesnik (Eds.), *Assessing and screening preschoolers* (2nd ed.). Boston: Allyn and Bacon.

American Psychological Association (1985). *Standards for educational and psychological testing* (p. 19). Washington, DC: Author.

American Psychological Association (1990). *Guidelines for providers of psychological services to ethnic, linguistic, and culturally diverse populations*. Washington, DC: Author.

Anastasi, A., & Urbina, S. (1997). *Psychological testing* (7th ed.). Upper Saddle River, NJ: Prentice-Hall.

Bagnato, S. J., & Neisworth, J. T. (1994). A national study of the social and treatment "invalidity" of intelligence testing for early intervention. *School Psychology Quarterly, 9*(2), 81–102.

Boehm, A. E. (1991). Assessment of basic relational concepts. In B. Bracken (Ed.), *The psychoeducational assessment of preschool children* (2nd ed., pp. 86–106). Boston: Allyn and Bacon.

Bracken, B. A. (1986). Incidence of basic concepts in the directions of five commonly used American tests of intelligence. *School Psychology International, 7*, 1–10.

Bracken, B. A. (1987). Limitations of preschool instruments and standards for minimal levels of technical adequacy. *Journal of Psychoeducational Assessment, 4*, 313–326.

Bracken, B. A. (Ed.) (1991). *The psychoeducational assessment of preschool children* (2nd ed.). Boston: Allyn and Bacon.

Bracken, B. A. (1994). Advocating for effective preschool assessment practices: A comment on Bagnato and Neisworth. *School Psychology Quarterly, 9*(2), 103–108.

Bracken, B. A., & Fagan, T. K. (Eds.). (1990). Intelligence: Theories and practice (Special Issue). *Journal of Psychoeducational Assessment, 8*(3).

Bracken, B. A., & McCallum, S. A. (1998). *Universal Nonverbal Intelligence Test*. Chicago: Riverside.

Bracken, B. A., & Walker, K. C. (1997). The utility of intelligence tests for preschool children. In D. P. Flanagan, J. Genshaft, & P. Harrison (Eds.), *Contemporary intellectual assessment: Theories, tests, and issues* (pp. 484–502). New York: Guilford Press.

Briggs, S. R., & Cheek, J. M. (1986). The role of factor analysis in the development and evaluation of personality scales. Special Issue: Methodological developments in personality research. *Journal of Personality, 54*, 106–148.

Bruning, R. H., Schraw, G. J., & Ronning, R. R. (1995). *Cognitive psychology and instruction* (2nd ed.). Englewood Cliffs, NJ: Merrill.

Carroll, J. B. (1993a). *Human cognitive abilities: A survey of factor-analytic studies*. Cambridge, England: Cambridge University Press.

Carroll, J. B. (1993b). What abilities are measure by the WIC-III? *Journal of Psychoeducational Assessment* [Monograph Series: WISC-III Monograph], 134–143.

Carroll, J. B. (1997). The three-stratum theory of cognitive abilities. In D. P. Flanagan, J. L. Genshaft, & P. L. Harrison (Eds.), *Contemporary intellectual as-sessment: Theories, tests, and issues* (pp. 122–130). New York: Guilford Press.

Cattell, R. B. (1941). Some theoretical issues in adult intelligence testing. *Psychological Bulletin, 38*, 592.

Cervantes, H. T. (1988). Nondiscriminatory assessment and informal data gathering: The case of Gonzaldo L. In R. L. Jones (Ed.), *Psychoeducational assessment of minority group children: A casebook*. Berkeley, CA: Cobb and Henry.

Chafouleas, S. M., Lewandowski, L. J., Smith, C. R., & Blachman, B. A. (1997). Phonological awareness skills in children: Examining performance across tasks and ages. *Journal of Psychoeducational Assessment, 15*, 334–347.

Comrey, A. L. (1988). Factor-analytic methods of scaled development in personality and clinical psychology. *Journal of Consulting and Clinical Psychology, 56*, 754–761.

Dana, R. H. (1993). *Multicultural assessment perspectives for professional psychology*. Boston: Allyn and Bacon.

Daniel, M. H. (1997). Intelligence testing: Status and trends. *American Psychologist, 52*, 1038–1045.

Dunn, L. (1968). Special education for the mildly retarded—Is much of it justifiable? *Exceptional Children, 35*, 5–22.

Eggen, P., & Kauchak, D. (1997). *Educational psychology* (3rd ed.). Upper Saddle River, NJ: Prentice-Hall.

Elliot, C. D. (1990). *Differential Ability Scales: Introductory and technical handbook*. San Antonio, TX: Psychological Corporation.

Esters, E. G., Ittenbach, R. F., & Han, K. (1997). Today's IQ tests: Are they really better than their historical predecessors? *School Psychology Review, 26*, 211–223.

Flanagan, D. P., & Alfonso, V. C. (1995). A critical review of the technical characteristics of new and recently revised intelligence tests for preschool children. *Journal of Psychoeducational Assessment, 13*, 66–90.

Flanagan, D. P., Alfonso, V. C., Kaminer, T., & Rader, D. E. (1995). Incidence of basic concepts in the directions of new and revised American intelligence tests for preschool children. *School Psychology International, 16*, 345–364.

Flanagan, D. P., Andrews, T. J., & Genshaft, J. L. (1997). The functional utility of intelligence tests with special education populations. In D. P. Flanagan, J. L. Genshaft, & P. L. Harrison (Eds.), *Con-

temporary intellectual assessment: Theories, tests, and issues (pp. 457–483). New York: Guilford Press.

Flanagan, D. P., & Genshaft, J. L. (1997). Guest editors' comments: Mini-series on issues related to the use and interpretation of intelligence testing in the schools. *School Psychology Review, 26,* 146–149.

Flanagan, D. P., & McGrew, K. S. (1997). A cross-battery approach to assessing and interpreting cognitive abilities: Narrowing the gap between practice and cognitive science. In D. P. Flanagan, J. L. Genshaft, & P. L. Harrison (Eds.), *Contemporary intellectual assessment: Theories, tests, and issues* (pp. 314–325). New York: Guilford Press.

Flanagan, D. P., McGrew, K. S., & Ortiz, S. O. (in press). *The Wechsler intelligence scales and* Gf-Gc *theory. A contemporary approach to interpretation.* Boston: Allyn and Bacon.

French, J. L., & Hale, R. L. (1990). A history of the development of psychological and educational testing. In C. R. Reynolds & R. W. Kamphaus (Eds.), *Handbook of psychological and educational assessment of children: Intelligence and achievement* (pp. 3–28). New York: Guilford Press.

Gagne, E. D. (1985). *The cognitive psychology of school learning.* Boston: Little, Brown.

Genshaft, J. L., & Gerner, M. (1998). *Gf-Gc* cross battery assessment: Implications for school psychologists. *Communique, 26*(8), 24–27.

Glutting, J. J., & Kaplan, D. (1990). Stanford-Binet Intelligence Scale, Fourth Edition: Making the case for reasonable interpretations. In C. R. Reynolds & R. W. Kamphaus (Eds.), *Handbook of psychological and educational assessment of children: Intelligence and achievement* (pp. 277–296). New York: Guilford Press.

Gustafsson, J. E., & Undheim, J. O. (1996). Individual differences in cognitive functions. In D. C. Berliner & R. C. Calfee (Eds.), *Handbook of educational psychology* (pp. 186–242). New York: Macmillan Library Reference USA.

Gyurke, J. S., Stone, B., & Beyer, M. (1990). A confirmatory factor analysis of the WPPSI-R. *Journal of Psychoeducational Assessment, 8,* 15–21.

Harrison, P. L. (1990). *AGS Early Screening Profiles manual.* Circle Pines, MN: American Guidance Service.

Harrison, P. L., Flanagan, D. P., & Genshaft, J. L. (1997). An integration and synthesis of contemporary theories, tests, and issues in the field of intellectual as-

sessment. In D. P. Flanagan, J. L. Genshaft, & P. L. Harrison (Eds.), *Contemporary intellectual assessment: Theories, tests, and issues* (pp. 533–562). New York: Guilford Press.

Hobbs, N. (1975). *The futures of children.* San Francisco: Jossey-Bass.

Horn, J. L. (1988). Thinking about human abilities. In J. R. Nesselroade & R. B. Cattell (Eds.), *Handbook of multivariate psychology* (Rev. ed., pp. 645–685). New York: Academic Press.

Horn, J. L. (1991). Measurement of intellectual capabilities: A review of theory. In K. S. McGrew, J. K. Werder, & R. W. Woodcock, *Woodcock-Johnson technical manual* (pp. 197–232). Chicago: Riverside.

Horn, J. L. (1994). Theory of fluid and crystallized intelligence. In R. J. Sternberg (Ed.), *Encyclopedia of human intelligence* (pp. 443–451). New York: Macmillan.

Horn, J. L., & Noll, J. (1997). Human cognitive capabilities: *Gf-Gc* theory. In D. P. Flanagan, J. L. Genshaft, & P. L. Harrison (Eds.), *Contemporary intellectual assessment: Theories, tests, and issues* (pp. 53–91). New York: Guilford Press.

Jensen, A. R. (1974). How biased are culture-loaded tests? *Genetic Psychology Monographs, 90,* 185–244.

Jensen, A. R. (1984). Test validity: *g* versus the specificity doctrine. *Journal of Social and Biological Structures, 7,* 93–118.

Jones, R. (1972). Labels and stigma in special education. *Exceptional Children, 38,* 546–553.

Kamphaus, R. W. (1993). *Clinical assessment of children's intelligence.* Boston: Allyn and Bacon.

Kamphaus, R. W., Petoskey, M. D., & Morgan, A. (1997). A history of intelligence test interpretation. In D. P. Flanagan, J. Genshaft, & P. Harrison (Eds.), *Contemporary intellectual assessment: Theories, tests, and issues* (pp. 32–47). New York: Guilford Press.

Kaufman, A. S. (1978). The importance of basic concepts in individual assessment of preschool children. *Journal of School Psychology, 16,* 207–211.

Kaufman, A. S. (1979). *Intelligent testing with the WISC-R.* New York: Wiley.

Kaufman, A. S. (1990a). *Assessing adolescent and adult intelligence.* Boston: Allyn and Bacon.

Kaufman, A. S. (1990b). The WPPSI-R: You can't judge a test by its colors. *Journal of School Psychology, 28,* 387–394.

Kaufman, A. S., & Kaufman, N. L. (1983). *Interpretive manual for the Kaufman Assessment Battery for*

Children. Circle Pines, MN: American Guidance Service.

Kaufman, A. S., & Kaufman, N. L. (1994). *Kaufman short neuropsychological assessment procedure.* Circle Pines, MN: American Guidance Service.

Keith, T. Z. (1985). Questioning the K-ABC: What does it measure? *School Psychology Review, 14,* 9–20.

Keith, T. Z. (1990). Confirmatory and hierarchical confirmatory analysis of the Differential Ability Scales. *Journal of Psychoeducational Assessment, 8,* 391–405.

Keith, T. Z. (1997). Using confirmatory factor analysis to aid in understanding the constructs measured by intelligence tests. In D. P. Flanagan, J. L. Genshaft, & P. L. Harrison (Eds.), *Contemporary intellectual assessment: Theories, tests, and issues* (pp. 373–402). New York: Guilford Press.

Kline, R. B. (1989). Is the Fourth Edition Stanford-Binet a four-factor test? Confirmatory factor analyses of alternative models for ages 2 through 23. *Journal of Psychoeducational Assessment, 7,* 4–13.

Kranzler, J. H. (1997). Educational and policy issues related to the use and interpretation of intelligence tests in the schools. *School Psychology Review, 26,* 150–162.

Lidz, C. S. (1991). Issues in the assessment of preschool children. In B. A. Bracken (Ed.), *The psychoeducational assessment of preschool children* (pp. 18–29). Boston: Allyn and Bacon.

Mather, N. (1991). *An instructional guide to the Woodcock-Johnson Psycho-Educational Battery—Revised.* Brandon, VT: Clinical Psychology.

McCallum, S. A., & Bracken, B. A. (1997). The Universal Nonverbal Intelligence Test. In D. P. Flanagan, J. L. Genshaft, & P. L. Harrison (Eds.), *Contemporary intellectual assessment: Theories, tests, and issues* (pp. 268–280). New York: Guilford Press.

McGrew, K. S. (1984). Normative-based guides for subtest profile interpretation of the Woodcock-Johnson Tests of Cognitive Ability. *Journal of Psychoeducational Assessment, 2,* 325–332.

McGrew, K. S. (1997). Analysis of the major intelligence batteries according to a proposed comprehensive Gf-Gc framework. In D. P. Flanagan, J. L. Genshaft, & P. L. Harrison (Eds.), *Contemporary intellectual assessment: Theories, tests, and issues* (pp. 151–180). New York: Guilford Press.

McGrew, K. S., & Flanagan, D. P. (1998). *The Intelligence Test Desk Reference (ITDR) Gf-Gc cross-battery assessment.* Boston: Allyn and Bacon.

McGrew, K. S., Untiedt, S. A., & Flanagan, D. P. (1996). General factor and uniqueness characteristics of the Kaufman Adolescent and Adult Intelligence Scale (KAIT). *Journal of Psychoeducational Assessment, 14,* 208–209.

Messick, S. (1992). Multiple intelligences or multilevel intelligence? Selective emphasis on distinctive properties of hierarchy: On Gardner's *Frames of Mind* and Sternberg's *Beyond IQ* in the context of theory and research on the structure of human abilities. *Psychological Inquiry, 3*(4), 365–384.

Naglieri, J. A., (1997). Planning, attention, simultaneous, and successive theory and the cognitive assessment system: A new theory-based measure of intelligence. In D. P. Flanagan, J. L. Genshaft, & P. L. Harrison (Eds.), *Contemporary intellectual assessment: Theories, tests, and issues* (pp. 247–267). New York: Guilford Press.

Ortiz, S. O., & Flanagan, D. P. (1998). Enhancing cognitive assessment of culturally and linguistically diverse individuals: Selective *Gf-Gc* cross-battery assessment. *The School Psychologist, 52,* 6–9.

Ortiz, S. O., Flanagan, D. P., & McGrew, K. S. (1998). *Gf-Gc* cross-battery interpretation and selective cross-battery assessment: Considering referral concerns and the needs of culturally and linguistically diverse populations. In K. S. McGrew & D. P. Flanagan, *The intelligence test desk reference (ITDR): Gf-Gc cross-battery assessment.* Boston: Allyn and Bacon.

Paget, K. (1991). The individual assessment situation: Basic considerations for preschool-age children. In B. A. Bracken (Ed.), *The psychoeducational assessment of preschool children* (pp. 32–39). Boston: Allyn and Bacon.

Perfetti, C. A., Beck, I., Bell, L. C., & Hughes, C. (1987). Phonemic knowledge and learning to read are reciprocal: A longitudinal study of first grade children. *Merrill-Palmer Quarterly, 33,* 283–319.

Reynolds, C. R., & Kaufman, A. S. (1990). Assessment of children's intelligence with the Wechsler Intelligence Scale for Children—Revised (WISC-R). In C. R. Reynolds & R. W. Kamphaus (Eds.), *Handbook of psychological and educational assessment of children: Intelligence and achievement* (pp. 127–165). New York: Guilford Press.

Roberts, R. D., Pallier, G., & Goff, G. N. (in press). Sensory processes within the structure of human cognitive abilities. To appear in P. L. Ackerman, P. C. Kyllonen, & R. D. Roberts (Eds.), *The future of learning and individual differences research: processes, traits, and content.* Washington, DC: American Pscyhological Association.

Roid, G. H., & Gyurke, J. (1991). General-factor and specific variance in the WPPSI-R. *Journal of Psychoeducational Assessment, 9,* 209–223.

Salvia, J., & Ysseldyke, J. (1991). *Assessment in special and remedial education* (5th ed.). Boston: Houghton-Mifflin.

Sattler, J. (1988). *Assessment of children's intelligence and special abilities* (2nd ed.). San Diego, CA: Author.

Sattler, J. (1992). *Assessment of children* (Rev. 3rd ed.). San Diego, CA: Author.

Shaw, S. R., Swerdlik, M. E., & Laurent, J. (1993). A review of the WISC-III. *Journal of Psychoeducational Assessment,* [WISC-III Monograph], 151–160.

Sternberg, R. J. (1993). Rocky's back again: A review of the WISC-III. *Journal of Psychoeducational Assessment* [WISC-III Monograph], 161–164.

Thorndike, R. M., Hagen, E. P., & Sattler, J. M. (1986). *Stanford-Binet Intelligence Scale, Fourth Edition.* Chicago: Riverside.

Thorndike, R. M., & Lohman, D. F. (1990). *A century of ability testing.* Chicago: Riverside.

Valdes, G., & Figueroa, R. A. (1994). *Bilingualism and testing: A special case of bias.* Norwood, NJ: Ablex.

Wagner, R. & Sternber, R. J. (1985). Practical intelligence in real-world pursuits: The role of tacit knowledge. *Journal of Personality and Social Psychology, 52,* 1236–1247.

Wechsler, D. (1989). *Manual for the Wechsler Preschool and Primary Scale of Intelligence—Revised.* San Antonio, TX: Psychological Corporation.

Wilson, B. (1992). The neuropsychological assessment of the preschool child: a branching model. *Handbook of Neuropsychology, 6,* 377–394.

Woodcock, R. W. (1990). Theoretical foundations of the WJ-R measures of cognitive ability. *Journal of Psychoeducational Assessment, 9,* 231–258.

Woodcock, R. W., & Johnson, M. B. (1989, 1990). *Woodcock-Johnson Psycho-Educational Battery—Revised.* Allen, TX: DLM Teaching Resources.

Ysseldyke, J. (1990). Goodness of fit of the Woodcock-Johnson Psycho-Educational Battery-Revised to the Horn-Cattell *Gf-Gc* theory. *Journal of Psychoeducational Assessment, 9,* 268–275.

Name Index